# The World's Best Poetry

Supplement VIII
## Cumulative Index

Poetry Anthology Press

**Survey of American Poetry**
Ten Volumes + 2 supplements


**Survey of British Poetry**
Four Volumes


**The World's Best Poetry**
Foundation Volumes I-X


Supplements

# The World's Best Poetry

## Supplement VIII
## Cumulative Index

An Author, Title, First Line, Translator, Subject,
and Keyword Index to the World's Best Poetry,
Volumes I-X and Supplements I-VII

940006

Prepared by
The Editorial Board, Roth Publishing, Inc.

 **Poetry Anthology Press**
Great Neck, New York

Library of Congress Catalog Number 82-84763
International Standard Book Number 0-89609-327-1

Manufactured in the U.S.A.

Poetry Anthology Press is a
division of Roth Publishing, Inc.

# CONTENTS

# *PREFACE*

The publications of **Poetry Anthology Press**, a division of Roth Publishing, Inc., constitute a comprehensive conspectus of international verse in English designed to form the core of a library's poetry collection. Covering the entire range of poetic literature, these anthologies encompass all topics and national literatures.

Each collection, published in a multivolume continuing series format, is devoted to a major area of the whole undertaking and contains complete author, title, and first line indexes. Biographical data is also provided.

*The World's Best Poetry*, with coverage through the 19th century, it topically classified and arranged by subject matter. Supplements keep the 10 volume foundation collection current and complete.

Survey of American Poetry is an anthology of American verse arranged chronologically in 10 volumes. Each volume presents a significant period of American poetic history, from 1607 to 1984. *Annual Survey of American Poetry* continues the coverage and maintains the currency of the collection.

*Survey of British Poetry: Anthology & Criticism* traces English language poetry chronologically in 4 volumes. The volumes explore the major periods in the English poetic tradition from the 5th century to the 20th.

# INTRODUCTION

The first ten foundation volumes of **THE WORLD'S BEST POETRY** and its seven supplements represent a substantial and significant collection of poetry from the earliest times to the present.

The foundation volumes are unified in their approach and format. The purpose is to have a subject based collection, wherein each volume is devoted to major topics, the whole being tied together in a general index in Volume X. The supplements are intended to augment and amplify the collection by focusing on chronology (20th century material), nationality (Asian, African, and Latin American), and previously neglected poets (African Americans, Hispanic Americans, Native Americans, and women).

The additional supplements, bringing the entire collection to a total of 4000 poems by over 1200 named poets, has created a need to access the whole in one single resource. Librarians have asked us to provide such a reference, and we have done so in this volume with two indexes.

*Index to Poems* contains five entries: title, author, first line, translator, and subject. Each entry is complete in itself and contains the volume or supplement ("supp") number and page where the poem is located (this information appears in brackets at the end of the entry). As this is a dictionary index, all entries are interfiled in one alphabetical sequence.

*1. Title Entry.* This entry contains the title of the poem, its author, and source information. The first word of the title is printed in bold face; the title appears in quotation marks when it is the first line.

*2. Author Entry.* Author, title, translator and source information are given in this entry. The author's name is printed in bold face.

*3. First Line Entry.* First line access to a poem is given when it is not the title. Title, author, and source information is provided.

The first line is always given in quotation marks; the first word is printed in bold face.

*4. Translator Entry.* Translated poems are indexed by a separate translator entry in which title, author, and source are provided.

*5. Subject Entry.* Title, author, and source data are given in this entry. The subject is printed in bold italics.

***Keyword Index.*** Entries in this separate index organize titles by significant word. For example, all titles with the word. For example, all titles containing the word "spring" are grouped together in the following fashion:

> **Spring.** Early [S. Keyes. Supp 2/411]
> in Carolina. [H. Timrod. Volume 5/86]
> __. Return of [p. Ronsard. Volume 5/78]

Notice that the titles have been inverted to bring the keyword into the first position, where necessary. Also note that after the first instance of the keyword, succeeding titles use an underline to indicate the repetition of the keyword. Thus the titles of the above examples read:

> Early spring.
> Spring in Carolina.
> Return of spring.

# INDEX TO POEMS

**Author, Title, First Line, Translator and Subject Index**

The Death of Sophocles. S. Kunitz (tr.). [Supp 5/11]

The Last Toast. S. Kunitz (tr.). [Supp 5/8]

Lot's Wife. S. Kunitz (tr.). [Supp 5/7]

Reading Hamlet. S. Kunitz (tr.). [Supp 5/6]

"This Cruel Age Has Deflected Me" S. Kunitz (tr.). [Supp 5/10]

"Why Is This Age Worse Than Earlier Ages?" S. Kunitz (tr.). [Supp 5/7]

Willow. S. Kunitz (tr.). [Supp 5/9]

*Akhmatova, Anna*

Poems for Akhmatova: 001. M. Tsvetayeva. [Supp 5/300]

Poems for Akhmatova: 002. M. Tsvetayeva. [Supp 5/300]

Poems for Akhmatova: 003. M. Tsvetayeva. [Supp 5/301]

Poems for Akhmatova: 004. M. Tsvetayeva. [Supp 5/301]

"al amanecer el monstruo del mar dormia." Bronchitis: The Rosario Beach House, 001. A. Rodriguez. [Supp 4/279]

**Al-Haydari, Buland**

Barrenness. M. Khouri and Hamid Algar (tr.). [Supp 7/229]

A False Step. M. Khouri and Hamid Algar (tr.). [Supp 7/227]

Mailman. M. Khouri and Hamid Algar (tr.). [Supp 7/226]

Old Age. M. Khouri and Hamid Algar (tr.). [Supp 7/230]

**Al-Sayyab, Badr Shakir**

"For I Am a Stranger" M. Khouri and Hamid Algar (tr.). [Supp 7/232]

The River an Death. M. Khouri and Hamid Algar (tr.). [Supp 7/233]

**al-Udhari, Abdullah (tr.)**

The Minaret. Adonis. [Supp 7/283]

A Mirror for the Twentieth Century. Adonis. [Supp 7/278]

The New Noah. Adonis. [Supp 7/280]

The Pearl. Adonis. [Supp 7/282]

Prophecy. Adonis. [Supp 7/280]

Song. Adonis. [Supp 7/278]

Alarm. T. Sayigh. [Supp 7/293]

"Alas, Fra Giacomo, %too late! - but follow me." Fra Giacomo. R. Buchanan. [Volume 9/76]

" Alas! How Light a Cause May Move", fr. Light of the Harem. T. Moore. [Volume 3/80]

"Alas, I have nor hope nore health." Stanza. P. Shelley. [Volume 3/164]

"Alas! that men must see." Love and Death. M. Deland. [Volume 3/394]

"Alas, that my heart is a lute." My Heart Is A Lute. L. Lindsay. [Volume 2/424]

"Alas! the weary hours pass slow." The Countersign. Unknown. [Volume 8/352]

"Alas! what pity 't is that regularity." Toby Tosspot. G. Colman. [Volume 9/257]

Albert, Prince Consort of England, fr. Idyls of the King. A. Tennyson. [Volume 7/34]

**Aldrich, James**

A Death-Bed. [Volume 3/306]

**Aldrich, Thomas Bailey**

After the Rain. [Volume 5/123]

Baby Bell. [Volume 1/60]

Before the Rain. [Volume 5/117]

Broken Music. [Volume 6/346]

Guiliemus Rex. [Volume 7/53]

On an Intaglio Head of Minerva. [Volume 6/383]

Outward Bound. [Volume 6/123]

Palabras Carinosas. [Volume 2/281]

Tennyson. [Volume 7/83]

**Alegria, Claribel**

Letter to Time. C. Forche (tr.). [Supp 5/14]

We Were Three. C. Forche (tr.). [Supp 5/12]

**Alexander, Cecil Frances**

Burial of Moses. [Volume 4/365]

**Alexander's** Feast; or, the Power of Music. J. Dryden. [Volume 6/372]

Alexis, Here She Stayed. W. Drummond of Hawthornden. [Volume 2/224]

"Alexis, here she stayed; among these pines." Alexis, Here She Stayed. W. Drummond of Hawthornden. [Volume 2/224]

Alfred the harper. J. Sterling. [Volume 8/238]

**Algarin, Miguel**

Sunday, August 11, 1974. [Supp 4/283]

**Alger, William R. (tr.)**

The Parting Lovers. Unknown. [Volume 3/104]

"To Heaven Approached a Sufi Saint" J. Rumi. [Volume 4/405]

Alice in Nightmareland. E. Lihn. [Supp 6/122]

*Alienation*

The Little Boy Lost. S. Smith. [Supp 2/103]

"Alike for those who for to-day prepare." Rubaiyat: 025. O. Khayyam. [Volume 6/208]

**Alisjahbana; S. Thorton and B. Raffell, S. T. (tr.)**

Because of You. A. Hamzah. [Supp 7/88]

Palace of Grace. A. Hamzah. [Supp 7/90]

**All.** F. Durivage. [Volume 8/415]

"All beauty, granted as a boon to earth." To Mary Stuart. P. Ronsard. [Volume 7/4]

"All day long roved Hiawatha." The Death of Minnehaha, fr. The Song of Hiawatha. H. Longfellow. [Volume 3/319]

"All day long the storm of battle through the." The Drummer-boy's Burial. Unknown. [Volume 9/172]

All Goats. E. Coatsworth. [Supp 1/85]

"All goats have a wild-brier grace." All Goats. E. Coatsworth. [Supp 1/85]

All Gone. C. Day Lewis. [Supp 2/109]

"All Greece hates." Helen. H. Doolittle. [Supp 2/4]

"All grim and soiled and brown and tan." The Reformer. J. Whittier. [Volume 8/157]

"All hail, remembrance and forgetfulness!" Memory and Oblivion. Macedonius. [Volume 6/321]

"All hail; thou noble land." America to Great Britain. W. Allston. [Volume 8/27]

"All I could see from where I stood." Renascence. E. Millay. [Supp 1/214]

"All in green went my love riding." Song. E. Cummings. [Supp 1/101]

"All in our marriage garden." Our Wee White Rose. G. Massey. [Volume 1/64]

"All in the April evening." Sheep and Lambs. K. Hinkson. [Volume 1/121]

"All in the downs the fleet was moored." Black-eyed Susan. J. Gay. [Volume 3/102]

"All is bright and clear and still." Venice, fr. View from the Euganean Hills. P. Shelley. [Volume 7/192]

"All my life %they have told me." Notes Found Near a Suicide: To You. F. Horne. [Supp 4/115]

"All my waiting %was for the past." Present. J. Das. [Supp 7/49]

"All night the cocks crew, under a moon like day." Tears in Sleep. L. Bogan. [Supp 1/61]

"All of a sudden." Past the Ice Age. M. Waddington. [Supp 5/314]

"All Quiet Along the Potomac" E. Beers. [Volume 8/350]

"All service ranks the same with God." Service, fr. Pippa Passes. R. Browning. [Volume 4/156]

"All that time there was thunder in the air." O Dreams, O Destinations: 005. C. Day Lewis. [Supp 2/120]

"All the stones %unturned say." Lost in Sulphur Canyons. J. Barnes. [Supp 4/299]

"All the things I speak of lie in the city." Things

"And again I was like one of those girls." Time
Caught in a Net. D. Ravikovitch. [Supp 5/232]

"And are ye sure the news is true?" There's Nae Luck
About The House. J. Adam. [Volume 2/442]

"And as the cock crew, those who stood before."
Rubaiyat: 003. O. Khayyam. [Volume 6/204]

"And David's lips are lockt; but in divine."
Rubaiyat: 006. O. Khayyam. [Volume 6/205]

"And Doth Not a Meting Like This" T. Moore. [Volume
1/366]

"'And even our women,' lastly grumbles Ben." The Girl
of All Periods. C. Patmore. [Volume 1/242]

"And fear not lest existence, closing your."
Rubaiyat: 046. O. Khayyam. [Volume 6/213]

"And from the windy west came two-gunned Gabriel."
Altarwise by Owl-light: 005. D. Thomas. [Supp
2/350]

"And God called Moses from the burning bush." Let My
People Go. J. Johnson. [Supp 4/68]

"And has not such a story from the old." Rubaiyat:
038. O. Khayyam. [Volume 6/211]

"And here face down beneath the sun." You, Andrew
Marvell. A. MacLeish. [Volume 1/204]

"And I am the one that must shed the blood." The
Cross. T. Ojaide. [Supp 6/56]

"And if our tormentors walk, we have to run." When We
Have to Fly. T. Ojaide. [Supp 6/52]

"And if the wine you drink, the lip you press."
Rubaiyat: 042. O. Khayyam. [Volume 6/212]

"And is here care in heaven? And is there love." The
Ministry of Angels, fr. The Faerie Queen. E.
Spenser. [Volume 4/415]

"And is the swallow gone?" The Departure of the
Swallow. W. Howitt. [Volume 5/331]

"And last night a man came in." Spring Street Bar. M.
Berssenbrugge. [Supp 4/12]

"And lately, by the tavern door agape." Rubaiyat: 058.
O. Khayyam. [Volume 6/215]

"And lo! forthwith there rose up round about."
Paradise: The Triumph of Christ, fr. The Diving
Comedy. Dante Alighieri. [Volume 4/443]

"And much as wine has played the infidel." Rubaiyat:
095. O. Khayyam. [Volume 6/222]

"And not a drop that from our cups we throw."
Rubaiyat: 039. O. Khayyam. [Volume 6/211]

"And now behold your tender nurse, the air." The
Dancing of the Air. S. Davies. [Volume 5/125]

"And now she cleans her teeth into the lake." Camping
Out. W. Empson. [Supp 2/140]

"And now the downpour ceases." The Return: 003. A.
Bontemps. [Supp 4/124]

"And now, unveiled, the toilet stands displayed." The
Toilet, fr. The Rape of the Lock. A. Pope.
[Volume 7/135]

"And now we're going to the unanimous minute." It Can
Happen. V. Huidobro. [Supp 6/120]

"And one morning while in the woods I stumbled
suddenly upon the." Between the World and Me. R.
Wright. [Supp 2/212]

"And said I that my limbs were old." Love, fr. Lay of
the Last Minstrel. S. Scott. [Volume 2/70]

"And several strengths from drowsiness campaigned."
The Sermon on the Warpland. G. Brooks. [Supp
4/159]

"And so for nights." The Night-Blooming Cereus. R.
Hayden. [Supp 4/139]

"And that inverted bowl they call the sky." Rubaiyat:
072. O. Khayyam. [Volume 6/218]

"And the just man trailed God's shining agent." Lot's
Wife. A. Akhmatova. [Supp 5/7]

**And** Then? T. Sayigh. [Supp 7/295]

"And then? %The question makes a tragedy out of a
comedy." And Then? T. Sayigh. [Supp 7/295]

"And then I turned unto their side my eyes."
Francesca Da Rimini, fr. Divina Commedia:

Inferno. Dante Alighieri. [Volume 2/99]

"And there they sat, a-popping corn." Poppin Corn.
Unknown. [Volume 2/193]

"And there two runners did the sign abide."
Atalanta's Race, fr. The Earthly Paradise. W.
Morris. [Volume 2/142]

"And this I know: whether the one true light."
Rubaiyat: 077. O. Khayyam. [Volume 6/219]

"And this reviving herb whose tender green."
Rubaiyat: 020. O. Khayyam. [Volume 6/207]

"And those who husbanded the golden grain." Rubaiyat:
015. O. Khayyam. [Volume 6/206]

"And thou hast walked aobut (how strange a story!)"
Address to the Mummy at Belzoni's Exhibition. H.
Smith. [Volume 6/235]

"And we, that now make merry in the room." Rubaiyat:
023. O. Khayyam. [Volume 6/208]

"And What Will Happen" K. Molodowsky. [Supp 5/175]

"And when like her, O Saki, you shall pass."
Rubaiyat: 101. O. Khayyam. [Volume 6/224]

"And when you have forgotten the bright bedclothes."
When You Have Forgotten Sunday: The Love Story.
G. Brooks. [Supp 4/156]

"And where have you been, my Mary." The Fairies of
the Caldon Low. M. Howitt. [Volume 1/148]

"And ye shall walk in silk attire." The Siller Croun.
S. Blamire. [Volume 2/177]

"And yet - and yet - in these our ghostly lives."
Dream-life, fr. Such Stuff as Dreams Are Made
Of. P. Calderon. [Volume 6/324]

**Anderson, Alexander**
Cuddle Doon. [Volume 1/44]

The **Angel** of Patience. J. Whittier. [Volume 3/402]

"The **angel** of the flowers, one day." The Moss Rose. F.
Krummacher. [Volume 5/281]

"The **angel** of the nation's peace." Our Fallen Heroes.
G. Griffith. [Volume 8/449]

"**Angel** or deamon! thou - whether of light." Napoleon.
V. Hugo. [Volume 7/8]

**Angelo, Michael**
"If It Be True That Any Beauteous Thing" J. Taylor
(tr.). [Volume 2/72]
The Might Of One Fair Face. J. Taylor (tr.).
[Volume 2/329]

*Angels*
Song of the East. A. Mutis. [Supp 6/133]

The **Angel's** Whisper. S. Lover. [Volume 1/10]

The **Angels'** Song. E. Sears. [Volume 4/48]

**Angira, Jared**
If. [Supp 6/21]
A Look in the Past. [Supp 6/23]

The **Angler**. J. Chalkhill. [Volume 5/139]

The **Angler's** Wish. I. Walton. [Volume 5/138]

**Anglesey, Zoe (tr.)**
I Want to Find Desperately I Look. B. Peralta.
[Supp 6/184]
It Is Certain That We are Constructing a World. R.
Murillo. [Supp 6/176]
The Man Who Boxes. A. Istaru. [Supp 6/136]
Uncertainty. B. Reyna. [Supp 6/146]

*Animals*
Dark Song, fr. Facade. E. Sitwell. [Supp 2/12]
Hunter Mountain. F. Lima. [Supp 4/245]

*Animate Nature*
The Arab to His Favorite Steed. C. Norton. [Volume
5/366]
Asian Birds. R. Bridges. [Volume 5/328]
The Belfry Pigeon. N. Willis. [Volume 5/325]
Beth Gelert. W. Spencer. [Volume 5/360]
Birds, fr. The Pelican Island. J. Montgomery.
[Volume 5/288]
The Blackbird. A. Tennyson. [Volume 5/320]
The Blood Horse. B. Procter. [Volume 5/369]
The Bobolinks. C. Cranch. [Volume 5/316]
Chariot of Cuchullin, fr. Breach of the Plain of

Philomena. [Volume 5/308]
Requiescat. [Volume 3/307]
The Slaying of Sohrab, fr. Sohrab and Rustum.
　[Volume 9/28]
The World and the Quietest. [Volume 6/430]
**Arnold, Sir Edwin**
After Death, fr. Pearls of the Faith. [Volume
　3/452]
The Secret of Death. [Volume 3/434]
"**Around** the corner %an invisible angel." Song of the
　East. A. Mutis. [Supp 6/133]
"**Arrayed** in snow-white pants and vest." The
　Compliment. E. Field. [Volume 9/342]
"**Arrested** like marble horses." A Frieze. J. Bishop.
　[Supp 2/24]
The **Arsenal** at Springfield. H. Longfellow. [Volume
　8/444]
**Art**. G. Parker. [Volume 6/345]
*Art*
Art Criticism. W. Landor. [Volume 7/110]
The Artist. A. Grissom. [Volume 6/384]
Boats in a Fog. R. Jeffers. [Supp 1/173]
Cousin Lucrece. E. Stedman. [Volume 7/131]
The Cuckoo Clock, fr. The Birthday. C. Southey.
　[Volume 7/148]
Delight in Disorder. R. Herrick. [Volume 7/135]
An Etruscan Ring. J. Mackail. [Volume 7/149]
Freedom is Dress, fr. Epicoene; or, the Silent
　Woman. B. Jonson. [Volume 7/131]
Laus Veneris. L. Moulton. [Volume 7/138]
Leonardo's "Mona Lisa" E. Dowden. [Volume 7/150]
The Monument. E. Bishop. [Supp 2/243]
Ode on a Grecian Urn. J. Keats. [Volume 7/136]
On an Intaglio Head of Minerva. T. Aldrich.
　[Volume 6/383]
The Toilet, fr. The Rape of the Lock. A. Pope.
　[Volume 7/135]
Art Criticism. W. Landor. [Volume 7/110]
Art of Book-keeping. T. Hood. [Volume 9/305]
"**Art** thou poor, yet hast thou golden slumbers?" The
　Happy Heart, fr. Patient Grissell. T. Dekker.
　[Volume 6/409]
"**Art** thou wear, art thou languid." Art Thou Weary. S.
　Stephen the Sabaite. [Volume 4/87]
Art Thou Weary. S. Stephen the Sabaite. [Volume 4/87]
*Arthurian Legend*
The Grail. S. Keyes. [Supp 2/413]
The **Artist**. A. Grissom. [Volume 6/384]
"**Art's** use; what is it but to touch the springs." Art.
　G. Parker. [Volume 6/345]
**Arvio, Sarah (tr.)**
It Can Happen. V. Huidobro. [Supp 6/120]
"**As** a child holds a pet." Port Bou. S. Spender. [Supp
　2/231]
"**As** a naked man I go." In Waste Places. J. Stephens.
　[Supp 1/286]
As a Plane Tree by the Water. R. Lowell. [Supp 2/387]
"**As** a young woman, who had known her? Tripping."
　Burial: 004. A. Walker. [Supp 4/226]
"**As** beautiful Kitty one morning was tripping." Kitty
　of Coleraine. C. Shanly. [Volume 2/132]
"**As** bust and hips." African China: 002. M. Tolson.
　[Supp 4/101]
"**As** By the Shore at Break of Day" T. Moore. [Volume
　8/138]
"**As** chimes that flow o'er shining seas." Far-Away. G.
　Sigerson. [Volume 6/183]
"**As** down breaks on the horns of my ox." Occupation. N.
　Hikmet. [Supp 7/308]
"**As** far as you can see, all is glittering gold."
　Short Song on Autumn Harvest. Li Chi. [Supp
　7/11]
"**As** he trudged along to school." The Story of Johnny-
　Head-In-Air. H. Hoffmann. [Volume 1/173]
"**As** i came wandering down Glen Spean." The Emigrant

Lassie. J. Blackie. [Volume 3/280]
"**As** I was walking all alane." The Twa Corbies.
　Unknown. [Volume 9/126]
"**As** in a wheel, all sinks, to reascend." Matter and
　Man Immortal, fr. Night Thoughts. E. Young.
　[Volume 4/406]
"**As** Jesus and his followers." The Boy Out of Church.
　R. Graves. [Supp 1/152]
"**As** on my bed at dawn I mused and prayed." Sunrise. C.
　Turner. [Volume 4/20]
"**As** one that for a weary space has lain." The Odyssey.
　A. Lang. [Volume 6/342]
"**As** one who cons at evening o'er an album all." An
　Old Sweetheart Of Mine. J. Riley. [Volume
　2/372]
"**As** One Who Wanders into Old Workings" C. Day Lewis.
　[Supp 2/110]
"**As** ships, becalmed at eve, that lay." Qua Cursum
　Ventus. A. Clough. [Volume 3/107]
"**As** Slow Our Ship" T. Moore. [Volume 3/106]
"**As** some lone miser visiting his store." East, West,
　Home's Best, fr. The Traveller. O. Goldsmith.
　[Volume 8/7]
"**As** the blue wings." The Elephant & the Butterfly
　Meet on the Buddha's Birthday. D. Wakoski.
　[Supp 5/320]
"**As** the companion is dead." Vigil. C. Meireles. [Supp
　5/162]
"**As** the dark cloud passed, I." Tablet. A. Shamlu.
　[Supp 7/207]
"**As** the gook woman howls." In the Mourning Time. R.
　Hayden. [Supp 4/138]
"**As** then the tulip of her morning sup." Rubaiyat: 040.
　O. Khayyam. [Volume 6/211]
"**As** under cover of departing day." Rubaiyat: 082. O.
　Khayyam. [Volume 6/220]
"**As** when, on Carmel's sterile steep." The Little
　Cloud. J. Bryant. [Volume 8/168]
**Ascending** Scale. M. Piercy. [Supp 5/202]
**Ascending** the Wildgoose Tower. Feng Chih. [Supp 7/2]
The **Ascent** of Man. R. Raymond. [Volume 6/202]
**Ascription**. C. Roberts. [Volume 4/134]
**Ashes** of Roses. E. Eastman. [Volume 3/51]
**Asian** Birds. R. Bridges. [Volume 5/328]
"**Ask** me no more where Jove bestows." A Song. T. Carew
　[Volume 2/36]
**Askewe, Anne**
The Fight of Faith. [Volume 4/136]
**Asleep**, Asleep. L. Bennett. [Volume 3/396]
"**Asleep**! asleep! men talk of 'sleep'" Asleep, Asleep.
　L. Bennett. [Volume 3/396]
**Assasination**. D. Lee. [Supp 4/212]
**Assimilation**. E. Manner. [Supp 5/148]
"The **Assyrian** came down like the wolf on the." The
　Destruction of Sennacherib, r. Hebrew Melodies.
　G. Byron. [Volume 8/183]
*Astrology*
Peace on Earth. W. Williams. [Supp 1/319]
*Astronomy*
The Undiscovered Planet. L. Lee. [Supp 2/343]
"**At** Arles in the Carlovingian days." The Ballad of
　Guibour, fr. Calendau. F. Mistral. [Volume
　7/327]
"**At** dinner she is hostess, I am host." The Family
　Skeleton, fr. Modern Love. G. Meredith. [Volume
　6/247]
At Epidaurus. L. Durrell. [Supp 2/257]
"**At** evening when the lamp is lit." The Land of Story-
　Books. R. Stevenson. [Volume 1/140]
"**At** Flores in the Azores Sir Richard Grenville lay."
　The Revenge. A. Tennyson. [Volume 7/383]
At Gibraltar. G. Woodberry. [Volume 8/439]
At Last. D. Mattera. [Supp 6/82]
"**At** midnight, in his guarded tent." Marco Bozzaris. F.
　Halleck. [Volume 8/200]

The Axe, fr. Malcolm's Katie. I. Crawford. [Volume 6/388]

"Ay, but I know." Unrequited Love, fr. Twelfth Night. W. Shakespeare. [Volume 3/9]

"Ay, tear her tattered ensign down!" "Old Ironsides" O. Holmes. [Volume 8/96]

**Ayton, Sir Robert**
Woman's Inconstancy. [Volume 3/71]

**Aytoun, William Edmonstoune**
The Broken Pitcher. [Volume 7/325]
The Execution of Montrose. [Volume 8/43]
The Heart of the Bruce. [Volume 7/420]

Babel Falls. A. Branch. [Supp 1/68]

The **Babie**. J. Rankin. [Volume 1/9]

*Babies*
Descending Figure: 2. The Sick Child. L. Gluck. [Supp 5/103]
Descending Figure: 3. For My Sister. L. Gluck. [Supp 5/103]
The First Year. E. Scovell. [Supp 2/188]
For a Christening: 001. A. Ridler. [Supp 2/273]
For a Christening: 002. A. Ridler. [Supp 2/274]
For a Christening: 003. A. Ridler. [Supp 2/274]
In a Storm. Li Ying. [Supp 7/17]
Little Brown Baby. P. Dunbar. [Supp 4/77]

The **Baby**. Kalidasa. [Volume 1/1]

The **Baby**. G. Macdonald. [Volume 1/4]

**Baby** Bell. T. Aldrich. [Volume 1/60]

**Baby** Louise. M. Eytinge. [Volume 1/21]

**Baby** May. W. Bennett. [Volume 1/17]

"The **baby** sits in her cradle." Silent Baby. E. Currier. [Volume 1/22]

"A **baby** was sleeping." The Angel's Whisper. S. Lover. [Volume 1/10]

**Baby** Zulma's Christmas Carol. A. Requier. [Volume 1/67]

"A **baby's** feet, like sea-shells pink." Etude Realiste. A. Swinburne. [Volume 1/8]

**Baby's** Shoes. W. Bennett. [Volume 1/66]

**Bachmann, Ingeborg**
Curriculum Vitae. M. Hamburger (tr.). [Supp 5/25]
Exile. M. Hamburger (tr.). [Supp 5/24]
Fog Land. M. Hamburger (tr.). [Supp 5/23]

Back. S. Tanikawa. [Supp 7/131]

"**Back** in the years when Phlagstaff, the dane, was." National Anthem. R. Newell. [Volume 9/415]

"**Back** to the flower-town, side by side." In Memory of Walter Savage Landor. A. Swinburne. [Volume 7/75]

*Backs*
Back. S. Tanikawa. [Supp 7/131]

"**Backward**, turn backward, O time, in your flight." Rock Me to Sleep. E. Akers. [Volume 1/284]

**Bacon, Francis**
The World. [Volume 3/151]

**Bacon, Leonard**
Colorado Morton's Ride. [Supp 1/21]

*Bacteria*
The World of Bacteria. H. Sakutaro. [Supp 7/105]

"**Bacteria's** legs, %bacteria's mouths." The World of Bacteria. H. Sakutaro. [Supp 7/105]

A **Bad** Dream. K. Raine. [Supp 5/227]

"A **bag** which was left and not only taken but turned away was not." A Frightful Release. G. Stein. [Supp 5/292]

**Bahe, Liz Sohappy**
Farewell. [Supp 4/322]

**Bailey, Philip James**
Death in Youth, fr. Festus. [Volume 3/428]
Life, fr. Festus. [Volume 4/407]
The Poet of Nature, fr. Festus. [Volume 6/334]

Youth and Love, fr. Festus. [Volume 1/252]

The **Bailiff's** Daughter of Islington. Unknown. [Volume 2/153]

**Baillie, Joanna**
The Heath-cock. [Volume 5/324]
Morning Song. [Volume 5/39]
Song, fr. Woo'd And Married And A. [Volume 2/411]

"The **bairnies** cuddle doon at night." Cuddle Doon. A. Anderson. [Volume 1/44]

**Baker, George Augustus**
Thoughts On The Commandments. [Volume 2/125]

The **Baker's** Tale, fr. The Hunting of the Snark. C. Dodgson. [Volume 9/456]

"A **bale-fire** kindled in the night." Carlyle and Emerson. M. Schuyler. [Volume 7/97]

"The **ball** no question makes of ayes and noes." Rubaiyat: 070. O. Khayyam. [Volume 6/217]

"A **ball** of fire shoots through the tamarack." The Scarlet Tanager. J. Benton. [Volume 5/329]

The **Ballad** of Agincourt. M. Drayton. [Volume 8/264]

The **Ballad** of Bouillabaisse. W. Thackeray. [Volume 1/393]

The **Ballad** of Dead Ladies. F. Villon. [Volume 6/192]

The **Ballad** of Guibour, fr. Calendau. F. Mistral. [Volume 7/327]

The **Ballad** of Judas Iscariot. R. Buchanan. [Volume 6/90]

The **Ballad** of Prose and Rhyme. A. Dobson. [Volume 6/340]

**Ballad** of the Goodly Fere. E. Pound. [Supp 1/249]

**Ballad** of the Long-Legged Bait. D. Thomas. [Supp 2/353]

**Ballad** of the Ten Casino Dancers. C. Meireles. [Supp 5/163]

A **Ballad** of Trees and the Master. S. Lanier. [Volume 4/69]

**Ballade** of Midsummer Days and Nights. W. Henley. [Volume 5/112]

**Ballantine, James**
Ilka Blade O' Grass Keps Its Ain Drap O' Dew. [Volume 3/241]
Muckle-Mou'd Meg. [Volume 7/418]

"**Balow**, my babe, ly still and sleipe!" Lady Ann Bothwell's Lament. Unknown. [Volume 3/47]

"**Bananas** ripe and green, and ginger root." The Tropics in New York. C. McKay. [Supp 4/86]

**Banda, Innocent**
Lindedi Singing. [Supp 6/27]
Malawi. [Supp 6/25]
"May Bright Mushrooms Grow" [Supp 6/29]
"Where Is the Fruit" [Supp 6/26]

**Banim, John**
Soggarth Aroon. [Volume 4/170]

**Banks, George Linnaeus**
What I Live For. [Volume 4/186]

The **Banks** O' Doon. R. Burns. [Volume 3/12]

**Bannockburn**. R. Burns. [Volume 8/304]

**Banty** Tim. J. Hay. [Volume 9/366]

"The **banyan's** branching clerestories close." The Jungle: 003. A. Lewis. [Supp 2/376]

**Barbara** Frietchie. J. Whittier. [Volume 8/362]

**Barbauld, Anna Letitia**
Life. [Volume 3/400]
The Poor Man's Day, fr. The Sabbath. [Volume 4/193]
Praise to God. [Volume 4/40]

*Barbers*
Haircut. K. Shapiro. [Supp 2/321]

**Barbier, Auguste**
The Bronze Statue of Napoleon. [Volume 8/232]

**Barclay, Alexander (tr.)**
Of Hym That Togyder Wyll Serve Two Maysters. S. Brandt. [Volume 4/217]

**Barclay** of Ury. J. Whittier. [Volume 7/429]

The **Bard**. T. Gray. [Volume 8/34]

Folding the Flocks. [Volume 5/359]
**Beaumont, Francis**
  Inscription on Melrose Abbey. [Volume 3/269]
  On the Tombs in Westminster Abbey. [Volume 3/269]
"**Beautiful** Evelyn Hope is dead." Evelyn Hope. R.
  Browning. [Volume 3/310]
"**Beautiful!** Sir, you may say so. Thar isn't."
  Chiquita. B. Harte. [Volume 5/371]
**Beautiful** Snow. J. Watson. [Volume 3/205]
"**Beautiful**, sublime, and glorious." The Sea. B.
  Barton. [Volume 5/377]
"**Beautiful** was the night. Behind the black wall."
  Moonlight on the Prairie, fr. Evangeline. H.
  Longfellow. [Volume 5/61]
**Beauty**. L. Thurlow. [Volume 2/251]
*Beauty*
  Cold Term. L. Jones. [Supp 4/176]
  The Enamel Girl. G. Taggard. [Supp 1/292]
  Leisure. W. Davies. [Supp 1/105]
  Multitudinous Stars and Sping Waters: 002. Ping
    Hsin. [Supp 5/116]
  Romantic Fool. H. Monro. [Supp 1/224]
  You or I? I. Shabaka. [Supp 7/260]
**Beauty**, fr. An Hymne in Honor of Beautie. E. Spenser.
  [Volume 6/282]
**Beauty** Unadorned, fr. Elegies. S. Propertius. [Volume
  6/282]
"**Because** both dad and mom." Let Me Tell You About
  Myself. T. Tomioka. [Supp 7/138]
"**Because** he had spoken harshly to his mother."
  Revelation. R. Warren. [Supp 2/131]
"**Because** I breathe not love to eyerie one." Love's
  Silence. S. Sidney. [Volume 2/73]
**Because** of You. A. Hamzah. [Supp 7/88]
"**Because** the sadness pursued me." News. G. Fuertes.
  [Supp 5/98]
"**Because** there was a man somewhere in a candystripe
  silk shirt." Homage to the Empress of the Blues.
  R. Hayden. [Supp 4/136]
"**Because** we live in the browning season." Kopis'taya
  (A Gathering of Spirits). P. Allen. [Supp
  4/305]
**Beddoes, Thomas Lovell**
  To Sea! [Volume 5/410]
**Bedouin** Love-Song. B. Taylor. [Volume 2/264]
**Bedtime**. F. Erskine; Earl of Rosslyn. [Volume 1/39]
**Beers, Ethel Lynn**
  Weighing the Baby. [Volume 1/5]
**Beers, Ethelinda Elliott**
  "All Quiet Along the Potomac" [Volume 8/350]
**Beers, Henry Augustin**
  The Singer of One Song. [Volume 6/343]
**Beethoven's** Third Symphony. R. Hovey. [Volume 6/379]
"**Before** I sigh my last gasp, let me breathe." The
  Will. J. Donne. [Volume 6/295]
"**Before** I tell you." Yellowstone. F. Lima. [Supp
  4/247]
"**Before** I trust my fate to thee." A Woman's Question.
  A. Procter. [Volume 2/248]
"**Before** proud Rome's imperial throne." Caractacus. B.
  Barton. [Volume 8/190]
**Before** Sedan. A. Dobson. [Volume 9/101]
"**Before** she first had smiled or looked with calm."
  The First Year. E. Scovell. [Supp 2/188]
"**Before** the hand is recognized the door is secretly
  pushed." New-Born Blackness. Lo Fu. [Supp 7/26]
"**Before** the phantom of false morning died." Rubaiyat:
  002. O. Khayyam. [Volume 6/204]
**Before** the Rain. T. Aldrich. [Volume 5/117]
"**Before** the Roman came to Rye or out of Severn." The
  Rolling English Road. G. Chesterton. [Supp
  1/81]
"**Before** the spring had flowered away full summer
  burst." A Berkshire Holiday. C. Bax. [Supp
  1/29]

"**Before** this generous time." The Finding of Love. R.
  Graves. [Supp 1/150]
"**Before** thy throne we bow." The Nation's Prayer. C.
  Kennedy. [Volume 8/102]
The **Beggar**. T. Moss. [Volume 3/189]
The **Beginning**. D. Pagis. [Supp 7/251]
"**Begotten** by the meeting of rock with rock." Sea
  Holly. C. Aiken. [Supp 1/12]
"**Behave** Yoursel' Before Folk" A. Rodger. [Volume
  2/114]
**Behind** Bars, sel. F. Tuqan. [Supp 5/305]
"**Behold**, I have a weapon." Othello's Remorse, fr.
  Othello. W. Shakespeare. [Volume 9/67]
"**Behold** the mansion reared by daedal Jack." The
  Modern House that Jack Built. Unknown. [Volume
  9/396]
"**Behold** the sea." The Sea. R. Emerson. [Volume 5/374]
"**Behold** this ruin! 'T was a skull." To a Skeleton.
  Unknown. [Volume 6/298]
"**Behold** where beauty walks with peace!" A California
  Christmas. J. Miller. [Volume 6/279]
"A **being** cleaves the moonlit air." Hans Christian
  Andersen. E. Gosse. [Volume 7/43]
**Belagcholly** Days. Unknown. [Volume 9/420]
A **Belated** Violet. O. Herford. [Volume 1/154]
The **Belfry** Pigeon. N. Willis. [Volume 5/325]
"**Believe** Me, If All Those Endearing Young Charms" T.
  Moore. [Volume 2/336]
**Belinda**, fr. rape of the lock. A. Pope. [Volume 2/14]
**Bell, Lindolf**
  On a Poem's Circumstances. R. Zenith (tr.). [Supp
  6/109]
  Poem to a Young Man. W. Smith (tr.). [Supp 6/108]
"The **bell** strikes one: we take no note of time." Time
  of the Supreme, fr. Night Thoughts. E. Young.
  [Volume 6/187]
The **Belle** of the Ball. W. Praed. [Volume 9/207]
**Belli, Carlos German**
  "Tongue-Tied or Stuttering" M. Ahern (tr.). [Supp
  6/185]
**Belli, Gioconda**
  Dressed in Dynamite. R. McCarthy (tr.). [Supp
  6/152]
**Belloc, Hilaire**
  The Night. [Supp 1/33]
  Sonnet 018. [Supp 1/33]
  The South Country. [Supp 1/31]
The **Bells**. E. Poe. [Volume 7/141]
*Bells*
  "Bells of Grey Crystal" E. Sitwell. [Supp 5/271]
  Bredon hill. A. Housman. [Supp 1/166]
  The Golden Corpse. S. Benet. [Supp 1/42]
  King David. S. Benet. [Supp 1/34]
"**Bells** crack ice, white cattle." Mountain Abbey,
  Surrounded by Elk Horns. C. Forche. [Supp 5/83]
"**Bells** of Grey Crystal" E. Sitwell. [Supp 5/271]
The **Bells** of Shandon. F. Mahony. [Volume 7/145]
"The **bells** of the churches are ringing." The
  Children's Church. K. Gerrock. [Volume 1/115]
"**Beloved** %where I have been." Poem: On Your Love. J.
  Jordan. [Supp 5/127]
"**Belshazzar** had a letter." Found Wanting. E.
  Dickinson. [Volume 4/326]
"**Ben** Battle was a soldier bold." Faithless Nelly Gray.
  T. Hood. [Volume 9/268]
**Ben** Bolt. T. English. [Volume 1/222]
"**Bending**, I bow my head." Combing. G. Cardiff. [Supp
  4/247]
"**Beneath** a shivering canopy reclined." Noontide. J.
  Leyden. [Volume 5/46]
"**Beneath** an Indian Palm a girl." Palm and the Pine. H.
  Heine. [Volume 3/40]
"**Beneath** our consecrated elm." Washington, fr. Under
  the Elm. J. Lowell. [Volume 7/15]
"**Beneath** the poplars o'er the sacred pool." The

Suppliant. E. Gosse. [Supp 1/145]
"**Beneath** the shadow of dawn's aerial cope." Hope and
Fear. A. Swinburne. [Volume 1/256]
"**Beneath** the warrior's helm, behold." On an Intaglio
Head of Minerva. T. Aldrich. [Volume 6/383]
**Benedetti, Mario**
Against Drawbridges: 001. R. Marquez and Elinor
Randall (tr.). [Supp 6/191]
Against Drawbridges: 002. R. Marquez and Elinor
Randall (tr.). [Supp 6/192]
Against Drawbridges: 003. R. Marquez and Elinor
Randall (tr.). [Supp 6/193]
**Benedicite**. J. Whittier. [Volume 1/356]
**Benet, Stephen Vincent**
The Golden Corpse. [Supp 1/42]
King David. [Supp 1/34]
**Benet, William Rose**
The Falconer of God. [Supp 1/46]
"There Lived a Lady in Milan" [Supp 1/47]
**Benjamin, Park**
The Old Sexton. [Volume 3/282]
**Bennett, G.**
The Time for Prayer. [Volume 4/112]
**Bennett, Henry Holcomb**
The Flag Goes By. [Volume 8/108]
**Bennett, Lucy A.**
Asleep, Asleep. [Volume 3/396]
**Bennett, William Cox**
Baby May. [Volume 1/17]
Baby's Shoes. [Volume 1/66]
Invocation to Rain In Summer. [Volume 5/113]
The Worn Wedding-Ring. [Volume 2/438]
**Benton, Joel**
December. [Volume 5/175]
The Scarlet Tanager. [Volume 5/329]
**Benton, Myron B.**
The Mowers. [Volume 7/249]
The **Bereaved** Swan. S. Smith. [Supp 2/102]
**Berkeley, Bishop George**
On the Prospect of Planting Arts and Learning in
America. [Volume 8/91]
A **Berkshire** Holiday. C. Bax. [Supp 1/29]
**Bernardo** Del Carpio. F. Hemans. [Volume 9/85]
**Berryman, John**
Canto Amor. [Supp 2/327]
The Song of the Demented Priest. [Supp 2/329]
**Berssenbrugge, Mei-mei**
Fish and Swimmer and Lonely Birds Sweep Past Us.
[Supp 4/11]
Poor Mouse. [Supp 4/10]
Spring Street Bar. [Supp 4/12]
"**Beside** the dead i knelt for prayer." Christus
Consolator. R. Raymond. [Volume 3/432]
"**Beside** the old hall-fire - upon my nurse's knee."
Fairy Days. W. Thackeray. [Volume 1/141]
"**Besieged** by the deaths of all its afternoons
forever." The Uninhabited City: 001. E.
Cardenal. [Supp 6/153]
Beth Gelert. W. Spencer. [Volume 5/360]
**Bethune, George Washington**
"It Is Not Death To Die" [Volume 3/455]
**Betjeman, John**
Parliament Hill Fields. [Supp 2/136]
Upper Lambourne. [Supp 2/138]
Youth and Age on Beaulieu River, Hants. [Supp
2/138]
*Betrayals*
"It Was a Funky Deal" E. Knight. [Supp 4/173]
Song. S. Spender. [Supp 2/233]
Spirit's Song. L. Bogan. [Supp 5/34]
**Betrothed** Anew. E. Stedman. [Volume 5/92]
"**Better** to see your cheek grown hollow." Madman's
Song. E. Wylie. [Supp 5/336]
"**Better** trust all and be deceived." Faith. F. Kemble-
Butler. [Volume 3/95]

"**Between** nose and eyes a strange contest arose." The
Nose and the Eyes. W. Cowper. [Volume 9/310]
"**Between** Rita & my eyes is a gun." Rita & the Gun. M.
Darwish. [Supp 7/263]
"**Between** the falling leaf and rose-bud's breath." The
Term of Death. S. Piatt. [Volume 3/261]
"**Between** the sandhills and the sea." A Parable. M.
Blind. [Volume 1/95]
"**Between** the stag and the little gazelle." Wild
Ballad. G. Fuertes. [Supp 5/93]
**Between** the World and Me. R. Wright. [Supp 2/212]
"**Between** two golden tufts of summer grass." Lying in
the Grass. E. Gosse. [Volume 1/225]
**Beware**. Unknown. [Volume 1/235]
**Beyond** Ashes. Lo Fu. [Supp 7/28]
**Beyond** Good and Evil. G. Woodberry. [Supp 1/322]
**Beyond** the Sea. Lo Fu. [Supp 7/27]
"**Beyond** the Smiling and the Weeping" H. Bonar.
[Volume 3/378]
"**Beyond** the sunset and the amber sea." Ode to Sleep.
P. Hayne. [Volume 6/439]
"**Beyond** these chiling winds and gloomy skies." Heaven.
N. Priest. [Volume 4/410]
**Beyong** the Whip. Lo Fu. [Supp 7/29]
*Bible*
Babel Falls. A. Branch. [Supp 1/68]
Middle Passage. R. Hayden. [Supp 4/142]
Nimrod Wars with the Angels. A. Branch. [Supp
1/67]
**Bich; Burton Raffel and W.S. Merwin, Nguyen Ngoc
(tr.)**
Eternal Struggle. Tru Vu. [Supp 7/198]
Green Nostalgia. The Lu. [Supp 7/191]
Little Luom. To Huu. [Supp 7/196]
Necessity. Nguyen Sa. [Supp 7/189]
Nightmare. The Lu. [Supp 7/193]
No Time. Nguyen Sa. [Supp 7/190]
Road Sabotage. To Huu. [Supp 7/194]
Since Then. To Huu. [Supp 7/194]
The Statue of the Century. Tru Vu. [Supp 7/198]
Who Am I? Tru Vu. [Supp 7/199]
"The **bier** descends, the spotless roses too." Jeune
Fille Et Jeune Fleur. F. Auguste. [Volume
3/305]
**Bill** and Joe, fr. Poems of the Class of 'Twenty-nine.
O. Holmes. [Volume 1/341]
**Bingen** on the Rhine. C. Norton. [Volume 8/221]
**Binyon, Laurence**
John Winter. [Supp 1/50]
The Sirens, sel. [Supp 1/53]
**Bion**
I Dreamt I Saw Great Venus. L. Hunt (tr.). [Volume
2/98]
The **Birch** Stream. A. Tennyson. [Volume 5/199]
*Birch Trees*
Birches. R. Frost. [Supp 1/131]
The Turning of the Leaves. V. Watkins. [Supp
2/191]
**Birches**. R. Frost. [Supp 1/131]
The **Bird**. Adonis. [Supp 7/284]
"**Bird** of the wilderness." The Skylark. J. Hogg.
[Volume 5/301]
"The **bird** said: 'What smells what sunshine, ah'" The
Bird Was Only a Bird. F. Farrozkhzad. [Supp
7/220]
"The **bird** that soars on highest wing." Humility. J.
Montgomery. [Volume 4/148]
The **Bird** Was Only a Bird. F. Farrozkhzad. [Supp
7/220]
*Birds*
The Bird Was Only a Bird. F. Farrozkhzad. [Supp
7/220]
The Bird. Adonis. [Supp 7/284]
Crowned Crane. Unknown (African American). [Supp
6/2]

Brahma. R. Emerson. [Volume 4/6]
Brainard, John Gardiner Calkins
    The Fall of Niagara. [Volume 5/208]
    "I Saw Two Clouds At Morning" [Volume 2/259]
Branch, Anna Hempstead
    Babel Falls. [Supp 1/68]
    Nimrod Wars with the Angels. [Supp 1/67]
    "Shame on Thee, O Manhattan" [Supp 1/71]
Branch, Mary L. Bolles
    The Petrified Fern. [Volume 6/200]
"The branches break. the beaters." A World withing a
    War: 005. H. Read. [Supp 2/42]
Brandt, Sebastian
    Of Hym That Togyder Wyll Serve Two Maysters. A.
    Barclay (tr.). [Volume 4/217]
The Brave at Home. T. Read. [Volume 8/109]
The Brave Old Oak. H. Chorley. [Volume 5/220]
*Bread*
    Our Daily Bread. C. Vallejo. [Supp 6/188]
Bread-Word Giver. J. Wheelwright. [Supp 2/53]
"Break, Break, Break" A. Tennyson. [Volume 3/358]
"Break, fantasy, from the cave of cloud." Fantasy, fr.
    The Vision of Delight. B. Johnson. [Volume
    6/3]
"Breakfast at Cindy's place." Kicking Lego Blocks:
    008. S. Wong. [Supp 4/17]
"Breakfast is drunk ... moist earth." Our Daily Bread.
    C. Vallejo. [Supp 6/188]
"The breaking waves dashed high." The Landing of the
    Pilgrim Fathers in New England. F. Hemans.
    [Volume 8/150]
Breath. B. Diop. [Supp 6/67]
"The breath of dew, and twilight's grace." A Friend's
    Song for Simoisius. L. Guiney. [Supp 1/154]
"Breathe, trumpets, breathe." Requiem. G. Lunt.
    [Volume 8/388]
Breathes There the Man?, fr. The Lay of the Last
    Minstrel. S. Scott. [Volume 8/4]
"Breathes there the man with soul so dead." Breathes
    There the Man?, fr. The Lay of the Last
    Minstrel. S. Scott. [Volume 8/4]
"Breathing the thin breath through our nostrils, we."
    The Generous Air. Palladas. [Volume 6/229]
Bredon hill. A. Housman. [Supp 1/166]
Brenan, Joseph
    "Come To Me, Dearest" [Volume 3/144]
Breton, Nicholas
    "I Would I Were An Excellent Divine" [Volume
    4/312]
    Phillida and Corydon. [Volume 2/152]
The Bride, fr. A Ballad Upon A Wedding. S. Suckling.
    [Volume 2/410]
A Bride in the '30's. W. Auden. [Supp 2/154]
"The bride she is winsome and bonny." Song, fr. Woo'd
    And Married And A. J. Baillie. [Volume 2/411]
The Bridge. S. Murano. [Supp 7/120]
The Bridge of Sighs. T. Hood. [Volume 3/208]
*Bridges*
    The Bridge. S. Murano. [Supp 7/120]
Bridges, Madeline [pseud.] See De Vere, Mary Ainge
Bridges, Robert
    Dejection. [Supp 1/73]
    For a Novel of Hall Caine's. [Volume 9/460]
    "I Will Not Let Thee Go" [Supp 1/72]
    "So Sweet Love Seemed That April Morn" [Supp 1/75]
    "The Unillumined Verge" [Volume 3/308]
    The Windmill. [Supp 1/74]
Bridges, Robert Seymour
    Asian Birds. [Volume 5/328]
    The Sea-poppy. [Volume 5/285]
    So Sweet Love Seemed. [Volume 2/326]
Brief: The Widow's Mites. R. Crashaw. [Volume 4/306]
Brief: "Two Went Up to the Temple to Pray" R. Crashaw.
    [Volume 4/306]
Brief: Water Turned Into Wine. R. Crashaw. [Volume

4/306]
The Brier-wood Pipe. C. Shanly. [Volume 6/317]
"Bright drips the morning from its trophied nets."
    Sonnet of Fishes. G. Barker. [Supp 2/291]
"Bright moon-- %all grief, sorrow, loneliness
    completed." Multitudinous Stars and Spring
    Waters: 008. Ping Hsin. [Supp 5/117]
"Bright star! would I were steadfast as thou art."
    Keats's Last Sonnet. J. Keats. [Volume 2/360]
"Brightest and best of the sons of the morning."
    Epiphany. R. Heber. [Volume 4/50]
"The brilliant black eye." Black and Blue Eyes. T.
    Moore. [Volume 2/39]
"Bringer of wealth." To the Rain. Unknown (African
    American). [Supp 6/9]
*Britain*
    Mort D'Arthur. A. Tennyson. [Volume 7/352]
*British Museum*
    Homage to the British Museum. W. Empson. [Supp
    2/141]
Broken Mirror. Yung Tzu. [Supp 7/35]
Broken Music. T. Aldrich. [Volume 6/346]
The Broken Pitcher. W. Aytoun. [Volume 7/325]
Bronchitis: The Rosario Beach House, 001. A.
    Rodriguez. [Supp 4/279]
Bronchitis: The Rosario Beach House, 002. A.
    Rodriguez. [Supp 4/280]
Bronchitis: The Rosario Beach House, 003. A.
    Rodriguez. [Supp 4/280]
Bronchitis: The Rosario Beach House, 004. A.
    Rodriguez. [Supp 4/281]
Bronchitis: The Rosario Beach House, 005. A.
    Rodriguez. [Supp 4/282]
The Bronze Statue of Napoleon. A. Barbier. [Volume
    8/232]
Brooke, Rupert
    The Great Lover. [Supp 1/80]
    The Old Vicarage, Grantchester. [Supp 1/76]
    The Soldier. [Supp 1/76]
The Brooklyn Bridge. E. Proctor. [Volume 7/247]
*Brooks and Streams. See Inland Waters*
Brooks, Charles Timothy (tr.)
    The Fisher. J. Goethe. [Volume 6/78]
    Harvest Song. L. Holty. [Volume 5/150]
    Max and Maurice, sel. W. Busch. [Volume 1/184]
    Men and Boys. K. Korner. [Volume 8/78]
    The Nobleman and the Pensioner. G. Pfeffel.
    [Volume 7/303]
    Sword Song. K. Korner. [Volume 8/217]
    Winter. M. Claudius. [Volume 5/172]
    Winter Song. L. Holty. [Volume 5/186]
    The Wives of Weinsberg. G. Burger. [Volume 9/200]
Brooks, Gwendolyn
    The Bean Eaters. [Supp 4/158]
    Jessie Mitchell's Mother. [Supp 5/41]
    "Life for My Child Is Simple and Is Good" [Supp
    4/162]
    Mrs. Small. [Supp 5/39]
    The Murder. [Supp 5/37]
    The Second Sermon on the Warpland. [Supp 4/160]
    The Sermon on the Warpland. [Supp 4/159]
    A Song in the Front Yard. [Supp 5/36]
    "Strong Men, Riding Horses" [Supp 5/38]
    A Sunset of the City. [Supp 5/42]
    To a Winter Squirrel. [Supp 5/44]
    "We Real Cool" [Supp 5/39]
    When You Have Forgotten Sunday: The Love Story.
    [Supp 4/156]
Brooks, Maria Gowen ("Maria del Occidente")
    Song of Eglia. [Volume 3/138]
Brooks, Phillips
    "O Little Town of Bethlehem" [Volume 4/47]
The Brookside. R. Milnes. [Volume 2/156]
"Brother, consider as you go your way." Somebody and
    Somebody Else and You. E. Rolfe. [Supp 2/220]

When My Ship Comes In. [Volume 3/245]
**Burger, Gottfried August**
  The Wives of Weinsberg. C. Brooks (tr.). [Volume 9/200]
**Burgess, Gelett**
  Phycholophon. [Volume 9/456]
  The Purple Cow. [Volume 9/455]
**Burial:** 001. A. Walker. [Supp 4/225]
**Burial:** 002. A. Walker. [Supp 4/225]
**Burial:** 003. A. Walker. [Supp 4/226]
**Burial:** 004. A. Walker. [Supp 4/226]
**Burial:** 005. A. Walker. [Supp 4/227]
**Burial:** 006. A. Walker. [Supp 4/227]
Burial of Moses. C. Alexander. [Volume 4/365]
The **Burial** of Robert Browning. M. Field. [Volume 7/89]
Burial of Sir John Moore. C. Wolfe. [Volume 8/283]
**Burleigh, William H.**
  Deborah Lee. [Volume 9/400]
"Burly, dozing humblebee!" To the Humblebee. R. Emerson. [Volume 5/342]
Burning Oneself to Death. S. Takahashi. [Supp 7/126]
**Burns.** E. Elliott. [Volume 7/63]
**Burns.** J. Whittier. [Volume 7/64]
**Burns, Robert**
  Address to the Toothache. [Volume 9/307]
  "Ae Fond Kiss Before We Part" [Volume 3/98]
  Afton Water. [Volume 5/202]
  Auld Lang Syne. [Volume 1/405]
  The Banks O' Doon. [Volume 3/12]
  Bannockburn. [Volume 8/304]
  A Bard's Epitaph. [Volume 7/113]
  Comin' Through The Rye. [Volume 2/108]
  The Cotter's Saturday Night. [Volume 1/300]
  "The Day Returns, My Bosom Burns" [Volume 2/422]
  "Duncan Gray Cam' Here To Woo" [Volume 2/178]
  Elegy on Captain Matthew Henderson. [Volume 1/363]
  For A' That and A' That. [Volume 6/398]
  "Green Grow The Rashes O" [Volume 2/91]
  Highland Mary. [Volume 3/329]
  I Love My Jean. [Volume 3/126]
  John Anderson, My Jo. [Volume 2/460]
  "Let Not Woman E'er Complain" [Volume 2/219]
  "My Heart's in the Highlands" [Volume 8/39]
  My Wife's A Winsome Wee Thing. [Volume 2/420]
  "O, My Luve's Like a Red, Red Rose" [Volume 3/99]
  "O, Say Ye Bonnie Leslie?" [Volume 3/130]
  Tam O' Shanter. [Volume 6/70]
  To a Louse. [Volume 5/348]
  To a Mountain Daisy. [Volume 5/277]
  To a Mouse. [Volume 5/350]
  To Mary in Heaven. [Volume 3/339]
  To the Unco Guid. [Volume 4/320]
  Whistle, and I'll Come To You, My Lad. [Volume 2/109]
**Burroughs, John**
  To the Lapland Longspur. [Volume 5/314]
  Waiting. [Volume 3/238]
**Burton, Richard**
  The Polar Quest. [Volume 5/421]
**Busch, Wilhelm**
  Max and Maurice, sel. C. Brooks (tr.). [Volume 1/184]
"Busy, curious, thirsty fly." The Fly. W. Oldys. [Volume 5/341]
"The busy day is over." The Happy Hour. M. Butts. [Volume 1/12]
"The busy larke, messager of daye." Morning in May, fr. The Canterbury Pilgrims. G. Chaucer. [Volume 5/89]
"The busy routine kills the flowers." A World withing a War: 003. H. Read. [Supp 2/39]
"But chief - surpassing all - a cuckoo clock!" The Cuckoo Clock, fr. The Birthday. C. Southey. [Volume 7/148]

"But even as you wait." The Contrary Experience: 002. H. Read. [Supp 2/33]
But for Lust. R. Pitter. [Supp 2/48]
"But for lust we could be friends." But for Lust. R. Pitter. [Supp 2/48]
"But fortune, like some others of her sex." Fortune, fr. Fanny. F. Halleck. [Volume 6/266]
"But God sent forth a pale and spectral host." Nimrod Wars with the Angels. A. Branch. [Supp 1/67]
"But happy they! the happiest of their kind!" Connubial Life, fr. The Seasons: Spring. J. Thomson. [Volume 2/430]
But He Was Cool. D. Lee. [Supp 4/216]
"But helpless pieces of the game he plays." Rubaiyat: 069. O. Khayyam. [Volume 6/217]
"But i remained, whose hopes were dim." The Dead Friend: 84, fr. In Memoriam. A. Tennyson. [Volume 1/361]
"But if in vain, down on the stubborn floor." Rubaiyat: 053. O. Khayyam. [Volume 6/214]
"But it could never be true." Devil's Dream. K. Fearing. [Supp 2/98]
"But Look %But Look" N. Sachs. [Supp 5/251]
"But now a queen is walking by." The Waitress. B. Akhmadulina. [Supp 5/2]
"But now, my boys, leave off and." The School of War, fr. Tamburlaine. C. Marlowe. [Volume 8/185]
"But now our quacks are gamesters, and they play." Quack Medicines, fr. The Borough. G. Crabbe. [Volume 6/287]
"But the majestic river floated on." Oxus, fr. Sohrab and Rustum. M. Arnold. [Volume 5/207]
"But t' is not thus, - and 't is not here." Verse. G. Byron. [Volume 3/170]
"But to reach the archimedean point." Mysticism Has Not the Patience to Wait for God's Revelation R. Eberhart. [Supp 2/128]
"But what of this? are we not all in." Love and Woman, fr. Love's Labor's Lost. W. Shakespeare. [Volume 2/65]
"But who the melodies of morn can tell?" Morning, fr. The Minstrel. T. Heywood. [Volume 5/42]
"'But why do you go?' said the lady, while both." Lord Walter's Wife. E. Browning. [Volume 2/392]
**Butler, Samuel**
  Hudibras; Sword and Dagger, fr. Hudibras. [Volume 9/254]
  The Religion of Hudibras, fr. Hudibras. [Volume 4/228]
**Butler, William Allen**
  "Nothing to Wear" [Volume 9/213]
**Butts, Mary Frances**
  The Happy Hour. [Volume 1/12]
"Buwayb ... %Buwayb ... %bells in a tower lost on the seabed." The River an Death. B. Al-Sayyab. [Supp 7/233]
"The buzz-saw snarled and rattled in the yard." "Out, Out--" R. Frost. [Supp 1/133]
"By an alley lined with tumble-down shacks." Arizona Poems: Mexican Quarter. J. Fletcher. [Supp 1/127]
"By broad Potomac's silent shore." George Washington. Unknown. [Volume 7/15]
"By Cavite on the bay." The Battle of Manila. R. Hovey. [Volume 8/421]
"By chance I saw him die, stretched on the ground." Elegy for a Dead Soldier: 004. K. Shapiro. [Supp 2/315,War]
"By Cool Siloam's Shady Rill" R. Herber. [Volume 1/122]
"By divination came the Dorians." In Arcadia. L. Durrell. [Supp 2/259]
"By Nebo's lonely mountain." Burial of Moses. C. Alexander. [Volume 4/365]
"By night they haunted a thicket of April mist."

Spectral Lovers. J. Ransom. [Supp 1/258]
**By the Alma River.** D. Craik. [Volume 8/292]
"By the fire that loves to tint her." Her Guitar. F.
    Sherman. [Volume 2/44]
**By the Fireside.** L. Larcom. [Volume 1/293]
"By the flow of the inland river." The Blue and the
    Gray. F. Finch. [Volume 8/455]
"By the gate with star and moon." Medallion. S. Plath.
    [Supp 5/210]
"By the merest chance, in the twilight gloom." What
    My Lover Said. H. Greene. [Volume 2/279]
"By the old Moulein Pagoda, lookin' eastward to the."
    Mandalay. R. Kipling. [Supp 1/180]
"By the rude bridge that arched the flood." Hymn. R.
    Emerson. [Volume 8/326]
"By the wayside, on a mossy stone." Old. R. Hoyt.
    [Volume 3/180]
"By then your hands will be stiff." We're Ready. C.
    Anwar. [Supp 7/81]
**Byers, Samuel Hawkins Marshall**
    Sherman's March to the Sea. [Volume 8/406]
**Byrant, William Cullen**
    The Death of the Flowers. [Volume 5/255]
    The Planting of the Apple-tree. [Volume 5/232]
    The Snow-shower. [Volume 5/178]
    Song of Marion's Men. [Volume 8/330]
**Byron,** fr. The Course of Time. R. Pollok. [Volume
    7/59]
**Byron, George Gordon, 6th Baron**
    "Adieu, Adieu! My Native Shore" [Volume 3/108]
    Calm on Lake Leman, fr. Childe Harold. [Volume
        5/211]
    The Coliseum, fr. Childe Harold. [Volume 7/178]
    The Destruction of Sennacherib. r. Hebrew Melodies.
        [Volume 8/183]
    The Dream. [Volume 3/73]
    Evening, fr. Don Juan. [Volume 5/57]
    Fallen Greece, fr. The Giaour. [Volume 8/125]
    Farewell to His Wife. [Volume 3/109]
    First Love, fr. "Don Juan," Canto I. [Volume
        2/256]
    The Girl of Cadiz. [Volume 2/28]
    Greece Enslaved, fr. Childe Harold. [Volume 8/127]
    "Maid of Athens, Ere We Part" [Volume 3/100]
    Napoleon, fr. Childe Harold. [Volume 7/9]
    Night, fr. Childe Harold. [Volume 5/65]
    The Orient, fr. The Bride of Abydos. [Volume
        7/164]
    The Pantheon, fr. Childe Harold. [Volume 7/181]
    A Picture of Death, fr. The Giaour. [Volume 3/261]
    The Poet's Impulse, fr. Childe Harold's Pilgrimage.
        [Volume 6/335]
    The Prisoner of Chillon. [Volume 9/88]
    The Rhine, fr. Childe Harolde. [Volume 7/169]
    Saint Peter's at Rome, fr. Childe Harold. [Volume
        7/186]
    The Sea, fr. Childe Harold. [Volume 5/375]
    She Walks in Beauty. [Volume 2/32]
    Song of the Greek Poet, fr. Don Juan. [Volume
        8/130]
    Stanzas. [Volume 2/361]
    Storm in the Alps, fr. Childe Harold. [Volume
        5/213]
    Swimming, fr. The Two Foscari. [Volume 5/141]
    To Thomas Moore. [Volume 7/57]
    Verse. [Volume 3/169,Volume 3/170,Volume 3/171]
    Waterloo, fr. Childe Harold. [Volume 8/287]
    Wreck, fr. Don Juan. [Volume 5/416]
**Byron, George Gordon, 6th Baron (tr.)**
    Francesca Da Rimini, fr. Divina Commedia: Inferno.
        Dante Alighieri. [Volume 2/99]
**Byron, Lord (tr.)**
    Francesca Da Rimini, fr. Divina Commedia: Inferno.
        Dante Alighieri. [Volume 2/99]

C Stands for Civilization. K. Fearing. [Supp 2/97]
The **C. S.** Army's Commissary. E. Thompson. [Volume
    8/396]
"The **cactus** towers, straight and tall." In Mexico. E.
    Stein. [Volume 7/257]
**Caedmon.** L. Lee. [Supp 2/338]
**Calderon, Pedro**
    Dream-life, fr. Such Stuff as Dreams Are Made Of.
        E. Fitzgerald (tr.). [Volume 6/324]
**Caldwell, William W. (tr.)**
    The Rose-bush. Unknown. [Volume 6/233]
A **California** Christmas. J. Miller. [Volume 6/279]
**Caliph** and Satan. J. Clarke. [Volume 4/119]
The **Call.** G. Herbert. [Volume 4/144]
"Call it not vain: - they do not err." The Poet's
    Death, fr. The Lay of the Last Minstrel. S.
    Scott. [Volume 6/355]
"Call on, celebrate the beam." The Tears of a Muse
    in America: 001. F. Prince. [Supp 2/267]
"Call us islands in the river." Islands in the River.
    Agyeya. [Supp 7/45]
**Call, Wathen Marks Wilks**
    Summer Days. [Volume 2/341]
**Callimachus**
    The Dead Poet-friend. W. Cory (tr.). [Volume
        1/396]
"**Calm** is the morn witout a sound." The Peace of
    Sorrow, fr. In Memoriam. A. Tennyson. [Volume
    3/350]
**Calm** on Lake Leman, fr. Childe Harold. G. Byron.
    [Volume 5/211]
**Calvary** Song. R. Raymond. [Volume 8/366]
**Calvary** Song, fr. Alice of Monmouth. E. Stedman.
    [Volume 8/365]
**Calverley, Charles Stuart**
    The Arab. [Volume 9/413]
    The Auld Wife. [Volume 9/387]
    The Cock and the Bull. [Volume 9/402]
    Disaster. [Volume 9/441]
    "Forever" [Volume 9/424]
    Lovers, and a Reflections. [Volume 9/409]
    Motherhood. [Volume 9/440]
    Ode to Tobacco. [Volume 9/387]
    On the Brink. [Volume 9/443]
"The **Cambridge** ladies who live in furnished souls."
    Sonnet - Realities I. E. Cummings. [Volume 1/104]
"**Camoes,** alone, of all the lyric race." Louis De
    Camoes. R. Campbell. [Supp 2/94]
The **Camp** at Night, fr. The Illiad. Homer. [Volume
    5/62]
**Camp-bell.** W. Praed. [Volume 7/56]
**Campbell, Roy**
    Choosing a Mast. [Supp 2/92]
    Death of the Bull. [Supp 2/91]
    Louis De Camoes. [Supp 2/94]
    The Serf. [Supp 2/94]
    The Sisters. [Supp 2/95]
    Toledo, July 1936. [Supp 2/95]
**Campbell, Thomas**
    Battle of the Baltic. [Volume 8/281]
    Exile of Erin. [Volume 8/67]
    The First Kiss. [Volume 2/94]
    Hallowed Ground. [Volume 8/119]
    Hohenlinden. [Volume 8/225]
    Hope, fr. The Pleasures of Hope. [Volume 4/145]
    The Last Man. [Volume 4/361]
    Lord Ullin's Daughter. [Volume 7/399]
    Napoleon and the British Sailor. [Volume 7/347]
    Poland, fr. The Pleasures of Hope. [Volume 8/144]
    The Soldier's Dream. [Volume 1/280]
    Song of the Greeks. [Volume 8/197]
    To the Evening Star. [Volume 5/54]

"Ye Mariners of England!" [Volume 5/407]
*Camping*
　Camping Out. W. Empson. [Supp 2/140]
　"O Sister %Where Do You Pitch Your Tent?" N. Sachs.
　　[Supp 5/249]
**Camping** Out. W. Empson. [Supp 2/140]
**Campion, Thomas**
　Advice To A Girl. [Volume 2/242]
"**Can** we believe - by an effort." Cities. H. Doolittle.
　[Supp 5/68]
**Cana.** J. Clarke. [Volume 4/65]
**Canada.** C. Roberts. [Volume 8/71]
*Canada*
　At the Cedars. D. Scott. [Volume 9/178]
**Canada** Not Last. W. Schuyler-Lighthall. [Volume 8/70]
The **Cane-bottomed** Chair. W. Thackeray. [Volume 1/377]
**Canning, George**
　Epitaph. [Volume 9/292]
　The Friend of Humanity and the Knife-Grinder.
　　[Volume 9/398]
　Song of One Eleven Years in Prison. [Volume 9/294]
The **Canterbury** Pilgrims, fr. The Canterbury Tales. G.
　Chaucer. [Volume 7/363]
**Canto** Amor. J. Berryman. [Supp 2/327]
**Canton, William**
　Laus Infantium. [Volume 1/7]
**Caprice.** W. Howells. [Volume 2/110]
**Captain** Reece. W. Gilbert. [Volume 9/297]
"The **car**, light-moving, I behold." Chariot of
　Cuchullin, fr. Breach of the Plain of
　Muirhevney Unknown. [Volume 5/371]
**Caractacus.** B. Barton. [Volume 8/190]
**Carbery, Ethna [pseud.]** See MacManus, Anna
**Cardenal, Ernesto**
　Lights. M. Zimmerman (tr.). [Supp 6/158]
　Managua 6:30 P.M. S. White (tr.). [Supp 6/155]
　The Peasant Women from Cua. M. Zimmerman (tr.).
　　[Supp 6/156]
　The Uninhabited City: 001. S. White (tr.). [Supp
　　6/153]
　The Uninhabited City: 002. S. White (tr.). [Supp
　　6/154]
**Cardiff, Gladys**
　Combing. [Supp 4/321]
　Long Person. [Supp 4/319]
**Carducci, Giosue**
　The Ox, fr. Poesie. F. Sewall (tr.). [Volume
　　5/359]
　Roma, fr. Poesie. F. Sewall (tr.). [Volume 6/310]
"**Care-charmer** sleep, son of the sable night." To
　Delia. S. Daniel. [Volume 5/61]
**Carew, Thomas**
　Disdain Returned. [Volume 2/20]
　"Give Me More Love or More Disdain" [Volume 2/245]
　A Song. [Volume 2/36]
　"Sweetly Breathing, Vernal Air" [Volume 5/82]
**Carey, Alice**
　My Creed. [Volume 4/237]
**Carey, Henry**
　God Save the King. [Volume 8/18]
　A Maiden's Ideal of a Husband, fr. The
　　Contrivances. [Volume 2/89]
　Sally In Our Alley. [Volume 2/290]
*Cargo*
　Ode to a Lost Cargo in a Ship Called Save: 002. J.
　　Craveirinha. [Supp 6/38]
**Cargoes.** J. Masefield. [Supp 1/210]
**Carillon.** H. Longfellow. [Volume 7/166]
**Carleton, Will**
　The New Church Organ. [Volume 9/316]
　"Out of the Old House, Nancy" [Volume 1/268]
　"Over the Hill to the Poor-house" [Volume 3/175]
**Carlyle** and Emerson. M. Schuyler. [Volume 7/97]
**Carlyle, Thomas (tr.)**
　Mignon's Song, fr. Wilhelm Meister. J. Goethe.

　[Volume 6/313]
**Carman, Bliss**
　The Gravedigger. [Volume 5/383]
　Hack and Hew. [Volume 6/387]
　The Joys of the Road. [Volume 1/253]
　A More Ancient Mariner. [Volume 5/345]
　Spring Song. [Volume 1/248]
**Carmen** Bellicosum. G. McMaster. [Volume 8/332]
**Carmi, T.**
　Fragment. G. Schulman (tr.). [Supp 7/246]
　Inventory. G. Schulman (tr.). [Supp 7/241]
　Judgment. G. Schulman (tr.). [Supp 7/245]
　Lullaby. G. Schulman (tr.). [Supp 7/244,Supp
　　7/243]
　Model Lesson. G. Schulman (tr.). [Supp 7/242]
　My Beloved Is Mine and I Am His. G. Schulman (tr.)
　　[Supp 7/243]
　Vigils. G. Schulman (tr.). [Supp 7/241]
**Carnegie, Sir James, Earl of Southesk**
　Kate Temple's Song. [Volume 2/94]
**Carriers** of the Dream Wheel. N. Momaday. [Supp 4/30
"**Carry** Her Over the Water" W. Auden. [Supp 2/157]
"**Carry** me across!" Saint Christopher. D. Craik.
　[Volume 4/296]
"**Cartoon** of slashes on the tide-traced crater."
　Altarwise by Owl-light: 006. D. Thomas. [Supp
　2/350]
**Cary, Alice**
　Pictures of Memory. [Volume 1/76]
　A Spinster's Stint. [Volume 2/118]
**Cary, Henry Francis (tr.)**
　Fairest Thing in Mortal Eyes. D. Charles. [Volume
　　3/356]
　Hell: Inscription Over the Gate, fr. The Diving
　　Comedy. Dante Alighieri. [Volume 4/436]
　Paradise: Sin and Redemption, fr. The Diving
　　Comedy. Dante Alighieri. [Volume 4/441]
　Paradise: The Saints in Glory, fr. The Diving
　　Comedy. Dante Alighieri. [Volume 4/445]
　Paradise: The Triumph of Christ, fr. The Diving
　　Comedy. Dante Alighieri. [Volume 4/443]
　Purgatory: Fire of Purification, fr. The Diving
　　Comedy. Dante Alighieri. [Volume 4/439]
　Purgatory: Man's Free-will, fr. The Diving Comedy.
　　Dante Alighieri. [Volume 4/438]
　Purgatory: Prayer of Penitents, fr. The Diving
　　Comedy. Dante Alighieri. [Volume 4/437]
　Purgatory: Prayer, fr. The Diving Comedy. Dante
　　Alighieri. [Volume 4/436]
**Cary, Phoebe**
　Nearer Home. [Volume 4/393]
**Casabianca.** F. Hemans. [Volume 9/184]
**Casiano, Americo**
　"When Was the Last Time You Saw Miami Smile?"
　　[Supp 4/288]
**Casimir of Poland**
　"It Kindless All My Soul" [Volume 4/373]
**Casino.** W. Auden. [Supp 2/158]
**Cassian, Nina**
　"Hills Picking Up the Moonlight" S. Deligiorgis
　　(tr.). [Supp 5/45]
　A Man. R. MacGregor-Hastiek (tr.). [Supp 5/46]
　Self-Portrait. R. MacGregor-Hastiek (tr.). [Supp
　　5/47]
**Castellanos, Rosario**
　Empty House. M. Ahern (tr.). [Supp 5/50]
　Home Economics. M. Ahern (tr.). [Supp 5/53]
　Malinche. M. Ahern (tr.). [Supp 5/51]
　Silence near an Ancient Stone. M. Ahern (tr.).
　　[Supp 5/49]
The **Castle** of Indolence. J. Thomson. [Volume 6/115]
The **Castle** Ruins. W. Barnes. [Volume 7/213]
"The **castled** crag of Drachenfels." The Rhine, fr.
　Childe Harolde. G. Byron. [Volume 7/169]
*Castles*

"A **child** said what is the grass? fetching it to me."
  What is the Grass?, fr. The Song of Myself. W.
  Whitman. [Volume 6/198]
"A **child** sleeps under a rose-bush fair." The Rose-
  bush. Unknown. [Volume 6/233]
The **Children**. C. Dickinson. [Volume 1/286]
**Children**. W. Landor. [Volume 1/26]
*Children*
  The Angel's Whisper. S. Lover. [Volume 1/10]
  The Babie. J. Rankin. [Volume 1/9]
  Baby Bell. T. Aldrich. [Volume 1/60]
  Baby Louise. M. Eytinge. [Volume 1/21]
  Baby May. W. Bennett. [Volume 1/17]
  Baby Zulma's Christmas Carol. A. Requier. [Volume
    1/67]
  Baby's Shoes. W. Bennett. [Volume 1/66]
  The Baby. G. Macdonald. [Volume 1/4]
  The Baby. Kalidasa. [Volume 1/1]
  The Barefoot Boy. J. Whittier. [Volume 1/84]
  Bedtime. F. Erskine; Earl of Rosslyn. [Volume
    1/39]
  A Belated Violet. O. Herford. [Volume 1/154]
  Birth. A. Stillman. [Volume 1/3]
  Boyhood. W. Allston. [Volume 1/76]
  "By Cool Siloam's Shady Rill" R. Herber. [Volume
    1/122]
  The Child in the Garden. H. Van Dyke. [Volume
    1/55]
  A Child. S. Tanikawa. [Supp 7/134]
  Children. W. Landor. [Volume 1/26]
  The Children's Church. K. Gerrock. [Volume 1/115]
  Choosing a Name. M. Lamb. [Volume 1/97]
  A Cradle Hymn. I. Watts. [Volume 1/98]
  Cradle Song. Unknown. [Volume 1/13]
  Cradle Song, fr. Bitter-Sweet. J. Holland. [Volume
    1/13]
  Cuddle Doon. A. Anderson. [Volume 1/44]
  The Dancers. M. Field. [Volume 1/133]
  The Dead Doll. M. Vandergrift. [Volume 1/129]
  The Dreadful Story About Harriet and the Matches.
    H. Hoffmann. [Volume 1/171]
  A Dutch Lullaby. E. Field. [Volume 1/102]
  The Elf and the Dormouse. O. Herford. [Volume
    1/152]
  Etude Realiste. A. Swinburne. [Volume 1/8]
  The Fairies of the Caldon Low. M. Howitt. [Volume
    1/148]
  Fairy Days. W. Thackeray. [Volume 1/141]
  The First Rose of Summer. O. Herford. [Volume
    1/154]
  Foreign Children. R. Stevenson. [Volume 1/130]
  Foreign Lands. R. Stevenson. [Volume 1/138]
  The Frost. H. Gould. [Volume 1/156]
  The Gambols of Children. G. Darley. [Volume 1/55]
  Gild's Evening Hymn. S. Baring-Gould. [Volume
    1/117]
  Go Sleep, Ma Honey. E. Barker. [Volume 1/100]
  Good King Arthur. Unknown. [Volume 1/184]
  Good Night and Good Morning. R. Milnes. [Volume
    1/109]
  A Good Play. R. Stevenson. [Volume 1/127]
  Half-Waking. W. Allingham. [Volume 1/103]
  The Happy Hour. M. Butts. [Volume 1/12]
  The History Lesson. Unknown. [Volume 1/194]
  The Household Sovereign, fr. The Hanging of the
    Crane. H. Longfellow. [Volume 1/23]
  "How Doth the Little Busy Bee" I. Watts. [Volume
    1/108]
  "I Remember, I Remember" T. Hood. [Volume 1/83]
  In School-Days. J. Whittier. [Volume 1/163]
  "It is Finished" C. Rossetti. [Volume 1/119]
  Japanese Lullaby. E. Field. [Volume 1/15]
  The Jumblies. E. Lear. [Volume 1/192]
  The Land of Counterpane. R. Stevenson. [Volume
    1/107]

The Land of Story-Books. R. Stevenson. [Volume
  1/140]
Laus Infantium. W. Canton. [Volume 1/7]
"Let Dogs Delight to Bark and Bite" I. Watts.
  [Volume 1/114]
Letty's Globe. C. Turner. [Volume 1/31]
A Life-Lesson. J. Riley. [Volume 1/127]
Limerick. E. Lear. [Volume 1/196, Volume 1/197,
  Volume 1/198, Volume 1/199, Volume 1/200, Volume
  1/201]
Limerick. R. Kipling. [Volume 1/201]
Limerick. Unknown. [Volume 1/202]
Little Bell. T. Westwood. [Volume 1/135]
A Little Child's Hymn. F. Palgrave. [Volume 1/120]
A Little Dutch Garden. H. Durbin. [Volume 1/153]
Little Feet. E. Akers. [Volume 1/19]
Little Goldenhair. F. Smith. [Volume 1/42]
Little Orphant Annie. J. Riley. [Volume 1/159]
The Lost Heir. T. Hood. [Volume 1/49]
Lullaby, fr. The Princess. A. Tennyson. [Volume
  1/11]
The Man in the Moon. J. Riley. [Volume 1/146]
Max and Maurice, sel. W. Busch. [Volume 1/184]
The Mitherless Bairn. W. Thom. [Volume 1/78]
A Mortifying Mistake. A. Pratt. [Volume 1/166]
Mother and Child. W. Simms. [Volume 1/25]
The Mother's Hope. L. Blanchard. [Volume 1/37]
The Mother's Sacrifice. S. Smith. [Volume 1/24]
Mr. and Mrs. Spikky Sparrow. E. Lear. [Volume
  1/177]
"My Little Girl is Nested." S. Peck. [Volume 1/41]
My Mother's Picture. W. Cowper. [Volume 1/79]
My Shadow. R. Stevenson. [Volume 1/133]
"No Baby in the House" C. Dolliver. [Volume 1/101]
Nokondi. H. Riyong. [Supp 6/48]
The Old Arm-Chair. E. Cook. [Volume 1/93]
The 'Old Oaken Bucket. S. Woodworth. [Volume 1/91]
Old-School Punishment. Unknown. [Volume 1/162]
On the Death of an Infant. J. Lowell. [Volume
  1/70]
On the Picture of an Infant Playing Near a
  Precipice. Leonidas of Alexandria. [Volume
  1/24]
Our Wee White Rose. G. Massey. [Volume 1/64]
The Owl and the Pussy-cat. E. Lear. [Volume 1/175]
A Parable. M. Blind. [Volume 1/95]
Philip, My King. D. Craik. [Volume 1/16]
Pictures of Memory. A. Cary. [Volume 1/76]
The Piper. W. Blake. [Volume 1/96]
Polly. W. Rands. [Volume 1/27]
A Portrait. E. Browning. [Volume 1/56]
Pretty Cow. J. Taylor. [Volume 1/105]
Rain on the Roof. C. Kinney. [Volume 1/88]
The Romance of the Swan's Nest. E. Browning.
  [Volume 1/123]
Sage Counsel. A. Quiller-Couch. [Volume 1/195]
Seein' Things. E. Field. [Volume 1/164]
Seven Times Four; maternity. J. Ingelow. [Volume
  1/36]
Seven Times One. J. Ingelow. [Volume 1/48]
The Shadows. F. Sherman. [Volume 1/132]
Sheep and Lambs. K. Hinkson. [Volume 1/121]
Silent Baby. E. Currier. [Volume 1/22]
The Smack in School. W. Palmer. [Volume 1/167]
Small and Early. T. Jenks. [Volume 1/46]
The Spider and the Fly. M. Howitt. [Volume 1/110]
The Story of Cruel Fredderick, fr. The English
  Struwwelpeter. H. Hoffmann. [Volume 1/170]
The Story of Johnny-Head-In-Air. H. Hoffmann.
  [Volume 1/173]
"There was a Little Girl" H. Longfellow. [Volume
  1/169]
Thread and Song. J. Palmer. [Volume 1/113]
The Three Children. Unknown. [Volume 1/174]
The Three Little Kittens. E. Follen. [Volume

**Clarke, James Freeman**
Caliph and Satan. [Volume 4/119]
Cana. [Volume 4/65]
**Clarke, James Freeman (tr.)**
The Children's Church. K. Gerrock. [Volume 1/115]
**Claudius, Matthias**
The Hen. [Volume 9/436]
Winter. C. Brooks (tr.). [Volume 5/172]
*Cleanliness*
Home Economics. R. Castellanos. [Supp 5/53]
**Cleanthes**
Hymn to Zeus. [Volume 4/7]
"Clear and cool, clear and cool." Song of the River.
C. Kingsley. [Volume 5/201]
"Clear, placid Leman! thy contrasted lake." Calm on
Lake Leman, fr. Childe Harold. G. Byron.
[Volume 5/211]
Clear Skies. Nirala. [Supp 7/68]
"Clear the brown path to meet his coulter's." The
Ploughman. O. Holmes. [Volume 5/94]
Cleator Moor. L. Lee. [Supp 2/340]
**Cleland, William**
Hallo, My Fancy. [Volume 6/3]
Cleon and I. C. Mackay. [Volume 6/420]
"Cleon hath a million acres, ne'er a one have I."
Cleon and I. C. Mackay. [Volume 6/420]
Cleopatra. W. Story. [Volume 2/354]
Cleopatra, fr. Antony and Cleopatra. W. Shakespeare.
[Volume 7/127]
**Clephane, Elizabeth Cecilia**
The Lost Sheep. [Volume 4/66]
**Cleveland, John**
To the Memory of Ben Jonson. [Volume 7/46]
**Clifton, Lucille**
Good Times. [Supp 4/193]
"Climbing a long open flight of sandstone steps."
Ascending Scale. M. Piercy. [Supp 5/202]
"Clime of the unforgotten brave!" Fallen Greece, fr.
The Giaour. G. Byron. [Volume 8/125]
"Cling to thy home! if there the meanest shed." Home.
Leonidas of Alexandria. [Volume 4/15]
"Close his eyes; is work is done." Dirge for a
Soldier. G. Boker. [Volume 8/370]
Close Your Eyes! A. Bontemps. [Supp 4/122]
The Closing Scene. T. Read. [Volume 8/416]
The Closing Year. G. Prentice. [Volume 6/307]
The Cloud. P. Shelley. [Volume 5/133]
The Cloud Chorus, fr. The Clouds. Aristophanes.
[Volume 5/131]
"A cloud lay cradled near the setting sun." The
Evening Cloud. J. Wilson. [Volume 7/156]
"A cloud possessed the hollow field." The High Tide
at Gettysburg. W. Thompson. [Volume 8/398]
*Clouds*
Arizona Poems: Clouds Across the Canyon. J.
Fletcher. [Supp 1/129]
Arizona Poems: Windmills. J. Fletcher. [Supp
1/126]
Most Lovely Shade. E. Sitwell. [Supp 2/15]
"My House is Cloudy" N. Yushij. [Supp 7/204]
"The Clouds Race on the Sea's Face" Li Ying. [Supp
7/14]
**Clough, Arthur Hugh**
The Condola. [Volume 7/191]
Despondency Rebuked. [Volume 3/235]
In a Lecture-room. [Volume 4/132]
The Latest Decalogue. [Volume 9/315]
Qua Cursum Ventus. [Volume 6/231]
Where Lies the Land? [Volume 6/231]
Coal. A. Lorde. [Supp 4/180]
"Coal is the total black, being spoken." Coal. A.
Lorde. [Supp 4/180]
The Coasters. T. Day. [Volume 7/153]
The Coat of Fire. E. Sitwell. [Supp 2/10]
**Coatsworth, Elizabeth J.**

All Goats. [Supp 1/85]
Song of the Three Seeds in the Macaw's Beak. [Supp
1/85]
The **Cobbler** and the Financier. J. Fontaine. [Volume
6/410]
"A cobbler sang from morn till night." The Cobbler
and the Financier. J. Fontaine. [Volume 6/410]
The Cock and the Bull. C. Calverley. [Volume 9/402]
"The cock is crowing." March. W. Wordsworth. [Volume
5/77]
"A coffin bearing the face of a boy." A Mirror for
the Twentieth Century. Adonis. [Supp 7/278]
"The cold moves from the Thai-nguyen down to the Yen-
the." Road Sabotage. To Huu. [Supp 7/194]
Cold Term. L. Jones. [Supp 4/176]
"The cold wind swept the mountain's height." The
Mother's Sacrifice. S. Smith. [Volume 1/24]
**Coleridge, Hartley**
Ideality. [Volume 6/8]
Shakespeare. [Volume 7/52]
"She is not Fair to Outward View" [Volume 2/33]
Summer Rain. [Volume 5/43]
**Coleridge, Mary Elizabeth**
"I Saw a Stable, Low and Very Bare" [Supp 1/87]
The White Women. [Supp 1/87]
**Coleridge, Samuel Taylor**
Dallying with Temptation, fr. Wallenstein. [Volume
4/327]
Epigram: "Hoarse Maevius Reads His Hobbling Verse"
[Volume 9/287]
Epigram: "Sly Beelzebub Took All Occasions"
[Volume 9/286]
Epigram: "Swans Sing Before They Die" [Volume
9/287]
Epigram: Cologne. [Volume 9/286]
The Exchange. [Volume 2/164]
Fancy in Nubibus. [Volume 5/50]
The Good Great Man. [Volume 3/244]
Hymn. [Volume 4/15]
The Knight's Tomb. [Volume 8/428]
Kubla Khan. [Volume 6/163]
Love. [Volume 2/159]
Metrical Feet. [Volume 9/429]
On an Infant. [Volume 4/232]
Rime of the Ancient Mariner. [Volume 6/130]
Youth, fr. Youth and Age. [Volume 1/263]
**Coles, Abraham (tr.)**
Stabat Mater Dolorosa. F. Jacopone. [Volume 4/70]
The Coliseum, fr. Childe Harold. G. Byron. [Volume
7/178]
The Collegian to His Bride. Punch. [Volume 9/434]
The Collier. V. Watkins. [Supp 2/189]
**Collins, Mortimer**
Darwin. [Volume 9/383]
The Two Worlds. [Volume 4/400]
**Collins, William**
"How Sleep the Brave" [Volume 8/449]
The Passions. [Volume 6/367]
**Collins, William (tr.)**
Women's Chorus. Aristophanes. [Volume 9/200]
Colloquy in Black Rock. R. Lowell. [Supp 2/388]
Colloquy with a King-Crab. J. Bishop. [Supp 2/24]
**Colman, George**
Gluggity Glug, fr. The Myrtle and the Vine.
[Volume 9/245]
Toby Tosspot. [Volume 9/257]
"The colonel rode by his picket-line." The Two Wives.
W. Howells. [Volume 8/355]
"A color in shaving, a saloon is well placed in the
centre of an alley." Eye Glasses. G. Stein.
[Supp 5/293]
Colorado. R. Fitzgerald. [Supp 2/240]
Colorado Morton's Ride. L. Bacon. [Supp 1/21]
"Colorado Morton's riding far." Colorado Morton's
Ride. L. Bacon. [Supp 1/21]

Conscience, frm Saitire XIII. Juvenal. [Volume 4/329]
"The **conscious** water saw its god and blushed." Brief: Water Turned Into Wine. R. Crashaw. [Volume 4/306]
A **Conservative**. C. Gilman. [Volume 9/422]
"**Consider** the sea's listless chime." The Sea-limits. D. Rossetti. [Volume 5/441]
*Consolation*
    "Afar in the Desert" T. Pringle. [Volume 3/222]
    After Death, fr. Pearls of the Faith. S. Arnold. [Volume 3/452]
    The Angel of Patience. J. Whittier. [Volume 3/402]
    Aunt Phillis's Guest. W. Gannett. [Volume 3/239]
    Blessed Are They. R. Raymond. [Volume 3/425]
    Blessed Are They That Mourn. W. Bryant. [Volume 3/421]
    Blind. I. Zangwill. [Volume 3/460]
    The Bottom Drawer. A. Barr. [Volume 3/405]
    The Changed Cross. H. Hobart. [Volume 3/231]
    Christus Consolator. R. Raymond. [Volume 3/432]
    Comfort. E. Browning. [Volume 3/433]
    Compensation. C. Cranch. [Volume 3/229]
    The Conqueror's Grave. W. Bryant. [Volume 3/442]
    De Profundis. E. Browning. [Volume 3/421]
    Death in Youth, fr. Festus. P. Bailey. [Volume 3/428]
    The Death of Death. W. Shakespeare. [Volume 3/461]
    Despondency Rebuked. A. Clough. [Volume 3/235]
    The Flower. G. Herbert. [Volume 3/219]
    Footsteps of Angels. H. Longfellow. [Volume 3/438]
    For Charlie's Sake. J. Palmer. [Volume 3/411]
    God's Sure Help in Sorrow. A. Ulrich. [Volume 3/236]
    Going and Coming. E. Jenks. [Volume 3/458]
    The Good Great Man. S. Coleridge. [Volume 3/244]
    The Green Grass Under the Snow. A. Preston. [Volume 3/442]
    Grief for the Dead. Unknown. [Volume 3/408]
    Happy Are the Dead. H. Vaughan. [Volume 3/439]
    I Hold Still. J. Sturm. [Volume 3/243]
    Ilka Blade O' Grass Keps Its Ain Drap O' Dew. J. Ballantine. [Volume 3/241]
    In Memoriam F. A. S. R. Stevenson. [Volume 3/428]
    Invictus. W. Henley. [Volume 3/221]
    "It Is Not Death To Die" G. Bethune. [Volume 3/455]
    Lines. H. Stowe. [Volume 3/426]
    Lycidas. J. Milton. [Volume 3/446]
    My Child. J. Pierpont. [Volume 3/417]
    My Wife and Child. H. Jackson. [Volume 3/228]
    Never Despair. W. O'Brien. [Volume 3/246]
    "Only a Year" H. Stowe. [Volume 3/418]
    Over the River. N. Priest. [Volume 3/406]
    Peace. Unknown. [Volume 3/437]
    The Rainy Day. H. Longfellow. [Volume 3/228]
    The Reaper and the Flowers. H. Longfellow. [Volume 3/417]
    Resignation. H. Longfellow. [Volume 3/430]
    "Sad is Our Yourth, For It Is Ever Going" A. De Vere. [Volume 3/225]
    The Saddest Fate. Unknown. [Volume 3/247]
    The Secret of Death. S. Arnold. [Volume 3/434]
    Something Beyond. M. Hudson. [Volume 3/234]
    Song. R. Le Gallienne. [Volume 3/417]
    The Song of the Savoyards. H. Blood. [Volume 3/248]
    Sonnet. L. Labe. [Volume 3/237]
    Sonnet to Cyriak Skinner. J. Milton. [Volume 3/220]
    Tears. E. Browning. [Volume 3/429]
    "There Is No Death" J. M'Creery. [Volume 3/456]
    "They Are All Gone" H. Vaughan. [Volume 3/403]
    "Thou are Gone to the Grave" R. Herber. [Volume 3/446]
    Times Go by Turns. R. Southwell. [Volume 3/228]

    To Myself. P. Fleming. [Volume 3/218]
    The Two Waitings. J. Chadwick. [Volume 3/409]
    Unchanging. F. Von Bodenstedt. [Volume 3/242]
    Waiting. J. Burroughs. [Volume 3/238]
    Watching for Papa. Unknown. [Volume 3/414]
    When My Ship Comes In. R. Burdette. [Volume 3/245]
**Constancy**. S. Suckling. [Volume 2/23]
**Constancy**. Unknown. [Volume 2/235]
**Conte, Maria la**
    Somebody's Darling. [Volume 8/378]
**Content**, fr. Farewell to Follie. R. Greene. [Volume 6/418]
**Contentment**. O. Holmes. [Volume 6/423]
**Contentment**. J. Sylvester. [Volume 6/417]
*Contentment*
    "The Sunlight on the Garden" L. MacNeice. [Supp 2/185]
The **Contrary** Experience: 001. H. Read. [Supp 2/32]
The **Contrary** Experience: 002. H. Read. [Supp 2/33]
The **Contrary** Experience: 003. H. Read. [Supp 2/34]
**Conversation**. L. MacNeice. [Supp 2/173]
The **Conversion** of Saint Paul. J. Keble. [Volume 4/82]
**Cook, Eliza**
    Ganging To And Ganging Frae. [Volume 2/293]
    The Old Arm-Chair. [Volume 1/93]
**Cooke, Philip Pendleton**
    Life in the Autumn Woods. [Volume 5/151]
**Cooke, Roose Terry**
    Trailing Arbutus. [Volume 5/250]
**Cooking** and Courting. Unknown. [Volume 2/174]
"**Cooks** who'd roast a sucking-pig." A Recipe. S. Smith. [Volume 9/385]
**Coolbrith, Ina Donna**
    Copa De Oro. [Volume 5/281]
    The Mariposa Lily. [Volume 5/280]
**Coolidge, Susan [pseud.]** See Woolsey, Sarah
**Cooper, James Fenimore**
    My Brigantine, fr. The Water Witch. [Volume 5/402]
**Copa De Oro.** I. Coolbrith. [Volume 5/281]
**Cope and William Plomer, Jack (tr.)**
    Dark Stream. I. Jonker. [Supp 5/122]
The **Coral** Insect. L. Sigourney. [Volume 5/395]
The **Coral** Reef, fr. The Pelican Island. J. Montgomery. [Volume 5/396]
"The **core** of him is hate." Steel Mill. L. Untermeyer. [Supp 1/311]
"The **cormorant** still screams." Late. L. Bogan. [Supp 5/32]
**Corn-Law** Hymn. E. Eliot. [Volume 6/397]
**Corneille, Pierre**
    Paulina's Appeal, fr. Polyeucte. W. Nokes (tr.). [Volume 2/396]
"The **cornel-trees** %uplift from the furrows." Orion Dead. H. Doolittle. [Supp 5/71]
**Cornford, Frances**
    Autumn Morning at Cambridge. [Supp 1/91]
    The Old Witch in the Copse. [Supp 1/90]
**Cornwall, Barry [pseud.]** See Procter, Bryan Waller
"**Cornwallis** led a country dance." The Dance. Unknown. [Volume 8/334]
**Cornwell, Henry Sylvester**
    The Sunset City. [Volume 7/158]
**Coronach**, fr. The Lady of the Lake. S. Scott. [Volume 3/309]
*Corpses*
    The Worms at Heaven's Gate. W. Stevens. [Supp 1/291]
**Cory, W. (tr.)**
    The Dead Poet-friend. Callimachus. [Volume 1/396]
The **Cosmic** Egg. Unknown. [Volume 9/436]
The **Cost** of Worth, fr. Bitter Sweet. J. Holland. [Volume 4/300]
**Costello, Louise Stuart (tr.)**
    On the Death of Her Brother, Francis I. M. De Valois. [Volume 3/338]

The Cross. T. Ojaide. [Supp 6/56]
Cross, Marian Evans Lewes ("George Eliot")
  Day is Dying, fr. The Spanish Gypsy. [Volume 5/50]
  "O, May I Join The Choir Invisible!" [Volume 4/241]
  Two Lovers. [Volume 2/402]
Crossing the Bar. A. Tennyson. [Volume 4/375]
Crow, Mary (tr.)
  Alice in Nightmareland. E. Lihn. [Supp 6/122]
The Crowded Street. W. Bryant. [Volume 6/239]
A Crowded Trolley Car. E. Wylie. [Supp 5/337]
Crowds
  Yearing I Walk in a Crowd. H. Sakutaro. [Supp 7/107]
Crowned Crane. Unknown (African American). [Supp 6/2]
"Crowned crane %beautiful crowned crane of power."
  Crowned Crane. Unknown (African American).
  [Supp 6/2]
Crowquill, Alfred [pseud.] See Forrester, Alfred
Crucifixion
  Ecce Homo. D. Gascoyne. [Supp 2/380]
"Cruising these residential Sunday." The City
  Planners. M. Atwood. [Supp 5/18]
The Crusaders. J. Mastoraki. [Supp 5/157]
"The crusanders %knew the holy places." The Crusaders.
  J. Mastoraki. [Supp 5/157]
Cruz, Victor Hernandez
  Snag. [Supp 4/278]
  Today Is a Day of Great Joy. [Supp 4/276]
The Cry of the Human. E. Browning. [Volume 4/286]
A Cry to Arms. H. Timrod. [Volume 8/100]
"crystal drop on my left shoulder on my right the
  misty." The Triangular Window. Yung Tzu. [Supp 7/36]
The Crystal Skull. K. Raine. [Supp 2/196]
Cuadra, Pablo Antonio
  At the Heart of Two Burning Stars. S. White (tr.).
  [Supp 6/162]
  The Drowned Horse. S. White (tr.). [Supp 6/160]
  Written on a Roadside Stone During the First
  Eruption. S. White (tr.). [Supp 6/161]
Cuckoo Birds
  Cuckoos. M. Kaneko. [Supp 7/112]
The Cuckoo Clock, fr. The Birthday. C. Southey.
  [Volume 7/148]
Cuckoo Song. Unknown. [Volume 5/90]
Cuckoos. M. Kaneko. [Supp 7/112]
Cuddle Doon. A. Anderson. [Volume 1/44]
Cullen, Countee
  Heritage. [Supp 1/96]
  Tableau. [Supp 1/100]
  Yet Do I Marvel. [Supp 4/134]
The Culprit Fay. J. Drake. [Volume 6/35]
Cummings, E. E.
  Portrait - II. [Supp 1/102]
  Portrait - X. [Supp 1/103]
  Song. [Supp 1/101]
  Sonnet - Realities I. [Supp 1/104]
Cumnor Hall. W. Mickle. [Volume 3/41]
Cumpiano, Ina (tr.)
  Song of Other Lives. L. Marechal. [Supp 6/105]
Cunningham, Allan
  The Poet's Bridal-Day Song. [Volume 2/414]
  "Thou Hast Sworn By Thy God, My Jeanie" [Volume 2/416]
  "A Wet Sheet and a Flowing Sea" [Volume 5/399]
Cunningham, John
  Morning. [Volume 5/40]
Cupid and Campaspe, fr. Alexander and Campaspe. J.
  Lyly. [Volume 2/105]
"Cupid and my Campaspe played." Cupid and Campaspe,
  fr. Alexander and Campaspe. J. Lyly. [Volume 2/105]
Cupid Swallowed. L. Hunt. [Volume 2/91]
Curfew Must Not Ring To-Night. R. Thorpe. [Volume

2/303]
"The curfew tolls the knell of parting day." Elegy
  Written in a Country Churchyard. T. Gray.
  [Volume 3/270]
Curriculum Vitae. I. Bachmann. [Supp 5/25]
Currier, Ellen Bartlett
  Silent Baby. [Volume 1/22]
"Cursed by the gods and crowned with shame." The Wife
  Of Loki. L. Elliot. [Volume 2/398]
"Curtains of rock." Orpheus in the Underworld. D.
  Gascoyne. [Supp 2/385]
A Cutlet. G. Stein. [Supp 5/293]
Cynicism
  C Stands for Civilization. K. Fearing. [Supp 2/97]
  The King of Spain. M. Bodenheim. [Supp 1/56]
"Cyriack, this three year's day, these eyes, though."
  Sonnet to Cyriak Skinner. J. Milton. [Volume 3/220]


D.S. :For Her Album. C. Anwar. [Supp 7/82]
Da Vinci, Leonardo
  Perseverance. W. Story (tr.). [Volume 6/284]
"Daddy Neptune, one day, to freedom did say." The
  Snug Little Island. T. Dibdin. [Volume 8/15]
Daffodils. W. Wordsworth. [Volume 5/247]
A Dagger of the Mind, fr. Macbeth. W. Shakespeare.
  [Volume 9/120]
"A dagger pointed at me." April. Pak Tu-Jin. [Supp 7/153]
Daglarca, Fazil
  Ant from Sivas. T. Halman (tr.). [Supp 7/299]
  Gleam in Time. T. Halman (tr.). [Supp 7/298]
  Nation's Hand. T. Halman (tr.). [Supp 7/303]
  Paris, Buddha, Stars and i. T. Halman (tr.). [Supp 7/301]
  Poverty. T. Halman (tr.). [Supp 7/302]
  "Waters Are Wiser Than We" T. Halman (tr.). [Supp 7/298]
Daisies
  Stansaz in Meditation: Part 001, Stanza 013. G.
  Stein. [Supp 5/290]
"Daisies are broken." Love Song. W. Williams. [Supp 1/320]
Daisy. F. Thompson. [Volume 3/136]
The Daisy, fr. Legend of Good Women. G. Chaucer.
  [Volume 5/275]
Dallying with Temptation, fr. Wallenstein. S.
  Coleridge. [Volume 4/327]
"A damned thief dog." Sad Moonlit Night. H. Sakutaro.
  [Supp 7/104]
Dana, Doris (tr.)
  The Foreigner. G. Mistral. [Supp 6/129]
  Little Feet. G. Mistral. [Supp 6/125]
  Mexican Child. G. Mistral. [Supp 6/128]
  Midnight. G. Mistral. [Supp 6/127]
  The Useless Wait. G. Mistral. [Supp 6/124]
Dana, Richard Henry
  The Little Beach Bird. [Volume 5/302]
  The Pleasure-Boat. [Volume 5/142]
The Dance. Unknown. [Volume 8/304]
The Dancers. M. Field. [Volume 1/133]
Dancing and Dancers
  Ballad of the Ten Casino Dancers. C. Meireles.
  [Supp 5/163]
  The New Platform Dances. J. Mapanje. [Supp 6/34]
The Dancing of the Air. S. Davies. [Volume 5/125]
Daniel, Samuel
  Love is a Sickness. [Volume 2/62]
  To Delia. [Volume 5/61]
Daniel Webster. O. Holmes. [Volume 7/20]
A Danish Barrow. F. Palgrave. [Volume 8/213]
Danny Deever. R. Kipling. [Volume 8/299]

All Gone. [Supp 2/109]
"As One Who Wanders into Old Workings" [Supp 2/110]
Birthday Poem for Thomas Hardy. [Supp 2/111]
"Come, Live with Me and Be My Love" [Supp 2/112]
The Conflict. [Supp 2/112]
Departure in the Dark. [Supp 2/113]
"In heaven, I suppose, Lie Down Together" [Supp 2/115]
"In the Heart of Contemplation" [Supp 2/115]
Maple and Sumach. [Supp 2/117]
"Nearing Again the Legendary Isle" [Supp 2/117]
O Dreams, O Destinations: 001. [Supp 2/118]
O Dreams, O Destinations: 002. [Supp 2/118]
O Dreams, O Destinations: 003. [Supp 2/119]
O Dreams, O Destinations: 004. [Supp 2/119]
O Dreams, O Destinations: 005. [Supp 2/120]
O Dreams, O Destinations: 006. [Supp 2/120]
O Dreams, O Destinations: 007. [Supp 2/120]
O Dreams, O Destinations: 008. [Supp 2/122]
"Rest From Loving and Be Living" [Supp 2/122]
The Sitting. [Supp 2/122]
A Time to Dance. [Supp 2/124]
"You That Love England" [Supp 2/125]
**Day** of These Days. L. Lee. [Supp 2/335]
"**Day** of vengeance, without morrow!" Dies Irae. T. Celano. [Volume 4/100]
"The **Day** Returns, My Bosom Burns" R. Burns. [Volume 2/422]
"**Day** set on Norham's castled steep." The Knight, fr. Marmion. S. Scott. [Volume 7/201]
"**Day-stars!** that ope your frownless eyes to." Hymn to the Flowers. H. Smith. [Volume 5/242]
**Day, Thomas Fleming**
The Coasters. [Volume 7/153]
**Daybreak.** S. Davenant. [Volume 2/4]
**Daybreak.** H. Longfellow. [Volume 5/37]
"The **days** begin to set." For My Daughter. J. Wright. [Supp 5/329]
The **Days** Gone By. J. Riley. [Volume 1/203]
**De Beranger, Pierre-Jean**
The Old Vagabond. [Volume 3/188]
**De Camoens, Luis**
Blighted Love. L. Strangford (tr.). [Volume 3/81]
**De Campos, Haroldo**
Anamorphosis. [Supp 6/112]
**De fust Banjo.** I. Russell. [Volume 9/377]
"**De** gray owl sing fum de chimbly top." A Plantation Ditty. F. Stanton. [Volume 9/376]
**De La Mare, Walter**
The Listeners. [Supp 1/107]
The Riddlers. [Supp 1/108]
**De La Selva, Salomon**
Tropical Town. S. White (tr.). [Supp 6/172]
"**De** massa ob de sheepfol'" De sheepfol! S. Greene. [Volume 4/67]
**De Melo Neto, Joao Cabral**
The Table. [Supp 6/111]
**De Morlaix, Bernard**
Praise of the Celestial Country. J. Neale (tr.). [Volume 4/418]
**De Profundis.** E. Browning. [Volume 3/421]
**De sheepfol!** S. Greene. [Volume 4/67]
**De Valois, Marguerite, Queen of Navarre**
On the Death of Her Brother, Francis I. L. Costello (tr.). [Volume 3/338]
**De Vega, Lope**
To-morrow. [Volume 4/94]
**De Vere, Aubrey Thomas**
Early Friendship. [Volume 1/344]
"Sad is Our Yourth, For It Is Ever Going" [Volume 3/225]
**De Vere, Mary Ainge ("Madeline Bridges")**
Friend and Lover. [Volume 1/374]
The Spinner. [Volume 3/70]

**De Vere, Stephen (tr.)**
To Thaliarchus. Horace. [Volume 1/232]
The **Dead.** M. Blind. [Volume 3/279]
"The **dead** abide with us! Though stark and cold." The Dead. M. Blind. [Volume 3/279]
A **Dead** Child Speaks. N. Sachs. [Supp 5/247]
The **Dead** Crab. A. Young. [Supp 2/2]
The **Dead** Doll. M. Vandergrift. [Volume 1/129]
**Dead** Fly. E. Chuilleanain. [Supp 5/189]
The **Dead** Friend: 116, fr. In Memoriam. A. Tennyson. [Volume 1/362]
The **Dead** Friend: 22, fr. In Memoriam. A. Tennyson. [Volume 1/360]
The **Dead** Friend: 23, fr. In Memoriam. A. Tennyson. [Volume 1/360]
The **Dead** Friend: 25, fr. In Memoriam. A. Tennyson. [Volume 1/361]
The **Dead** Friend: 84, fr. In Memoriam. A. Tennyson. [Volume 1/361]
"The **dead** horse has it all." You'll Get Yours. G. Fuertes. [Supp 5/97]
**Dead,** In a Foreign Land, fr. In Memoriam. A. Tennyson. [Volume 3/349]
The **Dead** Man Asks for a Song. Unknown (African American). [Supp 6/3]
"A **dead** man I am who travels." Exile. I. Bachmann. [Supp 5/24]
"**Dead!** one of them shot by the sea in the east." Mother and Poet. E. Browning. [Volume 3/323]
The **Dead** Poet-friend. Callimachus. [Volume 1/396]
The **Dead** Ride Fast. R. Blackmur. [Supp 2/107]
"**Dear** boys, they've killed our woods: the ground." Ryton Firs. L. Abercrombie. [Supp 1/5]
"**Dear** Buddha, %you left, as you had to." Paris, Buddha, Stars and i. F. Daglarca. [Supp 7/301]
"**Dear** common flower, that grow'st beside the." To the Dandelion. J. Lowell. [Volume 5/248]
"**Dear** friend! whose presence in the house." Cana. J. Clarke. [Volume 4/65]
"**Dear** girl, what boots it thus to dress thy hair." Beauty Unadorned, fr. Elegies. S. Propertius. [Volume 6/282]
"**Dear** hearts, you wre waiting a year ago." The Two Waitings. J. Chadwick. [Volume 3/409]
"**Dear** Lord, let me recount to thee." "It is Finished" C. Rossetti. [Volume 1/119]
"**Dear** Ned, no doubt you'll be surprised." Cooking and Courting. Unknown. [Volume 2/174]
"**Dear,** secret greenness! nurst below." The Seed Growing Secretly. H. Vaughan. [Volume 4/343]
"**Dear** Sir: %I write this letter on my birthday." Letter to Time. C. Alegria. [Supp 5/14]
"**Dear** Sirmio, that art the very eye." Homeward Bound. Cattullus. [Volume 1/313]
"**Dearest** love, do you remember." When This Cruel War is Over. Unknown. [Volume 8/382]
**Death.** H. Riyong. [Supp 6/47]
*Death*
After Summer. P. Marston. [Volume 3/336]
Amen. A. Mutis. [Supp 6/133]
Annabel Lee. E. Poe. [Volume 3/312]
The Answer. Unknown. [Volume 4/402]
Antony and Cleopatra. W. Lytle. [Volume 3/380]
Apology. R. Pitter. [Supp 5/205]
Apres. A. Munby. [Volume 3/355]
Are the children at Home? M. Sangster. [Volume 3/288]
Asleep, Asleep. L. Bennett. [Volume 3/396]
August 6. J. Mirikitani. [Supp 4/39]
Awakening. W. Gladden. [Volume 3/375]
"Beyond the Smiling and the Weeping" H. Bonar. [Volume 3/378]
"Break, Break, Break" A. Tennyson. [Volume 3/358]
Breath. B. Diop. [Supp 6/67]
Burial of Moses. C. Alexander. [Volume 4/365]

"Only Waiting" F. Mace. [Volume 4/369]
The Other World. H. Stowe. [Volume 4/389]
"Out, Out--" R. Frost. [Supp 1/133]
Owl Song. M. Atwood. [Supp 5/20]
Paradise. F. Faber. [Volume 4/434]
Paradise: Sin and Redemption, fr. The Diving
   Comedy. Dante Alighieri. [Volume 4/441]
Paradise: The Saints in Glory, fr. The Diving
   Comedy. Dante Alighieri. [Volume 4/445]
Paradise: The Triumph of Christ, fr. The Diving
   Comedy. Dante Alighieri. [Volume 4/443]
The Passage. L. Uhland. [Volume 3/342]
Passing Away. J. Pierpont. [Volume 4/350]
Peace. H. Vaughan. [Volume 4/414]
The Peace of Sorrow, fr. In Memoriam. A. Tennyson.
   [Volume 3/350]
Personal Resurrection, fr. In Memoriam. A.
   Tennyson. [Volume 3/352]
A Picture of Death, fr. The Giaour. G. Byron.
   [Volume 3/261]
The Poet's Tribute, fr. In Memoriam. A. Tennyson.
   [Volume 3/354]
Praise of the Celestial Country. B. De Morlaix.
   [Volume 4/418]
The Prospect. E. Browning. [Volume 4/347]
Prospice. R. Browning. [Volume 3/392]
Purgatory: Fire of Purification, fr. The Diving
   Comedy. Dante Alighieri. [Volume 4/439]
Purgatory: Man's Free-will, fr. The Diving Comedy.
   Dante Alighieri. [Volume 4/438]
Purgatory: Prayer of Penitents, fr. The Diving
   Comedy. Dante Alighieri. [Volume 4/437]
Purgatory: Prayer, fr. The Diving Comedy. Dante
   Alighieri. [Volume 4/436]
The Quaker Graveyard. S. Mitchell. [Volume 3/278]
Requiescat. M. Arnold. [Volume 3/307]
The Resignation. T. Chatterton. [Volume 4/368]
Rest. M. Howland. [Volume 3/397]
"The Roosters Will Crow When We Die" C. Meireles.
   [Supp 5/160]
Saint Agnes. A. Tennyson. [Volume 4/416]
Salutation. T. Eliot. [Supp 1/114]
"She Died in Beauty" C. Sillery. [Volume 3/319]
Sic Vita. H. King. [Volume 3/253]
Sister Lou. S. Brown. [Supp 2/88]
"Sit Down, Sad Soul" B. Procter. [Volume 4/372]
The Sleep. E. Browning. [Volume 3/389]
Sleepy Hollow. W. Channing. [Volume 3/277]
"Softly Woo Away Here Breath" B. Procter. [Volume
   3/318]
Soliloquy on Death, fr. Hamlet. W. Shakespeare.
   [Volume 3/252]
Soliloquy: On Immortality, fr. Cato. J. Addison.
   [Volume 4/384]
Song of the Silent Land. J. Von Salis. [Volume
   4/388]
Song of the Three Seeds in the Macaw's Beak. E.
   Coatsworth. [Supp 1/85]
Sonnet. L. Lindsay. [Volume 3/304]
Sonnet. J. Masefield. [Supp 1/209]
Sonnet 018. H. Belloc. [Supp 1/33]
The Spirit-Land. J. Very. [Volume 4/410]
Spiritual Companionship, fr. In Memoriam. A.
   Tennyson. [Volume 3/352]
Star-Mist, fr. Stars. J. Keble. [Volume 4/415]
Swimmers. L. Untermeyer. [Supp 1/309]
"Tell Me, Ye Winged Winds" C. Mackay. [Volume
   4/411]
The Term of Death. S. Piatt. [Volume 3/261]
Thalatta! Thalatta! J. Brown. [Volume 3/389]
Thanatopsis. W. Bryant. [Volume 3/264]
"This Cruel Age Has Deflected Me" A. Akhmatova.
   [Supp 5/10]
Thoughts of Heaven. R. Nicoll. [Volume 4/391]
Thy Braes Were Bonny. J. Logan. [Volume 3/314]

Time and Eternity, fr. In Memoriam. A. Tennyson.
   [Volume 3/351]
To Death. Gluck. [Volume 3/395]
"To Heaven Approached a Sufi Saint" J. Rumi.
   [Volume 4/405]
To Mary in Heaven. R. Burns. [Volume 3/339]
Too Late. D. Craik. [Volume 3/335]
The Two Mysteries. M. Dodge. [Volume 3/262]
The Two Worlds. M. Collins. [Volume 4/400]
The Undiscovered Country. E. Stedman. [Volume
   4/387]
"The Unillumined Verge" R. Bridges. [Volume 3/308]
The Uninhabited City: 002. E. Cardenal. [Supp
   6/154]
Vam E;sem. F. Scott. [Volume 3/361]
The Vanishing Boat. E. Gosse. [Supp 1/146]
Vigil. C. Meireles. [Supp 5/162]
Virtue Immortal. G. Herbert. [Volume 3/254]
Waiting in the Children's Hospital. C. Major.
   [Supp 4/199]
Watch Any Day. W. Auden. [Supp 2/169]
We Assume: On the Death of Our Son, %Reuben Masai
   Harper. M. Harper. [Supp 4/205]
We Were Three. C. Alegria. [Supp 5/12]
What of the Darkness? R. Le Gallienne. [Volume
   3/360]
When. S. Woolsey. [Volume 4/363]
"When Lilacs Last in the Dooryard Bloomed" W.
   Whitman. [Volume 3/362]
The Widow's Mite. F. Locker-Lampson. [Volume
   3/287]
A **Death-Bed**. J. Aldrich. [Volume 3/306]
The **Death-Bed**. T. Hood. [Volume 3/306]
**Death** in Life's Prime, fr. In Memoriam. A. Tennyson.
   [Volume 3/354]
**Death** in Youth, fr. Festus. P. Bailey. [Volume 3/428]
"**Death** is all metaphors, shape in one history."
   Altarwise by Owl-light: 002. D. Thomas. [Supp
   2/349]
The **Death** of Death. W. Shakespeare. [Volume 3/461]
The **Death** of Leonidas. G. Croly. [Volume 8/194]
The **Death** of Minnehaha, fr. The Song of Hiawatha. H.
   Longfellow. [Volume 3/319]
The **Death** of My Grandfather. H. Riyong. [Supp 6/50]
The **Death** of Sophocles. A. Akhmatova. [Supp 5/11]
The **Death** of the Ball Turret Gunner. R. Jarrell.
   [Supp 2/330]
**Death** of the Bull. R. Campbell. [Supp 2/91]
The **Death** of the Flowers. W. Byrant. [Volume 5/255]
The **Death** of the Hired Man. R. Frost. [Supp 1/135]
The **Death** of the Old Year. A. Tennyson. [Volume
   6/196]
**Death** the Leveller. J. Shirley. [Volume 3/254]
**Deborah** Lee. W. Burleigh. [Volume 9/400]
The **Debt**. P. Dunbar. [Supp 4/76]
*Debt*
   The Debt. P. Dunbar. [Supp 4/76]
The **Deceased**. K. Douglas. [Supp 2/405]
**December**. J. Benton. [Volume 5/175]
The **Deck** That Pouts. M. Piercy. [Supp 5/198]
A **Deed** and a Word. C. Mackay. [Volume 4/169]
"**Deep** in a forest wehre it rains." Cuckoos. M. Kaneko.
   [Supp 7/112]
"**Deep** in the winter plain, two armies." Two Armies. S.
   Spender. [Supp 2/235]
"**Deep** on the convent-roof the snows." Saint Agnes. A.
   Tennyson. [Volume 4/416]
A **Deer**. S. Murano. [Supp 7/120]
*Deer*
   A Deer. S. Murano. [Supp 7/120]
   Song. E. Cummings. [Supp 1/101]
"A **deer** at the verge of the forest." A Deer. S.
   Murano. [Supp 7/120]
**Defiance** Against Force. D. Diop. [Supp 6/70]
**Definition**. E. Rolfe. [Supp 2/217]

6/364]
Under the Portrait of John Milton. [Volume 7/54]
**Dryden, John (tr.)**
Veni Creator Spiritus. S. Gregory. [Volume 4/104]
**Du Bois, W. E. B.**
The Song of the Smoke. [Supp 4/65]
*Ducks*
Flighting for Duck. W. Empson. [Supp 2/142]
"The **Dule's** I' This Bonnet O' Mine" E. Waugh. [Volume 2/116]
"**Dull** swish of runners." Landing. A. Pozzi. [Supp 5/221]
"**Dull** unwashed windows of eyes." A Poem Some People Will Have to Understand. L. Jones. [Supp 4/178]
**Dunbar, Paul Laurence**
Conscience and Remorse. [Volume 4/326]
The Debt. [Supp 4/76]
"Ere Sleep comes Down To Soothe the Weary Eyes" [Supp 4/78]
Harriet Beecher Stowe. [Volume 7/105]
Little Brown Baby. [Supp 4/77]
On The Road. [Volume 2/292]
"We Wear the Mask That Grins and Lies" [Supp 4/75]
When Malindy Sings. [Supp 4/79]
**Dunbar, William**
Advice. [Volume 1/401]
The True Philosophy of Life. [Volume 6/299]
"**Duncan** Gray Cam' Here To Woo" R. Burns. [Volume 2/178]
**Dunlop, John**
Dinna Ask Me. [Volume 2/100]
**Duran, Cheli (tr.)**
Heat. N. Guillen. [Supp 6/138]
Monterrey Sun. A. Reyes. [Supp 6/149]
**Durbin, Harriet Whitney**
A Little Dutch Garden. [Volume 1/153]
"**During** the day I play at drowning." Plena. F. Lima. [Supp 4/248]
"**During** the middle watch." Vigils. T. Carmi. [Supp 7/241]
**Durivage, Francis Alexander**
All. [Volume 8/415]
**Durrell, Lawrence**
At Epidaurus. [Supp 2/257]
In Arcadia. [Supp 2/259]
Nemea. [Supp 2/260]
On Ithaca Standing. [Supp 2/260]
A Water-Colour of Venice. [Supp 2/261]
**Dusk.** S. Tanikawa. [Supp 7/136]
"The **dusky** night rides down the sky." A Hunting We Will Go. H. Fielding. [Volume 5/158]
A **Dutch** Lullaby. E. Field. [Volume 1/102]
**Dutton and Igor Mezhakoff-Koriakin, Geoffrey (tr.)**
"I Swear %By That Summer Photo" B. Akhmadulina. [Supp 5/3]
The Waitress. B. Akhmadulina. [Supp 5/2]
**Duty.** E. Hooper. [Volume 4/277]
"The **dwarf** barefooted, chanting." The Peasants. A. Lewis. [Supp 2/377]
"**Dwarf** pines; the wild plum on the wind-grassed shore." Colloquy with a King-Crab. J. Bishop. [Supp 2/24]
**Dwellers** at the Hermitage. D. Levertov. [Supp 5/143]
**Dwight, J. S. (tr.)**
The Landlady's Daughter. L. Uhland. [Volume 2/335]
**Dwight, Timothy**
Columbia. [Volume 8/89]
**Dyer, Edward**
"My Minde To Me a Kingdom Is" [Volume 6/325]
The **Dying** Christian to His Sould. A. Pope. [Volume 4/376]
The **Dying** Swan. A. Tennyson. [Volume 5/323]

**Each** and All. R. Emerson. [Volume 5/9]
"**Each** day, when the glow of sunset." Are the children at Home? M. Sangster. [Volume 3/288]
"**Each** golden not of music greets." Moonlight Song of the Mocking-bird. W. Hayne. [Volume 6/179]
"**Each** morn a thousand roses brings, you say." Rubaiyat: 009. O. Khayyam. [Volume 6/205]
"**Each** nation %whose vanguard sees the light." Nation's Hand. F. Daglarca. [Supp 7/303]
The **Eagle.** A. Tennyson. [Volume 5/321]
The **Eagle** and the Mole. E. Wylie. [Supp 1/326]
*Eagles*
The Eagle and the Mole. E. Wylie. [Supp 1/326]
The Eagle. A. Tennyson. [Volume 5/321]
The **Earl** O' Quarterdeck. G. MacDonald. [Volume 2/209]
"**Early** Evening Moon" A. Yosano. [Supp 7/144]
**Early** Friendship. A. De Vere. [Volume 1/344]
**Early** June, fr. Thyrsis. M. Arnold. [Volume 5/252]
**Early** Night. C. Forche. [Supp 5/82]
"**Early** on a sunny morning, while the lark was." Fetching Water From The Well. Unknown. [Volume 2/298]
"**Early** one winter morn, in such a village as this." Ivan Ivanovitch. R. Browning. [Volume 9/102]
The **Early** Primrose. H. White. [Volume 5/245]
**Early** Recollections. E. Chuilleanain. [Supp 5/192]
**Early** Spring. S. Keyes. [Supp 2/411]
"**Early** sun on beaulieu water." Youth and Age on Beaulieu River, Hants. J. Betjeman. [Supp 2/138]
"**Ears** in the Turrets Hear" D. Thomas. [Supp 2/362]
*Earth*
The Milk of the Mothers. M. Waddington. [Supp 5/310]
On Living: 003. N. Hikmet. [Supp 7/308]
To the Earth. Unknown (African American). [Supp 6/8]
"**Earth** and I Gave You Turquoise" N. Momaday. [Supp 4/302]
"**Earth,** condolences %earth, condolences." To the Earth. Unknown (African American). [Supp 6/8]
"**Earth** could not answer; nor the seas that mourn." Rubaiyat: 033. O. Khayyam. [Volume 6/210]
The **Earth** Falls Down. A. Sexton. [Supp 5/259]
"The **earth** goes on the earth glittering in gold." Inscription on Melrose Abbey. F. Beaumont. [Volume 3/269]
"**Earth** has not anything to show more fair." Sonnet. W. Wordsworth. [Volume 7/229]
"The **earth** is my mother." We Wait, 2. The Earth. R. Conley. [Supp 4/309]
"**Earth** now is green, and heaven is blue." To the Spring, fr. Hymnes of Astraea, in Acrosticke Verse. S. Davies. [Volume 7/3]
"**Earth,** ocean, air, beloved brotherhood!" Earth, Ocean, Air, fr. Alastor. P. Shelley. [Volume 5/4]
**Earth,** Ocean, Air, fr. Alastor. P. Shelley. [Volume 5/4]
The **Earth** Worm. D. Levertov. [Supp 5/142]
"**Easily,** my dear, you move, easily your head." A Bride in the '30's. W. Auden. [Supp 2/154]
**East,** West, Home's Best, fr. The Traveller. O. Goldsmith. [Volume 8/7]
*Easter*
Isis Wanderer. K. Raine. [Supp 2/199]
**Eastman, Charles Gamage**
A Picture. [Volume 1/315]
A Snow-storm. [Volume 5/180]
**Eastman, Elaine Goodale**
Ashes of Roses. [Volume 3/51]
Goldenrod. [Volume 5/285]
**Eaton, Arthur Wentworth**
The Voyage of Sleep. [Volume 6/438]

**Eberhart, Richard**
    "The Goal of Intellectual Man" [Supp 2/126]
    The Groundhog. [Supp 2/127]
    "I Walked Out to the Graveyard to See the Dead" [Supp 2/128]
    Mysticism Has Not the Patience to Wait for God's Revelation [Supp 2/128]
Ecce Homo. D. Gascoyne. [Supp 2/380]
Echo. J. Saxe. [Volume 9/211]
Echo and Silence. S. Brydges. [Volume 6/180]
Echo and the Lover. Unknown. [Volume 9/210]
"Echo! mysterious nymph, declare." Echo and the Lover. Unknown. [Volume 9/210]
Echo of Mandela. Z. Mandela. [Supp 6/78]
Echoes. T. Moore. [Volume 2/327]
An Eclogue for Christmas. L. MacNeice. [Supp 2/174]
"Eddie hung a light globe with the best electric." West Coast Episode. J. Jordan. [Supp 5/128]
*Education*
    An Elementary School Classroom in a Slum. S. Spender. [Supp 2/227]
**Edwards, Amelia Blandford**
    "Give Me Three Grains of Corn, Mother" [Volume 3/197]
*Edwards, Jonathan*
    Mr. Edwards and the Spider. R. Lowell. [Supp 2/393]
Edwon and Paulinus. Unknown. [Volume 4/385]
"E'en such is time; that takes in trust." Lines Found in His Bible in the Gate-house at Westminster. S. Raleigh. [Volume 4/352]
The Eggs And The Horses. Unknown. [Volume 2/432]
*Egypt*
    "Go Down, Moses" Unknown (African American). [Supp 4/48]
"Egyptian banks, an avenue of clay." Flighting for Duck. W. Empson. [Supp 2/142]
"The elder folk shook hands at last." The Meeting. J. Whittier. [Volume 4/208]
An Elegy. D. Gascoyne. [Supp 2/382]
Elegy. S. Keyes. [Supp 2/411]
Elegy for a Dead Soldier: 001. K. Shapiro. [Supp 2/314]
Elegy for a Dead Soldier: 002. K. Shapiro. [Supp 2/314]
Elegy for a Dead Soldier: 003. K. Shapiro. [Supp 2/314]
Elegy for a Dead Soldier: 004. K. Shapiro. [Supp 2/315,War]
Elegy for a Dead Soldier: 005. K. Shapiro. [Supp 2/315]
Elegy for a Dead Soldier: 006. K. Shapiro. [Supp 2/316]
Elegy for a Dead Soldier: 007. K. Shapiro. [Supp 2/316]
Elegy for a Dead Soldier: 008. K. Shapiro. [Supp 2/316]
Elegy for a Dead Soldier: 009. K. Shapiro. [Supp 2/317]
Elegy for a Dead Soldier: 010. K. Shapiro. [Supp 2/317]
Elegy for a Dead Soldier: 011. K. Shapiro. [Supp 2/318]
Elegy of the Wind. C. Okigbo. [Supp 6/62]
Elegy on Captain Matthew Henderson. R. Burns. [Volume 1/363]
elegy on Madam Blaize. O. Goldsmith. [Volume 9/266]
Elegy on the Death of a Mad Dog. O. Goldsmith. [Volume 9/263]
Elegy Written in a Country Churchyard. T. Gray. [Volume 3/270]
Elegy Written on a Frontporch. K. Shapiro. [Supp 2/318]
An Elementary School Classroom in a Slum. S. Spender. [Supp 2/227]

The Elements. O. Williams. [Supp 2/78]
The Elephant & the Butterfly Meet on the Buddha's Birthday. D. Wakoski. [Supp 5/320]
"Elephant beaten with candy and little pops and chews all bolts." A Sound. G. Stein. [Supp 5/293]
*Elephants*
    The Elephant & the Butterfly Meet on the Buddha's Birthday. D. Wakoski. [Supp 5/320]
The Elf and the Dormouse. O. Herford. [Volume 1/152]
**Eliot, Ebenezer**
    Corn-Law Hymn. [Volume 6/397]
    Spring. [Volume 5/88]
Eliot, George [pseud.] See Cross, Marian Evans L.
**Eliot, Samuel Atkins (tr.)**
    Labor Done, fr. Song of the Bell. J. Schiller. [Volume 6/412]
**Eliot, T. S.**
    La Figlia Che Piange. [Supp 1/120]
    Portrait of a Lady. [Supp 1/116]
    Salutation. [Supp 1/114]
**Elliot, Lady Charlotte**
    The Wife Of Loki. [Volume 2/398]
**Elliott, Ebenezer**
    Burns. [Volume 7/63]
Emerson. S. Woolsey. [Volume 7/97]
**Emerson, Ralph Waldo**
    Brahma. [Volume 4/6]
    Each and All. [Volume 5/9]
    Friendship. [Volume 1/339]
    Friendship, fr. Night Thoughts. [Volume 1/340]
    Good-bye. [Volume 4/31]
    Hymn. [Volume 8/326]
    The Problem. [Volume 4/229]
    The Rhodora. [Volume 5/252]
    The Sea. [Volume 5/374]
    The Snow-Storm. [Volume 5/176]
    To the Humblebee. [Volume 5/342]
The Emigrant Lassie. J. Blackie. [Volume 3/280]
**Empson, William**
    Camping Out. [Supp 2/140]
    Flighting for Duck. [Supp 2/142]
    Four Legs, Three Legs, Two Legs. [Supp 2/143]
    Homage to the British Museum. [Supp 2/141]
    Invitation to Juno. [Supp 2/141]
    Legal Fiction. [Supp 2/144]
    Missing Dates. [Supp 2/144]
    Note on Local Flora. [Supp 2/145]
    This Last Pain. [Supp 2/145]
Empty House. R. Castellanos. [Supp 5/50]
"An empty sky, a world of heather." Divided. J. Ingelow. [Volume 3/64]
Empty Vessel. H. MacDiarmid. [Supp 2/29]
"The empty winds are creaking and the oak." The Quaker Graveyard in Nantucket: 007. R. Lowell. [Supp 2/398]
"E'n like two little bank-dividing brooks." A Mystical Ecstasy. F. Quarles. [Volume 4/142]
The Enamel Girl. G. Taggard. [Supp 1/292]
The Encounter. J. Wright. [Supp 5/333]
"The end has come. We must sleep." Lullaby. T. Carmi. [Supp 7/244,Supp 7/243]
End of the Civil War, fr. King Richard III. W. Shakespeare. [Volume 8/424]
The End of the Day. D. Scott. [Volume 5/51]
The End of the Play. W. Thackeray. [Volume 4/256]
The End of the World. A. MacLeish. [Supp 1/203]
"The engine is killing the track, the track is silver." Totem. S. Plath. [Supp 5/216]
England and Her Colonies. W. Watson. [Volume 8/32]
*England and the English*
    Autumn Morning at Cambridge. F. Cornford. [Supp 1/91]
    The Canterbury Pilgrims, fr. The Canterbury Tales. G. Chaucer. [Volume 7/363]
    The Dream of Eugene Aram. T. Hood. [Volume 9/157]

England, fr. King John. W. Shakespeare. [Volume 7/390]
Godiva. A. Tennyson. [Volume 7/361]
The Greenwood Shrift. R. Southey. [Volume 7/379]
High-tide on the Coast of Lincolnshire. J. Ingelow. [Volume 9/145]
In the Engine-shed. W. Wilkins. [Volume 9/165]
In the Train. C. Bax. [Supp 1/27]
Lord Lovel. Unknown. [Volume 7/373]
The Old Vicarage, Grantchester. R. Brooke. [Supp 1/76]
Parliament Hill Fields. J. Betjeman. [Supp 2/136]
Perhaps. W. Auden. [Supp 2/165]
Revelry of the Dying. B. Dowling. [Volume 9/170]
The Revenge. A. Tennyson. [Volume 7/383]
Rizpah. A. Tennyson. [Volume 9/151]
Robin Hood and Allan-A-Dale. Unknown. [Volume 7/375]
The Rolling English Road. G. Chesterton. [Supp 1/81]
The Rose and the Gauntlet. J. Sterling. [Volume 9/131]
Sonnet - Realities I. E. Cummings. [Supp 1/104]
The South Country. H. Belloc. [Supp 1/31]
Upper Lambourne. J. Betjeman. [Supp 2/138]
The Welsh Marches. A. Housman. [Supp 1/167]
The Young Gray Head. C. Southey. [Volume 9/132]
England, fr. King John. W. Shakespeare. [Volume 7/390]
England, fr. The Timepiece. W. Cowper. [Volume 8/10]
England, fr. The Traveller. O. Goldsmith. [Volume 7/199]
"England, I stand on thy imperial ground." At Gibraltar. G. Woodberry. [Volume 8/439]
England to America. S. Dobell. [Supp 8/92]
"England, with all thy faults, I love thee still." England, fr. The Timepiece. W. Cowper. [Volume 8/10]
*English Army*
    Lessons of the War: Judging Distances. H. Reed. [Supp 2/344]
The English Robin. H. Weir. [Volume 5/327]
English Sparrows. E. Millay. [Supp 5/168]
**English, Thomas Dunn**
    Ben Bolt. [Volume 1/222]
Enid's Song, fr. Idyls of the King. A. Tennyson. [Volume 6/266]
"Enter Harlem %to walke from the howiling cave." Walk with De Mayor of Harlem. D. Henderson. [Supp 4/207]
"Eors is missing. In the early morn." Eros Is Missing. Meleager. [Volume 2/17]
The Epicure. Anacreon. [Volume 6/248]
Epigram: Cologne. S. Coleridge. [Volume 9/286]
Epigram: "Hoarse Maevius Reads His Hobbling Verse" S. Coleridge. [Volume 9/286]
Epigram: "Sly Beelzebub Took All Occasions" S. Coleridge. [Volume 9/286]
Epigram: "Swans Sing Before They Die" S. Coleridge. [Volume 9/287]
Epilogue. R. Browning. [Volume 4/374]
Epilogue from Emblems of Love. L. Abercrombie. [Supp 1/1]
Epiphany. R. Heber. [Volume 4/50]
Epitaph. L. Abercrombie. [Supp 1/5]
Epitaph. G. Canning. [Volume 9/292]
Epitaph. K. Shapiro. [Supp 2/318]
An Epitaph on the Admirable Dramatic Poet, W. Shakespeare. J. Milton. [Volume 7/51]
*Epitaphs*
    "After the Funeral" D. Thomas. [Supp 2/347]
    Burial: 003. A. Walker. [Supp 4/226]
    Burial: 004. A. Walker. [Supp 4/226]
    Elegy. S. Keyes. [Supp 2/411]
    It Would Be Nice to Deserve this Epitaph. R.

Retamar. [Supp 6/144]
    Tombstone with Cherubim. H. Gregory. [Supp 2/66]
*Equality*
    "I, Too, Sing America" L. Hughes. [Supp 4/131]
    "Ere Sleep comes Down To Soothe the Weary Eyes" P. Dunbar. [Supp 4/78]
The Erl-King. J. Goethe. [Volume 6/58]
Erminia and the Wounded Tancred. T. Tasso. [Volume 7/319]
Eros Is Missing. Meleager. [Volume 2/17]
*Erotic Love*
    "O Wha's Been Here Afore Me, Lass" H. MacDiarmid. [Supp 2/30]
    23rd Street Runs into Heaven. K. Patchen. [Supp 2/255]
"Erratic soul of some great purpose, doomed." The Comet. C. Sangster. [Volume 6/88]
**Erskine; Earl of Rosslyn, Francis Robert St. Clair**
    Bedtime. [Volume 1/39]
**Erskine, Ralph**
    Smoking Spiritualized. [Volume 6/250]
"The essence of the matter." What Value Has the People Whose Tongue Is Tied?: 007. N. Qabbani. [Supp 7/287]
**Esteves, Sandra Maria**
    Blanket Weaver. [Supp 4/292]
The Eternal Goodness. J. Whittier. [Volume 4/42]
"Eternal spirit of the chainless mind!" The Prisoner of Chillon. G. Byron. [Volume 9/88]
Eternal Struggle. Tru Vu. [Supp 7/198]
*Eternity*
    Desire. K. Raine. [Supp 2/197]
    Iliad. H. Wolfe. [Supp 1/321]
"Ethereal minstrel! pilgrim of the sky!" To the Skylark. W. Wordsworth. [Volume 5/296]
"Ethereal power! who at the noon of night." Blest Memory, fr. The Pleasures of Memory. S. Rogers. [Volume 6/300]
An Etruscan Ring. J. Mackail. [Volume 7/149]
Etude Realiste. A. Swinburne. [Volume 1/8]
**Euripides**
    Choral Song, fr. The Bacchae. H. Milman (tr.). [Volume 5/215]
    Sacrifice of Polyxena, fr. Hecuba. J. Symonds (tr.). [Volume 9/5]
Eurydice in Hades. J. Wright. [Supp 5/334]
Euthanasia. W. Clark. [Volume 4/359]
Eve. R. Hodgson. [Supp 1/163]
The Eve of Saint Agnes. J. Keats. [Volume 2/312]
Eve to Adam, fr. Paradise Lost. J. Milton. [Volume 4/273]
"Eve, with her basket, was." Eve. R. Hodgson. [Supp 1/163]
Evelyn Hope. R. Browning. [Volume 3/310]
"Even for the wind there was no room." The Way the Bird Sat. R. Bear. [Supp 4/337]
"Even in the graveyard, sleek golden turf." Hymn to the Graveyard. Pak Tu-Jin. [Supp 7/151]
"Even is come; and from the dark Park, hark." Nocturnal Sketch. T. Hood. [Volume 9/430]
Evening. A. Lampman. [Volume 5/52]
The Evening Cloud. J. Wilson. [Volume 7/156]
Evening, fr. Don Juan. G. Byron. [Volume 5/57]
Evening in Paradise, fr. Paradise Lost. J. Milton. [Volume 5/56]
Evening Scene. E. Scovell. [Supp 2/187]
The Evening Wind. W. Bryant. [Volume 5/54]
"Ever eating, never cloying." Time. J. Swift. [Volume 6/224]
"Ever let the fancy roam." Fancy. J. Keats. [Volume 6/9]
"The evergreen shadow and the pale magnolia." Souls Lake. R. Fitzgerald. [Supp 2/241]
"Every one." The Coral Reef, fr. The Pelican Island. J. Montgomery. [Volume 5/396]

"**Everybody** give the big boy a hand." Dempsey, Dempsey. H. Gregory. [Supp 2/62]
"**Everybody** loved Chick Lorimer in our town." Gone. C. Sandburg. [Supp 1/281]
"**Everyone** walking everywhere goes in a glow." Sacred Elegy V: 002. G. Barker. [Supp 2/290]
"**Everywhere** the substance of earth is the gate that we cannot." The Locked Gates. K. Raine. [Supp 5/225]
Eve's Lament, fr. Paradise Lost. J. Milton. [Volume 4/272]
"**Eveyone** buys his own." Cazonetta. A. Pozzi. [Supp 5/220]
*Evolution*
    The Menagerie. W. Moody. [Supp 1/228]
**Example**. J. Keble. [Volume 4/309]
**Excelsior**. H. Longfellow. [Volume 6/257]
The **Exchange**. S. Coleridge. [Volume 2/164]
The **Execution** of Montrose. W. Aytoun. [Volume 8/43]
**Exhortation** to Prayer. M. Mercer. [Volume 4/116]
**Exile**. I. Bachmann. [Supp 5/24]
**Exile** of Erin. T. Campbell. [Volume 8/67]
The **Exile's** Song. R. Gilfillan. [Volume 8/51]
*Exodus from Egypt*
    Departure in the Dark. C. Day Lewis. [Supp 2/113]
"**Expect** Nothing. Live Frugally" A. Walker. [Supp 4/224]
*Experience*
    The Lost Son: 005. T. Roethke. [Supp 2/210]
    The Lost Son: The Flight. T. Roethke. [Supp 2/205]
    The Lost Son: The Gibber. T. Roethke. [Supp 2/207]
    The Lost Son: The Pit. T. Roethke. [Supp 2/207]
    The Lost Son: The Return. T. Roethke. [Supp 2/209]
An **Experience** and a Moral. F. Cozzens. [Volume 2/58]
**Explorations**. L. MacNeice. [Supp 2/178]
**Eye** Glasses. G. Stein. [Supp 5/293]
**Eye-Witness**. R. Torrence. [Supp 1/303]
"The **eyeless** labourer in the night." Woman to Man. J. Wright. [Supp 5/327]
**Eytinge, Margaret**
    Baby Louise. [Volume 1/21]
**Ezekiel, Nissim**
    Island. [Supp 7/54]
    Night of the Scorpion. [Supp 7/53]
    Torso of a Woman. [Supp 7/55]

**Faber, Frederick William**
    Low Spirits. [Volume 4/338]
    Paradise. [Volume 4/434]
    The Right Must Win. [Volume 4/299]
    The Will of God. [Volume 4/36]
    The Word. [Volume 4/284]
"**Fabric** of earth and wind and wave!" Ghazal No. 9. M. Iqbal. [Supp 7/57]
**Face**. S. Tanikawa. [Supp 7/133]
**Face** Lost in the Wilderness. F. Tuqan. [Supp 7/273]
The **Face** of Hunger. M. Mtshali. [Supp 6/84]
"The **face** which, duly as the sun." De Profundis. E. Browning. [Volume 3/421]
*Faces*
    Face. S. Tanikawa. [Supp 7/133]
"The **faces** of women long dead, of our family." Women Songs: 001. K. Molodowsky. [Supp 5/172]
**Fafnir** and the Knights. S. Smith. [Supp 5/282]
*Failure*
    To a Friend Whose Work Has Come to Nothing. W. Yeats. [Supp 1/329]
"**Fair** are the flowers and the children, but their." Indirection. R. Realf. [Volume 6/332]
"**Fair** Greece! sad relic of departed worth!" Greece Enslaved, fr. Childe Harold. G. Byron. [Volume 8/127]

**Fair** Helen. Unknown. [Volume 3/330]
**Fair** Ines. T. Hood. [Volume 3/10]
"**Fair** lady, when you see the grace." To a Lady Admiring Herself in a Looking-Glass. T. Randolph. [Volume 2/21]
"A **Fair** little girl sat under a tree." Good Night and Good Morning. R. Milnes. [Volume 1/109]
"**Fair** pledges of a fruitful tree." To Blossoms. R. Herrick. [Volume 5/279]
"**Fair** Portia's counterfeit? What demi-god." Portia's Picture, fr. The Merchant of Venice. W. Shakespeare. [Volume 2/11]
"**Fair** ship, that from the Italian shore." Dead, In a Foreign Land, fr. In Memoriam. A. Tennyson. [Volume 3/349]
"**Fair** stood the wind for France." The Ballad of Agincourt. M. Drayton. [Volume 8/264]
"**Faire** daffadills, we weep to see." To Daffodils. R. Herrick. [Volume 5/246]
**Fairest** Thing in Mortal Eyes. D. Charles. [Volume 3/356]
The **Fairies**. W. Allingham. [Volume 6/19]
*Fairies*
    Airy Nothings, fr. The Tempest. W. Shakespeare. [Volume 6/58]
    Compliment to Queen Elizabeth, fr. A Midsummer Night's Dream. W. Shakespeare. [Volume 6/17]
    The Culprit Fay. J. Drake. [Volume 6/35]
    The Djinns. V. Hugo. [Volume 6/60]
    The Erl-King. J. Goethe. [Volume 6/58]
    The Fairies' Lullaby, fr. A Midsummer Night's Dream. W. Shakespeare. [Volume 6/18]
    Fairies' Song. T. Randolph. [Volume 6/19]
    The Fairies. W. Allingham. [Volume 6/19]
    The Fairy Child. J. Anster. [Volume 6/32]
    Fairy's Song, fr. A Midsummer Night's Dream. W. Shakespeare. [Volume 6/16]
    The Flitting of the Fairies, fr. The End of Elfintown. J. Barlow. [Volume 6/85]
    The Forsaken Merman. M. Arnold. [Volume 6/80]
    Garden Fairies. P. Marston. [Volume 6/33]
    Kilmeny, fr. The Queen's Wake. J. Hogg. [Volume 6/21]
    The Lady Lost in the Wood, fr. Comus. J. Milton. [Volume 6/64]
    The Lore-Lei. H. Heine. [Volume 6/77]
    The Nymph of the Severn, fr. Comus. J. Milton. [Volume 6/66]
    Oberon's Feast. R. Herrick. [Volume 6/14]
    "Oh! Where Do Fairies Hide Their Heads?" T. Bayly. [Volume 6/56]
    Queen Mab, fr. Romeo and Juliet. W. Shakespeare. [Volume 6/13]
    The Sirens' Song, fr. Inner Temple Masque. W. Browne. [Volume 6/79]
    Songs of Ariel, fr. The Tempest. W. Shakespeare. [Volume 6/57]
    Tam O' Shanter. R. Burns. [Volume 6/70]
The **Fairies** of the Caldon Low. M. Howitt. [Volume 1/148]
The **Fairies'** Lullaby, fr. A Midsummer Night's Dream. W. Shakespeare. [Volume 6/18]
**Fairies'** Song. T. Randolph. [Volume 6/19]
*Fairs*
    Holstenwall. S. Keyes. [Supp 2/413]
The **Fairy** Child. J. Anster. [Volume 6/32]
**Fairy** Days. W. Thackeray. [Volume 1/141]
**Fairy's** Song, fr. A Midsummer Night's Dream. W. Shakespeare. [Volume 6/16]
**Faith**. F. Kemble-Butler. [Volume 3/95]
**Faith**. G. Santayana. [Volume 4/136]
*Faith*
    The Call. G. Herbert. [Volume 4/144]
    Deus Absconditus. A. Ridler. [Supp 2/272]
    Doubt and Faith, fr. In Memoriam. A. Tennyson.

[Volume 4/139]
Faith. G. Santayana. [Volume 4/136]
The Fight of Faith. A. Askewe. [Volume 4/136]
"It Is Time That I Wrote My Will" W. Yeats. [Supp 1/330]
"My Times Are In Thy Hand" C. Hall. [Volume 4/140]
A Mystical Ecstasy. F. Quarles. [Volume 4/142]
Mysticism Has Not the Patience to Wait for God's Revelation. R. Eberhart. [Supp 2/128]
The Mystics Vision. M. Blind. [Volume 4/142]
The Oxen. T. Hardy. [Supp 1/159]
A Winter's Tale. D. Thomas. [Supp 2/368]
Faith And Hope. R. Peale. [Volume 2/446]
The Faithful Angel, fr. Paradise Lost. J. Milton. [Volume 4/337]
The Faithful Lovers. Unknown. [Volume 2/231]
Faithless Nelly Gray. T. Hood. [Volume 9/268]
Faithless Sally Brown. T. Hood. [Volume 9/271]
Faiz, Faiz Ahmed
    Blackout. N. Lazard (tr.). [Supp 7/169]
    Introduction. N. Lazard (tr.). [Supp 7/169]
    My Visitors. N. Lazard (tr.). [Supp 7/174]
    Once Again the Mind. N. Lazard (tr.). [Supp 7/173]
    Prison Daybreak. N. Lazard (tr.). [Supp 7/171]
    We Were Commanded by This Heart. N. Lazard (tr.). [Supp 7/175]
    When Autumn Came. N. Lazard (tr.). [Supp 7/170]
The Falconer of God. W. Benet. [Supp 1/46]
Falconer, William
    The Shipwreck. [Volume 5/417]
The Fall. K. Raine. [Supp 2/198]
The Fall, fr. Paradise Lost. J. Milton. [Volume 4/268]
The Fall of Cardinal Wolsey, fr. King Henry VIII. W. Shakespeare. [Volume 3/161]
The Fall of Niagara. J. Brainard. [Volume 5/208]
The Fall of Troy, fr. Aeneid. Virgil (Publius Vergillius Maro). [Volume 7/261]
The Fallen. J. Cheney. [Volume 6/442]
"The fallen cause still waits." The Cause of the South, fr. Sentinel Songs. A. Ryan. [Volume 8/451]
Fallen Greece, fr. The Giaour. G. Byron. [Volume 8/125]
Falling Asleep over the Aeneid. R. Lowell. [Supp 2/390]
"False dreams, all false." Iliad. H. Wolfe. [Supp 1/321]
A False Step. B. Al-Haydari. [Supp 7/227]
"False world, thou ly'st: thou canst not lend." The Vanity of the World. F. Quarles. [Volume 3/153]
Fame, fr. An Essay on Man. A. Pope. [Volume 6/264]
*Family*
    The Idea of Ancestry. E. Knight. [Supp 4/169]
"The family has been ill for some time." Resurrection of the Daughter. N. Shange. [Supp 5/266]
The Family Skeleton, fr. Modern Love. G. Meredith. [Volume 6/247]
"A famous hen's my story's theme." The Hen. M. Claudius. [Volume 9/436]
Fancy. J. Keats. [Volume 6/9]
A Fancy from Frontenelle. A. Dobson. [Volume 6/198]
Fancy in Nubibus. S. Coleridge. [Volume 5/50]
*Fans*
    On a Fan. A. Dobson. [Volume 6/385]
    A Painted Fan. L. Moulton. [Volume 6/385]
Fanshawe, Catharine
    A Riddle. [Volume 9/450]
Fantasy, fr. The Vision of Delight. B. Johnson. [Volume 6/3]
Far-Away. G. Sigerson. [Volume 6/183]
"Far away my sister is moving in her crib." Descending Figure: 3. For My Sister. L. Gluck. [Supp 5/103]
"Far far from gusty waves these children's faces." An

Elementary School Classroom in a Slum. S. Spender. [Supp 2/227]
"Far off, above the plain the summer dries." Second Air Force. R. Jarrell. [Supp 2/332]
"Far out at sea - the sun was high." Genius. R. Horne. [Volume 6/352]
"Far poured past Broadway's lamps alight." The Song of the Savoyards. H. Blood. [Volume 3/248]
"Fare thee well, and if forever." Farewell to His Wife. G. Byron. [Volume 3/109]
Farewell. L. Bahe. [Supp 4/322]
A Farewell. C. Kingsley. [Volume 1/205]
Farewell. W. Landor. [Volume 3/394]
A Farewell. A. Tennyson. [Volume 5/199]
Farewell at the Hour of Parting. A. Neto. [Supp 6/13]
"Farewell! - But Whenever You Welcome the Hour" T. Moore. [Volume 3/116]
"Farewell, -- Farewell to thee, Araby's daughter!" Farewell to Thee, Araby's Daughter, fr. The Fire-Worshippers. T. Moore. [Volume 3/316]
"'Farewell! farewell!' is often heard." Good-bye. Unknown. [Volume 3/97]
Farewell, Life. T. Hood. [Volume 3/384]
"Farewell, life! my senses swim." Farewell, Life. T. Hood. [Volume 3/384]
"Farewell, my youth! for now we needs must part." Ave Atque Vale. R. Watson. [Volume 6/191]
"Farewell! since vain is all my care." To Diane de Poitiers. C. Marot. [Volume 3/69]
"Farewell! Thou Art Too Dear" W. Shakespeare. [Volume 3/112]
Farewell to His Wife. G. Byron. [Volume 3/109]
"Farewell to Lochaber! and farewell, my Jean." Lochaber No More. A. Ramsay. [Volume 3/105]
"Farewell to such a world! Too long I press." Among the Redwoods. E. Sill. [Volume 5/234]
Farewell to Thee, Araby's Daughter, fr. The Fire-Worshippers. T. Moore. [Volume 3/316]
"Farewell to this land of the earthbound, whose craving." The Hawk. M. Iqbal. [Supp 7/59]
A Farewell to Tobacco. C. Lamb. [Volume 9/389]
"The farmer sat in his easy-chair." A Picture. C. Eastman. [Volume 1/315]
"The farmer's wife sat at the door." "They Are Dear Fish to Me" Unknown. [Volume 3/195]
*Farming and Farmers*
    After Winter. S. Brown. [Supp 2/82]
    A Black Man Talks of Reaping. A. Bontemps. [Supp 4/126]
    Country Summer. L. Adams. [Supp 2/70]
    Foreclosure. S. Brown. [Supp 2/83]
Farrozkhzad, Forugh
    The Bird Was Only a Bird. A. Karimi-Hakkak (tr.). [Supp 7/220]
    I Pity the Garden. A. Karimi-Hakkak (tr.). [Supp 7/221]
    Those Days. A. Karimi-Hakkak (tr.). [Supp 7/214]
    The Wind Will Take Us. A. Karimi-Hakkak (tr.). [Supp 7/217]
    The Wind-Up Doll. A. Karimi-Hakkak (tr.). [Supp 7/219]
"Farther horizons evert year." Emerson. S. Woolsey. [Volume 7/97]
*Fascination*
    "I Was Always Fascinated" A. Villanueva. [Supp 4/266]
Fataher and Mother Tongue. S. Lover. [Volume 8/6]
*Fatalism*
    The Hero. R. Fuller. [Supp 2/263]
*Fate*
    The Fall. K. Raine. [Supp 2/198]
    A Proclamation. C. Anwar. [Supp 7/84]
*Fates, The (Mythology)*
    Foreclosure. S. Brown. [Supp 2/83]
    Ode. J. Bishop. [Supp 2/25]

First Cycle of Love Poems: 002. G. Barker. [Supp 2/279]
First Cycle of Love Poems: 003. G. Barker. [Supp 2/280]
First Cycle of Love Poems: 004. G. Barker. [Supp 2/280]
First Cycle of Love Poems: 005. G. Barker. [Supp 2/282]
"First drink a health, this solemn night." Hands All Round. A. Tennyson. [Volume 8/29]
"First, feel, then feel, then." Young Soul. L. Jones. [Supp 4/179]
The First Kiss. T. Campbell. [Volume 2/94]
The First Kiss. R. Tagore. [Supp 7/71]
First Love, fr. "Don Juan," Canto I. G. Byron. [Volume 2/256]
The First Morning in Vietnam. Ho Ch'i-Fang. [Supp 7/5]
The First of May. A. Housman. [Supp 1/169]
The First Rose of Summer. O. Herford. [Volume 1/154]
The First Snow-Fall. J. Lowell. [Volume 3/283]
"First there was the lamb on knocking knees." Altarwise by Owl-light: 003. D. Thomas. [Supp 2/349]
"The first time that I dreamed, we were in flight." The Lesson. W. Auden. [Supp 2/162]
The First Year. E. Scovell. [Supp 2/188]
Fish and Swimmer and Lonely Birds Sweep Past Us. M. Berssenbrugge. [Supp 4/11]
"Fish have no sound. Crickets sing long with their wings." Sound. Ho Ch'i-Fang. [Supp 7/7]
The Fisher. J. Goethe. [Volume 6/78]
*Fishing and Fishermen*
  Ballad of the Long-Legged Bait. D. Thomas. [Supp 2/353]
  The Drunken Fisherman. R. Lowell. [Supp 2/389]
  Lone Fisherman. T. Heraty. [Supp 7/97]
  Sonnet of Fishes. G. Barker. [Supp 2/291]
  The Trout Map. A. Tate. [Supp 2/76]
Fitz-Green Halleck. J. Whittier. [Volume 7/92]
Fitz-James and Ellen, fr. The Lady of the Lake. S. Scott. [Volume 7/413]
Fitz-James and Roderick Dhu, fr. The Lady of the Lake. S. Scott. [Volume 7/404]
Fitzgerald, Edward
  On Anne Allen. [Volume 3/303]
Fitzgerald, Edward (tr.)
  Dream-life, fr. Such Stuff as Dreams Are Made Of. P. Calderon. [Volume 6/324]
  Rubaiyat: 001. O. Khayyam. [Volume 6/204]
  Rubaiyat: 002. O. Khayyam. [Volume 6/204]
  Rubaiyat: 003. O. Khayyam. [Volume 6/204]
  Rubaiyat: 004. O. Khayyam. [Volume 6/204]
  Rubaiyat: 005. O. Khayyam. [Volume 6/204]
  Rubaiyat: 006. O. Khayyam. [Volume 6/205]
  Rubaiyat: 007. O. Khayyam. [Volume 6/205]
  Rubaiyat: 008. O. Khayyam. [Volume 6/205]
  Rubaiyat: 009. O. Khayyam. [Volume 6/205]
  Rubaiyat: 010. O. Khayyam. [Volume 6/205]
  Rubaiyat: 011. O. Khayyam. [Volume 6/206]
  Rubaiyat: 012. O. Khayyam. [Volume 6/206]
  Rubaiyat: 013. O. Khayyam. [Volume 6/206]
  Rubaiyat: 014. O. Khayyam. [Volume 6/206]
  Rubaiyat: 015. O. Khayyam. [Volume 6/206]
  Rubaiyat: 016. O. Khayyam. [Volume 6/207]
  Rubaiyat: 017. O. Khayyam. [Volume 6/207]
  Rubaiyat: 018. O. Khayyam. [Volume 6/207]
  Rubaiyat: 019. O. Khayyam. [Volume 6/207]
  Rubaiyat: 020. O. Khayyam. [Volume 6/207]
  Rubaiyat: 021. O. Khayyam. [Volume 6/208]
  Rubaiyat: 022. O. Khayyam. [Volume 6/208]
  Rubaiyat: 023. O. Khayyam. [Volume 6/208]
  Rubaiyat: 024. O. Khayyam. [Volume 6/208]
  Rubaiyat: 025. O. Khayyam. [Volume 6/208]
  Rubaiyat: 026. O. Khayyam. [Volume 6/209]
  Rubaiyat: 027. O. Khayyam. [Volume 6/209]
  Rubaiyat: 028. O. Khayyam. [Volume 6/209]
  Rubaiyat: 029. O. Khayyam. [Volume 6/209]
  Rubaiyat: 030. O. Khayyam. [Volume 6/209]
  Rubaiyat: 031. O. Khayyam. [Volume 6/210]
  Rubaiyat: 032. O. Khayyam. [Volume 6/210]
  Rubaiyat: 033. O. Khayyam. [Volume 6/210]
  Rubaiyat: 034. O. Khayyam. [Volume 6/210]
  Rubaiyat: 035. O. Khayyam. [Volume 6/210]
  Rubaiyat: 036. O. Khayyam. [Volume 6/211]
  Rubaiyat: 037. O. Khayyam. [Volume 6/211]
  Rubaiyat: 038. O. Khayyam. [Volume 6/211]
  Rubaiyat: 039. O. Khayyam. [Volume 6/211]
  Rubaiyat: 040. O. Khayyam. [Volume 6/211]
  Rubaiyat: 041. O. Khayyam. [Volume 6/212]
  Rubaiyat: 042. O. Khayyam. [Volume 6/212]
  Rubaiyat: 043. O. Khayyam. [Volume 6/212]
  Rubaiyat: 044. O. Khayyam. [Volume 6/212]
  Rubaiyat: 045. O. Khayyam. [Volume 6/212]
  Rubaiyat: 046. O. Khayyam. [Volume 6/213]
  Rubaiyat: 047. O. Khayyam. [Volume 6/213]
  Rubaiyat: 048. O. Khayyam. [Volume 6/213]
  Rubaiyat: 049. O. Khayyam. [Volume 6/213]
  Rubaiyat: 050. O. Khayyam. [Volume 6/213]
  Rubaiyat: 051. O. Khayyam. [Volume 6/214]
  Rubaiyat: 052. O. Khayyam. [Volume 6/214]
  Rubaiyat: 053. O. Khayyam. [Volume 6/214]
  Rubaiyat: 054. O. Khayyam. [Volume 6/214]
  Rubaiyat: 055. O. Khayyam. [Volume 6/214]
  Rubaiyat: 056. O. Khayyam. [Volume 6/215]
  Rubaiyat: 057. O. Khayyam. [Volume 6/215]
  Rubaiyat: 058. O. Khayyam. [Volume 6/215]
  Rubaiyat: 059. O. Khayyam. [Volume 6/215]
  Rubaiyat: 060. O. Khayyam. [Volume 6/215]
  Rubaiyat: 061. O. Khayyam. [Volume 6/216]
  Rubaiyat: 062. O. Khayyam. [Volume 6/216]
  Rubaiyat: 063. O. Khayyam. [Volume 6/216]
  Rubaiyat: 064. O. Khayyam. [Volume 6/216]
  Rubaiyat: 065. O. Khayyam. [Volume 6/216]
  Rubaiyat: 066. O. Khayyam. [Volume 6/217]
  Rubaiyat: 067. O. Khayyam. [Volume 6/217]
  Rubaiyat: 068. O. Khayyam. [Volume 6/217]
  Rubaiyat: 069. O. Khayyam. [Volume 6/217]
  Rubaiyat: 070. O. Khayyam. [Volume 6/217]
  Rubaiyat: 071. O. Khayyam. [Volume 6/218]
  Rubaiyat: 072. O. Khayyam. [Volume 6/218]
  Rubaiyat: 073. O. Khayyam. [Volume 6/218]
  Rubaiyat: 074. O. Khayyam. [Volume 6/218]
  Rubaiyat: 075. O. Khayyam. [Volume 6/218]
  Rubaiyat: 076. O. Khayyam. [Volume 6/219]
  Rubaiyat: 077. O. Khayyam. [Volume 6/219]
  Rubaiyat: 078. O. Khayyam. [Volume 6/219]
  Rubaiyat: 079. O. Khayyam. [Volume 6/219]
  Rubaiyat: 080. O. Khayyam. [Volume 6/219]
  Rubaiyat: 081. O. Khayyam. [Volume 6/220]
  Rubaiyat: 082. O. Khayyam. [Volume 6/220]
  Rubaiyat: 083. O. Khayyam. [Volume 6/220]
  Rubaiyat: 084. O. Khayyam. [Volume 6/220]
  Rubaiyat: 085. O. Khayyam. [Volume 6/220]
  Rubaiyat: 086. O. Khayyam. [Volume 6/221]
  Rubaiyat: 087. O. Khayyam. [Volume 6/221]
  Rubaiyat: 088. O. Khayyam. [Volume 6/221]
  Rubaiyat: 089. O. Khayyam. [Volume 6/221]
  Rubaiyat: 090. O. Khayyam. [Volume 6/221]
  Rubaiyat: 091. O. Khayyam. [Volume 6/222]
  Rubaiyat: 092. O. Khayyam. [Volume 6/222]
  Rubaiyat: 093. O. Khayyam. [Volume 6/222]
  Rubaiyat: 094. O. Khayyam. [Volume 6/222]
  Rubaiyat: 095. O. Khayyam. [Volume 6/222]
  Rubaiyat: 096. O. Khayyam. [Volume 6/223]
  Rubaiyat: 097. O. Khayyam. [Volume 6/223]
  Rubaiyat: 098. O. Khayyam. [Volume 6/223]
  Rubaiyat: 099. O. Khayyam. [Volume 6/223]
  Rubaiyat: 100. O. Khayyam. [Volume 6/223]
  Rubaiyat: 101. O. Khayyam. [Volume 6/224]

7/288]

"For I Am a Stranger" B. Al-Sayyab. [Supp 7/232]

"For I remember stopping by the way." Rubaiyat: 037. O. Khayyam. [Volume 6/211]

"For infants time is like a humming shell." O Dreams, O Destinations: 001. C. Day Lewis. [Supp 2/118]

"for 'is' and 'is-not' though with rule and." Rubaiyat: 056. O. Khayyam. [Volume 6/215]

"For it seems you wish to know." A Gage D'amour. A. Dobson. [Volume 2/56]

For Mrs N. C. Anwar. [Supp 7/85]

For My Daughter. J. Wright. [Supp 5/329]

For One Who Would Not Take His Life in His Hands. D. Schwartz. [Supp 2/307]

"For Scotland's and for freedom's right." Bruce and the Spider. B. Barton. [Volume 8/302]

"For some we loved, the loveliest and the best." Rubaiyat: 022. O. Khayyam. [Volume 6/208]

For St. Bartholomew's Eve. M. Cowley. [Supp 2/59]

"For that I never knew you, I only learned to dread you." St. Roach. M. Rukeyser. [Supp 5/244]

For the Record. Ping Hsin. [Supp 5/115]

"For this comradfe is dead, dead in the war." Elegy for a Dead Soldier: 003. K. Shapiro. [Supp 2/314]

"For this hold true - too true, alas!" The Flitting of the Fairies, fr. The End of Elfintown. J. Barlow. [Volume 6/85]

"For those had the power." A Time to Dance. C. Day Lewis. [Supp 2/124]

"For to die young is youth's divinest gift." Death in Youth, fr. Festus. P. Bailey. [Volume 3/428]

"For why, who writes such histories as these." Books. J. Higgins. [Volume 6/361]

Forche, Carolyn
    Departure. [Supp 5/87]
    Early Night. [Supp 5/82]
    The Island. [Supp 5/84]
    Mountain Abbey, Surrounded by Elk Horns. [Supp 5/83]

Forche, Carolyn (tr.)
    Letter to Time. C. Alegria. [Supp 5/14]
    We Were Three. C. Alegria. [Supp 5/12]

Foreclosure. S. Brown. [Supp 2/83]

Foreign Children. R. Stevenson. [Volume 1/130]

Foreign Lands. R. Stevenson. [Volume 1/138]

The Foreigner. G. Mistral. [Supp 6/129]

"Foremost of false philosophies." Sea, False Philosophy. L. Riding. [Supp 1/264]

A Forest Hymn. W. Bryant. [Volume 5/223]

"A forest rose from the earth." Lamentations: 2. Nocturne. L. Gluck. [Supp 5/106]

Forests
    Assimilation. E. Manner. [Supp 5/148]
    Civilization. H. Riyong. [Supp 6/49]
    The Little Boy Lost. S. Smith. [Supp 2/103]
    Orion Dead. H. Doolittle. [Supp 5/71]
    "Redeemed %From Sleep" N. Sachs. [Supp 5/253]

"Forever" C. Calverley. [Volume 9/424]

Forever Unconfessed. R. Milnes. [Volume 2/241]

"Forever with the Lord" J. Montgomery. [Volume 4/403]

"Forever! 'T is a single word!" "Forever" C. Calverley. [Volume 9/424]

Forget Thee? J. Moultrie. [Volume 2/337]

"'Forget thee?' - If to dream by night, and muse." Forget Thee? J. Moultrie. [Volume 2/337]

Forgetfulness
    "Let It Be Forgotten" S. Teasdale. [Supp 1/293]
    When You Have Forgotten Sunday: The Love Story. G. Brooks. [Supp 4/156]

The Forging of the Anchor. S. Ferguson. [Volume 7/234]

Form. C. Major. [Supp 4/201]

"Formalized %by middle age." The Song of Bullets. J. Hagedorn. [Supp 4/29]

Forms
    Form. C. Major. [Supp 4/201]

Forrester, Alfred A. ("Alfred Crowquill")
    To My Nose. [Volume 9/421]

A Forsaken Garden. A. Swinburne. [Volume 5/388]

The Forsaken Merman. M. Arnold. [Volume 6/80]

Fortune. Sophocles. [Volume 6/283]

Fortune, fr. Fanny. F. Halleck. [Volume 6/266]

"The Forward Violet Thus Did I Chide" W. Shakespeare. [Volume 2/9]

"Forward we fare." The Fall of Troy, fr. Aeneid. Virgil (Publius Vergillius Maro). [Volume 7/261]

Fosdick, William W.
    The Maize. [Volume 5/267]

Foss, Sam Walter
    He'd Had No Show. [Volume 9/351]

Foster, Stephen Collins
    My Old Kentucky Home. [Volume 3/147]

Foster, William Prescott
    The Silence of the Hills. [Volume 5/213]

Found Wanting. E. Dickinson. [Volume 4/326]

"The fountains mingle with the river." Love's Philosophy. P. Shelley. [Volume 2/106]

Four Legs, Three Legs, Two Legs. W. Empson. [Supp 2/143]

"Four pelicans went over the house." Pelicans. R. Jeffers. [Supp 1/173]

"Four straight brick walls, severely plain." The Quaker Graveyard. S. Mitchell. [Volume 3/278]

Fox, W. J. (tr.)
    The Martyrs' Hymn. M. Luther. [Volume 4/334]

Fra Giacomo. R. Buchanan. [Volume 9/76]

"Fragile blades of grass." The Stars: 048. Ping Hsin. [Supp 5/119]

Fragment. T. Carmi. [Supp 7/246]

The Fragments of the Night. J. Lima. [Supp 6/141]

France
    The Ballad of Guibour, fr. Calendau. F. Mistral. [Volume 7/327]
    Before Sedan. A. Dobson. [Volume 9/101]
    The Glove and the Lions. L. Hunt. [Volume 7/330]
    The Glove. R. Browning. [Volume 7/332]
    Herve Riel. R. Browning. [Volume 7/341]
    How They Brought the Good News from Ghent to Aix. R. Browning. [Volume 7/349]
    Louis XV. J. Sterling. [Volume 7/339]
    Napoleon and the British Sailor. T. Campbell. [Volume 7/347]
    Provincia Deserta. E. Pound. [Supp 1/251]

Francesca Da Rimini, fr. Divina Commedia: Inferno. Dante Alighieri. [Volume 2/99]

Frankford's Soliloquy, fr. A Woman Killed with Kindness. O. Huckel. [Volume 4/328]

Franklin, Benjamin
    Paper. [Volume 9/289]

Frederick Douglass. R. Hayden. [Supp 4/137]

Free Will
    Explorations. L. MacNeice. [Supp 2/178]

Freedom. L. Hughes. [Supp 4/133]

Freedom
    The American Flag. J. Drake. [Volume 8/152]
    The Antiquity of Freedom. W. Bryant. [Volume 8/115]
    "As By the Shore at Break of Day" T. Moore. [Volume 8/138]
    Battle-Hymn of the Republic. J. Howe. [Volume 8/172]
    Brown of Ossawatomie. J. Whittier. [Volume 8/169]
    A Certain Peace. N. Giovanni. [Supp 4/218]
    A Court Lady. E. Browning. [Volume 8/146]
    Dark Symphony: 5. Larghetto. M. Tolson. [Supp 4/99]
    Dark Symphony: 6. Tempo di Marcia. M. Tolson. [Supp 4/400]

Pastor's Reverie. [Volume 4/313]
Ultima Veritas. [Volume 4/255]
**Glaucus.** S. Keyes. [Supp 2/412]
**Gleam** in Time. F. Daglarca. [Supp 7/298]
**Gleason, Judith (tr.)**
    Crowned Crane. Unknown (African American). [Supp 6/2]
    To the Earth. Unknown (African American). [Supp 6/8]
    To the Rain. Unknown (African American). [Supp 6/9]
    Train. D. Segooa. [Supp 6/88]
    Voice of the Diving Herdsman. Unknown (African American). [Supp 6/10]
"**Glittering** eyelashes and behind them." The Ox. S. Murano. [Supp 7/121]
"The **Glories** of our blood and state." Death the Leveller. J. Shirley. [Volume 3/254]
**Gloucester** Moors. W. Moody. [Supp 1/225]
The **Glove.** R. Browning. [Volume 7/332]
The **Glove** and the Lions. L. Hunt. [Volume 7/330]
**Gluck**
    To Death. [Volume 3/395]
**Gluck, Louise**
    Descending Figure: 1. The Wanderer. [Supp 5/102]
    Descending Figure: 2. The Sick Child. [Supp 5/103]
    Descending Figure: 3. For My Sister. [Supp 5/103]
    Lamentations: 1. The Logos. [Supp 5/106]
    Lamentations: 2. Nocturne. [Supp 5/106]
    Lamentations: 3. The Covenant. [Supp 5/106]
    Lamentations: 4. The Clearing. [Supp 5/107]
    The Mirror. [Supp 5/104]
    Swans. [Supp 5/105]
**Gluggity** Glug, fr. The Myrtle and the Vine. G. Colman. [Volume 9/245]
"**Go** away, %the wild wastes." Hurricanes. J. Das. [Supp 7/51]
**Go** Down Death. J. Johnson. [Supp 1/176]
"**Go** Down, Moses" Unknown (African American). [Supp 4/48]
"**Go** from me. Yet I feel that I shall stand." Sonnets From The Portuguese. E. Browning. [Volume 2/377]
"**Go,** Lovely Rose" E. Waller. [Volume 2/37]
"**Go,** patter to lubbers and swabs, do ye see." Poor Jack. C. Dibdin. [Volume 5/436]
**Go** Sleep, Ma Honey. E. Barker. [Volume 1/100]
"**Go,** spend your penny, beauty, when you will." Sonnet. J. Masefield. [Supp 1/209]
"**Go** stand at night upon an ocean craft." Illusions. R. Johnson. [Volume 6/277]
"**Go** through the gates with your eyes closed." Close Your Eyes! A. Bontemps. [Supp 4/122]
"The **Goal** of Intellectual Man" R. Eberhart. [Supp 2/126]
*Goats*
    All Goats. E. Coatsworth. [Supp 1/85]
**God.** G. Dershavin. [Volume 4/24]
**God.** Ya Hsuan. [Supp 7/34]
*God*
    Deus Absconditus. A. Ridler. [Supp 2/272]
    The Dreamer. C. Bax. [Supp 1/27]
    First Cycle of Love Poems: 001. G. Barker. [Supp 2/278]
    First Cycle of Love Poems: 002. G. Barker. [Supp 2/279]
    First Cycle of Love Poems: 003. G. Barker. [Supp 2/280]
    First Cycle of Love Poems: 004. G. Barker. [Supp 2/280]
    First Cycle of Love Poems: 005. G. Barker. [Supp 2/282]
    The Hound of Heaven. F. Thompson. [Supp 1/295]
    Nimrod Wars with the Angels. A. Branch. [Supp 1/67]

Noon. R. Jeffers. [Supp 1/175]
Prayer. G. Fuertes. [Supp 5/95]
Recessional. R. Kipling. [Supp 1/179]
Renascence. E. Millay. [Supp 1/214]
Report on Experience. E. Blunden. [Supp 2/46]
Sacred Elegy V: 001. G. Barker. [Supp 2/290]
Sacred Elegy V: 002. G. Barker. [Supp 2/290]
Sacred Elegy V: 003. G. Barker. [Supp 2/291]
Sacred Elegy V: 004. G. Barker. [Supp 2/291]
We Wait, 3. (To Be Sung to the Tune ... R. Conley. [Supp 4/310]
"**God** alone %sits on the church's windowsill." God. Ya Hsuan. [Supp 7/34]
**God** and Man, fr. Essay on Man. A. Pope. [Volume 4/21]
"**God** called the nearest angels who dwell with him." The Two Angels. J. Whittier. [Volume 4/157]
**God** in Nature, fr. Paracelsus. R. Browning. [Volume 5/6]
**God** is Everywhere. R. Nicoll. [Volume 4/28]
"**God** is good." Hope of the Human Heart, fr. Anima Mundi. R. Milnes. [Volume 4/110]
"**God** makes sech nights, all white an' still." The Courtin' J. Lowell. [Volume 2/190]
"**God** might have bade the earth bring forth." The Use of Flowers. M. Howitt. [Volume 5/241]
"**God** moves in a mysterious way." Light Shining Out of Darkness. W. Cowper. [Volume 4/23]
**God** of Mercy. K. Molodowsky. [Supp 5/178]
"**God** of our fathers, known of old." Recessional. R. Kipling. [Supp 1/179]
"**God** of the thunder! from whose cloudy seat." Jewish Hymn in Babylon. H. Milman. [Volume 4/307]
"**God** Pity the wretched prisoners." In Prison. M. Smith. [Volume 4/323]
"**God** ploughed one day with an earthquake." The Hills of the Lord. W. Gannett. [Volume 4/19]
"**God** prosper long our noble king." Chevy-Chace. Unknown. [Volume 8/244]
"**God** save our gracious king!" God Save the King. H. Carey. [Volume 8/18]
**God** Save the King. H. Carey. [Volume 8/18]
"**God** sends his teachers unto every age." Rhoecus. J. Lowell. [Volume 6/103]
"**God** sheild ye, heralds of the spring!" Return of Spring. P. Ronsard. [Volume 5/78]
"**God** spake three times and saved Van Elsen's." Vam E;sem. F. Scott. [Volume 3/361]
"**God,** who gave iron, purposed ne'er." Patriotic Song. E. Arndt. [Volume 8/76]
The **Goddess.** K. Raine. [Supp 2/198]
**Godiva.** A. Tennyson. [Volume 7/361]
**God's-Acre.** H. Longfellow. [Volume 3/276]
**God's** Command to His Angels. M. Iqbal. [Supp 7/58]
**God's** Judgment on a Wicked Bishop. R. Southey. [Volume 9/52]
"**God's** love and peace be with thee, where." Benedicite. J. Whittier. [Volume 1/356]
**God's** Sure Help in Sorrow. A. Ulrich. [Volume 3/236]
"**Goe,** soule, the bodie's guest." The Lye. S. Raleigh. [Volume 6/227]
"**Goethe** in Weimar sleeps, and Greece." Memorial Verses. M. Arnold. [Volume 7/72]
**Goethe, Johann Wolfgang Von**
    The Erl-King. S. Martin and William E. Aytoun (tr.). [Volume 6/58]
    The Fisher. C. Brooks (tr.). [Volume 6/78]
    Haste Not! Rest Not! [Volume 6/414]
    Mignon's Song, fr. Wilhelm Meister. T. Carlyle (tr.). [Volume 6/313]
**Going** and Coming. E. Jenks. [Volume 3/458]
"**Going** - ther great round sun." Going and Coming. E. Jenks. [Volume 3/458]
**Gold.** J. Drinkwater. [Supp 1/110]
"The **gold-armoured** ghost from the Roman road." The Youth with Red-gold Hair. E. Sitwell. [Supp

004. A. Lewis. [Supp 2/377]
"The gray sea, and the long black laud." Meeting at
    Night. R. Browning. [Volume 2/364]
Gray, Thomas
    The Bard. [Volume 8/34]
    Elegy Written in a Country Churchyard. [Volume
        3/270]
    Ode on the Pleasure Arising from Vicissitude.
        [Volume 5/18]
    On a Distant Prospect of Eton College. [Volume
        1/244]
    Spring. [Volume 5/79]
"The great cup tumbled, ringing like a bell." The
    Grail. S. Keyes. [Supp 2/413]
The Great Lover. R. Brooke. [Supp 1/80]
"Great Nature is an Army Gay" R. Gilder. [Volume
    5/16]
"Great ocean! strongest of creation's sons." Ocean,
    fr. The Course of Time. R. Pollok. [Volume
    5/379]
"The great soft downy snow-storm like a cloak." The
    Snow-storm. E. Wetherald. [Volume 5/177]
"Great spirits now on earth are sojourning." To
    Benjamin Robert Haydon. J. Keats. [Volume 7/69]
"A great, still shape, alone." Ireland. J. Piatt.
    [Volume 8/66]
"The Great Wall, so tall." The Great Wall, Within and
    Beyond. Liang Shang Ch'uan. [Supp 7/19]
The Great Wall, Within and Beyond. Liang Shang Ch'uan.
    [Supp 7/19]
Greatness, fr. An Essay on Man. A. Pope. [Volume
    6/283]
*Greece*
    At Epidaurus. L. Durrell. [Supp 2/257]
    The Fall of Troy, fr. Aeneid. Virgil (Publius
        Vergillius Maro). [Volume 7/261]
    A Frieze. J. Bishop. [Supp 2/24]
    Glaucus. S. Keyes. [Supp 2/412]
    In Arcadia. L. Durrell. [Supp 2/259]
    Iphigeneia and Agamemnon. W. Landor. [Volume 9/3]
    Nemea. L. Durrell. [Supp 2/260]
    On Ithaca Standing. L. Durrell. [Supp 2/260]
    Parrhasius. N. Willis. [Volume 9/8]
    Sacrifice of Polyxena, fr. Hecuba. Euripides.
        [Volume 9/5]
    "Then They Paraded Pompey's Urn" J. Mastoraki.
        [Supp 5/156]
Greece Enslaved, fr. Childe Harold. G. Byron. [Volume
    8/127]
Green, Annie D. ("Marian Douglas")
    Two Pictures. [Volume 1/318]
"Green be the turf above thee." Joseph Rodman Drake.
    F. Halleck. [Volume 7/91]
"The green corn waving in the dale." The Windmill. R.
    Bridges. [Supp 1/74]
The Green Grass Under the Snow. A. Preston. [Volume
    3/442]
"Green Grow The Rashes O" R. Burns. [Volume 2/91]
Green Nostalgia. The Lu. [Supp 7/191]
"Green stream full of live." Dark Stream. I. Jonker.
    [Supp 5/122]
Greene, Albert G.
    The Baron's Last Banquet. [Volume 7/300]
    Old Grimes. [Volume 9/265]
Greene, Homer
    What My Lover Said. [Volume 2/279]
Greene, Robert
    Content, fr. Farewell to Follie. [Volume 6/418]
    Philomela's Ode. [Volume 2/79]
    The Shepherd and the King. [Volume 2/63]
Greene, Sarah Pratt M'Lean
    De sheepfol! [Volume 4/67]
Greenwood Cemetery. C. Kennedy. [Volume 3/279]
Greenwood, Grace [pseud.] See Lippincott, Sarah J.
The Greenwood Shrift. R. Southey. [Volume 7/379]

The Greenwood Tree, fr. As You Like It. W.
    Shakespeare. [Volume 5/219]
Gregory, Horace
    Dempsey, Dempsey. [Supp 2/62]
    Hagen. [Supp 2/63]
    Hellbabies. [Supp 2/64]
    Salvos for Randolph Bourne: 001. [Supp 2/65]
    Salvos for Randolph Bourne: 002. [Supp 2/65]
    Salvos for Randolph Bourne: 003. [Supp 2/66]
    Salvos for Randolph Bourne: 001. [Supp 2/65]
    Salvos for Randolph Bourne: 002. [Supp 2/65]
    Salvos for Randolph Bourne: 003. [Supp 2/66]
    Tombstone with Cherubim. [Supp 2/66]
    The Woman Who Disapproved of Music at the Bar.
        [Supp 2/67]
Gregory, Saint
    Darkness is Thinning. J. Neale (tr.). [Volume
        4/122]
    Veni Creator Spiritus. J. Dryden (tr.). [Volume
        4/104]
Grief for the Dead. Unknown. [Volume 3/408]
Grief, fr. Hamlet. W. Shakespeare. [Volume 3/348]
"Grief hath been known to turn the young head." The
    Young Gray Head. C. Southey. [Volume 9/132]
"Grief sinks and sinks." Dwellers at the Hermitage. D.
    Levertov. [Supp 5/143]
Grief Unspeakable, fr. In Memoriam. A. Tennyson.
    [Volume 3/349]
Griffen, Gerald Joseph
    The Sister of Charity. [Volume 4/183]
Griffin, Bartholomew
    To Fidessa. [Volume 2/364]
Griffith, George Bancroft
    Our Fallen Heroes. [Volume 8/449]
Griggsby's Station. J. Riley. [Volume 9/349]
Grimoald, Nicholas
    The Friend, fr. On Friendship. [Volume 1/402]
Grissom, Arthur
    The Artist. [Volume 6/384]
The Groundhog. R. Eberhart. [Supp 2/127]
"The groves were God's first temples. Ere man." A
    Forest Hymn. W. Bryant. [Volume 5/223]
"Grow old along with me!" Rabbi Ben Ezra. R. Browning
    [Volume 4/220]
Growing Gray. A. Dobson. [Volume 6/286]
*Growing Up*
    Autobiography. L. MacNeice. [Supp 2/171]
    The Enamel Girl. G. Taggard. [Supp 1/292]
    The Lost Son: 005. T. Roethke. [Supp 2/210]
    The Lost Son: The Flight. T. Roethke. [Supp 2/205]
    The Lost Son: The Gibber. T. Roethke. [Supp 2/207]
    The Lost Son: The Pit. T. Roethke. [Supp 2/207]
    The Lost Son: The Return. T. Roethke. [Supp 2/209]
    The Runner with the Lots. L. Adams. [Supp 2/71]
    "That's How I Was" C. Conde. [Supp 4/291]
Growth. S. Tanikawa. [Supp 7/130]
Gruach. G. Bottomley. [Supp 1/63]
Guerrilla. W. Rendra. [Supp 7/99]
Guilemus Rex. T. Aldrich. [Volume 7/53]
Guillar, Ferreira
    August 1964. W. Smith (tr.). [Supp 6/115]
    Things of the Earth. W. Smith (tr.). [Supp 6/114]
Guillen, Nicolas
    Heat. C. Duran (tr.). [Supp 6/138]
*Guilt*
    Number Five. J. Ransom. [Supp 1/259]
Guilty, or Not Guilty? Unknown. [Volume 3/212]
Guiney, Louise Imogen
    A Friend's Song for Simoisius. [Supp 1/154]
    The Kings. [Supp 1/153]
    To a Dog's Memory. [Volume 5/363]
    Tryste Noel. [Volume 4/61]
    The Wild Ride. [Volume 6/259]
Gulf-weed. C. Fenner. [Volume 5/392]
*Gulls*

A Talisman. M. Moore. [Supp 1/233]

*Guns*
Port Bou. S. Spender. [Supp 2/231]
"The **guns** are hushed, after roaring at Quemoy." After a Gun Duel at Quemoy. Li Ying. [Supp 7/14]
**Gupta, Nagendranath (tr.)**
The First Kiss. R. Tagore. [Supp 7/71]
The **Gushing** Blood. Adonis. [Supp 7/284]
"The **gusty** morns are here." To a Dog's Memory. L. Guiney. [Volume 5/363]
**Gutierrez, Ernesto**
The Colors. S. White (tr.). [Supp 6/173]
I Am Resuscitated Now. S. White (tr.). [Supp 6/174]
In Me and Far Away. S. White (tr.). [Supp 6/174]
"**Guvener** B. is a sensible man." What Mr. Robinson Thinks, fr. The Biglow Papers. J. Lowell. [Volume 9/339]
"**G'way** an' quit dat noise, Miss Lucy." When Malindy Sings. P. Dunbar. [Supp 4/79]
**Gypsy** Man. L. Hughes. [Supp 1/171]

"**Ha!** bully for me again, when my turn for picket." The Brier-wood Pipe. C. Shanly. [Volume 6/317]
"**Ha!** there comes he, with seat, with blood of." Hermann and Thusnelda. F. Klopstock. [Volume 8/215]
"**Ha!** whare ye gaun, ye crawlin' ferlie?" To a Louse. R. Burns. [Volume 5/348]
**Habeas** Corpus. H. Jackson. [Volume 3/382]
**Habington, William**
To Roses in the Bosom of Castara. [Volume 2/34]
**Hack** and Hew. B. Carman. [Volume 6/387]
"**Hack** and Hew were the sons of God." Hack and Hew. B. Carman. [Volume 6/387]
**Hagedorn, Jessica**
Song for My Father. [Supp 4/24]
The Song of Bullets. [Supp 4/29]
Sorcery. [Supp 4/22]
**Hagen** H. Gregory. [Supp 2/63]
"**Hagen** is dead." Hagen. H. Gregory. [Supp 2/63]
**Hahn, Kimiko**
The Bath: August 6, 1945. [Supp 4/36]
Daughter. [Supp 4/35]
"**Hail**, beauteous stranger of the grove!" To the Cuckoo. J. Logan. [Volume 5/289]
"**Hail**, holy light, offspring of heaven first-born!" Invocation to Light, fr. Paradise Lost. J. Milton. [Volume 5/30]
"**Hail** to thee, blithe spirit!" To the Skylark. P. Shelley. [Volume 5/297]
*Hair*
Combing. G. Cardiff. [Supp 4/321]
"**Hair** All Tangled This Morning" A. Yosano. [Supp 7/145]
**Hair** All Tangled This Morning" A. Yosano. [Supp 7/145]
"A **hair** perhaps divides the false and true." Rubaiyat: 050. O. Khayyam. [Volume 6/213]
**Haircut**. K. Shapiro. [Supp 2/321]
**Hakon's** Defiance, fr. Hakon Jarl. A. Oehlenschlager. [Volume 8/208]
"**Half** a league, half a league." Charge of the Light Brigade. A. Tennyson. [Volume 8/294]
The **half-seen** memories of childish days." Early Friendship. A. De Vere. [Volume 1/344]
**Half-Waking**. W. Allingham. [Volume 1/103]
**Halfbreed** Cry. W. Rose. [Supp 4/323]
**Hall, Christopher Newman**
"My Times Are In Thy Hand" [Volume 4/140]
**Hall, Gertrude (tr.)**
The Spell. P. Verlaine. [Volume 6/367]

**Hall, Joseph**
Hollow Hospitality, fr. Satires. [Volume 9/384]
**Halleck, Fitz-Greene**
Alnwick Castle. [Volume 9/312]
Fortune, fr. Fanny. [Volume 6/266]
Joseph Rodman Drake. [Volume 7/91]
Marco Bozzaris. [Volume 8/200]
Weehawken and the New York Bay, fr. Fanny. [Volume 7/244]
**Hallo**, My Fancy. W. Cleland. [Volume 6/3]
**Hallowed** Ground. T. Campbell. [Volume 8/119]
**Halman, Talat Sait (tr.)**
Ant from Sivas. F. Daglarca. [Supp 7/299]
Gleam in Time. F. Daglarca. [Supp 7/298]
Nation's Hand. F. Daglarca. [Supp 7/303]
Paris, Buddha, Stars and i. F. Daglarca. [Supp 7/301]
Poverty. F. Daglarca. [Supp 7/302]
"**Waters** Are Wiser Than We" F. Daglarca. [Supp 7/298]
**Hamburger, Michael (tr.)**
Curriculum Vitae. I. Bachmann. [Supp 5/25]
Exile. I. Bachmann. [Supp 5/24]
Fog Land. I. Bachmann. [Supp 5/23]
"**Hamelin** Town's in Brunswick." The Pied Piper of Hamelin. R. Browning. [Volume 6/169]
**Hamilton, Elizabeth**
My Ain Fireside. [Volume 1/295]
*Hamlet*
Reading Hamlet. A. Akhmatova. [Supp 5/6]
**Hampton** Beach. J. Whittier. [Volume 5/427]
**Hamzah, Amir**
Because of You. S. Alisjahbana; S. Thorton and B. Raffell (tr.). [Supp 7/88]
Garden of the World. B. Raffel and Nurdin Salam (tr.). [Supp 7/88]
I Step Down. B. Raffel and Nurdin Salam (tr.). [Supp 7/89]
I'm Drifting. B. Raffel and Nurdin Salam (tr.). [Supp 7/92]
Palace of Grace. S. Alisjahbana; S. Thorton and B. Raffell (tr.). [Supp 7/90]
The **Hand** of Lincoln. E. Stedman. [Volume 7/30]
*Hands*
Snow Upon Paris. L. Senghor. [Supp 6/73]
Two Hands. A. Sexton. [Supp 5/258]
**Hands** All Round. A. Tennyson. [Volume 8/29]
"**Hands** pressed to the ground." Silence. G. Senanayake. [Supp 7/180]
A **Hanging**. F. Chipasula. [Supp 6/31]
"**Hans** Breitmann gife a barty." Hans Breitmann's Party. C. Leland. [Volume 9/325]
**Hans** Breitmann's Party. C. Leland. [Volume 9/325]
**Hans** Christian Andersen. E. Gosse. [Volume 7/43]
"**Happed** in my rage." Landscape. A. Hebert. [Supp 5/112]
The **Happiest** Heart. J. Cheney. [Volume 1/268]
*Happiness*
Good Times. L. Clifton. [Supp 4/193]
**Happy** Are the Dead. H. Vaughan. [Volume 3/439]
"A **happy** bit hame this auld world would be." We Are Brethren A' R. Nicoll. [Volume 1/353]
"A **happy** day at Whitsuntide." The Castle Ruins. W. Barnes. [Volume 7/213]
The **Happy** Heart, fr. Patient Grissell. T. Dekker. [Volume 6/409]
The **Happy** Hour. M. Butts. [Volume 1/12]
"**Happy** insect! ever blest." A Soliloquy. W. Harte. [Volume 5/339]
The **Happy** Mother. A. Laing. [Volume 1/281]
"**Happy** the man, whose wish and care." Ode to Solitude. A. Pope. [Volume 1/265]
"**Har**, hark! the lark an heaven's gate sings." Hark, Hark! The Lark, fr. Cymbeline. W. Shakespeare. [Volume 5/292]

"The **hard** blue winds of March." The Three Winds. L.
   Lee. [Supp 2/337]
**Hardinge, William M. (tr.)**
   The Generous Air. Palladas. [Volume 6/229]
   The Grave of Sophochles. Simmias. [Volume 3/269]
   The Wreath. Meleager. [Volume 5/255]
**Hardy, Thomas**
   An Ancient to Ancients. [Supp 1/161]
   The Darling Thrush. [Supp 1/156]
   Friends Beyond. [Supp 1/157]
   Hussar's Song, fr. The Dynasts. [Supp 1/159]
   The Oxen. [Supp 1/159]
   "When I Set Out for Lyonnesse" [Supp 1/160]
*Hardy, Thomas*
   Birthday Poem for Thomas Hardy. C. Day Lewis.
   [Supp 2/111]
**Harjo, Joy**
   Someone Talking. [Supp 4/339]
   3 AM %in the albuquerque airport. [Supp 4/342]
"**Hark!** ah, the nightingale!" Philomena. M. Arnold.
   [Volume 5/308]
**Hark,** Hark! The Lark, fr. Cymbeline. W. Shakespeare.
   [Volume 5/292]
"**Hark!** the faint bells of the sunken city." The
   Sunken City. W. Mueller.
*Harlem, New York*
   Walk with De Mayor of Harlem. D. Henderson. [Supp
   4/207]
**Harmosan.** R. Trench. [Volume 8/203]
"**Harold,** are you asleep?" Harold's Leap. S. Smith.
   [Supp 5/284]
**Harold's** Leap. S. Smith. [Supp 5/284]
"**Harp** of New England Song." Hawthorne. E. Stedman.
   [Volume 7/103]
"The **Harp** That Once Through Tara's Halls" T. Moore.
   [Volume 8/138]
**Harper, Frances E. W.**
   The Salve Auction. [Supp 4/63]
**Harper, Michael**
   We Assume: On the Death of Our Son, %Reuben Masai
   Harper. [Supp 4/205]
**Harpur, Charles**
   A Midsummer's Noon in the Australian Forest.
   [Volume 5/44]
**Harriet** Beecher Stowe. P. Dunbar. [Volume 7/105]
**Harrington, Sir John**
   Of a Certaine Man. [Volume 9/199]
   On the Warres in Ireland, fr. Epigrams. [Volume
   8/237]
**Harrison, S. Frances ("Seranus")**
   Chateau Papineau. [Volume 7/253]
**Harte, Bret**
   Chiquita. [Volume 5/371]
   Dickens in Camp. [Volume 7/77]
   Dow's Flat. [Volume 9/368]
   Her Letter. [Volume 2/128]
   Jim. [Volume 9/364]
   Plain Language from Truthful James. [Volume 9/374]
   Ramon. [Volume 9/176]
   The Society Upon the Stanislaus. [Volume 9/372]
   To the Pliocene Skull. [Volume 9/360]
**Harte, Walter**
   A Soliloquy. [Volume 5/339]
**Harvest.** E. Sitwell. [Supp 2/18]
**Harvest** Song. L. Holty. [Volume 5/150]
*Harvesting*
   Short Song on Autumn Harvest. Li Chi. [Supp 7/11]
"**Has** Summer Come Without the Rose?" A. O'Shaughnessy.
   [Volume 3/54]
"**Has** there any old fellow got mixed with the boys?"
   The Boys, fr. Poems of the Class of 'Twenty-
   nine. O. Holmes. [Volume 1/375]
"**Hast** thou a charm to stay the morning star." Hymn. S.
   Coleridge. [Volume 4/15]
**Haste** Not! Rest Not! J. Goethe. [Volume 6/414]

"**Hats** off! %along the street there comes." The Flag
   Goes By. H. Bennett. [Volume 8/108]
The **Haunted** Palace. E. Poe. [Volume 6/164]
"**Have** I, you ask, my fate forgot." Apology. R. Pitter.
   [Supp 5/205]
"**Have** you heard of the wonderful one-hoss shay." The
   One-Hoss Shay. O. Holmes. [Volume 9/345]
"**Have** you not heard the poets tell." Baby Bell. T.
   Aldrich. [Volume 1/60]
"**haven't** I danced the big dance." The New Platform
   Dances. J. Mapanje. [Supp 6/34]
**Havergal, Frances Ridley**
   "I Gave My Life for Thee" [Volume 4/95]
   Peace. [Volume 4/250]
"**Ha'** we lost the goodliest fere o' all." Ballad of
   the Goodly Fere. E. Pound. [Supp 1/249]
The **Hawk.** M. Iqbal. [Supp 7/59]
**Hawker, Robert Stephen**
   Song of the Western Men. [Volume 8/136]
*Hawks*
   The Hawk. M. Iqbal. [Supp 7/59]
**Hawthorne.** H. Longfellow. [Volume 7/]
**Hawthorne.** E. Stedman. [Volume 7/103]
**Hawtrey, E. C. (tr.)**
   Hector to His Wife, fr. The Iliad. Homer. [Volume
   3/122]
**Hay, John**
   Banty Tim. [Volume 9/366]
   Jim Bludso of the Prairie Belle. [Volume 9/358]
   Liberty. [Volume 8/112]
   Little Breeches. [Volume 9/362]
   Religion and Doctrine. [Volume 4/219]
   A Woman's Love. [Volume 3/52]
**Haydar and Michael Beard, Adnan (tr.)**
   I Love You. I. Shabaka. [Supp 7/261]
   "This Is My Wine" I. Shabaka. [Supp 7/261]
   You or I? I. Shabaka. [Supp 7/260]
**Hayden, Robert**
   Frederick Douglass. [Supp 4/137]
   Homage to the Empress of the Blues. [Supp 4/136]
   In the Mourning Time. [Supp 4/138]
   Middle Passage. [Supp 4/142]
   The Night-Blooming Cereus. [Supp 4/139]
   O Daedalus, Fly Away Home. [Supp 4/135]
   The Prisoner. [Supp 4/153]
   Runagate Runagate. [Supp 4/150]
   Those Winter Sundays. [Supp 4/149]
**Hayes, Ednah Procter Clarke**
   An Opal. [Volume 2/105]
**Hayne, Paul Hamilton**
   In Harbor. [Volume 3/398]
   Love Scorns Degrees, fr. The Mountain of the
   Lovers. [Volume 2/77]
   Ode to Sleep. [Volume 6/439]
   Patience. [Volume 4/343]
   Pre-Existence. [Volume 6/303]
   Storm in the Distance. [Volume 5/123]
**Hayne, William Hamilton**
   An Autumn Breeze. [Volume 6/179]
   Moonlight Song of the Mocking-bird. [Volume 6/179]
   Night Mists. [Volume 6/179]
**Hays, H. R. (tr.)**
   The Black Messengers. C. Vallejo. [Supp 6/187]
   Our Daily Bread. C. Vallejo. [Supp 6/188]
   The Wheel of the Hungry. C. Vallejo. [Supp 6/189]
**Hazewell, Edward Wentworth**
   Weteran and Recruit. [Volume 8/19]
"**He** arrives thus with the ray of his intelligence."
   The Tears of a Muse in America: 003. F. Prince.
   [Supp 2/268]
"**He** awoke this morning uneasily from a dream." Chief
   Leschi of the Nisqually. D. Niatum. [Supp
   4/303]
"**He** came at the end of the night, at the season of
   old age." Song. Adonis. [Supp 7/278]

Our Hands in the Garden. A. Brown (tr.). [Supp 5/110]
Hebrew Wedding, fr. The Fall Of Jerusalem. H. Milman. [Volume 2/405]
Hector to His Wife, fr. The Iliad. Homer. [Volume 3/122]
He'd Had No Show. S. Foss. [Volume 9/351]
Hedge, Frederic Henry (tr.)
    "Might Fortress Is Our God" M. Luther. [Volume 4/33]
"Heighho! daisies and buttercups." Seven Times Four; maternity. J. Ingelow. [Volume 1/36]
"'Heigho,' yawned one day King Francis." The Glove. R. Browning. [Volume 7/332]
Heine, Heinrich
    The Lore-Lei. [Volume 6/77]
    Palm and the Pine. R. Houghton (tr.). [Volume 3/40]
Helen. H. Doolittle. [Supp 2/4]
"Helen, thy beauty is to me." To Helen. E. Poe. [Volume 2/35]
Hell
    Alice in Nightmareland. E. Lihn. [Supp 6/122]
    Poem of Autumn. R. Dario. [Supp 6/165]
    The Pythoness. K. Raine. [Supp 2/201]
    The Tunnel. H. Crane. [Supp 1/92]
Hell: Inscription Over the Gate, fr. The Diving Comedy. Dante Alighieri. [Volume 4/436]
Hellbabies. H. Gregory. [Supp 2/64]
"Hellbabies sitting in speakeasies." Hellbabies. H. Gregory. [Supp 2/64]
Hellman, George Sidney
    The Hudson. [Volume 1/314]
Heloise and Abelard
    Sic et Non: I. The Complaint of Heloise. H. Read. [Supp 2/34]
    Sic et Non: II. The Portrait of Abelard. H. Read. [Supp 2/35]
Helvellyn. S. Scott. [Volume 5/364]
Hemans, Felicia
    Bernardo Del Carpio. [Volume 9/85]
    Casabianca. [Volume 9/184]
    The Homes of England. [Volume 1/274]
    The Hour of Death. [Volume 3/259]
    The Landing of the Pilgrim Fathers in New England. [Volume 8/150]
    The Treasures of the Deep. [Volume 5/385]
The Hen. M. Claudius. [Volume 9/436]
"Hence, All Ye Vain Delights", fr. The Nice Valour. J. Fletcher. [Volume 3/160]
"Hence, loathed melancholy." L'allegro. J. Milton. [Volume 6/241]
"Hence, vain deluding joys." Il Penseroso. J. Milton. [Volume 6/251]
Henderson, David
    Walk with De Mayor of Harlem. [Supp 4/207]
Henley, William Ernest
    Ballade of Midsummer Days and Nights. [Volume 5/112]
    Invictus. [Volume 3/221]
Henry James
    At the Grave of Henry James. W. Auden. [Supp 2/150]
Henry Sidgwick
    The Vanishing Boat. E. Gosse. [Supp 1/146]
Henry Ward Beecher. C. Phelps. [Volume 7/24]
Henry, John
    John Henry. Unknown (African American). [Supp 4/54]
Her Creed. S. Bolton. [Volume 4/236]
"Her eyes the glow-worme lend thee." The Night-Piece. R. Herrick. [Volume 2/165]
Her Guitar. F. Sherman. [Volume 2/44]
"Her hair was tawny with gold, her eyes with purple." A Court Lady. E. Browning. [Volume 8/146]

Her Letter. B. Harte. [Volume 2/128]
Her Likeness. D. Craik. [Volume 2/32]
"Her master gave the signal, with a look." Sweet Nature's Voice, fr. Susan: A Poem of Degrees. A. Munby. [Volume 6/350]
"Her mist of primroses within her breast." A Summer Night. G. Russell. [Supp 1/274]
"Her suffering ended with the day." A Death-Bed. J. Aldrich. [Volume 3/306]
"Her window opens to the bay." To Her Absent Sailor, fr. The Tent on the Beach. J. Whittier. [Volume 3/124]
Heraty, Toeti
    Finished. H. Aveling (tr.). [Supp 7/96]
    Lone Fisherman. H. Aveling (tr.). [Supp 7/97]
    Man. H. Aveling (tr.). [Supp 7/93]
    New Year's Celebrations. H. Aveling (tr.). [Supp 7/94]
    "Now I Understand" H. Aveling (tr.). [Supp 7/95]
    Panta Rei. H. Aveling (tr.). [Supp 7/93]
Herber, Reginald
    "By Cool Siloam's Shady Rill" [Volume 1/122]
    "Thou are Gone to the Grave" [Volume 3/446]
Herbert, George
    The Call. [Volume 4/144]
    The Church Porch, sel. [Volume 4/304]
    The Flower. [Volume 3/219]
    The Gifts of God. [Volume 4/276]
    Life. [Volume 6/232]
    Peace. [Volume 4/248]
    Praise. [Volume 4/123]
    Said I Not So. [Volume 4/282]
    Virtue Immortal. [Volume 3/254]
Herbert, W. (tr.)
    Thor Recovers His Hammer from Thrym. S. Saemund. [Volume 7/284]
"Here, a sheer hulk, lies poor Tom Bowling." Tom Bowling. C. Dibdin. [Volume 5/406]
"Here are old trees, tall oaks and gnarled pines." The Antiquity of Freedom. W. Bryant. [Volume 8/115]
"Here at my hand at my heart lie still." First Cycle of Love Poems: 002. G. Barker. [Supp 2/279]
"Here Charmian, take my bracelets." Cleopatra. W. Story. [Volume 2/354]
"Here everyone is all arranged, but someone will probably die." Back. S. Tanikawa. [Supp 7/131]
"Here I come creeping, creeping everywhere;" The Voice of the Grass. S. Roberts. [Volume 5/237]
"Here in the country's heart." The Country Faith. M. Gale. [Volume 5/10]
"Here in the ditch my bones I'll lay." The Old Vagabond. P. De Beranger. [Volume 3/188]
"Here is cruel Frederick, see!" The Story of Cruel Fredderick, fr. The English Struwwelpeter. H. Hoffmann. [Volume 1/170]
"Here is my cell: here my houselings." A World withing a War: 004. H. Read. [Supp 2/41]
"Here is no peace, althought the air has fainted." Innocent Landscape. E. Wylie. [Supp 5/340]
"Here is one leaf reserved for me." Verses Written in an Album. T. Moore. [Volume 2/34]
"Here is this leafy place." Before Sedan. A. Dobson. [Volume 9/101]
"Here it is again." Torso of a Woman. N. Ezekiel. [Supp 7/55]
"Here let us leave him; for his shroud the snow." On a Grave at Grindelwald. F. Myers. [Volume 3/280]
"Here lived the soul enchanted." Poe's Cottage at Fordham. J. Boner. [Volume 7/94]
"Here rests, and let no saucy knave." Epitaph. G. Canning. [Volume 9/292]
"Here the foot prints stop." After Twenty Years. F. Tuqan. [Supp 5/306]

"here the jack-hammer jabs into the ocean." Colloquy in Black Rock. R. Lowell. [Supp 2/388]
"Here we go a-walking, so softly, so softly." Walking Song. C. Williams. [Supp 1/315]
"Here where the curfew." Cousin Lucrece. E. Stedman. [Volume 7/131]
"Here where the sunlight." The White Peacock, fr. Sospiri Di Roma. W. Sharp. [Volume 7/175]
*Heredity*
    Mother's Habits. N. Giovanni. [Supp 4/223]
**Herford, Oliver**
    A Belated Violet. [Volume 1/154]
    The Elf and the Dormouse. [Volume 1/152]
    The First Rose of Summer. [Volume 1/154]
**Heritage**. C. Cullen. [Supp 1/96]
The **Heritage**. J. Lowell. [Volume 1/256]
*Heritage*
    Senses of Heritage. N. Shange. [Supp 5/264]
**Hermann** and Thusnelda. F. Klopstock. [Volume 8/215]
**Hermes, Paul [pseud.] See Thayer, William Roscoe**
The **Hermit**, fr. The Vicar Of Wakefield. O. Goldsmith. [Volume 2/199]
**Hernandez, Amado V.**
    The Kingdom of Mammon. E. San Juan Jr. (tr.). [Supp 7/176]
    Rice Grains. E. San Juan Jr. (tr.). [Supp 7/178]
    Two Questions. E. San Juan Jr. (tr.). [Supp 7/177]
The **Hero**. R. Fuller. [Supp 2/263]
**Heroes**. E. Proctor. [Volume 8/174]
*Heroes*
    A Private View. D. Ravikovitch. [Supp 5/236]
**Hero's** Beauty, fr. The First Sestiad of "Hero and Leander" C. Marlowe. [Volume 2/15]
**Herrick, Robert**
    Delight in Disorder. [Volume 7/135]
    The Holy Spirit. [Volume 4/108]
    The Kiss. [Volume 2/104]
    My Home. [Volume 4/246]
    The Night-Piece. [Volume 2/165]
    Oberon's Feast. [Volume 6/14]
    Ode to Ben Jonson. [Volume 7/47]
    To Blossoms. [Volume 5/279]
    To Daffodils. [Volume 5/246]
    To Dianeme. [Volume 2/18]
    To the Virgins. [Volume 1/229]
    To Violets. [Volume 5/253]
    A True Lent. [Volume 4/303]
    "Whenas in Silks my Julia Goes" [Volume 2/38]
**Herve Riel**. R. Browning. [Volume 7/341]
**Hervey, Thomas Kibble**
    Love. [Volume 2/359]
**Herwegh, Georg**
    The Trooper's Death. R. Raymond (tr.). [Volume 8/220]
"He's gane, he's gane! he's frae us torn." Elegy on Captain Matthew Henderson. R. Burns. [Volume 1/363]
**Hesperia**. A. Swinburne. [Volume 2/267]
**Heywood, Thomas**
    Hierarch of Angels. [Volume 7/53]
    Morning, fr. The Minstrel. [Volume 5/42]
    Pack Clouds Away. [Volume 5/41]
    The Portrait. [Volume 2/5]
*Hibernation*
    Winter Sleep. E. Wylie. [Supp 5/338]
**Hickey, Emily Henrietta**
    A Sea Story. [Volume 9/192]
**Hierarch** of Angels. T. Heywood. [Volume 7/53]
**Higgins, John**
    Books. [Volume 6/361]
**Higginson, Thomas Wentworth**
    "The Snowing of the Pines" [Volume 5/180]
"**High** grew the snow beneath the low-hung sky." The Axe, fr. Malcolm's Katie. I. Crawford. [Volume 6/388]

"**High** the vanes of Shrewsbury gleam." The Welsh Marches. A. Housman. [Supp 1/167]
"**High** thoughts!" Thoughts of Heaven. R. Nicoll. [Volume 4/391]
The **High** Tide at Gettysburg. W. Thompson. [Volume 8/398]
**High-tide** on the Coast of Lincolnshire. J. Ingelow. [Volume 9/145]
"**High** walls and huge the body may confine." Freedom of the Mind. W. Garrison. [Volume 8/161]
The **Higher** Good. T. Parker. [Volume 4/133]
**Highland** Mary. R. Burns. [Volume 3/329]
**Hikmet, Nazim**
    About the Sea. R. Blasing and Mutlu Konuk (tr.). [Supp 7/310]
    Occupation. R. Blasing and Mutlu Konuk (tr.). [Supp 7/308]
    On Living: 001. R. Blasing and Mutlu Konuk (tr.). [Supp 7/306]
    On Living: 002. R. Blasing and Mutlu Konuk (tr.). [Supp 7/307]
    On Living: 003. R. Blasing and Mutlu Konuk (tr.). [Supp 7/308]
    "One Night of Knee-Deep Snow" R. Blasing and Mutlu Konuk (tr.). [Supp 7/304]
    This Journey. R. Blasing and Mutlu Konuk (tr.). [Supp 7/312]
    Two Questions. R. Blasing and Mutlu Konuk (tr.). [Supp 7/309]
    You. R. Blasing and Mutlu Konuk (tr.). [Supp 7/309]
**Hildegarde, Saint**
    "O Fire of God, the Comforter" R. Littledale (tr.). [Volume 4/107]
The **Hill** Above the Mine. M. Cowley. [Supp 2/60]
"The **hill** blast comes howling through leaf-rifted." A Christmas Scene. T. Davis. [Volume 2/262]
The **Hills** of the Lord. W. Gannett. [Volume 4/19]
"**Hills** Picking Up the Moonlight" N. Cassian. [Supp 5/45]
The **Hills** Were Made for Freedom. W. Brown. [Volume 8/139]
**Hinkson, Katharne Tynan**
    Sheep and Lambs. [Volume 1/121]
"**His** children would have known a heritage." Elegy for a Dead Soldier: 010. K. Shapiro. [Supp 2/317]
"**His** echoing axe the settler swung." The Settler. A. Street. [Volume 7/240]
"**His** hand at last! By his own fingers writ." Hope Deferred. Unknown. [Volume 2/368]
"**His** is gone on the mountain." Coronach, fr. The Lady of the Lake. S. Scott. [Volume 3/309]
"**His** naked skin clothed in the torrid mist." The Serf. R. Campbell. [Supp 2/94]
"**His** pendulous body tolled." A Hanging. F. Chipasula. [Supp 6/31]
"**His** puissant sowrd unot his side." Hudibras; Sword and Dagger, fr. Hudibras. S. Butler. [Volume 9/254]
"**His** righ hands holds his slingshot." For the Record. Ping Hsin. [Supp 5/115]
"**His** tongue was touched with sacred fire." Henry Ward Beecher. C. Phelps. [Volume 7/24]
*Hispanics*
    "I Am Joaquin", sels. R. Gonzales. [Supp 4/234]
    "When Raza? %When" Alurista. [Supp 4/275]
*History*
    The Bath: August 6, 1945. K. Hahn. [Supp 4/36]
    November, 1941. R. Fuller. [Supp 2/265]
The **History** Lesson. Unknown. [Volume 1/194]
**History** of a Life. B. Procter. [Volume 6/234]
"**Hither**, come hither, ye clouds renowned, and." The Cloud Chorus, fr. The Clouds. Aristophanes. [Volume 5/131]
**Ho Ch'i-Fang**
    Do Not Wash Away the Red. B. McDougall (tr.). [Supp 7/7]

The First Morning in Vietnam. B. McDougall (tr.). [Supp 7/5]

Reminiscence. B. McDougall (tr.). [Supp 7/6]

The Song. B. McDougall (tr.). [Supp 7/4]

Sound. B. McDougall (tr.). [Supp 7/7]

"Ho, giant! This is I." The Bean-Stalk. E. Millay. [Supp 5/167]

"Ho! pony. Down the lonely road." Army Correspondents Last Ride. G. Townsend. [Volume 8/408]

"Ho! pretty page, with the dimpled chin." The Age Of Wisdom. W. Thackeray. [Volume 2/236]

"Ho, sailor of the sea!" How's My Boy. S. Dobell. [Volume 5/434]

"Ho, there! Fisherman, hold your hand!" The Second Mate. F. O'Brien. [Volume 9/189]

"Ho, woodsmen of the mountain-side!" A Cry to Arms. H. Timrod. [Volume 8/100]

**Hobart, Hon. Mrs. Charles**
The Changed Cross. [Volume 3/231]

**Hodgson, Ralph**
Eve. [Supp 1/163]
A Wood Song. [Supp 1/165]

**Hoffman, Charles Fenno**
Monterey. [Volume 8/336]
Sparkling and Bright. [Volume 1/386]

**Hoffmann, Heinrich**
The Dreadful Story About Harriet and the Matches. [Volume 1/171]
The Story of Cruel Fredderick, fr. The English Struwwelpeter. [Volume 1/170]
The Story of Johnny-Head-In-Air. [Volume 1/173]

"**Hog** Butcher for the world." Chicago. C. Sandburg. [Supp 1/283]

**Hogg, James**
Jock Johnstone the Tinkler. [Volume 7/390]
Kilmeny, fr. The Queen's Wake. [Volume 6/21]
The Skylark. [Volume 5/301]
When The Kye Comes Hame. [Volume 2/283]
The Women Fo'K. [Volume 9/197]

**Hohenlinden**. T. Campbell. [Volume 8/225]

"A **holder**. %A cigarette holder." What Is the Name of a Ring. G. Stein. [Supp 5/295]

A **Holiday** for Me. K. Das. [Supp 5/58]

**Holland, Josiah Gilbert**
The Cost of Worth, fr. Bitter Sweet. [Volume 4/300]
Cradle Song, fr. Bitter-Sweet. [Volume 1/13]
In the Cellar, fr. Bitter Sweet. [Volume 1/317]

**Hollow** Hospitality, fr. Satires. J. Hall. [Volume 9/384]

"The **hollow** winds begin to blow." Signs of Rain. E. Jenner. [Volume 5/118]

The **Holly-tree**. R. Southey. [Volume 5/221]

**Holmes, Oliver Wendell**
Bill and Joe, fr. Poems of the Class of 'Twenty-nine. [Volume 1/341]
The Boys, fr. Poems of the Class of 'Twenty-nine. [Volume 1/375]
Brother Jonathan's Lament for Sister Caroline. [Volume 8/344]
The Chambered Nautilus. [Volume 5/398]
Contentment. [Volume 6/423]
Daniel Webster. [Volume 7/20]
The Last Leaf. [Volume 3/187]
The Living Temple. [Volume 4/215]
Ode for a Social Meeting. [Volume 9/383]
"Old Ironsides" [Volume 8/96]
The Old Man Dreams. [Volume 2/459]
The One-Hoss Shay. [Volume 9/345]
The Ploughman. [Volume 5/94]
Rudolph the Headsman, fr. This Is It. [Volume 9/293]
To an Insect. [Volume 5/340]
The Voiceless. [Volume 3/172]

**Holness, Marga (tr.)**

Farewell at the Hour of Parting. A. Neto. [Supp 6/13]

The Marketwoman. A. Neto. [Supp 6/14]

Western Civilization. A. Neto. [Supp 6/17]

**Holstenwall.** S. Keyes. [Supp 2/413]

**Holty, Ludwig H. C.**
Harvest Song. C. Brooks (tr.). [Volume 5/150]
Winter Song. C. Brooks (tr.). [Volume 5/186]

A **Holy** Nation. R. Realf. [Volume 8/178]

**Holy** Poems: 001. G. Barker. [Supp 2/284]

**Holy** Poems: 002. G. Barker. [Supp 2/284]

**Holy** Poems: 003. G. Barker. [Supp 2/285]

The **Holy** Spirit. R. Herrick. [Volume 4/108]

The **Holy** War. R. Kipling. [Supp 1/182]

**Homage** to the British Museum. W. Empson. [Supp 2/141]

**Homage** to the Empress of the Blues. R. Hayden. [Supp 4/136]

**Home**. Leonidas of Alexandria. [Volume 1/266]

*Home*
The Auld Folks. A. Park. [Volume 1/333]
The Auld House. C. Nairne. [Volume 1/275]
By the Fireside. L. Larcom. [Volume 1/293]
The Children. C. Dickinson. [Volume 1/286]
Christmas. G. Wither. [Volume 1/330]
The Cotter's Saturday Night. R. Burns. [Volume 1/300]
Country Life. R. Stoddard. [Volume 1/320]
The Day is Done. H. Longfellow. [Volume 1/266]
The Happiest Heart. J. Cheney. [Volume 1/268]
The Happy Mother. A. Laing. [Volume 1/281]
Heart-rest. S. Taylor. [Volume 1/312]
Home. Leonidas of Alexandria. [Volume 1/266]
Home Song. D. Scott. [Volume 1/325]
Home Sweet Home, fr. Clari, the Maid of Milan. J. Payne. [Volume 1/335]
The Homes of England. F. Hemans. [Volume 1/274]
Homeward Bound. Cattullus. [Volume 1/313]
The House Beautiful. R. Stevenson. [Volume 1/277]
The Hudson. G. Hellman. [Volume 1/314]
"I Knew By the Smoke That So Gracefully Curled" T. Moore. [Volume 1/292]
If We Knew; or, Blessings of To-day. M. Smith. [Volume 1/278]
In the Cellar, fr. Bitter Sweet. J. Holland. [Volume 1/317]
The Ingle-side. H. Ainslee. [Volume 1/293]
Labor Song, fr. The Bell-Founder. D. MacCarthy. [Volume 1/327]
The Light'ood Fire. J. Boner. [Volume 1/299]
The Means to Attain Happy Life. H. Howard. [Volume 1/312]
My Ain Fireside. E. Hamilton. [Volume 1/295]
A New England Home in Winter. J. Whittier. [Volume 1/308]
Not One to Spare. Unknown. [Volume 1/288]
Ode to Solitude. A. Pope. [Volume 1/265]
"Out of the Old House, Nancy" W. Carleton. [Volume 1/268]
A Petition to Time. B. Procter. [Volume 1/334]
A Picture. C. Eastman. [Volume 1/315]
Rock Me to Sleep. E. Akers. [Volume 1/284]
Seven Times Six. J. Ingelow. [Volume 1/290]
A Sheperd's Life, fr. Third Part of Henry VI. W. Shakespeare. [Volume 1/319]
The Soldier's Dream. T. Campbell. [Volume 1/280]
The Song of the Old Mother. W. Yeats. [Volume 1/284]
The Swiss Peasant, fr. The Traveller. O. Goldsmith. [Volume 1/321]
Tired Mothers. M. Smith. [Volume 1/282]
Two Pictures. A. Green. [Volume 1/318]
The Village Blacksmith. H. Longfellow. [Volume 1/328]
The Wanderer's Home. O. Goldsmith. [Volume 1/314]
When the Cows Come Home. A. Mitchell. [Volume

4/282]

The **Household** Sovereign, fr. The Hanging of the Crane.
H. Longfellow. [Volume 1/23]

*Housewives*
To Another Housewife. J. Wright. [Supp 5/332]

**Housman, A. E.**
Bredon hill. [Supp 1/166]
The First of May. [Supp 1/169]
Loveliest of Trees. [Supp 1/166]
The Welsh Marches. [Supp 1/167]
"When First My Way" [Supp 1/170]
"With Rue My Heart is Laden" [Supp 1/169]

**Hovey, Richard**
The Battle of Manila. [Volume 8/421]
Beethoven's Third Symphony. [Volume 6/379]
The Faun. [Volume 5/26]
Love In The Winds. [Volume 2/252]

"How beautiful is the rain!" Rain in Summer. H.
Longfellow. [Volume 5/114]

"How beautiful it was, that one bright day."
Hawthorne. H. Longfellow. [Volume 7/]

"How beautiful this night! the balmiest sigh." Night,
fr. Queen Mab. P. Shelley. [Volume 5/66]

"How calm they sleep beneath the shade." Greenwood
Cemetery. C. Kennedy. [Volume 3/279]

"How can I walk towards my people, towards myself?"
The Pearl. Adonis. [Supp 7/282]

"How dear to this heart are the scenes of my child."
The 'Old Oaken Bucket. S. Woodworth. [Volume
1/91]

"How delicious is the winning." The First Kiss. T.
Campbell. [Volume 2/94]

"How does the water." The Cataract of Lodore. R.
Southey. [Volume 7/170]

"How Doth The Little Busy Bee" I. Watts. [Volume
1/108]

"How fresh, O Lord, how sweet and clean." The Flower.
G. Herbert. [Volume 3/219]

"How happy is he born and taught." The Character of a
Happy Life. S. Wotton. [Volume 6/225]

"How hard, when those who do not wish." Art of Book-
keeping. T. Hood. [Volume 9/305]

How Hong Kong Was Destroyed. D. Ravikovitch. [Supp
5/235]

"'How, how,' he said. 'Friend Chang,' I said." The
Chinese Nightingale. V. Lindsay. [Supp 1/189]

"How like the leper, with his own sad cry." The Buoy-
bell. C. Turner. [Volume 5/423]

"How little recks it where men lie." The Place Where
Man Should Die. M. Barry. [Volume 8/111]

"How many a time have I." Swimming, fr. The Two
Foscari. G. Byron. [Volume 5/141]

"How many pounds does the baby weigh." Weighing the
Baby. E. Beers. [Volume 1/5]

"How many summers, love." The Poet's Song To His Wife.
B. Procter. [Volume 2/421]

"How many thousand of my poorest." Sleep, fr. Second
Part of Henry IV. W. Shakespeare. [Volume
6/433]

"How many verses have I thrown." Verses Why Burnt. W.
Landor. [Volume 6/350]

How Old Women Should Live. M. Waddington. [Supp
5/312]

How Paddy god "Under Government." Unknown. [Volume
9/238]

"How prone we are to hide the hoard." Lavender.
Unknown. [Volume 3/359]

"How pure at heart and sound in head." Spiritual
Companionship, fr. In Memoriam. A. Tennyson.
[Volume 3/352]

"How seldom, Friend! a good great man inherits." The
Good Great Man. S. Coleridge. [Volume 3/244]

"How shall I know thee in the sphere which keeps."
The Future Life. W. Bryant. [Volume 4/397]

"How Sleep the Brave" W. Collins. [Volume 8/449]

"How slight a thing may set on'es fancy drifting."
Honey Dripping From the Comb. J. Riley. [Volume
1/224]

"How small a tooth hath mined the season's." Frost. E.
Thomas. [Volume 5/173]

"How still the morning of the hallowed day!" The Poor
Man's Day, fr. The Sabbath. A. Barbauld.
[Volume 4/193]

"How sweet the answer Echo makes." Echoes. T. Moore.
[Volume 2/327]

"How sweet the manger smells! The cows all." Fodder-
time, fr. Songs of Toil. C. Sylva. [Volume
5/358]

"How sweet the moonlight sleeps upon." Music, fr. The
Merchant of Venice. W. Shakespeare. [Volume
6/362]

"How sweet the sound in the city an hour before
sunrise." English Sparrows. E. Millay. [Supp
5/168]

"'How sweetly,' said the trembling maid." Linda to
Hafed, fr. The Fire-worshipers. T. Moore.
[Volume 3/6]

"How the Days Passed" N. Zach. [Supp 7/253]

"How the earth burns! Each pebble under foot." The
Oasis of Sidi Khaled. W. Blunt. [Volume 5/44]

How They Brought the Good News from Ghent to Aix. R.
Browning. [Volume 7/349]

How To Ask And Have. S. Lover. [Volume 2/179]

"How to isolate the fragments of the night." The
Fragments of the Night. J. Lima. [Supp 6/141]

"How well you served me above ground." Spirit's Song.
L. Bogan. [Supp 5/34]

**How, William Walsham**
The Word. [Volume 4/199]

"How wonderful is death!" To Ianthe, Sleeping. P.
Shelley. [Volume 7/129]

**Howard, Henry, Earl of Surrey**
Give Place, Ye Lovers. [Volume 2/7]
The Means to Attain Happy Life. [Volume 1/312]

**Howarth, Elen Clementine**
"'T is But a Little Faded Flower" [Volume 6/317]

**Howe, Irving (tr.)**
God of Mercy. K. Molodowsky. [Supp 5/178]

**Howe, Julia Ward**
Battle-Hymn of the Republic. [Volume 8/172]
Our Orders. [Volume 8/381]

**Howells, William Dean**
Caprice. [Volume 2/110]
The Two Wives. [Volume 8/355]

"However much I praise, you do not listen." Second
Rose Motif. C. Meireles. [Supp 5/161]

"However much I try, I will always be just what I
am." Self-Portrait. N. Cassian. [Supp 5/47]

**Howitt, Mary**
The Fairies of the Caldon Low. [Volume 1/148]
The Spider and the Fly. [Volume 1/110]
The Use of Flowers. [Volume 5/241]

**Howitt, William**
The Departure of the Swallow. [Volume 5/331]
A Summer Noon. [Volume 5/46]
The Wind in a Frolic. [Volume 1/143]

**Howland, Mary Woolsey**
Rest. [Volume 3/397]

How's My Boy? S. Dobell. [Volume 5/434]

**Hoyt, Ralph**
Old. [Volume 3/180]

**Hsiung Hung**
Fire on the Sea Floor. A. Palandri (tr.). [Supp
7/10]
"Walking Out of Expectation" A. Palandri (tr.).
[Supp 7/9]

**Huckel, Oliver**
Frankford's Soliloquy, fr. A Woman Killed with
Kindness. [Volume 4/328]
My Quaker Grandmothers. [Volume 6/235]

W. Gilbert. [Volume 9/301]
"The **Hunchback** in the Park" D. Thomas. [Supp 2/364]
"The **hunchback** on the corner, with gum and
   shoelaces." Pursuit. R. Warren. [Supp 2/132]
"A **hundred** miles of river, a hundred miles of glen."
   A River of Colors. Liang Shang Ch'uan. [Supp
   7/21]
"**Hung** like a rich pomegranate o'er the sea." The
   Shore, fr. Ariadne. C. Roberts. [Volume 5/421]
*Hunger*
   The Face of Hunger. M. Mtshali. [Supp 6/84]
   Model Lesson. T. Carmi. [Supp 7/242]
   The Wheel of the Hungry. C. Vallejo. [Supp 6/189]
**Hunt, Leigh**
   Abou Ben Adhem. [Volume 4/188]
   Cupid Swallowed. [Volume 2/91]
   The Glove and the Lions. [Volume 7/330]
   The Grasshopper and Cricket. [Volume 5/339]
   Jaffar. [Volume 1/350]
   Jenny Kissed Me. [Volume 1/358]
   Mahmoud. [Volume 7/305]
   On Hearing A Little Music-box. [Volume 7/139]
   Sneezing. [Volume 9/421]
   To a Child During Sickness. [Volume 1/59]
   To J.H.; four years old: a nursery song. [Volume
   1/33]
**Hunt, Leigh (tr.)**
   Fairies' Song. T. Randolph. [Volume 6/19]
   I Dreamt I Saw Great Venus. Bion. [Volume 2/98]
The **Hunted** Squirrel, fr. Britannia's Pastorals. W.
   Browne. [Volume 5/157]
**Hunter** Mountain. F. Lima. [Supp 4/245]
"**Hunters** are back from beating the winter's face."
   The Woman Thing. A. Lorde. [Supp 4/184]
The **Hunter's** Song. B. Procter. [Volume 5/156]
*Hunting and Hunters*
   Father Elephant. Unknown (African American). [Supp
   6/4]
   Flighting for Duck. W. Empson. [Supp 2/142]
   Song. E. Cummings. [Supp 1/101]
   The Woman Thing. A. Lorde. [Supp 4/184]
**Hunting** Song. S. Scott. [Volume 5/154]
A **Hunting** We Will Go. H. Fielding. [Volume 5/158]
"The **hurdy-gurdy,** public piano of the past." The Road
   from Election to Christmas. O. Williams. [Supp
   2/80]
The **Hurricane**. W. Bryant. [Volume 7/151]
**Hurricanes**. J. Das. [Supp 7/51]
*Hurricanes*
   Hurricanes. J. Das. [Supp 7/51]
**Hush!** J. Dorr. [Volume 3/380]
"**Hush!** my dear, lie still, and slumber." A Cradle
   Hymn. I. Watts. [Volume 1/98]
**Hussaini, Hatem (tr.)**
   Behind Bars, sel. F. Tuqan. [Supp 5/305]
**Hussar's** Song, fr. The Dynasts. T. Hardy. [Supp
   1/159]
**Hymn**. S. Coleridge. [Volume 4/15]
**Hymn**. R. Emerson. [Volume 8/326]
A **Hymn**, fr. The Seasons. J. Thomson. [Volume 5/70]
**Hymn** of the West. E. Stedman. [Volume 8/458]
"**Hymn** the finders! Hymn the bold." The Sirens, sel. L.
   Binyon. [Supp 1/53]
**Hymn** to Light, sel. A. Cowley. [Volume 5/35]
An **Hymn** to the Evening. P. Wheatley. [Supp 4/62]
**Hymn** to the Flowers. H. Smith. [Volume 5/242]
**Hymn** to the Graveyard. Pak Tu-Jin. [Supp 7/151]
**Hymn** to the Night. H. Longfellow. [Volume 5/68]
**Hymn** to Zeus. Cleanthes. [Volume 4/7]

"**I** aged that Bo tree." Bo Tree. Lin Ling. [Supp 7/23]
"**I** aged that Bo tree %light stirring and peace."

Purple. Lin Ling. [Supp 7/24]
"**I** ain't afeard uv snakes, or toads or bugs, or."
   Seein' Things. E. Field. [Volume 1/164]
"**I** always was afraid of Some's Pond." Atavism. E.
   Wylie. [Supp 5/337]
"**I** am a convict. You won't fall behind." Poems for
   Akhmatova: 003. M. Tsvetayeva. [Supp 5/301]
"**I** am a Friar of Orders Gray", fr. Robin Hood. J.
   O'Keeffe. [Volume 9/247]
"**I** am a gentleman in a dustcoat trying." Piazza Piece.
   J. Ransom. [Supp 1/260]
"**I** Am a Red Slogan" R. Wright. [Supp 2/214]
"**I** Am a University Student" S. Wongthed. [Supp 7/185]
"**I** am a witch, and a kind old witch." The Old Witch
   in the Copse. F. Cornford. [Supp 1/90]
"**I** am always aware of my mother." Mother. N. Kiyoko.
   [Supp 5/135]
"**I** am black and I have seen black hands." I Have Seen
   Black Hands: 004. R. Wright. [Supp 2/216]
"**I** am black and I have seen black hands, millions and
   millions of." I Have Seen Black Hands: 001. R.
   Wright. [Supp 2/214]
"**I** am black and I have seen black hands, millions and
   millions of." I Have Seen Black Hands: 002. R.
   Wright. [Supp 2/215]
"**I** am black and I have seen black hands, millions and
   millions of." I Have Seen Black Hands: 003. R.
   Wright. [Supp 2/216]
"**I** am black and I have seen black hands, millions and
   millions of." I Have Seen Black Hands: 001. R.
   Wright. [Supp 2/214]
"**I** am black and I have seen black hands, millions and
   millions of." I Have Seen Black Hands: 002. R.
   Wright. [Supp 2/215]
"**I** am black and I have seen black hands, millions and
   millions of." I Have Seen Black Hands: 003. R.
   Wright. [Supp 2/216]
"**I** am black and I have seen black hands, millions and
   millions of." I Have Seen Black Hands: 001. R.
   Wright. [Supp 2/214]
"**I** am black and I have seen black hands, millions and
   millions of." I Have Seen Black Hands: 002. R.
   Wright. [Supp 2/215]
"**I** am black and I have seen black hands, millions and
   millions of." I Have Seen Black Hands: 003. R.
   Wright. [Supp 2/216]
"**I** am by promise tried." Fitz-James and Roderick Dhu,
   fr. The Lady of the Lake. S. Scott. [Volume
   7/404]
"**I** am dying, Egypt, dying." Antony and Cleopatra. W.
   Lytle. [Volume 3/380]
"**I** am here in." Poem No. 4. S. Sanchez. [Supp 4/191]
"**I** am holding this turquoise." The Serenity in Stones.
   S. Ortiz. [Supp 4/315]
"**I** am in the dark, beyond all light." Gleam in Time.
   F. Daglarca. [Supp 7/298]
"**I** Am Joaquin", sels. R. Gonzales. [Supp 4/234]
"**I** am like a foolish elk." Into the Silence of the
   Forest. E. Manner. [Supp 5/147]
"**I** am monarch of all I survey." Verses. W. Cowper.
   [Volume 6/311]
"**I** am neither a communist." Who Am I? Tru Vu. [Supp
   7/199]
"**I** am not daunted, no; I will engage." The Shell, fr.
   Gebir. W. Landor. [Volume 5/427]
"**I** am Pattiradjawane." A Tale for Dein Tamaela. C.
   Anwar. [Supp 7/83]
"**I** am rarely vindictive but." About the Reunion. J.
   Jordan. [Supp 4/197]
**I** Am Resuscitated Now. E. Gutierrez. [Supp 6/174]
"**I** am Saint John on Patmos of my heart." Holy Poems:
   001. G. Barker. [Supp 2/284]
"**I** am so happy." The Flowering of the Rod: 008. H.
   Doolittle. [Supp 5/78]
"**I** am that serpent-haunted cave." The Pythoness. K.

I Found it. F. Tuqan. [Supp 7/275]

"I found it on a radiant day." I Found it. F. Tuqan. [Supp 7/275]

"I Gave My Life for Thee" F. Havergal. [Volume 4/95]

"I Gazed upon the glorious sky." June. W. Bryant. [Volume 5/102]

"I grew assured, before I asked." Sweet Meeting Of Desires, fr. The Angel In The House. C. Patmore. [Volume 2/166]

"I had come to the house, in a cave of trees." Medusa. L. Bogan. [Supp 1/61]

"I had sworn to be a bachelor, she had sworn to." Platonic. W. Terrertt. [Volume 1/372]

"I hae see great anes and sat in great ha's." My Ain Fireside. E. Hamilton. [Volume 1/295]

"I haf von funny leedle poy." Leedle Yawcob Strauss. C. Adams. [Volume 9/327]

"I hammer the pain of separateness." The Statue of the Century. Tru Vu. [Supp 7/198]

"I have a little shadow that goes in and out with." My Shadow. R. Stevenson. [Volume 1/133]

"I have all %my mother's habits." Mother's Habits. N. Giovanni. [Supp 4/223]

"I have an absent look." In Me and Far Away. E. Gutierrez. [Supp 6/174]

"I have been here before." Sudden Light. D. Rossetti. [Volume 6/302]

"I have been so great a lover: filled my days." The Great Lover. R. Brooke. [Supp 1/80]

"I have been wandering in the lonely valleys." Mountain Laurell. A. Noyes. [Supp 1/243]

"I have been young, and now am not too old." Report on Experience. E. Blunden. [Supp 2/46]

"I have dispensed with reasoning." Of Reason and Discovery. D. Mattera. [Supp 6/80]

"I have done it again." Lady Lazarus. S. Plath. [Supp 5/213]

"I have fancied, sometimes, the bethel-bent beam." The Old Village Choir. B. Taylor. [Volume 4/202]

"I have got a new-born sister." Choosing a Name. M. Lamb. [Volume 1/97]

"I have great admiration for ships." Denouement. A. Prado. [Supp 6/117]

"I have grown tired of you." Notes Found Near a Suicide: To Alfred. F. Horne. [Supp 4/114]

"I have had playmates, I have had companions." The Old Familiar Faces. C. Lamb. [Volume 3/143]

"I have known the inexorable sandess of pencils." Dolor. T. Roethke. [Supp 2/204]

"I have learned not to worry about love." Ne Face. A. Walker. [Supp 4/228]

"I have nothing to give you, but my anger." Love Poem for My Country. F. Chipasula. [Supp 6/30]

"I have seen." The Sea Shell, fr. The Excursion. W. Wordsworth. [Volume 5/426]

I Have Seen Black Hands: 001. R. Wright. [Supp 2/214]

I Have Seen Black Hands: 002. R. Wright. [Supp 2/215]

I Have Seen Black Hands: 003. R. Wright. [Supp 2/216]

I Have Seen Black Hands: 004. R. Wright. [Supp 2/216]

"I have sown beside all waters in my day." A Black Man Talks of Reaping. A. Bontemps. [Supp 4/126]

"I have to go to buy the paints that I disguise myself with every." Dressed in Dynamite. G. Belli. [Supp 6/152]

"I hear a bewitching song." The Song. Ho Ch'i-Fang. [Supp 7/4]

"I Hear an Army Charging Upon the Land" J. Joyce. [Supp 2/1]

"I hear in my heart, I heare in its ominous pulses." The Wild Ride. L. Guiney. [Volume 6/259]

"I Hear Something Falling" N. Zach. [Supp 7/255]

"I hear the bells at eventide." The End of the Day. D. Scott. [Volume 5/51]

"I hear the low wind wash the softening snow." The

Flight of the Geese. C. Roberts. [Volume 5/332]

"I heard the trailing garments of the night." Hymn to the Night. H. Longfellow. [Volume 5/68]

I Hold Still. J. Sturm. [Volume 3/243]

"I hold that Christian grace abounds." My Creed. A. Carey. [Volume 4/237]

"I in these flowery meads would be." The Angler's Wish. I. Walton. [Volume 5/138]

"I Knew By the Smoke That So Gracefully Curled" T. Moore. [Volume 1/292]

"I knew, I felt, (perception, unexpressed." God in Nature, fr. Paracelsus. R. Browning. [Volume 5/6]

"I knew this long ago, when we first loved." Eurydice in Hades. J. Wright. [Supp 5/334]

"I know a maiden fair to see." Beware. Unknown. [Volume 1/235]

"I know not in what fashion she was made." Broken Music. T. Aldrich. [Volume 6/346]

"I know not whence it rises." The Lore-Lei. H. Heine. [Volume 6/77]

"I know not whether." Ceremony After a Fire Raid: 002. D. Thomas. [Supp 2/359]

"I know that deep within your heart of hearts." A Woman's Complaint. Unknown. [Volume 2/426]

"I know that this was life, --the track." The Dead Friend: 25, fr. In Memoriam. A. Tennyson. [Volume 1/361]

"I lay me down to sleep." Rest. M. Howland. [Volume 3/397]

"I leaned out of window, I smelt the white clover." Seven Times Three. J. Ingelow. [Volume 2/282]

"I leant upon a coppice gate." The Darling Thrush. T. Hardy. [Supp 1/156]

"I leave behind me the elm-shadowed square." Outward Bound. T. Aldrich. [Volume 6/123]

"I lent my love a book one day." An Experience and a Moral. F. Cozzens. [Volume 2/58]

"I like a church; I like a cowl." The Problem. R. Emerson. [Volume 4/229]

"I like that ancient Saxon phrase which calls." God's-Acre. H. Longfellow. [Volume 3/276]

"I like the hunting of the hare." The Old Squire. W. Blunt. [Volume 5/165]

"I listened: %a bird on Mount Sinnin." The Bird. Adonis. [Supp 7/284]

"I live for those who love me." What I Live For. G. Banks. [Volume 4/186]

"I lived in a house." Painted Windows. G. Fuertes. [Supp 5/96]

"I looked into my heart to write." Summer Song. G. Barker. [Supp 2/293]

"I love, and have some cause to love, the earth." Delight in God. F. Quarles. [Volume 4/34]

"I love at eventide to walk alone." Summer Moods. J. Clare. [Volume 5/136]

"I love contemplating - apart." Napoleon and the British Sailor. T. Campbell. [Volume 7/347]

"I love it, I love it! and who shall dare." The Old Arm-Chair. E. Cook. [Volume 1/93]

I Love My Jean. R. Burns. [Volume 3/126]

"I love my Lady; she is very fair." My Beautiful Lady. T. Woolner. [Volume 2/260]

"I love my little son, and yet when he was ill." The Two Parents. H. MacDiarmid. [Supp 2/31]

"I love thee, love thee, Giulio!" Parting Lovers. E. Browning. [8/85]

"I love thee, pious ox; a gentle feeling." The Ox, fr. Poesie. G. Carducci. [Volume 5/359]

"I love to hear thine earnest voice." To an Insect. O. Holmes. [Volume 5/340]

"I love to wander through the woodlands hoary." A Still Day in Autumn. S. Whitman. [Volume 7/157]

I Love You. I. Shabaka. [Supp 7/261]

"I love you first because your face is fair." V-

749

Letter. K. Shapiro. [Supp 2/323]
"I love you more than human heart can bear." I Love You. I. Shabaka. [Supp 7/261]
"I loved him in my dawning years." A Life's Love. Unknown. [Volume 9/382]
"I loved thee once, I'll love no more." Woman's Inconstancy. S. Ayton. [Volume 3/71]
"I made a posie, while the day ran by." Life. G. Herbert. [Volume 6/232]
"I may be smelly and I may be old." The River God. S. Smith. [Supp 2/104]
"I met ayont the cairney." Empty Vessel. H. MacDiarmid. [Supp 2/29]
"I must abjure the balm of life, I must." Rubaiyat: 062. O. Khayyam. [Volume 6/216]
"I must get far away from this city." No Time. Nguyen Sa. [Supp 7/190]
"I must hide in the intimate depths of my veins." Totem. L. Senghor. [Supp 6/75]
"I must not think of thee; and, tired yet strong." Renouncement. A. Meynell. [Volume 2/338]
"I Must Speak" D. Brutus. [Supp 6/100]
"I need not praise the sweetness of his song." To Henry Wadsworth Longfellow. J. Lowell. [Volume 7/106]
"I never saw a moor." Heaven. E. Dickinson. [Volume 4/390]
"I never saw a purple cow." The Purple Cow. G. Burgess. [Volume 9/455]
"I only knew she came and went." My Love. Unknown. [Volume 9/427]
"I passed by a garden, a little dutch garden." A Little Dutch Garden. H. Durbin. [Volume 1/153]
I Pity the Garden. F. Farrozkhzad. [Supp 7/221]
"I praised the speech, but cannot now abide it." On the Warres in Ireland, fr. Epigrams. S. Harrington. [Volume 8/237]
"I Prithee Send Me Back My Heart" S. Suckling. [Volume 2/187]
"I put those things there. - See them burn." The Song of the Demented Priest. J. Berryman. [Supp 2/329]
"I quarreled with kings till the Sabbath." Song of the Sabbath. K. Molodowsky. [Supp 5/173]
"I ran out in the morning, when the air was clean and." Autumn Morning at Cambridge. F. Cornford. [Supp 1/91]
"I read in a poem." Flame, Speech. O. Paz. [Supp 6/147]
"I reckon I git your drift, gents." Banty Tim. J. Hay. [Volume 9/366]
"I reflect on this desperate note." Waiting in the Children's Hospital. C. Major. [Supp 4/199]
I Remember. R. Sanchez. [Supp 4/254]
"I remember a house I left behind." Empty House. R. Castellanos. [Supp 5/50]
"I remember a strong old man." I Remember. R. Sanchez. [Supp 4/254]
"I remember former days reading at night in the attic." Reminiscence. Ho Ch'i-Fang. [Supp 7/6]
"I Remember, I Remember" T. Hood. [Volume 1/83]
"I remember the night my mother." Night of the Scorpion. N. Ezekiel. [Supp 7/53]
I Remembered. S. Teasdale. [Supp 1/294]
"I reside at table mountain, and my name is." The Society Upon the Stanislaus. B. Harte. [Volume 9/372]
"I rise in the dawn, and i kneel and blow." The Song of the Old Mother. W. Yeats. [Volume 1/284]
"I rode in the dark of the spirit." Beyond Good and Evil. G. Woodberry. [Supp 1/322]
"I sang as one." The Conflict. C. Day Lewis. [Supp 2/112]
"I sat with Doris, the shepherd-maiden." Doris: A Pastoral. A. Munby. [Volume 2/169]

"I Saw a Stable, Low and Very Bare" M. Coleridge. [Supp 1/87]
"I saw him kiss your cheek! - 'T is true." Sly Thoughts. C. Patmore. [Volume 2/112]
"I saw him once before." The Last Leaf. O. Holmes. [Volume 3/187]
"I saw the sky descending, black and white." Where the Rainbow Ends. R. Lowell. [Supp 2/398]
"I saw the spiders marching through the air." Mr. Edwards and the Spider. R. Lowell. [Supp 2/393]
I Saw Thee. R. Palmer. [Volume 4/340]
"I saw thee when, as twilight fell." I Saw Thee. R. Palmer. [Volume 4/340]
"I Saw Two Clouds At Morning" J. Brainard. [Volume 2/259]
"I saw you toss the kites on high." The Wind. R. Stevenson. [Volume 1/145]
"I seduce the entire tribe of words." Words. T. Ojaide. [Supp 6/54]
"I See Drops of Rain" A. Yosano. [Supp 7/143]
"I see sounds, %i hear sights." Crazy: 002. L. Devkota. [Supp 7/163]
"I see the blind man as the people's guide." Crazy: 006. L. Devkota. [Supp 7/167]
"I see the cloud-born squadrons of the gale." Storm in the Distance. P. Hayne. [Volume 5/123]
"I see the deep's untrampled floor." Stanza. P. Shelley. [Volume 3/164]
"I see thee, how beneath thy robe, O king." Sacrifice of Polyxena, fr. Hecuba. Euripides. [Volume 9/5]
"I see'd her in de springtime." She Hugged Me and Kissed Me. Unknown (African American). [Supp 4/59]
"I seet here and the earth is wrapped in snow." A Twilgiht Fancy. D. Goodale. [Volume 5/53]
"I selfish and forsaken do still long for you." Deus Absconditus. A. Ridler. [Supp 2/272]
"I send a shell from the ocean beach." With a Nantucket Shell. C. Webb. [Volume 5/425]
"I send my heart up to thee, all my heart." In A Gondola. R. Browning. [Volume 2/346]
"I sent my sould through the invisible." Rubaiyat: 066. O. Khayyam. [Volume 6/217]
"I shouted at him." At the Mosque. C. Anwar. [Supp 7/79]
"I sigh for the heavenly country." The Heavenly City. S. Smith. [Supp 2/103]
I Sing for You. Lin Ling. [Supp 7/24]
I Sit and Sew. A. Nelson. [Supp 4/82]
"I sit and sew - a useless task it seem." I Sit and Sew. A. Nelson. [Supp 4/82]
"I slept and dreamed that life was beauty." Duty. E. Hooper. [Volume 4/277]
"I sometimes hold it half a sin." Grief Unspeakable, fr. In Memoriam. A. Tennyson. [Volume 3/349]
"I sometimes think that never blows so red." Rubaiyat: 019. O. Khayyam. [Volume 6/207]
"I sprang to the stirrup, and Joris and he." How They Brought the Good News from Ghent to Aix. R. Browning. [Volume 7/349]
"I stand agaze." Paulina's Appeal, fr. Polyeucte. P. Corneille. [Volume 2/396]
"I stand head in my hands thinking how." Poems for Akhmatova: 002. M. Tsvetayeva. [Supp 5/300]
"I stand upon the summit of my life." Thalatta! Thalatta! J. Brown. [Volume 3/389]
I Step Down. A. Hamzah. [Supp 7/89]
"I stood beside the ocean." Solitude. M. Iqbal. [Supp 7/61]
"I stood, one Sunday morning." London Churches. R. Milnes. [Volume 3/207]
"I strove with none, for none was worth my strife." Farewell. W. Landor. [Volume 3/394]
"I studies my tables over and over, and backward." A

Mortifying Mistake. A. Pratt. [Volume 1/166]

"I Swear %By That Summer Photo" B. Akhmadulina. [Supp 5/3]

"I take advantage of inventing women." Summer Wish. F. Lima. [Supp 4/244]

"I take my son outside." What I Tell Him. S. Ortiz. [Supp 4/316]

"I talked to old Lem." Old Lem. S. Brown. [Supp 2/85]

"I tear off the calendar." Remembering. Ping Hsin. [Supp 5/114]

"I tell you, hopeless grief is passionless." Hopeless Grief. E. Browning. [Volume 3/217]

"I tell you this - when, started from the goal." Rubaiyat: 075. O. Khayyam. [Volume 6/218]

"I think it is over, over." In Harbor. P. Hayne. [Volume 3/398]

"I think the vessel, that with fugitive." Rubaiyat: 036. O. Khayyam. [Volume 6/211]

"I thought, beloved, to have brought to you." The Gift. G. Russell. [Supp 1/274]

"I thought I saw an angel flying low." Nocturne at Bethesda. A. Bontemps. [Supp 4/127]

"I thought it was the little red." Half-Waking. W. Allingham. [Volume 1/103]

"I thought of you." Snag. V. Cruz. [Supp 4/278]

"I too followed him." The Sermon on the Mount. T. Sayigh. [Supp 7/296]

"I too have thought of all this, dear wife, but I." Hector to His Wife, fr. The Iliad. Homer. [Volume 3/122]

"I, Too, Sing America" L. Hughes. [Supp 4/131]

"I took the crazy short-cut to the bay." Swimmers. L. Untermeyer. [Supp 1/309]

"I used to dream militant." Revolutionary Dreams. N. Giovanni. [Supp 4/222]

"I wadna gi'e my ain wife." My Ain Wife. A. Laing. [Volume 2/419]

"I waited for the train at Coventry." Godiva. A. Tennyson. [Volume 7/361]

"I wake with any two cats, victors." Mornings in Various Years: 003. M. Piercy. [Supp 5/201]

"I walk, I only." Nocturn. F. Thompson. [Supp 1/302]

"I Walked Out to the Graveyard to See the Dead" R. Eberhart. [Supp 2/128]

"I walked the other day, to spend my hour." Happy Are the Dead. H. Vaughan. [Volume 3/439]

"I wandered by the brookside." The Brookside. R. Milnes. [Volume 2/156]

"I wandered lonely as a cloud." Daffodils. W. Wordsworth. [Volume 5/247]

"I Want To Die While You Love Me" G. Johnson. [Supp 4/84]

I Want to Find Desperately I Look. B. Peralta. [Supp 6/184]

"I Was Always Fascinated" A. Villanueva. [Supp 4/266]

"I was asking for something specific and perfect for." Mannahatta. W. Whitman. [Volume 7/245]

"I was made chief for girls." My Name Blew Like a Horn Among the Payira. O. P'bitek. [Supp 6/98]

"I was raised in checkered silence." Willow. A. Akhmatova. [Supp 5/9]

"I was young and 'Harry' was strong." Aunt Phillis's Guest. W. Gannett. [Volume 3/239]

"I watched her as she stopped to pluck." On the Brink. C. Calverley. [Volume 9/443]

"I weigh not fortune's frown or smile." Contentment. J. Sylvester. [Volume 6/417]

"I will arise and go now, and go to Innisfree." The Lake Isle of Innisfree. W. Yeats. [Volume 5/211]

"I will go back to the great sweet mother--" The Disappointed Lover, fr. The Triumph of Time. A. Swinburne. [Volume 5/378]

"I will go out to grass with that old king." The Faun. R. Hovey. [Volume 5/26]

"I will look %at the mirror." Mirror. J. Das. [Supp 7/50]

"I will not have the mad Clytie." Flowers. T. Hood. [Volume 5/282]

"I Will Not Let Thee Go" R. Bridges. [Supp 1/72]

"I will not let you say a woman's part." A Woman's Answer. A. Procter. [Volume 2/221]

"I will paint her as I see her." A Portrait. E. Browning. [Volume 1/56]

"I will show you a way." Assimilation. E. Manner. [Supp 5/148]

"I wish I were where Helen lies." Fair Helen. Unknown. [Volume 3/330]

"I woke with a start." Revenge. C. Anwar. [Supp 7/80]

"I wonder if the hawk knew." The Different Day. G. Conkling. [Supp 1/88]

"I wonder where it could went to." Legend. J. Weaver. [Supp 1/314]

I Won't Sell His Love. F. Tuqan. [Supp 5/307]

"I worship thee, sweet will of God!" The Will of God. F. Faber. [Volume 4/36]

"I would be wandering in disant fields." In Bondage. C. McKay. [Supp 4/87]

"I Would I Were An Excellent Divine" N. Breton. [Volume 4/312]

"I would like a photograph of that said Captain Dyar." A Poetical Plea. G. Stein. [Supp 5/296]

"I Would Not Live Alway" W. Muhlenberg. [Volume 3/392]

"I would not speak for him who could not speak." Elegy for a Dead Soldier: 006. K. Shapiro. [Supp 2/316]

"I wrap myself in sheep leather." Early Night. C. Forche. [Supp 5/82]

"I wrought them like a targe of hammered gold." On His "Sonnets of the Wingless Hours" E. Lee-Hamilton. [Volume 6/338]

"I'd been away from her three years,--about that." The Faithful Lovers. Unknown. [Volume 2/231]

The Idea of Ancestry. E. Knight. [Supp 4/169]

Ideality. H. Coleridge. [Volume 6/8]

Identity. J. Das. [Supp 7/48]

*Identity*

Identity. J. Das. [Supp 7/48]

Who Am I? Tru Vu. [Supp 7/199]

"The idle dayseye, the laborious wheel." O. R. Wilbur. [Supp 2/409]

If. J. Angira. [Supp 6/21]

"If a squirrel crosses my way." If. J. Angira. [Supp 6/21]

"If all the world and love were young." The Nymph's Reply. S. Raleigh. [Volume 2/150]

"If Doughty Deeds My Lady Please" R. Graham. [Volume 2/102]

"If ever I render back your heart." Song For a Slight Voice. L. Bogan. [Supp 5/33]

"If every man's internal care." Without and Within. Metastasio. [Volume 6/251]

"if I culd Blame it all on the weather." The Earth Falls Down. A. Sexton. [Supp 5/259]

"If I go east." The Wind's Song. W. Rendra. [Supp 7/101]

"If I pour petrol on a white child's face." A Poem in Black and White. M. Serote. [Supp 6/91]

"If I produce paralysis in verse." Early Recollections. E. Chuilleanain. [Supp 5/192]

"If I should die, think only this of me." The Soldier. R. Brooke. [Supp 1/76]

"If I Should Die To-Night" B. Smith. [Volume 3/374]

"If I think myself." The Insidious Dr. Fu Manchu. L. Jones. [Supp 4/174]

"If I were inside you." I Step Down. A. Hamzah. [Supp 7/89]

"If I were told that I must die to-morrow." When. S. Woolsey. [Volume 4/363]

"**If** It Be True That Any Beauteous Thing" M. Angelo. [Volume 2/72]

"**If** love were what the rose is." A Match. A. Swinburne. [Volume 2/86]

"**If** sleep and death be truly one." Time and Eternity, fr. In Memoriam. A. Tennyson. [Volume 3/351]

"**If** solitude hath ever led thy steps." Sunset, fr. Queen Mab. P. Shelley. [Volume 5/48]

"**If** stores of dry and learned lore we gain." The Memory of the Heart. D. Webster. [Volume 1/346]

"**If** suddenly upon the street." Love. C. Richardson. [Volume 4/189]

"**If** the red slayer think he slays." Brahma. R. Emerson. [Volume 4/6]

"**If** this fair rose offend thy sight." The White Rose. Unknown. [Volume 2/36]

"**If** thou dost bid thy friend farewell." Parting. C. Patmore. [Volume 3/96]

"**If** thou regrett'st thy youth, - why live?" Verse. G. Byron. [Volume 3/171]

"**If** thou shouldst ever come by choice or chance." Ginevra. S. Rogers. [Volume 9/81]

"**If** Thou Wert By My Side, My Love" R. Heber. [Volume 2/441]

"**If** thou wouldst view fair Melrose aright." Melrose Abbey, fr. The Lay of the Last Minstrel. S. Scott. [Volume 7/208]

"**If** to be absent were to be." To lucasta. R. Lovelace. [Volume 3/124]

**If** We Had But a Day. M. Dickinson. [Volume 4/187]

"**If** we had not buried our unity in the dust." What Value Has the People Whose Tongue Is Tied?: 018. N. Qabbani. [Supp 7/290]

"**If** we have lost the war, it is not strange." What Value Has the People Whose Tongue is Tied?: 005. N. Qabbani. [Supp 7/287]

**If** We Knew; or, Blessings of To-day. M. Smith. [Volume 1/278]

"**If** we knew the woe and heart-ache." If We Knew; or, Blessings of To-day. M. Smith. [Volume 1/278]

"**If** women could be fair, and yet not fond." A Renunciation. E. Vere. [Volume 2/246]

"**If** ye would love and loved be." Advice. W. Dunbar. [Volume 1/401]

"**If** you bright stars which gem the night'" Meeting Above. W. Leggett. [Volume 4/395]

"**If** you come to mind I think of you." Song. Pak Tu-Jin. [Supp 7/154]

"**If** You Want To Know Me" N. Sousa. [Supp 5/59]

*Ignorance*
Festoons of Fishes. A. Kreymborg. [Supp 1/184]
No Credit. K. Fearing. [Supp 2/101]

Il Penseroso. J. Milton. [Volume 6/251]

Iliad. H. Wolfe. [Supp 1/321]

Ilka Blade O' Grass Keps Its Ain Drap O' Dew. J. Ballantine. [Volume 3/241]

"**I'll** sing you a good old song." The Fine Old English Gentleman. Unknown. [Volume 9/255]

"**I'll** wake and watch this autumn night." Tge King's Highway. H. Preston. [Volume 6/102]

*Illness*
Absalom. M. Rukeyser. [Supp 5/240]
For Christopher. J. Jordan. [Supp 4/195]

Illusions. R. Johnson. [Volume 6/277]

"The **illustration** %is nothing to you without the application." To a Steam Roller. M. Moore. [Supp 5/185]

"**I'm** Alone %I See" Nirala. [Supp 7/68]

**I'm** Drifting. A. Hamzah. [Supp 7/92]

"**I'm** drifting, my darling." I'm Drifting. A. Hamzah. [Supp 7/92]

"**I'm** far frae my hame, an' I'm weary afternwhiles." My Ain Countree. M. Demarest. [Volume 4/353]

"**I'm** going to be a pirate ;with a bright brass pivot-gun." The Tarry Buccaneer. J. Masefield. [Supp 1/207]

"**I'm** in Hong Kong." How Hong Kong Was Destroyed. D. Ravikovitch. [Supp 5/235]

"**I'm** in love with you, Baby Louise!" Baby Louise. M. Eytinge. [Volume 1/21]

**I'm** Not Myself At All. S. Lover. [Volume 2/185]

"**I'm** Only a Woman, And That's Enough" G. Fuertes. [Supp 5/94]

"**I'm** sitting alone by the fire." Her Letter. B. Harte. [Volume 2/128]

"**I'm** sitting here with all my words intact." Silence near an Ancient Stone. R. Castellanos. [Supp 5/49]

"**I'm** sittin' on the stile, Mary." Lament of the Irish Emigrant. H. Sheridan. [Volume 3/343]

"**I'm** wearing awa', Jean." The Land O' the Leal. C. Nairne. [Volume 3/380]

*Imagination*
Fancy. J. Keats. [Volume 6/9]
Fantasy, fr. The Vision of Delight. B. Johnson. [Volume 6/3]
Hallo, My Fancy. W. Cleland. [Volume 6/3]
Ideality. H. Coleridge. [Volume 6/8]
Imagination, fr. A Midsummer Night's Dream. W. Shakespeare. [Volume 6/12]
Nehru. S. Takahashi. [Supp 7/126]
Walking Song. C. Williams. [Supp 1/315]

**Imagination**, fr. A Midsummer Night's Dream. W. Shakespeare. [Volume 6/12]

"The **Immediate** %Clear and Fleeting" J. Palaez. [Supp 6/198]

"The **immortal** gods." Devotion. P. Massinger. [Volume 4/252]

*Immortality*
A Frieze. J. Bishop. [Supp 2/24]
"In heaven, I suppose, Lie Down Together" C. Day Lewis. [Supp 2/115]
A Song of Derivations. A. Meynell. [Supp 1/213]
They Eat Out. M. Atwood. [Supp 5/19]

The **Immortality** of a Genius. S. Propertius. [Volume 6/357]

"The **imperfection** of the world." Jitterbugs. L. Jones. [Supp 4/177]

**Impression**. E. Gosse. [Volume 6/335]

"**In** a chariot of light from the regions of day." Liberty Tree. T. Paine. [Volume 8/324]

"**In** a coign of the cliff between lowland and highland." A Forsaken Garden. A. Swinburne. [Volume 5/388]

**In** a Copy of Omar Khayyam. J. Lowell. [Volume 7/39]

"**In** a dirty old house lived a dirty old man." The Dirty Old Man. W. Allingham. [Volume 3/55]

"**In** a garden shady this holy lady." Song for St. Cecilia's Day. W. Auden. [Supp 2/167]

**In** A Gondola. R. Browning. [Volume 2/346]

**In** a Lecture-room. A. Clough. [Volume 4/132]

"**In** a small chamber, friendless and unseen." William Lloyd Garrison. J. Lowell. [Volume 7/22]

**In** a Storm. Li Ying. [Supp 7/17,Supp 7/1,Supp 7/17]

"**In** a valley, centuries ago." The Petrified Fern. M. Branch. [Volume 6/200]

"**In** an instant %what falls from me is a matter of no concern." In Medias Res. F. Lima. [Supp 4/241]

**In** Arcadia. L. Durrell. [Supp 2/259]

"**In** Biafra this year, hunger killed." Model Lesson. T. Carmi. [Supp 7/242]

**In** Bondage. C. McKay. [Supp 4/87]

"**In** broad street building (on a winter night)" The Gouty Merchant and the Stranger. H. Smith. [Volume 9/275]

"**In** Chicago we push buttons to make love, ride mechanical." Chicago. Ya Hsuan. [Supp 7/30]

"**In** Deya when the mist." The Island. C. Forche. [Supp 5/84]

"**In** dream, again within the clean, cold hell." The

Gorse. W. Gibson. [Supp 1/141]
"In early days methought that all must last."
   Unchanging. F. Von Bodenstedt. [Volume 3/242]
"In eddying course when leaves began to fly." Echo
   and Silence. S. Brydges. [Volume 6/180]
"In either hand the hastening angel caught." The
   Departure from Paradise, Book XII, fr. Paradise
   Lost. J. Milton. [Volume 4/273]
"In facile natures fancies quickly grow."
   Perseverance. L. Da Vinci. [Volume 6/284]
"In fashion, as a snow-white rose, lay then."
   Paradise: The Saints in Glory, fr. The Diving
   Comedy. Dante Alighieri. [Volume 4/445]
"In front of the stove the dog, brown, is sleeping."
   Age. T. Tomioka. [Volume 7/140]
"In good King Charles's golden days." The Vicar of
   Bray. Unknown. [Volume 9/251]
In Harbor. P. Hayne. [Volume 3/398]
"In heaven, I suppose, Lie Down Together" C. Day
   Lewis. [Supp 2/115]
"In heavy sleep the caliph lay." Caliph and Satan. J.
   Clarke. [Volume 4/119]
"In his own image the creator made." Man. W. Landor.
   [Volume 3/151]
"In ;his tall senatorial." The Drum. E. Sitwell.
   [Supp 2/12]
"In Hong Kong we smile politely." Hong Kong. W.
   Rendra. [Supp 7/103]
In January. G. Bottomley. [Supp 1/62]
"In June, amid the golden fields." The Groundhog. R.
   Eberhart. [Supp 2/127]
"In June the early signs." For a Christening: 001. A.
   Ridler. [Supp 2/273]
"In Koln, a town of monks and bones." Epigram:
   Cologne. S. Coleridge. [Volume 9/286]
"In life there are blows so heavy. 'I don't know.'"
   The Black Messengers. C. Vallejo. [Supp 6/187]
"In life there is an ordinary question." Two
   Questions. A. Hernandez. [Supp 7/177]
"In Love, if Love be Love, if Love be ours." Not At
   All, Or All In All, fr. Merlin and Vivien. A.
   Tennyson. [Volume 2/250]
"In May, when sea-winds pierced our solitudes." The
   Rhodora. R. Emerson. [Volume 5/252]
"In me (the worm) clearly." The Walls Do Not Fall:
   006. H. Doolittle. [Supp 5/72]
In Me and Far Away. E. Gutierrez. [Supp 6/174]
In Medias Res. F. Lima. [Supp 4/241]
"In melancholic fancy." Hallo, My Fancy. W. Cleland.
   [Volume 6/3]
In Memoriam. L. Senghor. [Supp 6/76]
In Memoriam F. A. S. R. Stevenson. [Volume 3/428]
In Memory of Sigmund Freud. W. Auden. [Supp 2/158]
In Memory of Walter Savage Landor. A. Swinburne.
   [Volume 7/75]
In Mexico. E. Stein. [Volume 7/257]
"In mole-blue indolence the sun." The Jungle: 001. A.
   Lewis. [Supp 2/375]
"In moss-prankt dels which the sunbeams flatter."
   Lovers, and a Reflections. C. Calverley.
   [Volume 9/409]
"In my childhood trees were green." Autobiography. L.
   MacNeice. [Supp 2/171]
"In my safety were promised me." What Value Has the
   People Whose Tongue Is Tied?: 017. N. Qabbani.
   [Supp 7/290]
"In my sleep I was fain of their fellowship, fain."
   Sunrise: A Hymn of the Marshes. S. Lanier.
   [Volume 5/257]
"In my small night, ah." The Wind Will Take Us. F.
   Farrozkhzad. [Supp 7/217]
"In nightmareland, poor Alice." Alice in
   Nightmareland. E. Lihn. [Supp 6/122]
In Poets' Defence. J. Wheelwright. [Supp 2/54]
In Praise of Angling. S. Wotton. [Volume 5/136]

"In praise of little children I will say." Laus
   Infantium. W. Canton. [Volume 1/7]
In Prison. S. L'Estrange. [Volume 6/420]
In Prison. M. Smith. [Volume 4/323]
"In restaurants we argue." They Eat Out. M. Atwood.
   [Supp 5/19]
"In Saint Luke's Gospel we are told." The Sifting of
   Peter. H. Longfellow. [Volume 4/290]
"In Sana, O, in Sana, God the Lord." Prince Adeb. G.
   Boker. [Volume 7/308]
In School-Days. J. Whittier. [Volume 1/163]
"In silence %the distant heroes bow their." Echo of
   Mandela. Z. Mandela. [Supp 6/78]
"In slumbers of midnight the sailor-boy lay." The
   Mariner's Dream. W. Dimond. [Volume 5/438]
In State. F. Willson. [Volume 8/338]
"In summer, when the days were long." Summer Days. W.
   Call. [Volume 2/341]
"In summertime on Bredon." Bredon hill. A. Housman.
   [Supp 1/166]
"In tattered old slippers that toast at the bars."
   The Cane-bottomed Chair. W. Thackeray. [Volume
   1/377]
"In the afternoons the neon lights are sweet."
   Managua 6:30 P.M. E. Cardenal. [Supp 6/155]
In the Aging City. F. Tuqan. [Supp 7/269]
"In the ancient town of Bruges." Carillon. H.
   Longfellow. [Volume 7/166]
"In the Bario" Alurista. [Supp 4/274]
"In the barn the tenant cock." Morning. J. Cunningham.
   [Volume 5/40]
"In the beginning there was nought." Creation. A.
   Noyes. [Supp 1/245]
"In the best chamber of the house." The Bottom Drawer.
   A. Barr. [Volume 3/405]
"In the bitter waves of woe." Ultima Veritas. W.
   Gladden. [Volume 4/255]
"In the Blue Distance" N. Sachs. [Supp 5/248]
"In the bowl of buildings alias the back yard." Milk
   at the Bottom of the Sea. O. Williams. [Supp
   2/79]
In the Cellar, fr. Bitter Sweet. J. Holland. [Volume
   1/317]
"In the cold of the month of Magh." Crazy: 004. L.
   Devkota. [Supp 7/165]
"In the Course of Time" N. Zach. [Supp 7/255]
"In the days that tried our fathers." National Anthem.
   R. Newell. [Volume 9/418]
In the Engine-shed. W. Wilkins. [Volume 9/165]
"In the fair gardens of celestial peace." Lines. H.
   Stowe. [Volume 3/426]
"In the first year of the last disgrace." News of the
   World II. G. Barker. [Supp 2/285]
In the Flux. F. Tuqan. [Supp 7/272]
"In the gloomy ocean bed." The Kearsarge. J. Roche.
   [Volume 5/422]
"In the greenest of our valleys." The Haunted Palace.
   E. Poe. [Volume 6/164]
"In the Heart of Contemplation" C. Day Lewis. [Supp
   2/115]
"In the hollow tree, in the old gray tower." The Owl.
   B. Procter. [Volume 5/321]
"In the hour of my distress." The Holy Spirit. R.
   Herrick. [Volume 4/108]
"In the huge, rectangular room the ceiling." My
   Mother, Who Came from China, Where She Never
   Saw Snow. L. Mar. [Supp 4/34]
"In the ice-filled chaos before the end of creation."
   The Beginning. D. Pagis. [Supp 7/251]
"In the low-rafted garret, stooping." Dorothy in the
   Garret. J. Throwbridge. [Volume 3/89]
"In the merry month of May." Phillida and Corydon. N.
   Breton. [Volume 2/152]
In the Mourning Time. R. Hayden. [Supp 4/138]
"In the prison cell I sit." Tramp, Tramp, Tramp.

The **Insidious** Dr. Fu Manchu. L. Jones. [Supp 4/174]
*Instruments*
  Song For a Slight Voice. L. Bogan. [Supp 5/33]
*Intellect*
  Solutions. E. Blunden. [Supp 2/46]
**Intercession** and Redeoption, Book XI, fr. Paradise Lost. J. Milton. [Volume 4/270]
"**Into** a ward of the whitewashed halls." Somebody's Darling. M. Conte. [Volume 8/378]
"**Into** her mother's bedroom to wash the ballooning body." Jessie Mitchell's Mother. G. Brooks. [Supp 5/41]
"**Into** the organpipes and steeples." Ceremony After a Fire Raid: 003. D. Thomas. [Supp 2/361]
**Into** the Silence of the Forest. E. Manner. [Supp 5/147]
"**Into** the silent land." Song of the Silent Land. J. Von Salis. [Volume 4/388]
"**Into** the silver night." Revelation. E. Gosse. [Supp 1/145]
"**Into** the woods my master went." A Ballad of Trees and the Master. S. Lanier. [Volume 4/69]
"**Into** this universe, and why not knowing." Rubaiyat: 029. O. Khayyam. [Volume 6/209]
**Introduction**. F. Faiz. [Supp 7/169]
**Inventory**. T. Carmi. [Supp 7/241]
**Invictus**. W. Henley. [Volume 3/221]
**Invitation** to Juno. W. Empson. [Supp 2/141]
**Invocation**, fr. the Davideis. A. Cowley. [Volume 6/371]
**Invocation** to Light, fr. Paradise Lost. J. Milton. [Volume 5/30]
**Invocation** to Rain In Summer. W. Bennett. [Volume 5/113]
**Invocation** to Sleep, fr. Valentinian. J. Fletcher. [Volume 6/432]
**Iphigeneia** and Agamemnon. W. Landor. [Volume 9/3]
"**Iphigeneia**, when she heard her doom." Iphigeneia and Agamemnon. W. Landor. [Volume 9/3]
**Iqbal, Muhammed**
  Ghazal No. 9. V. Kiernan (tr.). [Supp 7/57]
  God's Command to His Angels. V. Kiernan (tr.). [Supp 7/58]
  The Hawk. V. Kiernan (tr.). [Supp 7/59]
  Political Leaders. V. Kiernan (tr.). [Supp 7/61]
  Reproach. V. Kiernan (tr.). [Supp 7/60]
  Solitude. V. Kiernan (tr.). [Supp 7/61]
  Two Planets. V. Kiernan (tr.). [Supp 7/57]
  The Way of Islam. V. Kiernan (tr.). [Supp 7/60]
"**Iram** indeed is gone with all his rose." Rubaiyat: 005. O. Khayyam. [Volume 6/204]
**Ireland**. D. MacCarthy. [Volume 8/62]
**Ireland**. J. Piatt. [Volume 8/66]
*Ireland and the Irish*
  "It Is Time That I Wrote My Will" W. Yeats. [Supp 1/330]
  Netrality. L. MacNeice. [Supp 2/181]
  The Sack of Baltimore. T. Davis. [Volume 9/127]
  September, 1913. W. Yeats. [Supp 1/328]
The **Irish** Spinning-Wheel. A. Graves. [Volume 2/53]
The **Irishman**. J. Orr. [Volume 8/52]
The **Irishman** and the Lady. W. Maginn. [Volume 9/320]
**Irwin, Wallace**
  Love sonnets of a Hoodlum, sel. [Volume 9/394]
"**I's** boun' to see my gal to-night." On The Road. P. Dunbar. [Volume 2/292]
"**Is** it a wish - that tiny tin whistle." Peewee. A. Kreymborg. [Supp 1/185]
"**Is** it possible?" Dallying with Temptation, fr. Wallenstein. S. Coleridge. [Volume 4/327]
"**Is** it the palm, the cocoa-palm." The Palm-tree. J. Whittier. [Volume 5/229]
"**Is** there a whim-inspired fool." A Bard's Epitaph. R. Burns. [Volume 7/113]
"'**Is** there anybody there?' said the traveller." The

Listeners. W. De La Mare. [Supp 1/107]
"**Is** there for honest poverty." For A' That and A' That. R. Burns. [Volume 6/398]
"**Is** there, when the winds are singing." The Mother's Hope. L. Blanchard. [Volume 1/37]
"**Is** this a dagger which I see before me." A Dagger of the Mind, fr. Macbeth. W. Shakespeare. [Volume 9/120]
"**Is** this a fast, - to keep." A True Lent. R. Herrick. [Volume 4/303]
"**Is** this the peace of God, this strange sweet." Peace. F. Havergal. [Volume 4/250]
**Isatou** Died. L. Peters. [Supp 6/18]
"**Isatou** died %when she was only five." Isatou Died. L. Peters. [Supp 6/18]
**Isis** Wanderer. K. Raine. [Supp 2/199]
**Island**. N. Ezekiel. [Supp 7/54]
The **Island**. C. Forche. [Supp 5/84]
*Islands*
  Island. N. Ezekiel. [Supp 7/54]
  Islands in the River. Agyeya. [Supp 7/45]
  Multitudinous Stars and Spring Waters: 006. Ping Hsin. [Supp 5/117]
**Islands** in the River. Agyeya. [Supp 7/45]
"The **islands** which whisper to the ambitious." At Epidaurus. L. Durrell. [Supp 2/257]
"The **isles** of Greece, the isles of Greece!" Song of the Greek Poet, fr. Don Juan. G. Byron. [Volume 8/130]
**Istaru, Ana**
  The Man Who Boxes. Z. Anglesey (tr.). [Supp 6/136]
"**It** almost maes me cry to tell." The Dreadful Story About Harriet and the Matches. H. Hoffmann. [Volume 1/171]
"**It** came upon the midnight clear." The Angels' Song. E. Sears. [Volume 4/48]
**It** Can Happen. V. Huidobro. [Supp 6/120]
"**It** can't be called red, it's not color but apple." Adherence to Apples. S. Tanikawa. [Supp 7/135]
"**It** chanced of late a shepherd's swain." A Fiction. Unknown. [Volume 2/81]
"**It** chanced to me upon a time to sail." My Native Land. J. O'Reilly. [Volume 8/59]
"**It** crawls, the underground snake." Readers of Newspapers. M. Tsvetayeva. [Supp 5/302]
"**It** don't seem hardly right, John." Jonathan to John. J. Lowell. [Volume 8/346]
"**It** flows through old, hushed Aegypt and its." The Nile. P. Shelley. [Volume 7/160]
"**It** is a castle of forbears." Life in the Castle. A. Hebert. [Supp 5/111]
"**It** is a hollow garden, under the cloud." Winter Swan. L. Bogan. [Supp 5/31]
"**It** is a new America." Brown River, Smile. J. Toomer. [Supp 4/91]
"**It** is a winter's tale." A Winter's Tale. D. Thomas. [Supp 2/368]
"**It** is birthday weather for you, dear soul?" Birthday Poem for Thomas Hardy. C. Day Lewis. [Supp 2/111]
**It** Is Certain That We are Constructing a World. R. Murillo. [Supp 6/176]
"**It** is done!" Laus Deo! J. Whittier. [Volume 8/176]
"**It** is Finished" C. Rossetti. [Volume 1/119]
"**It** is midnight." Poem at Thirty. S. Sanchez. [Supp 4/190]
"**It** is no madness to say." The Flowering of the Rod: 010. H. Doolittle. [Supp 5/79]
"**It** is not Beauty I demand." The Loveliness Of Love. G. Darley. [Volume 2/370]
"**It** Is Not Death To Die" G. Bethune. [Volume 3/455]
"**It** is not growing like a tree." Good Life, Long Life. B. Jonson. [Volume 6/230]
"**It** is not interesting to see." Thoughts About the Christian Doctrine of Eternal Hell. S. Smith.

**Jackson, Henry R.**
My Wife and Child. [Volume 3/228]
The **Jacobite** on Tower Hill. G. Thornbury. [Volume 8/17]
**Jacoby, Russell Powell**
My Love. [Volume 2/261]
**Jacopone, Fra**
Stabat Mater Dolorosa. A. Coles (tr.). [Volume 4/70]
**Jaffar**. L. Hunt. [Volume 1/350]
"**Jaffar**, the Barmecide, the good vizier." Jaffar. L. Hunt. [Volume 1/350]
**Japanese** Lullaby. E. Field. [Volume 1/15]
**Japp, Alexander Hay**
Shelley. [Volume 7/58]
**Jardin** Du Palais Royal. D. Gascoyne. [Supp 2/384]
**Jarrell, Randall**
The Death of the Ball Turret Gunner. [Supp 2/330]
Losses. [Supp 2/331]
A Pilot from the Carrier. [Supp 2/332]
Second Air Force. [Supp 2/332]
**Jarvenpa, Aili (tr.)**
Assimilation. E. Manner. [Supp 5/148]
"From My Life I Make a Poem" E. Manner. [Supp 5/149]
Into the Silence of the Forest. E. Manner. [Supp 5/147]
"**Jason**, that cunning old sailor." Jason's Grave in Jerusalem. D. Pagis. [Supp 7/250]
**Jason's** Grave in Jerusalem. D. Pagis. [Supp 7/250]
"**Jazz** notes and Brahms intermittently." To My Contemporaries: 001. E. Rolfe. [Supp 2/222]
**Jazzonia**. L. Hughes. [Supp 4/129]
**Jeanie** Morrison. W. Motherwell. [Volume 3/127]
**Jeffers, Robinson**
Boats in a Fog. [Supp 1/173]
Noon. [Supp 1/175]
Pelicans. [Supp 1/173]
Tamar, sel. [Supp 1/174]
**Jenks, Edward A.**
Going and Coming. [Volume 3/458]
**Jenks, Tudor**
Small and Early. [Volume 1/46]
**Jenner, Edward**
Signs of Rain. [Volume 5/118]
**Jenny** Kissed Me. L. Hunt. [Volume 1/358]
"**Jenny** kissed me when we met." Jenny Kissed Me. L. Hunt. [Volume 1/358]
**Jessie** Mitchell's Mother. G. Brooks. [Supp 5/41]
"**Jest** rain and snow! and rain again!" The First Blue-Bird. J. Riley. [Volume 5/287]
"The **jester** shook his hood and bells, and leaped." The Jester's Sermon. G. Thornbury. [Volume 6/272]
The **Jester's** Plea. F. Locker-Lampson. [Volume 6/350]
The **Jester's** Sermon. G. Thornbury. [Volume 6/272]
*Jesus Christ*
"All the World Moved" J. Jordan. [Supp 4/194]
Ballad of the Goodly Fere. E. Pound. [Supp 1/249]
The Drunken Fisherman. R. Lowell. [Supp 2/389]
Eye-Witness. R. Torrence. [Supp 1/303]
"I Saw a Stable, Low and Very Bare" M. Coleridge. [Supp 1/87]
"The Starlight's Intuitions Pierced the Twelve" D. Schwartz. [Supp 2/309]
Steal Away. Unknown (African American). [Supp 4/51]
"Still Falls the Rain" E. Sitwell. [Supp 2/21]
To a Contemporary Bunkshooter. C. Sandburg. [Supp 1/279]
"Were You There When They Crucified My Lord?" Unknown (African American). [Supp 4/60]
"**Jesus**, Estrella, Esperanza, Mercy." Middle Passage. R. Hayden. [Supp 4/142]
**Jesus** Shall Reign. I. Watts. [Volume 4/96]

"**Jesus** shall reign where'er the sun." Jesus Shall Reign. I. Watts. [Volume 4/96]
**Jet** Flight. Agyeya. [Supp 7/40]
**Jeune** Fille Et Jeune Fleur. F. Auguste. [Volume 3/305]
**Jewish** Hymn in Babylon. H. Milman. [Volume 4/307]
"The **Jews** did not cross the borders." What Value Has the People Whose Tongue Is Tied?: 012. N. Qabbani. [Supp 7/288]
**Jim**. B. Harte. [Volume 9/364]
**Jim** Bludso of the Prairie Belle. J. Hay. [Volume 9/358]
"**Jim** was a fisherman, up on the hill." Jim's Kids. E. Field. [Volume 3/290]
**Jim's** Kids. E. Field. [Volume 3/290]
"**Jingle**, jingle, clear the way." Sleigh Song. G. Pettee. [Volume 5/189]
**Jitterbugs**. L. Jones. [Supp 4/177]
"**Joao** was young like us." The Poem of Joao. N. Sousa. [Supp 5/61]
**Jock** Johnstone the Tinkler. J. Hogg. [Volume 7/390]
"**Joe** Beall 'ud set upon a keg." He'd Had No Show. S. Foss. [Volume 9/351]
**Joe** Hill Listens to the Praying. K. Patchen. [Supp 2/248]
*Johannesburg*
City Johannesburgh. M. Serote. [Supp 6/90]
**John** Anderson, My Jo. R. Burns. [Volume 2/460]
"**John** Anderson, my jo, John." John Anderson, My Jo. R. Burns. [Volume 2/460]
"**John** begins like Genesis." The World is Deed. J. Wheelwright. [Supp 2/57]
"**John** Brown of Ossawatomie spake on his dying." Brown of Ossawatomie. J. Whittier. [Volume 8/169]
"**John** Brown's body lies a-moldering in the grave." Words for the "Hallelujah Chorus" H. Brownell. [Volume 8/171]
**John** Charles Fremont. J. Whittier. [Volume 8/173]
"**John** Dobbins was so captivated." The Eggs And The Horses. Unknown. [Volume 2/432]
"**John**, founder of towns, - dweller in none." Bread-Word Giver. J. Wheelwright. [Supp 2/53]
"**John** Gilpin was a citizen." The Diverting History of John Gilpin. W. Cowper. [Volume 9/276]
**John** Henry. Unknown (African American). [Supp 4/54]
**John** Winter. L. Binyon. [Supp 1/50]
**Johnson, Ben**
Fantasy, fr. The Vision of Delight. [Volume 6/3]
**Johnson, Fenton**
Tired. [Supp 4/85]
**Johnson, Georgia Douglas**
The Heart of a Woman. [Supp 4/83]
"I Want To Die While You Love Me" [Supp 4/84]
**Johnson, James Weldon**
Go Down Death. [Supp 1/176]
Let My People Go. [Supp 4/68]
"O Black and Unknown Bards" [Supp 4/67]
**Johnson, Robert Underwood**
Illusions. [Volume 6/277]
A September Violet. [Volume 5/254]
**Johnson, Samuel**
Charles XII, fr. The Vanity of Human Wishes. [Volume 7/7]
Shakespeare, fr. Prologue. [Volume 7/51]
To-Morrow, fr. Irene. [Volume 6/189]
"A **Jolly** fat friar loved liquor good store." Gluggity Glug, fr. The Myrtle and the Vine. G. Colman. [Volume 9/245]
**Jonathan** to John. J. Lowell. [Volume 8/346]
**Jones, Ebenezer**
Rain. [Volume 5/124]
**Jones, Ernest Charles**
The Song of the Lower Classes. [Volume 6/391]
**Jones, Leroi**
Cold Term. [Supp 4/176]

Harold's Leap. S. Smith. [Supp 5/284]
**Lear, Edward**
  The Jumblies. [Volume 1/192]
  Limerick. [Volume 1/196,Volume 1/197,Volume 1/198, Volume 1/199,Volume 1/200,Volume 1/201]
  Mr. and Mrs. Spikky Sparrow. [Volume 1/177]
  The Owl and the Pussy-cat. [Volume 1/175]
"**Leave** all to God." God's Sure Help in Sorrow. A. Ulrich. [Volume 3/236]
"**Leaves** have their time to fall." The Hour of Death. F. Hemans. [Volume 3/259]
**Leavetaking.** W. Watson. [Supp 1/313]
"**Leaving** a jumble of jagged mountains in the west." About the Sea. N. Hikmet. [Supp 7/310]
**Lecky, William E. H.**
  The Sower and His Seed. [Volume 6/330]
  Undeveloped Lives. [Volume 6/268]
**Lee, Don L.**
  Assaination. [Supp 4/212]
  But He Was Cool. [Supp 4/216]
  Mixed Sketches. [Supp 4/210]
  We Walk the Way of the New World: 001. [Supp 4/213]
  We Walk the Way of the New World: 002. [Supp 4/214]
**Lee-Hamilton, Eugene**
  On His "Sonnets of the Wingless Hours" [Volume 6/338]
**Lee, Laurie**
  Caedmon. [Supp 2/338]
  Cleator Moor. [Supp 2/340]
  Day of These Days. [Supp 2/335]
  Michaelmas. [Supp 2/341]
  Milkmaid. [Supp 2/336]
  Song at Night. [Supp 2/341]
  The Tame Hare. [Supp 2/342]
  The Three Winds. [Supp 2/337]
  The Undiscovered Planet. [Supp 2/343]
**Lee, Peter H. (tr.)**
  Channel. Chong Chi-Yong. [Supp 7/150]
  Fever. Chong Chi-Yong. [Supp 7/147]
  Grandpa. Chong Chi-Yong. [Supp 7/147]
  Moon. Chong Chi-Yong. [Supp 7/149]
  Summit. Chong Chi-Yong. [Supp 7/148]
**Lee** to the Rear. J. Thompson. [Volume 8/401]
**Leedle** Yawcob Strauss. C. Adams. [Volume 9/327]
**Left** on the Battle-field. S. Bolton. [Volume 8/386]
*Legacies*
  Strange Legacies. S. Brown. [Supp 4/117]
**Legacy:** My South. D. Randall. [Supp 4/154]
**Legal** Fiction. W. Empson. [Supp 2/144]
**Legend.** J. Weaver. [Supp 1/314]
The **Legendar** Storm. L. Inada. [Supp 4/3]
"A **legendary** storm - that's." The Legendar Storm. L. Inada. [Supp 4/3]
**Leggett, William**
  Meeting Above. [Volume 4/395]
**Leisure.** W. Davies. [Supp 1/105]
**Leland, Charles Godfrey**
  Hans Breitmann's Party. [Volume 9/325]
  Ritter Hugo. [Volume 9/324]
  Tom Mooney. [Supp 1/186]
*Leonardo da Vinci*
  "There Lived a Lady in Milan" W. Benet. [Supp 1/47]
**Leonardo's** "Mona Lisa" E. Dowden. [Volume 7/150]
**Leonidas of Alexandria**
  Home. R. Bland (tr.). [Volume 1/266]
  On the Picture of an Infant Playing Near a Precipice. S. Rogers (tr.). [Volume 1/24]
The **Leper.** N. Willis. [Volume 7/315]
**Leroux, Guiraud**
  The Nun and Harp. H. Preston (tr.). [Volume 3/93]
**Les** Sylphides. L. MacNeice. [Supp 2/185]
The **Lesson.** W. Auden. [Supp 2/162]

**Lessons** of the War: Judging Distances. H. Reed. [Supp 2/344]
"**Lest** the magic %of silence crack." Fear. J. Das. [Supp 7/48]
**L'Estrange, Sir Roger**
  In Prison. [Volume 6/420]
"**Let** Dogs Delight to Bark and Bite" I. Watts. [Volume 1/114]
"**Let** her lie naked here, my hand resting." News of the World III. G. Barker. [Supp 2/286]
"**Let** It Be Forgotten" S. Teasdale. [Supp 1/293]
"**Let** Liberty run onward with the years." A Holy Nation. R. Realf. [Volume 8/178]
"**Let** me be your servant." Healthful Old Age, fr. As You Like It. W. Shakespeare. [Volume 6/287]
"**Let** me but do my work from day to day." Work. H. Van Dyke. [Volume 6/415]
"**Let** me move slowly through the street." The Crowded Street. W. Bryant. [Volume 6/239]
"**Let** Me Not To The Marriage Of True Minds" W. Shakespeare. [Volume 2/376]
"**Let** me play love's last card." Poem to a Young Man. L. Bell. [Supp 6/108]
**Let** Me Tell You About Myself. T. Tomioka. [Supp 7/138]
**Let** My People Go. J. Johnson. [Supp 4/68]
"**Let** Not ambition mock their useful toil." The Cotter's Saturday Night. R. Burns. [Volume 1/300]
"**Let** not soft slumber close my eyes." Self-Inquiry. I. Watts. [Volume 4/280]
"**Let** Not Woman E'er Complain" R. Burns. [Volume 2/219]
"**Let** nothing make thee sad or fretful." To Myself. P. Fleming. [Volume 3/218]
"**Let** Taylor preach, upon a morning breezy." Moning Meditations. T. Hood. [Volume 9/261]
"**Let** the desert be the world's forehead." Face. S. Tanikawa. [Supp 7/133]
"**Let** the tale's sailor from a Christian voyage." Altarwise by Owl-light: 010. D. Thomas. [Supp 2/352]
"'**Let** there be light,' God said; and forthwith." Light, fr. Paradise Lost. J. Milton. [Volume 5/30]
"**Let** us glance for a moment, 't is well worth the." The Grave-yard, fr. A Fable for Critics. J. Lowell. [Volume 9/267]
"**Let** us go back into the dusk again." The Return: 004. A. Bontemps. [Supp 4/125]
"**Let** Us Have Madness Openly" K. Patchen. [Supp 2/254]
"**Let** us live, then, and be glad." Gaudeamus Igitur. Unknown. [Volume 1/231]
"**Let** us remember Hernandez de Cordoba on the striden coast." The Uninhabited City: 002. E. Cardenal. [Supp 6/154]
"**Let** us sit on the green grass." A Moment on Green Grass. Agyeya. [Supp 7/41]
"**Let** us walk in the white snow." Velvet Shoes. E. Wylie. [Supp 1/326]
"**Let** us with care observe." Labor Done, fr. Song of the Bell. J. Schiller. [Volume 6/412]
"**Let's** Leave Here" C. Anwar. [Supp 7/86]
"**Let's** open a road in the air." The Blind Indians. J. Pasos. [Supp 6/181]
"**Let's** say we're seriously ill, need surgery." On Living: 002. N. Hikmet. [Supp 7/307]
"**Let's** sleep outside." Night. J. Das. [Supp 7/50]
A **Letter** on the Use of Machine Guns at Weddings. K. Patchen. [Supp 2/252]
A **Letter** to a Policeman in Kansas City. K. Patchen. [Supp 2/253]
**Letter** to Time. C. Alegria. [Supp 5/14]
**Letty's** Globe. C. Turner. [Volume 1/31]
**Lever, Charles**

A Sunrise Song. S. Lanier. [Volume 6/277]

A Tear. S. Rogers. [Volume 6/271]

This Life. W. Drummond of Hawthornden. [Volume 6/225]

The Three Warnings. H. Thrale. [Volume 6/289]

To a Skeleton. Unknown. [Volume 6/298]

Train Ride. J. Wheelwright. [Supp 2/56]

The True Philosophy of Life. W. Dunbar. [Volume 6/299]

Undeveloped Lives. W. Lecky. [Volume 6/268]

The Vagabonds. J. Trowbridge. [Volume 6/260]

The Valley of the Shadow. E. Robinson. [Supp 1/267]

Where Lies the Land? A. Clough. [Volume 6/231]

The Wild Ride. L. Guiney. [Volume 6/259]

The Will. J. Donne. [Volume 6/295]

Without and Within. Metastasio. [Volume 6/251]

Yussouf. J. Lowell. [Volume 6/279]

"Life: %a wailing and a bawling." Hopeless. Nirala. [Supp 7/63]

"Life for My Child Is Simple and Is Good" G. Brooks. [Supp 4/162]

Life, fr. Festus. P. Bailey. [Volume 4/407]

"Life! I know not what thou art." Life. A. Barbauld. [Volume 3/400]

"Life in a day: he took his girl to the ballet." Les Sylphides. L. MacNeice. [Supp 2/185]

Life in the Autumn Woods. P. Cooke. [Volume 5/151]

Life in the Castle. A. Hebert. [Supp 5/111]

A Life-Lesson. J. Riley. [Volume 1/127]

"Life, like a romping school-boy full of glee." Life. E. Wilcox. [Volume 6/233]

"Life may be given in many ways." Abraham Lincoln. J. Lowell. [Volume 7/32]

The Life of Flowers. W. Landor. [Volume 5/244]

"A Life on the Ocean Wave" E. Sargent. [Volume 5/409]

A Life's Love. Unknown. [Volume 9/382]

Light. F. Bourdillon. [Volume 2/78]

Light. G. Macdonald. [Volume 5/32]

*Light Bulbs*

West Coast Episode. J. Jordan. [Supp 5/128]

Light, fr. Paradise Lost. J. Milton. [Volume 5/30]

Light Shining Out of Darkness. W. Cowper. [Volume 4/23]

"Light stretches out its hand filled with light." Eternal Struggle. Tru Vu. [Supp 7/198]

"Light-winged smoke! Icarian bird." Smoke. H. Thoreau. [Volume 7/156]

"A lighter scarf of richer fold." Baby Zulma's Christmas Carol. A. Requier. [Volume 1/67]

The Light'ood Fire. J. Boner. [Volume 1/299]

Lights. E. Cardenal. [Supp 6/158]

*Lights*

Lights. E. Cardenal. [Supp 6/158]

Managua 6:30 P.M. E. Cardenal. [Supp 6/155]

Purple. Lin Ling. [Supp 7/24]

Soul Lamp. Li Chi. [Supp 7/12]

Lihn, Enrique

Alice in Nightmareland. M. Crow (tr.). [Supp 6/122]

"Like a hound with nose to the trail." Michaelmas. L. Lee. [Supp 2/341]

Like A Laverock In The Lift. J. Ingelow. [Volume 2/399]

"Like as the armed knighte." The Fight of Faith. A. Askewe. [Volume 4/136]

"Like as the damask rose you see." Man's Mortality. S. Wastell. [Volume 3/254]

"Like souls that balance joy and pain." Sir Launcelot And Queen Guinevere. A. Tennyson. [Volume 2/257]

"Like the soldier in the anecdote." It's Better to Light a Candle Than to Curse the Darkness. R. Retamar. [Supp 6/143]

"Like the soldier, like the sailor, like the bib and

tuck and bailer." A Letter on the Use of Machine Guns at Weddings. K. Patchen. [Supp 2/252]

"Like to the clear in highest sphere." Rosalynd. T. Lodge. [Volume 2/19]

"Like to the falling of a star." Sic Vita. H. King. [Volume 3/253]

"Like two little doves in gray." My Quaker Grandmothers. O. Huckel. [Volume 6/235]

Lilacs. A. Lowell. [Supp 1/195]

"Lilacs %false blue, %white." Lilacs. A. Lowell. [Supp 1/195]

Lima, Frank

Hunter Mountain. [Supp 4/245]

In Medias Res. [Supp 4/241]

159 John Street. [Supp 4/242]

Plena. [Supp 4/248]

Summer Wish. [Supp 4/244]

Vacations. [Supp 4/243]

Yellowstone. [Supp 4/247]

Lima, Jose Lezama

"A Dark Meadow Invites Me" [Supp 6/140]

The Fragments of the Night. [Supp 6/141]

Limerick. R. Kipling. [Volume 1/201]

Limerick. E. Lear. [Volume 1/196,Volume 1/197,Volume 1/198,Volume 1/199,Volume 1/200,Volume 1/201]

Limerick. Unknown. [Volume 1/202]

"Limping to this spreading portrait." Portrait of a Negative. A. Kuo. [Supp 4/7]

Lin Ling

Bo Tree. A. Palandri (tr.). [Supp 7/23]

I Sing for You. A. Palandri (tr.). [Supp 7/24]

Purple. A. Palandri (tr.). [Supp 7/24]

*Lincoln, Abraham*

Abraham Lincoln. T. Taylor. [Volume 7/25]

Abraham Lincoln. J. Lowell. [Volume 7/32]

The Hand of Lincoln. E. Stedman. [Volume 7/30]

O Captain! My Captain! W. Whitman. [Volume 7/28]

On the Life-Mask of Lincoln. R. Gilder. [Volume 7/29]

Linda to Hafed, fr. The Fire-worshipers. T. Moore. [Volume 3/6]

Lindedi Singing. I. Banda. [Supp 6/27]

Lindsay, Lady

My Heart Is A Lute. [Volume 2/424]

Sonnet. [Volume 3/304]

Lindsay, Vachel

The Chinese Nightingale. [Supp 1/189]

"Line Like %Living Hair" N. Sachs. [Supp 5/252]

Lines. H. Stowe. [Volume 3/426]

Lines. C. Ticheborne. [Volume 3/159]

Lines Found in His Bible in the Gate-house at Westminster. S. Raleigh. [Volume 4/352]

Lines To An Indian Air. P. Shelley. [Volume 2/254]

Lines to Miss Florence Huntington. Unknown. [Volume 9/453]

Lines to the Storymy Petrel. Unknown. [Volume 5/332]

Lines Written in an Album. W. Gaylord. [Volume 9/443]

"Linger not long. Home is not home without." The Wife to Her Husband. Unknown. [Volume 3/146]

Linton, William James

Patience, fr. Poems of Freedom. [Volume 8/114]

"The lion is the beast to fight." Sage Counsel. A. Quiller-Couch. [Volume 1/195]

"The lion is the desert's king; through his domain." The Lion's Ride. F. Freiligrath. [Volume 5/355]

The Lion's Ride. F. Freiligrath. [Volume 5/355]

Lippincott, Sarah Jane ("Grace Greenwood")

The Poet of To-day. [Volume 6/338]

Lisle, Claude Joseph Rouget de

The Marseillaise. [Volume 8/145]

"Listen more to things." Breath. B. Diop. [Supp 6/67]

"Listen. Put on Morning" W. Graham. [Supp 2/401]

The Listeners. W. De La Mare. [Supp 1/107]

Litany. S. Grant. [Volume 4/74]

"Lithe and long as the serpent train." The Grape-vine
  Swing. W. Simms. [Volume 5/231]
The **Little** Beach Bird. R. Dana. [Volume 5/302]
**Little Bell.** T. Westwood. [Volume 1/135]
**Little Billee.** W. Thackeray. [Volume 9/296]
"A **Little** Boat, %A Golden Evening" Nirala. [Supp
  7/70]
The **Little** Boy Lost. S. Smith. [Supp 2/103]
**Little** Breeches. J. Hay. [Volume 9/362]
**Little** Brown Baby. P. Dunbar. [Supp 4/77]
"**Little** brown baby wif spa'klin' eyes." Little Brown
  Baby. P. Dunbar. [Supp 4/77]
"**little** brown squirrel hops in the corn." National
  Anthem. R. Newell. [Volume 9/419]
A **Little** Child's Hymn. F. Palgrave. [Volume 1/120]
The **Little** Cloud. J. Bryant. [Volume 4/21]
A **Little** Dutch Garden. H. Durbin. [Volume 1/153]
"A **little** elbow leans upon your knee." Tired Mothers.
  M. Smith. [Volume 1/282]
"**Little** Ellie sits alone." The Romance of the Swan's
  Nest. E. Browning. [Volume 1/123]
**Little** Feet. E. Akers. [Volume 1/19]
**Little** Feet. G. Mistral. [Supp 6/125]
"**Little** feet of children." Little Feet. G. Mistral.
  [Supp 6/125]
"The **little** gate was reached at last." Auf
  Weidersehen, Summer. J. Lowell. [Volume 3/114]
**Little** Goldenhair. F. Smith. [Volume 1/42]
"**Little** I ask; my wants are few." Contentment. O.
  Holmes. [Volume 6/423]
"**Little** Indian, Sioux or Crow." Foreign Children. R.
  Stevenson. [Volume 1/130]
**Little, Lizzie M**
  Life. [Volume 2/93]
**Little** Luom. To Huu. [Supp 7/196]
The **Little** Milliner. R. Buchanan. [Volume 2/135]
"A **little** more toward the light." Growing Gray. A.
  Dobson. [Volume 6/286]
"**Little** orphant Annie's come to our house to." Little
  Orphant Annie. J. Riley. [Volume 1/159]
**Little** Orphant Annie. J. Riley. [Volume 1/159]
"**Little** poppies, little hell flames." Poppies in July.
  S. Plath. [Supp 5/218]
The **Little** Red Lark. A. Graves. [Volume 2/158]
"A **little** stream has lost its way." A Deed and a Word.
  C. Mackay. [Volume 4/169]
"**Little** thinks, in the field, you red-cloaked." Each
  and All. R. Emerson. [Volume 5/9]
"A **little** way below her chin." On Some Buttercups. F.
  Sherman. [Volume 2/46]
**Littledale, R. F. (tr.)**
  "O Fire of God, the Comforter" S. Hildegarde.
  [Volume 4/107]
**Live** In My Heart And Pay No Rent. S. Lover. [Volume
  2/180]
"**Living** in a wide landscape are the flowers." Desert
  Flowers. K. Douglas. [Supp 2/406]
"**Living** is no laughing matter." On Living: 001. N.
  Hikmet. [Supp 7/306]
The **Living** Temple. O. Holmes. [Volume 4/215]
**Living** Waters. C. Spencer. [Volume 4/251]
**Lo Fu**
  Beyond Ashes. A. Palandri (tr.). [Supp 7/28]
  Beyond the Sea. A. Palandri (tr.). [Supp 7/27]
  Beyong the Whip. A. Palandri (tr.). [Supp 7/29]
  New-Born Blackness. A. Palandri (tr.). [Supp 7/26]
"**Lo**, the poor Indian! whose untutored mind." God and
  Man, fr. Essay on Man. A. Pope. [Volume 4/21]
"**Lo** Venice, gay with color, lights and song." Canada
  Not Last. W. Schuyler-Lighthall. [Volume 8/70]
"**Lo!** where the rosy-bosomed hours." Spring. T. Gray.
  [Volume 5/79]
**Lochaber** No More. A. Ramsay. [Volume 3/105]
**Lochinvar**, fr. Marmion. S. Scott. [Volume 2/276]
"**Locked** arm in arm they cross the way." Tableau. C.

  Cullen. [Supp 1/100]
The **Locked** Gates. K. Raine. [Supp 5/225]
**Locker-Lampson, Frederick**
  The Jester's Plea. [Volume 6/350]
  On an Old Muff. [Volume 9/235]
  To My Grandmother. [Volume 1/210]
  The Widow's Mite. [Volume 3/287]
**Lockhart, John Gibson**
  Zara's Ear-Rings, fr. The Spanish. [Volume 2/265]
**Lockhart, John Gibson (tr.)**
  The Lord of Butrago. Unknown. [Volume 8/206]
**Locksley** Hall. A. Tennyson. [Volume 3/17]
**Lodge, Thomas**
  Rosalynd. [Volume 2/19]
  Rosalynd's Complaint. [Volume 2/89]
**Logan, John**
  Thy Braes Were Bonny. [Volume 3/314]
  To the Cuckoo. [Volume 5/289]
**Logau, Frederick Von**
  Retribution. H. Longfellow (tr.). [Volume 6/226]
**London.** J. Davidson. [Volume 7/230]
*London*
  Walking Song. C. Williams. [Supp 1/315]
**London** Bridge. F. Weatherly. [Volume 6/238]
**London** Churches. R. Milnes. [Volume 3/207]
**Lone** Fisherman. T. Heraty. [Supp 7/97]
The **Lonely** Bugel Grieves. G. Mellen. [Volume 8/327]
"The **lonely** sound of the pounding stone scatters over
  the cold." Do Not Wash Away the Red. Ho Ch'i-
  Fang. [Supp 7/7]
"**Long** is the night." Curriculum Vitae. I. Bachmann.
  [Supp 5/25]
**Long** Person. G. Cardiff. [Supp 4/319]
"**Long** pored Saint Austin o'er the sacred page."
  Passage in the Life of Saint Augustine. Unknown.
  [Volume 4/1]
"**Long** steel grass-- %the white soldiers pass." Trio
  for Two Cats and a Trombone. E. Sitwell. [Supp
  5/269]
**Longfellow.** A. Dobson. [Volume 7/107]
**Longfellow, Henry Wadsworth**
  The Arsenal at Springfield. [Volume 8/444]
  Carillon. [Volume 7/166]
  The Day is Done. [Volume 1/266]
  Daybreak. [Volume 5/37]
  The Death of Minnehaha, fr. The Song of Hiawatha.
  [Volume 3/319]
  Excelsior. [Volume 6/257]
  Flowers. [Volume 5/238]
  Footsteps of Angels. [Volume 3/438]
  God's-Acre. [Volume 3/276]
  Hawthorne. [Volume 7/]
  The Household Sovereign, fr. The Hanging of the
  Crane. [Volume 1/23]
  Hymn to the Night. [Volume 5/68]
  King Robert of Sicily. [Volume 4/148]
  The Ladder of Saint Augustine. [Volume 4/294]
  Maidenhood. [Volume 1/214]
  Moonlight on the Prairie, fr. Evangeline. [Volume
  5/61]
  My Lost Youth. [Volume 1/260]
  The Old Bridge at Florence. [Volume 7/174]
  The Primeval Forest, fr. Evangeline. [Volume
  5/218]
  A Psalm of Life. [Volume 4/275]
  Rain in Summer. [Volume 5/114]
  The Rainy Day. [Volume 3/228]
  The Reaper and the Flowers. [Volume 3/417]
  The Republic, fr. The Building of the Ship.
  [Volume 8/94]
  Resignation. [Volume 3/430]
  Santa Filomena. [Volume 4/166]
  Sea-weed. [Volume 5/393]
  Serenade, fr. The Spanish Student. [Volume 2/255]
  The Sifting of Peter. [Volume 4/290]

The Skeleton in Armor. [Volume 7/295]
Snow-flakes. [Volume 5/174]
"There was a Little Girl" [Volume 1/169]
The Village Blacksmith. [Volume 1/328]
The Wreck of the Hesperus. [Volume 9/186]
**Longfellow, Henry Wadsworth (tr.)**
Beware. Unknown. [Volume 1/235]
Retribution. F. Logau. [Volume 6/226]
Song of the Silent Land. J. Von Salis. [Volume 4/388]
**Longfellow, Samuel**
Vesper Hymn. [Volume 4/195]
*Longing*
John Winter. L. Binyon. [Supp 1/50]
*Lonliness*
Behind Bars, sel. F. Tuqan. [Supp 5/305]
In Me and Far Away. E. Gutierrez. [Supp 6/174]
Miranda's Song. W. Auden. [Supp 2/164]
The Mixer. L. MacNeice. [Supp 2/180]
Necessity. Nguyen Sa. [Supp 7/189]
A Poem Some People Will Have to Understand. L. Jones. [Supp 4/178]
"**Look** at me with thy large brown eyes." Philip, My King. D. Craik. [Volume 1/16]
"**Look** at the steady rifles, Joe." Joe Hill Listens to the Praying. K. Patchen. [Supp 2/248]
"**Look** at this man in the room before you." Room with Revolutionists. E. Rolfe. [Supp 2/218]
"**Look** in my face; my name is might-have-been." The Nevermore. D. Rossetti. [Volume 3/82]
A **Look** in the Past. J. Angira. [Supp 6/23]
"**Look** on this cast, and know the hand." The Hand of Lincoln. E. Stedman. [Volume 7/30]
"**Look** to the blowing rose about us - lo." Rubaiyat: 014. O. Khayyam. [Volume 6/206]
"The **lopped** tree in time may grow again." Times Go by Turns. R. Southwell. [Volume 3/228]
"**Lor,** thou hast given me a cell." My Home. R. Herrick. [Volume 4/246]
"**Lord** %rise up and forgive my sin, lord." The Sin. G. Senanayake. [Supp 7/182]
"**Lord!** call thy pallid angel." Corn-Law Hymn. E. Eliot. [Volume 6/397]
"**Lord,** how the creatures bully me!" The Encounter. J. Wright. [Supp 5/333]
**Lord** Lovel. Unknown. [Volume 7/373]
"**Lord** Lovel he stood at his castle gate." Lord Lovel. Unknown. [Volume 7/373]
The **Lord** of Butrago. Unknown. [Volume 8/206]
"**Lord** of the winds! I fell the nigh." The Hurricane. W. Bryant. [Volume 7/151]
**Lord** Ullin's Daughter. T. Campbell. [Volume 7/399]
**Lord** Walter's Wife. E. Browning. [Volume 2/392]
"**Lord,** what am I, that, with unceasing care." To-morrow. L. De Vega. [Volume 4/94]
"**Lord!** When Those Glorious Lights I See" G. Wither. [Volume 4/14]
"**Lord,** you have visited Paris on this day of your birth." Snow Upon Paris. L. Senghor. [Supp 6/73]
**Lorde, Audre**
Coal. [Supp 4/180]
Summer Oracle. [Supp 4/182]
The Woman Thing. [Supp 4/184]
The **Lore-Lei**. H. Heine. [Volume 6/77]
**Loreine**: A Horse. A. Ficke. [Supp 1/121]
*Loss*
The Golden Journey to Samarkand. J. Flecker. [Supp 1/122]
The Runner with the Lots. L. Adams. [Supp 2/71]
Sea Holly. C. Aiken. [Supp 1/12]
"When You Are Old" W. Yeats. [Supp 1/332]
**Losse** in Delayes. R. Southwell. [Volume 4/341]
**Losses**. R. Jarrell. [Supp 2/331]
A **Lost** Chord. A. Procter. [Volume 6/306]

The **Lost** Heir. T. Hood. [Volume 1/49]
**Lost** in Sulphur Canyons. J. Barnes. [Supp 4/299]
The **Lost** Leader. R. Browning. [Volume 7/70]
The **Lost** Pleiad. W. Simms. [Volume 4/347]
The **Lost** Sheep. E. Clephane. [Volume 4/66]
The **Lost** Son: 005. T. Roethke. [Supp 2/210]
The **Lost** Son: Moss-Gathering. T. Roethke. [Supp 2/210]
The **Lost** Son: The Flight. T. Roethke. [Supp 2/205]
The **Lost** Son: The Gibber. T. Roethke. [Supp 2/207]
The **Lost** Son: The Pit. T. Roethke. [Supp 2/207]
The **Lost** Son: The Return. T. Roethke. [Supp 2/209]
"A **lot** of men and armies stand to take." A Letter to a Policeman in Kansas City. K. Patchen. [Supp 2/253]
**Lot's** Wife. A. Akhmatova. [Supp 5/7]
The **Lotus-Eaters**. A. Tennyson. [Volume 6/402]
"**Loud** a hundred clansmen raise." Song of Clan-Alpine, fr. The Lady of the Lake. S. Scott. [Volume 8/305]
"**Loud** and clear %from the Saint Nicholas tower, on the listening." City Bells, fr. The Lay of St. Aloy's. R. Barham. [Volume 7/147]
"**Loud** roared the dreadful thunder." The Bay of Biscay. A. Cherry. [Volume 5/405]
**Louis** De Camoes. R. Campbell. [Supp 2/94]
**Louis** XV. J. Sterling. [Volume 7/339]
*Love*
& Then. N. Shange. [Supp 5/263]
**Love**. R. Browning. [Volume 2/339]
**Love**. S. Coleridge. [Volume 2/159]
**Love**. T. Hervey. [Volume 2/359]
**Love**. C. Richardson. [Volume 4/189]
*Love*
Ah, How Sweet, fr. Tyrannic Love. J. Dryden. [Volume 2/68]
The Annoyer. N. Willis. [Volume 2/75]
Beauty. E. Thurlow. [Volume 2/251]
Because of You. A. Hamzah. [Supp 7/88]
Bedouin Love-Song. B. Taylor. [Volume 2/264]
"Believe Me, If All Those Endearing Young Charms" T. Moore. [Volume 2/336]
Charlie Machree. W. Hoppin. [Volume 2/365]
A Christmas Scene. T. Davis. [Volume 2/262]
Cleopatra. W. Story. [Volume 2/354]
"Come Into The Garden, Maud" A. Tennyson. [Volume 2/273]
Come, Rest In This Bosom, fr. Irish Melodies. T. Moore. [Volume 2/332]
Cupid Swallowed. L. Hunt. [Volume 2/91]
Curfew Must Not Ring To-Night. R. Thorpe. [Volume 2/303]
Dialogue. Adonis. [Supp 7/285]
Echoes. T. Moore. [Volume 2/327]
The Eve of Saint Agnes. J. Keats. [Volume 2/312]
Fetching Water From The Well. Unknown. [Volume 2/298]
A Fiction. Unknown. [Volume 2/81]
The Finding of Love. R. Graves. [Supp 1/150]
First Love, fr. "Don Juan," Canto I. G. Byron. [Volume 2/256]
Fish and Swimmer and Lonely Birds Sweep Past Us. M. Berssenbrugge. [Supp 4/11]
"Fly To The Desert, Fly With Me" T. Moore. [Volume 2/343]
For One Who Would Not Take His Life in His Hands. D. Schwartz. [Supp 2/307]
Forget Thee? J. Moultrie. [Volume 2/337]
Ganging To And Ganging Frae. E. Cook. [Volume 2/293]
The Gift. G. Russell. [Supp 1/274]
The Gillyflower of Gold. W. Morris. [Volume 2/333]
Girl's Song. L. Bogan. [Supp 5/32]
Gold. J. Drinkwater. [Supp 1/110]
The Great Lover. R. Brooke. [Supp 1/80]

LOVE-

WORLD'S BEST POETRY, SUPPLEMENT VIII

Athulf and Ethilda. S. Taylor. [Volume 2/96]
"Behave Yoursel' Before Folk" A. Rodger. [Volume 2/114]
Blest as the Immortal Gods. Sappho. [Volume 2/97]
Caprice. W. Howells. [Volume 2/110]
The Chess-Board. O. Meredith. [Volume 2/127]
Comin' Through The Rye. R. Burns. [Volume 2/108]
Cupid and Campaspe, fr. Alexander and Campaspe. J. Lyly. [Volume 2/105]
Dinna Ask Me. J. Dunlop. [Volume 2/100]
"The Dule's I' This Bonnet O' Mine" E. Waugh. [Volume 2/116]
The First Kiss. T. Campbell. [Volume 2/94]
Francesca Da Rimini, fr. Divina Commedia: Inferno. Dante Alighieri. [Volume 2/99]
Her Letter. B. Harte. [Volume 2/128]
I Dreamt I Saw Great Venus. Bion. [Volume 2/98]
"If Doughty Deeds My Lady Please" R. Graham. [Volume 2/102]
Kate Temple's Song. S. Carnegie. [Volume 2/94]
The Kiss. R. Herrick. [Volume 2/104]
Kisses. W. Strode. [Volume 2/106]
Kissing's No Sin. Unknown. [Volume 2/107]
Kitty Neil. J. Waller. [Volume 2/133]
Kitty of Coleraine. C. Shanly. [Volume 2/132]
The Little Milliner. R. Buchanan. [Volume 2/135]
Love In The Valley. G. Meredith. [Volume 2/121]
Love's Philosophy. P. Shelley. [Volume 2/106]
The Love-Knot. N. Perry. [Volume 2/126]
O Swallow, Swallow, Flying South, fr. The Princess. A. Tennyson. [Volume 2/100]
An Opal. E. Hayes. [Volume 2/105]
The Plaidie. C. Sibley. [Volume 2/131]
Sly Thoughts. C. Patmore. [Volume 2/112]
Smile and Never Heed Me. C. Swain. [Volume 2/115]
Song of the Milkmaid, fr. Queen Mary. A. Tennyson. [Volume 2/107]
Song, fr. The Miller's Daughter. A. Tennyson. [Volume 2/102]
Sonnet Upon A Stolen Kiss. G. Wither. [Volume 2/110]
A Spinster's Stint. A. Cary. [Volume 2/118]
Tell Me, My Heart, If This Be Love. L. Lyttelton. [Volume 2/95]
The Telltale. E. Akers. [Volume 2/119]
Thoughts On The Commandments. G. Baker. [Volume 2/125]
Whistle, and I'll Come To You, My Lad. R. Burns. [Volume 2/109]
The Whistle. R. Story. [Volume 2/112]

*Love- Complaints*
Advice To A Girl. T. Campion. [Volume 2/242]
Affaire D'amour. M. Deland. [Volume 2/245]
The Age Of Wisdom. W. Thackeray. [Volume 2/236]
Alexis, Here She Stayed. W. Drummond of Hawthornden. [Volume 2/224]
Answer To Master Wither's Song,"Shall I, Wasting In Despair" B. Jonson. [Volume 2/239]
The Author's Resolution, In A Sonnet, fr. Fair Virtue. G. Wither. [Volume 2/238]
Bitterness. V. Sackville-West. [Supp 1/277]
The Chronicle. A. Cowley. [Volume 2/232]
The Common Doom. J. Shirley. [Volume 2/237]
Constancy. Unknown. [Volume 2/235]
Epilogue from Emblems of Love. L. Abercrombie. [Supp 1/1]
The Faithful Lovers. Unknown. [Volume 2/231]
Forever Unconfessed. R. Milnes. [Volume 2/241]
"Full Many A Glorious Morning" W. Shakespeare. [Volume 2/224]
"Give Me More Love or More Disdain" T. Carew. [Volume 2/245]
"I Will Not Let Thee Go" R. Bridges. [Supp 1/72]
The Lesson. W. Auden. [Supp 2/162]
"Let Not Woman E'er Complain" R. Burns. [Volume

2/219]
Love Song. W. Williams. [Supp 1/320]
Love's Blindness. W. Shakespeare. [Volume 2/223]
My Dear And Only Love. J. Graham. [Volume 2/226]
A Renunciation. E. Vere. [Volume 2/246]
Rivalry In Love. W. Walsh. [Volume 2/225]
Si Jeunesse Savait! E. Stedman. [Volume 2/242]
Summer Song. G. Barker. [Supp 2/293]
The Suppliant. E. Gosse. [Supp 1/145]
To Chloe. J. Wolcott. [Volume 2/220]
To the Unimplored Beloved. E. Shanks. [Supp 1/284]
Waiting for the Grapes. W. Maginn. [Volume 2/243]
Why So Pale And Wan? S. Suckling. [Volume 2/247]
A Woman's Answer. A. Procter. [Volume 2/221]
A Woman's Question. A. Procter. [Volume 2/248]

*Love- Courtship*
Among The Heather. W. Allingham. [Volume 2/171]
Aux Italiens. O. Meredith. [Volume 2/214]
The Bailiff's Daughter of Islington. Unknown. [Volume 2/153]
The Brookside. R. Milnes. [Volume 2/156]
Ca' The Yowes. I. Pagan. [Volume 2/176]
Cooking and Courting. Unknown. [Volume 2/174]
The Courtin' J. Lowell. [Volume 2/190]
Doris: A Pastoral. A. Munby. [Volume 2/169]
"Duncan Gray Cam' Here To Woo" R. Burns. [Volume 2/178]
The Earl O' Quarterdeck. G. MacDonald. [Volume 2/209]
The Exchange. S. Coleridge. [Volume 2/164]
The Friar Of Orders Gray. T. Percy. [Volume 2/195]
Golden Eyes. Rufinus. [Volume 2/151]
The Hermit, fr. The Vicar Of Wakefield. O. Goldsmith. [Volume 2/199]
How To Ask And Have. S. Lover. [Volume 2/179]
"I Prithee Send Me Back My Heart" S. Suckling. [Volume 2/187]
I'm Not Myself At All. S. Lover. [Volume 2/185]
The Laird O' Cockpen. C. Nairne. [Volume 2/205]
The Little Red Lark. A. Graves. [Volume 2/158]
Live In My Heart And Pay No Rent. S. Lover. [Volume 2/180]
Love. S. Coleridge. [Volume 2/159]
"Love Me Little, Love Me Long" Unknown. [Volume 2/188]
Love's Logic. Unknown. [Volume 2/164]
"My Eyes! How I Love You" J. Saxe. [Volume 2/155]
The Night-Piece. R. Herrick. [Volume 2/165]
The Nymph's Reply. S. Raleigh. [Volume 2/150]
Othello's Defence, fr. Othello. W. Shakespeare. [Volume 2/207]
The Passionate Shepherd To His Love. C. Marlowe. [Volume 2/149]
Phillida and Corydon. N. Breton. [Volume 2/152]
Poppin Corn. Unknown. [Volume 2/193]
Rory O'More. S. Lover. [Volume 2/172]
The Siller Croun. S. Blamire. [Volume 2/177]
Somebody. Unknown. [Volume 2/162]
Story Of The Gate. T. Robertson. [Volume 2/167]
Sweet Meeting Of Desires, fr. The Angel In The House. C. Patmore. [Volume 2/166]
"Where Are You Going, My Pretty Maid?" Unknown. [Volume 2/155]
Widow Machree. S. Lover. [Volume 2/181]
Widow Malone. C. Lever. [Volume 2/183]
Love Dissembled, fr. As You Like It. W. Shakespeare. [Volume 2/31]
Love, fr. Hero and Leander. C. Marlowe. [Volume 2/64]
Love, fr. Lay of the Last Minstrel. S. Scott. [Volume 2/70]
Love, fr. The Merchant of Venice. W. Shakespeare. [Volume 2/62]
"Love in my bosom, like a bee." Rosalynd's Complaint. T. Lodge. [Volume 2/89]
Love in the Ether. A. Prado. [Supp 6/118]

[Volume 7/100]
**Lowell, Robert Trail Spence**
After the Surprising Conversions. [Supp 2/386]
As a Plane Tree by the Water. [Supp 2/387]
Colloquy in Black Rock. [Supp 2/388]
The Drunken Fisherman. [Supp 2/389]
Falling Asleep over the Aeneid. [Supp 2/390]
Mr. Edwards and the Spider. [Supp 2/393]
The Quaker Graveyard in Nantucket: 001. [Supp 2/394]
The Quaker Graveyard in Nantucket: 002. [Supp 2/395]
The Quaker Graveyard in Nantucket: 003. [Supp 2/395]
The Quaker Graveyard in Nantucket: 004. [Supp 2/396]
The Quaker Graveyard in Nantucket: 005. [Supp 2/397]
The Quaker Graveyard in Nantucket: 006. [Supp 2/397]
The Quaker Graveyard in Nantucket: 007. [Supp 2/398]
The Relief of Lucknow. [Volume 8/296]
Where the Rainbow Ends. [Supp 2/398]
"**Lucina** Schynning in Silence of the Night" E. Chuilleanain. [Supp 5/190]
**Lucius** Junius Brutus Over the Body of Lucretia, fr. Brutus. J. Payne. [Volume 9/14]
"**Lucretius** could not credit centaurs." Invitation to Juno. W. Empson. [Supp 2/141]
*Lullabies*
Lullaby. T. Carmi. [Supp 7/244]
**Lullaby.** T. Carmi. [Supp 7/244,Supp 7/243]
**Lullaby,** fr. The Princess. A. Tennyson. [Volume 1/11]
"The **lunatic,** the lover, and the poet." Imagination, fr. A Midsummer Night's Dream. W. Shakespeare. [Volume 6/12]
**Lunt, George**
Requiem. [Volume 8/388]
*Lust*
But for Lust. R. Pitter. [Supp 2/48]
Peter Quince at the Clavier. W. Stevens. [Supp 1/289]
Sic et Non: I. The Complaint of Heloise. H. Read. [Supp 2/34]
Sic et Non: II. The Portrait of Abelard. H. Read. [Supp 2/35]
**Luther, Martin**
The Martyrs' Hymn. W. Fox (tr.). [Volume 4/334]
"Might Fortress Is Our God" F. Hedge (tr.). [Volume 4/33]
**Lyall, Sir Alfred Comyns**
Meditations of a Hindu Prince. [Volume 4/3]
"**Lybia,** Egypt, Hellas." The Contrary Experience: 003. H. Read. [Supp 2/34]
**Lycidas.** J. Milton. [Volume 3/446]
The **Lye.** S. Raleigh. [Volume 6/227]
**Lying** in the Grass. E. Gosse. [Volume 1/225]
**Lyly, John**
Cupid and Campaspe, fr. Alexander and Campaspe. [Volume 2/105]
**Lyte, Henry Francis**
Abide wth Me. [Volume 4/76]
**Lytle, William Haines**
Antony and Cleopatra. [Volume 3/380]
**Lyttelton, Lord George**
Tell Me, My Heart, If This Be Love. [Volume 2/95]
**Lytton, Lord Edward**
"When Stars Are In The Quiet Skies" [Volume 2/331]


**Macandrew, Barbara Miller**
Coming. [Volume 4/355]

**Macaulay** as Poet. W. Landor. [Volume 7/61]
**Macaulay; Thomas Babington, Lord**
Horatius at the Bridge. [Volume 7/265]
Ivry. [Volume 8/226]
Naseby. [Volume 8/272]
The Roman Father, fr. Virginia. [Volume 9/16]
**MacCarthy, Denis Florence**
"Bless the Dear Old Verdant Land" [Volume 8/60]
Ireland. [Volume 8/62]
Labor Song, fr. The Bell-Founder. [Volume 1/327]
Summer Longings. [Volume 5/81]
**McCarthy, Regina (tr.)**
Dressed in Dynamite. G. Belli. [Supp 6/152]
**Maccartney, Louisa [pseud.]** See Crawford, Julia
**MacDiarmid, Hugh**
At the Centoph. [Supp 2/29]
Empty Vessel. [Supp 2/29]
"O Wha's Been Here Afore Me, Lass" [Supp 2/30]
Reflections in an Iron Workds. [Supp 2/30]
Scunner. [Supp 2/31]
The Two Parents. [Supp 2/31]
**MacDonald, Elizabeth Roberts**
A Song of Seasons. [Volume 5/191]
**Macdonald, George**
The Baby. [Volume 1/4]
**MacDonald, George**
The Earl O' Quarterdeck. [Volume 2/209]
**Macdonald, George**
Light. [Volume 5/32]
**McDougall, Bonnie (tr.)**
Do Not Wash Away the Red. Ho Ch'i-Fang. [Supp 7/7]
The First Morning in Vietnam. Ho Ch'i-Fang. [Supp 7/5]
Reminiscence. Ho Ch'i-Fang. [Supp 7/6]
The Song. Ho Ch'i-Fang. [Supp 7/4]
Sound. Ho Ch'i-Fang. [Supp 7/7]
**Mace, Francis Laughton**
"Only Waiting" [Volume 4/369]
**Macedonius**
Memory and Oblivion. R. Bland (tr.). [Volume 6/321]
**MacGregor-Hastiek, Roy (tr.)**
A Man. N. Cassian. [Supp 5/46]
Self-Portrait. N. Cassian. [Supp 5/47]
**Mackail, John William**
An Etruscan Ring. [Volume 7/149]
**Mackay, Charles**
Cleon and I. [Volume 6/420]
Day Breaks. [Volume 4/244]
A Deed and a Word. [Volume 4/169]
The Good Time Coming. [Volume 6/399]
Small Beginnings. [Volume 4/309]
"Tell Me, Ye Winged Winds" [Volume 4/411]
Tubal Cain. [Volume 8/426]
**McKay, Claude**
America. [Supp 1/203]
In Bondage. [Supp 4/87]
The Tropics in New York. [Supp 4/86]
**MacLeish, Archibald**
The End of the World. [Supp 1/203]
You, Andrew Marvell. [Supp 1/204]
**McLellan, Isaac**
"New England Dead!" [Volume 8/156]
**MacManus, Anna ("Ethna Carbery")**
Thinkin' Long. [Volume 3/141]
Turlough MacSweeney. [Volume 8/54]
**McMaster, Guy Humphrey**
Carmen Bellicosum. [Volume 8/332]
**MacNeice, Louis**
Autobiography. [Supp 2/171]
Brother Fire. [Supp 2/172]
Conversation. [Supp 2/173]
An Eclogue for Christmas. [Supp 2/174]
Explorations. [Supp 2/178]
June Thunder. [Supp 2/179]

Les Sylphides. [Supp 2/185]
The Mixer. [Supp 2/180]
Museums. [Supp 2/180]
Netrality. [Supp 2/181]
Perseus. [Supp 2/182]
Slow Movement. [Supp 2/182]
Stylite. [Supp 2/183]
Sunday Morning. [Supp 2/184]
"The Sunlight on the Garden" [Supp 2/185]
**Madgett, Naomi Long**
Black Woman. [Supp 4/166]
Midway. [Supp 4/164]
Mortality. [Supp 4/163]
Simple. [Supp 4/165]
**Madman's** Song. E. Wylie. [Supp 5/336]
*Magicians*
Valentine for Ben Franklin Who Drives a Truck in
California. D. Wakoski. [Supp 5/322]
**Maginn, William**
The Irishman and the Lady. [Volume 9/320]
Waiting for the Grapes. [Volume 2/243]
**Mahmoud.** L. Hunt. [Volume 7/305]
The **Mahogany-tree.** W. Thackeray. [Volume 1/391]
**Mahony, Francis ("Father Prout")**
The Bells of Shandon. [Volume 7/145]
The Flight Into Egypt. [Volume 4/62]
"The **maid,** and thereby hangs a tale." The Bride, fr.
A Ballad Upon A Wedding. S. Suckling. [Volume
2/410]
"The **maid,** as by the papers doth appear." Too Great a
Sacrifice. Unknown. [Volume 9/394]
"**Maid** of Athens, Ere We Part" G. Byron. [Volume
3/100]
"The **maid** who binds her warrior's sash." The Brave at
Home. T. Read. [Volume 8/109]
"**Maiden,** with the meek brown eyes." Maidenhood. H.
Longfellow. [Volume 1/214]
**Maidenhood.** H. Longfellow. [Volume 1/214]
A **Maiden's** Ideal of a Husband, fr. The Contrivances.
H. Carey. [Volume 2/89]
**Mailman.** B. Al-Haydari. [Supp 7/226]
The **Maize.** W. Fosdick. [Volume 5/267]
**Major, Clarence**
Dismal Moment, Passing. [Supp 4/203]
Form. [Supp 4/201]
None of It Was. [Supp 4/202]
Vietnam. [Supp 4/204]
Waiting in the Children's Hospital. [Supp 4/199]
"**Make** me over, mother April." Spring Song. B. Carman.
[Volume 1/248]
"**Make** thyself known, Sibyl, or let despair."
Leonardo's "Mona Lisa" E. Dowden. [Volume
7/150]
"**Make** Way for Liberty!" J. Montgomery. [Volume 8/140]
**Malawi.** I. Banda. [Supp 6/25]
"**Malawi,** your secret flame." Malawi. I. Banda. [Supp
6/25]
**Malinche.** R. Castellanos. [Supp 5/51]
A **Man.** N. Cassian. [Supp 5/46]
**Man.** T. Heraty. [Supp 7/93]
**Man.** W. Landor. [Volume 3/151]
"**Man** and the water buffalo have been companions
from." Rice Grains. A. Hernandez. [Supp 7/178]
"**Man** has surrounded himself." Concerning a Room. S.
Tanikawa. [Supp 7/132]
The **Man** in the Moon. J. Riley. [Volume 1/146]
"**Man** is a sacred city, built of marvellous earth."
The Chief Centurions. J. Masefield. [Supp
1/208]
"A **man** said unot his angel." The Kings. L. Guiney.
[Supp 1/153]
"**Man** wants but little here below." The Wants of Man.
J. Adams. [Volume 6/421]
The **Man** Who Boxes. A. Istaru. [Supp 6/136]
The **Man** with the Hoe. J. Cheney. [Volume 6/395]

The **Man** with the Hoe. E. Markham. [Volume 6/393,Supp
1/205]
"The **management** area of Cherokee." The Trout Map. A.
Tate. [Supp 2/76]
**Managua** 6:30 P.M. E. Cardenal. [Supp 6/155]
**Manchuria.** W. Rendra. [Supp 7/102]
**Mandalay.** R. Kipling. [Supp 1/180]
**Mandela, Zindzi**
Echo of Mandela. [Supp 6/78]
**Mandela's** Sermon. K. Kgositsile. [Supp 6/77]
**Mangan, James Clarence (tr.)**
The Sunken City. W. Mueller.
"**Manking,** %let us love one another." The Stars: 012.
Ping Hsin. [Supp 5/119]
**Mannahatta.** W. Whitman. [Volume 7/245]
**Manner, Eeva-Liisa**
Assimilation. A. Jarvenpa (tr.). [Supp 5/148]
At the Street Corner. M. Allwood (tr.). [Supp
5/153]
"From My Life I Make a Poem" A. Jarvenpa (tr.).
[Supp 5/149]
Into the Silence of the Forest. A. Jarvenpa (tr.).
[Supp 5/147]
Strontium. M. Allwood (tr.). [Supp 5/150]
"The Trees Are Naked" M. Allwood (tr.). [Supp
5/154]
"The Women Thought Christ Risen" M. Allwood (tr.).
[Supp 5/155]
**Man's** Mortality. S. Wastell. [Volume 3/254]
"**Many** a long, long year ago." The Nantucket Skipper.
J. Fields. [Volume 9/343]
**Many** a Thousand Die. Unknown (African American).
[Supp 4/52]
"**Many** a year is in its grave." The Passage. L. Uhland.
[Volume 3/342]
"**Many** know you now by virtue of that music." Musician.
C. Bax. [Supp 1/28]
**Mapanje, Jack A.**
The New Platform Dances. [Supp 6/34]
When This Carnival Finally Closes. [Supp 6/35]
**Maple** and Sumach. C. Day Lewis. [Supp 2/117]
"**Maple** and sumach down this autumn ride." Maple and
Sumach. C. Day Lewis. [Supp 2/117]
**Mar, Laureen**
Black Rocks. [Supp 4/33]
My Mother, Who Came from China, Where She Never
Saw Snow. [Supp 4/34]
The Window Frames the Moon. [Supp 4/32]
**March.** A. Swinburne. [Volume 5/74]
**March.** W. Wordsworth. [Volume 5/77]
"**March,** march, Ettrick and Teviotdale!" Border Ballad.
S. Scott. [Volume 8/50]
**March-Patrol** of the Naked Heroes. H. Gorman. [Supp
1/143]
**Marco** Bozzaris. F. Halleck. [Volume 8/200]
**Marechal, Leopoldo**
Song of Other Lives. I. Cumpiano (tr.). [Supp
6/105]
"**Margarita** first possessed." The Chronicle. A. Cowley.
[Volume 2/232]
**Mariner** man. E. Sitwell. [Supp 5/271]
The **Mariner's** Dream. W. Dimond. [Volume 5/438]
The **Mariposa** Lily. I. Coolbrith. [Volume 5/280]
**Mark** Antony, Over the Body of Caesar, fr. Julius
Caesar. W. Shakespeare. [Volume 9/20]
The **Marketwoman.** A. Neto. [Supp 6/14]
"The **marketwoman** %strong sun." The Marketwoman. A.
Neto. [Supp 6/14]
**Markham, Edwin**
The Man with the Hoe. [Volume 6/393,Supp 1/205]
**Marlowe, Christopher**
Hero's Beauty, fr. The First Sestiad of "Hero and
Leander" [Volume 2/15]
Love, fr. Hero and Leander. [Volume 2/64]
The Passionate Shepherd To His Love. [Volume

2/149]
The School of War, fr. Tamburlaine. [Volume 8/185]
**Marmion** and Douglas, fr. Marmion. S. Scott. [Volume 7/401]
**Marot, Clement**
To Diane de Poitiers. L. Costello (tr.). [Volume 3/69]
**Marquez and Elinor Randall, Robert (tr.)**
Against Drawbridges: 001. M. Benedetti. [Supp 6/191]
Against Drawbridges: 002. M. Benedetti. [Supp 6/192]
Against Drawbridges: 003. M. Benedetti. [Supp 6/193]
**Marquez, Robert (tr.)**
It Would Be Nice to Deserve this Epitaph. R. Retamar. [Supp 6/144]
*Marriage*
Adam Describing Eve, fr. Paradise Lost. J. Milton. [Volume 2/385]
Adam To Eve, fr. Paradise Lost. J. Milton. [Volume 2/368]
The Bride, fr. A Ballad Upon A Wedding. S. Suckling. [Volume 2/410]
Brutus And Portia, fr. Julius Cesar. W. Shakespeare. [Volume 2/389]
Canto Amor. J. Berryman. [Supp 2/327]
"Carry Her Over the Water" W. Auden. [Supp 2/157]
Connubial Life, fr. The Seasons: Spring. J. Thomson. [Volume 2/430]
Darby And Joan. F. Weatherly. [Volume 2/447]
"The Day Returns, My Bosom Burns" R. Burns. [Volume 2/422]
Dolcino To Margaret. C. Kingsley. [Volume 2/445]
The Eggs And The Horses. Unknown. [Volume 2/432]
Faith And Hope. R. Peale. [Volume 2/446]
The Fire Of Love, fr. The Examen Miscellaneum. C. Sackville. [Volume 2/449]
The Golden Wedding. D. Gray. [Volume 2/448]
Hebrew Wedding, fr. The Fall Of Jerusalem. H. Milman. [Volume 2/405]
"If Thou Wert By My Side, My Love" R. Heber. [Volume 2/441]
In Twos. W. Gannett. [Volume 2/403]
Invitation to Juno. W. Empson. [Supp 2/141]
John Anderson, My Jo. R. Burns. [Volume 2/460]
Laodamia. W. Wordsworth. [Volume 2/451]
Les Sylphides. L. MacNeice. [Supp 2/185]
"Let Me Not To The Marriage Of True Minds" W. Shakespeare. [Volume 2/376]
Like A Laverock In The Lift. J. Ingelow. [Volume 2/399]
Lord Walter's Wife. E. Browning. [Volume 2/392]
Love Lightens Labor. Unknown. [Volume 2/428]
My Ain Wife. A. Laing. [Volume 2/419]
My Heart Is A Lute. L. Lindsay. [Volume 2/424]
My Love. J. Lowell. [Volume 2/383]
My Wife's A Winsome Wee Thing. R. Burns. [Volume 2/420]
The Newly-Wedded. W. Praed. [Volume 2/413]
Not Ours the Vows. B. Barton. [Volume 2/450]
"O Lay Thy Hand In Mine, Dear!" G. Massey. [Volume 2/445]
The Old Man Dreams. O. Holmes. [Volume 2/459]
Paulina's Appeal, fr. Polyeucte. P. Corneille. [Volume 2/396]
The Poet's Bridal-Day Song. A. Cunningham. [Volume 2/414]
The Poet's Song To His Wife. B. Procter. [Volume 2/421]
Possession. B. Taylor. [Volume 2/418]
Possession. O. Meredith. [Volume 2/424]
The Retort. G. Morris. [Volume 2/431]
Reunited Love. R. Blackmore. [Volume 2/425]
"She Was A Phantom Of Delight" W. Wordsworth.

[Volume 2/422]
Song, fr. Woo'd And Married And A. J. Baillie. [Volume 2/411]
A Sonnet. G. Stein. [Supp 5/297]
Sonnets. J. Lowell. [Volume 2/382]
Sonnets From The Portuguese. E. Browning. [Volume 2/377]
There's Nae Luck About The House. J. Adam. [Volume 2/442]
"Thou Hast Sworn By Thy God, My Jeanie" A. Cunningham. [Volume 2/416]
"Till Death Us Part." A. Stanley. [Volume 2/458]
Two Lovers. M. Cross. [Volume 2/402]
The Wedding-Day, fr. Epithalamion. E. Spenser. [Volume 2/4068]
Were I But His Own Wife. M. Downing. [Volume 2/400]
The Wife Of Loki. L. Elliot. [Volume 2/398]
A Woman's Complaint. Unknown. [Volume 2/426]
Woman's Will. J. Saxe. [Volume 2/438]
The Worn Wedding-Ring. W. Bennett. [Volume 2/438]
The **Marseillaise**. C. Lisle. [Volume 8/145]
**Marston.** S. Spender. [Supp 2/229]
**"Marston,** dropping it in the grate, broke his pipe." Marston. S. Spender. [Supp 2/229]
**Marston, Philip Bourke**
After Summer. [Volume 3/336]
Garden Fairies. [Volume 6/33]
To All in Haven. [Volume 6/428]
**Martial**
To One Who Had Scoffed at the Poet's Poverty. [Volume 6/327]
**"Martial,** the things that do attain." The Means to Attain Happy Life. H. Howard. [Volume 1/312]
**Martin and William E. Aytoun, Sir Theodore (tr.)**
The Erl-King. J. Goethe. [Volume 6/58]
**Martin, Edward Sanford**
A Girl of Pompeii. [Volume 1/208]
**Martin, Hardie St. (tr.)**
No One. N. Parra. [Supp 6/180]
**Martin, Sir Theodore (tr.)**
Homeward Bound. Cattullus. [Volume 1/313]
**Martley, John**
A Budget of Paradoxes. [Volume 2/30]
The **Martyr**. Adonis. [Supp 7/285]
The **Martyrs'** Hymn. M. Luther. [Volume 4/334]
**Marvell, Andrew**
A Drop of Dew. [Volume 5/100]
Song of the Emigrants in Bermuda. [Volume 5/400]
"The **marvellous** clouds %pass by the moon long accustomed." Lone Fisherman. T. Heraty. [Supp 7/97]
**"Mary** sat musing on the lamp-flame at the table." The Death of the Hired Man. R. Frost. [Supp 1/135]
**Marzials, Theophile (tr.)**
Last Night. Unknown. [Volume 2/339]
**Masefield, John**
Cargoes. [Supp 1/210]
The Chief Centurions. [Supp 1/208]
Sonnet. [Supp 1/209]
The Tarry Buccaneer. [Supp 1/207]
**Masks.** J. Das. [Supp 7/47]
*Masks*
Masks. J. Das. [Supp 7/47]
Prayer to Masks. L. Senghor. [Supp 6/74]
"**Masks!** Masks! %black mas red mask, your white-and-black masks." Prayer to Masks. L. Senghor. [Supp 6/74]
**Mason, Caroline Atherton**
The Voyage. [Volume 4/38]
**Massey, Gerald**
"O Lay Thy Hand In Mine, Dear!" [Volume 2/445]
Our Wee White Rose. [Volume 1/64]
**Massinger, Philip**
Devotion. [Volume 4/252]

[Supp 5/163]
Pyrargyrite Metal, 9. C. Meireles. [Supp 5/164]
Second Rose Motif. C. Meireles. [Supp 5/161]
Vigil. C. Meireles. [Supp 5/162]
"The merry brown hares came leaping." A Rough Rhyme
on a Rough Matter. C. Kingsley. [Volume 3/191]
Mersa. K. Douglas. [Supp 2/406]
Merwin, William Stanley (tr.)
Parting. J. Borges. [Supp 6/104]
"Tonight I Can Write the Saddest Lines" P. Neruda.
[Supp 6/131]
A Message from the Crane. Pak Tu-Jin. [Supp 7/154]
Messiah. A. Pope. [Volume 4/97]
Messinger, Robert Hinckley
A Winter Wish. [Volume 1/389]
Metastasio
Without and Within. [Volume 6/251]
"Methinks it were no pain to die." To Death. Gluck.
[Volume 3/395]
"Methinks we do as fretful children do." The Prospect.
E. Browning. [Volume 4/347]
"Methinks, when on the languid eye." Euthanasia. W.
Clark. [Volume 4/359]
Metrical Feet. S. Coleridge. [Volume 9/429]
Mexican Child. G. Mistral. [Supp 6/128]
*Mexico nd Mexicans*
Arizona Poems: Windmills. J. Fletcher. [Supp
1/126]
Meynell, Alice
Cradle-song at Twilight. [Supp 1/212]
The Lady Poverty. [Supp 1/212]
The Modern Poet. [Volume 6/347]
Renouncement. [Volume 2/338]
The Shepherdess. [Supp 1/210]
A Song of Derivations. [Supp 1/213]
To the Beloved. [Supp 1/211]
*Mice*
Poor Mouse. M. Berssenbrugge. [Supp 4/10]
Michaelmas. L. Lee. [Supp 2/341]
*Michael, Saint*
Michaelmas. L. Lee. [Supp 2/341]
Mickle, William Julius
Cumnor Hall. [Volume 3/41]
"Mid pleasures and palaces though we may roam." Home
Sweet Home, fr. Clari, the Maid of Milan. J.
Payne. [Volume 1/335]
"'Mid white sierras, that slope to the sea." Above
the Clouds. J. Miller. [Volume 6/334]
"The midday sun, with fiercest glare." The Conversion
of Saint Paul. J. Keble. [Volume 4/82]
"The middle part of the day." Bronchitis: The Rosario
Beach House, 002. A. Rodriguez. [Supp 4/280]
Middle Passage. R. Hayden. [Supp 4/142]
"The Midges Dance Aboon the Burn" R. Tannahill.
[Volume 5/47]
Midnight. G. Mistral. [Supp 6/127]
"Midnight past! Not a sound of aught." The Portrait.
O. Meredith. [Volume 3/82]
The Midnight Skaters. E. Blunden. [Supp 2/45]
A Midsummer's Noon in the Australian Forest. C.
Harpur. [Volume 5/44]
Midway. N. Madgett. [Supp 4/164]
"Might Fortress Is Our God" M. Luther. [Volume 4/33]
"The might Mahmud, Allah-breathing Lord." Rubaiyat:
060. O. Khayyam. [Supp 6/215]
The Might Of One Fair Face. M. Angelo. [Volume 2/329]
"The might of one fair face sublimes my love." The
Might Of One Fair Face. M. Angelo. [Volume
2/329]
"The mighty Red river surged." Ant from Sivas. F.
Daglarca. [Supp 7/299]
Mignon's Song, fr. Wilhelm Meister. J. Goethe.
[Volume 6/313]
"Mild offspring of a dark and sullen sire." The Early
Primrose. H. White. [Volume 5/245]

"A mile behind is Cloucester town." Gloucester Moors.
W. Moody. [Supp 1/225]
A Mile from Eden. A. Ridler. [Supp 2/275]
The Military Harpist. R. Pitter. [Supp 2/48]
*Milk and Milking*
Milkmaid. L. Lee. [Supp 2/336]
Milk at the Bottom of the Sea. O. Williams. [Supp
2/79]
The Milk of the Mothers. M. Waddington. [Supp 5/310]
The Milking-Maid. C. Rossetti. [Volume 2/49]
Milkmaid. L. Lee. [Supp 2/336]
The Milkmaid. J. Taylor. [Volume 9/259]
"A milkmaid, who poised a full pail on her head." The
Milkmaid. J. Taylor. [Volume 9/259]
The Milkmaid's Song. S. Dobell. [Volume 2/285]
Millay, Edna St. Vincent
The Bean-Stalk. [Supp 5/167]
English Sparrows. [Supp 5/168]
The Poet and His Book. [Supp 1/219]
The Rabbit. [Supp 5/169]
Renascence. [Supp 1/214]
Sonnet from Second April. [Supp 1/224]
Spring. [Supp 5/166]
Weeds. [Supp 1/223]
Miller, Joaquin
Above the Clouds. [Volume 6/334]
A California Christmas. [Volume 6/279]
Proem, fr. The Isles of the Amazons. [Volume
6/278]
Miller, William
Willie Winkie. [Volume 1/31]
*Mills and Millers*
Arizona Poems: Windmills. J. Fletcher. [Supp
1/126]
Steel Mill. L. Untermeyer. [Supp 1/311]
The Windmill. R. Bridges. [Supp 1/74]
Milman, Henry Hart
Hebrew Wedding, fr. The Fall Of Jerusalem. [Volume
2/405]
Jewish Hymn in Babylon. [Volume 4/307]
Milman, Henry Hart (tr.)
Choral Song, fr. The Bacchae. Euripides. [Volume
5/215]
Milnes, Richard Monckton, 1st Baron Houghton
The Brookside. [Volume 2/156]
Forever Unconfessed. [Volume 2/241]
Good Night and Good Morning. [Volume 1/109]
Hope of the Human Heart, fr. Anima Mundi. [Volume
4/110]
London Churches. [Volume 3/207]
To Thackeray. [Volume 7/83]
Milton, John
Adam and Eve, fr, Paradise Lost. [Volume 7/124]
Adam Describing Eve, fr. Paradise Lost. [Volume
2/385]
Adam To Eve, fr. Paradise Lost. [Volume 2/368]
Battle of the Angels, fr. Paradise Lost. [Volume
8/179]
The Departure from Paradise, Book XII, fr.
Paradise Lost. [Volume 4/273]
An Epitaph on the Admirable Dramatic Poet, W.
Shakespeare. [Volume 7/51]
Eve to Adam, fr. Paradise Lost. [Volume 4/273]
Eve's Lament, fr. Paradise Lost. [Volume 4/272]
Evening in Paradise, fr. Paradise Lost. [Volume
5/56]
The Faithful Angel, fr. Paradise Lost. [Volume
4/337]
The Fall, fr. Paradise Lost. [Volume 4/268]
Il Penseroso. [Volume 6/251]
Intercession and Redeoption, Book XI, fr. Paradise
Lost. [Volume 4/270]
Invocation to Light, fr. Paradise Lost. [Volume
5/30]
L'allegro. [Volume 6/241]

The Lady Lost in the Wood, fr. Comus. [Volume 6/64]
Light, fr. Paradise Lost. [Volume 5/30]
Lycidas. [Volume 3/446]
The Nymph of the Severn, fr. Comus. [Volume 6/66]
On His Blindness. [Volume 4/333]
On the Morning of Christ's Nativity. [Volume 4/51]
Paradise Lost, sels. [Volume 4/262]
The Poet's Theme, Book I, fr. Paradise Lost. [Volume 4/262]
Samson On His Blindness, fr. Samson Agonistes. [Volume 3/158]
Song: On May Morning. [Volume 5/85]
Sonnet to Cyriak Skinner. [Volume 3/220]
The Temptation, Book IX, fr. Paradise Lost. [Volume 4/263]
To the Lord-General Cromwell. [Volume 7/5]
To the Nightingale. [Volume 5/305]
"**Milton!** thou shouldst be living at this hour." To Milton. W. Wordsworth. [Volume 7/54]
The **Minaret.** Adonis. [Supp 7/283]
"**Mine** eyes have seen the glory of the coming of." Battle-Hymn of the Republic. J. Howe. [Volume 8/172]
"**Mine** eyes he closed, but open left the cell." Adam Describing Eve, fr. Paradise Lost. J. Milton. [Volume 2/385]
"**Mine** Is the Silent Face" L. Peters. [Supp 6/19]
*Mining and Miners*
Cleator Moor. L. Lee. [Supp 2/340]
The Collier. V. Watkins. [Supp 2/189]
The **Ministry** of Angels, fr. The Faerie Queen. E. Spenser. [Volume 4/415]
**Minstrel's** Song. T. Chatterton. [Volume 3/340]
**Minstrels'** Marriage-Song, fr. Cella: A Tragical Interlude. T. Chatterton. [Volume 2/340]
**Mintz, Ruth Finer (tr.)**
The Abandoned. N. Alterman. [Supp 7/238]
Memento of Roads. N. Alterman. [Supp 7/235]
Moon. N. Alterman. [Supp 7/237]
Red Ridinghood. N. Alterman. [Supp 7/236]
The **Minute-Gun.** R. Sharpe. [Volume 5/403]
**Miranda's** Song. W. Auden. [Supp 2/164]
**Mirikitani, Janice**
August 6. [Supp 4/39]
Desert Flowers. [Supp 4/44]
Hospitals Are to Die In. [Supp 4/42]
**Mirror.** J. Das. [Supp 7/50]
The **Mirror.** L. Gluck. [Supp 5/104]
A **Mirror** for the Twentieth Century. Adonis. [Supp 7/278]
*Mirrors*
Life in the Castle. A. Hebert. [Supp 5/111]
Mirror. J. Das. [Supp 7/50]
"**Miss** Flora, McFlimsey, of Madison Square." "Nothing to Wear" W. Butler. [Volume 9/213]
**Missing** Dates. W. Empson. [Supp 2/144]
"**Missing** from the map, the abandoned roads." Old Roads. E. Chuilleanain. [Supp 5/191]
*Missouri River*
Foreclosure. S. Brown. [Supp 2/83]
**Mist.** H. Thoreau. [Volume 7/153]
**Mr.** and Mrs. Spikky Sparrow. E. Lear. [Volume 1/177]
**Mr.** Edwards and the Spider. R. Lowell. [Supp 2/393]
**Mistral, Frederic**
The Ballad of Guibour, fr. Calendau. H. Preston (tr.). [Volume 7/327]
**Mistral, Gabriela**
The Foreigner. D. Dana (tr.). [Supp 6/129]
Little Feet. D. Dana (tr.). [Supp 6/125]
Mexican Child. D. Dana (tr.). [Supp 6/128]
Midnight. D. Dana (tr.). [Supp 6/127]
The Useless Wait. D. Dana (tr.). [Supp 6/124]
**Mrs.** Small. G. Brooks. [Supp 5/39]
**Mitchell, Agnes E.**

When the Cows Come Home. [Volume 1/323]
**Mitchell, Silas Weir**
The Quaker Graveyard. [Volume 3/278]
**Mitchell, Stephen (tr.)**
The Beginning. D. Pagis. [Supp 7/251]
Brothers. D. Pagis. [Supp 7/247]
The Caveman Is Not About to Talk. D. Pagis. [Supp 7/248]
Jason's Grave in Jerusalem. D. Pagis. [Supp 7/250]
Snake. D. Pagis. [Supp 7/250]
The Story. D. Pagis. [Supp 7/249]
Sudden Heart. D. Pagis. [Supp 7/252]
**Mitchell, Walter**
Tacking Ship Off Shore. [Volume 5/411]
**Mitford, Mary Russell**
Rienzi to the Romans, fr. Rienzi. [Volume 8/123]
The **Mitherless** Bairn. W. Thom. [Volume 1/78]
**Mixed** Sketches. D. Lee. [Supp 4/210]
The **Mixer.** L. MacNeice. [Supp 2/180]
"**Moan,** Moan, Ye Dying Gales" H. Neele. [Volume 3/152]
The **Mocking-bird.** F. Stanton. [Volume 5/319]
**Model** Lesson. T. Carmi. [Supp 7/242]
The **Modern** Hiawatha. Unknown. [Volume 9/414]
The **Modern** House that Jack Built. Unknown. [Volume 9/396]
The **Modern** Poet. A. Meynell. [Volume 6/347]
"**Moe** and more stars! behold yon hazy arch." Star-Mist, fr. Stars. J. Keble. [Volume 4/415]
**Moir, David Macbeth**
The Rustic Lad's Lament in the Town. [Volume 3/131]
*Moles*
The Eagle and the Mole. E. Wylie. [Supp 1/326]
**Molodowsky, Kadia**
"And What Will Happen" J. Valentine (tr.). [Supp 5/175]
God of Mercy. I. Howe (tr.). [Supp 5/178]
Song of the Sabbath. J. Valentine (tr.). [Supp 5/173]
White Night. A. Rich (tr.). [Supp 5/176]
Women Songs: 001. A. Rich (tr.). [Supp 5/172]
Women Songs: 002. A. Rich (tr.). [Supp 5/172]
**Momaday, N. Scott**
Carriers of the Dream Wheel. [Supp 4/301]
"Earth and I Gave You Turquoise" [Supp 4/302]
"A **moment** guessed - then back behind the told." Rubaiyat: 052. O. Khayyam. [Volume 6/214]
A **Moment** on Green Grass. Agyeya. [Supp 7/41]
"A **moment** then Lord Marmion stayed." Flodden Field, fr. Marmion. S. Scott. [Volume 8/312]
"A **moment's** halt - a momentary tast." Rubaiyat: 048. O. Khayyam. [Volume 6/213]
**Moments** of Initiation. K. Kerpi. [Supp 6/45]
"The **monarch** who wears a shrieking crown." Holy Poems: 003. G. Barker. [Supp 2/285]
*Money*
Dividends. K. Fearing. [Supp 2/100]
A Poetical Plea. G. Stein. [Supp 5/296]
**Moning** Meditations. T. Hood. [Volume 9/261]
"The **monk** sat in his den." The Weak Monk. S. Smith. [Supp 2/106]
"**Monnlight's** flowing %a worm is glowing." Moonlight. N. Yushij. [Supp 7/202]
**Monro, Harold**
"A Flower is Looking Through the Ground" [Supp 1/225]
Romantic Fool. [Supp 1/224]
"**Mont** Blanc yet gleams on high: - the power is." From Mont Blanc. P. Shelley. [Volume 5/217]
**Monterey.** C. Hoffman. [Volume 8/336]
**Monterrey** Sun. A. Reyes. [Supp 6/149]
**Montgomery, James**
Birds, fr. The Pelican Island. [Volume 5/288]
The Coral Reef, fr. The Pelican Island. [Volume 5/396]

"Forever with the Lord" [Volume 4/403]
Humility. [Volume 4/148]
"Make Way for Liberty!" [Volume 8/140]
My Country. [Volume 8/5]
Parted Friends. [Volume 1/347]
What is Prayer? [Volume 4/111]
*Montreal*
Lady in Blue: Homage to Montreal. M. Waddington.
[Supp 5/315]
**Montreuil, Mathieu de**
To Madame De Sevigne. [Volume 7/40]
The **Monument**. E. Bishop. [Supp 2/243]
"The **monument** outlasting bronze." The Ancient and
Modern Muses. F. Palgrave. [Volume 6/337]
**Moody, William Vaughn**
Gloucester Moors. [Supp 1/225]
The Menagerie. [Supp 1/228]
**Moon**. N. Alterman. [Supp 7/237]
**Moon**. Chong Chi-Yong. [Supp 7/149]
*Moon*
After Twenty Years. F. Tuqan. [Supp 5/306]
"Hills Picking Up the Moonlight" N. Cassian. [Supp
5/45]
Moon. Chong Chi-Yong. [Supp 7/149]
Moonlit Apples. J. Drinkwater. [Supp 1/109]
Revenge. C. Anwar. [Supp 7/80]
The Window Frames the Moon. L. Mar. [Supp 4/32]
"The **moon** has ascended between us." Love Apart. C.
Okigbo. [Supp 6/62]
"**Moon** moon, %shout the excited children." Nokondi. H.
Riyong. [Supp 6/48]
**Moonlight**. N. Yushij. [Supp 7/202]
"**Moonlight**, clear as water." Deliverance. Ping Hsin.
[Supp 5/118]
**Moonlight** on the Prairie, fr. Evangeline. H.
Longfellow. [Volume 5/61]
**Moonlight** Song of the Mocking-bird. W. Hayne. [Volume
6/179]
**Moonlit** Apples. J. Drinkwater. [Supp 1/109]
**Moore, Clement Clarke**
A Visit from St. Nicholas. [Volume 1/157]
**Moore, Marianne**
"He Made This Screen" [Supp 1/233]
Nevertheless. [Supp 5/186]
Sojourn in the Whale. [Supp 5/185]
A Talisman. [Supp 1/233]
That Harp You Play So Well. [Supp 1/234]
Those Various Scalpels. [Supp 5/183]
To a Prize Bird. [Supp 5/182]
To a Steam Roller. [Supp 5/185]
To Statecraft Embalmed. [Supp 5/182]
**Moore, T. Sturge**
Theseus. [Supp 1/235]
**Moore, Thomas**
" Alas! How Light a Cause May Move", fr. Light of
the Harem. [Volume 3/80]
"And Doth Not a Meting Like This" [Volume 1/366]
"As By the Shore at Break of Day" [Volume 8/138]
"As Slow Our Ship" [Volume 3/106]
"Believe Me, If All Those Endearing Young Charms"
[Volume 2/336]
Black and Blue Eyes. [Volume 2/39]
Come, Rest In This Bosom, fr. Irish Melodies.
[Volume 2/332]
Echoes. [Volume 2/327]
Farewell to Thee, Araby's Daughter, fr. The Fire-
Worshippers. [Volume 3/316]
"Farewell! - But Whenever You Welcome the Hour"
[Volume 3/116]
"Fly To The Desert, Fly With Me" [Volume 2/343]
The Garret. [Volume 1/369]
"The Harp That Once Through Tara's Halls" [Volume
8/138]
"I Knew By the Smoke That So Gracefully Curled"
[Volume 1/292]

Linda to Hafed, fr. The Fire-worshipers. [Volume
3/6]
Love's Young Dream, fr. Irish Melodies. [Volume
2/327]
Nonsense. [Volume 9/455]
"O, Breathe Not His Name!" [Volume 7/6]
"Oft in the Stilly Night" [Volume 6/314]
Orator Puff. [Volume 9/273]
"'T is the Last Rose of Summer", fr. Irish
Melodies. [Volume 5/283]
"Those Evening Bells" [Volume 7/141]
The Vale of Avoca. [Volume 1/351]
The Vale of Cashmere, fr. The Light of the Harem.
[Volume 7/165]
Verses Written in an Album. [Volume 2/34]
"Wreathe the Bowl" [Volume 1/387]
*Morality*
Beyond Good and Evil. G. Woodberry. [Supp 1/322]
A More Ancient Mariner. B. Carman. [Volume 5/345]
"**More** beautiful and soft than any moth." The
Landscape near an Aerodome. S. Spender. [Supp
2/228]
"**More** beautiful than any gift you gave." The Token. F.
Prince. [Supp 2/270]
**More** of a Corpse Than a Woman. M. Rukeyser. [Supp
2/303]
"**More** than once I have heard." Lindedi Singing. I.
Banda. [Supp 6/27]
"**More** than the soul of ancient song is given." The
Poet of To-day. S. Lippincott. [Volume 6/338]
"**More** than the wind, more than the snow." Rain. E.
Jones. [Volume 5/124]
"**More** than this, yes." The Wind-Up Doll. F.
Farrozkhzad. [Supp 7/219]
**Morike, Eduard**
My River. [Volume 5/205]
**Morning**. J. Cunningham. [Volume 5/40]
*Morning*
Dawn. L. Devkota. [Supp 7/157]
Day of These Days. L. Lee. [Supp 2/335]
Prelude. J. Drinkwater. [Supp 1/110]
A Wood Song. R. Hodgson. [Supp 1/165]
**Morning**, fr. The Minstrel. T. Heywood. [Volume 5/42]
The **Morning-Glory**. M. Lowell. [Volume 3/285]
**Morning** in May, fr. The Canterbury Pilgrims. G.
Chaucer. [Volume 5/89]
**Morning** Song. J. Baillie. [Volume 5/39]
**Morning** Song. S. Plath. [Supp 5/212]
A **Morning** Thought. E. Sill. [Volume 3/267]
**Mornings** in Various Years: 001. M. Piercy. [Supp
5/200]
**Mornings** in Various Years: 002. M. Piercy. [Supp
5/200]
**Mornings** in Various Years: 003. M. Piercy. [Supp
5/201]
**Morris, George Pope**
My mother's Bible. [Volume 1/228]
The Retort. [Volume 2/431]
"Woodman, Spare that Tree" [Volume 1/94]
**Morris, William**
Atalanta's Race, fr. The Earthly Paradise. [Volume
2/142]
The Day is coming. [Volume 8/431]
The Gillyflower of Gold. [Volume 2/333]
**Mors Et Vita**. S. Waddington. [Volume 1/396]
**Mort D'Arthur**. A. Tennyson. [Volume 7/352]
**Mortality**. W. Knox. [Volume 3/256]
**Mortality**. N. Madgett. [Supp 4/163]
*Mortality*
"The Heavy Bear Who Goes with Me" D. Schwartz.
[Supp 2/308]
O Dreams, O Destinations: 001. C. Day Lewis. [Supp
2/118]
"**Mortality**, behold and fear." On the Tombs in
Westminster Abbey. F. Beaumont. [Volume 3/269]

"The **muse,** disgusted at an age and clime." On the Prospect of Planting Arts and Learning in America. B. Berkeley. [Volume 8/91]

"**Muse** of lament, you are the most beautiful of." Poems for Akhmatova: 001. M. Tsvetayeva. [Supp 5/300]

**Musee** des Beaux Arts. W. Auden. [Supp 2/164]

"The **muse's** fairest light in no dark time." To the Memory of Ben Jonson. J. Cleveland. [Volume 7/46]

"**Muses,** that sing Love's sensual empirie." Sonnet. G. Chapman. [Volume 2/73]

**Museum.** S. Tanikawa. [Supp 7/131]

**Museums.** L. MacNeice. [Supp 2/180]

*Museums*

Museum. S. Tanikawa. [Supp 7/131]

"**Museums** offer us, running from among the buses." Museums. L. MacNeice. [Supp 2/180]

*Mushrooms*

"May Bright Mushrooms Grow" I. Banda. [Supp 6/29]

*Music and Musicians*

Alexander's Feast; or, the Power of Music. J. Dryden. [Volume 6/372]

Beethoven's Third Symphony. R. Hovey. [Volume 6/379]

The Bells of Shandon. F. Mahony. [Volume 7/145]

The Bells. E. Poe. [Volume 7/141]

The Cello. R. Gilder. [Volume 6/364]

Chopin. E. Lazarus. [Volume 7/114]

City Bells, fr. The Lay of St. Aloy's. R. Barham. [Volume 7/147]

Influence of Music, fr. King Henry Eighth. W. Shakespeare. [Volume 6/362]

Invocation, fr. the Davideis. A. Cowley. [Volume 6/371]

The Military Harpist. R. Pitter. [Supp 2/48]

Music, fr. The Merchant of Venice. W. Shakespeare. [Volume 6/362]

On Hearing A Little Music-box. L. Hunt. [Volume 7/139]

The Passions. W. Collins. [Volume 6/367]

Peter Quince at the Clavier. W. Stevens. [Supp 1/289]

Plucking Out a Rhythm. L. Inada. [Supp 4/4]

Pyrargyrite Metal, 9. C. Meireles. [Supp 5/164]

Song at Night. L. Lee. [Supp 2/341]

A Song for Saint Cecilia's Day, 1687. J. Dryden. [Volume 6/364]

Song for St. Cecilia's Day. W. Auden. [Supp 2/167]

The Spell. P. Verlaine. [Volume 6/367]

"Those Evening Bells" T. Moore. [Volume 7/141]

To--- P. Shelley. [Volume 6/363]

The Weary Blues. L. Hughes. [Supp 1/171]

"**Music** for a while." Song at Night. L. Lee. [Supp 2/341]

**Music,** fr. The Merchant of Venice. W. Shakespeare. [Volume 6/362]

**Music** in Camp. J. Thompson. [Volume 8/389]

"A **music-stand** of crimson lacquer, long since brough." The Red Lacquer Music-Stand. A. Lowell. [Supp 1/198]

"**Music,** when soft voices die." To--- P. Shelley. [Volume 6/363]

A **Musical** Instrument. E. Browning. [Volume 6/86]

**Musician.** C. Bax. [Supp 1/28]

**Mutis, Alvaro**

Amen. [Supp 6/133]

Song of the East. [Supp 6/133]

A Word. [Supp 6/134]

**My Ain** Countree. M. Demarest. [Volume 4/353]

**My Ain** Fireside. E. Hamilton. [Volume 1/295]

**My Ain** Wife. A. Laing. [Volume 2/419]

**My** beautiful **Lady.** T. Woolner. [Volume 2/260]

"**My** beautiful! my beautiful! that standest meekly." The Arab to His Favorite Steed. C. Norton.

[Volume 5/366]

**My** Beloved Is Mine and I Am His. T. Carmi. [Supp 7/243]

"**My** boat is on the shore." To Thomas Moore. G. Byron. [Volume 7/57]

"**My** body, eh? Friend death, how now?" Habeas Corpus. H. Jackson. [Volume 3/382]

**My** Bondange and My Freedom, 1853. F. Douglass. [Supp 4/52]

**My** Brigantine, fr. The Water Witch. J. Cooper. [Volume 5/402]

**My** Child. J. Pierpont. [Volume 3/417]

**My** Choice. W. Browne. [Volume 2/87]

**My** Country. J. Montgomery. [Volume 8/5]

"**My** country, 't is of thee." America. S. Smith. [Volume 8/95]

**My** Creed. A. Carey. [Volume 4/237]

"**My** curse upon thy venomed stang." Address to the Toothache. R. Burns. [Volume 9/307]

"**My** daddy has paid the rent." Good Times. L. Clifton. [Supp 4/193]

"**My** daughters, the old woman says, the weaver." The Soothsayer. D. Levertov. [Supp 5/144]

"**My** Days Among the Dead" R. Southey. [Volume 4/396]

"**My** days are in the yellow leaf." Verse. G. Byron. [Volume 3/170]

**My** Dear And Only Love. J. Graham. [Volume 2/226]

"**My** dear and only love, I pray." My Dear And Only Love. J. Graham. [Volume 2/226]

"**My** dear, be sensible! Upon my word." Love's Logic. Unknown. [Volume 2/164]

"**My** dear one is mine as mirrors are lonely." Miranda's Song. W. Auden. [Supp 2/164]

"**My** deck is furious." The Deck That Pouts. M. Piercy. [Supp 5/198]

"**My** ear-rings! my ear-rings! they've dropt into." Zara's Ear-Rings, fr. The Spanish. J. Lockhart. [Volume 2/265]

"**My** Eyes! How I Love You" J. Saxe. [Volume 2/155]

"**My** fairest child, i have no song to give you." A Farewell. C. Kingsley. [Volume 1/205]

"**My** fields lie dry, and all my schemes." Woe and Wellaway. N. Yushij. [Supp 7/205]

"**My** first vivid memory of you." To Jesus Villaneuva, with Love. A. Villanueva. [Supp 4/259]

"**My** gentle Puck, come hither. Thou." Compliment to Queen Elizabeth, fr. A Midsummer Night's Dream. W. Shakespeare. [Volume 6/17]

"**My** girl hath violet eyes and yellow hair." The Little Milliner. R. Buchanan. [Volume 2/135]

"**My** God, I Love Thee" S. Xavier. [Volume 4/103]

"**My** good blade carves the casques of me." Sir Galahad. A. Tennyson. [Volume 4/164]

"**My** grandpa waz a doughboy from carolina." Senses of Heritage. N. Shange. [Supp 5/264]

"**My** hair is springy like the forest grasses." Black Woman. N. Madgett. [Supp 4/166]

"**My** heart aches, and a drowsy numbness pains." Ode to a Nightingale. J. Keats. [Volume 3/166]

**My** Heart Is A Lute. L. Lindsay. [Volume 2/424]

"**My** Heart Leaps Up" W. Wordsworth. [Volume 5/8]

"**My** Heart's in the Highlands" R. Burns. [Volume 8/39]

"**My** Heid is Like to Rend, Willie" W. Motherwell. [Volume 3/49]

**My** Home. R. Herrick. [Volume 4/246]

"**My** House is Cloudy" N. Yushij. [Supp 7/204]

"**My** joy, my jockey, my Gabriel." First Cycle of Love Poems: 005. G. Barker. [Supp 2/282]

"**My** kingdom is my sweetheart's face." My Sweetheart's Face. J. Wyeth. [Volume 2/43]

**My** Lady. Dante Alighieri. [Volume 2/24]

"**My** life is like the summer rose." Life. R. Wilde. [Volume 6/230]

"**My** Little Girl is Nested." S. Peck. [Volume 1/41]

"**My** little love, do you remember." The Chess-Board. O.

"Nae shoon to hide her tiny taes." The Babie. J.
Rankin. [Volume 1/9]
"Nae star was glintin' out aboon." Ganging To And
Ganging Frae. E. Cook. [Volume 2/293]
**Nairne, Carolina Oliphant, Baroness**
The Auld House. [Volume 1/275]
The Laird O' Cockpen. [Volume 2/205]
The Land O' the Leal. [Volume 3/380]
"A **naked** house, a naked moor." The House Beautiful. R.
Stevenson. [Volume 1/277]
The **Nantucket** Skipper. J. Fields. [Volume 9/343]
**Naples**, fr. Italy. S. Rogers. [Volume 7/194]
**Napoleon.** V. Hugo. [Volume 7/8]
**Napoleon** and the British Sailor. T. Campbell. [Volume
7/347]
**Napoleon**, fr. Childe Harold. G. Byron. [Volume 7/9]
*Napoleon I*
Napoleon. V. Hugo. [Volume 7/8]
Napoleon, fr. Childe Harold. G. Byron. [Volume
7/9]
**Naseby.** L. Macaulay; Thomas Babington. [Volume 8/272]
**Nash, Thomas**
Spring, the Sweet Spring. [Volume 5/77]
**Nathan** Hale. F. Finch. [Volume 8/328]
**Nathan, L. E. (tr.)**
About Returning. Agyeya. [Supp 7/39]
Jet Flight. Agyeya. [Supp 7/40]
**National** Anthem. R. Newell. [Volume 9/415, Volume
9/417, Volume 9/416, Volume 9/418, Volume 9/419]
**Nation's** Hand. F. Daglarca. [Supp 7/303]
The **Nation's** Prayer. C. Kennedy. [Volume 8/102]
*Native Americans*
Chief Leschi of the Nisqually. D. Niatum. [Supp
4/303]
Farewell. L. Bahe. [Supp 4/322]
Halfbreed Cry. W. Rose. [Supp 4/323]
Kopis'taya (A Gathering of Spirits). P. Allen.
[Supp 4/305]
March-Patrol of the Naked Heroes. H. Gorman. [Supp
1/143]
Ossawatomie. C. Sandburg. [Supp 1/282]
We Wait, 5. The Old Prophecy. R. Conley. [Supp
4/311]
**Nature.** J. Very. [Volume 5/20]
*Nature*
Adam and Eve, fr, Paradise Lost. J. Milton.
[Volume 7/124]
After the Rain. T. Aldrich. [Volume 5/123]
An Indian Song. W. Yeats. [Volume 5/22]
The Angler's Wish. I. Walton. [Volume 5/138]
The Angler. J. Chalkhill. [Volume 5/139]
Ballade of Midsummer Days and Nights. W. Henley.
[Volume 5/112]
Before the Rain. T. Aldrich. [Volume 5/117]
Betrothed Anew. E. Stedman. [Volume 5/92]
Boats in a Fog. R. Jeffers. [Supp 1/173]
The Camp at Night, fr. The Illiad. Homer. [Volume
5/62]
Charles XII, fr. The Vanity of Human Wishes. S.
Johnson. [Volume 7/7]
Cleopatra, fr. Antony and Cleopatra. W.
Shakespeare. [Volume 7/127]
The Cloud Chorus, fr. The Clouds. Aristophanes.
[Volume 5/131]
The Cloud. P. Shelley. [Volume 5/133]
The Coasters. T. Day. [Volume 7/153]
"Come to These Scenes of Peace" W. Bowles. [Volume
5/17]
The Country Faith. M. Gale. [Volume 5/10]
Cuckoo Song. Unknown. [Volume 5/90]
The Dancing of the Air. S. Davies. [Volume 5/125]
Dawn. R. Gilder. [Volume 5/38]
Day is Dying, fr. The Spanish Gypsy. M. Cross.

Daybreak. H. Longfellow. [Volume 5/37]
December. J. Benton. [Volume 5/175]
"Die down, O Dismal Day" D. Gray. [Volume 5/88]
Dismal Moment, Passing. C. Major. [Supp 4/203]
A Drop of Dew. A. Marvell. [Volume 5/100]
Each and All. R. Emerson. [Volume 5/9]
Earth, Ocean, Air, fr. Alastor. P. Shelley.
[Volume 5/4]
The Encounter. J. Wright. [Supp 5/333]
The End of the Day. D. Scott. [Volume 5/51]
Evening. A. Lampman. [Volume 5/52]
The Evening Cloud. J. Wilson. [Volume 7/156]
Evening in Paradise, fr. Paradise Lost. J. Milton.
[Volume 5/56]
The Evening Wind. W. Bryant. [Volume 5/54]
Evening, fr. Don Juan. G. Byron. [Volume 5/57]
Fancy in Nubibus. S. Coleridge. [Volume 5/50]
The Faun. R. Hovey. [Volume 5/26]
Frost. E. Thomas. [Volume 5/173]
God in Nature, fr. Paracelsus. R. Browning.
[Volume 5/6]
"Great Nature is an Army Gay" R. Gilder. [Volume
5/16]
Harvest Song. L. Holty. [Volume 5/150]
Home Thoughts from Abroad. R. Browning. [Volume
5/83]
The Hunted Squirrel, fr. Britannia's Pastorals. W.
Browne. [Volume 5/157]
The Hunter's Song. B. Procter. [Volume 5/156]
Hunting Song. S. Scott. [Volume 5/154]
A Hunting We Will Go. H. Fielding. [Volume 5/158]
The Hurricane. W. Bryant. [Volume 7/151]
Hymn to Light, sel. A. Cowley. [Volume 5/35]
Hymn to the Night. H. Longfellow. [Volume 5/68]
A Hymn, fr. The Seasons. J. Thomson. [Volume 5/70]
I Found it. F. Tuqan. [Supp 7/275]
In Praise of Angling. S. Wotton. [Volume 5/136]
"In the Blue Distance" N. Sachs. [Supp 5/248]
"In the Wide Awe and Wisdom of the Night" C.
Roberts. [Volume 5/69]
Indian Summer. J. Tabb. [Volume 5/167]
Indolence. V. Watkins. [Supp 2/190]
Influence of Natural Objects, fr. The Prelude. W.
Wordsworth. [Volume 5/20]
Invocation to Light, fr. Paradise Lost. J. Milton.
[Volume 5/30]
Invocation to Rain In Summer. W. Bennett. [Volume
5/113]
June. W. Bryant. [Volume 5/102]
Knee-deep in June. J. Riley. [Volume 5/108]
The Latter Rain. J. Very. [Volume 5/148]
Life in the Autumn Woods. P. Cooke. [Volume 5/151]
Light. G. Macdonald. [Volume 5/32]
Light, fr. Paradise Lost. J. Milton. [Volume 5/30]
The Locked Gates. K. Raine. [Supp 5/225]
March. A. Swinburne. [Volume 5/74]
March. W. Wordsworth. [Volume 5/77]
May Morning. C. Thaxter. [Volume 5/84]
"The Midges Dance Aboon the Burn" R. Tannahill.
[Volume 5/47]
A Midsummer's Noon in the Australian Forest. C.
Harpur. [Volume 5/44]
Mist. H. Thoreau. [Volume 7/153]
Moonlight on the Prairie, fr. Evangeline. H.
Longfellow. [Volume 5/61]
Morning. J. Cunningham. [Volume 5/40]
Morning in May, fr. The Canterbury Pilgrims. G.
Chaucer. [Volume 5/89]
Morning Song. J. Baillie. [Volume 5/39]
Morning, fr. The Minstrel. T. Heywood. [Volume
5/42]
"My Heart Leaps Up" W. Wordsworth. [Volume 5/8]
Nature. J. Very. [Volume 5/20]
Night. J. White. [Volume 5/64]
Night, fr. Childe Harold. G. Byron. [Volume 5/65]

Never Despair. W. O'Brien. [Volume 3/246]
"Never despair! Let the feeble in spirit." Never
    Despair. W. O'Brien. [Volume 3/246]
"Never love unless you can." Advice To A Girl. T.
    Campion. [Volume 2/242]
"Never until the manking making." A Refusal to Mourn
    the Death, by Fire of a Child in London. D.
    Thomas. [Supp 2/368]
The Nevermore. D. Rossetti. [Volume 3/82]
Nevertheless. M. Moore. [Supp 5/186]
New-Born Blackness. Lo Fu. [Supp 7/26]
The New Church Organ. W. Carleton. [Volume 9/316]
*New England*
    Lilacs. A. Lowell. [Supp 1/195]
"New England Dead!" I. McLellan. [Volume 8/156]
A New England Home in Winter. J. Whittier. [Volume
    1/308]
*New Jersey*
    Legend. J. Weaver. [Supp 1/314]
The New Jerusalem. Unknown. [Volume 4/426]
"The New Negro strides upon the continent." Dark
    Symphony: 4. Tempo Primo. M. Tolson. [Supp
    4/98]
The New Noah. Adonis. [Supp 7/280]
The New Platform Dances. J. Mapanje. [Supp 6/34]
The New Year, fr. In Memoriam. A. Tennyson. [Volume
    4/260]
*New Years*
    New Year's Celebrations. T. Heraty. [Supp 7/94]
New Year's Celebrations. T. Heraty. [Supp 7/94]
*New York*
    "There Is Nothing In New York" A. Villanueva.
    [Supp 4/268]
*New York City*
    "Shame on Thee, O Manhattan" A. Branch. [Supp
    1/71]
    The Tunnel. H. Crane. [Supp 1/92]
Newell, Robert Henry
    National Anthem. [Volume 9/415, Volume 9/417, Volume
    9/416, Volume 9/418, Volume 9/419]
    "Picciola" [Volume 8/285]
The Newly-Wedded. W. Praed. [Volume 2/413]
Newman, John Henry
    Lead, Kindly Light. [Volume 4/41]
Newport-Beach. H. Tuckerman. [Volume 7/239]
News. G. Fuertes. [Supp 5/98]
News of the World II. G. Barker. [Supp 2/285]
News of the World III. G. Barker. [Supp 2/286]
"The newspaper folded." The Table. J. De Melo Neto.
    [Supp 6/111]
*Newspapers*
    Readers of Newspapers. M. Tsvetayeva. [Supp 5/302]
"Next to thee, O fair gazelle." The Arab to the Palm.
    B. Taylor. [Volume 5/227]
"Next year the grave grass will cover us." Street
    Corner College. K. Patchen. [Supp 2/255]
Nguyen Sa
    Necessity. N. Bich; Burton Raffel and W.S. Merwin
    (tr.). [Supp 7/189]
    No Time. N. Bich; Burton Raffel and W.S. Merwin
    (tr.). [Supp 7/190]
Niatum, Duane
    Chief Leschi of the Nisqually. [Supp 4/303]
Nichols, Rebecca S.
    The Philosopher Toad. [Volume 4/234]
Nicoll, Robert
    God is Everywhere. [Volume 4/28]
    Thoughts of Heaven. [Volume 4/391]
    We Are Brethren A' [Volume 1/353]
*Nietzsche, Friedrich*
    Beyond Good and Evil. G. Woodberry. [Supp 1/322]
The Night. H. Belloc. [Supp 1/33]
Night. J. Das. [Supp 7/50]
Night. J. White. [Volume 5/64]
*Night*

Awakening. A. Pozzi. [Supp 5/219]
Cradle-song at Twilight. A. Meynell. [Supp 1/212]
The Fragments of the Night. J. Lima. [Supp 6/141]
An Hymn to the Evening. P. Wheatley. [Supp 4/62]
Midnight. G. Mistral. [Supp 6/127]
Night. J. Das. [Supp 7/50]
O Daedalus, Fly Away Home. R. Hayden. [Supp 4/135]
Poem at Thirty. S. Sanchez. [Supp 4/190]
The Return: 002. A. Bontemps. [Supp 4/124]
Souls Lake. R. Fitzgerald. [Supp 2/241]
You, Andrew Marvell. A. MacLeish. [Supp 1/204]
"Night and we heard heavy and cadenced hoofbeats."
    The Return. J. Bishop. [Supp 2/27]
The Night-Blooming Cereus. R. Hayden. [Supp 4/139]
Night, fr. Childe Harold. G. Byron. [Volume 5/65]
Night, fr. Queen Mab. P. Shelley. [Volume 5/66]
"The night has a thousand eyes." Light. F. Bourdillon.
    [Volume 2/78]
"The night is late, the house is still." For
    Charlie's Sake. J. Palmer. [Volume 3/411]
Night Mists. W. Hayne. [Volume 6/179]
Night of the Scorpion. N. Ezekiel. [Supp 7/53]
The Night-Piece. R. Herrick. [Volume 2/165]
Night Storm. S. Murano. [Supp 7/118]
"Night to a grave that was newly made." The Old
    Sexton. P. Benjamin. [Volume 3/282]
"The night was a corpse." Dawn. L. Devkota. [Supp
    7/157]
"The night was dark, though sometimes a faint." Dawn.
    R. Gilder. [Volume 5/38]
The Nightingales' Song, fr. Music's Duel. R. Crashaw.
    [Volume 5/306]
Nightmare. The Lu. [Supp 7/193]
*Nightmares*
    Nightmare. The Lu. [Supp 7/193]
"Night's Fall Unlocks the Dirge of the Sea" W. Graham.
    [Supp 2/402]
The Nile. P. Shelley. [Volume 7/160]
Nimrod Wars with the Angels. A. Branch. [Supp 1/67]
Nirala
    Clear Skies. D. Rubin (tr.). [Supp 7/68]
    "Flower Garden %Like %a Fragrant Sare" D. Rubin
    (tr.). [Supp 7/70]
    Hopeless. D. Rubin (tr.). [Supp 7/63]
    "I'm Alone %I See" D. Rubin (tr.). [Supp 7/68]
    "It's True, %This Is the Gift You Gave" D. Rubin
    (tr.). [Supp 7/63]
    "A Little Boat, %A Golden Evening" D. Rubin (tr.).
    [Supp 7/70]
    Paradise. D. Rubin (tr.). [Supp 7/67]
    Stump?A. D. Rubin (tr.). [Supp 7/65]
    To a Waterfall. D. Rubin (tr.). [Supp 7/66]
    To Love. D. Rubin (tr.). [Supp 7/66]
Nist and Yoland Leite, John (tr.)
    "The Roosters Will Crow When We Die" C. Meireles.
    [Supp 5/160]
No. T. Hood. [Volume 5/167]
"No %don't look for me." Where I Am. M. Dos Santos.
    [Supp 6/42]
"No abbey's gloom, nor dark cathedral stoops." Sleepy
    Hollow. W. Channing. [Volume 3/277]
"No Baby in the House" C. Dolliver. [Volume 1/101]
No Credit. K. Fearing. [Supp 2/101]
"No history deceived him, for he knew." Elegy for a
    Dead Soldier: 007. K. Shapiro. [Supp 2/316]
"No more driver call for me." Many a Thousand Die.
    Unknown (African American). [Supp 4/52]
"No more the battle or the chase." Indian Summer. J.
    Tabb. [Volume 5/167]
"No more these simple flowers." Burns. J. Whittier.
    [Volume 7/64]
"No more with overflowing light." For a Dead Lady. E.
    Robinson. [Supp 1/271]
"No, no! Go from me. I have left her lately." A
    Virginal. E. Pound. [Supp 1/251]

"No notice in the papers." Tombstone with Cherubim. H. Gregory. [Supp 2/66]

No One. N. Parra. [Supp 6/180]

"No one thinks of the flowers." I Pity the Garden. F. Farrozkhzad. [Supp 7/221]

"No poetic phantasy." The Flowering of the Rod: 009. H. Doolittle. [Supp 5/78]

"No shadow of doubt; the sun." Monterrey Sun. A. Reyes. [Supp 6/149]

"No stir in the air, no stir in the sea." The Inchcape Rock. R. Southey. [Volume 5/431]

"No sun - no moon!" No. T. Hood. [Volume 5/167]

No Time. Nguyen Sa. [Supp 7/190]

*Noah*
    Still, Citizen Sparrow. R. Wilbur. [Supp 2/409]

The **Nobleman** and the Pensioner. G. Pfeffel. [Volume 7/303]

"**Nobody** comes to the graveyard on the hill." The Hill Above the Mine. M. Cowley. [Supp 2/60]

"**Nobody** ever gallped on this road." The Dead Ride Fast. R. Blackmur. [Supp 2/107]

**Nocturn.** F. Thompson. [Supp 1/302]

**Nocturnal** Sketch. T. Hood. [Volume 9/430]

**Nocturne** at Bethesda. A. Bontemps. [Supp 4/127]

**Nocturne** in a Deserted Brickyard. C. Sandburg. [Supp 1/278]

**Noel, Thomas**
    The Pauper's Drive. [Volume 3/202]

"A **noisette** on my garden path." The Shadow Rose. R. Rogers. [Volume 3/53]

**Nokes, W. F. (tr.)**
    Paulina's Appeal, fr. Polyeucte. P. Corneille. [Volume 2/396]

**Nokondi.** H. Riyong. [Supp 6/48]

"**None** in the land can say." Dark Symphony: 5. Larghetto. M. Tolson. [Supp 4/99]

**None** of It Was. C. Major. [Supp 4/202]

**Nonsense.** T. Moore. [Volume 9/455]

*Nonsense*
    The Baker's Tale, fr. The Hunting of the Snark. C. Dodgson. [Volume 9/456]
    For a Novel of Hall Caine's. R. Bridges. [Volume 9/460]
    Jabberwocky. C. Dodgson. [Volume 9/459]
    Nonsense. T. Moore. [Volume 9/455]
    Phycholophon. G. Burgess. [Volume 9/456]
    The Purple Cow. G. Burgess. [Volume 9/455]

**Noon.** R. Jeffers. [Supp 1/175]

**Noontide.** J. Leyden. [Volume 5/46]

"**Nor** force nor fraud shall sunder us! O ye." England to America. S. Dobell. [Volume 8/92]

*Norseland*
    Frithiof at the court of Angantyr, fr. Frithiof Saga. E. Tegner. [Volume 7/289]
    The Skeleton in Armor. H. Longfellow. [Volume 7/295]
    Thor Recovers His Hammer from Thrym. S. Saemund. [Volume 7/284]

**North, Christopher [pseud.] See Wilson, John**

*North Pole*
    Polar Exploration. S. Spender. [Supp 2/230]

The **Northern** Lights. B. Taylor. [Volume 5/34]

**Norton, Caroline Elizabeth Sarah Sheridan**
    The Arab to His Favorite Steed. [Volume 5/366]
    Bingen on the Rhine. [Volume 8/221]
    The King of Denmark's Ride. [Volume 3/346]
    Love Not. [Volume 3/8]
    "We Have Been Friends Together" [Volume 1/351]

**Norton, Charles Eliot (tr.)**
    My Lady. Dante Alighieri. [Volume 2/24]

The **Nose** and the Eyes. W. Cowper. [Volume 9/310]

**Nostalgia.** K. Shapiro. [Supp 2/322]

*Nostalgia*
    A Berkshire Holiday. C. Bax. [Supp 1/29]

"**Not** a drum was heard, not a funeral note." Burial of Sir John Moore. C. Wolfe. [Volume 8/283]

"**Not** a sound disurbs the air." A Midsummer's Noon in the Australian Forest. C. Harpur. [Volume 5/44]

"**Not** as all other women are." My Love. J. Lowell. [Volume 2/383]

"**Not** as you meant, O learned man, and good!" Hopefully Waiting. A. Randolph. [Volume 4/371]

**Not** At All, Or All In All, fr. Merlin and Vivien. A. Tennyson. [Volume 2/250]

"**Not** 'common speech' %a dead level." A Common Ground: 003. D. Levertov. [Supp 5/139]

"**Not** every thought can find its words." Undeveloped Lives. W. Lecky. [Volume 6/268]

"**Not** far advanced was morning day." Marmion and Douglas, fr. Marmion. S. Scott. [Volume 7/401]

"**Not** for the dead, but for memories. None of." Burial: 006. A. Walker. [Supp 4/227]

**Not** Honey. H. Doolittle. [Supp 2/5]

"**Not** honey %not the plunder of the bee." Not Honey. H. Doolittle. [Supp 2/5]

"**Not** in the sky." The Lost Pleiad. W. Simms. [Volume 4/347]

"**Not** in the world of light alone." The Living Temple. O. Holmes. [Volume 4/215]

"**Not** Marble, Not the Gilded Monuments" W. Shakespeare. [Volume 1/359]

**Not** Men Alone. E. Rolfe. [Supp 2/217]

"**Not** on a prayerless bed, not on a prayerless bed." Exhortation to Prayer. M. Mercer. [Volume 4/116]

**Not** on the Battle-field. J. Pierpont. [Volume 8/429]

**Not** One to Spare. Unknown. [Volume 1/288]

"**Not** only how far away, but the way that you say it." Lessons of the War: Judging Distances. H. Reed. [Supp 2/344]

**Not** Ours the Vows. B. Barton. [Volume 2/450]

"**Not** ours the vows of such as plight." Not Ours the Vows. B. Barton. [Volume 2/450]

"**Not** picnics or pageants or the improbable." Terror. R. Warren. [Supp 2/133]

"**Not** through heaven but unformed light." Jet Flight. Agyeya. [Supp 7/40]

"**Not** to be tuneless in old age!" Longfellow. A. Dobson. [Volume 7/107]

"**Not** to understand a treasure's worth." The Present Good, fr. The Task. W. Cowper. [Volume 3/150]

"**Not** what we would, but what we must." Country Life. R. Stoddard. [Volume 1/320]

"**Not** yet! Do not yet touch." The Turning of the Leaves. V. Watkins. [Supp 2/191]

**Note** on Local Flora. W. Empson. [Supp 2/145]

**Notes** Found Near a Suicide: To Alfred. F. Horne. [Supp 4/114]

**Notes** Found Near a Suicide: To All of You. F. Horne. [Supp 4/108]

**Notes** Found Near a Suicide: To Caroline. F. Horne. [Supp 4/114]

**Notes** Found Near a Suicide: To Catalina. F. Horne. [Supp 4/108]

**Notes** Found Near a Suicide: To "Chick" F. Horne. [Supp 4/109]

**Notes** Found Near a Suicide: To Henry. F. Horne. [Supp 4/113]

**Notes** Found Near a Suicide: To James. F. Horne. [Supp 4/111]

**Notes** Found Near a Suicide: To Mother. F. Horne. [Supp 4/108]

**Notes** Found Near a Suicide: To Telie. F. Horne. [Supp 4/109]

**Notes** Found Near a Suicide: To the One Who Called Me Nigger. F. Horne. [Supp 4/114]

**Notes** Found Near a Suicide: To the Poets. F. Horne. [Supp 4/112]

**Notes** Found Near a Suicide: To Wanda. F. Horne. [Supp 4/110]

Notes Found Near a Suicide: To You. F. Horne. [Supp 4/115]
Nothing But Leaves. L. Akerman. [Volume 4/283]
"Nothing but leaves; the spirit grieves." Nothing But Leaves. L. Akerman. [Volume 4/283]
"Nothing so sharply remnds a man he is mortal." Departure in the Dark. C. Day Lewis. [Supp 2/113]
"Nothing to Wear" W. Butler. [Volume 9/213]
November, 1941. R. Fuller. [Supp 2/265]
Now. A. Yosano. [Supp 7/143]
"Now %thinking back." Now. A. Yosano. [Supp 7/143]
"Now all the truth is out." To a Friend Whose Work Has Come to Nothing. W. Yeats. [Supp 1/329]
Now and Afterwards. D. Craik. [Volume 3/268]
"Now as I was young and easy under the apole boughs." Fern Hill. D. Thomas. [Supp 2/363]
"Now came still evening on, and twilight gray." Evening in Paradise, fr. Paradise Lost. J. Milton. [Volume 5/56]
"Now can you see the monument? It is of wood." The Monument. E. Bishop. [Supp 2/243]
"Now fades the last long streak of snow." Spring: 114, fr. In Memoriam. A. Tennyson. [Volume 5/91]
"Now gentle sleep hath closed up those eyes." Sonnet Upon A Stolen Kiss. G. Wither. [Volume 2/110]
"Now glory to the lord of hosts, from whom all." Ivry. L. Macaulay; Thomas Babington. [Volume 8/226]
"'Now I lay,' - repeat it, darling." The Unfinished Prayer. Unknown. [Volume 1/43]
"Now I Understand" T. Heraty. [Supp 7/95]
"Now I'll tell you about the cries from Cua." The Peasant Women from Cua. E. Cardenal. [Supp 6/156]
"Now is my love all ready forth to come." The Wedding-Day, fr. Epithalamion. E. Spenser. [Volume 2/4068]
"Now is the winter of our discontent." End of the Civil War, fr. King Richard III. W. Shakespeare. [Volume 8/424]
"Now, on sea and land descending." Vesper Hymn. S. Longfellow. [Volume 4/195]
"Now one and all, you roses." A Wood Song. R. Hodgson. [Supp 1/165]
"Now Philippa is Gone" A. Ridler. [Supp 2/276]
"Now Pine-Needles" S. Smith. [Supp 5/286]
"Now stamp the Lord's prayer on a grain of rice." Altarwise by Owl-light: 007. D. Thomas. [Supp 2/351]
"Now that the young buds are tipped with a falling sun." Early Spring. S. Keyes. [Supp 2/411]
"Now That Your Eyes Are Shut" E. Wylie. [Supp 5/339]
"Now the ambassadors have gone, refusing." Meditation. R. Fuller. [Supp 2/264]
"Now the bright crocus flames, and now." Spring. Meleager. [Volume 2/26]
"Now the bright morning star, day's harbinger." Song: On May Morning. J. Milton. [Volume 5/85]
"Now the day is over." Gild's Evening Hymn. S. Baring-Gould. [Volume 1/117]
"Now the golden morn aloft." Ode on the Pleasure Arising from Vicissitude. T. Gray. [Volume 5/18]
"Now the joys of the road are chiefly these." The Joys of the Road. B. Carman. [Volume 1/253]
"Now the new year reviving old desires." Rubaiyat: 004. O. Khayyam. [Volume 6/204]
"Now the plains come to adore the mountain wall." Colorado. R. Fitzgerald. [Supp 2/240]
"Now the rich cherry, whose sleek wood." Country Summer. L. Adams. [Supp 2/70]
"Now the rite is duly done." The Newly-Wedded. W. Praed. [Volume 2/413]
"Now the third and fatal conflict for the Persian." Harmosan. R. Trench. [Volume 8/203]

"Now this particular girl." Spinster. S. Plath. [Supp 5/211]
"Now unto yonder wood-pile go." A Saddened Tramp. Unknown. [Volume 9/395]
"Now was the sun so stationed, as when first." Purgatory: Fire of Purification, fr. The Diving Comedy. Dante Alighieri. [Volume 4/439]
"Now went forth the morn." Battle of the Angels, fr. Paradise Lost. J. Milton. [Volume 8/179]
"Now westward sol had spent the richest beams." The Nightingales' Song, fr. Music's Duel. R. Crashaw. [Volume 5/306]
"Now, when my life is more than half consumed." Gruach. G. Bottomley. [Supp 1/63]
"Now will I weave violets, daffodils." The Wreath. Meleager. [Volume 5/255]
Noyes, Alfred
   Creation. [Supp 1/245]
   The May-tree. [Supp 1/242]
   Mountain Laurell. [Supp 1/243]
   Sherwood. [Volume 6/181]
Number Five. J. Ransom. [Supp 1/259]
The Nun and Harp. G. Leroux. [Volume 3/93]
The Nymph of the Severn, fr. Comus. J. Milton. [Volume 6/66]
The Nymph's Reply. S. Raleigh. [Volume 2/150]

O. R. Wilbur. [Supp 2/409]
"O, a dainty plant is the ivy green." The Ivy Green. C. Dickens. [Volume 5/263]
"Oh Achilles of the moleskins." Notes Found Near a Suicide: To "Chick" F. Horne. [Supp 4/109]
"O bitterness never spoken, the death mask etched in." Salvos for Randolph Bourne: 001. H. Gregory. [Supp 2/65]
"O Black and Unknown Bards" J. Johnson. [Supp 4/67]
"O blackbird! sing me something well." The Blackbird. A. Tennyson. [Volume 5/320]
"O blithe new-comer@ I have heard." To the Cuckoo. W. Wordsworth. [Volume 5/290]
"O, Breathe Not His Name!" T. Moore. [Volume 7/6]
"O Caledonia! stern and wild." Scotland, fr. The Lay of the Last Minstrel. S. Scott. [Volume 8/33]
"O, came ye owner by the yoke-burn ford." Jock Johnstone the Tinkler. J. Hogg. [Volume 7/390]
O Captain! My Captain! W. Whitman. [Volume 7/28]
"O captain! my captain! our fearful trip is done." O Captain! My Captain! W. Whitman. [Volume 7/28]
"O child of nations, giant-limbed." Canada. C. Roberts. [Volume 8/71]
"O children %from Atlantic Ocean to Arabian Gulf." What Value Has the People Whose Tongue Is Tied?: 020. N. Qabbani. [Supp 7/291]
O Daedalus, Fly Away Home. R. Hayden. [Supp 4/135]
"O David, if I had." That Harp You Play So Well. M. Moore. [Supp 1/234]
"O days and hours, your work is this." The Dead Friend: 116, fr. In Memoriam. A. Tennyson. [Volume 1/362]
"Oh dear! is summer over?" The First Rose of Summer. O. Herford. [Volume 1/154]
"O, Dinna ask me gin I lo'e ye." Dinna Ask Me. J. Dunlop. [Volume 2/100]
"O, Do Not Wanton With Those Eyes" B. Jonson. [Volume 2/39]
"O, don't be sorrowful, darling!" Faith And Hope. R. Peale. [Volume 2/446]
O Dreams, O Destinations: 001. C. Day Lewis. [Supp 2/118]
O Dreams, O Destinations: 002. C. Day Lewis. [Supp 2/118]
O Dreams, O Destinations: 003. C. Day Lewis. [Supp

"O Sister %Where Do You Pitch Your Tent?" N. Sachs. [Supp 5/249]

"O Swallow, Swallow, flying, flying South." O Swallow, Swallow, Flying South, fr. The Princess. A. Tennyson. [Volume 2/100]

O Swallow, Swallow, Flying South, fr. The Princess. A. Tennyson. [Volume 2/100]

"O swan of slenderness." The Little Red Lark. A. Graves. [Volume 2/158]

"O swiftness of the swallow and strengh." Tamar, sel. R. Jeffers. [Supp 1/174]

O Taste and See. D. Levertov. [Supp 5/140]

"O, terribly proud was Miss MacBride." The Proud Miss MacBride. J. Saxe. [Volume 9/228]

"O, that last day in Lucknow fort!" The Relief of Lucknow. R. Lowell. [Volume 8/296]

"O that the chemist's magic art." A Tear. S. Rogers. [Volume 6/271]

"O that those lips had language! Life has passed." My Mother's Picture. W. Cowper. [Volume 1/79]

"Oh That 'T Were Possible", fr. Maud. A. Tennyson. [Volume 3/331]

"O the Chimneys" N. Sachs. [Supp 5/246]

"O the days are gone when beauty bright." Love's Young Dream, fr. Irish Melodies. T. Moore. [Volume 2/327]

"O the days gone by! O the days gone by!" The Days Gone By. J. Riley. [Volume 1/203]

"O the gallant fisher's life." The Angler. J. Chalkhill. [Volume 5/139]

"O, The Pleasant Days of Old" F. Browne. [Volume 7/206]

"O the snow, the beautiful snow." Beautiful Snow. J. Watson. [Volume 3/205]

"Oh the wonder of our life." A Query. Unknown. [Volume 4/146]

"O, then, I see, Queen Mab hath been with you." Queen Mab, fr. Romeo and Juliet. W. Shakespeare. [Volume 6/13]

"Oh thinkin' long's the weary work!" Thinkin' Long. A. MacManus. [Volume 3/141]

"O, those little, those little blue shoes!" Baby's Shoes. W. Bennett. [Volume 1/66]

"O thou almight father! who dost make." Purgatory: Prayer of Penitents, fr. The Diving Comedy. Dante Alighieri. [Volume 4/437]

"O thou eternal one! whose presence bright." God. G. Dershavin. [Volume 4/24]

"O thou great friend to all the sons of men." The Way, the Truth, and the Life. T. Parker. [Volume 4/92]

"O thou of home the guardian Lar." A Winter-evening Hymn to My Fire. J. Lowell. [Volume 1/297]

"O thou vast ocean! ever-sounding sea!" Address to the Ocean. B. Procter. [Volume 5/381]

"Oh thou, who didst with pitfall and gin." Rubaiyat: 080. O. Khayyam. [Volume 6/219]

"O thou who hast beneath thy hand." Ascription. C. Roberts. [Volume 4/134]

"O thou who lovest not alone." The Aim. C. Roberts. [Volume 4/129]

"Oh thou, who man of baser earth didst make." Rubaiyat: 081. O. Khayyam. [Volume 6/220]

"O thou whose fancies from afar are brought." To Hartley Coleridge; six years old. W. Wordsworth. [Volume 1/40]

"O thou, whose glorious orbs on high." Hymn of the West. E. Stedman. [Volume 8/458]

"O unexpected stroke, worse than of death!" Eve's Lament, fr. Paradise Lost. J. Milton. [Volume 4/272]

"O unhatched bird, so high preferred." Ode to the Roc. W. Courthope. [Volume 9/437]

"O unseen spirit! now a calm divine." On a Beautiful Day. J. Sterling. [Volume 5/6]

"O veauteous God! uncircumscribed treasure." Heaven. J. Taylor. [Volume 4/408]

"O Vocables of Love" L. Riding. [Supp 1/265]

"O, wad that my time were owre but." The Rustic Lad's Lament in the Town. D. Moir. [Volume 3/131]

"O waly, waly, up the bank." Wally, Waly. Unknown. [Volume 3/45]

"O wanderer in the southern weather." An Indian Song. W. Yeats. [Volume 5/22]

"O Wha's Been Here Afore Me, Lass" H. MacDiarmid. [Supp 2/30]

"O, wherefore come ye forth, in triumph from the." Naseby. L. Macaulay; Thomas Babington. [Volume 8/272]

"O which is more, the pleasure or the pain." The Serious Child. R. Pitter. [Supp 5/207]

"O whistle, and I'll come to you, my lad." Whistle, and I'll Come To You, My Lad. R. Burns. [Volume 2/109]

"O who will walk a mile with me." A Wayfaring Song. H. Van Dyke. [Volume 1/347]

"O why should the spirit of mortal be proud?" Mortality. W. Knox. [Volume 3/256]

"O wild west wind, thou breath of autumn's." Ode to the West Wind. P. Shelley. [Volume 5/128]

"O Winter! Wilt Thou Never Go?" D. Gray. [Volume 5/191]

"O wonderful nonsense of lotion of lucky tiger." Haircut. K. Shapiro. [Supp 2/321]

"O word, of God incarnate." The Word. W. How. [Volume 4/199]

"'O world-god, give me wealth!' the Egyptian." Gifts. E. Lazarus. [Volume 8/8]

"O world! O life! O time!" A Lament. P. Shelley. [Volume 3/172]

"O world, thou choosest not the better part!" Faith. G. Santayana. [Volume 4/136]

"O ye wha are sae guid yoursel'" To the Unco Guid. R. Burns. [Volume 4/320]

"O Yet We Trust That Somehow", fr. In Memoriam. A. Tennyson. [Volume 4/243]

"O, young Lochinvar is come out of the west." Lochinvar, fr. Marmion. S. Scott. [Volume 2/276]

The Oasis of Sidi Khaled. W. Blunt. [Volume 5/44]

Oberon's Feast. R. Herrick. [Volume 6/14]

Obeyesekere, Ranjini (tr.)
Killing One's Gods. G. Senanayake. [Supp 7/183]
Silence. G. Senanayake. [Supp 7/180]
The Sin. G. Senanayake. [Supp 7/182]

"The objects are disposed: the sky is suitable." November, 1941. R. Fuller. [Supp 2/265]

O'Brien, Fitz-James
Kane. [Volume 7/120]
The Second Mate. [Volume 9/189]

O'Brien, William Smith
Never Despair. [Volume 3/246]

*Obscurity*
Portrait - II. E. Cummings. [Supp 1/102]
Portrait - X. E. Cummings. [Supp 1/103]
The Weak Monk. S. Smith. [Supp 2/106]

Occidente, Maria del [pseud.] See Brooks, Maria G.

Occupation. N. Hikmet. [Supp 7/308]

Ocean, fr. The Course of Time. R. Pollok. [Volume 5/379]

O'Connor, Joseph
The General's Death. [Volume 8/369]

Ode. J. Bishop. [Supp 2/25]

Ode. H. Timrod. [Volume 8/454]

Ode. W. Wordsworth. [Volume 4/377]

Ode for a Social Meeting. O. Holmes. [Volume 9/383]

Ode, fr. The Spectator. J. Addison. [Volume 4/13]

Ode on a Grecian Urn. J. Keats. [Volume 7/136]

Ode on the Pleasure Arising from Vicissitude. T. Gray. [Volume 5/18]

Ode to a Lost Cargo in a Ship Called Save: 001. J. Craveirinha. [Supp 6/37]
Ode to a Lost Cargo in a Ship Called Save: 002. J. Craveirinha. [Supp 6/38]
Ode to a Lost Cargo in a Ship Called Save: 003. J. Craveirinha. [Supp 6/39]
Ode to a Lost Cargo in a Ship Called Save: 004. J. Craveirinha. [Supp 6/41]
Ode to a Nightingale. J. Keats. [Volume 3/166]
Ode to Ben Jonson. R. Herrick. [Volume 7/47]
Ode to Duty. W. Wordsworth. [Volume 4/278]
Ode to Mother Carey's Chicken. T. Watts. [Volume 5/333]
Ode to Peace. W. Tennant. [Volume 8/423]
Ode to Sleep. P. Hayne. [Volume 6/439]
Ode to Solitude. A. Pope. [Volume 1/265]
Ode to the Confederate Dead. A. Tate. [Supp 2/73]
Ode to the Human Heart. L. Blanchard. [Volume 9/428]
Ode to the Roc. W. Courthope. [Volume 9/437]
Ode to the West Wind. P. Shelley. [Volume 5/128]
Ode to Tobacco. C. Calverley. [Volume 9/387]
**O'Donnell, John Francis**
   A Spinning Song. [Volume 8/56]
"The **odor** of a rose: light of a star." Shelley. A. Japp. [Volume 7/58]
"**Odysseus** rested on his oar and saw." The Second Voyage. E. Chuilleanain. [Supp 5/193]
The **Odyssey**. A. Lang. [Volume 6/342]
**Oehlenschlager, Adam Gottlob**
   Hakon's Defiance, fr. Hakon Jari. S. Lascelles (tr.). [Volume 8/208]
"O'er a low couch the setting sun." The Baron's Last Banquet. A. Greene. [Volume 7/300]
"O'er the wet sands an insect crept." An Autograph. J. Lowell. [Volume 6/344]
Of a Certaine Man. S. Harrington. [Volume 9/199]
Of a Contented Spirit. L. Thomas. [Volume 6/328]
"of all men poverty pursued him least." Elegy for a Dead Soldier: 009. K. Shapiro. [Supp 2/317]
"Of all the floures in the mede." The Daisy, fr. Legend of Good Women. G. Chaucer. [Volume 5/275]
"Of all the girls that are so smart." Sally In Our Alley. H. Carey. [Volume 2/290]
"Of all the heavenly gifts that mortal men commend." The Friend, fr. On Friendship. N. Grimoald. [Volume 1/402]
"Of all the ships upon the blue." Captain Reece. W. Gilbert. [Volume 9/297]
"Of all the thoughs of god that are." The Sleep. E. Browning. [Volume 3/389]
"Of all the torments, all the cares." Rivalry In Love. W. Walsh. [Volume 2/225]
"Of a' the airts the wind can blaw." I Love My Jean. R. Burns. [Volume 3/126]
Of Blue China. A. Lang. [Volume 9/448]
"of eviden invisibles %exquisite the hovering." Portrait - II. E. Cummings. [Supp 1/102]
Of Hym That Togyder Wyll Serve Two Maysters. S. Brandt. [Volume 4/217]
"Of man's first disobedience and the fruit." The Poet's Theme, Book I, fr. Paradise Lost. J. Milton. [Volume 4/262]
"Of Nelson and the north." Battle of the Baltic. T. Campbell. [Volume 8/281]
Of Reason and Discovery. D. Mattera. [Supp 6/80]
"Oft in the Stilly Night" T. Moore. [Volume 6/314]
"Often i think of the beautiful town." My Lost Youth. H. Longfellow. [Volume 1/260]
**Ogden, Eva L.**
   The Sea. [Volume 9/227]
"Oh, deem not they are blest alone." Blessed Are They That Mourn. W. Bryant. [Volume 3/421]
"Oh, did you see him riding down." Riding Down. N. Perry. [Volume 1/206]

"Oh, good gigantic smile o' the brown old earth." Among the Rocks. R. Browning. [Volume 5/430]
"Oh, hush thee, earth! Fold thou thy weary." Hush! J. Dorr. [Volume 3/400]
"Oh, I'm not myself at all." I'm Not Myself At All. S. Lover. [Volume 2/185]
"Oh, it's twenty gallant gentlemen." The Last Hunt. W. Thayer. [Volume 8/262]
"Oh, never talk again to me." The Girl of Cadiz. G. Byron. [Volume 2/28]
"Oh, not more subtly silence strays." To the Beloved. A. Meynell. [Supp 1/211]
"Oh, silver tree!" Jazzonia. L. Hughes. [Supp 4/129]
"Oh, talk not to me of a name great in story." Stanzas. G. Byron. [Volume 2/361]
"Oh! Temple, Temple of Bot!" S. Wongthed. [Supp 7/186]
"Oh, the auld house, the auld house." The Auld House. C. Nairne. [Volume 1/275]
"Oh, the fern, the fern, the Irish hill fern." The Mountain Fern. A. Geoghegan. [Volume 5/264]
"Oh, the shambling sea is a sexton old." The Gravedigger. B. Carman. [Volume 5/383]
"Oh, the wind from the desert blew in!" Khamsin. C. Scollard. [Volume 9/42]
"Oh! there is." Life, fr. Festus. P. Bailey. [Volume 4/407]
"Oh, thou great Babel - out of nothing reared." Babel Falls. A. Branch. [Supp 1/68]
"Oh, thou northland bobolink." To the Lapland Longspur. J. Burroughs. [Volume 5/314]
"Oh, threats of hell and hopes of paradise!" Rubaiyat: 063. O. Khayyam. [Volume 6/216]
"Oh, to be in England now that April's there." Home Thoughts from Abroad. R. Browning. [Volume 5/83]
"Oh, wha hae ye brought us hame now, my." Muckle-Mou'd Meg. J. Ballantine. [Volume 7/418]
"Oh! Where Do Fairies Hide Their Heads?" T. Bayly. [Volume 6/56]
"Oh, where is the knight or the squire so bold." The Diver. J. Schiller. [Volume 9/44]
"Oh! why left I my hame?" The Exile's Song. R. Gilfillan. [Volume 8/51]
"Oh, yes, friend! I'm crazy." Crazy: 001. L. Devkota. [Supp 7/163]
"Oh, yes we mean all kind words that we say." We Love But Few. Unknown. [Volume 1/368]
**O'Hara, Theodore**
   The Bivouac of the Dead. [Volume 8/441]
"Oh, 't is time I should talk to your mother." How To Ask And Have. S. Lover. [Volume 2/179]
**Ojaide, Tanure**
   Africa Now. [Supp 6/53]
   The Cross. [Supp 6/56]
   "In the Struggle to Be Free" [Supp 6/56]
   When We Have to Fly. [Supp 6/52]
   Words. [Supp 6/54]
**Okara, Gabriel**
   "Once Upon a Time, Son" [Supp 6/58]
   You Laughed and Laughed and Laughed. [Supp 6/59]
**O'Keeffe, John**
   "I am a Friar of Orders Gray", fr. Robin Hood. [Volume 9/247]
**Okigbo, Christopher**
   Elegy of the Wind. [Supp 6/62]
   Love Apart. [Supp 6/62]
**Old**. R. Hoyt. [Volume 3/180]
Old Age. B. Al-Haydari. [Supp 7/230]
*Old Age*
   After Ronsard. C. Williams. [Supp 1/315]
   An Ancient to Ancients. T. Hardy. [Supp 1/161]
   Old Age. B. Al-Haydari. [Supp 7/230]
   "The Old Couple %Sitting Hand In Hand" N. Sachs. [Supp 5/254]

The Old Indians. J. Pasos. [Supp 6/181]
An Old Woman. E. Sitwell. [Supp 2/16]
Piazza Piece. J. Ransom. [Supp 1/260]
"When You Are Old" W. Yeats. [Supp 1/332]
Old Age and Death, fr. Verses Upon His Divine Poesy.
    E. Waller. [Volume 6/293]
The Old Arm-Chair. E. Cook. [Volume 1/93]
An Old Battle-flield. F. Stanton. [Volume 8/446]
"Old Birch, who taught the village school." The
    Retort. G. Morris. [Volume 2/431]
The Old Bridge at Florence. H. Longfellow. [Volume
    7/174]
"The Old Couple %Sitting Hand In Hand" N. Sachs.
    [Supp 5/254]
The Old Familiar Faces. C. Lamb. [Volume 3/143]
"An old farm-house with meadows wide." Two Pictures.
    A. Green. [Volume 1/318]
Old Folks at Home. W. Cowper. [Volume 3/149]
Old Grimes. A. Greene. [Volume 9/265]
"Old Grimes is dead, that good old man." Old Grimes.
    A. Greene. [Volume 9/265]
The Old Indians. J. Pasos. [Supp 6/181]
"Old Ironsides" O. Holmes. [Volume 8/96]
Old Lem. S. Brown. [Supp 2/85]
The Old Maid. G. Barlow. [Volume 2/369]
The Old Man and Jim. J. Riley. [Volume 8/357]
The Old Man Dreams. O. Holmes. [Volume 2/459]
"Old man, God bless you! does your pipe taste." The
    Nobleman and the Pensioner. G. Pfeffel. [Volume
    7/303]
"Old man never had much to say." The Old Man and Jim.
    J. Riley. [Volume 8/357]
"Old Master Brown brought his ferule down." Old-
    School Punishment. Unknown. [Volume 1/162]
"The old mayor climbed the belfry tower." High-tide
    on the Coast of Lincolnshire. J. Ingelow.
    [Volume 9/145]
"The old men, very old, are sitting.' The Old Indians.
    J. Pasos. [Supp 6/181]
The 'Old Oaken Bucket. S. Woodworth. [Volume 1/91]
The "Old, Old Song" C. Kingsley. [Volume 1/230]
Old Roads. E. Chuilleanain. [Supp 5/191]
Old Roads
    Old Roads. E. Chuilleanain. [Supp 5/191]
Old-School Punishment. Unknown. [Volume 1/162]
The Old Sexton. P. Benjamin. [Volume 3/282]
The Old Squire. W. Blunt. [Volume 5/165]
An Old Sweetheart Of Mine. J. Riley. [Volume 2/372]
An Old time Christmas, fr. Marmion. S. Scott. [Volume
    7/210]
"Old tubal cain was a man of might." Tubal Cain. C.
    Mackay. [Volume 8/426]
The Old Vagabond. P. De Beranger. [Volume 3/188]
The Old Vicarage, Grantchester. R. Brooke. [Supp
    1/76]
The Old Village Choir. B. Taylor. [Volume 4/202]
"Old wine to drink." A Winter Wish. R. Messinger.
    [Volume 1/389]
"Old winter is the man for me." Winter. M. Claudius.
    [Volume 5/172]
The Old Witch in the Copse. F. Cornford. [Supp 1/90]
An Old Woman. E. Sitwell. [Supp 2/16]
"Old women %should live like worms." How Old Women
    Should Live. M. Waddington. [Supp 5/312]
"The old women move quietly up." Burial: 003. A.
    Walker. [Supp 4/226]
The Old Year and the New. W. Wilkinson. [Volume
    6/194]
"Older, we build a road where once our active." O
    Dreams, O Destinations: 007. C. Day Lewis.
    [Supp 2/120]
Oldys, William
    The Fly. [Volume 5/341]
The O'Lincoln Family. W. Flagg. [Volume 5/312]
Oliphant, Carolina. See Nairne, Baroness

Oliphant, Thomas (tr.)
    Where Are the Men? Taliessin. [Volume 8/301]
Olivia, fr. Twelfth Night. W. Shakespeare. [Volume
    2/10]
On a Beautiful Day. J. Sterling. [Volume 5/6]
On a Bust of Dante. T. Parsons. [Volume 7/41]
"On a deserted islet in the ocean." A Message from
    the Crane. Pak Tu-Jin. [Supp 7/154]
On a Distant Prospect of Eton College. T. Gray.
    [Volume 1/244]
On a Fan. A. Dobson. [Volume 6/385]
On a Grave at Grindelwald. F. Myers. [Volume 3/280]
On a Griddle. E. Waller. [Volume 2/35]
"On a ground beaten gold by running and." A Game of
    Ball. M. Rukeyser. [Supp 5/242]
"On a little piece of wood." Mr. and Mrs. Spikky
    Sparrow. E. Lear. [Volume 1/177]
"On a lone barren sile, where the wild roaring." The
    Grave of Bonaparte. L. Heath. [Volume 8/435]
On a Poem's Circumstances. L. Bell. [Supp 6/109]
On a Portrait of Wordsworth. E. Browning. [Volume
    7/69]
"On a sheer bluff." Summit. Chong Chi-Yong. [Supp
    7/148]
On an Infant. S. Coleridge. [Volume 4/232]
On an Intaglio Head of Minerva. T. Aldrich. [Volume
    6/383]
On an Old Muff. F. Locker-Lampson. [Volume 9/235]
On Anne Allen. E. Fitzgerald. [Volume 3/303]
On Being Brought from Africa to America. P. Wheatley.
    [Supp 4/61]
"On either side the river lie." The Lady of Shalott.
    A. Tennyson. [Volume 6/124]
On First Looking Into Chapman's Homer. J. Keats.
    [Volume 6/341]
On Hearing A Little Music-box. L. Hunt. [Volume
    7/139]
"On Hellespont, guilty of true love's blood." Hero's
    Beauty, fr. The First Sestiad of "Hero and
    Leander" C. Marlowe. [Volume 2/15]
"On her white breast a sparkling cross she wore."
    Belinda, fr. rape of the lock. A. Pope. [Volume
    2/14]
On His Blindness. J. Milton. [Volume 4/333]
On His "Sonnets of the Wingless Hours" E. Lee-
    Hamilton. [Volume 6/338]
On Ithaca Standing. L. Durrell. [Supp 2/260]
"On Linden, when the sun was low." Hohenlinden. T.
    Campbell. [Volume 8/225]
On Living: 001. N. Hikmet. [Supp 7/306]
On Living: 002. N. Hikmet. [Supp 7/307]
On Living: 003. N. Hikmet. [Supp 7/308]
"On ochre wall in ice-formed caves shaggy
    Neanderthals." To My Son Parker, Asleep in the
    Next Room. B. Kaufman. [Supp 4/185]
"On, on, my brown Arab, away, away!" The Arab. C.
    Calverley. [Volume 9/413]
"On parents' knees, a naked, new-born child." The
    Baby. Kalidasa. [Volume 1/1]
"On political leaders what hopes can we fix?"
    Political Leaders. M. Iqbal. [Supp 7/61]
On Some Buttercups. F. Sherman. [Volume 2/46]
On Suicide. S. Murano. [Supp 7/117]
On the Brink. C. Calverley. [Volume 9/443]
"On the cross-beam under the old south bell." The
    Belfry Pigeon. N. Willis. [Volume 5/325]
"On the day when the lotus bloomed, alas, my mind
    was." Gitanjali: 020. R. Tagore. [Supp 7/75]
On the Death of an Infant. J. Lowell. [Volume 1/70]
On the Death of Her Brother, Francis I. M. De Valois.
    [Volume 3/338]
On the Death of Thomas Carlyle and George Eliot. A.
    Swinburne. [Volume 7/96]
On the Departure of Sir Walter Scott from Abbotsford .
    .. W. Wordsworth. [Volume 7/61]

Khamsin. C. Scollard. [Volume 9/42]
The Leper. N. Willis. [Volume 7/315]
Mahmoud. L. Hunt. [Volume 7/305]
The Nobleman and the Pensioner. G. Pfeffel.
[Volume 7/303]
Prince Adeb. G. Boker. [Volume 7/308]
The Sack of the City. V. Hugo. [Volume 9/26]
The Slaying of Sohrab, fr. Sohrab and Rustum. M.
Arnold. [Volume 9/28]
Orion Dead. H. Doolittle. [Supp 5/71]
Ormsby, John (tr.)
Battle Scene, fr. The Cid. Unknown. [Volume 8/205]
"The orphan boat of my heart." Multitudinous Stars
and Spring Waters: 004. Ping Hsin. [Supp 5/116]
*Orpheus (Mythology)*
Orpheus in the Underworld. D. Gascoyne. [Supp
2/385]
Orpheus in the Underworld. D. Gascoyne. [Supp 2/385]
"Orpheus, with his lute, made trees." Influence of
Music, fr. King Henry Eighth. W. Shakespeare.
[Volume 6/362]
"Orpheus, 't is said, the Thracian lyre-strings
sweeping." The Immortality of a Genius. S.
Propertius. [Volume 6/357]
Orr, James
The Irishman. [Volume 8/52]
Ortiz, Simon
The Serenity in Stones. [Supp 4/315]
Survival This Way. [Supp 4/314]
To Insure Survival. [Supp 4/317]
What I Tell Him. [Supp 4/316]
Osgood, Frances Sargent
Labor. [Volume 6/389]
Osgood, Kate Putnam
Driving Home the Cows. [Volume 8/404]
O'Shaughnessy, Arthur
"Has Summer Come Without the Rose?" [Volume 3/54]
Ossawatomie. C. Sandburg. [Supp 1/282]
Othello's Defence, fr. Othello. W. Shakespeare.
[Volume 2/207]
Othello's Remorse, fr. Othello. W. Shakespeare.
[Volume 9/67]
The Other Half. J. Wright. [Supp 5/331]
The Other World. H. Stowe. [Volume 4/389]
"Our band is few, but true and tried." Song of
Marion's Men. W. Byrant. [Volume 8/330]
"Our Boat to the Waves" W. Channing. [Volume 5/409]
"Our bugles sang truce, - for the night-cloud had."
The Soldier's Dream. T. Campbell. [Volume
1/280]
"OUr bugles sound gayly. To horse and away!" Calvary
Song. R. Raymond. [Volume 8/366]
"Our camp-fires shone bright on the mountains."
Sherman's March to the Sea. S. Byers. [Volume
8/406]
Our Country's Call. W. Bryant. [Volume 8/98]
Our Daily Bread. C. Vallejo. [Supp 6/188]
Our Fallen Heroes. G. Griffith. [Volume 8/449]
"Our father land! and wouldst thou know." Fataher and
Mother Tongue. S. Lover. [Volume 8/6]
"Our Father who I know is on earth." Prayer. G.
Fuertes. [Supp 5/95]
"Our fathers' God! from out whose hand." Centennial
Hymn. J. Whittier. [Volume 8/457]
Our Garden. C. Anwar. [Supp 7/78]
"Our garden %doesn't spread out very far, it's a
little affair." Our Garden. C. Anwar. [Supp
7/78]
"Our god, Our help in Ages Past" I. Watts. [Volume
4/32]
"Our good steeds snuff the evening air." Calvary Song,
fr. Alice of Monmouth. E. Stedman. [Volume
8/365]
Our Hands in the Garden. A. Hebert. [Supp 5/110]
"Our life is twofold; sleep hath its own world." The

Dream. G. Byron. [Volume 3/73]
"Our oil gushing forth in the desert." What Value Has
the People Whose Tongue Is Tied?: 015. N.
Qabbani. [Supp 7/289]
Our Orders. J. Howe. [Volume 8/381]
"Our revels now are ended. These our actors." Airy
Nothings, fr. The Tempest. W. Shakespeare.
[Volume 6/58]
"Our single purpose was to walk through snow." Polar
Exploration. S. Spender. [Supp 2/230]
Our Skater Belle. Unknown. [Volume 5/190]
"Our skins are numbed, unfeeling." What Value Has the
People Whose Tongue Is Tied?: 014. N. Qabbani.
[Supp 7/289]
Our State. J. Whittier. [Volume 8/93]
Our Wee White Rose. G. Massey. [Volume 1/64]
"Our youthtime passes down a colonnade." O Dreams, O
Destinations: 004. C. Day Lewis. [Supp 2/119]
"Out from behind this bending, rough-cut mask." Out
from Behind This Mask. W. Whitman. [Volume
7/100]
Out from Behind This Mask. W. Whitman. [Volume 7/100]
"Out of abysses o illiteracy." Dark Symphony: 6.
Tempo di Marcia. M. Tolson. [Supp 4/400]
"Out of fear, they built a dwelling place."
Lamentations: 3. The Covenant. L. Gluck. [Supp
5/106]
"Out of her own body she pushed." Grandmother. P.
Allen. [Supp 4/304]
"Out of the bosom of the air." Snow-flakes. H.
Longfellow. [Volume 5/174]
"Out of the clover and blue-eyed grass." Driving Home
the Cows. K. Osgood. [Volume 8/404]
"Out of the golden remote wild west where the sea."
Hesperia. A. Swinburne. [Volume 2/267]
"Out of the hills of Habersham." Song of the
Chattahoochee. S. Lanier. [Volume 7/242]
"Out of the night that covers me." Invictus. W.
Henley. [Volume 3/221]
"Out of the Old House, Nancy" W. Carleton. [Volume
1/268]
"Out of the tomb we bring Badroulbadour." The Worms
at Heaven's Gate. W. Stevens. [Supp 1/291]
"Out on the furthest tether let it run." The
Undiscovered Planet. L. Lee. [Supp 2/343]
"Out, Out--" R. Frost. [Supp 1/133]
"Out upon it. I have loved." Constancy. S. Suckling.
[Volume 2/23]
"Outstretched beneath the leafy shade." The Greenwood
Shrift. R. Southey. [Volume 7/379]
Outward Bound. T. Aldrich. [Volume 6/123]
"Over hill, over dale." Fairy's Song, fr. A Midsummer
Night's Dream. W. Shakespeare. [Volume 6/16]
"Over his keys the musing organist." The Vision of
Sir Launfal. J. Lowell. [Volume 4/172]
"Over the dumb campagna-sea." A View Across the roman
Campagna. E. Browning. [Volume 7/187]
"Over the Hill to the Poor-house" W. Carleton.
[Volume 3/175]
Over the River. N. Priest. [Volume 3/406]
"Over the river they beckon to me." Over the River. N.
Priest. [Volume 3/406]
"Over the snows." The Snows. C. Sangster. [Volume
5/203]
"Overloaded, undermanned, %trusting to a lee." The
Coasters. T. Day. [Volume 7/153]
Ovid (Publius Ovidius Naso)
A Transformation, fr. The Metamorphoses. H. King
(tr.). [Volume 6/87]
The Owl. B. Procter. [Volume 5/321]
The Owl and the Pussy-cat. E. Lear. [Volume 1/175]
"The owl and the pussy-cat went to sea." The Owl and
the Pussy-cat. E. Lear. [Volume 1/175]
Owl Song. M. Atwood. [Supp 5/20]
The Ox. S. Murano. [Supp 7/121]

The **Ox**, fr. Poesie. G. Carducci. [Volume 5/359]
"The **ox** he openeth wide the doore." Tryste Noel. L.
   Guiney. [Volume 4/61]
The **Oxen**. T. Hardy. [Supp 1/159]
**Oxus**, fr. Sohrab and Rustum. M. Arnold. [Volume
   5/207]

**Pack** Clouds Away. T. Heywood. [Volume 5/41]
"**Pack** clouds away, and welcome day." Pack Clouds Away.
   T. Heywood. [Volume 5/41]
**Pagan, Isabel**
   Ca' The Yowes. [Volume 2/176]
*Paganism*
   Stylite. L. MacNeice. [Supp 2/183]
**Pagis, Dan**
   The Beginning. S. Mitchell (tr.). [Supp 7/251]
   Brothers. S. Mitchell (tr.). [Supp 7/247]
   The Caveman Is Not About to Talk. S. Mitchell
      (tr.). [Supp 7/248]
   Jason's Grave in Jerusalem. S. Mitchell (tr.).
      [Supp 7/250]
   Snake. S. Mitchell (tr.). [Supp 7/250]
   The Story. S. Mitchell (tr.). [Supp 7/249]
   Sudden Heart. S. Mitchell (tr.). [Supp 7/252]
**Pain** for a Daughter. A. Sexton. [Supp 5/260]
"**Pain** is something useless." A Private View. D.
   Ravikovitch. [Supp 5/236]
**Paine, Thomas**
   Liberty Tree. [Volume 8/324]
"**Pain's** furnace heat withing me quivers." I Hold
   Still. J. Sturm. [Volume 3/243]
A **Painted** Fan. L. Moulton. [Volume 6/385]
**Painted** Windows. G. Fuertes. [Supp 5/96]
*Painting and Painters*
   Musee des Beaux Arts. W. Auden. [Supp 2/164]
   The Sitting. C. Day Lewis. [Supp 2/122]
**Pak Tu-Jin**
   April. S. Solberg (tr.). [Supp 7/153]
   Heavenly Lake. S. Solberg (tr.). [Supp 7/155]
   Hymn to the Graveyard. S. Solberg (tr.). [Supp
      7/151]
   A Message from the Crane. S. Solberg (tr.). [Supp
      7/154]
   Song. S. Solberg (tr.). [Supp 7/154]
   Stars. S. Solberg (tr.). [Supp 7/151]
   Sun. S. Solberg (tr.). [Supp 7/152]
**Palabras** Carinosas. T. Aldrich. [Volume 2/281]
**Palace** of Grace. A. Hamzah. [Supp 7/90]
**Palaez, Juan Sanchez**
   Dark Bond. [Supp 6/197]
   Depth of Love. [Supp 6/196]
   "The Immediate %Clear and Fleeting" [Supp 6/198]
**Palandri, Angela C. Y. Jung (tr.)**
   Beyond Ashes. Lo Fu. [Supp 7/28]
   Beyond the Sea. Lo Fu. [Supp 7/27]
   Beyong the Whip. Lo Fu. [Supp 7/29]
   Bo Tree. Lin Ling. [Supp 7/23]
   Broken Mirror. Yung Tzu. [Supp 7/35]
   Chicago. Ya Hsuan. [Supp 7/30]
   Fire on the Sea Floor. Hsiung Hung. [Supp 7/10]
   God. Ya Hsuan. [Supp 7/34]
   I Sing for You. Lin Ling. [Supp 7/24]
   New-Born Blackness. Lo Fu. [Supp 7/26]
   Purple. Lin Ling. [Supp 7/24]
   San-Kan River. Ya Hsuan. [Supp 7/31]
   The Triangular Window. Yung Tzu. [Supp 7/36]
   "Walking Out of Expectation" Hsiung Hung. [Supp
      7/9]
   Winter Fancy. Yung Tzu. [Supp 7/37]
**Palgrave, Francis Turner**
   The Ancient and Modern Muses. [Volume 6/337]
   A Danish Barrow. [Volume 8/213]

A Little Child's Hymn. [Volume 1/120]
**Palinode**, Autumn. J. Lowell. [Volume 3/115]
**Palladas**
   The Generous Air. W. Hardinge (tr.). [Volume
      6/229]
"**Pallid** with too much longing." Laus Veneris. L.
   Moulton. [Volume 7/138]
**Palm** and the Pine. H. Heine. [Volume 3/40]
The **Palm-tree**. J. Whittier. [Volume 5/229]
**Palmer, John Williamson**
   For Charlie's Sake. [Volume 3/411]
   Stonewall Jackson's Way. [Volume 8/360]
   Thread and Song. [Volume 1/113]
**Palmer, Ray**
   I Saw Thee. [Volume 4/340]
**Palmer, William Pitt**
   The Smack in School. [Volume 1/167]
**Pan** in Wall Street. E. Stedman. [Volume 6/381]
**Panta** Rei. T. Heraty. [Supp 7/93]
The **Pantheon**, fr. Childe Harold. G. Byron. [Volume
   7/181]
**Paper**. B. Franklin. [Volume 9/289]
*Paper Houses*
   The Deck That Pouts. M. Piercy. [Supp 5/198]
"**Pap's** got his patent right, and rich as all
   creation." Griggsby's Station. J. Riley.
   [Volume 9/349]
A **Parable**. M. Blind. [Volume 1/95]
**Paracas**. A. Cisneros. [Supp 6/186]
**Paradise**. F. Faber. [Volume 4/434]
**Paradise**. Nirala. [Supp 7/67]
**Paradise** Lost, sels. J. Milton. [Volume 4/262]
**Paradise**: Sin and Redemption, fr. The Diving Comedy.
   Dante Alighieri. [Volume 4/441]
**Paradise**: The Saints in Glory, fr. The Diving Comedy.
   Dante Alighieri. [Volume 4/445]
**Paradise**: The Triumph of Christ, fr. The Diving
   Comedy. Dante Alighieri. [Volume 4/443]
*Paranoia*
   The Woman Who Disapproved of Music at the Bar. H.
   Gregory. [Supp 2/67]
*Parenthood*
   The Two Parents. H. MacDiarmid. [Supp 2/31]
   The Voice. W. Gibson. [Supp 1/141]
*Parents*
   Lamentations: 3. The Covenant. L. Gluck. [Supp
   5/106]
**Paris**, Buddha, Stars and i. F. Daglarca. [Supp 7/301]
**Park, Andrew**
   The Auld Folks. [Volume 1/333]
"The **park**, the heart, you see at town's center is
   soft." Last Look at La Plata, Missouri. J.
   Barnes. [Supp 4/298]
**Parker, Dorothy**
   Somebody's Song. [Supp 1/248]
**Parker, Gilbert**
   Art. [Volume 6/345]
**Parker, Theodore**
   The Higher Good. [Volume 4/133]
   The Way, the Truth, and the Life. [Volume 4/92]
*Parks*
   An Autumn Park. D. Gascoyne. [Supp 2/379]
**Parliament** Hill Fields. J. Betjeman. [Supp 2/136]
**Parnell, Frances Isabel**
   After Death. [Volume 8/68]
**Parnell, Thomas**
   "When Your Beauty Appears" [Volume 2/278]
*Parodies*
   The Arab. C. Calverley. [Volume 9/413]
   The Auld Wife. C. Calverley. [Volume 9/387]
   Belagcholly Days. Unknown. [Volume 9/420]
   The Cock and the Bull. C. Calverley. [Volume
   9/402]
   A Conservative. C. Gilman. [Volume 9/422]
   Deborah Lee. W. Burleigh. [Volume 9/400]

041. O. Khayyam. [Volume 6/212]
**Perry, Nora**
    The Love-Knot. [Volume 2/126]
    Riding Down. [Volume 1/206]
**Perseus**. L. MacNeice. [Supp 2/182]
**Perseverance**. L. Da Vinci. [Volume 6/284]
*Perseverance*
    The Conflict. C. Day Lewis. [Supp 2/112]
    The Dead Ride Fast. R. Blackmur. [Supp 2/107]
    Homage to the British Museum. W. Empson. [Supp 2/141]
    "Rest From Loving and Be Living" C. Day Lewis. [Supp 2/122]
    This Last Pain. W. Empson. [Supp 2/145]
**Personal Resurrection**, fr. In Memoriam. A. Tennyson. [Volume 3/352]
**Peter Quince at the Clavier**. W. Stevens. [Supp 1/289]
**Peters, Lenrie**
    Isatou Died. [Supp 6/18]
    "Mine Is the Silent Face" [Supp 6/19]
**Petition**. W. Auden. [Supp 2/167]
**A Petition** to Time. B. Procter. [Volume 1/334]
The **Petrified Fern**. M. Branch. [Volume 6/200]
**Pettee, G. W.**
    Sleigh Song. [Volume 5/189]
**Pfeffel, Gotlieb Conrad**
    The Nobleman and the Pensioner. C. Brooks (tr.). [Volume 7/303]
**Phelps, Charles Henry**
    Henry Ward Beecher. [Volume 7/24]
**Philip, My King**. D. Craik. [Volume 1/16]
**Phillida** and Corydon. N. Breton. [Volume 2/152]
**Phillips, Ambrose (tr.)**
    Blest as the Immortal Gods. Sappho. [Volume 2/97]
**Phillips and Vinita Atmiyanandana Lalwer, Herbert (tr.)**
    "I Am a University Student" S. Wongthed. [Supp 7/185]
    "Oh! Temple, Temple of Bot!" S. Wongthed. [Supp 7/186]
**"Phillis Is My Only Joy"** J. Sedley. [Volume 2/22]
**Philomela's Ode**. R. Greene. [Volume 2/79]
**Philomena**. M. Arnold. [Volume 5/308]
The **Philosopher** Toad. R. Nichols. [Volume 4/234]
**Philostratus**
    "Drink To Me Only With Thine Eyes." fr. The Forest. B. Jonson (tr.). [Volume 2/16]
*Photographs*
    Portrait of a Negative. A. Kuo. [Supp 4/7]
*Photos*
    "I Swear %By That Summer Photo" B. Akhmadulina. [Supp 5/3]
**Phycholophon**. G. Burgess. [Volume 9/456]
**Physics**. W. Whewell. [Volume 9/434]
"The **piano** tuner spoke to me, that tenderest." Pyrargyrite Metal, 9. C. Meireles. [Supp 5/164]
**Piatt, John James**
    Ireland. [Volume 8/66]
    To a Lady. [Volume 2/47]
**Piatt, Sarah M. B.**
    The Witch in the Glass. [Volume 1/46]
**Piatt, Sarah Morgan Bryan**
    The Term of Death. [Volume 3/261]
**Piazza** Piece. J. Ransom. [Supp 1/260]
**"Pibroch** of Donuil Dhu" S. Scott. [Volume 8/311]
**"Picciola"** R. Newell. [Volume 8/285]
A **Picture**. C. Eastman. [Volume 1/315]
A **Picture** of Death, fr. The Giaour. G. Byron. [Volume 3/261]
**Pictures** of Memory. A. Cary. [Volume 1/76]
The **Pied** Piper of Hamelin. R. Browning. [Volume 6/169]
**Piercy, Marge**
    Ascending Scale. [Supp 5/202]
    The Deck That Pouts. [Supp 5/198]

Mornings in Various Years: 001. [Supp 5/200]
Mornings in Various Years: 002. [Supp 5/200]
Mornings in Various Years: 003. [Supp 5/201]
The Window of the Woman Burning. [Supp 5/197]
The World comes Back Like an Old Cat. [Supp 5/200]
**Piero Della Francesca**. A. Ridler. [Supp 2/276]
**Pierpont, John**
    My Child. [Volume 3/417]
    Not on the Battle-field. [Volume 8/429]
    Passing Away. [Volume 4/350]
    Warren's Address. [Volume 8/326]
    Whittling. [Volume 1/89]
**Pietri, Pedro**
    "Do Not Let" [Supp 4/258]
    Song Without Words. [Supp 4/256]
**Pike, Albert**
    Dixie. [Volume 8/106]
The **Pilgrimage**. S. Raleigh. [Volume 4/335]
The **Pilgrims** and the Peas. J. Wolcott. [Volume 9/249]
A **Pilot** from the Carrier. R. Jarrell. [Supp 2/332]
**Pindar, Peter [pseud.]** See Wolcott, John
*Pine Trees*
    Choosing a Mast. R. Campbell. [Supp 2/92]
    "Now Pine-Needles" S. Smith. [Supp 5/286]
**Ping Hsin**
    Deliverance. Kai-yu Hsu (tr.). [Supp 5/118]
    For the Record. K. Rexroth and Ling Chung (tr.). [Supp 5/115]
    Multitudinous Stars and Sping Waters: 001. K. Rexroth and Ling Chung (tr.). [Supp 5/116]
    Multitudinous Stars and Sping Waters: 002. K. Rexroth and Ling Chung (tr.). [Supp 5/116]
    Multitudinous Stars and Spring Waters: 003. K. Rexroth and Ling Chung (tr.). [Supp 5/116]
    Multitudinous Stars and Spring Waters: 004. K. Rexroth and Ling Chung (tr.). [Supp 5/116]
    Multitudinous Stars and Spring Waters: 005. K. Rexroth and Ling Chung (tr.). [Supp 5/116]
    Multitudinous Stars and Spring Waters: 006. K. Rexroth and Ling Chung (tr.). [Supp 5/117]
    Multitudinous Stars and Spring Waters: 007. K. Rexroth and Ling Chung (tr.). [Supp 5/117]
    Multitudinous Stars and Spring Waters: 008. K. Rexroth and Ling Chung (tr.). [Supp 5/117]
    Multitudinous Stars and Spring Waters: 009. K. Rexroth and Ling Chung (tr.). [Supp 5/117]
    Remembering. K. Rexroth and Ling Chung (tr.). [Supp 5/114]
    The Stars: 002. Kai-yu Hsu (tr.). [Supp 5/119]
    The Stars: 012. Kai-yu Hsu (tr.). [Supp 5/119]
    The Stars: 034. Kai-yu Hsu (tr.). [Supp 5/119]
    The Stars: 048. Kai-yu Hsu (tr.). [Supp 5/119]
    The Stars: 052. Kai-yu Hsu (tr.). [Supp 5/119]
**Pinkney, Edward Coate**
    A Health. [Volume 2/41]
**"The Pipe."** Nehru. S. Takahashi. [Supp 7/127]
**"Piped** the blackbird, on the beechwood spray." Little Bell. T. Westwood. [Volume 1/135]
The **Piper**. W. Blake. [Volume 1/96]
**"Piping** down the valleys wild." The Piper. W. Blake. [Volume 1/96]
*Pirates*
    The Tarry Buccaneer. J. Masefield. [Supp 1/207]
**Pitt, William**
    The Sailor's Consolation. [Volume 5/435]
**Pitter, Ruth**
    Apology. [Supp 5/205]
    But for Lust. [Supp 2/48]
    The Difference. [Supp 5/205]
    The Military Harpist. [Supp 2/48]
    The Serious Child. [Supp 5/207]
    The Tigress. [Supp 2/50]
    The Viper. [Supp 2/51]
    Vision of the Cuckoo. [Supp 5/206]
**"Pity** the sorrows of a poor old man!" The Beggar. T.

The Immortality of a Genius. J. Cranstoun (tr.).
[Volume 6/357]
**Prophecy.** Adonis. [Supp 7/280]
The **Prospect.** E. Browning. [Volume 4/347]
**Prospice.** R. Browning. [Volume 3/392]
**Protea.** D. Mattera. [Supp 6/80]
"The **protea** is not a flower." Protea. D. Mattera.
[Supp 6/80]
"**Proud** and lowly, beggar and lord." London Bridge. F.
Weatherly. [Volume 6/238]
The **Proud** Miss MacBride. J. Saxe. [Volume 9/228]
**Prout, Father [pseud.]** See Mahony, Francis
**Provincia** Deserta. E. Pound. [Supp 1/251]
"A **prowling** wolf, whose shaggy skin." The Wolf and
the Dog. J. Fontaine. [Volume 8/121]
A **Psalm** of Life. H. Longfellow. [Volume 4/275]
"A **public** haunt they found her in." A Girl of Pompeii.
E. Martin. [Volume 1/208]
*Puerto Rico*
  Song for My Father. J. Hagedorn. [Supp 4/24]
*Puffballs*
  The Giant Puffball. E. Blunden. [Supp 2/44]
The **Pumpkin.** J. Whittier. [Volume 5/270]
**Punch**
  The Collegian to His Bride. [Volume 9/434]
"The **pure** air trembles, O pitiless God." Noon. R.
Jeffers. [Supp 1/175]
**Purgatory:** Fire of Purification, fr. The Diving
Comedy. Dante Alighieri. [Volume 4/439]
**Purgatory:** Man's Free-will, fr. The Diving Comedy.
Dante Alighieri. [Volume 4/438]
**Purgatory:** Prayer, fr. The Diving Comedy. Dante
Alighieri. [Volume 4/436]
**Purgatory:** Prayer of Penitents, fr. The Diving Comedy.
Dante Alighieri. [Volume 4/437]
**Purple.** Lin Ling. [Supp 7/24]
The **Purple** Cow. G. Burgess. [Volume 9/455]
A **Purse.** G. Stein. [Supp 5/292]
"A **purse** was not green, it was not straw color, it
was hardly seen." A Purse. G. Stein. [Supp
5/292]
**Pursuit.** R. Warren. [Supp 2/132]
**Pushkin, Aleksander Sergyevich**
  The Last Leaf. J. Pollen (tr.). [Volume 3/187]
"'**Put** up the sword!' the voice of Christ once."
Disarmament. J. Whittier. [Volume 8/425]
**Pyrargyrite** Metal, 9. C. Meireles. [Supp 5/164]
The **Pythoness.** K. Raine. [Supp 2/201]


**Qabbani, Nizzar**
  What Value Has the People Whose Tongue is Tied?:
  001. M. Khouri and Hamid Algar (tr.). [Supp
  7/286]
  What Value Has the People Whose Tongue is Tied?:
  002. M. Khouri and Hamid Algar (tr.). [Supp
  7/286]
  What Value Has the People Whose Tongue is Tied?:
  003. M. Khouri and Hamid Algar (tr.). [Supp
  7/286]
  What Value Has the People Whose Tongue is Tied?:
  004. M. Khouri and Hamid Algar (tr.). [Supp
  7/287]
  What Value Has the People Whose Tongue is Tied?:
  005. M. Khouri and Hamid Algar (tr.). [Supp
  7/287]
  What Value Has the People Whose Tongue is Tied?:
  006. M. Khouri and Hamid Algar (tr.). [Supp
  7/287]
  What Value Has the People Whose Tongue Is Tied?:
  007. M. Khouri and Hamid Algar (tr.). [Supp
  7/287]
  What Value Has the People Whose Tongue Is Tied?:

008. M. Khouri and Hamid Algar (tr.). [Supp
7/287]
What Value Has the People Whose Tongue Is Tied?:
009. M. Khouri and Hamid Algar (tr.). [Supp
7/288]
What Value Has the People Whose Tongue Is Tied?:
010. M. Khouri and Hamid Algar (tr.). [Supp
7/288]
What Value Has the People Whose Tongue Is Tied?:
011. M. Khouri and Hamid Algar (tr.). [Supp
7/288]
What Value Has the People Whose Tongue Is Tied?:
012. M. Khouri and Hamid Algar (tr.). [Supp
7/288]
What Value Has the People Whose Tongue Is Tied?:
013. M. Khouri and Hamid Algar (tr.). [Supp
7/288]
What Value Has the People Whose Tongue Is Tied?:
014. M. Khouri and Hamid Algar (tr.). [Supp
7/289]
What Value Has the People Whose Tongue Is Tied?:
015. M. Khouri and Hamid Algar (tr.). [Supp
7/289]
What Value Has the People Whose Tongue Is Tied?:
016. M. Khouri and Hamid Algar (tr.). [Supp
7/289]
What Value Has the People Whose Tongue Is Tied?:
017. M. Khouri and Hamid Algar (tr.). [Supp
7/290]
What Value Has the People Whose Tongue Is Tied?:
018. M. Khouri and Hamid Algar (tr.). [Supp
7/290]
What Value Has the People Whose Tongue Is Tied?:
019. M. Khouri and Hamid Algar (tr.). [Supp
7/291]
What Value Has the People Whose Tongue Is Tied?:
020. M. Khouri and Hamid Algar (tr.). [Supp
7/291]
**Qua** Cursum Ventus. A. Clough. [Volume 3/107]
**Quack** Medicines, fr. The Borough. G. Crabbe. [Volume
6/287]
The **Quaker** Graveyard. S. Mitchell. [Volume 3/278]
The **Quaker** Graveyard in Nantucket: 001. R. Lowell.
[Supp 2/394]
The **Quaker** Graveyard in Nantucket: 002. R. Lowell.
[Supp 2/395]
The **Quaker** Graveyard in Nantucket: 003. R. Lowell.
[Supp 2/395]
The **Quaker** Graveyard in Nantucket: 004. R. Lowell.
[Supp 2/396]
The **Quaker** Graveyard in Nantucket: 005. R. Lowell.
[Supp 2/397]
The **Quaker** Graveyard in Nantucket: 006. R. Lowell.
[Supp 2/397]
The **Quaker** Graveyard in Nantucket: 007. R. Lowell.
[Supp 2/398]
**Quarles, Francis**
  Delight in God. [Volume 4/34]
  A Mystical Ecstasy. [Volume 4/142]
  The Vanity of the World. [Volume 3/153]
**Quarrel** of Brutus and Cassius, fr. Julius Caesar. W.
Shakespeare. [Volume 1/381]
The **Queen** Forgets. G. Sterling. [Supp 1/287]
"The **queen** looked up, and said." The Foolish Virgins,
fr. Idyls of the KingL Guinevere. A. Tennyson.
[Volume 4/331]
**Queen** Mab, fr. Romeo and Juliet. W. Shakespeare.
[Volume 6/13]
**Queen Mary of Hungary**
  Prayer. [Volume 4/124]
**Quennell, Peter**
  Leviathan. [Supp 1/254]
A **Query.** Unknown. [Volume 4/146]
The **Question.** P. Shelley. [Volume 5/272]
**Quevedo Y. Villegas, Francisco de**

A Private View. W. Bargad and Stanley Chyet (tr.). [Supp 5/236]
Time Caught in a Net. W. Bargad and Stanley Chyet (tr.). [Supp 5/232]
Tirzah and the Wide World. W. Bargad and Stanley Chyet (tr.). [Supp 5/233]
**Raymond, Grace [pseud.] See Stillman, Annie R.**
**Raymond, Rossiter Worthington**
The Ascent of Man. [Volume 6/202]
Blessed Are They. [Volume 3/425]
Calvary Song. [Volume 8/366]
Christus Consolator. [Volume 3/432]
**Raymond, Rossiter Worthington (tr.)**
The Trooper's Death. G. Herwegh. [Volume 8/220]
The **Razor-seller.** J. Wolcott. [Volume 9/287]
**"Reaching** down arm-deep into bright water." Shells. K. Raine. [Supp 5/224]
**Read, Herbert**
Bombing Casualties in Spain. [Supp 2/32]
The Contrary Experience: 001. [Supp 2/32]
The Contrary Experience: 002. [Supp 2/33]
The Contrary Experience: 003. [Supp 2/34]
Sic et Non: I. The Complaint of Heloise. [Supp 2/34]
Sic et Non: II. The Portrait of Abelard. [Supp 2/35]
A World Within a War: 001. [Supp 2/36]
A World withing a War: 002. [Supp 2/38]
A World withing a War: 003. [Supp 2/39]
A World withing a War: 004. [Supp 2/41]
A World withing a War: 005. [Supp 2/42]
**Read, Thomas Buchanan**
The Brave at Home. [Volume 8/109]
The Closing Scene. [Volume 8/416]
Drifting. [Volume 7/195]
Sheridan's Ride. [Volume 8/383]
**Readers** of Newspapers. M. Tsvetayeva. [Supp 5/302]
*Reading*
The Story. D. Pagis. [Supp 7/249]
**Reading** Hamlet. A. Akhmatova. [Supp 5/6]
**Reading Time:** 1 Minute 26 Seconds. M. Rukeyser. [Supp 2/304]
**Realf, Richard**
A Holy Nation. [Volume 8/178]
Indirection. [Volume 6/332]
*Reality*
The Flowering of the Rod: 009. H. Doolittle. [Supp 5/78]
The **Reaper** and the Flowers. H. Longfellow. [Volume 3/417]
**Reapers.** J. Toomer. [Supp 4/88]
*Reapers*
Reapers. J. Toomer. [Supp 4/88]
*Reason*
Killing One's Gods. G. Senanayake. [Supp 7/183]
Of Reason and Discovery. D. Mattera. [Supp 6/80]
Rebecca's Hymn, fr. Ivanhoe. S. Scott. [Volume 4/205]
**"Rebel** poets, who've given vicar aid." In Poets' Defence. J. Wheelwright. [Supp 2/54]
**Recessional.** R. Kipling. [Supp 1/179]
A **Recipe.** S. Smith. [Volume 9/385]
*Recollection*
Early Recollections. E. Chuilleanain. [Supp 5/192]
**"Recovery** - daughter of creation too." My Recovery. F. Klopstock. [Volume 4/293]
The **Recruit.** R. Chambers. [Volume 9/321]
**"Red** fool, laughing comrade." To a Comrade in Arms. A. Lewis. [Supp 2/378]
The **Red** Lacquer Music-Stand. A. Lowell. [Supp 1/198]
**Red** Ridinghood. N. Alterman. [Supp 7/236]
**"The red-tiled** towers of the old Chateau." Chateau Papineau. S. Harrison. [Volume 7/253]
**"Redeemed** %From Sleep" N. Sachs. [Supp 5/253]
**Rediscovery.** K. Awoonor. [Supp 6/20]
**Reed and Clive Wake, John (tr.)**

In Memoriam. L. Senghor. [Supp 6/76]
Prayer to Masks. L. Senghor. [Supp 6/74]
Snow Upon Paris. L. Senghor. [Supp 6/73]
Totem. L. Senghor. [Supp 6/75]
**Reed, Henry**
Lessons of the War: Judging Distances. [Supp 2/344]
**Reflections** in an Iron Workds. H. MacDiarmid. [Supp 2/30]
The **Reformer.** J. Whittier. [Volume 8/157]
A **Refusal** to Mourn the Death, by Fire of a Child in London. D. Thomas. [Supp 2/368]
*Regret*
La Figlia Che Piange. T. Eliot. [Supp 1/120]
*Rejection*
Letter to Time. C. Alegria. [Supp 5/14]
The **Relief** of Lucknow. R. Lowell. [Volume 8/296]
*Religion*
Abide wth Me. H. Lyte. [Volume 4/76]
After the Surprising Conversions. R. Lowell. [Supp 2/386]
The Angels' Song. E. Sears. [Volume 4/48]
Art Thou Weary. S. Stephen the Sabaite. [Volume 4/87]
A Ballad of Trees and the Master. S. Lanier. [Volume 4/69]
Brahma. R. Emerson. [Volume 4/6]
Brief: "Two Went Up to the Temple to Pray" R. Crashaw. [Volume 4/306]
Brief: The Widow's Mites. R. Crashaw. [Volume 4/306]
Brief: Water Turned Into Wine. R. Crashaw. [Volume 4/306]
Caedmon. L. Lee. [Supp 2/338]
Cana. J. Clarke. [Volume 4/65]
The Christ. R. Trench. [Volume 4/75]
A Christmas Hymn. A. Domett. [Volume 4/59]
The Church Porch, sel. G. Herbert. [Volume 4/304]
Conscience and Remorse. P. Dunbar. [Volume 4/326]
Conscience, frm Saitire XIII. Juvenal. [Volume 4/329]
The Conversion of Saint Paul. J. Keble. [Volume 4/82]
The Cost of Worth, fr. Bitter Sweet. J. Holland. [Volume 4/300]
The Cry of the Human. E. Browning. [Volume 4/286]
Dallying with Temptation, fr. Wallenstein. S. Coleridge. [Volume 4/327]
De sheepfol! S. Greene. [Volume 4/67]
Delight in God. F. Quarles. [Volume 4/34]
The Departure from Paradise, Book XII, fr. Paradise Lost. J. Milton. [Volume 4/273]
Dies Irae. T. Celano. [Volume 4/100]
The Disciples After the Ascension. A. Stanley. [Volume 4/77]
Duty. E. Hooper. [Volume 4/277]
Epiphany. R. Heber. [Volume 4/50]
The Eternal Goodness. J. Whittier. [Volume 4/42]
Eve to Adam, fr. Paradise Lost. J. Milton. [Volume 4/273]
Eve's Lament, fr. Paradise Lost. J. Milton. [Volume 4/272]
Example. J. Keble. [Volume 4/309]
The Faithful Angel, fr. Paradise Lost. J. Milton. [Volume 4/337]
The Fall, fr. Paradise Lost. J. Milton. [Volume 4/268]
Father, Thy Will Be Done! S. Adams. [Volume 4/34]
The Flight Into Egypt. F. Mahony. [Volume 4/62]
The Foolish Virgins, fr. Idyls of the KingL Guinevere. A. Tennyson. [Volume 4/331]
Found Wanting. E. Dickinson. [Volume 4/326]
Frankford's Soliloquy, fr. A Woman Killed with Kindness. O. Huckel. [Volume 4/328]
The Gifts of God. G. Herbert. [Volume 4/276]

God. G. Dershavin. [Volume 4/24]

God and Man, fr. Essay on Man. A. Pope. [Volume 4/21]

God is Everywhere. R. Nicoll. [Volume 4/28]

The Good Shepherd with the Kid. M. Arnold. [Volume 4/68]

Good-bye. R. Emerson. [Volume 4/31]

Heritage. C. Cullen. [Supp 1/96]

The Hills of the Lord. W. Gannett. [Volume 4/19]

Holy Poems: 001. G. Barker. [Supp 2/284]

Holy Poems: 002. G. Barker. [Supp 2/284]

Holy Poems: 003. G. Barker. [Supp 2/285]

The Holy Spirit. R. Herrick. [Volume 4/108]

Hope of the Human Heart, fr. Anima Mundi. R. Milnes. [Volume 4/110]

Hymn. S. Coleridge. [Volume 4/15]

Hymn to Zeus. Cleanthes. [Volume 4/7]

"I Gave My Life for Thee" F. Havergal. [Volume 4/95]

I Saw Thee. R. Palmer. [Volume 4/340]

"I Would I Were An Excellent Divine" N. Breton. [Volume 4/312]

In Prison. M. Smith. [Volume 4/323]

Intercession and Redeoption, Book XI, fr. Paradise Lost. J. Milton. [Volume 4/270]

Jesus Shall Reign. I. Watts. [Volume 4/96]

Jewish Hymn in Babylon. H. Milman. [Volume 4/307]

Judge Not. A. Proctor. [Volume 4/319]

Knocking, Ever Knocking. H. Stowe. [Volume 4/92]

The Laborer. W. Gallagher. [Volume 4/302]

The Ladder of Saint Augustine. H. Longfellow. [Volume 4/294]

The Landscape near an Aerodome. S. Spender. [Supp 2/228]

Lead, Kindly Light. J. Newman. [Volume 4/41]

Light Shining Out of Darkness. W. Cowper. [Volume 4/23]

Litany. S. Grant. [Volume 4/74]

"Lord! When Those Glorious Lights I See" G. Wither. [Volume 4/14]

Losse in Delayes. R. Southwell. [Volume 4/341]

The Lost Sheep. E. Clephane. [Volume 4/66]

The Love of God. E. Scudder. [Volume 4/39]

Love to Christ, fr. An Hymne of Heavenly Love. E. Spenser. [Volume 4/90]

Low Spirits. F. Faber. [Volume 4/338]

The Martyrs' Hymn. M. Luther. [Volume 4/334]

The Masters' Touch. H. Bonar. [Volume 4/337]

Meditations of a Hindu Prince. S. Lyall. [Volume 4/3]

Messiah. A. Pope. [Volume 4/97]

"Might Fortress Is Our God" M. Luther. [Volume 4/33]

"My God, I Love Thee" S. Xavier. [Volume 4/103]

My Recovery. F. Klopstock. [Volume 4/293]

Myrrh-Bearers. M. Preston. [Volume 4/72]

Nothing But Leaves. L. Akerman. [Volume 4/283]

"O Fire of God, the Comforter" S. Hildegarde. [Volume 4/107]

"O Little Town of Bethlehem" P. Brooks. [Volume 4/47]

Ode to Duty. W. Wordsworth. [Volume 4/278]

Ode, fr. The Spectator. J. Addison. [Volume 4/13]

On His Blindness. J. Milton. [Volume 4/333]

On the Morning of Christ's Nativity. J. Milton. [Volume 4/51]

"Our god, Our help in Ages Past" I. Watts. [Volume 4/32]

Paradise Lost, sels. J. Milton. [Volume 4/262]

Passage in the Life of Saint Augustine. Unknown. [Volume 4/1]

Pastor's Reverie. W. Gladden. [Volume 4/313]

Patience. P. Hayne. [Volume 4/343]

Per Pacem Ad Lucem. A. Procter. [Volume 4/333]

The Pilgrimage. S. Raleigh. [Volume 4/335]

The Poet's Theme, Book I, fr. Paradise Lost. J. Milton. [Volume 4/262]

Praise to God. A. Barbauld. [Volume 4/40]

A Psalm of Life. H. Longfellow. [Volume 4/275]

The Right Must Win. F. Faber. [Volume 4/299]

The Rise of Man. J. Chadwick. [Volume 4/311]

"Rock of Ages" E. Rice. [Volume 4/85]

"Rocked in the Cradle of the Deep" E. Willard. [Volume 4/30]

Said I Not So. G. Herbert. [Volume 4/282]

Saint Christopher. D. Craik. [Volume 4/296]

Scorn Not the Least. R. Southwell. [Volume 4/298]

The Seed Growing Secretly. H. Vaughan. [Volume 4/343]

Self-Inquiry. I. Watts. [Volume 4/280]

The Sifting of Peter. H. Longfellow. [Volume 4/290]

Small Beginnings. C. Mackay. [Volume 4/309]

Sometime. M. Smith. [Volume 4/344]

Song, fr. Pippa Passes. R. Browning. [Volume 4/1]

Stabat Mater Dolorosa. F. Jacopone. [Volume 4/70]

The Star of Bethlehem. H. White. [Volume 4/89]

"Stone the Woman, Let the Man Go Free" Unknown. [Volume 4/322]

"Strong Son of God, Immortal Love", fr. In Memoriam. A. Tennyson. [Volume 4/45]

Sunrise. C. Turner. [Volume 4/20]

Te Deum Laudamus. American Episcopal Church Prayer-Book. [Volume 4/9]

The Temptation, Book IX, fr. Paradise Lost. J. Milton. [Volume 4/263]

The Three Enemies. C. Rossetti. [Volume 4/280]

To the Unco Guid. R. Burns. [Volume 4/320]

To-morrow. L. De Vega. [Volume 4/94]

A True Lent. R. Herrick. [Volume 4/303]

Tryste Noel. L. Guiney. [Volume 4/61]

The Two Rabbis. J. Whittier. [Volume 4/316]

Two Sayings. E. Browning. [Volume 4/68]

The Universal Prayer. A. Pope. [Volume 4/11]

Up Hill. C. Rossetti. [Volume 4/332]

Vanity. R. Trench. [Volume 4/292]

Veni Creator Spiritus. S. Gregory. [Volume 4/104]

Veni Sancte Spiritus. Robert II; King of France. [Volume 4/105]

The Voyage. C. Mason. [Volume 4/38]

The Way, the Truth, and the Life. T. Parker. [Volume 4/92]

"When Gathering Clouds Around I View" S. Grant. [Volume 4/88]

The Will of God. F. Faber. [Volume 4/36]

The Word. F. Faber. [Volume 4/284]

Wrestling Jacob. C. Wesley. [Volume 4/79]

**Religion** and Doctrine. J. Hay. [Volume 4/219]

The **Religion** of Hudibras, fr. Hudibras. S. Butler. [Volume 4/228]

"**Remain**, for me, chaste, unapproached, unstirred." To the Unimplored Beloved. E. Shanks. [Supp 1/284]

**Remembering**. Ping Hsin. [Supp 5/114]

**Remembering** Nat Turner. S. Brown. [Supp 2/87]

**Reminiscence**. Ho Ch'i-Fang. [Supp 7/6]

*Reminiscence*

Reminiscence. Ho Ch'i-Fang. [Supp 7/6]

**Remonstrance** with the Snails. Unknown. [Volume 5/352]

"**Remote**, unfriended, melancholy, slow." The Wanderer's Home. O. Goldsmith. [Volume 1/314]

**Renascence**. E. Millay. [Supp 1/214]

**Rendra**, W. S.

    Black Bird. B. Raffel; Harry Aveling and Derwent May (tr.). [Supp 7/100]

    Guerrilla. B. Raffel; Harry Aveling and Derwent May (tr.). [Supp 7/99]

    Hong Kong. B. Raffel; Harry Aveling and Derwent May (tr.). [Supp 7/103]

    Manchuria. B. Raffel; Harry Aveling and Derwent May (tr.). [Supp 7/102]

"She's Singing in the Rain" B. Raffel; Harry
Aveling and Derwent May (tr.). [Supp 7/101]
The Wind's Song. B. Raffel; Harry Aveling and
Derwent May (tr.). [Supp 7/101]
**Renouncement**. A. Meynell. [Volume 2/338]
A **Renunciation**. E. Vere. [Volume 2/246]
**Report** on Experience. E. Blunden. [Supp 2/46]
*Repression*
The Weed. E. Bishop. [Supp 2/245]
**Reproach**. M. Iqbal. [Supp 7/60]
The **Republic**, fr. The Building of the Ship. H.
Longfellow. [Volume 8/94]
A **Request**. K. Das. [Supp 5/58]
**Requiem**. G. Lunt. [Volume 8/388]
**Requier, Augustus Julian**
Baby Zulma's Christmas Carol. [Volume 1/67]
**Requiescat**. M. Arnold. [Volume 3/307]
The **Resignation**. T. Chatterton. [Volume 4/368]
**Resignation**. H. Longfellow. [Volume 3/430]
**Resolution** of Dependence. G. Barker. [Supp 2/288]
"**Respected** wife: by these few lines my whereabouts."
The Mystified Quaker in New York. Unknown.
[Volume 9/352]
*Responsibilities*
"In the Heart of Contemplation" C. Day Lewis.
[Supp 2/115]
**Rest**. M. Howland. [Volume 3/397]
**Rest**. M. Woods. [Volume 6/431]
*Rest*
The Fallen. J. Cheney. [Volume 6/442]
Invocation to Sleep, fr. Valentinian. J. Fletcher.
[Volume 6/432]
Ode to Sleep. P. Hayne. [Volume 6/439]
Rest. M. Woods. [Volume 6/431]
Sleep. J. Wolcott. [Volume 6/433]
Sleep, fr. Astrophel and Stella. S. Sidney.
[Volume 6/433]
Sleep, fr. Second Part of Henry IV. W. Shakespeare.
[Volume 6/433]
Sleeplessness. W. Wordsworth. [Volume 6/434]
To All in Haven. P. Marston. [Volume 6/428]
The Two Oceans. J. Sterling. [Volume 6/439]
The Voyage of Sleep. A. Eaton. [Volume 6/438]
Watching. E. Judson. [Volume 6/435]
A Woman's Wish. M. Townsend. [Volume 6/429]
The World and the Quietest. M. Arnold. [Volume
6/430]
"**Rest** From Loving and Be Living" C. Day Lewis. [Supp
2/122]
"**Restless** little waterfall." To a Waterfall. Nirala.
[Supp 7/66]
**Resurrection** of the Daughter. N. Shange. [Supp 5/266]
**Retamar, Roberto Fernandez**
It Would Be Nice to Deserve this Epitaph. R.
Marquez (tr.). [Supp 6/144]
It's Better to Light a Candle Than to Curse the
Darkness. M. Randal and Robert Cohen (tr.).
[Supp 6/143]
*Retirement*
Swineherd. E. Chuilleanain. [Supp 5/188]
The **Retort**. G. Morris. [Volume 2/431]
**Retribution**. F. Logau. [Volume 6/226]
The **Return**. J. Bishop. [Supp 2/27]
The **Return**: 001. A. Bontemps. [Supp 4/124]
The **Return**: 002. A. Bontemps. [Supp 4/124]
The **Return**: 003. A. Bontemps. [Supp 4/124]
The **Return**: 004. A. Bontemps. [Supp 4/125]
**Return** of Spring. P. Ronsard. [Volume 5/78]
**Reunited** Love. R. Blackmore. [Volume 2/425]
**Revelation**. E. Gosse. [Supp 1/145]
**Revelation**. R. Warren. [Supp 2/131]
"The **revelations** of devout and learned." Rubaiyat:
065. O. Khayyam. [Volume 6/216]
**Revelry** of the Dying. B. Dowling. [Volume 9/170]
**Revenge**. C. Anwar. [Supp 7/80]

The **Revenge**. A. Tennyson. [Volume 7/383]
*Revolution*
Bread-Word Giver. J. Wheelwright. [Supp 2/53]
In Poets' Defence. J. Wheelwright. [Supp 2/54]
Room with Revolutionists. E. Rolfe. [Supp 2/218]
The Serf. R. Campbell. [Supp 2/94]
Tom Mooney. C. Leland. [Supp 1/186]
"You That Love England" C. Day Lewis. [Supp 2/125]
**Revolutionary** Dreams. N. Giovanni. [Supp 4/222]
**Rexroth and Ikuko Atsumi, Kenneth (tr.)**
A Chinese Ulysses. S. Kazuko. [Supp 5/132]
"I Fire at the Face of the Country Where I Was
Born" S. Kazuko. [Supp 5/130]
Mother. N. Kiyoko. [Supp 5/135]
**Rexroth and Ling Chung, Kenneth (tr.)**
For the Record. Ping Hsin. [Supp 5/115]
Multitudinous Stars and Sping Waters: 001. Ping
Hsin. [Supp 5/116]
Multitudinous Stars and Sping Waters: 002. Ping
Hsin. [Supp 5/116]
Multitudinous Stars and Spring Waters: 003. Ping
Hsin. [Supp 5/116]
Multitudinous Stars and Spring Waters: 004. Ping
Hsin. [Supp 5/116]
Multitudinous Stars and Spring Waters: 005. Ping
Hsin. [Supp 5/116]
Multitudinous Stars and Spring Waters: 006. Ping
Hsin. [Supp 5/117]
Multitudinous Stars and Spring Waters: 007. Ping
Hsin. [Supp 5/117]
Multitudinous Stars and Spring Waters: 008. Ping
Hsin. [Supp 5/117]
Multitudinous Stars and Spring Waters: 009. Ping
Hsin. [Supp 5/117]
Remembering. Ping Hsin. [Supp 5/114]
**Reyes, Alfonso**
Monterrey Sun. C. Duran (tr.). [Supp 6/149]
**Reyna, Bessy**
Uncertainty. Z. Anglesey (tr.). [Supp 6/146]
The **Rhine**, fr. Childe Harolde. G. Byron. [Volume
7/169]
The **Rhodora**. R. Emerson. [Volume 5/252]
**Rhoecus**. J. Lowell. [Volume 6/103]
**Rhubarb**. G. Stein. [Supp 5/295]
"**Rhubard** is susan not susan not seat in bunch toys
not wild and." Rhubarb. G. Stein. [Supp 5/295]
**Rice, Edward H.**
"Rock of Ages" [Volume 4/85]
**Rice** Grains. A. Hernandez. [Supp 7/178]
**Rich, Adrienne (tr.)**
White Night. K. Molodowsky. [Supp 5/176]
Women Songs: 001. K. Molodowsky. [Supp 5/172]
Women Songs: 002. K. Molodowsky. [Supp 5/172]
"The **rich** man's son inherits lands." The Heritage. J.
Lowell. [Volume 1/256]
**Richard** Cory. E. Robinson. [Supp 1/266]
**Richardson, Charles Francis**
Love. [Volume 4/189]
A **Riddle**. C. Fanshawe. [Volume 9/450]
The **Riddlers**. W. De La Mare. [Supp 1/108]
**Riding** Down. N. Perry. [Volume 1/206]
"**Riding** from Coleraine." Peg of Limavaddy. W.
Thackeray. [Volume 1/236]
**Riding, Laura**
"O Vocables of Love" [Supp 1/265]
Sea, False Philosophy. [Supp 1/264]
**Ridler, Anne**
Christmas and Common Birth. [Supp 2/271]
Deus Absconditus. [Supp 2/272]
For a Christening: 001. [Supp 2/273]
For a Christening: 002. [Supp 2/274]
For a Christening: 003. [Supp 2/274]
A Mile from Eden. [Supp 2/275]
"Now Philippa is Gone" [Supp 2/276]
Piero Della Francesca. [Supp 2/276]

To My Contemporaries: 002. [Supp 2/223]
To My Contemporaries: 003. [Supp 2/225]
"**Roll** on, thou ball, roll on!" To the Terrestrial
Globe. W. Gilbert. [Volume 9/309]
The **Rolling** English Road. G. Chesterton. [Supp 1/81]
**Roma**, fr. Poesie. G. Carducci. [Volume 6/310]
The **Roman** Father, fr. Virginia. L. Macaulay; Thomas
Babington. [Volume 9/16]
**Roman** Poem Number Thirteen. J. Jordan. [Supp 4/196]
**Roman** Poem Number Two. J. Jordan. [Supp 5/124]
"**Roman** Virgil, thou that singest." To Virgil. A.
Tennyson. [Volume 7/37]
The **Romance** of the Swan's Nest. E. Browning. [Volume
1/123]
**Romantic** Fool. H. Monro. [Supp 1/224]
"**Romantic** fool who cannot speak!" Romantic Fool. H.
Monro. [Supp 1/224]
*Rome*
Horatius at the Bridge. L. Macaulay; Thomas
Babington. [Volume 7/265]
Lucius Junius Brutus Over the Body of Lucretia, fr.
Brutus. J. Payne. [Volume 9/14]
Mark Antony, Over the Body of Caesar, fr. Julius
Caesar. W. Shakespeare. [Volume 9/20]
The Roman Father, fr. Virginia. L. Macaulay;
Thomas Babington. [Volume 9/16]
**Ronsard, Pierre de**
Return of Spring. [Volume 5/78]
To Mary Stuart. L. Costello (tr.). [Volume 7/4]
"'**Room** for the leper! room!' and as he came." The
Leper. N. Willis. [Volume 7/315]
**Room** with Revolutionists. E. Rolfe. [Supp 2/218]
*Rooms*
Concerning a Room. S. Tanikawa. [Supp 7/132]
**Rooney, John Jerome**
The Men Behind the Guns. [Volume 8/419]
"The **Roosters** Will Crow When We Die" C. Meireles.
[Supp 5/160]
**Rory** O'More. S. Lover. [Volume 2/172]
**Rosalind**. T. Lodge. [Volume 2/19]
**Rosalynd's** Complaint. T. Lodge. [Volume 2/89]
The **Rose** and the Gauntlet. J. Sterling. [Volume
9/131]
**Rose, Aurobindo (tr.)**
"The Meandering Current of the Jhelum" R. Tagore.
[Supp 7/71]
"When You Were Alone" R. Tagore. [Supp 7/74]
**Rose** Aylmer. W. Landor. [Volume 2/375]
The **Rose-bush**. Unknown. [Volume 6/233]
"**Rose**, hash rose %marred and with stints of petals."
Sea Rose. H. Doolittle. [Supp 5/66]
"The **rose** in the garden slipped her bud." A Fancy
from Frontenelle. A. Dobson. [Volume 6/198]
"A **rose** of fire shut in a veil of snow." An Opal. E.
Hayes. [Volume 2/105]
"The **rose** of heaven." Multitudinous Stars and Spring
Waters: 007. Ping Hsin. [Supp 5/117]
**Rose, Wendy**
Halfbreed Cry. [Supp 4/323]
Story Keeper. [Supp 4/325]
*Roses*
Multitudinous Stars and Spring Waters: 007. Ping
Hsin. [Supp 5/117]
Sea Rose. H. Doolittle. [Supp 5/66]
Sonnet. J. Masefield. [Supp 1/209]
"**Roses** and butterflies snared on a fan." A Painted
Fan. L. Moulton. [Volume 6/385]
"**Roses** are beauty, but I never see." Sonnet. J.
Masefield. [Supp 1/209]
**Rossetti, Christina Georgina**
"It is Finished" [Volume 1/119]
The Milking-Maid. [Volume 2/49]
The Three Enemies. [Volume 4/280]
Up Hill. [Volume 4/332]
**Rossetti, Dante Gabriel**

The Blessed Damozel. [Volume 6/97]
The Nevermore. [Volume 3/82]
The Sea-limits. [Volume 5/441]
Sudden Light. [Volume 6/302]
When Do I See Thee Most? fr. The House of Life.
[Volume 2/251]
The Woodspurge. [Volume 5/251]
**Rossetti, Dante Gabriel (tr.)**
The Ballad of Dead Ladies. F. Villon. [Volume
6/192]
"A **rosy** shield upon its back." The Dead Crab. A.
Young. [Supp 2/2]
A **Rough** Rhyme on a Rough Matter. C. Kingsley. [Volume
3/191]
"**Row** after row with strict impunity." Ode to the
Confederate Dead. A. Tate. [Supp 2/73]
**Rowing**. A. Sexton. [Supp 5/256]
"The **royal** feast was done; the king." The Fool's
Prayer. E. Sill. [Volume 6/275]
**Royden, Matthew**
Sir Philip Sidney. [Volume 7/45]
**Rubaiyat**: 001. O. Khayyam. [Volume 6/204]
**Rubaiyat**: 002. O. Khayyam. [Volume 6/204]
**Rubaiyat**: 003. O. Khayyam. [Volume 6/204]
**Rubaiyat**: 004. O. Khayyam. [Volume 6/204]
**Rubaiyat**: 005. O. Khayyam. [Volume 6/204]
**Rubaiyat**: 006. O. Khayyam. [Volume 6/205]
**Rubaiyat**: 007. O. Khayyam. [Volume 6/205]
**Rubaiyat**: 008. O. Khayyam. [Volume 6/205]
**Rubaiyat**: 009. O. Khayyam. [Volume 6/205]
**Rubaiyat**: 010. O. Khayyam. [Volume 6/205]
**Rubaiyat**: 011. O. Khayyam. [Volume 6/206]
**Rubaiyat**: 012. O. Khayyam. [Volume 6/206]
**Rubaiyat**: 013. O. Khayyam. [Volume 6/206]
**Rubaiyat**: 014. O. Khayyam. [Volume 6/206]
**Rubaiyat**: 015. O. Khayyam. [Volume 6/206]
**Rubaiyat**: 016. O. Khayyam. [Volume 6/207]
**Rubaiyat**: 017. O. Khayyam. [Volume 6/207]
**Rubaiyat**: 018. O. Khayyam. [Volume 6/207]
**Rubaiyat**: 019. O. Khayyam. [Volume 6/207]
**Rubaiyat**: 020. O. Khayyam. [Volume 6/207]
**Rubaiyat**: 021. O. Khayyam. [Volume 6/208]
**Rubaiyat**: 022. O. Khayyam. [Volume 6/208]
**Rubaiyat**: 023. O. Khayyam. [Volume 6/208]
**Rubaiyat**: 024. O. Khayyam. [Volume 6/208]
**Rubaiyat**: 025. O. Khayyam. [Volume 6/208]
**Rubaiyat**: 026. O. Khayyam. [Volume 6/209]
**Rubaiyat**: 027. O. Khayyam. [Volume 6/209]
**Rubaiyat**: 028. O. Khayyam. [Volume 6/209]
**Rubaiyat**: 029. O. Khayyam. [Volume 6/209]
**Rubaiyat**: 030. O. Khayyam. [Volume 6/209]
**Rubaiyat**: 031. O. Khayyam. [Volume 6/210]
**Rubaiyat**: 032. O. Khayyam. [Volume 6/210]
**Rubaiyat**: 033. O. Khayyam. [Volume 6/210]
**Rubaiyat**: 034. O. Khayyam. [Volume 6/210]
**Rubaiyat**: 035. O. Khayyam. [Volume 6/210]
**Rubaiyat**: 036. O. Khayyam. [Volume 6/211]
**Rubaiyat**: 037. O. Khayyam. [Volume 6/211]
**Rubaiyat**: 038. O. Khayyam. [Volume 6/211]
**Rubaiyat**: 039. O. Khayyam. [Volume 6/211]
**Rubaiyat**: 040. O. Khayyam. [Volume 6/211]
**Rubaiyat**: 041. O. Khayyam. [Volume 6/212]
**Rubaiyat**: 042. O. Khayyam. [Volume 6/212]
**Rubaiyat**: 043. O. Khayyam. [Volume 6/212]
**Rubaiyat**: 044. O. Khayyam. [Volume 6/212]
**Rubaiyat**: 045. O. Khayyam. [Volume 6/212]
**Rubaiyat**: 046. O. Khayyam. [Volume 6/213]
**Rubaiyat**: 047. O. Khayyam. [Volume 6/213]
**Rubaiyat**: 048. O. Khayyam. [Volume 6/213]
**Rubaiyat**: 049. O. Khayyam. [Volume 6/213]
**Rubaiyat**: 050. O. Khayyam. [Volume 6/213]
**Rubaiyat**: 051. O. Khayyam. [Volume 6/214]
**Rubaiyat**: 052. O. Khayyam. [Volume 6/214]
**Rubaiyat**: 053. O. Khayyam. [Volume 6/214]
**Rubaiyat**: 054. O. Khayyam. [Volume 6/214]

"Line Like %Living Hair" [Supp 5/252]
"O Sister %Where Do You Pitch Your Tent?" [Supp 5/249]
"O the Chimneys" [Supp 5/246]
"The Old Couple %Sitting Hand In Hand" [Supp 5/254]
"Redeemed %From Sleep" [Supp 5/253]
You. [Supp 5/254]
The Sack of Baltimore. T. Davis. [Volume 9/127]
The Sack of the City. V. Hugo. [Volume 9/26]
Sackville, Charles, Earl Of Dorset
The Fire Of Love, fr. The Examen Miscellaneum. [Volume 2/449]
Sackville-West, V.
Bitterness. [Supp 1/277]
The Land, sel. [Supp 1/276]
Sacred Elegy V: 001. G. Barker. [Supp 2/290]
Sacred Elegy V: 002. G. Barker. [Supp 2/290]
Sacred Elegy V: 003. G. Barker. [Supp 2/291]
Sacred Elegy V: 004. G. Barker. [Supp 2/291]
Sacrifice
Colorado Morton's Ride. L. Bacon. [Supp 1/21]
Sacrifice of Polyxena, fr. Hecuba. Euripides. [Volume 9/5]
"Sad is Our Yourth, For It Is Ever Going" A. De Vere. [Volume 3/225]
Sad Moonlit Night. H. Sakutaro. [Supp 7/104]
A Saddened Tramp. Unknown. [Volume 9/395]
The Saddest Fate. Unknown. [Volume 3/247]
Sadness
"Away, Melancholy %Away With It, Let It Go" S. Smith. [Supp 5/281]
Cazonetta. A. Pozzi. [Supp 5/220]
Saemund, Sigfusson
Thor Recovers His Hammer from Thrym. W. Herbert (tr.). [Volume 7/284]
Sage Counsel. A. Quiller-Couch. [Volume 1/195]
"Sages %walk %barefoot %sometimes." George Washington Sends a Pair of Shoebuckles ... D. Wakoski. [Supp 5/319]
Sahara Desert
Mersa. K. Douglas. [Supp 2/406]
Said I Not So. G. Herbert. [Volume 4/282]
"Said I not som - that i would sin no more?" Said I Not So. G. Herbert. [Volume 4/282]
"Said one among them - surely not in vain." Rubaiyat: 084. O. Khayyam. [Volume 6/220]
"Said the lion to the lioness-- %'when you are amber." Heart and Mind. E. Sitwell. [Supp 2/14]
"Said the raggedy man on a hot afternoon." The Man in the Moon. J. Riley. [Volume 1/146]
Sailors and Sailing
I Sing for You. Lin Ling. [Supp 7/24]
John Winter. L. Binyon. [Supp 1/50]
The Quaker Graveyard in Nantucket: 001. R. Lowell. [Supp 2/394]
The Sailor's Consolation. W. Pitt. [Volume 5/435]
Saint Agnes. A. Tennyson. [Volume 4/416]
"Saint Agnes' Eve,--ah, bitter chill it was!" The Eve of Saint Agnes. J. Keats. [Volume 2/312]
"Saint Anthony at church." Saint Anthony's Sermon to the Fishes. Unknown. [Volume 9/239]
Saint Anthony's Sermon to the Fishes. Unknown. [Volume 9/239]
"Saint Augustine! well hast thou said." The Ladder of Saint Augustine. H. Longfellow. [Volume 4/294]
Saint Christopher. D. Craik. [Volume 4/296]
"The saint on the pillar stands." Stylite. L. MacNeice. [Supp 2/183]
Saint Peter's at Rome, fr. Childe Harold. G. Byron. [Volume 7/186]
St. Roach. M. Rukeyser. [Supp 5/244]
Sakutaro, Hagiwara
The Army. H. Sato (tr.). [Supp 7/110]
Blue Cat. H. Sato (tr.). [Supp 7/108]

Frog's Death. H. Sato (tr.). [Supp 7/104]
It Thought a Design. H. Sato (tr.). [Supp 7/109]
Sad Moonlit Night. H. Sato (tr.). [Supp 7/104]
White Moon. H. Sato (tr.). [Supp 7/106]
The World of Bacteria. H. Sato (tr.). [Supp 7/105]
The World of Fantasy the Buddha Saw. H. Sato (tr.). [Supp 7/108]
Yearing I Walk in a Crowd. H. Sato (tr.). [Supp 7/107]
"The sale began - young girls were there." The Salve Auction. F. Harper. [Supp 4/63]
Sally In Our Alley. H. Carey. [Volume 2/290]
Salutation. T. Eliot. [Supp 1/114]
The Salve Auction. F. Harper. [Supp 4/63]
Salvos for Randolph Bourne: 001. H. Gregory. [Supp 2/65]
Salvos for Randolph Bourne: 002. H. Gregory. [Supp 2/65]
Salvos for Randolph Bourne: 003. H. Gregory. [Supp 2/66]
"The same as stacked lunchboxes." Mount Fuji. M. Kaneko. [Supp 7/113]
"The same road, %the same houses." Barrenness. B. Al-Haydari. [Supp 7/229]
Samson On His Blindness, fr. Samson Agonistes. J. Milton. [Volume 3/158]
San Juan Jr., E. (tr.)
The Kingdom of Mammon. A. Hernandez. [Supp 7/176]
Rice Grains. A. Hernandez. [Supp 7/178]
Two Questions. A. Hernandez. [Supp 7/177]
San-Kan River. Ya Hsuan. [Supp 7/31]
Sanchez, Ricardo
I Remember. [Supp 4/254]
Toward. [Supp 4/249]
Sanchez, Sonia
Last Poem i'm Gonna Write About Us. [Supp 4/189]
Pennsylvania Dutch Country. [Supp 4/192]
Poem at Thirty. [Supp 4/190]
Poem No. 4. [Supp 4/191]
Right On: Wite America. [Supp 4/187]
"The sand is swift, overflowing." Snake. D. Pagis. [Supp 7/250]
Sandburg, Carl
Chicago. [Supp 1/283]
Gone. [Supp 1/281]
Nocturne in a Deserted Brickyard. [Supp 1/278]
Ossawatomie. [Supp 1/282]
To a Contemporary Bunkshooter. [Supp 1/279]
The Sandpiper. C. Thaxter. [Volume 5/303]
The Sands O' Dee. C. Kingsley. [Volume 9/181]
Sangster, Charles
The Comet. [Volume 6/88]
The Snows. [Volume 5/203]
Sangster, Margaret E. M.
Are the children at Home? [Volume 3/288]
Santa Filomena. H. Longfellow. [Volume 4/166]
Santayana, George
Faith. [Volume 4/136]
Sappho
Blest as the Immortal Gods. A. Phillips (tr.). [Volume 2/97]
Sargent, Epes
"A Life on the Ocean Wave" [Volume 5/409]
Sassafras. S. Peck. [Volume 5/274]
Sato, Hiroaki (tr.)
Age. T. Tomioka. [Supp 7/140]
The Army. H. Sakutaro. [Supp 7/110]
Blue Cat. H. Sakutaro. [Supp 7/108]
Frog's Death. H. Sakutaro. [Supp 7/104]
It Thought a Design. H. Sakutaro. [Supp 7/109]
Let Me Tell You About Myself. T. Tomioka. [Supp 7/138]
Sad Moonlit Night. H. Sakutaro. [Supp 7/104]
We Do Not Know the Name of the King. M. Takahashi. [Supp 7/122]

"The **scullion** of the queen was grieved because." The
Scullion of the Queen. M. Bodenheim. [Supp
1/56]

**Scunner.** H. MacDiarmid. [Supp 2/31]

"**Scuttle** %your world. Imagination has already done
it." Strontium. E. Manner. [Supp 5/150]

**Scythe** Song. A. Lang. [Volume 7/248]

The Sea. B. Barton. [Volume 5/377]

The Sea. R. Emerson. [Volume 5/374]

The Sea. E. Ogden. [Volume 9/227]

The Sea. B. Procter. [Volume 5/380]

*Sea*
  About the Sea. N. Hikmet. [Supp 7/310]
  Address to the Ocean. B. Procter. [Volume 5/381]
  All's Well, fr. The British Fleet. T. Dibdin.
    [Volume 5/404]
  Among the Rocks. R. Browning. [Volume 5/430]
  "At Whose Sheltering Shall the Day Sea" W. Graham.
    [Supp 2/400]
  The Bay of Biscay. A. Cherry. [Volume 5/405]
  Beyond the Sea. Lo Fu. [Supp 7/27]
  The Buoy-bell. C. Turner. [Volume 5/423]
  Casabianca. F. Hemans. [Volume 9/184]
  The Chambered Nautilus. O. Holmes. [Volume 5/398]
  The Coral Insect. L. Sigourney. [Volume 5/395]
  The Coral Reef, fr. The Pelican Island. J.
    Montgomery. [Volume 5/396]
  Denouement. A. Prado. [Supp 6/117]
  The Disappointed Lover, fr. The Triumph of Time. A.
    Swinburne. [Volume 5/378]
  Dover Beach. M. Arnold. [Volume 5/423]
  Ferryboat. E. Chuilleanain. [Supp 5/193]
  Flotsam and Jetsam. Unknown. [Volume 5/387]
  A Forsaken Garden. A. Swinburne. [Volume 5/388]
  Gigha. W. Graham. [Supp 2/401]
  The Gravedigger. B. Carman. [Volume 5/383]
  Gulf-weed. C. Fenner. [Volume 5/392]
  Hampton Beach. J. Whittier. [Volume 5/427]
  The Heaving of the Lead. C. Dibdin. [Volume 5/402]
  How's My Boy. S. Dobell. [Volume 5/434]
  The Inchcape Rock. R. Southey. [Volume 5/431]
  It Can Happen. V. Huidobro. [Supp 6/120]
  The Kearsarge. J. Roche. [Volume 5/422]
  "A Life on the Ocean Wave" E. Sargent. [Volume
    5/409]
  Mariner man. E. Sitwell. [Supp 5/271]
  The Mariner's Dream. W. Dimond. [Volume 5/438]
  A Message from the Crane. Pak Tu-Jin. [Supp 7/154]
  The Minute-Gun. R. Sharpe. [Volume 5/403]
  My Brigantine, fr. The Water Witch. J. Cooper.
    [Volume 5/402]
  "Night's Fall Unlocks the Dirge of the Sea" W.
    Graham. [Supp 2/402]
  Ocean, fr. The Course of Time. R. Pollok. [Volume
    5/379]
  On the Loss of the Royal George. W. Cowper.
    [Volume 9/182]
  "Our Boat to the Waves" W. Channing. [Volume
    5/409]
  Paracas. A. Cisneros. [Supp 6/186]
  The Polar Quest. R. Burton. [Volume 5/421]
  Poor Jack. C. Dibdin. [Volume 5/436]
  The Rock and the Sea. C. Gilman. [Volume 5/418]
  The Sailor's Consolation. W. Pitt. [Volume 5/435]
  The Sands O' Dee. C. Kingsley. [Volume 9/181]
  The Sea Shell, fr. The Excursion. W. Wordsworth.
    [Volume 5/426]
  A Sea Story. E. Hickey. [Volume 9/192]
  Sea, False Philosophy. L. Riding. [Supp 1/264]
  The Sea, fr. Childe Harold. G. Byron. [Volume
    5/375]
  The Sea-limits. D. Rossetti. [Volume 5/441]
  Sea-weed. H. Longfellow. [Volume 5/393]
  The Sea. R. Emerson. [Volume 5/374]
  The Sea. B. Barton. [Volume 5/377]

  The Sea. B. Procter. [Volume 5/380]
  The Second Mate. F. O'Brien. [Volume 9/189]
  The Second Voyage. E. Chuilleanain. [Supp 5/193]
  The Shell, fr. Gebir. W. Landor. [Volume 5/427]
  Shells. K. Raine. [Supp 5/224]
  The Shipwreck. W. Falconer. [Volume 5/417]
  The Shore, fr. Ariadne. C. Roberts. [Volume 5/421]
  Song of the Emigrants in Bermuda. A. Marvell.
    [Volume 5/400]
  Stars. Pak Tu-Jin. [Supp 7/151]
  The Storm. G. Stevens. [Volume 5/414]
  Tacking Ship Off Shore. W. Mitchell. [Volume
    5/411]
  The Three Fishers. C. Kingsley. [Volume 9/183]
  To Sea! T. Beddoes. [Volume 5/410]
  Tom Bowling. C. Dibdin. [Volume 5/406]
  The Treasures of the Deep. F. Hemans. [Volume
    5/385]
  The Triangular Window. Yung Tzu. [Supp 7/36]
  Twilight at Sea. A. Welby. [Volume 5/411]
  "A Wet Sheet and a Flowing Sea" A. Cunningham.
    [Volume 5/399]
  The White Squall. B. Procter. [Volume 5/408]
  The Wind Sleepers. H. Doolittle. [Supp 5/67]
  With a Nantucket Shell. C. Webb. [Volume 5/425]
  The Wreck of the Hesperus. H. Longfellow. [Volume
    9/186]
  Wreck, fr. Don Juan. G. Byron. [Volume 5/416]
  "Ye Mariners of England!" T. Campbell. [Volume
    5/407]

"The **sea** crahed over the grim gray rocks." Flotsam
  and Jetsam. Unknown. [Volume 5/387]

"The **sea** drained off, my poverty's uncovered." All
  Gone. C. Day Lewis. [Supp 2/109]

Sea, False Philosophy. L. Riding. [Supp 1/264]

The **Sea**, fr. Childe Harold. G. Byron. [Volume 5/375]

Sea Holly. C. Aiken. [Supp 1/12]

"The **sea** is calm to-night." Dover Beach. M. Arnold.
  [Volume 5/423]

The **Sea**-limits. D. Rossetti. [Volume 5/441]

The **Sea**-poppy. R. Bridges. [Volume 5/285]

"**sea** produced that town: Sete, which the boat turns
  to." Mediterranean: 006. M. Rukeyser. [Supp
  2/302]

Sea Rose. H. Doolittle. [Supp 5/66]

The **Sea** Shell, fr. The Excursion. W. Wordsworth.
  [Volume 5/426]

"The **sea**! the sea! the open sea!" The Sea. B. Procter.
  [Volume 5/380]

"The **sea** was bright, and the bark rode well." The
  White Squall. B. Procter. [Volume 5/408]

**Sea-weed.** H. Longfellow. [Volume 5/393]

"**Search** thou the ruling passion; there, alone." The
  Ruling Passion, fr. Moral Essays. A. Pope.
  [Volume 6/294]

*Searching*
  Late. L. Bogan. [Supp 5/32]

**Searle, Chris (tr.)**
  Ode to a Lost Cargo in a Ship Called Save: 001. J.
    Craveirinha. [Supp 6/37]
  Ode to a Lost Cargo in a Ship Called Save: 002. J.
    Craveirinha. [Supp 6/38]
  Ode to a Lost Cargo in a Ship Called Save: 003. J.
    Craveirinha. [Supp 6/39]
  Ode to a Lost Cargo in a Ship Called Save: 004. J.
    Craveirinha. [Supp 6/41]
  Where I Am. M. Dos Santos. [Supp 6/42]

**Sears, Edmund Hamilton**
  The Angels' Song. [Volume 4/48]

"The **seas** are quiet when the winds give o'er." Old
  Age and Death, fr. Verses Upon His Divine Poesy.
  E. Waller. [Volume 6/293]

Seascape. S. Spender. [Supp 2/232]

*Seashore*

Rowing. [Supp 5/256]
Two Hands. [Supp 5/258]
"Sez Corporal Madden to Private McFadden." The
Recruit. R. Chambers. [Volume 9/321]
Shabaka, Illyas Abu
I Love You. A. Haydar and Michael Beard (tr.).
[Supp 7/261]
"This Is My Wine" A. Haydar and Michael Beard
(tr.). [Supp 7/261]
You or I? A. Haydar and Michael Beard (tr.). [Supp
7/260]
The Shaded Water. W. Simms. [Volume 5/196]
"The shades of eve had crossed the glen." The Pretty
Girl of Loch Dan. S. Ferguson. [Volume 1/220]
"The shades of night were falling fast." Excelsior. H.
Longfellow. [Volume 6/257]
The Shadow Rose. R. Rogers. [Volume 3/53]
The Shadows. F. Sherman. [Volume 1/132]
"The shadows lay along Broadway." Unseen Spirits. N.
Willis. [Volume 3/204]
"Shadows of clouds." Arizona Poems: Clouds Across the
Canyon. J. Fletcher. [Supp 1/129]
Shakespeare. H. Coleridge. [Volume 7/52]
Shakespeare and John Fletcher, William
"Take, O, Take Those Lips Away" [Volume 3/71]
"Shakespeare and Milton - what third blazoned."
Tennyson. T. Aldrich. [Volume 7/83]
Shakespeare, fr. Prologue. S. Johnson. [Volume 7/51]
Shakespeare, William
Airy Nothings, fr. The Tempest. [Volume 6/58]
"Blow, Blow, Thou Winter Wind", fr. As You Like It.
[Volume 3/155]
Brutus And Portia, fr. Julius Cesar. [Volume
2/389]
Cleopatra, fr. Antony and Cleopatra. [Volume
7/127]
Compliment to Queen Elizabeth, fr. A Midsummer
Night's Dream. [Volume 6/17]
The Course of True Love, fr. Midsummer Night's
Dream. [Volume 3/3]
A Dagger of the Mind, fr. Macbeth. [Volume 9/120]
The Death of Death. [Volume 3/461]
Dover Cliff, fr. King Lear. [Volume 5/214]
End of the Civil War, fr. King Richard III.
[Volume 8/424]
England, fr. King John. [Volume 7/390]
The Fairies' Lullaby, fr. A Midsummer Night's
Dream. [Volume 6/18]
Fairy's Song, fr. A Midsummer Night's Dream.
[Volume 6/16]
The Fall of Cardinal Wolsey, fr. King Henry VIII.
[Volume 3/161]
"Farewell! Thou Art Too Dear" [Volume 3/112]
"Fear No More the Heat O' the Sun", fr. Cymbeline.
[Volume 3/328]
"The Forward Violet Thus Did I Chide" [Volume 2/9]
Friendship, fr. Hamlet. [Volume 1/345]
"Full Many A Glorious Morning" [Volume 2/224]
The Greenwood Tree, fr. As You Like It. [Volume
5/219]
Grief, fr. Hamlet. [Volume 3/348]
Hark, Hark! The Lark, fr. Cymbeline. [Volume
5/292]
Healthful Old Age, fr. As You Like It. [Volume
6/287]
Imagination, fr. A Midsummer Night's Dream.
[Volume 6/12]
Influence of Music, fr. King Henry Eighth. [Volume
6/362]
The King to His Soldiers Before Harfleur, fr. King
Henry V. [Volume 8/268]
"Let Me Not To The Marriage Of True Minds" [Volume
2/376]
Love and Woman, fr. Love's Labor's Lost. [Volume
2/65]

Love Dissembled, fr. As You Like It. [Volume 2/31]
Love's Blindness. [Volume 2/223]
Love's Memory, fr. All's Well That Ends Well.
[Volume 3/140]
Love, fr. The Merchant of Venice. [Volume 2/62]
Mark Antony, Over the Body of Caesar, fr. Julius
Caesar. [Volume 9/20]
The Murder, fr. Macbeth. [Volume 9/122]
Music, fr. The Merchant of Venice. [Volume 6/362]
"Not Marble, Not the Gilded Monuments" [Volume
1/359]
O Mistress Mine, fr. Twelfth Night. [Volume 2/79]
Olivia, fr. Twelfth Night. [Volume 2/10]
Othello's Defence, fr. Othello. [Volume 2/207]
Othello's Remorse, fr. Othello. [Volume 9/67]
Portia's Picture, fr. The Merchant of Venice.
[Volume 2/11]
Prayer and Repentance, fr. Hamlet. [Volume 4/118]
Quarrel of Brutus and Cassius, fr. Julius Caesar.
[Volume 1/381]
Queen Mab, fr. Romeo and Juliet. [Volume 6/13]
Seven Ages of Man, fr. As You Like It. [Volume
7/126]
Shall I compare thee? [Volume 2/4]
A Sheperd's Life, fr. Third Part of Henry VI.
[Volume 1/319]
Sleep, fr. Second Part of Henry IV. [Volume 6/433]
Soliloquy on Death, fr. Hamlet. [Volume 3/252]
Songs of Ariel, fr. The Tempest. [Volume 6/57]
Sonnet 12: The Approach of Age. [Volume 6/194]
Unrequited Love, fr. Twelfth Night. [Volume 3/9]
"When Icicles Hang by the Wall", fr. Love's Labor
's Lost. [Volume 5/171]
When in Disgrace. [Volume 1/358]
"When in the chronicle of wasted time." [Volume
2/3]
"When to the Sessions of Sweet Silent Thought"
[Volume 1/348]
Young Friends, fr. A Midsummer Night's Dream.
[Volume 1/344]
*Shakespeare, William*
Miranda's Song. W. Auden. [Supp 2/164]
Shall I compare thee? W. Shakespeare. [Volume 2/4]
"Shall I compare thee to a summer's day?" Shall I
compare thee? W. Shakespeare. [Volume 2/4]
"Shall I mine affections slack." Answer To Master
Wither's Song,"Shall I, Wasting In Despair" B.
Jonson. [Volume 2/239]
"Shall I sonnet-sing you about myself?" House. R.
Browning. [Volume 7/108]
"Shall I tell you whom I love?" My Choice. W. Browne.
[Volume 2/87]
"Shall I, wasting in despair." The Author's
Resolution, In A Sonnet, fr. Fair Virtue. G.
Wither. [Volume 2/238]
"Shall mine eyes behold thy glory, O my country?"
After Death. F. Parnell. [Volume 8/68]
"Shame on Thee, O Manhattan" A. Branch. [Supp 1/71]
"Shame upon you, Robin." Song of the Milkmaid, fr.
Queen Mary. A. Tennyson. [Volume 2/107]
Shamlu, Ahmad
"May My Prison Have No Enclosure" A. Karimi-Hakkak
(tr.). [Supp 7/213]
The Song of Abraham in Fire. A. Karimi-Hakkak
(tr.). [Supp 7/211]
Tablet. A. Karimi-Hakkak (tr.). [Supp 7/207]
Shange, Ntozake
& Then. [Supp 5/263]
For Colored Girls Who Have Considered Suicide ...,
sel. [Supp 4/230,Supp 4/231]
Inquiry. [Supp 5/265]
Resurrection of the Daughter. [Supp 5/266]
Senses of Heritage. [Supp 5/264]
Shanks, Edward
To the Unimplored Beloved. [Supp 1/284]

**Shanly, Charles Dawson**
The Brier-wood Pipe. [Volume 6/317]
Civil War. [Volume 8/353]
Kitty of Coleraine. [Volume 2/132]
The Walker of the Snow. [Volume 6/167]
"Shapcot! to thee the Fairy State." Oberon's Feast. R.
Herrick. [Volume 6/14]
"The **shape** alone let others prize." Song. M. Akenside.
[Volume 2/11]
"**Shapes** of all sorts and sizes, great and small."
Rubaiyat: 083. O. Khayyam. [Volume 6/220]
**Shapiro, Karl**
The Dome of Sunday. [Supp 2/312]
Elegy for a Dead Soldier: 001. [Supp 2/314]
Elegy for a Dead Soldier: 002. [Supp 2/314]
Elegy for a Dead Soldier: 003. [Supp 2/314]
Elegy for a Dead Soldier: 004. [Supp 2/315]
Elegy for a Dead Soldier: 005. [Supp 2/315]
Elegy for a Dead Soldier: 006. [Supp 2/316]
Elegy for a Dead Soldier: 007. [Supp 2/316]
Elegy for a Dead Soldier: 008. [Supp 2/316]
Elegy for a Dead Soldier: 009. [Supp 2/317]
Elegy for a Dead Soldier: 010. [Supp 2/317]
Elegy for a Dead Soldier: 011. [Supp 2/318]
Elegy for a Dead Soldier: 001. [Supp 2/314]
Elegy for a Dead Soldier: 002. [Supp 2/314]
Elegy for a Dead Soldier: 003. [Supp 2/314]
Elegy for a Dead Soldier: 004. [War]
Elegy for a Dead Soldier: 005. [Supp 2/315]
Elegy for a Dead Soldier: 006. [Supp 2/316]
Elegy for a Dead Soldier: 007. [Supp 2/316]
Elegy for a Dead Soldier: 008. [Supp 2/316]
Elegy for a Dead Soldier: 009. [Supp 2/317]
Elegy for a Dead Soldier: 010. [Supp 2/317]
Elegy for a Dead Soldier: 011. [Supp 2/318]
Elegy Written on a Frontporch. [Supp 2/318]
Epitaph. [Supp 2/318]
Haircut. [Supp 2/321]
Nostalgia. [Supp 2/322]
The Potomac. [Supp 2/323]
V-Letter. [Supp 2/323]
The **Sharing** of the Earth. J. Schiller. [Volume 6/356]
**Sharp, Elizabeth A**
Vision of a Fair Woman. [Volume 2/25]
**Sharp, William**
The White Peacock, fr. Sospiri Di Roma. [Volume
7/175]
**Sharpe, R. S.**
The Minute-Gun. [Volume 5/403]
"**She** always stood upon the steps." Watching for Papa.
Unknown. [Volume 3/414]
"**She** came to him in dreams - her ears." The Tame Hare.
L. Lee. [Supp 2/342]
"**She** Died in Beauty" C. Sillery. [Volume 3/319]
"**She** gave her life to love. She never knew." The Old
Maid. G. Barlow. [Volume 2/369]
"**She** goes by many names; Diana of the sacred wood."
The Goddess. K. Raine. [Supp 2/198]
"**she** has gone, -- she has left us in passion and."
Brother Jonathan's Lament for Sister Caroline.
O. Holmes. [Volume 8/344]
"**She** has no need to fear the fall." Portrait. L.
Bogan. [Supp 5/31]
"**She** hath no beauty in her face." Patience. P. Hayne.
[Volume 4/343]
"**She** hath no gems of lustre bright." A Knot of Blue.
S. Peck. [Volume 1/233]
**She** Hugged Me and Kissed Me. Unknown (African
American). [Supp 4/59]
"**She** hung the cage at the window." Caprice. W.
Howells. [Volume 2/110]
"**She** is a winsome wee thing." My Wife's A Winsome Wee
Thing. R. Burns. [Volume 2/420]
"'**She** is dead!' they said to him; 'come away'" The
Secret of Death. S. Arnold. [Volume 3/434]

"**She** is not Fair to Outward View" H. Coleridge.
[Volume 2/33]
"**She** laid it where the sunbeams fall." Motherhood. C.
Calverley. [Volume 9/440]
"**She** lifted up her head." Loreine: A Horse. A. Ficke.
[Supp 1/121]
"**She** may count three little daisies very well."
Stansaz in Meditation: Part 001, Stanza 013. G.
Stein. [Supp 5/290]
"**She** once was a lady of honor and wealth." The Sister
of Charity. G. Griffen. [Volume 4/183]
"**She** says, 'the cock crows, --hark!'" The Parting
Lovers. Unknown. [Volume 3/104]
"**She** shrank from all, and her silent mood." The
Female Convict. L. Landon. [Volume 3/215]
"**She** speaks with the moisture of her barbarous seas."
The Foreigner. G. Mistral. [Supp 6/129]
"**She** sports a witching gown." Dollie. S. Peck.
[Volume 1/234]
"**She** stands, a thousand-wintered tree." England and
Her Colonies. W. Watson. [Volume 8/32]
"**She** stood at the bar of justice." Guilty, or Not
Guilty? Unknown. [Volume 3/212]
"**She** stood before a chosen few." Her Creed. S. Bolton.
[Volume 4/236]
"**She** stood breast height amid the corn." Ruth. T.
Hood. [Volume 1/219]
"**She** told the story, and the whole world wept."
Harriet Beecher Stowe. P. Dunbar. [Volume
7/105]
**She** Walks in Beauty. G. Byron. [Volume 2/32]
"**She** walks in beauty, like the night." She Walks in
Beauty. G. Byron. [Volume 2/32]
"**She** walks, - the lady of my delight." The
Shepherdess. A. Meynell. [Supp 1/210]
"**She** wanders in the April woods." Agatha. A. Austin.
[Volume 3/13]
"**She** Was A Phantom Of Delight" W. Wordsworth. [Volume
2/422]
"**She** was rich and of high degree." The Sea. E. Ogden.
[Volume 9/227]
"**She,** who but late in beauty's flower was seen."
Time's Revenge. Agathias. [Volume 3/72]
**Sheep** and Lambs. K. Hinkson. [Volume 1/121]
The **Shell,** fr. Gebir. W. Landor. [Volume 5/427]
**Shelley.** A. Japp. [Volume 7/58]
**Shelley, Percy Bysshe**
Autumn: A Dirge. [Volume 5/170]
The Cloud. [Volume 5/133]
Earth, Ocean, Air, fr. Alastor. [Volume 5/4]
From Mont Blanc. [Volume 5/217]
"I Fear Thy Kisses, Gentle Maiden" [Volume 2/30]
A Lament. [Volume 3/172]
Lines To An Indian Air. [Volume 2/254]
Love's Philosophy. [Volume 2/106]
Night, fr. Queen Mab. [Volume 5/66]
The Nile. [Volume 7/160]
Ode to the West Wind. [Volume 5/128]
The Question. [Volume 5/272]
Stanza. [Volume 3/164, Volume 3/165]
Sunset, fr. Queen Mab. [Volume 5/48]
To Ianthe, Sleeping. [Volume 7/129]
To Night. [Volume 5/63]
To the Skylark. [Volume 5/297]
To--- [Volume 6/363]
The Trial of Beatrice, fr. The Cenci. [Volume
9/68]
Venice, fr. View from the Euganean Hills. [Volume
7/192]
**Shells.** K. Raine. [Supp 5/224]
**Shenstone, William**
The Village Schoolmistress, fr. The Schoolmaster.
[Volume 7/231]
A **Sheperd's** Life, fr. Third Part of Henry VI. W.
Shakespeare. [Volume 1/319]

The **Shepherd** and the King. R. Greene. [Volume 2/63]
The **Shepherdess**. A. Meynell. [Supp 1/210]
"**Shepherds** all, and maidens fair." Folding the Flocks.
    F. Beaumont and Joseph Fletcher. [Volume
    5/359]
*Shepherds and Shepherdesses*
    In January. G. Bottomley. [Supp 1/62]
    The Shepherdess. A. Meynell. [Supp 1/210]
**Sheridan, Helen Selina, Lady Dufferin**
    Lament of the Irish Emigrant. [Volume 3/343]
**Sheridan's** Ride. T. Read. [Volume 8/383]
**Sherman, Frank Dempster**
    Her Guitar. [Volume 2/44]
    On Some Buttercups. [Volume 2/46]
    The Shadows. [Volume 1/132]
**Sherman's** March to the Sea. S. Byers. [Volume 8/406]
**Sherwood**. A. Noyes. [Volume 6/181]
"**Sherwood** in the twilight, is Robin Hood awake?"
    Sherwood. A. Noyes. [Volume 6/181]
"**She's** Singing in the Rain" W. Rendra. [Supp 7/101]
"**She's** somewhere in the sunlight strong." Song. R. Le
    Gallienne. [Volume 3/417]
**Shiffert and Yuki Sawa, Edith Marcombe (tr.)**
    The Bridge. S. Murano. [Supp 7/120]
    Cuckoos. M. Kaneko. [Supp 7/112]
    A Deer. S. Murano. [Supp 7/120]
    Diving. S. Murano. [Supp 7/115]
    Horse on a City Street. S. Murano. [Supp 7/116]
    Mount Fuji. M. Kaneko. [Supp 7/113]
    Night Storm. S. Murano. [Supp 7/118]
    On Suicide. S. Murano. [Supp 7/117]
    The Ox. S. Murano. [Supp 7/121]
    A Small Bird's Sky. S. Murano. [Supp 7/118]
"A **ship** sailed from the back of Nehru's head." Nehru.
    S. Takahashi. [Supp 7/126]
"The **ship** was large." Ode to a Lost Cargo in a Ship
    Called Save: 001. J. Craveirinha. [Supp 6/37]
*Ships*
    Ode to a Lost Cargo in a Ship Called Save: 001. J.
    Craveirinha. [Supp 6/37]
The **Shipwreck**. W. Falconer. [Volume 5/417]
**Shirley, James**
    The Common Doom. [Volume 2/237]
    Death the Leveller. [Volume 3/254]
"A **shoal** of idlers, from a merchant craft." Pelters
    of Pyramids. R. Horne. [Volume 6/264]
The **Shore**, fr. Ariadne. C. Roberts. [Volume 5/421]
**Short** Song on Autumn Harvest. Li Chi. [Supp 7/11]
"**Should** all acquaintance be forgot." Auld Lang Syne.
    R. Burns. [Volume 1/405]
"**Show** me a sight." The Irish Spinning-Wheel. A.
    Graves. [Volume 2/53]
"**Shun** delays, they breed remorse." Losse in Delayes.
    R. Southwell. [Volume 4/341]
Si Jeunesse Savait! E. Stedman. [Volume 2/242]
**Sibley, Charles**
    The Plaidie. [Volume 2/131]
*Siblings*
    Daughter. K. Hahn. [Supp 4/35]
Sic et Non: I. The Complaint of Heloise. H. Read.
    [Supp 2/34]
Sic et Non: II. The Portrait of Abelard. H. Read.
    [Supp 2/35]
Sic Vita. H. King. [Volume 3/253]
"**Sickles** sound." Harvest Song. L. Holty. [Volume
    5/150]
**Sidney, Sir Philip**
    Love's Silence. [Volume 2/73]
    My True-Love Hath My Heart. [Volume 2/330]
    Sleep, fr. Astrophel and Stella. [Volume 6/433]
    Sonnet, fr. Astrophel and Stella. [Volume 3/13,
    Volume 6/342]
Siege of Belgrade. Unknown. [Volume 9/426]
The **Sifting** of Peter. H. Longfellow. [Volume 4/290]
**Sigerson, George**

Far-Away. [Volume 6/183]
**Signs** of Rain. E. Jenner. [Volume 5/118]
**Sigourney, Lydia Huntley**
    The Coral Insect. [Volume 5/395]
Silence. G. Senanayake. [Supp 7/180]
*Silence*
    Silence. G. Senanayake. [Supp 7/180]
    Song of Other Lives. L. Marechal. [Supp 6/105]
    Willow. A. Akhmatova. [Supp 5/9]
    "With My Customary Restraint" D. Brutus. [Supp
    6/101]
"**Silence**, %dead bells' blood." Song of Other Lives. L.
    Marechal. [Supp 6/105]
"**Silence** before %sound." Zacchaeus in the Leaves. V.
    Watkins. [Supp 2/192]
**Silence** near an Ancient Stone. R. Castellanos. [Supp
    5/49]
"The **silence** of a ladder leaning against a wall."
    Inventory. T. Carmi. [Supp 7/241]
The **Silence** of the Hills. W. Foster. [Volume 5/213]
"**Silence**. A while go." A Sea Story. E. Hickey.
    [Volume 9/192]
**Silent** Baby. E. Currier. [Volume 1/22]
**Silko, Leslie Marmon**
    Indian Song: Survival. [Supp 4/331]
    Love Poem. [Supp 4/336]
    The Time We Climbed Snake Mountain. [Supp 4/334]
    Toe'osh: A Lagune Coyote Story. [Supp 4/328]
    Where Mountain Lion Lay Down with Deer, February
    1973. [Supp 4/335]
**Sill, Edward Rowland**
    Among the Redwoods. [Volume 5/234]
    The Fool's Prayer. [Volume 6/275]
    A Morning Thought. [Volume 3/267]
The **Siller** Croun. S. Blamire. [Volume 2/177]
**Sillery, Charles Doyne**
    "She Died in Beauty" [Volume 3/319]
The **Silver** Stag. K. Raine. [Supp 2/201]
**Simmias**
    The Grave of Sophocles. W. Hardinge (tr.).
    [Volume 3/269]
**Simmons, Bartholomew**
    To the Memory of Thomas Hood. [Volume 7/62]
**Simms, William Gilmore**
    The Grape-vine Swing. [Volume 5/231]
    The Lost Pleiad. [Volume 4/347]
    Mother and Child. [Volume 1/25]
    The Shaded Water. [Volume 5/196]
**Simple**. N. Madgett. [Supp 4/165]
"A **simple** child." We Are Seven. W. Wordsworth.
    [Volume 1/73]
"**Simple**, erect, severe, austere, sublime." The
    Pantheon, fr. Childe Harold. G. Byron. [Volume
    7/181]
The **Sin**. G. Senanayake. [Supp 7/182]
*Sin*
    Ballad of the Long-Legged Bait. D. Thomas. [Supp
    2/353]
    King David. S. Benet. [Supp 1/34]
    The Sin. G. Senanayake. [Supp 7/182]
"**Since** early morning." Paracas. A. Cisneros. [Supp
    6/186]
**Since** Then. To Huu. [Supp 7/194]
"**Since** then summer light has burned in me." Since
    Then. To Huu. [Supp 7/194]
"**Since** there's no helpe, --come, let us kisse and."
    Come, Let Us Kisse and Parte. M. Drayton.
    [Volume 3/111]
"**Since** your lights were extinguished." Blackout. F.
    Faiz. [Supp 7/169]
"**Sing** me a song of the dead." The Dead Man Asks for a
    Song. Unknown (African American). [Supp 6/3]
"**Sing** of song of spring-time!" A Song of Seasons. E.
    MacDonald. [Volume 5/191]
"**Sing** thou my songs for me when I am dead!" Thy songs

"**Slowly** the poison the whole blood stream fills." Missing Dates. W. Empson. [Supp 2/144]
"**Slowly** the topography emerges, a pile." The World comes Back Like an Old Cat. M. Piercy. [Supp 5/200]
**Sly** Thoughts. C. Patmore. [Volume 2/112]
The **Smack** in School. W. Palmer. [Volume 1/167]
**Small** and Early. T. Jenks. [Volume 1/46]
**Small** Beginnings. C. Mackay. [Volume 4/309]
A **Small** Bird's Sky. S. Murano. [Supp 7/118]
"The **small** bue Arab stallion dances on the hill." Blue Arab. J. Wright. [Supp 5/327]
"A **small** child %is ill, has awakened." Descending Figure: 2. The Sick Child. L. Gluck. [Supp 5/103]
**Smile** and Never Heed Me. C. Swain. [Volume 2/115]
*Smiling*
   "When Was the Last Time You Saw Miami Smile?" A. Casiano. [Supp 4/288]
**Smith, Belle E.**
   "If I Should Die To-Night" [Volume 3/374]
**Smith, F. Burge**
   Little Goldenhair. [Volume 1/42]
**Smith, Goldwin (tr.)**
   Beauty Unadorned, fr. Elegies. S. Propertius. [Volume 6/282]
**Smith, Horace**
   Address to the Mummy at Belzoni's Exhibition. [Volume 6/235]
   The Gouty Merchant and the Stranger. [Volume 9/275]
   Hymn to the Flowers. [Volume 5/242]
**Smith, May Riley**
   If We Knew; or, Blessings of To-day. [Volume 1/278]
   In Prison. [Volume 4/323]
   Sometime. [Volume 4/344]
   Tired Mothers. [Volume 1/282]
**Smith, Samuel Francis**
   America. [Volume 8/95]
**Smith, Seba**
   The Mother's Sacrifice. [Volume 1/24]
**Smith, Stevie**
   "Away, Melancholy %Away With It, Let It Go" [Supp 5/281]
   The Bereaved Swan. [Supp 2/102]
   Fafnir and the Knights. [Supp 5/282]
   Harold's Leap. [Supp 5/284]
   The Heavenly City. [Supp 2/103]
   The Little Boy Lost. [Supp 2/103]
   Love Me! [Supp 5/285]
   "Now Pine-Needles" [Supp 5/286]
   The River God. [Supp 2/104]
   Thoughts About the Christian Doctrine of Eternal Hell. [Supp 5/279]
   To the Tune of the Coventry Carol. [Supp 2/105]
   The Wanderer. [Supp 5/285]
   The Weak Monk. [Supp 2/106]
**Smith, Sydney**
   A Recipe. [Volume 9/385]
**Smith, Walter C.**
   The Self-exiled. [Volume 4/158]
**Smith, William Jay (tr.)**
   August 1964. F. Guillar. [Supp 6/115]
   Poem to a Young Man. L. Bell. [Supp 6/108]
   Things of the Earth. F. Guillar. [Supp 6/114]
**Smoke.** H. Thoreau. [Volume 7/156]
**Smoking** Spiritualized. R. Erskine. [Volume 6/250]
**Snag.** V. Cruz. [Supp 4/278]
**Snake.** D. Pagis. [Supp 7/250]
*Snakes*
   Snake. D. Pagis. [Supp 7/250]
   The Viper. R. Pitter. [Supp 2/51]
**Sneezing.** L. Hunt. [Volume 9/421]
*Snow*

Early Night. C. Forche. [Supp 5/82]
   Milk at the Bottom of the Sea. O. Williams. [Supp 2/79]
   Velvet Shoes. E. Wylie. [Supp 1/326]
**Snow-flakes.** M. Dodge. [Volume 5/176]
**Snow-flakes.** H. Longfellow. [Volume 5/174]
"The **snow** had begun in the gloaming." The First Snow-Fall. J. Lowell. [Volume 3/283]
"The **snow**, less intransigeant than their marble." At the Grave of Henry James. W. Auden. [Supp 2/150]
The **Snow-shower.** W. Byrant. [Volume 5/178]
A **Snow-storm.** C. Eastman. [Volume 5/180]
The **Snow-Storm.** R. Emerson. [Volume 5/176]
The **Snow-storm.** E. Wetherald. [Volume 5/177]
**Snow** Upon Paris. L. Senghor. [Supp 6/73]
*Snowflakes*
   Winter Poem. N. Giovanni. [Supp 5/100]
"The **Snowing** of the Pines" T. Higginson. [Volume 5/180]
The **Snows.** C. Sangster. [Volume 5/203]
The **Snug** Little Island. T. Dibdin. [Volume 8/15]
"'**So** ...' they said." The Dinner-party. A. Lowell. [Supp 1/201]
"**So** all day long the noise of battle rolled." Mort D'Arthur. A. Tennyson. [Volume 7/352]
"**So** every spirit, as it is most pure." Beauty, fr. An Hymne in Honor of Beautie. E. Spenser. [Volume 6/282]
"**So** gentle and so gracious doth appear." My Lady. Dante Alighieri. [Volume 2/24]
"**So** I would rather drown, remembering." The Flowering of the Rod: 006. H. Doolittle. [Supp 5/76]
"**So** like a god I sit here." The Sitting. C. Day Lewis. [Supp 2/122]
"**So** many worlds, so much to do." Death in Life's Prime, fr. In Memoriam. A. Tennyson. [Volume 3/354]
"**So** much to do: so little done!" Three Days. J. Gilmore. [Volume 6/189]
"**So** now is come our joyful's feast." Christmas. G. Wither. [Volume 1/330]
"**So**, some tempestuous morn in early June." Early June, fr. Thyrsis. M. Arnold. [Volume 5/252]
**So** Sweet Love Seemed. R. Bridges. [Volume 2/326]
"**So** Sweet Love Seemed That April Morn" R. Bridges. [Supp 1/75]
"**So** sweet love seemed that April morn." So Sweet Love Seemed. R. Bridges. [Volume 2/326]
"**So** that soldierly legend is still on its journey." Kearny at Seven Pines. E. Stedman. [Volume 8/367]
"**So**, the truth's out. I'll grasp it like a snake." Only a Woman. D. Craik. [Volume 3/86]
"**So** when that angel of the darker drink." Rubaiyat: 043. O. Khayyam. [Volume 6/212]
"**So** you keep looking back." Heat and Sweat. M. Serote. [Supp 6/92]
*Social Problems*
   I Have Seen Black Hands: 001. R. Wright. [Supp 2/214]
   I Have Seen Black Hands: 002. R. Wright. [Supp 2/215]
   I Have Seen Black Hands: 003. R. Wright. [Supp 2/216]
   I Have Seen Black Hands: 004. R. Wright. [Supp 2/216]
   Joe Hill Listens to the Praying. K. Patchen. [Supp 2/248]
   A Letter on the Use of Machine Guns at Weddings. K. Patchen. [Supp 2/252]
   A Letter to a Policeman in Kansas City. K. Patchen. [Supp 2/253]
   Salvos for Randolph Bourne: 001. H. Gregory. [Supp 2/65]

Salvos for Randolph Bourne: 002. H. Gregory. [Supp 2/65]

Salvos for Randolph Bourne: 003. H. Gregory. [Supp 2/66]

Somebody and Somebody Else and You. E. Rolfe. [Supp 2/220]

Street Corner College. K. Patchen. [Supp 2/255]

The Society Upon the Stanislaus. B. Harte. [Volume 9/372]

"Soft on the sunset sky." Ashes of Roses. E. Eastman. [Volume 3/51]

"Softer than silence, stiller than still air." "The Snowing of the Pines" T. Higginson. [Volume 5/180]

"The softest whisperings of the scented south." An Old Battle-field. F. Stanton. [Volume 8/446]

"Softly Woo Away Here Breath" B. Procter. [Volume 3/318]

Soggarth Aroon. J. Banim. [Volume 4/170]

Sojourn in the Whale. M. Moore. [Supp 5/185]

Solberg, S. E. (tr.)
April. Pak Tu-Jin. [Supp 7/153]
Heavenly Lake. Pak Tu-Jin. [Supp 7/155]
Hymn to the Graveyard. Pak Tu-Jin. [Supp 7/151]
A Message from the Crane. Pak Tu-Jin. [Supp 7/154]
Song. Pak Tu-Jin. [Supp 7/154]
Stars. Pak Tu-Jin. [Supp 7/151]
Sun. Pak Tu-Jin. [Supp 7/152]

The Soldier. R. Brooke. [Supp 1/76]

A Soldier Dreaming of White Lilies. M. Darwish. [Supp 7/265]

"A soldier of the legion lay dying in Algiers." Bingen on the Rhine. C. Norton. [Volume 8/221]

*Soldiers*
Elegy for a Dead Soldier: 001. K. Shapiro. [Supp 2/314]

Elegy for a Dead Soldier: 002. K. Shapiro. [Supp 2/314]

Elegy for a Dead Soldier: 003. K. Shapiro. [Supp 2/314]

Elegy for a Dead Soldier: 004. K. Shapiro. [Supp 2/315,War]

Elegy for a Dead Soldier: 005. K. Shapiro. [Supp 2/315]

Elegy for a Dead Soldier: 006. K. Shapiro. [Supp 2/316]

Elegy for a Dead Soldier: 007. K. Shapiro. [Supp 2/316]

Elegy for a Dead Soldier: 008. K. Shapiro. [Supp 2/316]

Elegy for a Dead Soldier: 009. K. Shapiro. [Supp 2/317]

Elegy for a Dead Soldier: 010. K. Shapiro. [Supp 2/317]

Elegy for a Dead Soldier: 011. K. Shapiro. [Supp 2/318]

Hussar's Song, fr. The Dynasts. T. Hardy. [Supp 1/159]

A Man. N. Cassian. [Supp 5/46]

Two Armies. S. Spender. [Supp 2/235]

The Soldier's Dream. T. Campbell. [Volume 1/280]

A Soliloquy. W. Harte. [Volume 5/339]

Soliloquy on Death, fr. Hamlet. W. Shakespeare. [Volume 3/252]

Soliloquy: On Immortality, fr. Cato. J. Addison. [Volume 4/384]

The Solitary Woodsman. C. Roberts. [Volume 5/145]

Solitude. M. Iqbal. [Supp 7/61]

*Solitude*
"I'm Alone %I See" Nirala. [Supp 7/68]
Souls Lake. R. Fitzgerald. [Supp 2/241]
Tearing Up My Mother's Letters. D. Wakoski. [Supp 5/324]

Solutions. E. Blunden. [Supp 2/46]

"Some %times I dream bout." Last Poem i'm Gonna Write

About Us. S. Sanchez. [Supp 4/189]

"Some find Love late, some find him soon." When Will Love Come? P. Beatty. [Volume 2/74]

"Some might lament that I were cold." Stanza. P. Shelley. [Volume 3/165]

"Some nights the moon is the curve of a comb." The Window Frames the Moon. L. Mar. [Supp 4/32]

"Some of the glories of this world, and some." Rubaiyat: 013. O. Khayyam. [Volume 6/206]

"Some say that kissing's a sin." Kissing's No Sin. Unknown. [Volume 2/107]

"Some time on must leave." Finished. T. Heraty. [Supp 7/96]

"Some wit of old - such wits of old there were." Paper. B. Franklin. [Volume 9/289]

Somebody. Unknown. [Volume 2/162]

Somebody and Somebody Else and You. E. Rolfe. [Supp 2/220]

"somebody knew Lincoln somebody Xerxes." Portrait - X. E. Cummings. [Supp 1/103]

"Somebody's courting somebody." Somebody. Unknown. [Volume 2/162]

Somebody's Darling. M. Conte. [Volume 8/378]

Somebody's Song. D. Parker. [Supp 1/248]

"Someday perhaps, the poem." Introduction. F. Faiz. [Supp 7/169]

Someone Talking. J. Harjo. [Supp 4/339]

Something Beyond. M. Hudson. [Volume 3/234]

"Something beyond! though now, with joy unfound." Something Beyond. M. Hudson. [Volume 3/234]

"Something hangs in back of me." The Wings. D. Levertov. [Supp 5/141]

"Something there is that doesn't love a wall." Mending Wall. R. Frost. [Supp 1/130]

Sometime. M. Smith. [Volume 4/344]

"Sometime, when all life's lessons have been." Sometime. M. Smith. [Volume 4/344]

"Sometimes, apart in sleep, by chance." The Trance. S. Spender. [Supp 2/234]

"Sometimes in summer months, the matrix earth." Summer Idyll. G. Barker. [Supp 2/292]

"Sometimes the living dead." African China: 004. M. Tolson. [Supp 4/103]

"Sometimes, when nature falls asleep." Night Mists. W. Hayne. [Volume 6/179]

"Sometimes you hear a question like 'what is'" Categories. N. Giovanni. [Supp 5/100]

"Somewhere in the world there hide." In Twos. W. Gannett. [Volume 2/403]

"Somewhere, out on the blue seas sailing." When My Ship Comes In. R. Burdette. [Volume 3/245]

Song. Adonis. [Supp 7/278]

Song. M. Akenside. [Volume 2/11]

Song. J. Bunyan. [Volume 6/418]

A Song. T. Carew. [Volume 2/36]

Song. E. Cummings. [Supp 1/101]

The Song. Ho Ch'i-Fang. [Supp 7/4]

Song. R. Le Gallienne. [Volume 3/417]

Song. Pak Tu-Jin. [Supp 7/154]

Song. S. Scott. [Volume 3/31]

Song. S. Sedley. [Volume 2/71]

Song. E. Sitwell. [Supp 5/277]

Song. S. Spender. [Supp 2/233]

Song. Walther Von Der Vogelweide. [Volume 2/26]

Song at Night. L. Lee. [Supp 2/341]

Song For a Slight Voice. L. Bogan. [Supp 5/33]

Song for My Father. J. Hagedorn. [Supp 4/24]

A Song for Saint Cecilia's Day, 1687. J. Dryden. [Volume 6/364]

Song for St. Cecilia's Day. W. Auden. [Supp 2/167]

"A song for the plant of my own native west." The Maize. W. Fosdick. [Volume 5/267]

Song, fr. Pippa Passes. R. Browning. [Volume 4/1]

Song, fr. The Lady of the Lake. S. Scott. [Volume 3/101]

Song, fr. The Miller's Daughter. A. Tennyson. [Volume 2/102]
Song, fr. Woo'd And Married And A. J. Baillie. [Volume 2/411]
A Song in the Front Yard. G. Brooks. [Supp 5/36]
"A song in the valley of Nemea." Nemea. L. Durrell. [Supp 2/260]
The Song of Abraham in Fire. A. Shamlu. [Supp 7/211]
The Song of Bullets. J. Hagedorn. [Supp 4/29]
Song of Clan-Alpine, fr. The Lady of the Lake. S. Scott. [Volume 8/305]
A Song of Derivations. A. Meynell. [Supp 1/213]
Song of Eglia. M. Brooks. [Volume 3/138]
Song of Marion's Men. W. Byrant. [Volume 8/330]
Song of One Eleven Years in Prison. G. Canning. [Volume 9/294]
Song of Other Lives. L. Marechal. [Supp 6/105]
A Song of Seasons. E. MacDonald. [Volume 5/191]
Song of the Brook, fr. The Brook: An Idyl. A. Tennyson. [Volume 5/194]
The Song Of The Camp. B. Taylor. [Volume 2/362]
Song of the Chattahoochee. S. Lanier. [Volume 7/242]
The Song of the Demented Priest. J. Berryman. [Supp 2/329]
Song of the East. A. Mutis. [Supp 6/133]
Song of the Emigrants in Bermuda. A. Marvell. [Volume 5/400]
Song of the Greek Poet, fr. Don Juan. G. Byron. [Volume 8/130]
Song of the Greeks. T. Campbell. [Volume 8/197]
The Song of the Lower Classes. E. Jones. [Volume 6/391]
Song of the Milkmaid, fr. Queen Mary. A. Tennyson. [Volume 2/107]
The Song of the Old Mother. W. Yeats. [Volume 1/284]
Song of the River. C. Kingsley. [Volume 5/201]
Song of the Sabbath. K. Molodowsky. [Supp 5/173]
The Song of the Savoyards. H. Blood. [Volume 3/248]
The Song of the Shirt. T. Hood. [Volume 3/199]
Song of the Silent Land. J. Von Salis. [Volume 4/388]
The Song of the Smoke. W. Du Bois. [Supp 4/65]
Song of the Summer Winds. G. Darley. [Volume 5/99]
Song of the Sun. J. Toomer. [Supp 4/90]
Song of the Three Seeds in the Macaw's Beak. E. Coatsworth. [Supp 1/85]
Song of the Western Men. R. Hawker. [Volume 8/136]
Song: On May Morning. J. Milton. [Volume 5/85]
"The song that I came to sing remains unsung to this day." Gitanjali: 013. R. Tagore. [Supp 7/75]
Song to the Argentine, sel. R. Dario. [Supp 6/169]
"A song to the oak, the brave old oak." The Brave Old Oak. H. Chorley. [Volume 5/220]
Song to the Runaway Slave. Unknown (African American). [Supp 4/53]
Song Without Words. P. Pietri. [Supp 4/256]
Songs and Singing
    The Dead Man Asks for a Song. Unknown (African American). [Supp 6/3]
    Empty Vessel. H. MacDiarmid. [Supp 2/29]
    Flower Bridge. Liang Shang Ch'uan. [Supp 7/22]
    Georgia Dusk. J. Toomer. [Supp 4/89]
    Homage to the Empress of the Blues. R. Hayden. [Supp 4/136]
    "She's Singing in the Rain" W. Rendra. [Supp 7/101]
    The Song. Ho Ch'i-Fang. [Supp 7/4]
    When Malindy Sings. P. Dunbar. [Supp 4/79]
    Songs of Ariel, fr. The Tempest. W. Shakespeare. [Volume 6/57]
"Songs on this side, the other side responds." Flower Bridge. Liang Shang Ch'uan. [Supp 7/22]
Sonnet. G. Chapman. [Volume 2/73]
The Sonnet. R. Gilder. [Volume 6/344]
Sonnet. L. Labe. [Volume 3/237]
Sonnet. L. Lindsay. [Volume 3/304]

Sonnet. J. Masefield. [Supp 1/209]
A Sonnet. G. Stein. [Supp 5/297]
The Sonnet. W. Wordsworth. [Volume 7/55]
Sonnet. W. Wordsworth. [Volume 7/229]
Sonnet 018. H. Belloc. [Supp 1/33]
Sonnet 12: The Approach of Age. W. Shakespeare. [Volume 6/194]
Sonnet, fr. Astrophel and Stella. S. Sidney. [Volume 3/13,Volume 6/342]
Sonnet from Second April. E. Millay. [Supp 1/224]
Sonnet of Fishes. G. Barker. [Supp 2/291]
Sonnet - Realities I. E. Cummings. [Supp 1/104]
Sonnet to Cyriak Skinner. J. Milton. [Volume 3/220]
Sonnet Upon A Stolen Kiss. G. Wither. [Volume 2/110]
Sonnets. J. Lowell. [Volume 2/382]
Sonnets From The Portuguese. E. Browning. [Volume 2/377]
"Soon as the sun forsook the eastern main." An Hymn to the Evening. P. Wheatley. [Supp 4/62]
The Soothsayer. D. Levertov. [Supp 5/144]
Sophocles
    The Death of Sophocles. A. Akhmatova. [Supp 5/11]
Sophocles
    Fortune. R. Garnett (tr.). [Volume 6/283]
Sorcerers
    Sorcery. J. Hagedorn. [Supp 4/22]
Sorcery. J. Hagedorn. [Supp 4/22]
Sorrow
    Dolor. T. Roethke. [Supp 2/204]
    The Riddlers. W. De La Mare. [Supp 1/108]
    "We Wear the Mask That Grins and Lies" P. Dunbar. [Supp 4/75]
Sorrows of Werther. W. Thackeray. [Volume 9/204]
Soul
    The Eagle and the Mole. E. Wylie. [Supp 1/326]
Soul Lamp. Li Chi. [Supp 7/12]
"The soul of man is larger than the sky." Shakespeare. H. Coleridge. [Volume 7/52]
Souls Lake. R. Fitzgerald. [Supp 2/241]
Sound. Ho Ch'i-Fang. [Supp 7/7]
A Sound. G. Stein. [Supp 5/293]
Sound of the Flute. Li Ying. [Supp 7/16]
"Sounds all to arms!" Catiline to the Roman Army, fr. Catiline. G. Croly. [Volume 8/188]
The Source. L. Inada. [Supp 4/2]
Sousa, Noemia de
    "If You Want To Know Me" M. Dickinson (tr.). [Supp 5/59]
    The Poem of Joao. M. Dickinson (tr.). [Supp 5/61]
South Africa
    Echo of Mandela. Z. Mandela. [Supp 6/78]
    Protea. D. Mattera. [Supp 6/80]
The South Country. H. Belloc. [Supp 1/31]
"The south-land boasts its teeming cane." Our State. J. Whittier. [Volume 8/93]
Southern Mansion. A. Bontemps. [Supp 4/123]
The Southern Road. D. Randall. [Supp 4/155]
Southey, Caroline Bowles
    The Cuckoo Clock, fr. The Birthday. [Volume 7/148]
    The Young Gray Head. [Volume 9/132]
Southey, Robert
    The Battle of Blenheim. [Volume 8/437]
    The Cataract of Lodore. [Volume 7/170]
    God's Judgment on a Wicked Bishop. [Volume 9/52]
    The Holly-tree. [Volume 5/221]
    The Inchcape Rock. [Volume 5/431]
    "My Days Among the Dead" [Volume 4/396]
    Well of St. Keyne. [Volume 9/204]
Southey, Robert and Caroline
    The Greenwood Shrift. [Volume 7/379]
"Southrons, hear your country call you!" Dixie. A. Pike. [Volume 8/106]
South, The
    The Southern Road. D. Randall. [Supp 4/155]
Southwell, Robert

Spring Street Bar. M. Berssenbrugge. [Supp 4/12]
Spring, the Sweet Spring. T. Nash. [Volume 5/77]
"Spring, the sweet spring, is the year's pleasant."
    Spring, the Sweet Spring. T. Nash. [Volume
    5/77]
"Spring, with that nameless pathos in the air."
    Spring in Carolina. H. Timrod. [Volume 5/86]
Squire, John Collings
    The Discovery. [Supp 1/285]
Stabat Mater Dolorosa. F. Jacopone. [Volume 4/70]
"Stady, boys, steady!" Wounded to Death. J. Watson.
    [Volume 8/375]
"The stag at eve had drunk his fill." The Stag Hunt,
    fr. The Lady of the Lake. S. Scott. [Volume
    5/159]
The Stag Hunt, fr. The Lady of the Lake. S. Scott.
    [Volume 5/159]
The Stag Hunt, fr. The Seasons: Autumn. J. Thomson.
    [Volume 5/163]
"The stag too, singled from the herd where long." The
    Stag Hunt, fr. The Seasons: Autumn. J. Thomson.
    [Volume 5/163]
"Stand here by my side and turn, I pray." The Snow-
    shower. W. Bryant. [Volume 5/178]
"Stand on the highest pavement of the stair." La
    Figlia Che Piange. T. Eliot. [Supp 1/120]
"Stand! the ground's your own, my braves!" Warren's
    Address. J. Pierpont. [Volume 8/326]
"Stand up - erect! Thou hast the form." The Laborer.
    W. Gallagher. [Volume 4/302]
"Standing, emptying %myself to the endless flow of
    flies." Civilization. H. Riyong. [Supp 6/49]
Stanley, Arthur Penrhyn
    The Disciples After the Ascension. [Volume 4/77]
    "Till Death Us Part." [Volume 2/458]
Stansaz in Meditation: Part 001, Stanza 013. G. Stein.
    [Supp 5/290]
Stansaz in Meditation: Part 002, Stanza 001. G. Stein.
    [Supp 5/290]
Stansaz in Meditation: Part 005, Stanza 041. G. Stein.
    [Supp 5/291]
Stanton, Frank Lebby
    The Mocking-bird. [Volume 5/319]
    An Old Battle-field. [Volume 8/446]
    A Plantation Ditty. [Volume 9/376]
Stanza. P. Shelley. [Volume 3/164, Volume 3/165]
Stanzas. G. Byron. [Volume 2/361]
The Star-Bangled Banner. F. Key. [Volume 8/154]
Star-Mist, fr. Stars. J. Keble. [Volume 4/415]
The Star of Bethlehem. H. White. [Volume 4/89]
Star Talk. R. Graves. [Supp 1/149]
"Star that bringest home the bee." To the Evening
    Star. T. Campbell. [Volume 5/54]
"The Starlight's Intuitions Pierced the Twelve" D.
    Schwartz. [Supp 2/309]
Stars. Pak Tu-Jin. [Supp 7/151]
Stars
    Peace on Earth. W. Williams. [Supp 1/319]
    Star Talk. R. Graves. [Supp 1/149]
    Stars. Pak Tu-Jin. [Supp 7/151]
The Stars: 002. Ping Hsin. [Supp 5/119]
The Stars: 012. Ping Hsin. [Supp 5/119]
The Stars: 034. Ping Hsin. [Supp 5/119]
The Stars: 048. Ping Hsin. [Supp 5/119]
The Stars: 052. Ping Hsin. [Supp 5/119]
"Stars of the summer night!" Serenade, fr. The
    Spanish Student. H. Longfellow. [Volume 2/255]
"Stars, stars, %lean down and speak." The Milk of the
    Mothers. M. Waddington. [Supp 5/310]
"Start with a simple room." Plucking Out a Rhythm. L.
    Inada. [Supp 4/4]
"Start with the itch and there will be no scratch.
    Study." We Walk the Way of the New World: 002.
    D. Lee. [Supp 4/214]
"The stately homes of England." The Homes of England.

F. Hemans. [Volume 1/274]
The Statue of the Century. Tru Vu. [Supp 7/198]
Statues
    The Statue of the Century. Tru Vu. [Supp 7/198]
Stay, Spring. A. Young. [Supp 2/3]
"Stay, spring, for by this ruthless haste." Stay,
    Spring. A. Young. [Supp 2/3]
Steal Away. Unknown (African American). [Supp 4/51]
"Steal away, steal away, steal away to Jesus." Steal
    Away. Unknown (African American). [Supp 4/51]
Stedman, Edmund Clarence
    Betrothed Anew. [Volume 5/92]
    Calvary Song, fr. Alice of Monmouth. [Volume
        8/365]
    Cousin Lucrece. [Volume 7/131]
    The Hand of Lincoln. [Volume 7/30]
    Hawthorne. [Volume 7/103]
    Hymn of the West. [Volume 8/458]
    Kearny at Seven Pines. [Volume 8/367]
    Pan in Wall Street. [Volume 6/381]
    Si Jeunesse Savait! [Volume 2/242]
    The Undiscovered Country. [Volume 4/387]
"A steed! a steed of matchlesse speed." The
    Cavalier's Song. W. Motherwell. [Volume 8/270]
Steel. J. Auslander. [Supp 1/16]
"Steel doors - guillontine gates." The Prisoner. R.
    Hayden. [Supp 4/153]
Steel Mill. L. Untermeyer. [Supp 1/311]
"Steer hither, steer your winged pines." The Sirens'
    Song, fr. Inner Temple Masque. W. Browne.
    [Volume 6/79]
Stein, Evaleen
    In Mexico. [Volume 7/257]
Stein, Gertrude
    A Cutlet. [Supp 5/293]
    Eye Glasses. [Supp 5/293]
    A Frightful Release. [Supp 5/292]
    A Mounted Umbrella. [Supp 5/292]
    A Poetical Plea. [Supp 5/296]
    A Purse. [Supp 5/292]
    Rhubarb. [Supp 5/295]
    A Sonnet. [Supp 5/297]
    A Sound. [Supp 5/293]
    Stansaz in Meditation: Part 001, Stanza 013. [Supp
        5/290]
    Stansaz in Meditation: Part 002, Stanza 001. [Supp
        5/290]
    Stansaz in Meditation: Part 005, Stanza 041. [Supp
        5/291]
    Suppose and Eyes. [Supp 5/294]
    A Table. [Supp 5/294]
    Water Raining. [Supp 5/293]
    What Is the Name of a Ring. [Supp 5/295]
Stephen, James Kenneth
    Lapsus calami. [Volume 9/422]
Stephen the Sabaite, Saint
    Art Thou Weary. J. Neale (tr.). [Volume 4/87]
Stephens, James
    In Waste Places. [Supp 1/286]
Sterling, George
    The Black Vulture. [Supp 1/288]
    The Queen Forgets. [Supp 1/287]
Sterling, John
    Alfred the harper. [Volume 8/238]
    Louis XV. [Volume 7/339]
    On a Beautiful Day. [Volume 5/6]
    The Rose and the Gauntlet. [Volume 9/131]
    The Two Oceans. [Volume 6/439]
"Stern daughter of the voice of God!" Ode to Duty. W.
    Wordsworth. [Volume 4/278]
Stevens, George Alexander
    The Storm. [Volume 5/414]
Stevens, Wallace
    Peter Quince at the Clavier. [Supp 1/289]
    The Worms at Heaven's Gate. [Supp 1/291]

**Stevenson, Robert Louis**
  Foreign Children. [Volume 1/130]
  Foreign Lands. [Volume 1/138]
  A Good Play. [Volume 1/127]
  Heather Ale: A Galloway Legend. [Volume 8/40]
  The House Beautiful. [Volume 1/277]
  In Memoriam F. A. S. [Volume 3/428]
  In the Season. [Volume 1/209]
  The Land of Counterpane. [Volume 1/107]
  The Land of Story-Books. [Volume 1/140]
  My Shadow. [Volume 1/133]
  The Unseen Playmate. [Volume 1/131]
  The Wind. [Volume 1/145]
**Still**, Citizen Sparrow. R. Wilbur. [Supp 2/409]
"**Still**, citizen sparrow, this vulture which you
    call." Still, Citizen Sparrow. R. Wilbur. [Supp
    2/409]
A **Still** Day in Autumn. S. Whitman. [Volume 7/157]
"**Still** Falls the Rain" E. Sitwell. [Supp 2/21]
**Still, John**
  Good Ale. [Volume 9/248]
"**Still** sits the school-house by the road." In School-
    Days. J. Whittier. [Volume 1/163]
"**Still** thirteen years: 't is autumn now." Palinode,
    Autumn. J. Lowell. [Volume 3/115]
"**Still** to be neat, still to be drest." Freedom is
    Dress, fr. Epicoene; or, the Silent Woman. B.
    Jonson. [Volume 7/131]
**Stillman, Annie R. ("Grace Raymond")**
  Birth. [Volume 1/3]
**Stoddard, Richard Henry**
  Country Life. [Volume 1/320]
  The Flight of Youth. [Volume 1/264]
  "Men of the North and West" [Volume 8/97]
"**Ston** axes and the like." Museum. S. Tanikawa. [Supp
    7/131]
"**Stone** the Woman, Let the Man Go Free" Unknown.
    [Volume 4/322]
*Stones*
  Lost in Sulphur Canyons. J. Barnes. [Supp 4/299]
  The Serenity in Stones. S. Ortiz. [Supp 4/315]
**Stonewall** Jackson's Way. J. Palmer. [Volume 8/360]
"**Stood** the afflicted mother weeping." Stabat Mater
    Dolorosa. F. Jacopone. [Volume 4/70]
"**Stop**, mortal! Here thy brother lies." Burns. E.
    Elliott. [Volume 7/63]
*Stories*
  Rowing. A. Sexton. [Supp 5/256]
  Story Keeper. W. Rose. [Supp 4/325]
"The **stories** %would be braided in my hair." Story
    Keeper. W. Rose. [Supp 4/325]
The **Storm**. G. Stevens. [Volume 5/414]
**Storm** in the Alps, fr. Childe Harold. G. Byron.
    [Volume 5/213]
**Storm** in the Distance. P. Hayne. [Volume 5/123]
"The **storm** is out; the land is roused." Men and Boys.
    K. Korner. [Volume 8/78]
*Storms*
  Night Storm. S. Murano. [Supp 7/118]
The **Story**. D. Pagis. [Supp 7/249]
"A **story**, a story." Rowing. A. Sexton. [Supp 5/256]
**Story** Keeper. W. Rose. [Supp 4/325]
The **Story** of a Summer Day. A. Hume. [Volume 5/104]
The **Story** of Cruel Fredderick, fr. The English
    Struwwelpeter. H. Hoffmann. [Volume 1/170]
The **Story** of Johnny-Head-In-Air. H. Hoffmann. [Volume
    1/173]
**Story** Of The Gate. T. Robertson. [Volume 2/167]
**Story, Robert**
  The Whistle. [Volume 2/112]
**Story, William Wetmore**
  Cleopatra. [Volume 2/354]
**Story, William Wetmore (tr.)**
  Perseverance. L. Da Vinci. [Volume 6/284]
**Stowe, Harriet Beecher**

A **Day** in the Pamfili Doria. [Volume 7/182]
  Knocking, Ever Knocking. [Volume 4/92]
  Lines. [Volume 3/426]
  "Only a Year" [Volume 3/418]
  The Other World. [Volume 4/389]
"**Straightway** Virginius led the maid." The Roman
    Father, fr. Virginia. L. Macaulay; Thomas
    Babington. [Volume 9/16]
**Strand, Mark (tr.)**
  Flame, Speech. O. Paz. [Supp 6/147]
"**Strange**, is it not? that of the myriads who."
    Rubaiyat: 064. O. Khayyam. [Volume 6/216]
**Strange** Legacies. S. Brown. [Supp 4/117]
"**Strangely** assorted, the shape of song and the
    bloody." The Military Harpist. R. Pitter. [Supp
    2/48]
"A **stranger** arrived." The Minaret. Adonis. [Supp
    7/283]
"A **stranger** came one night to Yussouf's tent."
    Yussouf. J. Lowell. [Volume 6/279]
"**Stranger**, you who hide my love." Song. S. Spender.
    [Supp 2/233]
"**Stranger**, 't is vain! midst Rome thou seek'st for."
    To Rome. F. Quevedo Y. Villegas. [Volume 7/177]
**Strangford, Lord (tr.)**
  Blighted Love. L. De Camoens. [Volume 3/81]
"**Strapped** at the center of the blazing wheel." A
    Pilot from the Carrier. R. Jarrell. [Supp
    2/332]
**Street, Alfred B.**
  The Settler. [Volume 7/240]
**Street** Corner College. K. Patchen. [Supp 2/255]
"A **street** there is in Paris famous." The Ballad of
    Bouillabaisse. W. Thackeray. [Volume 1/393]
"**Strew** on her roses, roses." Requiescat. M. Arnold.
    [Volume 3/307]
*Strikes and Strikers*
  Not Men Alone. E. Rolfe. [Supp 2/217]
"**Stripped** country, shrunken as a beggar's heart." The
    Golden Corpse. S. Benet. [Supp 1/42]
**Strode, William**
  Kisses. [Volume 2/106]
**Strong** Men. S. Brown. [Supp 4/119]
"**Strong** Men, Riding Horses" G. Brooks. [Supp 5/38]
"**Strong** Son of God, Immortal Love", fr. In Memoriam.
    A. Tennyson. [Volume 4/45]
**Strong, William (tr.)**
  Frithiof at the court of Angantyr, fr. Frithiof
    Saga. E. Tegner. [Volume 7/289]
**Strontium**. E. Manner. [Supp 5/150]
**Stryk and Takashi Ikemoto, Lucien (tr.)**
  Burning Oneself to Death. S. Takahashi. [Supp
    7/126]
  Nehru. S. Takahashi. [Supp 7/126, Supp 7/127]
  Time. S. Takahashi. [Supp 7/125]
  What is Moving. S. Takahashi. [Supp 7/128]
  Words. S. Takahashi. [Supp 7/129]
*Students*
  "I Am a University Student" S. Wongthed. [Supp
    7/185]
"**Stuff** of the moon." Nocturne in a Deserted Brickyard.
    C. Sandburg. [Supp 1/278]
**Stump?A**. Nirala. [Supp 7/65]
**Sturm, Julius**
  I Hold Still. [Volume 3/243]
**Stylite**. L. MacNeice. [Supp 2/183]
*Subways*
  The Tunnel. H. Crane. [Supp 1/92]
"**Such** a morning it is when love." Day of These Days.
    L. Lee. [Supp 2/335]
"**Such** a starved bank of moss." Love. R. Browning.
    [Volume 2/339]
**Suckling, Sir John**
  The Bride, fr. A Ballad Upon A Wedding. [Volume
    2/410]

Constancy. [Volume 2/23]
"I Prithee Send Me Back My Heart" [Volume 2/187]
Why So Pale And Wan? [Volume 2/247]
**Sudden** Heart. D. Pagis. [Supp 7/252]
**"Sudden** heart, tightrope walker with no rope." Sudden
Heart. D. Pagis. [Supp 7/252]
**Sudden** Light. D. Rossetti. [Volume 6/302]
**"Suddenly** from a wayside station." In the Train. C.
Bax. [Supp 1/27]
*Suicide*
Dirge. K. Fearing. [Supp 2/99]
An Elegy. D. Gascoyne. [Supp 2/382]
For Colored Girls Who Have Considered Suicide ...,
sel. N. Shange. [Supp 4/230,Supp 4/231]
Notes Found Near a Suicide: To "Chick" F. Horne.
[Supp 4/109]
Notes Found Near a Suicide: To Alfred. F. Horne.
[Supp 4/114]
Notes Found Near a Suicide: To All of You. F.
Horne. [Supp 4/108]
Notes Found Near a Suicide: To Caroline. F. Horne.
[Supp 4/114]
Notes Found Near a Suicide: To Catalina. F. Horne.
[Supp 4/108]
Notes Found Near a Suicide: To Henry. F. Horne.
[Supp 4/113]
Notes Found Near a Suicide: To James. F. Horne.
[Supp 4/111]
Notes Found Near a Suicide: To Mother. F. Horne.
[Supp 4/108]
Notes Found Near a Suicide: To Telic. F. Horne.
[Supp 4/109]
Notes Found Near a Suicide: To the One Who Called
Me Nigger. F. Horne. [Supp 4/114]
Notes Found Near a Suicide: To the Poets. F. Horne.
[Supp 4/112]
Notes Found Near a Suicide: To Wanda. F. Horne.
[Supp 4/110]
Notes Found Near a Suicide: To You. F. Horne.
[Supp 4/115]
On Suicide. S. Murano. [Supp 7/117]
Richard Cory. E. Robinson. [Supp 1/266]
Steel. J. Auslander. [Supp 1/16]
*Summer*
Country Summer. L. Adams. [Supp 2/70]
Summer Idyll. G. Barker. [Supp 2/292]
Summer Night, Riverside. S. Teasdale. [Supp 1/294]
Summer Song. G. Barker. [Supp 2/293]
"The **summer** and autumn had been so wet." God's
Judgment on a Wicked Bishop. R. Southey.
[Volume 9/52]
**Summer** Days. W. Call. [Volume 2/341]
**"Summer** has gone." Life in the Autumn Woods. P. Cooke.
[Volume 5/151]
**Summer** Idyll. G. Barker. [Supp 2/292]
**Summer** in Calcutta. K. Das. [Supp 5/56]
**"Summer** is icumen in." Cuckoo Song. Unknown. [Volume
5/90]
**"Summer** joys are o'er." Winter Song. L. Holty.
[Volume 5/186]
**Summer** Longings. D. MacCarthy. [Volume 5/81]
**Summer** Moods. J. Clare. [Volume 5/136]
A **Summer** Night. G. Russell. [Supp 1/274]
**Summer** Night, Riverside. S. Teasdale. [Supp 1/294]
A **Summer** Noon. W. Howitt. [Volume 5/46]
**Summer** Oracle. A. Lorde. [Supp 4/182]
**Summer** Rain. H. Coleridge. [Volume 5/43]
**Summer** Song. G. Barker. [Supp 2/293]
**Summer** Storm. J. Lowell. [Volume 5/119]
"The **summer** sun if falling soft on Carbery's." The
Sack of Baltimore. T. Davis. [Volume 9/127]
"The **summer** sun was sinking." The Fairy Child. J.
Anster. [Volume 6/32]
**Summer** Wish. F. Lima. [Supp 4/244]
**Summit**. Chong Chi-Yong. [Supp 7/148]

**Sun**. Pak Tu-Jin. [Supp 7/152]
*Sun*
Monterrey Sun. A. Reyes. [Supp 6/149]
Multitudinous Stars and Spring Waters: 005. Ping
Hsin. [Supp 5/116]
Sun. Pak Tu-Jin. [Supp 7/152]
Sun Gods Have Sun Spots. D. Wakoski. [Supp 5/321]
Sunrise Over the Gobi. Li Ying. [Supp 7/15]
The Youth with Red-gold Hair. E. Sitwell. [Supp
2/22]
"The **sun** burns on its sultry wick." Elegy Written on
a Frontporch. K. Shapiro. [Supp 2/318]
"The **sun** comes up and the sun goes down." Vanity. R.
Trench. [Volume 4/292]
The **Sun-dial**. A. Dobson. [Volume 3/15]
**Sun** Gods Have Sun Spots. D. Wakoski. [Supp 5/321]
"The **sun** is blue and scarlet on my page." Falling
Asleep over the Aeneid. R. Lowell. [Supp 2/390]
"The **sun** is warm, the sky is clear." Stanza. P.
Shelley. [Volume 3/164]
**"Sun**, moon and stars come down to talk old stories."
Heavenly Lake. Pak Tu-Jin. [Supp 7/155]
"The **sun** shines bright on our old Kentucky home." My
Old Kentucky Home. S. Foster. [Volume 3/147]
"The **sun** sinks softly to his evening post." National
Anthem. R. Newell. [Volume 9/417]
"The **sun** that brief December day." A New England Home
in Winter. J. Whittier. [Volume 1/308]
"The **sun** was shining on the sea." The Walrus and the
Carpenter, fr. Alice in Wonderland. C. Dodgson.
[Volume 1/180]
"The **sun** was sunk, and after him the star." The
Temptation, Book IX, fr. Paradise Lost. J.
Milton. [Volume 4/263]
"The **sunburnt** mowers are in the swath." The Mowers. M.
Benton. [Volume 7/249]
**"Sunday** afternoon and it is one-thirty and all the."
Sunday, August 11, 1974. M. Algarin. [Supp
4/283]
**Sunday**, August 11, 1974. M. Algarin. [Supp 4/283]
**Sunday** Morning. L. MacNeice. [Supp 2/184]
**Sunday** Morning Bells. D. Craik. [Volume 4/190]
**"Sunday** shuts down on this twentieth-century
evening." Boy with His Hair Cut Short. M.
Rukeyser. [Supp 2/295]
**"Sunday**. %The crowding stony faces of my fellows make
me afraid." In Memoriam. L. Senghor. [Supp
6/76]
**"Sundays** too my father got up early." Those Winter
Sundays. R. Hayden. [Supp 4/149]
The **Sunken** City. W. Mueller.
"The **sunlight** fills the trembling air." Betrothed
Anew. E. Stedman. [Volume 5/92]
"The **sunlight** glitters keen and bright." Hampton
Beach. J. Whittier. [Volume 5/427]
"The **Sunlight** on the Garden" L. MacNeice. [Supp
2/185]
**Sunrise**. C. Turner. [Volume 4/20]
**Sunrise**: A Hymn of the Marshes. S. Lanier. [Volume
5/257]
**Sunrise** Over the Gobi. Li Ying. [Supp 7/15]
A **Sunrise** Song. S. Lanier. [Volume 6/277]
**"Sunset** and evening star." Crossing the Bar. A.
Tennyson. [Volume 4/375]
The **Sunset** City. H. Cornwell. [Volume 7/158]
**Sunset**, fr. Queen Mab. P. Shelley. [Volume 5/48]
"The **sunset** light is on the sail." Wings. M. Ritter.
[Volume 1/137]
A **Sunset** of the City. G. Brooks. [Supp 5/42]
The **Suppliant**. E. Gosse. [Supp 1/145]
**Suppose** and Eyes. G. Stein. [Supp 5/294]
**"Suppose** it is within a gate which opens is open at
the hour of." Suppose and Eyes. G. Stein. [Supp
5/294]
*Survival*

"If It Be True That Any Beauteous Thing" M. Angelo. [Volume 2/72]

The Might Of One Fair Face. M. Angelo. [Volume 2/329]

**Taylor, Sir Henry**
Athulf and Ethilda. [Volume 2/96]
Heart-rest. [Volume 1/312]
The Wind and the Pine-tree, fr. Edwin the Fair. [Volume 5/219]

**Taylor, Tom**
Abraham Lincoln. [Volume 7/25]

**Taylor, W. (tr.)**
My Recovery. F. Klopstock. [Volume 4/293]

Te Deum Laudamus. American Episcopal Church Prayer-Book. [Volume 4/9]

A Tear. S. Rogers. [Volume 6/271]

**Tearing** Up My Mother's Letters. D. Wakoski. [Supp 5/324]

Tears. E. Browning. [Volume 3/429]

"Tears for my lady dead." Lament for Heliodore. Meleager. [Volume 3/337]

"Tears, Idle Tears", fr. The Princess. A. Tennyson. [Volume 3/142]

Tears in Sleep. L. Bogan. [Supp 1/61]

The **Tears** of a Muse in America: 001. F. Prince. [Supp 2/267]

The **Tears** of a Muse in America: 002. F. Prince. [Supp 2/267]

The **Tears** of a Muse in America: 003. F. Prince. [Supp 2/268]

The **Tears** of a Muse in America: 004. F. Prince. [Supp 2/269]

"Tears wash away the atoms in the eye." Compensation. C. Cranch. [Volume 3/229]

**Teasdale, Sara**
I Remembered. [Supp 1/294]
"Let It Be Forgotten" [Supp 1/293]
Summer Night, Riverside. [Supp 1/294]

**Tegner, Elias**
Frithiof at the court of Angantyr, fr. Frithiof Saga. W. Strong (tr.). [Volume 7/289]

**Telephone** Conversation. W. Soyinka. [Supp 6/65]

Tell Me, My Heart, If This Be Love. L. Lyttelton. [Volume 2/95]

"tell me not, in mournful numbers." A Psalm of Life. H. Longfellow. [Volume 4/275]

"Tell me not, sweet, I am unkinde." To Lucasta. R. Lovelace. [Volume 3/97]

"Tell me now in what hidden way is." The Ballad of Dead Ladies. F. Villon. [Volume 6/192]

"Tell me where is fancy bred." Love, fr. The Merchant of Venice. W. Shakespeare. [Volume 2/62]

"Tell Me, Ye Winged Winds" C. Mackay. [Volume 4/411]

"Tell the story to your sons." The Fight of the "Armstrong" Privateer. J. Roche. [Volume 7/433]

"Tell us some of the charms of the stars." Vision of a Fair Woman. E. Sharp. [Volume 2/25]

"Tell you what I like the best." Knee-deep in June. J. Riley. [Volume 5/108]

The **Telltale**. E. Akers. [Volume 2/119]

The **Temptation**, Book IX, fr. Paradise Lost. J. Milton. [Volume 4/263]

"Ten dancers glide." Ballad of the Ten Casino Dancers. C. Meireles. [Supp 5/163]

"Ten thousand warblers cheer the day, and one." Unmusical Birds, fr. The Task. W. Cowper. [Volume 5/309]

Ten Yen Coin. S. Tanikawa. [Supp 7/134]

"Tenderly, ivy, on Sophocles' grave - right tenderly." The Grave of Sophochles. Simmias. [Volume 3/269]

*Tenderness*
"Where Does This Tenderness Come From?" M. Tsvetayeva. [Supp 5/299]

**Tennant, William**
Ode to Peace. [Volume 8/423]

**Tennyson**. T. Aldrich. [Volume 7/83]

**Tennyson, Alfred Lord**
Albert, Prince Consort of England, fr. Idyls of the King. [Volume 7/34]
The Birch Stream. [Volume 5/199]
The Blackbird. [Volume 5/320]
"Break, Break, Break" [Volume 3/358]
The Bugle, fr. The Princess. [Volume 5/210]
Charge of the Light Brigade. [Volume 8/294]
"Come Into The Garden, Maud" [Volume 2/273]
Crossing the Bar. [Volume 4/375]
The Dead Friend: 116, fr. In Memoriam. [Volume 1/362]
The Dead Friend: 22, fr. In Memoriam. [Volume 1/360]
The Dead Friend: 23, fr. In Memoriam. [Volume 1/360]
The Dead Friend: 25, fr. In Memoriam. [Volume 1/361]
The Dead Friend: 84, fr. In Memoriam. [Volume 1/361]
Dead, In a Foreign Land, fr. In Memoriam. [Volume 3/349]
Death in Life's Prime, fr. In Memoriam. [Volume 3/354]
The Death of the Old Year. [Volume 6/196]
Doubt and Faith, fr. In Memoriam. [Volume 4/139]
The Dying Swan. [Volume 5/323]
The Eagle. [Volume 5/321]
Enid's Song, fr. Idyls of the King. [Volume 6/266]
A Farewell. [Volume 5/199]
The Foolish Virgins, fr. Idyls of the KingL Guinevere. [Volume 4/331]
Godiva. [Volume 7/361]
Grief Unspeakable, fr. In Memoriam. [Volume 3/349]
Hands All Round. [Volume 8/29]
Home They Brought Her Warrior Dead, fr. The Princess. [Volume 3/345]
L., fr. In Memoriam. [Volume 3/353]
"Lady Clara Vere De Vere" [Volume 3/4]
Lady Clare. [Volume 2/300]
The Lady of Shalott. [Volume 6/124]
Locksley Hall. [Volume 3/17]
The Lotus-Eaters. [Volume 6/402]
Lullaby, fr. The Princess. [Volume 1/11]
The May Queen. [Volume 3/292]
Mort D'Arthur. [Volume 7/352]
The New Year, fr. In Memoriam. [Volume 4/260]
Not All, Or All In All, fr. Merlin and Vivien. [Volume 2/250]
O Swallow, Swallow, Flying South, fr. The Princess. [Volume 2/100]
"Oh That 'T Were Possible", fr. Maud. [Volume 3/331]
"O Yet We Trust That Somehow", fr. In Memoriam. [Volume 4/243]
The Peace of Sorrow, fr. In Memoriam. [Volume 3/350]
Personal Resurrection, fr. In Memoriam. [Volume 3/352]
The Poet's Tribute, fr. In Memoriam. [Volume 3/354]
The Revenge. [Volume 7/383]
Rizpah. [Volume 9/151]
Saint Agnes. [Volume 4/416]
Sir Galahad. [Volume 4/164]
Sir Launcelot And Queen Guinevere. [Volume 2/257]
The Sleeping Beauty, fr. The Day Dream. [Volume 2/307]
Song of the Brook, fr. The Brook: An Idyl. [Volume 5/194]
Song of the Milkmaid, fr. Queen Mary. [Volume 2/107]

Song, fr. The Miller's Daughter. [Volume 2/102]
Spiritual Companionship, fr. In Memoriam. [Volume 3/352]
Spring: 083, fr. In Memoriam. [Volume 5/91]
Spring: 114, fr. In Memoriam. [Volume 5/91]
"Strong Son of God, Immortal Love", fr. In Memoriam. [Volume 4/45]
"Tears, Idle Tears", fr. The Princess. [Volume 3/142]
Time and Eternity, fr. In Memoriam. [Volume 3/351]
To Victor Hugo. [Volume 7/41]
To Virgil. [Volume 7/37]
Ulysses. [Volume 6/426]
"What Does Little Birdie Say?" [Volume 1/98]
The **Term** of Death. S. Piatt. [Volume 3/261]
**Terrertt, William B.**
Platonic. [Volume 1/372]
**Terror**. R. Warren. [Supp 2/133]
**Tersteegen, Gerhard**
The Love of God Supreme. J. Wesley (tr.). [Volume 4/130]
**Thackeray, William Makepeace**
The Age Of Wisdom. [Volume 2/236]
At the Church Gate. [Volume 2/60]
The Ballad of Bouillabaisse. [Volume 1/393]
The Cane-bottomed Chair. [Volume 1/377]
The End of the Play. [Volume 4/256]
Fairy Days. [Volume 1/141]
Little Billee. [Volume 9/296]
The Mahogany-tree. [Volume 1/391]
Peg of Limavaddy. [Volume 1/236]
Sorrows of Werther. [Volume 9/204]
**Thalatta!** Thalatta! J. Brown. [Volume 3/389]
**Thanatopsis**. W. Bryant. [Volume 3/264]
"**Thank** God, bless God, all ye who suffer not." Tears. E. Browning. [Volume 3/429]
"**Thank** God my brain is not inclined to cut." The Menagerie. W. Moody. [Supp 1/228]
"**Thank** heaven! the crisis." For Annie. E. Poe. [Volume 3/385]
"**Thank** you, pretty cow, that made." Pretty Cow. J. Taylor. [Volume 1/105]
"**That** clandestine night flight." Lights. E. Cardenal. [Supp 6/158]
"**That** clime is not like this dull clime of ours." Heaven. Unknown. [Volume 4/398]
"**That** each, who seems a separate whole." Personal Resurrection, fr. In Memoriam. A. Tennyson. [Volume 3/352]
"**That** e'en my buried ashed such a snare." Rubaiyat: 092. O. Khayyam. [Volume 6/222]
**That** England, fr. Aurora Leigh. E. Browning. [Volume 7/200]
"**That** evening %faces faded around us." In the Flux. F. Tuqan. [Supp 7/272]
"**That** firewood pale with salt and burning green." Gigha. W. Graham. [Supp 2/401]
**That** Harp You Play So Well. M. Moore. [Supp 1/234]
"**That** I love thee, charming maid, I a thousand." Waiting for the Grapes. W. Maginn. [Volume 2/243]
"**That** is the way God made you." To a Winter Squirrel. G. Brooks. [Supp 5/44]
"**That** night an eagle swooped down from the skies onto." The Death of Sophocles. A. Akhmatova. [Supp 5/11]
"**That** was a steady light not a low flying firefly." Winter Fancy. Yung Tzu. [Supp 7/37]
"**That** was the best moment of the monk's life." Burning Oneself to Death. S. Takahashi. [Supp 7/126]
"**That** was the fatal move, the ruination." O Dreams, O Destinations: 003. C. Day Lewis. [Supp 2/119]
"**That** was too high a mountain, last year." For Mrs N. C. Anwar. [Supp 7/85]

"**That** which hath made them." The Murder, fr. Macbeth. W. Shakespeare. [Volume 9/122]
"**That** which her slender waist confined." On a Griddle. E. Waller. [Volume 2/35]
"**That** you have wronged me doth appear." Quarrel of Brutus and Cassius, fr. Julius Caesar. W. Shakespeare. [Volume 1/381]
"**That's** How I Was" C. Conde. [Supp 4/291]
**Thaxter, Celia**
May Morning. [Volume 5/84]
The Sandpiper. [Volume 5/303]
**Thayer, William Roscoe ("Paul Hermes")**
The Last Hunt. [Volume 8/262]
**The Lu**
Green Nostalgia. N. Bich; Burton Raffel and W.S. Merwin (tr.). [Supp 7/191]
Nightmare. N. Bich; Burton Raffel and W.S. Merwin (tr.). [Supp 7/193]
*Theater*
At Epidaurus. L. Durrell. [Supp 2/257]
"**Then** as a nimble squirrel from the wood." The Hunted Squirrel, fr. Britannia's Pastorals. W. Browne. [Volume 5/157]
"**Then** cried my Cid - 'in charity, as to the'" Battle Scene, fr. The Cid. Unknown. [Volume 8/205]
"**Then** die! %outside the prison gawks." For St. Bartholomew's Eve. M. Cowley. [Supp 2/59]
**Then** I Saw What the Calling Was. M. Rukeyser. [Supp 5/243]
"**Then** like the ship at rest in the bay." First Cycle of Love Poems: 004. G. Barker. [Supp 2/280]
"**Then** of the thee in me who works behind." Rubaiyat: 034. O. Khayyam. [Volume 6/210]
"**Then** rose from sea to sky the wild farewell." Wreck, fr. Don Juan. G. Byron. [Volume 5/416]
"**Then** said a second - ne'er a peevish boy." Rubaiyat: 085. O. Khayyam. [Volume 6/220]
"**Then** They Paraded Pompey's Urn" J. Mastoraki. [Supp 5/156]
"**Then** to the lip of this poor earthen urn." Rubaiyat: 035. O. Khayyam. [Volume 6/210]
"**There** are gains of all our losses." The Flight of Youth. R. Stoddard. [Volume 1/264]
"**There** are no colors in the fairest sky." Walton's Book of Lives, fr. Ecclesiastical Sonnets. W. Wordsworth. [Volume 7/55]
"**There** are people who know how to love." Poem of Explanations. D. Ravikovitch. [Supp 5/237]
"**There** are some days the happy ocean lies." Seascape. S. Spender. [Supp 2/232]
"**There** are some hearts like wells, green-mossed." Living Waters. C. Spencer. [Volume 4/251]
"**There** are some people I know." Sorcery. J. Hagedorn. [Supp 4/22]
"**There** are such spring-like nights here." Women Songs: 002. K. Molodowsky. [Supp 5/172]
"**There** are things lovely and dangerous still." Poem: Of Nightsong and Flight. J. Jordan. [Supp 5/129]
"**There** are times for dreaming." Times. D. Diop. [Supp 6/71]
"**There** are truths you Americans need to be told." America, fr. A Fable for Critics. J. Lowell. [Volume 9/337]
"**There** are who say the lover's heart." Love. T. Hervey. [Volume 2/359]
"**There** came a man, making his hasty moan." Mahmoud. L. Hunt. [Volume 7/305]
"**There** came a soul to the gate of heaven." The Self-exiled. W. Smith. [Volume 4/158]
"**There** came to the beach a poor exile of Erin." Exile of Erin. T. Campbell. [Volume 8/67]
"**There** hangs a sabre, and there a rein." All. F. Durivage. [Volume 8/415]
"**There** in the field hear the voice of the lark day-

long." The Difference. R. Pitter. [Supp 5/205]

"There is a castle on a hill." Gold. J. Drinkwater. [Supp 1/110]

"There Is A Garden In Her Face" Unknown. [Volume 2/9]

"There is a gentle nymph not far from hence." The Nymph of the Severn, fr. Comus. J. Milton. [Volume 6/66]

"There is a glorious city in the sea." Venice, fr. Italy. S. Rogers. [Volume 7/189]

"There is a land, of every land the pride." My Country. J. Montgomery. [Volume 8/5]

"There is a land of pure delight." Heaven. I. Watts. [Volume 4/413]

"There is a pleasure in the pathless woods." The Sea, fr. Childe Harold. G. Byron. [Volume 5/375]

"There is a reaper whose name is death." The Reaper and the Flowers. H. Longfellow. [Volume 3/417]

"There Is a Spell, for Instance" H. Doolittle. [Supp 2/6]

"There is a supreme God in the ethnological section." Homage to the British Museum. W. Empson. [Supp 2/141]

"There is a tree native in Turkestan." Note on Local Flora. W. Empson. [Supp 2/145]

"There is delight in singing, though none hear." Robert Browning. W. Landor. [Volume 7/89]

"There is Lowell, who's striving Parnassus to." Lowell on Himself, fr. A Fable for Critics. J. Lowell. [Volume 7/100]

"There is no breeze upon the fern." Beal' an Dhuine, fr. The Lady of the Lake. S. Scott. [Volume 8/307]

"There Is No Death" J. M'Creery. [Volume 3/456]

"There is no flock, however watched and tended." Resignation. H. Longfellow. [Volume 3/430]

"There is no force however great." Physics. W. Whewell. [Volume 9/434]

"'There is no God,' the foolish saith." The Cry of the Human. E. Browning. [Volume 4/286]

"There is no rhyme that is half so sweet." Proem. M. Cawein. [Volume 6/333]

"There is not in this wide world a valley so sweet." The Vale of Avoca. T. Moore. [Volume 1/351]

"There Is Nothing In New York" A. Villanueva. [Supp 4/268]

"There is nothing to be said for you. Guard." To Statecraft Embalmed. M. Moore. [Supp 5/182]

"There is rain upon the window." Home Song. D. Scott. [Volume 1/325]

"there is such power even in smallest things." There is Such Powerm fr. Sonnets in Shadow. A. Bates. [Volume 6/310]

There is Such Powerm fr. Sonnets in Shadow. A. Bates. [Volume 6/310]

"There is the peace that cometh after sorrow." Peace. Unknown. [Volume 3/437]

"There! little girl, don't cry!" A Life-Lesson. J. Riley. [Volume 1/127]

"There Lived a Lady in Milan" W. Benet. [Supp 1/47]

"There never was a mood of mine." I Remembered. S. Teasdale. [Supp 1/294]

"There once the penitents took off their shoes." The Quaker Graveyard in Nantucket: 006. R. Lowell. [Supp 2/397]

"There stood an unsold captive in the mart." Parrhasius. N. Willis. [Volume 9/8]

"There sunk the greatest, nor the worst of men." Napoleon, fr. Childe Harold. G. Byron. [Volume 7/9]

"There the black river, boundary to hell." The Southern Road. D. Randall. [Supp 4/155]

"There the most daintie paradise on ground." The Bower of Bliss, fr. The Faerie Queene. E. Spenser. [Volume 6/112]

"There was (not certaine when) a certaine." Of a

Certaine Man. S. Harrington. [Volume 9/199]

"There was a lady lived at Leith." The Irishman and the Lady. W. Maginn. [Volume 9/320]

"There was a Little Girl" H. Longfellow. [Volume 1/169]

"There was a mall boy of Quebec." Limerick. R. Kipling. [Volume 1/201]

"There was a monkey climbed up a tree." The History Lesson. Unknown. [Volume 1/194]

"There was a sound of revelry by night." Waterloo, fr. Childe Harold. G. Byron. [Volume 8/287]

"There was a time when meadow, grove and." Ode. W. Wordsworth. [Volume 4/377]

"There was a young lady in blue." Limerick. E. Lear. [Volume 1/201]

"There was a young lady of Clare." Limerick. E. Lear. [Volume 1/198]

"There was a young lady of Greenwich." Limerick. E. Lear. [Volume 1/201]

"There was a young lady of Niger." Limerick. R. Kipling. [Volume 1/201]

"There was a young lady of Norway." Limerick. E. Lear. [Volume 1/200]

"There was a young maid who said, 'why'" Limerick. Unknown. [Volume 1/202]

"There was a young person of smyrna." Limerick. E. Lear. [Volume 1/200]

"There was a youthe, and a well-beloved youthe." The Bailiff's Daughter of Islington. Unknown. [Volume 2/153]

"There was an ape in the days that were earlier." Darwin. M. Collins. [Volume 9/383]

"There was an Indian, who had known no change." The Discovery. J. Squire. [Supp 1/285]

"There was an old man in a boat." Limerick. E. Lear. [Volume 1/197]

"There was an old man in a tree." Limerick. E. Lear. [Volume 1/197]

"There was an old man of Aosta." Limerick. E. Lear. [Volume 1/197]

"There was an old man of Kamschatka." Limerick. E. Lear. [Volume 1/197]

"There was an old man of Marseilles." Limerick. E. Lear. [Volume 1/200]

"There was an old man of the Dee." Limerick. E. Lear. [Volume 1/198]

"There was an old man of the Nile." Limerick. E. Lear. [Volume 1/198]

"There was an old man of the west." Limerick. E. Lear. [Volume 1/200]

"There was an old man of Toulouse." Limerick. E. Lear. [Volume 1/198]

"There was an old man on some rocks." Limerick. E. Lear. [Volume 1/199]

"There was an old man who said 'how'" Limerick. E. Lear. [Volume 1/199]

"There was an old man who said 'hush!'" Limerick. E. Lear. [Volume 1/199]

"There was an old man, who when little." Limerick. E. Lear. [Volume 1/201]

"There was an old man with a beard." Limerick. E. Lear. [Volume 1/200]

"There was an old man with a nose." Limerick. E. Lear. [Volume 1/196]

"There was an old person of Buda." Limerick. E. Lear. [Volume 1/197]

"There was an old person of Chili." Limerick. E. Lear. [Volume 1/197]

"There was an old person of Cromer." Limerick. E. Lear. [Volume 1/198]

"There was an old person of Hurst." Limerick. E. Lear. [Volume 1/199]

"There was an old person of philae." Limerick. E. Lear. [Volume 1/200]

"There was an old person of Ware." Limerick. E. Lear.

[Volume 1/200]

"There was an old person whose habits." Limerick. E. Lear. [Volume 1/199]

"There was the door to which I found no key." Rubaiyat: 032. O. Khayyam. [Volume 6/210]

"There were faces to remember in the valley of the." The Valley of the Shadow. E. Robinson. [Supp 1/267]

"There were just meant as covers." My Mother Pieced Quilts. T. Acosta. [Supp 4/285]

"There were ninety and ine that safely lay." The Lost Sheep. E. Clephane. [Volume 4/66]

"There were three maidens who loved a king." Three Lovers. L. Hooper. [Volume 2/77]

"there were three sailors of Bristol City." Little Billee. W. Thackeray. [Volume 9/296]

"Therefore all things, in all three tenses." Sacred Elegy V: 003. G. Barker. [Supp 2/291]

"There's a city that lies in the kingdom of." The Sunset City. H. Cornwell. [Volume 7/158]

"There's a good time coming, boys." The Good Time Coming. C. Mackay. [Volume 6/399]

"There's a grim one-horse hearse in a jolly round." The Pauper's Drive. T. Noel. [Volume 3/202]

"There's a joy without canker or cark." Of Blue China. A. Lang. [Volume 9/448]

"There's a landscape inside me." Love in the Ether. A. Prado. [Supp 6/118]

"There's a legend that's told of a gypsy who dwelt." The Flight Into Egypt. F. Mahony. [Volume 4/62]

There's Nae Luck About The House. J. Adam. [Volume 2/442]

"There's no dew left on the daisies and clover." Seven Times One. J. Ingelow. [Volume 1/48]

"There's no way I can fall asleep." No One. N. Parra. [Supp 6/180]

"These, as they change, almighty Father, these." A Hymn, fr. The Seasons. J. Thomson. [Volume 5/70]

"These errors loved no less than the saint loves arrows." Sacred Elegy V: 001. G. Barker. [Supp 2/290]

"These fragmented verses %are only drops of sprays." Multitudinous Stars and Spring Waters: 003. Ping Hsin. [Supp 5/116]

"These pearls of thought in Persian gulfs were." In a Copy of Omar Khayyam. J. Lowell. [Volume 7/39]

"These to him Memory - since he held them dear." Albert, Prince Consort of England, fr. Idyls of the King. A. Tennyson. [Volume 7/34]

"These, who desired to live, went out to death." Epitaph. L. Abercrombie. [Supp 1/5]

Theseus. T. Moore. [Supp 1/235]

"They are able, with science, to measure the millionth of an." C Stands for Civilization. K. Fearing. [Supp 2/97]

"They Are All Gone" H. Vaughan. [Volume 3/403]

"They Are Dear Fish to Me" Unknown. [Volume 3/195]

"They are dying! they are dying! where the golden." Ireland. D. MacCarthy. [Volume 8/62]

"They came in the berths." Ode to a Lost Cargo in a Ship Called Save: 004. J. Craveirinha. [Supp 6/41]

"They Come! The Merry Summer Months" W. Motherwell. [Volume 5/97]

"They dragged you from the homeland." Strong Men. S. Brown. [Supp 4/119]

"They eat beans mostly, this old yellow pair." The Bean Eaters. G. Brooks. [Supp 4/158]

They Eat Out. M. Atwood. [Supp 5/19]

"They finally %had to take obachan." Hospitals Are to Die In. J. Mirikitani. [Supp 4/42]

"They have fenced in the dirt road." Burial: 001. A. Walker. [Supp 4/225]

"They named it Aultgraat - ugly burn." The Black Rock

of Kiltearen. A. Young. [Supp 2/2]

"They roused him with muffins - they roused hom." The Baker's Tale, fr. The Hunting of the Snark. C. Dodgson. [Volume 9/456]

"They say the lion and the lizard keep." Rubaiyat: 018. O. Khayyam. [Volume 6/207]

"They seemed to those who saw them meet." Forever Unconfessed. R. Milnes. [Volume 2/241]

"They tell us to forget." Dark Symphony: 3. Andante Sostenuto. M. Tolson. [Supp 4/97]

"They tell you that Death's at the turn of the." "The Unillumined Verge" R. Bridges. [Volume 3/308]

"They told me, Heracleitus, they told me you." The Dead Poet-friend. Callimachus. [Volume 1/396]

"They went to sea in a sieve, they did." The Jumblies. E. Lear. [Volume 1/192]

"They were both still." Lamentations: 1. The Logos. L. Gluck. [Supp 5/106]

"They're always abusing the women." Women's Chorus. Aristophanes. [Volume 9/200]

"They've got a bran new organ, Sue." The New Church Organ. W. Carleton. [Volume 9/316]

"Thick lay the dust, uncomfortably white." Summer Rain. H. Coleridge. [Volume 5/43]

"Thin, in this battered Caravanserai." Rubaiyat: 017. O. Khayyam. [Volume 6/207]

"The thin Potomac scarcely moves." The Potomac. K. Shapiro. [Supp 2/323]

"A Thing of Beauty is a Joy Forever", fr. Endymion. J. Keats. [Volume 6/329]

Things of the Earth. F. Guillar. [Supp 6/114]

Things to Welcome Love. J. Pasos. [Supp 6/182]

"Think not I love him, though I ask for him." Love Dissembled, fr. As You Like It. W. Shakespeare. [Volume 2/31]

"Think not that mystery has place." Mystery. J. Drinkwater. [Supp 1/113]

"Thinking reason my friend." Killing One's Gods. G. Senanayake. [Supp 7/183]

Thinkin' Long. A. MacManus. [Volume 3/141]

"This advantage to be seized; and here, an escape prepared against an." Dividends. K. Fearing. [Supp 2/100]

"This beauty, is it your or is it mine?" You or I? I. Shabaka. [Supp 7/260]

"This black tower drinks the blinding light." The Drunkard. E. Sitwell. [Supp 5/272]

"This blue half circle of sea." Mersa. K. Douglas. [Supp 2/406]

"This book is all that's left me now." My mother's Bible. G. Morris. [Volume 1/228]

"This bronze doth keep the very form and mould." On the Life-Mask of Lincoln. R. Gilder. [Volume 7/29]

"This county might have." Right On: Wite America. S. Sanchez. [Supp 4/187]

"This Cruel Age Has Deflected Me" A. Akhmatova. [Supp 5/10]

"This day at leat." At Least. D. Mattera. [Supp 6/82]

"This earth will grow cold." On Living: 003. N. Hikmet. [Supp 7/308]

"This England never did, nor never shall." England, fr. King John. W. Shakespeare. [Volume 7/390]

"This figure, that thou here seest put." On the Portrait of Shakespeare. B. Jonson. [Volume 7/48]

"This gentle and half melancholy breeze." An Autumn Breeze. W. Hayne. [Volume 6/179]

"This I got on the day that Goring." The Three Scars. G. Thornbury. [Volume 8/276]

"This Indian weed, now withered quite." The Indian Weed. Unknown. [Volume 6/249]

"This is combat, from land to sky." Poverty. F. Daglarca. [Supp 7/302]

"This is has to be here." Dismal Moment, Passing. C.

"Those horns, the envy of the moon." Death of the Bull. R. Campbell. [Supp 2/91]

Those Various Scalpels. M. Moore. [Supp 5/183]

"Those were good times, in olden days." Written on a Fly-leaf of Theocritus. M. Thompson. [Volume 6/358]

Those Winter Sundays. R. Hayden. [Supp 4/149]

"Thou are Gone to the Grave" R. Herber. [Volume 3/446]

"Thou art the joy of age." Light. G. Macdonald. [Volume 5/32]

"Thou blossom, bright with autumn dew." To the Fringed Gentian. W. Bryant. [Volume 5/284]

"Thou for whose birth the whole creation yearned." The Rise of Man. J. Chadwick. [Volume 4/311]

"Thou grace divine, encircling all." The Love of God. E. Scudder. [Volume 4/39]

"Thou happy, happy elf." To My Infant Son. T. Hood. [Volume 1/29]

"Thou Hast Sworn By Thy God, My Jeanie" A. Cunningham. [Volume 2/416]

"Thou hidden love of God, whose height." The Love of God Supreme. G. Tersteegen. [Volume 4/130]

"Thou lingering star, with lessening ray." To Mary in Heaven. R. Burns. [Volume 3/339]

"Thou little bird, thou dweller by the sea." The Little Beach Bird. R. Dana. [Volume 5/302]

"Thou shalt have one God only: who." The Latest Decalogue. A. Clough. [Volume 9/315]

"'Thou solitary!' the blackbird cried." The Riddlers. W. De La Mare. [Supp 1/108]

"Thou still unravished bride of quietness!" Ode on a Grecian Urn. J. Keats. [Volume 7/136]

"Thou that once, on mother's knee." A Little Child's Hymn. F. Palgrave. [Volume 1/120]

"Thou, too, sail on, O ship of state!" The Republic, fr. The Building of the Ship. H. Longfellow. [Volume 8/94]

"Thou wast all that to me, love." To One In Paradise. E. Poe. [Volume 2/371]

"Thou, who dost dwell alone." Desire. M. Arnold. [Volume 4/125]

"Thou who, when fears attack." Ode to Tobacco. C. Calverley. [Volume 9/387]

"Thou whose sweet youth and early hopes enhance." The Church Porch, sel. G. Herbert. [Volume 4/304]

"Though black the night, I know upon the sky." Prelude. J. Drinkwater. [Supp 1/110]

"Though it was still night." Prison Daybreak. F. Faiz. [Supp 7/171]

"Though the hills are cold and snowy." A Day in the Pamfili Doria. H. Stowe. [Volume 7/182]

"Though the mills of God grind slowly, yet they." Retribution. F. Logau. [Volume 6/226]

"Though, when other maids stand by." Smile and Never Heed Me. C. Swain. [Volume 2/115]

Thought. C. Cranch. [Volume 6/322]

Thought

Above the Clouds. J. Miller. [Volume 6/334]

Aesop. A. Lang. [Volume 6/330]

The Ancient and Modern Muses. F. Palgrave. [Volume 6/337]

Art. G. Parker. [Volume 6/345]

An Autograph. J. Lowell. [Volume 6/344]

The Ballad of Prose and Rhyme. A. Dobson. [Volume 6/340]

Broken Music. T. Aldrich. [Volume 6/346]

Dream-life, fr. Such Stuff as Dreams Are Made Of. P. Calderon. [Volume 6/324]

Genius. R. Horne. [Volume 6/352]

The Immortality of a Genius. S. Propertius. [Volume 6/357]

Impression. E. Gosse. [Volume 6/335]

Indirection. R. Realf. [Volume 6/332]

The Inner Vision. W. Wordsworth. [Volume 6/322]

The Jester's Plea. F. Locker-Lampson. [Volume 6/350]

The Modern Poet. A. Meynell. [Volume 6/347]

"My Minde To Me a Kingdom Is" E. Dyer. [Volume 6/325]

The Odyssey. A. Lang. [Volume 6/342]

Of a Contented Spirit. L. Thomas. [Volume 6/328]

On First Looking Into Chapman's Homer. J. Keats. [Volume 6/341]

On His "Sonnets of the Wingless Hours" E. Lee-Hamilton. [Volume 6/338]

"One Day I Wrote Her Name", fr. Amoretti. E. Spenser. [Volume 6/353]

The Poet of Nature, fr. Festus. P. Bailey. [Volume 6/334]

The Poet of To-day. S. Lippincott. [Volume 6/338]

The Poet's Death, fr. The Lay of the Last Minstrel. S. Scott. [Volume 6/355]

The Poet's Impulse, fr. Childe Harold's Pilgrimage. G. Byron. [Volume 6/335]

Proem. M. Cawein. [Volume 6/333]

The Sharing of the Earth. J. Schiller. [Volume 6/356]

The Singer of One Song. H. Beers. [Volume 6/343]

Sonnet, fr. Astrophel and Stella. S. Sidney. [Volume 6/342]

The Sonnet. R. Gilder. [Volume 6/344]

The Sower and His Seed. W. Lecky. [Volume 6/330]

Sweet Nature's Voice, fr. Susan: A Poem of Degrees. A. Munby. [Volume 6/350]

"A Thing of Beauty is a Joy Forever", fr. Endymion. J. Keats. [Volume 6/329]

Thought. C. Cranch. [Volume 6/322]

Thy songs and Mine. J. Dorr. [Volume 6/355]

To One Who Had Scoffed at the Poet's Poverty. Martial. [Volume 6/327]

Unknown Poets, fr. The Excursion. W. Wordsworth. [Volume 6/339]

Verses Why Burnt. W. Landor. [Volume 6/350]

Written on a Fly-leaf of Theocritus. M. Thompson. [Volume 6/358]

"Thought is deeper than all speech." Thought. C. Cranch. [Volume 6/322]

Thoughts About the Christian Doctrine of Eternal Hell. S. Smith. [Supp 5/279]

"The thoughts are strange that crowd into my." The Fall of Niagara. J. Brainard. [Volume 5/208]

Thoughts of Heaven. R. Nicoll. [Volume 4/391]

Thoughts On The Commandments. G. Baker. [Volume 2/125]

Thrale, Hester Lynch

The Three Warnings. [Volume 6/289]

Thread and Song. J. Palmer. [Volume 1/113]

"Thread those reviving passions down." Verse. G. Byron. [Volume 3/171]

3 AM %in the albuquerque airport. J. Harjo. [Supp 4/342]

The Three Children. Unknown. [Volume 1/174]

"The Three children sliding on the ice." The Three Children. Unknown. [Volume 1/174]

Three Days. J. Gilmore. [Volume 6/189]

The Three Enemies. C. Rossetti. [Volume 4/280]

The Three Fishers. C. Kingsley. [Volume 9/183]

"Three fishers went sailing out into the west." The Three Fishers. C. Kingsley. [Volume 9/183]

"Three horsemen galloped the dusty way." On the Road to Chorrera. A. Bates. [Volume 2/47]

"Three hundred nights like three hundred walls." Parting. J. Borges. [Supp 6/104]

Three Hundred Thousand More. Unknown. [Volume 8/356]

The Three Little Kittens. E. Follen. [Volume 1/106]

"Three little kittens lost their mittens." The Three Little Kittens. E. Follen. [Volume 1/106]

Three Lovers. L. Hooper. [Volume 2/77]

"Three poets, in three distant ages born." Under the

"**Today** I love you so much I mistrust you." Fish and Swimmer and Lonely Birds Sweep Past Us. M. Berssenbrugge. [Supp 4/11]

**Today** Is a Day of Great Joy. V. Cruz. [Supp 4/276]

"**Today** Is Sunday" G. Fuertes. [Supp 5/95]

**Toe'osh:** A Lagune Coyote Story. L. Silko. [Supp 4/328]

"**Toil** on! toil on! ye emphemeral train." The Coral Insect. L. Sigourney. [Volume 5/395]

The **Toilet,** fr. The Rape of the Lock. A. Pope. [Volume 7/135]

The **Token.** F. Prince. [Supp 2/270]

**Told** In a Dream. K. Raine. [Supp 5/230]

**Toledo,** July 1936. R. Campbell. [Supp 2/95]

"**Toledo,** when I saw you die." Toledo, July 1936. R. Campbell. [Supp 2/95]

*Toledo, Ohio*
   Not Men Alone. E. Rolfe. [Supp 2/217]

*Toledo, Spain*
   Toledo, July 1936. R. Campbell. [Supp 2/95]

"**Toll** for the brave." On the Loss of the Royal George. W. Cowper. [Volume 9/182]

"**Toll** the slow bell." The Fallen. J. Cheney. [Volume 6/442]

**Tolson, Melvin B.**
   African China: 001. [Supp 4/101]
   African China: 002. [Supp 4/101]
   African China: 003. [Supp 4/102]
   African China: 004. [Supp 4/103]
   African China: 005. [Supp 4/104]
   African China: 006. [Supp 4/104]
   Dark Symphony: 1. Allegro Moderato. [Supp 4/96]
   Dark Symphony: 2. Lento Grave. [Supp 4/97]
   Dark Symphony: 3. Andante Sostenuto. [Supp 4/97]
   Dark Symphony: 4. Tempo Primo. [Supp 4/98]
   Dark Symphony: 5. Larghetto. [Supp 4/99]
   Dark Symphony: 6. Tempo di Marcia. [Supp 4/400]

**Tom** Bowling. C. Dibdin. [Volume 5/406]

**Tom** Mooney. C. Leland. [Supp 1/186]

"**Tom** Mooney sits behind a grating." Tom Mooney. C. Leland. [Supp 1/186]

**Tombstone** with Cherubim. H. Gregory. [Supp 2/66]

**Tomioka, Taeko**
   Age. H. Sato (tr.). [Supp 7/140]
   Let Me Tell You About Myself. H. Sato (tr.). [Supp 7/138]

"**Tongue!** never cease to sing Fidessa's praise." To Fidessa. B. Griffin. [Volume 2/364]

"**Tongue-Tied** or Stuttering" C. Belli. [Supp 6/185]

"**Tonight** %the machinery of shadow." For Christopher. J. Jordan. [Supp 4/195]

"**Tonight** I Can Write the Saddest Lines" P. Neruda. [Supp 6/131]

**Tonis** Ad Resto Mare. J. Swift. [Volume 9/319]

"**Too** daring prince! ah whither dost thou run?" Parting of Hector and Andromache, fr. The Iliad. Homer. [Volume 3/118]

**Too** Great a Sacrifice. Unknown. [Volume 9/394]

**Too** Late. D. Craik. [Volume 3/335]

"**Too** Late I Stayed" W. Spencer. [Volume 1/352]

*Tools*
   The World is Deed. J. Wheelwright. [Supp 2/57]

**Toomer, Jean**
   Brown River, Smile. [Supp 4/91]
   Georgia Dusk. [Supp 4/89]
   Reapers. [Supp 4/88]
   Song of the Sun. [Supp 4/90]

**Torrence, Ridgely**
   Eye-Witness. [Supp 1/303]

**Torso** of a Woman. N. Ezekiel. [Supp 7/55]

**Totem.** S. Plath. [Supp 5/216]

**Totem.** L. Senghor. [Supp 6/75]

"**T**" other day, as I was twining." Cupid Swallowed. L. Hunt. [Volume 2/91]

"**Touch** us gently, time!" A Petition to Time. B.

Procter. [Volume 1/334]

**Toward.** R. Sanchez. [Supp 4/249]

"**Toward** the end of twenty minutes." Roman Poem Number Two. J. Jordan. [Supp 5/124]

"**Toward,** toward, ever toward." Toward. R. Sanchez. [Supp 4/249]

"**Town,** tower, %shore, deep." The Djinns. V. Hugo. [Volume 6/60]

**Townsend, George Alfred**
   Army Correspondents Last Ride. [Volume 8/408]

**Townsend, Mary Ashley**
   A Woman's Wish. [Volume 6/429]

**Trailing** Arbutus. R. Cooke. [Volume 5/250]

**Train.** D. Segooa. [Supp 6/88]

**Train** Ride. J. Wheelwright. [Supp 2/56]

*Trains*
   Train. D. Segooa. [Supp 6/88]

**Tramp,** Tramp, Tramp. Unknown. [Volume 8/380]

The **Trance.** S. Spender. [Supp 2/234]

A **Transformation,** fr. The Metamorphoses. Ovid (Publius Ovidius Naso). [Volume 6/87]

The **Translation.** M. Doren. [Supp 1/312]

*Travel*
   Amagoduka at Glencoe station. M. Mtshali. [Supp 6/84]
   Marston. S. Spender. [Supp 2/229]
   Sweet Stay-at-Home. W. Davies. [Supp 1/106]
   "When I Set Out for Lyonnesse" T. Hardy. [Supp 1/160]

"A **traveller** through a dusty road stewed acorns." Small Beginnings. C. Mackay. [Volume 4/309]

"**Tread** softly, for here you stand." On Ithaca Standing. L. Durrell. [Supp 2/260]

The **Treasures** of the Deep. F. Hemans. [Volume 5/385]

"The **tree** of deepest root is found." The Three Warnings. H. Thrale. [Volume 6/289]

"The **Tree** Sleeps in the Winter" N. Russell. [Supp 4/296]

*Trees*
   Among the Redwoods. E. Sill. [Volume 5/234]
   The Arab to the Palm. B. Taylor. [Volume 5/227]
   Bo Tree. Lin Ling. [Supp 7/23]
   The Brave Old Oak. H. Chorley. [Volume 5/220]
   "Did You Not See" A. Kuo. [Supp 4/6]
   The Flowering of the Rod: 010. H. Doolittle. [Supp 5/79]
   A Forest Hymn. W. Bryant. [Volume 5/223]
   The GGreengage Tree. E. Sitwell. [Supp 5/274]
   The Grape-vine Swing. W. Simms. [Volume 5/231]
   The Greenwood Tree, fr. As You Like It. W. Shakespeare. [Volume 5/219]
   The Holly-tree. R. Southey. [Volume 5/221]
   Jazzonia. L. Hughes. [Supp 4/129]
   The Mountain. H. Riyong. [Supp 6/47]
   The Palm-tree. J. Whittier. [Volume 5/229]
   The Planting of the Apple-tree. W. Byrant. [Volume 5/232]
   The Primeval Forest, fr. Evangeline. H. Longfellow. [Volume 5/218]
   Ryton Firs. L. Abercrombie. [Supp 1/5]
   Stump?A. Nirala. [Supp 7/65]
   "The Tree Sleeps in the Winter" N. Russell. [Supp 4/296]
   The Voice of the Grass. S. Roberts. [Volume 5/237]
   The Wind and the Pine-tree, fr. Edwin the Fair. S. Taylor. [Volume 5/219]

"The **Trees** Are Naked" E. Manner. [Supp 5/154]

"A **trellis** of sticks." Multitudinous Stars and Spring Waters: 009. Ping Hsin. [Supp 5/117]

**Trench, Richard Chenevix**
   The Christ. [Volume 4/75]
   Harmosan. [Volume 8/203]
   Vanity. [Volume 4/292]

The **Trial** of Beatrice, fr. The Cenci. P. Shelley. [Volume 9/68]

The **Two** Oceans. J. Sterling. [Volume 6/439]
"**Two** of far nobler shape, erect and tall." Adam and Eve, fr, Paradise Lost. J. Milton. [Volume 7/124]
The **Two** Parents. H. MacDiarmid. [Supp 2/31]
**Two** Pictures. A. Green. [Volume 1/318]
**Two** Planets. M. Iqbal. [Supp 7/57]
"**Two** planets meeting face to face." Two Planets. M. Iqbal. [Supp 7/57]
**Two** Questions. A. Hernandez. [Supp 7/177]
The **Two** Rabbis. J. Whittier. [Volume 4/316]
**Two** Sayings. E. Browning. [Volume 4/68]
"**Two** sayings of the Holy Scriptures beat." Two Sayings. E. Browning. [Volume 4/68]
"**Two** seas, amid the night." The Two Oceans. J. Sterling. [Volume 6/439]
"**Two** souls diverse out of our human sight." On the Death of Thomas Carlyle and George Eliot. A. Swinburne. [Volume 7/96]
The **Two** Waitings. J. Chadwick. [Volume 3/409]
The **Two** Wives. W. Howells. [Volume 8/355]
The **Two** Worlds. M. Collins. [Volume 4/400]
"**Two** worlds there are. To one our eyes we strain." The Two Worlds. M. Collins. [Volume 4/400]
"**Tying** her bonnet under her chin." The Love-Knot. N. Perry. [Volume 2/126]


"**U** feel that way sometimes." Mixed Sketches. D. Lee. [Supp 4/210]
**Uhland, Ludwig**
   The Landlady's Daughter. J. Dwight (tr.). [Volume 2/335]
   The Passage. S. Austin (tr.). [Volume 3/342]
**Ulalume**. E. Poe. [Volume 6/152]
**Ulrich, Anton, Duke of Brunswick**
   God's Sure Help in Sorrow. [Volume 3/236]
**Ultima** Veritas. W. Gladden. [Volume 4/255]
**Ulysses**. A. Tennyson. [Volume 6/426]
*Ulysses*
   A Chinese Ulysses. S. Kazuko. [Supp 5/132]
*Umbrellas*
   A Mounted Umbrella. G. Stein. [Supp 5/292]
**Una** and the Lion, fr. The Faerie Queene. E. Spenser. [Volume 6/110]
**Una** and the Red Crosse Knight, fr. The Faerie Queene. E. Spenser. [Volume 6/108]
*Uncertainity*
   Uncertainty. B. Reyna. [Supp 6/146]
**Uncertainty**. B. Reyna. [Supp 6/146]
"**Uncertainty** can have your name." Uncertainity. B. Reyna. [Supp 6/146]
**Unchanging**. F. Von Bodenstedt. [Volume 3/242]
"**Unconquerably**, men venture on the quest." The Polar Quest. R. Burton. [Volume 5/421]
*Unconscious*
   The Trance. S. Spender. [Supp 2/234]
"**Under** a bridge of stone the river shuddered by." The Dreamer. C. Bax. [Supp 1/27]
"**Under** a splintered mast." A Talisman. M. Moore. [Supp 1/233]
"**Under** a spreading chestnut-tree." The Village Blacksmith. H. Longfellow. [Volume 1/328]
"**Under** a toadstool." The Elf and the Dormouse. O. Herford. [Volume 1/152]
"**Under** my Window" T. Westwood. [Volume 1/139]
"**Under** the bloody tumbling of twilight." The Song of Abraham in Fire. A. Shamlu. [Supp 7/211]
"**Under** the greenwood tree." The Greenwood Tree, fr. As You Like It. W. Shakespeare. [Volume 5/219]
**Under** the Portrait of John Milton. J. Dryden. [Volume 7/54]
**Under** the Shade of the Trees. M. Preston. [Volume

8/392]
"**Under** yonder beech-tree standing on the green." Love In The Valley. G. Meredith. [Volume 2/121]
"**Underneath** this wooden cross there lies." Epitaph. K. Shapiro. [Supp 2/318]
**Undeveloped** Lives. W. Lecky. [Volume 6/268]
The **Undiscovered** Country. E. Stedman. [Volume 4/387]
The **Undiscovered** Planet. L. Lee. [Supp 2/343]
*Unemployment*
   Boy with His Hair Cut Short. M. Rukeyser. [Supp 2/295]
"**Unfading** hope! when life's last embers burn." Hope, fr. The Pleasures of Hope. T. Campbell. [Volume 4/145]
The **Unfinished** Prayer. Unknown. [Volume 1/43]
"The **Unillumined** Verge" R. Bridges. [Volume 3/308]
The **Uninhabited** City: 001. E. Cardenal. [Supp 6/153]
The **Uninhabited** City: 002. E. Cardenal. [Supp 6/154]
*United States*
   America. C. McKay. [Supp 1/203]
   The Tears of a Muse in America: 001. F. Prince. [Supp 2/267]
   The Tears of a Muse in America: 002. F. Prince. [Supp 2/267]
   The Tears of a Muse in America: 003. F. Prince. [Supp 2/268]
   The Tears of a Muse in America: 004. F. Prince. [Supp 2/269]
The **Universal** Prayer. A. Pope. [Volume 4/11]
**Unknown** Poets, fr. The Excursion. W. Wordsworth. [Volume 6/339]
**Unmusical** Birds, fr. The Task. W. Cowper. [Volume 5/309]
**Unrequited** Love, fr. Twelfth Night. W. Shakespeare. [Volume 3/9]
The **Unseen** Playmate. R. Stevenson. [Volume 1/131]
**Unseen** Spirits. N. Willis. [Volume 3/204]
"**Unsuitable** for song as well as sense." Island. N. Ezekiel. [Supp 7/54]
**Untermeyer, Louis**
   Steel Mill. [Supp 1/311]
   Swimmers. [Supp 1/309]
"**Until** the last veil was cast aside." Poem 22. T. Sayigh. [Supp 7/294]
"**Untremulous** in the river clear." Summer Storm. J. Lowell. [Volume 5/119]
"**Up** from earth's centre through the seventh gate." Rubaiyat: 031. O. Khayyam. [Volume 6/210]
"**Up** from the meadows rich with corn." Barbara Frietchie. J. Whittier. [Volume 8/362]
"**Up** from the south at break of day." Sheridan's Ride. T. Read. [Volume 8/383]
**Up** Hill. C. Rossetti. [Volume 4/332]
"**Up** into the cherry tree." Foreign Lands. R. Stevenson. [Volume 1/138]
"**Up!** quit thy bower! late wears the hour." Morning Song. J. Baillie. [Volume 5/39]
"**Up** the airy mountain." The Fairies. W. Allingham. [Volume 6/19]
"**Up** the ash tree climbs the ivy." Upper Lambourne. J. Betjeman. [Supp 2/138]
"**Up** the dale and down the bourne." Song of the Summer Winds. G. Darley. [Volume 5/99]
"**Up** the streets of Aberdeen." Barclay of Ury. J. Whittier. [Volume 7/429]
"**Up!** up, my friend! and quit you books." The Tables Turned. W. Wordsworth. [Volume 5/23]
"**Upon** a rock yet uncreate." The Cosmic Egg. Unknown [Volume 9/436]
"**Upon** ane stormy Sunday." The Plaidie. C. Sibley. [Volume 2/131]
"**Upon** St. Michael's Isle." The Burial of Robert Browning. M. Field. [Volume 7/89]
**Upper** Lambourne. J. Betjeman. [Supp 2/138]
**Upstate**. D. Walcott. [Supp 4/167]

The Use of Flowers. M. Howitt. [Volume 5/241]
The Useless Wait. G. Mistral. [Supp 6/124]

The V-A-S-E. J. Roche. [Volume 9/446]
V-Letter. K. Shapiro. [Supp 2/323]
Vacations. F. Lima. [Supp 4/243]
*Vacations*
    A Holiday for Me. K. Das. [Supp 5/58]
    Vacations. F. Lima. [Supp 4/243]
The Vagabonds. J. Trowbridge. [Volume 6/260]
*Vagabonds*
    "The Hunchback in the Park" D. Thomas. [Supp 2/364]
    Street Corner College. K. Patchen. [Supp 2/255]
The Vale of Avoca. T. Moore. [Volume 1/351]
The Vale of Cashmere, fr. The Light of the Harem. T. Moore. [Volume 7/165]
"The vale of tempe had in vain been fair." Ideality. H. Coleridge. [Volume 6/8]
Valentine for Ben Franklin Who Drives a Truck in California. D. Wakoski. [Supp 5/322]
Valentine, Jean (tr.)
    "And What Will Happen" K. Molodowsky. [Supp 5/175]
    Song of the Sabbath. K. Molodowsky. [Supp 5/173]
Vallejo, Cesar
    The Black Messengers. H. Hays (tr.). [Supp 6/187]
    Our Daily Bread. H. Hays (tr.). [Supp 6/188]
    The Wheel of the Hungry. H. Hays (tr.). [Supp 6/189]
The Valley Brook. J. Bryant. [Volume 5/193]
The Valley of the Shadow. E. Robinson. [Supp 1/267]
Vam E;sem. F. Scott. [Volume 3/361]
Van Dyk, H. S. (tr.)
    On the Death of an Infant. J. Lowell. [Volume 1/70]
Van Dyke, Henry
    The Child in the Garden. [Volume 1/55]
    A Wayfaring Song. [Volume 1/347]
    Work. [Volume 6/415]
*Vancouver*
    "I Fire at the Face of the Country Where I Was Born" S. Kazuko. [Supp 5/130]
Vandergrift, Margaret
    The Dead Doll. [Volume 1/129]
The Vanishing Boat. E. Gosse. [Supp 1/146]
Vanity. R. Trench. [Volume 4/292]
The Vanity of the World. F. Quarles. [Volume 3/153]
"The various voices are his poem now." Glaucus. S. Keyes. [Supp 2/412]
"Vastness which grows, but grows to harmonize." Saint Peter's at Rome, fr. Childe Harold. G. Byron. [Volume 7/186]
Vaughan, Henry
    Happy Are the Dead. [Volume 3/439]
    Peace. [Volume 4/414]
    The Seed Growing Secretly. [Volume 4/343]
    "They Are All Gone" [Volume 3/403]
Velvet Shoes. E. Wylie. [Supp 1/326]
Venable, William Henry
    The School Girl. [Volume 1/213]
    A Welcome to "Boz" [Volume 7/77]
Veni Creator Spiritus. S. Gregory. [Volume 6/104]
Veni Sancte Spiritus. Robert II; King of France. [Volume 4/105]
Venice. J. Symonds. [Volume 7/188]
Venice, fr. Italy. S. Rogers. [Volume 7/189]
Venice, fr. View from the Euganean Hills. P. Shelley. [Volume 7/192]
"Venice, thou siren of sea cities, wrought." Venice. J. Symonds. [Volume 7/188]
*Venice, Italy*
    A Water-Colour of Venice. L. Durrell. [Supp 2/261]

Vere, Edward, Earl of Oxford
    A Renunciation. [Volume 2/246]
Verlaine, Paul
    The Spell. G. Hall (tr.). [Volume 6/367]
Verse. G. Byron. [Volume 3/169, Volume 3/170, Volume 3/171]
"Verse, a breeze 'mid blossoms straying." Youth, fr. Youth and Age. S. Coleridge. [Volume 1/263]
Verses. W. Cowper. [Volume 6/311]
Verses Why Burnt. W. Landor. [Volume 6/350]
Verses Written in an Album. T. Moore. [Volume 2/34]
"Very dark the autumn sky." A Belated Violet. O. Herford. [Volume 1/154]
Very, Jones
    The Latter Rain. [Volume 5/148]
    Life. [Volume 4/261]
    Nature. [Volume 5/20]
    The Spirit-Land. [Volume 4/410]
Vesper Hymn. S. Longfellow. [Volume 4/195]
Vesper Hymn. E. Scudder. [Volume 4/196]
The Vicar of Bray. Unknown. [Volume 9/251]
"Victor in poesy! Victor in romance!" To Victor Hugo. A. Tennyson. [Volume 7/41]
"Victorious men of earth, no more." The Common Doom. J. Shirley. [Volume 2/237]
*Victory*
    What Value Has the People Whose Tongue Is Tied?: 008. N. Qabbani. [Supp 7/287]
Vietnam. C. Major. [Supp 4/204]
*Vietnam*
    The First Morning in Vietnam. Ho Ch'i-Fang. [Supp 7/5]
A View Across the roman Campagna. E. Browning. [Volume 7/187]
Vigil. C. Meireles. [Supp 5/162]
Vigils. T. Carmi. [Supp 7/241]
The Village Blacksmith. H. Longfellow. [Volume 1/328]
The Village Schoolmistress, fr. The Schoolmaster. W. Shenstone. [Volume 7/231]
Villanueva, Alma
    "I Was Always Fascinated" [Supp 4/266]
    "There Is Nothing In New York" [Supp 4/268]
    To Jesus Villaneuva, with Love. [Supp 4/259]
    "You Cannot Leave" [Supp 4/263]
Villon, Francois
    The Ballad of Dead Ladies. D. Rossetti (tr.). [Volume 6/192]
"The vine had struck a fibre; which about." Rubaiyat: 076. O. Khayyam. [Volume 6/219]
"A Violet in Her Hair" C. Swain. [Volume 2/17]
The Viper. R. Pitter. [Supp 2/51]
Virgil (Publius Vergillius Maro)
    The Fall of Troy, fr. Aeneid. S. Bowen (tr.). [Volume 7/261]
A Virginal. E. Pound. [Supp 1/251]
Virtue Immortal. G. Herbert. [Volume 3/254]
Vision of a Fair Woman. E. Sharp. [Volume 2/25]
A Vision of Beauty. B. Jonson. [Volume 2/23]
The Vision of Sir Launfal. J. Lowell. [Volume 4/172]
Vision of the Cuckoo. R. Pitter. [Supp 5/206]
A Visit from St. Nicholas. C. Moore. [Volume 1/157]
The Visitants. M. Waddington. [Supp 5/317]
"Vital moments come." Moments of Initiation. K. Kerpi. [Supp 6/45]
"Vital spark of heavenly flame!" The Dying Christian to His Sould. A. Pope. [Volume 4/376]
The Voice. W. Gibson. [Supp 1/141]
Voice of the Diving Herdsman. Unknown (African American). [Supp 6/10]
The Voice of the Grass. S. Roberts. [Volume 5/237]
"A voice resounds like thunder-pearl." The Watch on the Rhine. M. Schneckenburger. [Volume 8/80]
"The voice that would reach you, hunter, must speak." To Roosevelt. R. Dario. [Supp 6/163]
The Voiceless. O. Holmes. [Volume 3/172]

"Void only %take away your veil of stars."
  Multitudinous Stars and Sping Waters: 002. Ping
  Hsin. [Supp 5/116]
*Volcanoes*
  The Different Day. G. Conkling. [Supp 1/88]
  Written on a Roadside Stone During the First
  Eruption. P. Cuadra. [Supp 6/161]
**Von Bodenstedt, Friedrich Martin**
  Unchanging. [Volume 3/242]
**Von Salis, Johann Gaudenz**
  Song of the Silent Land. H. Longfellow (tr.).
  [Volume 4/388]
"'Vourneen, when your days were bright." Live In My
  Heart And Pay No Rent. S. Lover. [Volume 2/180]
The Vowels: an Enigma. J. Swift. [Volume 9/311]
The Voyage. C. Mason. [Volume 4/38]
The Voyage of Sleep. A. Eaton. [Volume 6/438]
*Vultures*
  The Black Vulture. G. Sterling. [Supp 1/288]
  Still, Citizen Sparrow. R. Wilbur. [Supp 2/409]


**Waddington, Miriam**
  How Old Women Should Live. [Supp 5/312]
  Lady in Blue: Homage to Montreal. [Supp 5/315]
  The Milk of the Mothers. [Supp 5/310]
  Past the Ice Age. [Supp 5/314]
  The Visitants. [Supp 5/317]
**Waddington, Samuel**
  Mors Et Vita. [Volume 1/396]
The Wail of Prometheus Bound, fr. Prometheus.
  Aeschylus. [Volume 3/156]
"Wailing, wailing, wailing, the wind over land and."
  Rizpah. A. Tennyson. [Volume 9/151]
Waiting. J. Burroughs. [Volume 3/238]
*Waiting*
  Present. J. Das. [Supp 7/49]
Waiting for the Grapes. W. Maginn. [Volume 2/243]
Waiting in the Children's Hospital. C. Major. [Supp
  4/199]
The Waitress. B. Akhmadulina. [Supp 5/2]
"Wake! for the sun, who scattered into flight."
  Rubaiyat: 001. O. Khayyam. [Volume 6/204]
"Waken, lords and ladies gay." Hunting Song. S. Scott.
  [Volume 5/154]
"Waking alone I would marshal my tasks." Mornings in
  Various Years: 002. M. Piercy. [Supp 5/200]
"Waking, he found himself in a train, andante." Slow
  Movement. L. MacNeice. [Supp 2/182]
**Wakoski, Diane**
  The Elephant & the Butterfly Meet on the Buddha's
  Birthday. [Supp 5/320]
  George Washington Sends a Pair of Shoebuckles ...
  [Supp 5/319]
  The Ring. [Supp 5/323]
  Sun Gods Have Sun Spots. [Supp 5/321]
  Tearing Up My Mother's Letters. [Supp 5/324]
  Valentine for Ben Franklin Who Drives a Truck in
  California [Supp 5/322]
**Walcott, Derek**
  Upstate. [Supp 4/167]
Walk. F. Horne. [Supp 4/106]
Walk with De Mayor of Harlem. D. Henderson. [Supp
  4/207]
**Walker, Alice**
  Burial: 001. [Supp 4/225]
  Burial: 002. [Supp 4/225]
  Burial: 003. [Supp 4/226]
  Burial: 004. [Supp 4/226]
  Burial: 005. [Supp 4/227]
  Burial: 006. [Supp 4/227]
  "Expect Nothing. Live Frugally" [Supp 4/224]
  Medicine. [Supp 4/229]

Ne Face. [Supp 4/228]
The Walker of the Snow. C. Shanly. [Volume 6/167]
*Walking*
  Walk. F. Horne. [Supp 4/106]
"Walking Out of Expectation" Hsiung Hung. [Supp 7/9]
Walking Song. C. Williams. [Supp 1/315]
"wall, no! I can't tell whar he lives." Jim Bludso of
  the Prairie Belle. J. Hay. [Volume 9/358]
**Waller, Edmund**
  "Go, Lovely Rose" [Volume 2/37]
  Old Age and Death, fr. Verses Upon His Divine
  Poesy. [Volume 6/293]
  On a Griddle. [Volume 2/35]
**Waller, John Francis**
  Kitty Neil. [Volume 2/133]
  The Spinning-Wheel Song. [Volume 2/294]
"Wallowing in this bloody sty." The Drunken Fisherman.
  R. Lowell. [Supp 2/389]
*Walls*
  Mending Wall. R. Frost. [Supp 1/130]
The Walls Do Not Fall: 006. H. Doolittle. [Supp 5/72]
The Walls Do Not Fall: 013. H. Doolittle. [Supp 5/73]
The Walls Do Not Fall: 014. H. Doolittle. [Supp 5/74]
Wally, Waly. Unknown. [Volume 3/45]
The Walrus and the Carpenter, fr. Alice in Wonderland.
  C. Dodgson. [Volume 1/180]
**Walsh, William**
  Rivalry In Love. [Volume 2/225]
**Walther Von Der Vogelweide**
  Song. E. Taylor (tr.). [Volume 2/26]
**Walton, Izaak**
  The Angler's Wish. [Volume 5/138]
Walton's Book of Lives, fr. Ecclesiastical Sonnets. W.
  Wordsworth. [Volume 7/55]
"Wan %swan %on the lake." The Bereaved Swan. S. Smith.
  [Supp 2/102]
The Wanderer. S. Smith. [Supp 5/285]
The Wanderer's Home. O. Goldsmith. [Volume 1/314]
"Wandering and fortuitous the paths." The Jungle: 002.
  A. Lewis. [Supp 2/375]
The Wants of Man. J. Adams. [Volume 6/421]
*War*
  Alfred the harper. J. Sterling. [Volume 8/238]
  All. F. Durivage. [Volume 8/415]
  "All Quiet Along the Potomac" E. Beers. [Volume
  8/350]
  Army Correspondents Last Ride. G. Townsend.
  [Volume 8/408]
  At the Centoph. H. MacDiarmid. [Supp 2/29]
  At the Heart of Two Burning Stars. P. Cuadra.
  [Supp 6/162]
  The Ballad of Agincourt. M. Drayton. [Volume
  8/264]
  Bannockburn. R. Burns. [Volume 8/304]
  Barbara Frietchie. J. Whittier. [Volume 8/362]
  The Battle of Manila. R. Hovey. [Volume 8/421]
  Battle of the Angels, fr. Paradise Lost. J. Milton.
  [Volume 8/179]
  Battle of the Baltic. T. Campbell. [Volume 8/281]
  Battle Scene, fr. The Cid. Unknown. [Volume 8/205]
  The Battle-Song of Gustavus Adolphus. M. Altenburg.
  [Volume 8/216]
  Bay Billy. F. Gassaway. [Volume 8/373]
  Beal' an Dhuine, fr. The Lady of the Lake. S.
  Scott. [Volume 8/307]
  Bingen on the Rhine. C. Norton. [Volume 8/221]
  The Black Regiment. G. Boker. [Volume 8/393]
  The Bonnets of Bonnie Dundee. S. Scott. [Volume
  8/322]
  The Bronze Statue of Napoleon. A. Barbier. [Volume
  8/232]
  Brother Jonathan's Lament for Sister Caroline. O.
  Holmes. [Volume 8/344]
  Bruce and the Spider. B. Barton. [Volume 8/302]
  Burial of Sir John Moore. C. Wolfe. [Volume 8/283]

"The **warm** sun is failing, the bleak wind is wailing."
Autumn: A Dirge. P. Shelley. [Volume 5/170]
"**Warm**, wild, rainy wind, blowing fitfully." May
Morning. C. Thaxter. [Volume 5/84]
**Warren, Robert Penn**
Pursuit. [Supp 2/132]
Revelation. [Supp 2/131]
Terror. [Supp 2/133]
**Warren's** Address. J. Pierpont. [Volume 8/326]
"The **warrior** bowed his crested head, and tamed."
Bernardo Del Carpio. F. Hemans. [Volume 9/85]
"A **warrior** so bold, and a virgin so bright." Alonzo
the Brave and the Fair Imogine. M. Lewis.
[Volume 7/321]
"**Was** it the chime of a tiny bell." Passing Away. J.
Pierpont. [Volume 7/84]
"**Was** this small plant for thee cut down?" Smoking
Spiritualized. R. Erskine. [Volume 6/250]
**Washington**, fr. Under the Elm. J. Lowell. [Volume
7/15]
*Washington, D.C.*
The Potomac. K. Shapiro. [Supp 2/323]
*Washington, George*
George Washington. Unknown. [Volume 7/15]
Washington, fr. Under the Elm. J. Lowell. [Volume
7/15]
"**Waste** not your hour, nor in the vain pursuit."
Rubaiyat: 054. O. Khayyam. [Volume 6/214]
**Wastell, Simon**
Man's Mortality. [Volume 3/254]
**Watch** Any Day. W. Auden. [Supp 2/169]
"**Watch** any day his nonchalant pauses, see." Watch Any
Day. W. Auden. [Supp 2/169]
The **Watch** on the Rhine. M. Schneckenburger. [Volume
8/80]
**Watching**. E. Judson. [Volume 6/435]
**Watching** for Papa. Unknown. [Volume 3/414]
"**Watching** you in the mirror I wonder." The Mirror. L.
Gluck. [Supp 5/104]
*Water*
Water Raining. G. Stein. [Supp 5/293]
"**Water** astonishing and difficult altogether makes a
meadow and a %stroke." Water Raining. G. Stein.
[Supp 5/293]
A **Water-Colour** of Venice. L. Durrell. [Supp 2/261]
The **Water-lily**. J. Tabb. [Volume 5/280]
"The **water** purled, the waters swelled." The Fisher. J.
Goethe. [Volume 6/78]
**Water** Raining. G. Stein. [Supp 5/293]
*Waterfalls*
The Black Rock of Kiltearen. A. Young. [Supp 2/2]
To a Waterfall. Nirala. [Supp 7/66]
**Waterloo**, fr. Childe Harold. G. Byron. [Volume 8/287]
"**Waters** Are Wiser Than We" F. Daglarca. [Supp 7/298]
**Watkins, Vernon**
The Collier. [Supp 2/189]
Indolence. [Supp 2/190]
The Turning of the Leaves. [Supp 2/191]
Zacchaeus in the Leaves. [Supp 2/192]
**Watson, Ellen (tr.)**
Denouement. A. Prado. [Supp 6/117]
Love in the Ether. A. Prado. [Supp 6/118]
**Watson, John Whittaker**
Beautiful Snow. [Volume 3/205]
Wounded to Death. [Volume 8/375]
**Watson, Rosamund Marriott**
Ave Atque Vale. [Volume 6/191]
**Watson, William**
England and Her Colonies. [Volume 8/32]
Lachrymae Musarum. [Volume 7/84]
Leavetaking. [Supp 1/313]
The Turk in Armenia, fr. The Purple East. [Volume
8/22]
Wordsworth's Grave, sel. [Volume 7/74]
**Watts, Isaac**

A Cradle Hymn. [Volume 1/98]
Heaven. [Volume 4/413]
"How Doth the Little Busy Bee" [Volume 1/108]
Jesus Shall Reign. [Volume 4/96]
"Let Dogs Delight to Bark and Bite" [Volume 1/114]
"Our god, Our help in Ages Past" [Volume 4/32]
Self-Inquiry. [Volume 4/280]
**Watts, Theodore**
Ode to Mother Carey's Chicken. [Volume 5/333]
**Waugh, Edwin**
"The Dule's I' This Bonnet O' Mine" [Volume 2/116]
"**Wave** after wave of greenness rolling down." Perished.
M. Ritter. [Volume 3/169]
"**Wave** after wave successively rolls on." Newport-
Beach. H. Tuckerman. [Volume 7/239]
**Waves**. D. Diop. [Supp 6/70]
"The **waves** lay down their trail." Evening Scene. E.
Scovell. [Supp 2/187]
"**Way** down upon de Swanne Ribber." Old Folks at Home.
W. Cowper. [Volume 3/149]
The **Way** of Islam. M. Iqbal. [Supp 7/60]
The **Way** the Bird Sat. R. Bear. [Supp 4/337]
The **Way**, the Truth, and the Life. T. Parker. [Volume
4/92]
"The **way** to the boiler was dark." The Lost Son: The
Return. T. Roethke. [Supp 2/209]
A **Wayfaring** Song. H. Van Dyke. [Volume 1/347]
"**We** are born; we laugh; we weep." Life. B. Procter.
[Volume 3/251]
**We** Are Brethren A' R. Nicoll. [Volume 1/353]
"**We** are coming, Father Abraham, three hundred." Three
Hundred Thousand More. Unknown. [Volume 8/356]
"**We** are little airy creatures." The Vowels: an Enigma.
J. Swift. [Volume 9/311]
"**We** are no other than a moving row." Rubaiyat: 068. O.
Khayyam. [Volume 6/217]
**We** Are Seven. W. Wordsworth. [Volume 1/73]
"**We** are two travellers, Roger and I." The Vagabonds.
J. Trowbridge. [Volume 6/260]
"**We** ask for no statistics of the killed." Elegy for a
Dead Soldier: 005. K. Shapiro. [Supp 2/315]
"**We** assume %that in 28 hours." We Assume: On the
Death of Our Son, %Reuben Masai Harper. M.
Harper. [Supp 4/205]
**We** Assume: On the Death of Our Son, %Reuben Masai
Harper. M. Harper. [Supp 4/205]
"**We** built a ship upon the stairs." A Good Play. R.
Stevenson. [Volume 1/127]
"**We** count the broken lyres that rest." The Voiceless.
O. Holmes. [Volume 3/172]
**We** Do Not Know the Name of the King. M. Takahashi.
[Supp 7/122]
"**We** had this idea." Our Hands in the Garden. A.
Hebert. [Supp 5/110]
"**We** Have Been Friends Together" C. Norton. [Volume
1/351]
"**We** have lost the planet to the block party."
Vacations. F. Lima. [Supp 4/243]
"**We** have paid for our love and improvision." What
Value Has the People Whose Tongue Is Tied?: 009.
N. Qabbani. [Supp 7/288]
"**We** heard her speaking of chinese musicians." The
Woman Who Disapproved of Music at the Bar. H.
Gregory. [Supp 2/67]
"**We** knew it would rain, for all the morn." Before the
Rain. T. Aldrich. [Volume 5/117]
"**We** know not what it is, dear, this sleep so deep."
The Two Mysteries. M. Dodge. [Volume 3/262]
"**We** know not yet what life shall be." Mors Et Vita. S.
Waddington. [Volume 1/396]
"**We** know what trembles on the scales." Courage. A.
Akhmatova. [Supp 5/9]
"**We** listen, wind from where." The Runner with the
Lots. L. Adams. [Supp 2/71]
**We** Love But Few. Unknown. [Volume 1/368]

Rubaiyat: 010. O. Khayyam. [Volume 6/205]
"We'll not weep for summer over." After Summer. P. Marston. [Volume 3/336]
Well of St. Keyne. R. Southey. [Volume 9/204]
"A well there is in the West country." Well of St. Keyne. R. Southey. [Volume 9/204]
"'Well, this is bad!' we sighing said." The C. S. Army's Commissary. E. Thompson. [Volume 8/396]
"'Well,' murmured one, 'let whoso make or buy'" Rubaiyat: 089. O. Khayyam. [Volume 6/221]
The Welsh Marches. A. Housman. [Supp 1/167]
"we're going to the fair at holstenwall." Holstenwall. S. Keyes. [Supp 2/413]
"Were I As Base As Is The Lowly Plain" J. Sylvester. [Volume 2/330]
Were I But His Own Wife. M. Downing. [Volume 2/400]
"Were I but his own wife, to guard and to guide." Were I But His Own Wife. M. Downing. [Volume 2/400]
We're Ready. C. Anwar. [Supp 7/81]
"Were You There When They Crucified My Lord?" Unknown (African American). [Supp 4/60]
"Werther had a love for Charlotte." Sorrows of Werther. W. Thackeray. [Volume 9/204]
Wesley, Charles
     Wrestling Jacob. [Volume 4/79]
Wesley, John (tr.)
     The Love of God Supreme. G. Tersteegen. [Volume 4/130]
West Coast Episode. J. Jordan. [Supp 5/128]
Western Civilization. A. Neto. [Supp 6/17]
Westwood, Thomas
     Little Bell. [Volume 1/135]
     "Under my Window" [Volume 1/139]
"A Wet Sheet and a Flowing Sea" A. Cunningham. [Volume 5/399]
Weteran and Recruit. E. Hazewell. [Volume 8/19]
Wetherald, Ethelwyn
     The Snow-storm. [Volume 5/177]
"We've all of us been told." Against Drawbridges: 001. M. Benedetti. [Supp 6/191]
"The whale butting through scarps of moving marble." Explorations. L. MacNeice. [Supp 2/178]
Whales
     Sojourn in the Whale. M. Moore. [Supp 5/185]
"Whan that Aprille with hise shoures soote." The Canterbury Pilgrims, fr. The Canterbury Tales. G. Chaucer. [Volume 7/363]
"What a moment, what a doubt!" Sneezing. L. Hunt. [Volume 9/421]
"What a season's here!" Spring. L. Devkota. [Supp 7/156]
"What ails John Winter, that so oft." John Winter. L. Binyon. [Supp 1/50]
"What Ails This Heart O' Mine?" S. Blamire. [Volume 3/139]
"What am I? O thou sea, with all thy noise." Theseus. T. Moore. [Supp 1/235]
"'What are the bugles blowin' for?' said." Danny Deever. R. Kipling. [Volume 8/299]
"What are the thoughts that are stirring him." Under the Shade of the Trees. M. Preston. [Volume 8/392]
"What are you staring at, mariner man." Mariner man. E. Sitwell. [Supp 5/271]
"What came before and afterward." The Queen Forgets. G. Sterling. [Supp 1/287]
"What Can An Old Man Do But Die?" T. Hood. [Volume 3/174]
"What chance %sweet dreamlike chance." I Won't Sell His Love. F. Tuqan. [Supp 5/307]
"What Constitutes a State?" S. Jones. [Volume 8/3]
"What desperate nightmare rapts me to this land." Legacy: My South. D. Randall. [Supp 4/154]
"What Does Little Birdie Say?" A. Tennyson. [Volume

1/98]
"What does thou see, lone watcher on the tower." Day Breaks. C. Mackay. [Volume 4/244]
What For?/Pa' Victor hara. Alurista. [Supp 4/270]
"What for the rush." What For?/Pa' Victor hara. Alurista. [Supp 4/270]
"What! from his helpless creature be repaid." Rubaiyat: 079. O. Khayyam. [Volume 6/219]
"What gift for passionate lovers shall we find?" Perfume. E. Goose. [Volume 2/]
"What happens to a dream deferred?" Dream Deferred. L. Hughes. [Supp 4/132]
"What hid'st thou in thy treasure-caves and cells?" The Treasures of the Deep. F. Hemans. [Volume 5/385]
"What hope is here for modern rhyme." The Poet's Tribute, fr. In Memoriam. A. Tennyson. [Volume 3/354]
"What I Expected" S. Spender. [Supp 2/236]
"What I have heard." Paradise: Sin and Redemption, fr. The Diving Comedy. Dante Alighieri. [Volume 4/441]
What I Live For. G. Banks. [Volume 4/186]
What I Tell Him. S. Ortiz. [Supp 4/316]
"What I thought was love." The Liar. L. Jones. [Supp 4/175]
"What if some morning, when the stars were." A Morning Thought. E. Sill. [Volume 3/267]
"What is a sonnet? 'T is the pearly shell." The Sonnet. R. Gilder. [Volume 6/344]
"What is Africa to me." Heritage. C. Cullen. [Supp 1/96]
"What is it fades and flickers in the fire." By the Fireside. L. Larcom. [Volume 1/293]
What is Moving. S. Takahashi. [Supp 7/128]
What is Prayer? J. Montgomery. [Volume 4/111]
"What is the German's Fatherland?" E. Arndt. [Volume 8/74]
What is the Grass?, fr. The Song of Myself. W. Whitman. [Volume 6/198]
"What is the little one thinking about?" Cradle Song, fr. Bitter-Sweet. J. Holland. [Volume 1/13]
"What is the metre of the dictionary?" Altarwise by Owl-light: 004. D. Thomas. [Supp 2/349]
What Is the Name of a Ring. G. Stein. [Supp 5/295]
"What is this drink but." Summer in Calcutta. K. Das. [Supp 5/56]
"What is this life if, full of care." Leisure. W. Davies. [Supp 1/105]
"What man is there so bold that he should say." Liberty. J. Hay. [Volume 8/112]
"What memory fired her pallid face." The Nun and Harp. G. Leroux. [Volume 3/93]
What Mr. Robinson Thinks, fr. The Biglow Papers. J. Lowell. [Volume 9/339]
What My Lover Said. H. Greene. [Volume 2/279]
"What need you, being come to sense." September, 1913. W. Yeats. [Supp 1/328]
"What needs my Shakespeare for his honored." An Epitaph on the Admirable Dramatic Poet, W. Shakespeare. J. Milton. [Volume 7/51]
"What of the bow?" The Bowman's Song, fr. The White Company. S. Doyle. [Volume 8/12]
What of the Darkness? R. Le Gallienne. [Volume 3/360]
"What of the darkness? Is it very fair?" What of the Darkness? R. Le Gallienne. [Volume 3/360]
"What! out of senseless nothing to provoke." Rubaiyat: 078. O. Khayyam. [Volume 6/219]
"What profits it, O England, to prevail." The Turk in Armenia, fr. The Purple East. W. Watson. [Volume 8/22]
"What shall I do with all the days and hours." Absence. F. Kemble-Butler. [Volume 3/133]
"What, shall I tell you then, is a Muslim's life?" The Way of Islam. M. Iqbal. [Supp 7/60]

Arthur. Unknown. [Volume 1/184]
"**When** grandpa %goes out to the field." Grandpa. Chong Chi-Yong. [Supp 7/147]
"**When** hath wind or rain." The Life of Flowers. W. Landor. [Volume 5/244]
"**When** I am living in the midlands." The South Country. H. Belloc. [Supp 1/31]
"**When** I am standing on a mountain crest." Love In The Winds. R. Hovey. [Volume 2/252]
"**When** I consider how my light is spent." On His Blindness. J. Milton. [Volume 4/333]
"**When** I die %do not throw the meat and bones away." A Request. K. Das. [Supp 5/58]
"**When** I do count the clock that tells the time." Sonnet 12: The Approach of Age. W. Shakespeare. [Volume 6/194]
"**When** I Hear Your Name" G. Fuertes. [Supp 5/91]
"**When** I Nap" N. Giovanni. [Supp 4/219]
"**When** I saw the night in his blazing eyelids." The Martyr. Adonis. [Supp 7/285]
"**When** I see birches bend to left and right." Birches. R. Frost. [Supp 1/131]
"**When** I Set Out for Lyonnesse" T. Hardy. [Supp 1/160]
"**When** I think on the happy days." Absence. Unknown. [Volume 3/141]
"**When** I turned to look back." What is Moving. S. Takahashi. [Supp 7/128]
"**When** I was born on Amman hill." The Collier. V. Watkins. [Supp 2/189]
"**When** I was freed." Purgatory: Prayer, fr. The Diving Comedy. Dante Alighieri. [Volume 4/436]
"**When** i was sick and lay a-bed." The Land of Counterpane. R. Stevenson. [Volume 1/107]
"**When** I would think of you, my mind holds only." The Kestrels. K. Keyes. [Supp 2/414]
"**When** Icicles Hang by the Wall", fr. Love's Labor 's Lost. W. Shakespeare. [Volume 5/171]
**When** in Disgrace. W. Shakespeare. [Volume 1/358]
"**When** in disgrace with fortune and men's eyes." When in Disgrace. W. Shakespeare. [Volume 1/358]
"**When** in the chronicle of wasted time." W. Shakespeare. [Volume 2/3]
"**When** in the storm on Albion's coast." The Minute-Gun. R. Sharpe. [Volume 5/403]
"**When** is the time for prayer?" The Time for Prayer. G. Bennett. [Volume 4/112]
"**When** Israel, of the Lord beloved." Rebecca's Hymn, fr. Ivanhoe. S. Scott. [Volume 4/205]
"**When** John Henry was a little fellow." John Henry. Unknown (African American). [Supp 4/54]
"**When** late I heard the trembling cello play." The Cello. R. Gilder. [Volume 6/364]
"**When** learning's triumph o'er her barbarous." Shakespeare, fr. Prologue. S. Johnson. [Volume 7/51]
"**When** Letty had scarce passed her third year." Letty's Globe. C. Turner. [Volume 1/31]
"**When** Lilacs Last in the Dooryard Bloomed" W. Whitman. [Volume 3/362]
"**When** love with unconfined wings." To Althea from Prison. R. Lovelace. [Volume 8/133]
**When** Malindy Sings. P. Dunbar. [Supp 4/79]
"**When**, marshalled on the nightly plain." The Star of Bethlehem. H. White. [Volume 4/89]
"**When** mighty roast beef was the Englishman's." The Roast Beef of Old England. H. Fielding. [Volume 8/13]
"**When** music, heavenly maid, was young." The Passions. W. Collins. [Volume 6/367]
**When** My Ship Comes In. R. Burdette. [Volume 3/245]
"**When** my time comes." Me. C. Anwar. [Supp 7/77]
"**When** nature had made all her birds." The Bobolinks. C. Cranch. [Volume 5/316]
"**When** our brother fire was having his dog's day." Brother Fire. L. MacNeice. [Supp 2/172]

"**When** our tears are dry on the shore." Rediscovery. K. Awoonor. [Supp 6/20]
"**When** our wild day is wiped like a tear." Red Ridinghood. N. Alterman. [Supp 7/236]
"**When** Psyche's friend becomes her lover." Friend and Lover. M. De Vere. [Volume 1/374]
"**When** Raza? %When" Alurista. [Supp 4/275]
"**When** Roman fields are red with cyclamen." February in Rome. E. Gosse. [Volume 7/185]
"**When** Stars Are In The Quiet Skies" L. Lytton. [Volume 2/331]
"**When**, stricken by the freezing blast." Daniel Webster. O. Holmes. [Volume 7/20]
"**When** suddenly in the middle of life a word arrives that one." A Word. A. Mutis. [Supp 6/134]
"**When** that my mood is sad, and in the noise." The Shaded Water. W. Simms. [Volume 5/196]
"**When** the black-lettered list to the gods was presented." Wife, Children, and Friends. W. Spencer. [Volume 1/354]
**When** the Cows Come Home. A. Mitchell. [Volume 1/323]
"**When** the feud of hot and cold." December. J. Benton. [Volume 5/175]
"**When** the Frost is on the Punkin" J. Riley. [Volume 5/168]
"**When** the gray lake-water rushes." The Solitary Woodsman. C. Roberts. [Volume 5/145]
"**When** the heart is laden." Masks. J. Das. [Supp 7/47]
"**When** the hero's task was done." The Hero. R. Fuller. [Supp 2/263]
"**When** the hours of day are numbered." Footsteps of Angels. H. Longfellow. [Volume 3/438]
"**When** the humid shadows hover." Rain on the Roof. C. Kinney. [Volume 1/88]
**When** The Kye Comes Hame. J. Hogg. [Volume 2/283]
"**When** the lessons and tasks are all ended." The Children. C. Dickinson. [Volume 1/286]
"**When** the sea is saltiest." Beyond the Sea. Lo Fu. [Supp 7/27]
"**When** the sheep are in the fauld and the kye a'" Auld Robin Gray. L. Barnard. [Volume 3/32]
"**When** the veil from the eyes is lifted." Si Jeunesse Savait! E. Stedman. [Volume 2/242]
"**When** the ways are heavy with mire and rut." The Ballad of Prose and Rhyme. A. Dobson. [Volume 6/340]
"**When** the wayside tangles blaze." Goldenrod. E. Eastman. [Volume 5/285]
"**When** the whale's viscera go and the roll." The Quaker Graveyard in Nantucket: 005. R. Lowell. [Supp 2/397]
"**When** there are so many we shall have to mourn." In Memory of Sigmund Freud. W. Auden. [Supp 2/158]
"**When** they stop poems." Today Is a Day of Great Joy. V. Cruz. [Supp 4/276]
"**When** they woke me." Coming Back. J. Bruchac. [Supp 4/318]
**When** This Carnival Finally Closes. J. Mapanje. [Supp 6/35]
**When** This Cruel War is Over. Unknown. [Volume 8/382]
"**When** this frothful carnival finally closes, brother." When This Carnival Finally Closes. J. Mapanje. [Supp 6/35]
"**When** to the garden of untroubled thought." The Child in the Garden. H. Van Dyke. [Volume 1/55]
"**When** to the Sessions of Sweet Silent Thought" W. Shakespeare. [Volume 1/348]
"**When** Was the Last Time You Saw Miami Smile?" A. Casiano. [Supp 4/288]
**When** We Have to Fly. T. Ojaide. [Supp 6/52]
"**When** we lay where Budmouth Beach is." Hussar's Song, fr. The Dynasts. T. Hardy. [Supp 1/159]
"**When** we shut our eyes what will they give us?" Paradise. Nirala. [Supp 7/67]
**When** Will Love Come? P. Beatty. [Volume 2/74]

The Uninhabited City: 001. E. Cardenal. [Supp 6/153]
The Uninhabited City: 002. E. Cardenal. [Supp 6/154]
Written on a Roadside Stone During the First Eruption. P. Cuadra. [Supp 6/161]
"White with daisies and red with sorrel." Weeds. E. Millay. [Supp 1/223]
The White Women. M. Coleridge. [Supp 1/87]
"Whiter %than the crust." The Wind Sleepers. H. Doolittle. [Supp 5/67]
"Whiter, midst falling dew." To a Waterfowl. W. Bryant. [Volume 5/304]
Whitman, Sarah Helen
A Still Day in Autumn. [Volume 7/157]
Whitman, Walt
Mannahatta. [Volume 7/245]
Myself, fr. The Song of Myself. [Volume 7/102]
O Captain! My Captain! [Volume 7/28]
Out from Behind This Mask. [Volume 7/100]
What is the Grass?, fr. The Song of Myself. [Volume 6/198]
"When Lilacs Last in the Dooryard Bloomed" [Volume 3/362]
Whittier, John Greenleaf
The Angel of Patience. [Volume 3/402]
Barbara Frietchie. [Volume 8/362]
Barclay of Ury. [Volume 7/429]
The Barefoot Boy. [Volume 1/84]
Benedicite. [Volume 1/356]
Brown of Ossawatomie. [Volume 8/169]
Burns. [Volume 7/64]
Centennial Hymn. [Volume 8/457]
Disarmament. [Volume 8/425]
The Eternal Goodness. [Volume 4/42]
Fitz-Green Halleck. [Volume 7/92]
Hampton Beach. [Volume 5/427]
In School-Days. [Volume 1/163]
John Charles Fremont. [Volume 8/173]
Laus Deo! [Volume 8/176]
Maud Muller. [Volume 3/35]
The Meeting. [Volume 4/208]
A New England Home in Winter. [Volume 1/308]
Our State. [Volume 8/93]
The Palm-tree. [Volume 5/229]
The Prayer of Agassiz. [Volume 7/116]
The Pumpkin. [Volume 5/270]
The Reformer. [Volume 8/157]
To Her Absent Sailor, fr. The Tent on the Beach. [Volume 3/124]
The Two Angels. [Volume 4/157]
The Two Rabbis. [Volume 4/316]
Whittling. J. Pierpont. [Volume 1/89]
Who Am I? Tru Vu. [Supp 7/199]
"Who Cried Out?" Ode to a Lost Cargo in a Ship Called Save: 002. J. Craveirinha. [Supp 6/38]
"Who drives the horses of the sun." The Happiest Heart. J. Cheney. [Volume 1/268]
"Who has not dreamed a world of bliss." A Summer Noon. W. Howitt. [Volume 5/46]
"Who has not heard of the Vale of Cashmere." The Vale of Cashmere, fr. The Light of the Harem. T. Moore. [Volume 7/165]
"Who is masked?" New Year's Celebrations. T. Heraty. [Supp 7/94]
"Who is this whose feet." The Swan's Feet. E. Scovell. [Supp 2/188]
"Who knows if we can land on tomorrow." Broken Mirror. Yung Tzu. [Supp 7/35]
"Who rides so late through the midnight blast?" The Erl-King. J. Goethe. [Volume 6/58]
"Who says: %'picked flowers quickly fade'" Man. T. Heraty. [Supp 7/93]
"Who will give me permission right now." It Is Certain That We are Constructing a World. R.

Murillo. [Supp 6/176]
"Who would not go." The Answer. Unknown. [Volume 4/402]
"Whoe'er she be." Wishes For The Supposed Mistress. R. Crashaw. [Volume 2/83]
"Whoever lives true life, will love true love." That England, fr. Aurora Leigh. E. Browning. [Volume 7/200]
"Whose is this horrifying face." Ecce Homo. D. Gascoyne. [Supp 2/380]
"Whose secret presence, through creation's veins." Rubaiyat: 051. O. Khayyam. [Volume 6/214]
"Whre once we danced, where once we sang." An Ancient to Ancients. T. Hardy. [Supp 1/161]
Why? M. Ritter. [Volume 2/75]
"Why, all the saints and sages who discussed." Rubaiyat: 026. O. Khayyam. [Volume 6/209]
"Why, be this juice the growth of god, who dare." Rubaiyat: 061. O. Khayyam. [Volume 6/216]
"Why came the rose? Because the sun, is shining." Why? M. Ritter. [Volume 2/75]
"Why do poets %like to die." Notes Found Near a Suicide: To the Poets. F. Horne. [Supp 4/112]
"Why, if the soul can fling the dust aside." Rubaiyat: 044. O. Khayyam. [Volume 6/212]
"Why Is This Age Worse Than Earlier Ages?" A. Akhmatova. [Supp 5/7]
Why So Pale And Wan? S. Suckling. [Volume 2/247]
"Why so pale and wan, fond lover?" Why So Pale And Wan? S. Suckling. [Volume 2/247]
Why Thus Longing? H. Seawall. [Volume 4/127]
"Why thus longing, thus forever singing." Why Thus Longing? H. Seawall. [Volume 4/127]
"Why, when the world's great mind." The World and the Quietest. M. Arnold. [Volume 6/430]
"Why will they never sleep." Ode. J. Bishop. [Supp 2/25]
"'Why,' said another, 'some there are to tell'" Rubaiyat: 088. O. Khayyam. [Volume 6/221]
"Wichever way the wind doth blow." The Voyage. C. Mason. [Volume 4/38]
Wicklow Winds, fr. Wicklow. G. Savage-Armstrong. [Volume 5/127]
Widow Machree. S. Lover. [Volume 2/181]
"Widow Machree, it's no wonder you frown." Widow Machree. S. Lover. [Volume 2/181]
Widow Malone. C. Lever. [Volume 2/183]
The Widow's Mite. F. Locker-Lampson. [Volume 3/287]
Wife, Children, and Friends. W. Spencer. [Volume 1/354]
The Wife Of Loki. L. Elliot. [Volume 2/398]
The Wife to Her Husband. Unknown. [Volume 3/146]
Wiffen, Benjamin B. (tr.)
To Rome. F. Quevedo Y. Villegas. [Volume 7/177]
Wilbur, Richard
O. [Supp 2/409]
Still, Citizen Sparrow. [Supp 2/409]
Wilcox, Ella Wheeler
Life. [Volume 6/233]
Wild Ballad. G. Fuertes. [Supp 5/93]
"The wild boars are grubbing for acorns." Sic et Non: II. The Portrait of Abelard. H. Read. [Supp 2/35]
"The wild breakers of freedom." Waves. D. Diop. [Supp 6/70]
Wild Honey. M. Thompson. [Volume 5/344]
The Wild Ride. L. Guiney. [Volume 6/259]
"Wild strawberries, gooseberries, trampled." Ave Eva. J. Wheelwright. [Supp 2/52]
Wilde, Oscar
Ave Imperatrix. [Volume 8/22]
Wilde, Richard Henry
Life. [Volume 6/230]
The Wilderness. K. Das. [Supp 5/57]
The Wilderness. K. Raine. [Supp 5/227]

Mixer. L. MacNeice. [Supp 2/180]

"With a ripple of leaves and a tinkle of streams."
Ballade of Midsummer Days and Nights. W. Henley.
[Volume 5/112]

"With alien sweetmeats trucked to our homes." Africa
Now. T. Ojaide. [Supp 6/53]

"With all thy hart, with all thy soule and mind."
Love to Christ, fr. An Hymne of Heavenly Love.
E. Spenser. [Volume 4/90]

"With buds embalmed alive in ice." A Mile from Eden.
A. Ridler. [Supp 2/275]

"With deep affection." The Bells of Shandon. F.
Mahony. [Volume 7/145]

"With earth's first clay they did the last man
knead." Rubaiyat: 073. O. Khayyam. [Volume
6/218]

"With echoing steps the worshippers." Give Me Thy
Heart. A. Proctor. [Volume 4/238]

"With fingers weary and worn." The Song of the Shirt.
T. Hood. [Volume 3/199]

"With focus sharp as Flemish-painted face." The Dome
of Sunday. K. Shapiro. [Supp 2/312]

"With his last ten yen coin." Ten Yen Coin. S.
Tanikawa. [Supp 7/134]

"With how sad steps, o moon! thous climb'st the."
Sonnet, fr. Astrophel and Stella. S. Sidney.
[Volume 3/13]

"With klingle, klangle, klingle." When the Cows Come
Home. A. Mitchell. [Volume 1/323]

"With me along the strip of herbage strown."
Rubaiyat: 011. O. Khayyam. [Volume 6/206]

"With My Customary Restraint" D. Brutus. [Supp 6/101]

"With pensive eyes the little room I view." The
Garret. T. Moore. [Volume 1/369]

"With pipe and flute." What Value Has the People
Whose Tongue Is Tied?: 008. N. Qabbani. [Supp
7/287]

"With Rue My Heart is Laden" A. Housman. [Supp 1/169]

"With sacrifice, before the rising morn." Laodamia. W.
Wordsworth. [Volume 2/451]

"With silent awe I hail the sacred morn." The Sabbath
Morning. J. Leyden. [Volume 4/192]

"With sorrow and heart's distress." Eve to Adam, fr.
Paradise Lost. J. Milton. [Volume 4/273]

"With the gulls' hysteria above me." Galway Bay. G.
Barker. [Supp 2/283]

"With them the seed of wisdom did I sow." Rubaiyat:
028. O. Khayyam. [Volume 6/209]

Wither, George
The Author's Resolution, In A Sonnet, fr. Fair
Virtue. [Volume 2/238]
Christmas. [Volume 1/330]
"Lord! When Those Glorious Lights I See" [Volume
4/14]
Sonnet Upon A Stolen Kiss. [Volume 2/110]

"Within my head, aches the perpetual winter." Winter
and Summer. S. Spender. [Supp 2/237]

"Within the sober realm of leafless trees." The
Closing Scene. T. Read. [Volume 1/369]

"Within these woods of Arcadia." Sir Philip Sidney. M.
Royden. [Volume 7/45]

"Within this lowly grave a Conqueror lies." The
Conqueror's Grave. W. Bryant. [Volume 3/442]

Without and Within. Metastasio. [Volume 6/251]

"Without expectation %there is no end." Summer Oracle.
A. Lorde. [Supp 4/182]

"Without haste! without rest!" Haste Not! Rest Not! J.
Goethe. [Volume 6/414]

"Without you, who is going to walk me home."
Necessity. Nguyen Sa. [Supp 7/189]

The Wives of Weinsberg. G. Burger. [Volume 9/200]

Woe and Wellaway. N. Yushij. [Supp 7/205]

Wolcott, John ("Peter Pindar")
The Pilgrims and the Peas. [Volume 9/249]
The Razor-seller. [Volume 9/287]

Sleep. [Volume 6/433]
To Chloe. [Volume 2/220]

The Wolf and the Dog. J. Fontaine. [Volume 8/121]

Wolfe, Charles
Burial of Sir John Moore. [Volume 8/283]

Wolfe, Humbert
Iliad. [Supp 1/321]

woman. Unknown. [Volume 9/197]

"Woman dancing with hair." The Window of the Woman
Burning. M. Piercy. [Supp 5/197]

The Woman Thing. A. Lorde. [Supp 4/184]

Woman to Child. J. Wright. [Supp 5/328]

Woman to Man. J. Wright. [Supp 5/327]

The Woman Who Disapproved of Music at the Bar. H.
Gregory. [Supp 2/67]

A Woman's Answer. A. Procter. [Volume 2/221]

A Woman's Complaint. Unknown. [Volume 2/426]

Woman's Inconstancy. S. Ayton. [Volume 3/71]

A Woman's Love. J. Hay. [Volume 3/52]

A Woman's Question. A. Procter. [Volume 2/248]

Woman's Will. J. Saxe. [Volume 2/438]

A Woman's Wish. M. Townsend. [Volume 6/429]

Women
Anne Hathaway. Unknown. [Volume 7/110]
The Belle of the Ball. W. Praed. [Volume 9/207]
Echo. J. Saxe. [Volume 9/211]
Echo and the Lover. Unknown. [Volume 9/210]
Gone. C. Sandburg. [Supp 1/281]
The Heart of a Woman. G. Johnson. [Supp 4/83]
How Paddy god "Under Government." Unknown. [Volume
9/238]
"I'm Only a Woman, And That's Enough" G. Fuertes.
[Supp 5/94]
Jessie Mitchell's Mother. G. Brooks. [Supp 5/41]
"Nothing to Wear" W. Butler. [Volume 9/213]
Of a Certaine Man. S. Harrington. [Volume 9/199]
On an Old Muff. F. Locker-Lampson. [Volume 9/235]
The Peasant Women from Cua. E. Cardenal. [Supp
6/156]
The Proud Miss MacBride. J. Saxe. [Volume 9/228]
Remembering. Ping Hsin. [Supp 5/114]
The Sea. E. Ogden. [Volume 9/227]
Sorrows of Werther. W. Thackeray. [Volume 9/204]
Summer Wish. F. Lima. [Supp 4/244]
"There Lived a Lady in Milan" W. Benet. [Supp
1/47]
Time Caught in a Net. D. Ravikovitch. [Supp 5/232]
Well of St. Keyne. R. Southey. [Volume 9/204]
The Window of the Woman Burning. M. Piercy. [Supp
5/197]
The Wives of Weinsberg. G. Burger. [Volume 9/200]
woman. Unknown. [Volume 9/197]
The Women Fo'K. J. Hogg. [Volume 9/197]
"The Women Gather" N. Giovanni. [Supp 4/220]
Women Songs: 001. K. Molodowsky. [Supp 5/172]
Women Songs: 002. K. Molodowsky. [Supp 5/172]
Women's Chorus. Aristophanes. [Volume 9/200]

Women - Bourgeoisie
More of a Corpse Than a Woman. M. Rukeyser. [Supp
2/303]

The Women Fo'K. J. Hogg. [Volume 9/197]

"The Women Gather" N. Giovanni. [Supp 4/220]

Women Songs: 001. K. Molodowsky. [Supp 5/172]

Women Songs: 002. K. Molodowsky. [Supp 5/172]

"The Women Thought Christ Risen" E. Manner. [Supp
5/155]

Women's Chorus. Aristophanes. [Volume 9/200]

Wonders
Mystery. J. Drinkwater. [Supp 1/113]

Wong, Shawn
Kicking Lego Blocks: 001. [Supp 4/14]
Kicking Lego Blocks: 002. [Supp 4/15]
Kicking Lego Blocks: 008. [Supp 4/17]
Love among Friends. [Supp 4/13]

Wongthed, Suchit

*Yen (Money)*
Ten Yen Coin. S. Tanikawa. [Supp 7/134]
"Yes as alike as entirely." To My Father. W. Graham. [Supp 2/403]
"Yes, - I am poor, callistratus! I own." To One Who Had Scoffed at the Poet's Poverty. Martial. [Volume 6/327]
"Yes, stone thw woman, let the man go free." "Stone the Woman, Let the Man Go Free" Unknown. [Volume 4/322]
"Yes, they were king exceedingly; most mild." Bitterness. V. Sackville-West. [Supp 1/277]
"Yes, this is wicklow; round our feet." Wicklow Winds, fr. Wicklow. G. Savage-Armstrong. [Volume 5/127]
"Yesterday %a thousand cranes." August 6. J. Mirikitani. [Supp 4/39]
"Yesterday this day's madness did prepare." Rubaiyat: 074. O. Khayyam. [Volume 6/218]
Yet Do I Marvel. C. Cullen. [Supp 4/134]
"Yet now despair itself is mild." Stanza. P. Shelley. [Volume 3/165]
"Yet, O stricken heart, remember, O remember." In Memoriam F. A. S. R. Stevenson. [Volume 3/428]
"Yet once more, O ye laurels, and once more." Lycidas. J. Milton. [Volume 3/446]
"Yet resurrection is a sense of direction." The Flowering of the Rod: 007. H. Doolittle. [Supp 5/77]
"Yet we, the latter-day twice-born." The Walls Do Not Fall: 014. H. Doolittle. [Supp 5/74]
"Yon rising moon that looks for us again." Rubaiyat: 100. O. Khayyam. [Volume 6/223]
Yosano, Akiko
    "Early Evening Moon" S. Goldstein and Seishi Shinoda (tr.). [Supp 7/144]
    "Hair All Tangled This Morning" S. Goldstein and Seishi Shinoda (tr.). [Supp 7/145]
    "I See Drops of Rain" S. Goldstein and Seishi Shinoda (tr.). [Supp 7/143]
    Now. S. Goldstein and Seishi Shinoda (tr.). [Supp 7/143]
    Slipping. S. Goldstein and Seishi Shinoda (tr.). [Supp 7/144]
    "Through These Pines" S. Goldstein and Seishi Shinoda (tr.). [Supp 7/145]
    Whispering Goodnight. S. Goldstein and Seishi Shinoda (tr.). [Supp 7/144]
    Wind. S. Goldstein and Seishi Shinoda (tr.). [Supp 7/146]
You. N. Hikmet. [Supp 7/309]
You. N. Sachs. [Supp 5/254]
"You %in the night." You. N. Sachs. [Supp 5/254]
You, Andrew Marvell. A. MacLeish. [Supp 1/204]
"You are a field." You. N. Hikmet. [Supp 7/309]
"You are our darling and your foreign guest." For a Christening: 002. A. Ridler. [Supp 2/274]
"You are power %and send steel ships hurtling." Notes Found Near a Suicide: To the One Who Called Me Nigger F. Horne. [Supp 4/114]
"You ask a verse, to sing (ah, laughing face!)" To a Lady. J. Piatt. [Volume 2/47]
"You bells in the steeple, ring out your changes." Seven Times Two. J. Ingelow. [Volume 1/204]
"You block out everything, even the sun." Poems for Akhmatova: 004. M. Tsvetayeva. [Supp 5/301]
"You, bowing, youm crying." Defiance Against Force. D. Diop. [Supp 6/70]
"You Cannot Leave" A. Villanueva. [Supp 4/263]
"You charm when you talk, walk, or move." To Madame De Sevigne. M. Montreuil. [Volume 7/40]
"You come along ... tearing your shirt ... yelling about." To a Contemporary Bunkshooter. C. Sandburg. [Supp 1/279]
"You come forth." To Insure Survival. S. Ortiz. [Supp 4/317]

"You cry as the gull cries." The Contrary Experience: 001. H. Read. [Supp 2/32]
"You, Funaroff - where's the victory?" To My Contemporaries: 002. E. Rolfe. [Supp 2/223]
"You had two girls - baptiste." At the Cedars. D. Scott. [Volume 9/178]
"'You have a hundred months to live,' I was told in a dream." Told In a Dream. K. Raine. [Supp 5/230]
"'You have heard,' said a youth to his sweetheart." The Whistle. R. Story. [Volume 2/112]
"You have made my voice." Notes Found Near a Suicide: To Telic. F. Horne. [Supp 4/109]
"You know, my friends, with what a brave carouse." Rubaiyat: 055. O. Khayyam. [Volume 6/214]
"You know we French stormed Ratisbon." Incident of the French Camp. R. Browning. [Volume 8/230]
You Laughed and Laughed and Laughed. G. Okara. [Supp 6/59]
"You lay a wreath on murdered Lincoln's bier." Abraham Lincoln. T. Taylor. [Volume 7/25]
"You meaner beauties of the night." To His Mistress. S. Wotton. [Volume 2/8]
"You mother poses on black rocks." Black Rocks. L. Mar. [Supp 4/33]
"You must wake and call me early, call me early." The May Queen. A. Tennyson. [Volume 3/292]
"You, Nebuchadnessah, whoa, sah!" Nebuchadnezzar. I. Russell. [Volume 9/380]
"You needn't be trying to comfort me - i tell you." The Dead Doll. M. Vandergrift. [Volume 1/129]
You or I? I. Shabaka. [Supp 7/260]
"You sang round-dance songs." Farewell. L. Bahe. [Supp 4/322]
"You say, but with no touch of scorn." Doubt and Faith, fr. In Memoriam. A. Tennyson. [Volume 4/139]
"You see, the problem is." Blue Like Death. J. Welch. [Supp 4/312]
"You see this pebble-stone? It's a thing I." The Cock and the Bull. C. Calverley. [Volume 9/402]
"You stand near the window as lights wink." 23rd Street Runs into Heaven. K. Patchen. [Supp 2/255]
"You suit me well; for you can make me laugh." To a Prize Bird. M. Moore. [Supp 5/182]
"You take me into the garden of the world, my darling!" Garden of the World. A. Hamzah. [Supp 7/88]
"You That Love England" C. Day Lewis. [Supp 2/125]
"You were both quiet, looking out over the water." Swans. L. Gluck. [Supp 5/105]
"You were yourself." Beyond Ashes. Lo Fu. [Supp 7/28]
"You who were darkness warmed my flesh." Woman to Child. J. Wright. [Supp 5/328]
"You, with your head beard in your hand, meditating." Poem of Autumn. R. Dario. [Supp 6/165]
You'll Get Yours. G. Fuertes. [Supp 5/97]
Young, Andrew
    The Black Rock of Kiltearen. [Supp 2/2]
    The Dead Crab. [Supp 2/2]
    The Scarecrow. [Supp 2/3]
    Stay, Spring. [Supp 2/3]
"Young Ben he was a nice young man." Faithless Sally Brown. T. Hood. [Volume 9/271]
Young, Edward
    Matter and Man Immortal, fr. Night Thoughts. [Volume 4/406]
    Procrastination, fr. Night Thoughts. [Volume 6/190]
    Time of the Supreme, fr. Night Thoughts. [Volume 6/187]
Young Friends, fr. A Midsummer Night's Dream. W. Shakespeare. [Volume 1/344]
The Young Gray Head. C. Southey. [Volume 9/132]

# KEYWORD INDEX

**Abandoned.** The [N. Alterman. Supp 7/238]
**Abbey.** Inscription on Melrose [F. Beaumont. Volume 3/269]
___. On the Tombs in Westminster [F. Beaumont. Volume 3/269]
___. Tintern [W. Wordsworth. Volume 5/11]
**Abbot** of Canterbury, fr. Percy's Reliques. King John and the [Unknown. Volume 9/241]
**Abbotsford** ... On the Departure of Sir Walter Scott from [W. Wordsworth. Volume 7/61]
**Abelard.** Sic et Non: II. The Portrait of [H. Read. Supp 2/35]
**Abide** with Me. [H. Lyte. Volume 4/76]
**Abou Ben Adhem.** [L. Hunt. Volume 4/188]
**Abraham** in Fire. The Song of [A. Shamlu. Supp 7/211]
___ Lincoln. [J. Lowell. Volume 7/32]
___ Lincoln. [T. Taylor. Volume 7/25]
**Abroad.** Home Thoughts from [R. Browning. Volume 5/83]
**Absalom.** [M. Rukeyser. Supp 5/240]
**Absconditus.** Deus [A. Ridler. Supp 2/272]
**Absence.** [F. Kemble-Butler. Volume 3/133]
___ [Unknown. Volume 3/141]
**Absent** Sailor, fr. The Tent on the Beach. To Her [J. Whittier. Volume 3/124]
**Abydos.** The Orient, fr. The Bride of [G. Byron. Volume 7/164]
**Acrosticke** Verse. To the Spring, fr. Hymnes of Astraea, in [S. Davies. Volume 7/3]
**Adair.** Robin [L. Keppel. Volume 3/134]
**Adam** and Eve, fr, Paradise Lost. [J. Milton. Volume 7/124]
___ Describing Eve, fr. Paradise Lost [J. Milton. Volume 2/385]
___ To Eve, fr. Paradise Lost [J. Milton. Volume 2/368]
**Adam,** fr. Paradise Lost. Eve to [J. Milton. Volume 4/273]
**Address.** Warren's [J. Pierpont. Volume 8/326]
___ to the Mummy at Belzoni's Exhibition. [H. Smith. Volume 6/235]
___ to the Ocean. [B. Procter. Volume 5/381]
___ to the Toothache. [R. Burns. Volume 9/307]
**Adeb.** Prince [G. Boker. Volume 7/308]
**Adhem.** Abou Ben [L. Hunt. Volume 4/188]
**Adherence** to Apples. [S. Tanikawa. Supp 7/135]
**Adieu!** My Native Shore" " Adieu, [G. Byron. Volume 3/108]
**Adieu,** Adieu! My Native Shore" " [G. Byron. Volume 3/108]
**Admiring** Herself in a Looking-Glass. To a Lady [T. Randolph. Volume 2/21]
**Adolphus.** The Battle-Song of Gustavus [M. Altenburg. Volume 8/216]
**Advice.** [W. Dunbar. Volume 1/401]
___ To A Girl. [T. Campion. Volume 2/242]
**Aeneid.** Falling Asleep over the [R. Lowell. Supp 2/390]
___. The Fall of Troy, fr. [Virgil (Publius Vergilius Maro). Volume 7/261]
**Aerodome.** The Landscape near an [S. Spender. Supp 2/228]
**Aesop.** [A. Lang. Volume 6/330]
**Afar** in the Desert" " [T. Pringle. Volume 3/222]
**Affaire** D'amour. [M. Deland. Volume 2/245]
**Africa.** [D. Diop. Supp 6/71]
___ Now. [T. Ojaide. Supp 6/53]
___ to America. On Being Brought from [P. Wheatley. Supp 4/61]
**African** China: 001. [M. Tolson. Supp 4/101]
___ China: 002. [M. Tolson. Supp 4/101]
___ China: 003. [M. Tolson. Supp 4/102]
___ China: 004. [M. Tolson. Supp 4/103]
___ China: 005. [M. Tolson. Supp 4/104]

___ China: 006. [M. Tolson. Supp 4/104]
**Afterwards.** Now and [D. Craik. Volume 3/268]
**Afton** Water. [R. Burns. Volume 5/202]
**Agamemnon.** Iphigeneia and [W. Landor. Volume 9/3]
**Agassiz.** The Prayer of [J. Whittier. Volume 7/116]
**Agatha.** [A. Austin. Volume 3/13]
**Age.** [T. Tomioka. Supp 7/140]
___. Old [B. Al-Haydari. Supp 7/230]
___. Past the Ice [M. Waddington. Supp 5/314]
___. Sonnet 12: The Approach of [W. Shakespeare. Volume 6/194]
___. Youth, fr. Youth and [S. Coleridge. Volume 1/263]
___ and Death, fr. Verses Upon His Divine Poesy. Old [E. Waller. Volume 6/293]
___ Has Deflected Me" " This Cruel [A. Akhmatova. Supp 5/10]
___ Of Wisdom. The [W. Thackeray. Volume 2/236]
___ on Beaulieu River, Hants. Youth and [J. Betjeman. Supp 2/138]
___ Worse Than Earlier Ages?" " Why Is This [A. Akhmatova. Supp 5/7]
**Age,** fr. As You Like It. Healthful Old [W. Shakespeare. Volume 6/287]
___ fr. Tales of the Hall. The Approach of [G. Crabbe. Volume 3/163]
**Ages** of Man, fr. As You Like It. Seven [W. Shakespeare. Volume 7/126]
___ Past" " Our god, Our help in [I. Watts. Volume 4/32]
**Ages"** " Rock of [E. Rice. Volume 4/85]
**Ages?"** " Why Is This Age Worse Than Earlier [A. Akhmatova. Supp 5/7]
**Agincourt.** The Ballad of [M. Drayton. Volume 8/264]
**Aging** City. In the [F. Tuqan. Supp 7/269]
**Agnes.** Saint [A. Tennyson. Volume 4/416]
___. The Eve of Saint [J. Keats. Volume 2/312]
**Agonistes.** Samson On His Blindness, fr. Samson [J. Milton. Volume 3/158]
**Ails** This Heart O' Mine?" " What [S. Blamire. Volume 3/139]
**Aim.** The [C. Roberts. Volume 4/129]
**Air.** Lines To An Indian [P. Shelley. Volume 2/254]
___ Force. Second [R. Jarrell. Supp 2/332]
**Air"** " Sweetly Breathing, Vernal [T. Carew. Volume 5/82]
**Air,** fr. Alastor. Earth, Ocean, [P. Shelley. Volume 5/4]
**Airman's** Alphabet. The [W. Auden. Supp 2/148]
**airport.** 3 AM %in the albuquerque [J. Harjo. Supp 4/342]
**Aix.** How They Brought the Good News from Ghent to [R. Browning. Volume 7/349]
**Akhmatova:** 001. Poems for [M. Tsvetayeva. Supp 5/300]
___ 002. Poems for [M. Tsvetayeva. Supp 5/300]
___ 003. Poems for [M. Tsvetayeva. Supp 5/301]
___ 004. Poems for [M. Tsvetayeva. Supp 5/301]
**Alarm.** [T. Sayigh. Supp 7/293]
**Alastor.** Earth, Ocean, Air, fr. [P. Shelley. Volume 5/4]
**Albert,** Prince Consort of England, fr. Idyls of the King [A. Tennyson. Volume 7/34]
**Album.** D.S. :For Her [C. Anwar. Supp 7/82]
___. Lines Written in an [W. Gaylord. Volume 9/443]
___. Verses Written in an [T. Moore. Volume 2/34]
**albuquerque** airport. 3 AM %in the [J. Harjo. Supp 4/342]
**Ale.** Good [J. Still. Volume 9/248]

Ale: A Galloway Legend. Heather    [R. Stevenson.
    Volume 8/40]
Alexander and Campaspe. Cupid and Campaspe, fr.
    [J. Lyly. Volume 2/105]
Alexander's Feast; or, the Power of Music.    [J.
    Dryden. Volume 6/372]
Alexis, Here She Stayed.    [W. Drummond of
    Hawthornden. Volume 2/224]
Alfred. Notes Found Near a Suicide: To    [F. Horne.
    Supp 4/114]
___. Rule, Britannia, fr.    [J. Thomson. Volume
    8/11]
___ the harper.    [J. Sterling. Volume 8/238]
Allan-A-Dale. Robin Hood and    [Unknown. Volume
    7/375]
Allegro Moderato. Dark Symphony: 1.    [M. Tolson.
    Supp 4/96]
Allen. On Anne    [E. Fitzgerald. Volume 3/303]
Alley. Sally In Our    [H. Carey. Volume 2/290]
Alligator. The    [B. Ravenel. Supp 1/261]
Alma River. By the    [D. Craik. Volume 8/292]
Alnwick Castle.    [F. Halleck. Volume 9/312]
Alone %I See"  " I'm    [Nirala. Supp 7/68]
___. Not Men    [E. Rolfe. Supp 2/217]
Alone"  " When You Were    [R. Tagore. Supp 7/74]
Alonzo the Brave and the Fair Imogine.    [M. Lewis.
    Volume 7/321]
Aloy's. City Bells, fr. The Lay of St.    [R. Barham.
    Volume 7/147]
Alphabet. The Airman's    [W. Auden. Supp 2/148]
Alpine Descent. An    [S. Rogers. Volume 5/216]
Alps, fr. Childe Harold. Storm in the    [G. Byron.
    Volume 5/213]
Altarwise by Owl-light: 001.    [D. Thomas. Supp
    2/348]
___ by Owl-light: 002.    [D. Thomas. Supp 2/349]
___ by Owl-light: 003.    [D. Thomas. Supp 2/349]
___ by Owl-light: 004.    [D. Thomas. Supp 2/349]
___ by Owl-light: 005.    [D. Thomas. Supp 2/350]
___ by Owl-light: 006.    [D. Thomas. Supp 2/350]
___ by Owl-light: 007.    [D. Thomas. Supp 2/351]
___ by Owl-light: 008.    [D. Thomas. Supp 2/351]
___ by Owl-light: 009.    [D. Thomas. Supp 2/352]
___ by Owl-light: 010.    [D. Thomas. Supp 2/352]
Althea from Prison. To    [R. Lovelace. Volume
    8/133]
Always Fascinated"  " I Was    [A. Villanueva. Supp
    4/266]
Always"  " I Would Not Live    [W. Muhlenberg.
    Volume 3/392]
Amagoduka at Glencoe station.    [M. Mtshali. Supp
    6/84]
Amazing, Beauteous Change!"  "    [P. Doddridge.
    Volume 4/197]
Amazons. Proem, fr. The Isles of the    [J. Miller.
    Volume 6/278]
Amen.    [A. Mutis. Supp 6/133]
America.    [W. Bryant. Volume 8/88]
___    [C. McKay. Supp 1/203]
___    [S. Smith. Volume 8/95]
___. England to    [S. Dobell. Volume 8/92]
___. On Being Brought from Africa to    [P.
    Wheatley. Supp 4/61]
___. On the Prospect of Planting Arts and Learning
    in    [B. Berkeley. Volume 8/91]
___. Right On: Wite    [S. Sanchez. Supp 4/187]
___ to Great Britain.    [W. Allston. Volume
    8/27]
America"  " I, Too, Sing    [L. Hughes. Supp 4/131]
America, fr. A Fable for Critics    [J. Lowell.
    Volume 9/337]
America: 001. The Tears of a Muse in    [F. Prince.
    Supp 2/267]
___ 002. The Tears of a Muse in    [F. Prince.
    Supp 2/267]

___ 003. The Tears of a Muse in    [F. Prince.
    Supp 2/268]
___ 004. The Tears of a Muse in    [F. Prince.
    Supp 2/269]
American Flag. The    [J. Drake. Volume 8/152]
Amor. Canto    [J. Berryman. Supp 2/327]
Amoretti. " One Day I Wrote Her Name", fr.    [E.
    Spenser. Volume 6/353]
Anamorphosis.    [H. De Campos. Supp 6/112]
Ancestry. The Idea of    [E. Knight. Supp 4/169]
Anchor. The Forging of the    [S. Ferguson. Volume
    7/234]
Ancient and Modern Muses. The    [F. Palgrave.
    Volume 6/337]
___ Mariner. A More    [B. Carman. Volume 5/345]
___ Mariner. Rime of the    [S. Coleridge. Volume
    6/130]
___ Stone. Silence near an    [R. Castellanos.
    Supp 5/49]
___ to Ancients. An    [T. Hardy. Supp 1/161]
Ancients. An Ancient to    [T. Hardy. Supp 1/161]
Andersen. Hans Christian    [E. Gosse. Volume 7/43]
Anderson, My Jo. John    [R. Burns. Volume 2/460]
Andrew Marvell. You,    [A. MacLeish. Supp 1/204]
Andromache, fr. The Iliad. Parting of Hector and
    [Homer. Volume 3/118]
Anew. Betrothed    [E. Stedman. Volume 5/92]
Angantyr, fr. Frithiof Saga. Frithiof at the court of
    [E. Tegner. Volume 7/289]
Angel In The House. Sweet Meeting Of Desires, fr. The
    [C. Patmore. Volume 2/166]
___ of Patience. The    [J. Whittier. Volume
    3/402]
Angel, fr. Paradise Lost. The Faithful    [J. Milton.
    Volume 4/337]
Angels' Song. The    [E. Sears. Volume 4/48]
Angels. Footsteps of    [H. Longfellow. Volume
    3/438]
___. God's Command to His    [M. Iqbal. Supp 7/58]
___. Hierarch of    [T. Heywood. Volume 7/53]
___. Nimrod Wars with the    [A. Branch. Supp
    1/67]
___. The Two    [J. Whittier. Volume 4/157]
Angel's Whisper. The    [S. Lover. Volume 1/10]
Angels, fr. Paradise Lost. Battle of the    [J.
    Milton. Volume 8/179]
___ fr. The Faerie Queen. The Ministry of    [E.
    Spenser. Volume 4/415]
Angler. The    [J. Chalkhill. Volume 5/139]
Angler's Wish. The    [I. Walton. Volume 5/138]
Angling. In Praise of    [S. Wotton. Volume 5/136]
Anima Mundi. Hope of the Human Heart, fr.    [R.
    Milnes. Volume 4/110]
Annoyer. The    [N. Willis. Volume 2/75]
Answer. A Woman's    [A. Procter. Volume 2/221]
___. Prayer and    [O. Huckel. Volume 4/128]
___. The    [Unknown. Volume 4/402]
___. To Master Wither's Song, Shall I, Wasting In
    Despair.    [B. Jonson. Volume 2/239]
Ant from Sivas.    [F. Daglarca. Supp 7/299]
Anthem. National    [R. Newell. Volume 9/415]
___. National    [R. Newell. Volume 9/416]
___. National    [R. Newell. Volume 9/417]
___. National    [R. Newell. Volume 9/418]
___. National    [R. Newell. Volume 9/419]
Anthony's Sermon to the Fishes. Saint    [Unknown.
    Volume 9/239]
Antiquity of Freedom. The    [W. Bryant. Volume
    8/115]
Antony and Cleopatra.    [W. Lytle. Volume 3/380]
___ and Cleopatra. Cleopatra, fr.    [W.
    Shakespeare. Volume 7/127]
Antony, Over the Body of Caesar, fr. Julius Caesar.
    Mark    [W. Shakespeare. Volume 9/20]
Apology.    [R. Pitter. Supp 5/205]

4/67]
— and White. A Poem in    [M. Serote. Supp 6/91]
— Bird.    [W. Rendra. Supp 7/100]
— Hands: 001. I Have Seen    [R. Wright. Supp 2/214]
— Hands: 002. I Have Seen    [R. Wright. Supp 2/215]
— Hands: 003. I Have Seen    [R. Wright. Supp 2/216]
— Hands: 004. I Have Seen    [R. Wright. Supp 2/216]
— Man Talks of Reaping. A    [A. Bontemps. Supp 4/126]
— Messengers. The    [C. Vallejo. Supp 6/187]
— Regiment. The    [G. Boker. Volume 8/393]
— Rock. Colloquy in    [R. Lowell. Supp 2/388]
— Rock of Kiltearen. The    [A. Young. Supp 2/2]
— Rocks.    [L. Mar. Supp 4/33]
— Vulture. The    [G. Sterling. Supp 1/288]
— Woman.    [N. Madgett. Supp 4/166]
Black-eyed Susan.    [J. Gay. Volume 3/102]
Blackbird. The    [A. Tennyson. Volume 5/320]
Blackness. New-Born    [Lo Fu. Supp 7/26]
Blackout.    [F. Faiz. Supp 7/169]
Blacksmith. The Village    [H. Longfellow. Volume 1/328]
Blade O' Grass Keps Its Ain Drap O' Dew. Ilka    [J. Ballantine. Volume 3/241]
Blaize. elegy on Madam    [O. Goldsmith. Volume 9/266]
Blanc. From Mont    [P. Shelley. Volume 5/217]
Blanket Weaver.    [S. Esteves. Supp 4/292]
Blenheim. The Battle of    [R. Southey. Volume 8/437]
Bless the Dear Old Verdant Land"  "    [D. MacCarthy. Volume 8/60]
Blessed Are They.    [R. Raymond. Volume 3/425]
— Are They That Mourn.    [W. Bryant. Volume 3/421]
— Damozel. The    [D. Rossetti. Volume 6/97]
Blessings of To-day. If We Knew; or,    [M. Smith. Volume 1/278]
Blest as the Immortal Gods.    [Sappho. Volume 2/97]
— Memory, fr. The Pleasures of Memory    [S. Rogers. Volume 6/300]
Blew Like a Horn Among the Payira. My Name    [O. P'bitek. Supp 6/98]
Blight. We Wait, 1. White    [R. Conley. Supp 4/309]
Blighted Love.    [L. De Camoens. Volume 3/81]
Blind.    [I. Zangwill. Volume 3/460]
— Indians. The    [J. Pasos. Supp 6/181]
Blindness. Love's    [W. Shakespeare. Volume 2/223]
—. On His    [J. Milton. Volume 4/333]
Blindness, fr. Samson Agonistes. Samson On His    [J. Milton. Volume 3/158]
Bliss, fr. The Faerie Queene. The Bower of    [E. Spenser. Volume 6/112]
Blocks: 001. Kicking Lego    [S. Wong. Supp 4/14]
— 002. Kicking Lego    [S. Wong. Supp 4/15]
— 008. Kicking Lego    [S. Wong. Supp 4/17]
Blood. The Gushing    [Adonis. Supp 7/284]
— Horse. The    [B. Procter. Volume 5/369]
Bloomed"  " When Lilacs Last in the Dooryard    [W. Whitman. Volume 3/362]
Blossoms. To    [R. Herrick. Volume 5/279]
Blow, Blow, Thou Winter Wind", fr. As You Like It. "    [W. Shakespeare. Volume 3/155]
— Thou Winter Wind", fr. As You Like It. " Blow,    [W. Shakespeare. Volume 3/155]
Bludso of the Prairie Belle. Jim    [J. Hay. Volume 9/358]
Blue. A Knot of    [S. Peck. Volume 1/233]
— and the Gray. The    [F. Finch. Volume 8/455]

— Arab.    [J. Wright. Supp 5/327]
— Cat.    [H. Sakutaro. Supp 7/108]
— China. Of    [A. Lang. Volume 9/448]
— Distance"  " In the    [N. Sachs. Supp 5/248]
— Eyes.    [J. Keats. Volume 2/40]
— Eyes. Black and    [T. Moore. Volume 2/39]
— Like Death.    [J. Welch. Supp 4/312]
Blue-Bird. The First    [J. Riley. Volume 5/287]
Blue: Homage to Montreal. Lady in    [M. Waddington. Supp 5/315]
Blues. Homage to the Empress of the    [R. Hayden. Supp 4/136]
—. The Weary    [L. Hughes. Supp 1/171]
Boat. The Vanishing    [E. Gosse. Supp 1/146]
— to the Waves"  " Our    [W. Channing. Volume 5/409]
Boat, %A Golden Evening"  "A Little    [Nirala. Supp 7/70]
Boats in a Fog.    [R. Jeffers. Supp 1/173]
Bobolinks. The    [C. Cranch. Volume 5/316]
Body is Stars"  " Your    [S. Spender. Supp 2/238]
— of Caesar, fr. Julius Caesar. Mark Antony, Over the    [W. Shakespeare. Volume 9/20]
— of Lucretia, fr. Brutus. Lucius Junius Brutus Over the    [J. Payne. Volume 9/14]
Bolt. Ben    [T. English. Volume 1/222]
Bombing Casualties in Spain.    [H. Read. Supp 2/32]
Bonaparte. The Grave of    [L. Heath. Volume 8/435]
Bond. Dark    [J. Palaez. Supp 6/197]
Bondage. In    [C. McKay. Supp 4/87]
Bondange and My Freedom, 1853. My    [F. Douglass. Supp 4/52]
Bonnet O' Mine"  "The Dule's I' This    [E. Waugh. Volume 2/116]
Bonnets of Bonnie Dundee. The    [S. Scott. Volume 8/322]
Bonnie Dundee. The Bonnets of    [S. Scott. Volume 8/322]
— Leslie?"  " O, Say Ye    [R. Burns. Volume 3/130]
Bonny. Thy Braes Were    [J. Logan. Volume 3/314]
Book. The Poet and His    [E. Millay. Supp 1/219]
— I, fr. Paradise Lost. The Poet's Theme,    [J. Milton. Volume 4/262]
— IX, fr. Paradise Lost. The Temptation,    [J. Milton. Volume 4/263]
— of God. The    [H. Bonar. Volume 4/206]
— of Lives, fr. Ecclesiastical Sonnets. Walton's    [W. Wordsworth. Volume 7/55]
— XI, fr. Paradise Lost. Intercession and Redeoption,    [J. Milton. Volume 4/270]
— XII, fr. Paradise Lost. The Departure from Paradise,    [J. Milton. Volume 4/273]
Book-keeping. Art of    [T. Hood. Volume 9/305]
Book-stall. The    [C. Scollard. Volume 6/360]
Books.    [J. Higgins. Volume 6/361]
Books, fr. The Kaleder of Sheperdes    [Unknown. Volume 6/359]
Border Ballad.    [S. Scott. Volume 8/50]
Born"  " I Fire at the Face of the Country Where I Was    [S. Kazuko. Supp 5/130]
Borough. Quack Medicines, fr. The    [G. Crabbe. Volume 6/287]
Bosom Burns"  "The Day Returns, My    [R. Burns. Volume 2/422]
— of Castara. To Roses in the    [W. Habington. Volume 2/34]
Bosom, fr. Irish Melodies. Come, Rest In This    [T. Moore. Volume 2/332]
Bot!"  " Oh! Temple, Temple of    [S. Wongthed. Supp 7/186]
Bothwell's Lament. Lady Ann    [Unknown. Volume 3/47]
Bottom Drawer. The    [A. Barr. Volume 3/405]

of the Sea. Milk at the   [O. Williams. Supp 2/79]

**Bouillabaisse.** The Ballad of   [W. Thackeray. Volume 1/393]

**Bound.** Homeward   [Cattullus. Volume 1/313]

__. Outward   [T. Aldrich. Volume 6/123]

**Bound,** fr. Prometheus. The Wail of Prometheus [Aeschylus. Volume 3/156]

**Bourne:** 001. Salvos for Randolph   [H. Gregory. Supp 2/65]

— 002. Salvos for Randolph   [H. Gregory. Supp 2/65]

— 003. Salvos for Randolph   [H. Gregory. Supp 2/66]

**Bower** of Bliss, fr. The Faerie Queene. The   [E. Spenser. Volume 6/112]

**Bowl"** " Wreathe the   [T. Moore. Volume 1/387]

**Bowling.** Tom   [C. Dibdin. Volume 5/406]

**Bowman's** Song, fr. The White Company. The   [S. Doyle. Volume 8/12]

**Boxes.** The Man Who   [A. Istaru. Supp 6/136]

**Boy.** How's My   [S. Dobell. Volume 5/434]

__. The Barefoot   [J. Whittier. Volume 1/84]

— Lost. The Little   [S. Smith. Supp 2/103]

— on a Swing.   [M. Mtshali. Supp 6/83]

— Out of Church. The   [R. Graves. Supp 1/152]

— with His Hair Cut Short.   [M. Rukeyser. Supp 2/295]

**Boyhood.**   [W. Allston. Volume 1/76]

**Boys.** Men and   [K. Korner. Volume 8/78]

**Boys,** fr. Poems of the Class of 'Twenty-nine. The [O. Holmes. Volume 1/375]

**Bozzaris.** Marco   [F. Halleck. Volume 8/200]

**Braes** Were Bonny. Thy   [J. Logan. Volume 3/314]

**Brahma.**   [R. Emerson. Volume 4/6]

**Brave** and the Fair Imogine. Alonzo the   [M. Lewis. Volume 7/321]

— at Home. The   [T. Read. Volume 8/109]

— Old Oak. The   [H. Chorley. Volume 5/220]

**Brave"** " How Sleep the   [W. Collins. Volume 8/449]

**Bray.** The Vicar of   [Unknown. Volume 9/251]

**Breach** of the Plain of Muirhevney. Chariot of Cuchullin, fr.   [Unknown. Volume 5/371]

**Bread.** Our Daily   [C. Vallejo. Supp 6/188]

**Bread-Word** Giver.   [J. Wheelwright. Supp 2/53]

**Break** of Day" " As By the Shore at   [T. Moore. Volume 8/138]

**Break"** " Break, Break,   [A. Tennyson. Volume 3/358]

**Break,** Break" " Break,   [A. Tennyson. Volume 3/358]

— Break, Break" "   [A. Tennyson. Volume 3/358]

**Breaks.** Day   [C. Mackay. Volume 4/244]

**Breath.**   [B. Diop. Supp 6/67]

**Breath"** " Softly Woo Away Here   [B. Procter. Volume 3/318]

**Breathe** Not His Name!" " O,   [T. Moore. Volume 7/6]

**Breathes** There the Man?, fr. The Lay of the Last Minstrel   [S. Scott. Volume 5/157]

**Breathing,** Vernal Air" " Sweetly   [T. Carew. Volume 5/82]

**Bredon** hill.   [A. Housman. Supp 1/166]

**Breeches.** Little   [J. Hay. Volume 9/362]

**Breeze.** An Autumn   [W. Hayne. Volume 6/179]

**Breitmann's** Party. Hans   [C. Leland. Volume 9/325]

**Brethren** A' We Are   [R. Nicoll. Volume 1/353]

**Brickyard.** Nocturne in a Deserted   [C. Sandburg. Supp 1/278]

**Bridal-Day** Song. The Poet's   [A. Cunningham. Volume 2/414]

**Bride.** The Collegian to His   [Punch. Volume 9/434]

— in the '30's. A   [W. Auden. Supp 2/154]

— of Abydos. The Orient, fr. The   [G. Byron. Volume 7/164]

**Bride,** fr. A Ballad Upon A Wedding. The   [S. Suckling. Volume 2/410]

**Bridge.** Flower   [Liang Shang Ch'uan. Supp 7/22]

__. Horatius at the   [L. Macaulay; Thomas Babington. Volume 7/265]

__. London   [F. Weatherly. Volume 6/238]

__. The   [S. Murano. Supp 7/120]

__. The Brooklyn   [E. Proctor. Volume 7/247]

— at Florence. The Old   [H. Longfellow. Volume 7/174]

— of Sighs. The   [T. Hood. Volume 3/208]

**Brief:** "Two Went Up to the Temple to Pray".   [R. Crashaw. Volume 4/306]

— The Widow's Mites.   [R. Crashaw. Volume 4/306]

— Water Turned Into Wine.   [R. Crashaw. Volume 4/306]

**Brier-wood** Pipe. The   [C. Shanly. Volume 6/317]

**Brigade.** Charge of the Light   [A. Tennyson. Volume 8/294]

**Brigantine,** fr. The Water Witch. My   [J. Cooper. Volume 5/402]

**Bright.** Sparkling and   [C. Hoffman. Volume 1/386]

— Mushrooms Grow" " May   [I. Banda. Supp 6/29]

**Brink.** On the   [C. Calverley. Volume 9/443]

**Britain.** America to Great   [W. Allston. Volume 8/27]

**Britannia,** fr. Alfred. Rule,   [J. Thomson. Volume 8/11]

**Britannia's** Pastorals. The Hunted Squirrel, fr. [W. Browne. Volume 5/157]

**British** Fleet. All's Well, fr. The   [T. Dibdin. Volume 5/404]

— Museum. Homage to the   [W. Empson. Supp 2/141]

— Sailor. Napoleon and the   [T. Campbell. Volume 7/347]

— Soldier in China. The Private of the Buffsl or The   [S. Doyle. Volume 8/20]

**Broken** Mirror.   [Yung Tzu. Supp 7/35]

— Music.   [T. Aldrich. Volume 6/346]

— Pitcher. The   [W. Aytoun. Volume 7/325]

**Bronchitis:** The Rosario Beach House, 001.   [A. Rodriguez. Supp 4/279]

— The Rosario Beach House, 002.   [A. Rodriguez. Supp 4/280]

— The Rosario Beach House, 003.   [A. Rodriguez. Supp 4/280]

— The Rosario Beach House, 004.   [A. Rodriguez. Supp 4/281]

— The Rosario Beach House, 005.   [A. Rodriguez. Supp 4/282]

**Bronze** Statue of Napoleon. The   [A. Barbier. Volume 8/232]

**Brook,** fr. The Brook: An Idyl. Song of the   [A. Tennyson. Volume 5/194]

**Brook:** An Idyl. Song of the Brook, fr. The   [A. Tennyson. Volume 5/194]

**Brooklyn** Bridge. The   [E. Proctor. Volume 7/247]

**Brookside.** The   [R. Milnes. Volume 2/156]

**Brother** Fire.   [L. MacNeice. Supp 2/172]

— Jonathan's Lament for Sister Caroline.   [O. Holmes. Volume 8/344]

**Brother,** Francis I. On the Death of Her   [M. De Valois. Volume 3/338]

**Brothers.**   [D. Pagis. Supp 7/247]

**Brought** from Africa to America. On Being   [P. Wheatley. Supp 4/61]

— Her Warrior Dead, fr. The Princess. Home They [A. Tennyson. Volume 3/345]

— the Good News from Ghent to Aix. How They

[R. Browning. Volume 7/349]
**Brown.** Faithless Sally    [T. Hood. Volume 9/271]
— Baby. Little    [P. Dunbar. Supp 4/77]
— of Ossawatomie.    [J. Whittier. Volume 8/169]
— River, Smile.    [J. Toomer. Supp 4/91]
**Bruce.** The Heart of the    [W. Aytoun. Volume 7/420]
— and the Spider.    [B. Barton. Volume 8/302]
**Brutus.** Lucius Junius Brutus Over the Body of
    Lucretia, fr.    [J. Payne. Volume 9/14]
— and Cassius, fr. Julius Caesar. Quarrel of
    [W. Shakespeare. Volume 1/381]
— And Portia, fr. Julius Caesar    [W.
    Shakespeare. Volume 2/389]
— Over the Body of Lucretia, fr. Brutus. Lucius
    Junius    [J. Payne. Volume 9/14]
**Buccaneer.** The Tarry    [J. Masefield. Supp 1/207]
**Bucket.** The ' Old Oaken    [S. Woodworth. Volume 1/91]
**Buddha** Saw. The World of Fantasy the    [H. Sakutaro.
    Supp 7/108]
**Buddha,** Stars and i. Paris,    [F. Daglarca. Supp 7/301]
**Buddha's** Birthday. The Elephant & the Butterfly Meet
    on the    [D. Wakoski. Supp 5/320]
**Budget** of Paradoxes. A    [J. Martley. Volume 2/30]
**Buffsl** or The British Soldier in China. The Private
    of the    [S. Doyle. Volume 8/20]
**Bugel** Grieves. The Lonely    [G. Mellen. Volume 8/327]
**Bugle,** fr. The Princess. The    [A. Tennyson. Volume 5/210]
**Building** of the Ship. The Republic, fr. The    [H.
    Longfellow. Volume 8/94]
**Built.** The Modern House that Jack    [Unknown.
    Volume 9/396]
**Bull.** Death of the    [R. Campbell. Supp 2/91]
**Bullets.** The Song of    [J. Hagedorn. Supp 4/29]
**Bunkshooter.** To a Contemporary    [C. Sandburg. Supp 1/279]
**Burial.** The Drummer-boy's    [Unknown. Volume 9/172]
— of Moses.    [C. Alexander. Volume 4/365]
— of Robert Browning. The    [M. Field. Volume 7/89]
— of Sir John Moore.    [C. Wolfe. Volume 8/283]
**Burial:** 001.    [A. Walker. Supp 4/225]
— 002.    [A. Walker. Supp 4/225]
— 003.    [A. Walker. Supp 4/226]
— 004.    [A. Walker. Supp 4/226]
— 005.    [A. Walker. Supp 4/227]
— 006.    [A. Walker. Supp 4/227]
**Burn"** "The Midges Dance Aboon the    [R. Tannahill.
    Volume 5/47]
**Burning.** The Window of the Woman    [M. Piercy. Supp 5/197]
— Oneself to Death.    [S. Takahashi. Supp 7/126]
— Stars. At the Heart of Two    [P. Cuadra.
    Supp 6/162]
**Burns.**    [E. Elliott. Volume 7/63]
    [J. Whittier. Volume 7/64]
**Burns"** "The Day Returns, My Bosom    [R. Burns.
    Volume 2/422]
**Burnt.** Verses Why    [W. Landor. Volume 6/350]
**Bust** of Dante. On a    [T. Parsons. Volume 7/41]
**Busy** Bee" " How Doth the Little    [I. Watts.
    Volume 1/108]
**Butrago.** The Lord of    [Unknown. Volume 8/206]
**Buttercups.** On Some    [F. Sherman. Volume 2/46]
**Butterfly** Meet on the Buddha's Birthday. The Elephant
    & the    [D. Wakoski. Supp 5/320]
**Byron,** fr. The Course of Time    [R. Pollok. Volume 7/59]

**Cadiz.** The Girl of    [G. Byron. Volume 2/28]
**Caedmon.**    [L. Lee. Supp 2/338]
**Caesar.** Brutus And Portia, fr. Julius    [W.
    Shakespeare. Volume 2/389]
— . Mark Antony, Over the Body of Caesar, fr.
    Julius    [W. Shakespeare. Volume 9/20]
— . Quarrel of Brutus and Cassius, fr. Julius
    [W. Shakespeare. Volume 1/381]
**Caesar,** fr. Julius Caesar. Mark Antony, Over the Body
    of    [W. Shakespeare. Volume 9/20]
**Cain.** Tubal    [C. Mackay. Volume 8/426]
**Caine's.** For a Novel of Hall    [R. Bridges. Volume 9/460]
**calami.** Lapsus    [J. Stephen. Volume 9/422]
**Calcutta.** Summer in    [K. Das. Supp 5/56]
**Caldon** Low. The Fairies of the    [M. Howitt. Volume 1/148]
**Calendau.** The Ballad of Guibour, fr.    [F. Mistral.
    Volume 7/327]
**California.** Valentine for Ben Franklin Who Drives a
    Truck in    [D. Wakoski. Supp 5/322]
— Christmas. A    [J. Miller. Volume 6/279]
**Caliph** and Satan.    [J. Clarke. Volume 4/119]
**Called** Me Nigger. Notes Found Near a Suicide: To the
    One Who    [F. Horne. Supp 4/114]
— Save: 001. Ode to a Lost Cargo in a Ship
    [J. Craveirinha. Supp 6/37]
— Save: 002. Ode to a Lost Cargo in a Ship
    [J. Craveirinha. Supp 6/38]
— Save: 003. Ode to a Lost Cargo in a Ship
    [J. Craveirinha. Supp 6/39]
— Save: 004. Ode to a Lost Cargo in a Ship
    [J. Craveirinha. Supp 6/41]
**Calling** Was. Then I Saw What the    [M. Rukeyser.
    Supp 5/243]
**Calm** on Lake Leman, fr. Childe Harold    [G. Byron.
    Volume 5/211]
**Calvary** Song.    [R. Raymond. Volume 8/366]
— Song, fr. Alice of Monmouth    [E. Stedman.
    Volume 8/366]
**Cambridge.** Autumn Morning at    [F. Cornford. Supp 1/91]
**Camoes.** Louis De    [R. Campbell. Supp 2/94]
**Camp.** Dickens in    [B. Harte. Volume 7/77]
— . Incident of the French    [R. Browning.
    Volume 8/230]
— . Music in    [J. Thompson. Volume 8/389]
— . The Song Of The    [B. Taylor. Volume 2/362]
— at Night, fr. The Illiad. The    [Homer.
    Volume 5/62]
**Camp-bell.**    [W. Praed. Volume 7/56]
**Campagna.** A View Across the roman    [E. Browning.
    Volume 7/187]
**Campaspe.** Cupid and Campaspe, fr. Alexander and
    [J. Lyly. Volume 2/105]
**Campaspe,** fr. Alexander and Campaspe. Cupid and
    [J. Lyly. Volume 2/105]
**Camping** Out.    [W. Empson. Supp 2/140]
**Cana.**    [J. Clarke. Volume 4/65]
**Canada.**    [C. Roberts. Volume 8/71]
— Not Last.    [W. Schuyler-Lighthall. Volume 8/70]
**Candle** Than to Curse the Darkness. It's Better to
    Light a    [R. Retamar. Supp 6/143]
**Cane-bottomed** Chair. The    [W. Thackeray. Volume 1/377]
**Canterbury** Pilgrims. Morning in May, fr. The    [G.
    Chaucer. Volume 5/89]
— Pilgrims, fr. The Canterbury Tales. The    [G.
    Chaucer. Volume 7/363]
— Tales. The Canterbury Pilgrims, fr. The    [G.
    Chaucer. Volume 7/363]

Chevy-Chace.  [Unknown. Volume 8/244]
Chicago.  [C. Sandburg. Supp 1/283]
___  [Ya Hsuan. Supp 7/30]
Chicken. Ode to Mother Carey's  [T. Watts. Volume 5/333]
Chide" "The Forward Violet Thus Did I  [W. Shakespeare. Volume 2/9]
Chief Centurions. The  [J. Masefield. Supp 1/208]
___  Leschi of the Nisqually.  [D. Niatum. Supp 4/303]
Child. A  [S. Tanikawa. Supp 7/134]
___.  Descending Figure: 2. The Sick  [L. Gluck. Supp 5/103]
___.  Mexican  [G. Mistral. Supp 6/128]
___.  Mother and  [W. Simms. Volume 1/25]
___.  My  [J. Pierpont. Volume 3/417]
___.  My Wife and  [H. Jackson. Volume 3/228]
___.  The Fairy  [J. Anster. Volume 6/32]
___.  The Serious  [R. Pitter. Supp 5/207]
___.  Woman to  [J. Wright. Supp 5/328]
___  During Sickness. To a  [L. Hunt. Volume 1/59]
___  in London. A Refusal to Mourn the Death, by Fire of a  [D. Thomas. Supp 2/368]
___  in the Garden. The  [H. Van Dyke. Volume 1/55]
___  Is Simple and Is Good"  " Life for My  [G. Brooks. Supp 4/162]
___  Speaks. A Dead  [N. Sachs. Supp 5/247]
Childe Harold. Calm on Lake Leman, fr.  [G. Byron. Volume 5/211]
___  Harold. Greece Enslaved, fr.  [G. Byron. Volume 8/127]
___  Harold. Napoleon, fr.  [G. Byron. Volume 7/9]
___  Harold. Night, fr.  [G. Byron. Volume 5/65]
___  Harold. Saint Peter's at Rome, fr.  [G. Byron. Volume 7/186]
___  Harold. Storm in the Alps, fr.  [G. Byron. Volume 5/213]
___  Harold. The Coliseum, fr.  [G. Byron. Volume 7/178]
___  Harold. The Pantheon, fr.  [G. Byron. Volume 7/181]
___  Harold. The Sea, fr.  [G. Byron. Volume 5/375]
___  Harold. Waterloo, fr.  [G. Byron. Volume 8/287]
___  Harolde. The Rhine, fr.  [G. Byron. Volume 7/169]
___  Harold's Pilgrimage. The Poet's Impulse, fr.  [G. Byron. Volume 6/335]
Children.  [W. Landor. Volume 1/26]
___.  Foreign  [R. Stevenson. Volume 1/130]
___.  The  [C. Dickinson. Volume 1/286]
___.  The Gambols of  [G. Darley. Volume 1/55]
___.  The Three  [Unknown. Volume 1/174]
children at Home? Are the  [M. Sangster. Volume 3/288]
Children, and Friends. Wife,  [W. Spencer. Volume 1/354]
Children's Church. The  [K. Gerrock. Volume 1/115]
___  Hospital. Waiting in the  [C. Major. Supp 4/199]
Child's Hymn. A Little  [F. Palgrave. Volume 1/120]
Chillon. The Prisoner of  [G. Byron. Volume 9/88]
Chimes of England. The  [A. Coxe. Volume 4/200]
Chimneys"  " O the  [N. Sachs. Supp 5/246]
China. Of Blue  [A. Lang. Volume 9/448]
___.  The Private of the Buffsl or The British Soldier in  [S. Doyle. Volume 8/20]
China, Where She Never Saw Snow. My Mother, Who Came from  [L. Mar. Supp 4/34]
China: 001. African  [M. Tolson. Supp 4/101]

___  002. African  [M. Tolson. Supp 4/101]
___  003. African  [M. Tolson. Supp 4/102]
___  004. African  [M. Tolson. Supp 4/103]
___  005. African  [M. Tolson. Supp 4/104]
___  006. African  [M. Tolson. Supp 4/104]
Chinese Nightingale. The  [V. Lindsay. Supp 1/189]
___  Ulysses. A  [S. Kazuko. Supp 5/132]
Chiquita.  [B. Harte. Volume 5/371]
Chloe. To  [J. Wolcott. Volume 2/220]
___  is False.  [E. Gosse. Supp 1/145]
Choice. My  [W. Browne. Volume 2/87]
Choir. The Old Village  [B. Taylor. Volume 4/202]
___  Invisible!"  " O, May I Join The  [M. Cross. Volume 4/241]
Choosing a Mast.  [R. Campbell. Supp 2/92]
___  a Name.  [M. Lamb. Volume 1/97]
Chopin.  [E. Lazarus. Volume 7/114]
Choral Song, fr. The Bacchae  [Euripides. Volume 5/215]
Chord. A Lost  [A. Procter. Volume 6/306]
Chorrera. On the Road to  [A. Bates. Volume 2/47]
Chorus. Women's  [Aristophanes. Volume 9/200]
Chorus" Words for the "Hallelujah  [H. Brownell. Volume 8/171]
Chorus, fr. The Clouds. The Cloud  [Aristophanes. Volume 5/131]
Christ. The  [R. Trench. Volume 4/75]
___  Risen"  "The Women Thought  [E. Manner. Supp 5/155]
Christ, fr. An Hymne of Heavenly Love. Love to  [E. Spenser. Volume 4/90]
___  fr. The Diving Comedy. Paradise: The Triumph of  [Dante Alighieri. Volume 4/443]
Christening: 001. For a  [A. Ridler. Supp 2/273]
___  002. For a  [A. Ridler. Supp 2/274]
___  003. For a  [A. Ridler. Supp 2/274]
Christian Andersen. Hans  [E. Gosse. Volume 7/43]
___  Doctrine of Eternal Hell. Thoughts About the  [S. Smith. Supp 5/279]
___  to His Sould. The Dying  [A. Pope. Volume 4/376]
Christmas.  [G. Wither. Volume 1/330]
___.  A California  [J. Miller. Volume 6/279]
___.  An Eclogue for  [L. MacNeice. Supp 2/174]
___.  The Road from Election to  [O. Williams. Supp 2/80]
___  and Common Birth.  [A. Ridler. Supp 2/271]
___  Carol. Baby Zulma's  [A. Requier. Volume 1/67]
___  Hymn. A  [A. Domett. Volume 4/59]
___  in India.  [R. Kipling. Volume 7/161]
___  Scene. A  [T. Davis. Volume 2/262]
Christmas, fr. Marmion. An Old time  [S. Scott. Volume 7/210]
Christopher. For  [J. Jordan. Supp 4/195]
___  Saint  [D. Craik. Volume 4/296]
Christ's Nativity. On the Morning of  [J. Milton. Volume 4/51]
Christus Consolator.  [R. Raymond. Volume 3/432]
Chronicle. The  [A. Cowley. Volume 2/232]
chronicle of wasted time."  " When in the  [W. Shakespeare. Volume 2/3]
Church. The Boy Out of  [R. Graves. Supp 1/152]
___.  The Children's  [K. Gerrock. Volume 1/115]
___  Gate. At the  [W. Thackeray. Volume 2/60]
___  Organ. The New  [W. Carleton. Volume 9/316]
___  Porch, sel. The  [G. Herbert. Volume 4/304]
Churches. London  [R. Milnes. Volume 3/207]
Churchyard. Elegy Written in a Country  [T. Gray. Volume 3/270]
Cid. Battle Scene, fr. The  [Unknown. Volume 8/205]
Circumstances. On a Poem's  [L. Bell. Supp 6/109]
Cities.  [H. Doolittle. Supp 5/68]

Tennyson. Volume 1/361]
— Ladies. The Ballad of    [F. Villon. Volume 6/192]
— Lady. For a    [E. Robinson. Supp 1/271]
— Man Asks for a Song. The    [Unknown (African American). Supp 6/3]
— Poet-friend. The    [Callimachus. Volume 1/396]
— Ride Fast. The    [R. Blackmur. Supp 2/107]
— Soldier: 001. Elegy for a    [K. Shapiro. Supp 2/314]
— Soldier: 002. Elegy for a    [K. Shapiro. Supp 2/314]
— Soldier: 003. Elegy for a    [K. Shapiro. Supp 2/314]
— Soldier: 004. Elegy for a    [K. Shapiro. Supp 2/315]
— Soldier: 004. Elegy for a    [K. Shapiro. War]
— Soldier: 005. Elegy for a    [K. Shapiro. Supp 2/315]
— Soldier: 006. Elegy for a    [K. Shapiro. Supp 2/316]
— Soldier: 007. Elegy for a    [K. Shapiro. Supp 2/316]
— Soldier: 008. Elegy for a    [K. Shapiro. Supp 2/316]
— Soldier: 009. Elegy for a    [K. Shapiro. Supp 2/317]
— Soldier: 010. Elegy for a    [K. Shapiro. Supp 2/317]
— Soldier: 011. Elegy for a    [K. Shapiro. Supp 2/318]
**Dead!"** " New England    [I. McLellan. Volume 8/156]
**Dead"** " I Walked Out to the Graveyard to See the    [R. Eberhart. Supp 2/128]
— " My Days Among the    [R. Southey. Volume 4/396]
**Dead,** fr. The Princess. Home They Brought Her Warrior    [A. Tennyson. Volume 3/345]
— In a Foreign Land, fr. In Memoriam    [A. Tennyson. Volume 3/349]
**Deal"** " It Was a Funky    [E. Knight. Supp 4/173]
**Dear** And Only Love. My    [J. Graham. Volume 2/226]
— Fish to Me" " They Are    [Unknown. Volume 3/195]
— Old Verdant Land" " Bless the    [D. MacCarthy. Volume 8/60]
**Dear!"** " O Lay Thy Hand In Mine,    [G. Massey. Volume 2/445]
**Dear"** " Farewell! Thou Art Too    [W. Shakespeare. Volume 3/112]
**Dearest"** " Come To Me,    [J. Brenan. Volume 3/144]
**Death.**    [H. Riyong. Supp 6/47]
—. After    [F. Parnell. Volume 8/68]
—. Blue Like    [J. Welch. Supp 4/312]
—. Burning Oneself to    [S. Takahashi. Supp 7/126]
—. Frog's    [H. Sakutaro. Supp 7/104]
—. Go Down    [J. Johnson. Supp 1/176]
—. Love and    [M. Deland. Volume 3/394]
—. The Death of    [W. Shakespeare. Volume 3/461]
—. The General's    [J. O'Connor. Volume 8/369]
—. The Hour of    [F. Hemans. Volume 3/259]
—. The River an    [B. Al-Sayyab. Supp 7/233]
—. The Secret of    [S. Arnold. Volume 3/434]
—. The Term of    [S. Piatt. Volume 3/261]
—. The Trooper's    [G. Herwegh. Volume 8/220]
—. To    [Gluck. Volume 3/395]
—. Wounded to    [J. Watson. Volume 8/375]
— in Life's Prime, fr. In Memoriam    [A. Tennyson. Volume 3/354]
— in Youth, fr. Festus    [P. Bailey. Volume 3/428]

— of a Mad Dog. Elegy on the    [O. Goldsmith. Volume 9/263]
— of an Infant. On the    [J. Lowell. Volume 1/70]
— of Death. The    [W. Shakespeare. Volume 3/461]
— of Her Brother, Francis I. On the    [M. De Valois. Volume 3/338]
— of Leonidas. The    [G. Croly. Volume 8/194]
— of Minnehaha, fr. The Song of Hiawatha. The    [H. Longfellow. Volume 3/319]
— of My Grandfather. The    [H. Riyong. Supp 6/50]
— of Our Son, %Reuben Masai Harper. We Assume: On the    [M. Harper. Supp 4/205]
— of Sophocles. The    [A. Akhmatova. Supp 5/11]
— of the Ball Turret Gunner. The    [R. Jarrell. Supp 2/330]
— of the Bull.    [R. Campbell. Supp 2/91]
— of the Flowers. The    [W. Byrant. Volume 5/255]
— of the Hired Man. The    [R. Frost. Supp 1/135]
— of the Old Year. The    [A. Tennyson. Volume 6/196]
— of Thomas Carlyle and George Eliot. On the    [A. Swinburne. Volume 7/96]
— the Leveller.    [J. Shirley. Volume 3/254]
— To Die" " It Is Not    [G. Bethune. Volume 3/455]
— Us Part."    " Till    [A. Stanley. Volume 2/458]
**Death"** " There Is No    [J. M'Creery. Volume 3/456]
**Death,** by Fire of a Child in London. A Refusal to Mourn the    [D. Thomas. Supp 2/368]
— fr. Hamlet. Soliloquy on    [W. Shakespeare. Volume 3/252]
— fr. Pearls of the Faith. After    [S. Arnold. Volume 3/452]
— fr. The Giaour. A Picture of    [G. Byron. Volume 3/261]
— fr. The Lay of the Last Minstrel. The Poet's    [S. Scott. Volume 6/355]
— fr. Verses Upon His Divine Poesy. Old Age and    [E. Waller. Volume 6/293]
**Death-Bed. A**    [J. Aldrich. Volume 3/306]
— . The    [T. Hood. Volume 3/306]
**Deborah Lee.**    [W. Burleigh. Volume 9/400]
**Debt. The**    [P. Dunbar. Supp 4/76]
**Decalogue. The Latest**    [A. Clough. Volume 9/315]
**Deceased. The**    [K. Douglas. Supp 2/405]
**December.**    [J. Benton. Volume 5/175]
**Deck That Pouts. The**    [M. Piercy. Supp 5/198]
**Deed and a Word. A**    [C. Mackay. Volume 4/169]
**Deeds My Lady Please"** " If Doughty    [R. Graham. Volume 2/102]
**Deep. The Treasures of the**    [F. Hemans. Volume 5/385]
**Deep"** " Rocked in the Cradle of the    [E. Willard. Volume 4/30]
**Deer. A**    [S. Murano. Supp 7/120]
**Deer, February 1973. Where Mountain Lion Lay Down with**    [L. Silko. Supp 4/335]
**Deever. Danny**    [R. Kipling. Volume 8/299]
**Defence. In Poets'**    [J. Wheelwright. Supp 2/54]
**Defence, fr. Othello. Othello's**    [W. Shakespeare. Volume 2/207]
**Deferred. Dream**    [L. Hughes. Supp 4/132]
— . Hope    [Unknown. Volume 2/368]
**Defiance Against Force.**    [D. Diop. Supp 6/70]
**Defiance, fr. Hakon Jari. Hakon's**    [A. Oehlenschlager. Volume 8/208]
**Definition.**    [E. Rolfe. Supp 2/217]
**Deflected Me"** " This Cruel Age Has    [A. Akhmatova.

**Disdain"** " Give Me More Love or More   [T. Carew. Volume 2/245]

**Disgrace.** When in   [W. Shakespeare. Volume 1/358]

**Dismal** Day" " Die down, O   [D. Gray. Volume 5/88]
___ Moment, Passing.   [C. Major. Supp 4/203]

**Disorder.** Delight in   [R. Herrick. Volume 7/135]

**Dissembled,** fr. As You Like It. Love   [W. Shakespeare. Volume 2/31]

**Distance.** Storm in the   [P. Hayne. Volume 5/123]

**Distance"** " In the Blue   [N. Sachs. Supp 5/248]

**Distances.** Lessons of the War: Judging   [H. Reed. Supp 2/344]

**Distant** Prospect of Eton College. On a   [T. Gray. Volume 1/244]

**Ditty.** A Plantation   [F. Stanton. Volume 9/376]

**Diver.** The   [J. Schiller. Volume 9/44]

**Diverting** History of John Gilpin. The   [W. Cowper. Volume 9/276]

**Divided.**   [J. Ingelow. Volume 3/64]

**Dividends.**   [K. Fearing. Supp 2/100]

**Divina** Commedia: Inferno. Francesca Da Rimini, fr.   [Dante Alighieri. Volume 2/99]

**Divine** Poesy. Old Age and Death, fr. Verses Upon His   [E. Waller. Volume 6/293]

**Divine"** " I Would I Were An Excellent   [N. Breton. Volume 4/312]

**Diving.**   [S. Murano. Supp 7/115]
___ Comedy. Hell: Inscription Over the Gate, fr. The   [Dante Alighieri. Volume 4/436]
___ Comedy. Paradise: Sin and Redemption, fr. The   [Dante Alighieri. Volume 4/441]
___ Comedy. Paradise: The Saints in Glory, fr. The   [Dante Alighieri. Volume 4/445]
___ Comedy. Paradise: The Triumph of Christ, fr. The   [Dante Alighieri. Volume 4/443]
___ Comedy. Purgatory: Fire of Purification, fr. The   [Dante Alighieri. Volume 4/439]
___ Comedy. Purgatory: Man's Free-will, fr. The   [Dante Alighieri. Volume 4/438]
___ Comedy. Purgatory: Prayer of Penitents, fr. The   [Dante Alighieri. Volume 4/437]
___ Comedy. Purgatory: Prayer, fr. The   [Dante Alighieri. Volume 4/436]
___ Herdsman. Voice of the   [Unknown (African American). Supp 6/10]

**Dixie.**   [A. Pike. Volume 8/106]

**Djinns.** The   [V. Hugo. Volume 6/60]

**Dr.** Fu Manchu. The Insidious   [L. Jones. Supp 4/174]

**Doctrine.** Religion and   [J. Hay. Volume 4/219]
___ of Eternal Hell. Thoughts About the Christian   [S. Smith. Supp 5/279]

**Dog.** Elegy on the Death of a Mad   [O. Goldsmith. Volume 9/263]
___. The Wolf and the   [J. Fontaine. Volume 8/121]

**Dogs** Delight to Bark and Bite" " Let   [I. Watts. Volume 1/114]

**Dog's** Memory. To a   [L. Guiney. Volume 5/363]

**Dolcino** To Margaret.   [C. Kingsley. Volume 2/445]

**Doll.** The Dead   [M. Vandergrift. Volume 1/129]
___ The Wind-Up   [F. Farrozkhzad. Supp 7/219]

**Dollie.**   [S. Peck. Volume 1/234]

**Dolor.**   [T. Roethke. Supp 2/204]

**Dolorosa.** Stabat Mater   [F. Jacopone. Volume 4/70]

**Dome** of Sunday. The   [K. Shapiro. Supp 2/312]

**Don** Juan. Evening, fr.   [G. Byron. Volume 5/57]
___ Juan. Song of the Greek Poet, fr.   [G. Byron. Volume 8/130]
___ Juan. Wreck, fr.   [G. Byron. Volume 5/416]

**Done!** Father, Thy Will Be   [S. Adams. Volume 4/346]

**Done,** fr. Song of the Bell. Labor   [J. Schiller. Volume 6/412]

**Donkey.** The   [G. Chesterton. Supp 1/84]

**Donnelly.** Lovely Mary   [W. Allingham. Volume 2/50]

**Donuil** Dhu" " Pibroch of   [S. Scott. Volume 8/311]

**Doom.** The Common   [J. Shirley. Volume 2/237]

**Doon.** Cuddle   [A. Anderson. Volume 1/44]
___. The Banks O'   [R. Burns. Volume 3/12]

**Dooryard** Bloomed" " When Lilacs Last in the   [W. Whitman. Volume 3/362]

**Doria.** A Day in the Pamfili   [H. Stowe. Volume 7/182]

**Doris:** A Pastoral.   [A. Munby. Volume 2/169]

**Dormouse.** The Elf and the   [O. Herford. Volume 1/152]

**Dorothy** in the Garret.   [J. Throwbridge. Volume 3/89]

**Dot** Long-Handled Dipper.   [C. Adams. Volume 9/328]

**Doubt** and Faith, fr. In Memoriam   [A. Tennyson. Volume 4/139]

**Doubting** Heart. A   [A. Procter. Volume 3/171]

**Doughty** Deeds My Lady Please" " If   [R. Graham. Volume 2/102]

**Douglas** Tragedy. The   [Unknown. Volume 8/258]

**Douglas,** fr. Marmion. Marmion and   [S. Scott. Volume 7/401]

**Douglass.** Frederick   [R. Hayden. Supp 4/137]

**Dover** Beach.   [M. Arnold. Volume 5/423]
___ Cliff, fr. King Lear   [W. Shakespeare. Volume 5/214]

**Down,** Moses" " Go   [Unknown (African American). Supp 4/48]

**down,** O Dismal Day" " Die   [D. Gray. Volume 5/88]

**Down,** Sad Soul" " Sit   [B. Procter. Volume 4/372]

**Dow's** Flat.   [B. Harte. Volume 9/368]

**Doxology.** A Lancashire   [D. Craik. Volume 4/204]

**Drake.** Joseph Rodman   [F. Halleck. Volume 7/91]

**Dramatic** Poet, W. Shakespeare. An Epitaph on the Admirable   [J. Milton. Volume 7/51]

**Drap** O' Dew. Ilka Blade O' Grass Keps Its Ain   [J. Ballantine. Volume 3/241]

**Drawbridges:** 001. Against   [M. Benedetti. Supp 6/191]
___ 002. Against   [M. Benedetti. Supp 6/192]
___ 003. Against   [M. Benedetti. Supp 6/193]

**Drawer.** The Bottom   [A. Barr. Volume 3/405]

**Dreadful** Story About Harriet and the Matches. The   [H. Hoffmann. Volume 1/171]

**Dream.** A Bad   [K. Raine. Supp 5/227]
___. Compliment to Queen Elizabeth, fr. A Midsummer Night's   [W. Shakespeare. Volume 6/17]
___. Devil's   [K. Fearing. Supp 2/98]
___. Fairy's Song, fr. A Midsummer Night's   [W. Shakespeare. Volume 6/16]
___. Imagination, fr. A Midsummer Night's   [W. Shakespeare. Volume 6/12]
___. The   [G. Byron. Volume 3/73]
___. The Course of True Love, fr. Midsummer Night's   [W. Shakespeare. Volume 3/3]
___. The Fairies' Lullaby, fr. A Midsummer Night's   [W. Shakespeare. Volume 6/18]
___. The Mariner's   [W. Dimond. Volume 5/438]
___. The Sleeping Beauty, fr. The Day   [A. Tennyson. Volume 2/307]
___. The Soldier's   [T. Campbell. Volume 1/280]
___. Told In a   [K. Raine. Supp 5/230]
___. Young Friends, fr. A Midsummer Night's   [W. Shakespeare. Volume 1/344]
___ Deferred.   [L. Hughes. Supp 4/132]
___ of Eugene Aram. The   [T. Hood. Volume 9/157]
___ Wheel. Carriers of the   [N. Momaday. Supp 4/301]

**Dream,** fr. Irish Melodies. Love's Young   [T. Moore. Volume 2/327]

**Dream-life,** fr. Such Stuff as Dreams Are Made Of

— Near a Suicide: To Catalina. Notes  [F.
   Horne. Supp 4/108]
— Near a Suicide: To Henry. Notes  [F. Horne.
   Supp 4/113]
— Near a Suicide: To James. Notes  [F. Horne.
   Supp 4/111]
— Near a Suicide: To Mother. Notes  [F. Horne.
   Supp 4/108]
— Near a Suicide: To Telie. Notes  [F. Horne.
   Supp 4/109]
— Near a Suicide: To the One Who Called Me
   Nigger. Notes  [F. Horne. Supp 4/114]
— Near a Suicide: To the Poets. Notes  [F.
   Horne. Supp 4/112]
— Near a Suicide: To Wanda. Notes  [F. Horne.
   Supp 4/110]
— Near a Suicide: To You. Notes  [F. Horne.
   Supp 4/115]
— Wanting.  [E. Dickinson. Volume 4/326]
**Four; maternity.** Seven Times  [J. Ingelow. Volume
   1/36]
**Frae.** Ganging To And Ganging  [E. Cook. Volume
   2/293]
**Fragments** of the Night. The  [J. Lima. Supp 6/141]
**Fragrant Sare" " Flower** Garden %Like %a  [Nirala.
   Supp 7/70]
**Frames** the Moon. The Window  [L. Mar. Supp 4/32]
**Francesca.** Piero Della  [A. Ridler. Supp 2/276]
— Da Rimini, fr. Divina Commedia: Inferno
   [Dante Alighieri. Volume 2/99]
**Frankford's** Soliloquy, fr. A Woman Killed with
   Kindness  [O. Huckel. Volume 4/328]
**Franklin** Who Drives a Truck in California. Valentine
   for Ben  [D. Wakoski. Supp 5/322]
**Fredderick,** fr. The English Struwwelpeter. The Story
   of Cruel  [H. Hoffmann. Volume 1/170]
**Frederick** Douglass.  [R. Hayden. Supp 4/137]
**Free" "** In the Struggle to Be  [T. Ojaide. Supp
   6/56]
— " Stone the Woman, Let the Man Go
   [Unknown. Volume 4/322]
**Free-will,** fr. The Diving Comedy. Purgatory: Man's
   [Dante Alighieri. Volume 4/438]
**Freedom.**  [L. Hughes. Supp 4/133]
—. Patience, fr. Poems of  [W. Linton. Volume
   8/114]
—. The Antiquity of  [W. Bryant. Volume 8/115]
—. The Hills Were Made for  [W. Brown. Volume
   8/139]
— is Dress, fr. Epicoene; or, the Silent Woman
   [B. Jonson. Volume 7/131]
— of the Mind.  [W. Garrison. Volume 8/161]
**Freedom,** 1853. My Bondage and My  [F. Douglass.
   Supp 4/52]
**Fremont.** John Charles  [J. Whittier. Volume 8/173]
**French** Camp. Incident of the  [R. Browning. Volume
   8/230]
**Freud.** In Memory of Sigmund  [W. Auden. Supp
   2/158]
**Friar** Of Orders Gray. The  [T. Percy. Volume
   2/195]
— of Orders Gray", fr. Robin Hood. " I am a
   [J. O'Keeffe. Volume 9/247]
**Friday** Night Eleven O'Clock.  [L. Devkota. Supp
   7/160]
**Friend** and Lover.  [M. De Vere. Volume 1/374]
— of Humanity and the Knife-Grinder. The  [G.
   Canning. Volume 9/398]
— Whose Work Has Come to Nothing. To a  [W.
   Yeats. Supp 1/329]
**Friend,** fr. An Essay on Man. The Poet's  [A. Pope.
   Volume 7/112]
— fr. Friendship. To Seek a  [W. Cowper.
   Volume 1/397]
— fr. On Friendship. The  [N. Grimoald.

Volume 1/402]
**Friend:** 116, fr. In Memoriam. The Dead  [A.
   Tennyson. Volume 1/362]
— 22, fr. In Memoriam. The Dead  [A. Tennyson.
   Volume 1/360]
— 23, fr. In Memoriam. The Dead  [A. Tennyson.
   Volume 1/360]
— 25, fr. In Memoriam. The Dead  [A. Tennyson.
   Volume 1/361]
— 84, fr. In Memoriam. The Dead  [A. Tennyson.
   Volume 1/361]
**Friends.** Love among  [S. Wong. Supp 4/13]
—. Parted  [J. Montgomery. Volume 1/347]
—. The Prairie Fire, fr. The Song of Three  [J.
   Neihardt. Supp 1/240]
—. Wife, Children, and  [W. Spencer. Volume
   1/354]
— Beyond.  [T. Hardy. Supp 1/157]
— Together" " We Have Been  [C. Norton.
   Volume 1/351]
**Friend's** Song for Simoisius. A  [L. Guiney. Supp
   1/154]
**Friends,** fr. A Midsummer Night's Dream. Young  [W.
   Shakespeare. Volume 1/344]
**Friendship.**  [R. Emerson. Volume 1/339]
—. Early  [A. De Vere. Volume 1/344]
—. The Friend, fr. On  [N. Grimoald. Volume
   1/402]
—. To Seek a Friend, fr.  [W. Cowper. Volume
   1/397]
**Friendship,** fr. Hamlet  [W. Shakespeare. Volume
   1/345]
— fr. Night Thoughts  [R. Emerson. Volume
   1/340]
**Frietchie.** Barbara  [J. Whittier. Volume 8/362]
**Frieze.** A  [J. Bishop. Supp 2/24]
**Frightful** Release. A  [G. Stein. Supp 5/292]
**Fringed** Gentian. To the  [W. Bryant. Volume 5/284]
**Frithiof** at the court of Angantyr, fr. Frithiof Saga
   [E. Tegner. Volume 7/289]
— Saga. Frithiof at the court of Angantyr, fr.
   [E. Tegner. Volume 7/289]
**frm** Saitire XIII. Conscience,  [Juvenal. Volume
   4/329]
**Frog's** Death.  [H. Sakutaro. Supp 7/104]
**Frolic.** The Wind in a  [W. Howitt. Volume 1/143]
**From?" "** Where Does This Tenderness Come  [M.
   Tsvetayeva. Supp 5/299]
**Front** Yard. A Song in the  [G. Brooks. Supp 5/36]
**Frontenelle.** A Fancy from  [A. Dobson. Volume
   6/198]
**Frontporch.** Elegy Written on a  [K. Shapiro. Supp
   2/318]
**Frost.**  [E. Thomas. Volume 5/173]
—. The  [H. Gould. Volume 1/156]
— is on the Punkin" " When the  [J. Riley.
   Volume 5/168]
**Frugally" "** Expect Nothing. Live  [A. Walker.
   Supp 4/224]
**Fruit" "** Where Is the  [I. Banda. Supp 6/26]
**Fuji.** Mount  [M. Kaneko. Supp 7/113]
**Full** Many A Glorious Morning" "  [W. Shakespeare.
   Volume 2/224]
**Funeral" "** After the  [D. Thomas. Supp 2/347]
**Funky Deal" "** It Was a  [E. Knight. Supp 4/173]
**fust** Banjo. De  [I. Russell. Volume 9/377]
**Future** Life. The  [W. Bryant. Volume 4/397]

**Galahad.** Sir  [A. Tennyson. Volume 4/164]
**Gales" "** Moan, Moan, Ye Dying  [H. Neele. Volume
   3/152]
**Galloway** Legend. Heather Ale: A  [R. Stevenson.

Volume 8/40]
Galway Bay. [G. Barker. Supp 2/283]
Gambols of Children. The [G. Darley. Volume 1/55]
Game of Ball. A [M. Rukeyser. Supp 5/242]
Ganging Frae. Ganging To And [E. Cook. Volume 2/293]
__. To And Ganging Frae. [E. Cook. Volume 2/293]
Garden %Like %a Fragrant Sare" " Flower [Nirala. Supp 7/70]
__. A Forsaken [A. Swinburne. Volume 5/388]
__. A Little Dutch [H. Durbin. Volume 1/153]
__. I Pity the [F. Farrozkhzad. Supp 7/221]
__. Our [C. Anwar. Supp 7/78]
__. Our Hands in the [A. Hebert. Supp 5/110]
__. The Child in the [H. Van Dyke. Volume 1/55]
__ Fairies. [P. Marston. Volume 6/33]
__ In Her Face" " There Is A [Unknown. Volume 2/9]
__ of the World. [A. Hamzah. Supp 7/88]
Garden" "The Sunlight on the [L. MacNeice. Supp 2/185]
Garden, Maud" " Come Into The [A. Tennyson. Volume 2/273]
Gardens" " Down by the Salley [W. Yeats. Supp 1/328]
Garret. Dorothy in the [J. Throwbridge. Volume 3/89]
__. The [T. Moore. Volume 1/369]
Garrison. William Lloyd [J. Lowell. Volume 7/22]
Gate. At the Church [W. Thackeray. Volume 2/60]
__. Story Of The [T. Robertson. Volume 2/167]
__. The Worms at Heaven's [W. Stevens. Supp 1/291]
Gate, fr. The Diving Comedy. Hell: Inscription Over the [Dante Alighieri. Volume 4/436]
Gate-house at Westminster. Lines Found in His Bible in the [S. Raleigh. Volume 4/352]
Gates. The Locked [K. Raine. Supp 5/225]
Gather" "The Women [N. Giovanni. Supp 4/220]
Gathering Clouds Around I View" " When [S. Grant. Volume 4/88]
__ of Spirits). Kopis'taya (A [P. Allen. Supp 4/305]
Gaudeamus Igitur. [Unknown. Volume 1/231]
Gauntlet. The Rose and the [J. Sterling. Volume 9/131]
Gay" " Great Nature is an Army [R. Gilder. Volume 5/16]
Gebir. The Shell, fr. [W. Landor. Volume 5/427]
Geese. The Flight of the [C. Roberts. Volume 5/332]
Gelert. Beth [W. Spencer. Volume 5/360]
General's Death. The [J. O'Connor. Volume 8/369]
Generous Air. The [Palladas. Volume 6/229]
Genius. [R. Horne. Volume 6/352]
__. The Immortality of a [S. Propertius. Volume 6/357]
Genoa. On the Monument Erected to Mazzini at [A. Swinburne. Volume 7/13]
Gentian. To the Fringed [W. Bryant. Volume 5/284]
Gentle Maiden" " I Fear Thy Kisses, [P. Shelley. Volume 2/30]
Gentleman. The Fine Old English [Unknown. Volume 9/255]
George. On the Loss of the Royal [W. Cowper. Volume 9/182]
__ Eliot. On the Death of Thomas Carlyle and [A. Swinburne. Volume 7/96]
__ Sand. [E. Browning. Volume 7/40]
__ Washington. [Unknown. Volume 7/15]
__ Washington Sends a Pair of Shoebuckles ... [D. Wakoski. Supp 5/319]
Georgia Dusk. [J. Toomer. Supp 4/89]

German's Fatherland?" " What is the [E. Arndt. Volume 8/74]
Gettysburg. The High Tide at [W. Thompson. Volume 8/398]
Ghazal No. 9 [M. Iqbal. Supp 7/57]
Ghent to Aix. How They Brought the Good News from [R. Browning. Volume 7/349]
Giacomo. Fra [R. Buchanan. Volume 9/76]
Giant Puffball. The [E. Blunden. Supp 2/44]
Giaour. A Picture of Death, fr. The [G. Byron. Volume 3/261]
__. Fallen Greece, fr. The [G. Byron. Volume 8/125]
Gibber. The Lost Son: The [T. Roethke. Supp 2/207]
Gibraltar. At [G. Woodberry. Volume 8/439]
Gift. The [G. Russell. Supp 1/274]
__ You Gave" " It's True, %This Is the [Nirala. Supp 7/63]
Gifts. [E. Lazarus. Volume 8/8]
__ of God. The [G. Herbert. Volume 4/276]
Gigha. [W. Graham. Supp 2/401]
Gilded Monuments" " Not Marble, Not the [W. Shakespeare. Volume 1/359]
Gild's Evening Hymn. [S. Baring-Gould. Volume 1/117]
Gillyflower of Gold. The [W. Morris. Volume 2/333]
Gilpin. The Diverting History of John [W. Cowper. Volume 9/276]
Ginevra. [S. Rogers. Volume 9/81]
Girl. Advice To A [T. Campion. Volume 2/242]
__. The Enamel [G. Taggard. Supp 1/292]
__. The School [W. Venable. Volume 1/213]
__. To a Highland [W. Wordsworth. Volume 1/216]
__ is Nested." " My Little [S. Peck. Volume 1/41]
__ of All Periods. The [C. Patmore. Volume 1/242]
__ of Cadiz. The [G. Byron. Volume 2/28]
__ of Loch Dan. The Pretty [S. Ferguson. Volume 1/220]
__ of Pompeii. A [E. Martin. Volume 1/208]
Girl" " There was a Little [H. Longfellow. Volume 1/169]
Girls Who Have Considered Suicide ..., sel. For Colored [N. Shange. Supp 4/230]
__ Who Have Considered Suicide ..., sel. For Colored [N. Shange. Supp 4/231]
Girl's Song. [L. Bogan. Supp 5/32]
Gitanjali: 013. [R. Tagore. Supp 7/75]
__ 020. [R. Tagore. Supp 7/75]
__ 035. [R. Tagore. Supp 7/76]
__ 040. [R. Tagore. Supp 7/76]
Glass. The Witch in the [S. Piatt. Volume 1/46]
Glasses. Eye [G. Stein. Supp 5/293]
Glaucus. [S. Keyes. Supp 2/412]
Gleam in Time. [F. Daglarca. Supp 7/298]
Glencoe station. Amagoduka at [M. Mtshali. Supp 6/84]
Globe. Letty's [C. Turner. Volume 1/31]
__. To the Terrestrial [W. Gilbert. Volume 9/309]
Glorious Lights I See" " Lord! When Those [G. Wither. Volume 4/14]
__ Morning" " Full Many A [W. Shakespeare. Volume 2/224]
Glory, fr. The Diving Comedy. Paradise: The Saints in [Dante Alighieri. Volume 4/445]
Gloucester Moors. [W. Moody. Supp 1/225]
Glove. The [R. Browning. Volume 7/332]
__ and the Lions. The [L. Hunt. Volume 7/330]
Glug, fr. The Myrtle and the Vine. Gluggity [G. Colman. Volume 9/245]

195

199

**Heroes.** [E. Proctor. Volume 8/174]
___. March-Patrol of the Naked [H. Gorman. Supp 1/143]
___. Our Fallen [G. Griffith. Volume 8/449]
**Hero's Beauty,** fr. The First Sestiad of "Hero and Leander" [C. Marlowe. Volume 2/15]
**Herve Riel.** [R. Browning. Volume 7/341]
**Hesperia.** [A. Swinburne. Volume 2/267]
**Hesperus.** The Wreck of the [H. Longfellow. Volume 9/186]
**Hew.** Hack and [B. Carman. Volume 6/387]
**Hiawatha.** The Death of Minnehaha, fr. The Song of [H. Longfellow. Volume 3/319]
___. The Modern [Unknown. Volume 9/414]
**Hide** Their Heads?" " Oh! Where Do Fairies [T. Bayly. Volume 6/56]
**Hierarch** of Angels. [T. Heywood. Volume 7/53]
**High** Tide at Gettysburg. The [W. Thompson. Volume 8/398]
**High-tide** on the Coast of Lincolnshire. [J. Ingelow. Volume 9/145]
**Higher** Good. The [T. Parker. Volume 4/133]
**Highland** Girl. To a [W. Wordsworth. Volume 1/216]
___ Mary. [R. Burns. Volume 3/329]
**Highlands"** " My Heart's in the [R. Burns. Volume 8/39]
**Highway.** Tge King's [H. Preston. Volume 6/102]
**hill.** Bredon [A. Housman. Supp 1/166]
**Hill.** Fern [D. Thomas. Supp 2/363]
___. The Jacobite on Tower [G. Thornbury. Volume 8/17]
___. Up [C. Rossetti. Volume 4/332]
___ Above the Mine. The [M. Cowley. Supp 2/60]
___ Fields. Parliament [J. Betjeman. Supp 2/136]
___ Listens to the Praying. Joe [K. Patchen. Supp 2/248]
___ to the Poor-house" " Over the [W. Carleton. Volume 3/175]
**Hills.** The Silence of the [W. Foster. Volume 5/213]
___. Venice, fr. View from the Euganean [P. Shelley. Volume 7/192]
___ of the Lord. The [W. Gannett. Volume 4/19]
___ Picking Up the Moonlight" " [N. Cassian. Supp 5/45]
___ Were Made for Freedom. The [W. Brown. Volume 8/139]
**Hindu** Prince. Meditations of a [S. Lyall. Volume 4/3]
**Hired** Man. The Death of the [R. Frost. Supp 1/135]
**History** Lesson. The [Unknown. Volume 1/194]
___ of a Life. [B. Procter. Volume 6/234]
___ of John Gilpin. The Diverting [W. Cowper. Volume 9/276]
**Hobbling** Verse" Epigram: "Hoarse Maevius Reads His [S. Coleridge. Volume 9/287]
**Hoe.** The Man with the [J. Cheney. Volume 6/395]
___. The Man with the [E. Markham. Supp 1/205]
___. The Man with the [E. Markham. Volume 6/393]
**Hohenlinden.** [T. Campbell. Volume 8/225]
**Hold** Still. I [J. Sturm. Volume 3/243]
**Holiday.** A Berkshire [C. Bax. Supp 1/29]
___ for Me. A [K. Das. Supp 5/58]
**Hollow.** Sleepy [W. Channing. Volume 3/277]
___ Hospitality, fr. Satires [J. Hall. Volume 9/384]
**Holly-tree.** The [R. Southey. Volume 5/221]
**Holstenwall.** [S. Keyes. Supp 2/413]
**Holy** Nation. A [R. Realf. Volume 8/178]
___ Poems: 001. [G. Barker. Supp 2/284]
___ Poems: 002. [G. Barker. Supp 2/284]
___ Poems: 003. [G. Barker. Supp 2/285]

___ Spirit. The [R. Herrick. Volume 4/108]
___ War. The [R. Kipling. Supp 1/182]
**Homage** to Montreal. Lady in Blue: [M. Waddington. Supp 5/315]
___ to the British Museum. [W. Empson. Supp 2/141]
___ to the Empress of the Blues. [R. Hayden. Supp 4/136]
**Home.** [Leonidas of Alexandria. Volume 1/266]
___. My [R. Herrick. Volume 4/246]
___. My Old Kentucky [S. Foster. Volume 3/147]
___. Nearer [P. Cary. Volume 4/393]
___. O Daedalus, Fly Away [R. Hayden. Supp 4/135]
___. Old Folks at [W. Cowper. Volume 3/149]
___. The Brave at [T. Read. Volume 8/109]
___. The Wanderer's [O. Goldsmith. Volume 1/314]
___. When the Cows Come [A. Mitchell. Volume 1/323]
___ Economics. [R. Castellanos. Supp 5/53]
___ in Winter. A New England [J. Whittier. Volume 1/308]
___ Song. [D. Scott. Volume 1/325]
___ Sweet Home, fr. Clari, the Maid of Milan [J. Payne. Volume 1/335]
___ the Cows. Driving [K. Osgood. Volume 8/404]
___ They Brought Her Warrior Dead, fr. The Princess [A. Tennyson. Volume 3/345]
___ Thoughts from Abroad. [R. Browning. Volume 5/83]
**Home,** fr. Clari, the Maid of Milan. Home Sweet [J. Payne. Volume 1/335]
___ Wounded. [S. Dobell. Volume 3/58]
**Home?** Are the children at [M. Sangster. Volume 3/288]
**Homer.** On First Looking Into Chapman's [J. Keats. Volume 6/341]
**Homes** of England. The [F. Hemans. Volume 1/274]
**Home's** Best, fr. The Traveller. East, West, [O. Goldsmith. Volume 8/7]
**Homeward** Bound. [Cattullus. Volume 1/313]
**Homo.** Ecce [D. Gascoyne. Supp 2/380]
**Honey.** Go Sleep, Ma [E. Barker. Volume 1/100]
___. Not [H. Doolittle. Supp 2/5]
___. Wild [M. Thompson. Volume 5/344]
___ Dripping From the Comb. [J. Riley. Volume 1/224]
**Hong** Kong. [W. Rendra. Supp 7/103]
___ Kong Was Destroyed. How [D. Ravikovitch. Supp 5/235]
**Honor** of Beautie. Beauty, fr. An Hymne in [E. Spenser. Volume 6/282]
**Hood.** " I am a Friar of Orders Gray", fr. Robin [J. O'Keeffe. Volume 9/247]
___. To the Memory of Thomas [B. Simmons. Volume 7/62]
___ and Allan-A-Dale. Robin [Unknown. Volume 7/375]
**Hoodlum,** sel. Love sonnets of a [W. Irwin. Volume 9/394]
**Hope.** Evelyn [R. Browning. Volume 3/310]
___. Faith And [R. Peale. Volume 2/446]
___. Hope, fr. The Pleasures of [T. Campbell. Volume 4/145]
___. Poland, fr. The Pleasures of [T. Campbell. Volume 8/144]
___. The Mother's [L. Blanchard. Volume 1/37]
___ and Fear. [A. Swinburne. Volume 1/256]
___ Deferred. [Unknown. Volume 2/368]
___ of the Human Heart, fr. Anima Mundi [R. Milnes. Volume 4/110]
**Hope,** fr. The Pleasures of Hope [T. Campbell. Volume 4/145]

Hopefully Waiting.   [A. Randolph. Volume 4/371]
Hopeless.   [Nirala. Supp 7/63]
__   Grief.   [E. Browning. Volume 3/217]
Horatius. Lauriger   [Unknown. Volume 1/230]
__   at the Bridge.   [L. Macaulay; Thomas
     Babington. Volume 7/265]
Horn Among the Payira. My Name Blew Like a   [O.
     P'bitek. Supp 6/98]
Horns. Mountain Abbey, Surrounded by Elk   [C.
     Forche. Supp 5/83]
Horse. Loreine: A   [A. Ficke. Supp 1/121]
__.   The Blood   [B. Procter. Volume 5/369]
__.   The Drowned   [P. Cuadra. Supp 6/160]
__   on a City Street.   [S. Murano. Supp 7/116]
__   Then Said" "The Wooden   [J. Mastoraki.
     Supp 5/157]
Horses. The Eggs And The   [Unknown. Volume 2/432]
Horses" " Strong Men, Riding   [G. Brooks. Supp
     5/38]
Hospital. Waiting in the Children's   [C. Major.
     Supp 4/199]
Hospitality, fr. Satires. Hollow   [J. Hall. Volume
     9/384]
Hospitals Are to Die In.   [J. Mirikitani. Supp
     4/42]
Hound of Heaven. The   [F. Thompson. Supp 1/295]
Hour. The Happy   [M. Butts. Volume 1/12]
__   of Death. The   [F. Hemans. Volume 3/259]
__   of Parting. Farewell at the   [A. Neto. Supp
     6/13]
Hour" " Farewell! - But Whenever You Welcome the
     [T. Moore. Volume 3/116]
Hours" On His "Sonnets of the Wingless   [E. Lee-
     Hamilton. Volume 6/338]
House.   [R. Browning. Volume 7/108]
__.   Empty   [R. Castellanos. Supp 5/50]
__.   Open   [T. Roethke. Supp 2/211]
__.   Sweet Meeting Of Desires, fr. The Angel In The
     [C. Patmore. Volume 2/166]
__.   The Auld   [C. Nairne. Volume 1/275]
__.   There's Nae Luck About The   [J. Adam.
     Volume 2/442]
__   Beautiful. The   [R. Stevenson. Volume
     1/277]
__   is Cloudy" " My   [N. Yushij. Supp 7/204]
__   of Life. When Do I See Thee Most? fr. The
     [D. Rossetti. Volume 2/251]
__   that Jack Built. The Modern   [Unknown.
     Volume 9/396]
House" " Near the Wall of a   [Y. Amichai. Supp
     7/240]
__   " No Baby in the   [C. Dolliver. Volume
     1/101]
House, 001. Bronchitis: The Rosario Beach   [A.
     Rodriguez. Supp 4/279]
__   002. Bronchitis: The Rosario Beach   [A.
     Rodriguez. Supp 4/280]
__   003. Bronchitis: The Rosario Beach   [A.
     Rodriguez. Supp 4/280]
__   004. Bronchitis: The Rosario Beach   [A.
     Rodriguez. Supp 4/281]
__   005. Bronchitis: The Rosario Beach   [A.
     Rodriguez. Supp 4/282]
__   Nancy" " Out of the Old   [W. Carleton.
     Volume 1/268]
Household Sovereign, fr. The Hanging of the Crane.
     The   [H. Longfellow. Volume 1/23]
Housewife. To Another   [J. Wright. Supp 5/332]
How's My Boy.   [S. Dobell. Volume 5/434]
Hudibras. Hudibras; Sword and Dagger, fr.   [S.
     Butler. Volume 9/254]
__.   The Religion of Hudibras, fr.   [S. Butler.
     Volume 4/228]
Hudibras, fr. Hudibras. The Religion of   [S.
     Butler. Volume 4/228]

Hudibras; Sword and Dagger, fr. Hudibras   [S.
     Butler. Volume 9/254]
Hudson. The   [G. Hellman. Volume 1/314]
Hugged Me and Kissed Me. She   [Unknown (African
     American). Supp 4/59]
Human. The Cry of the   [E. Browning. Volume 4/286]
__   Heart. Ode to the   [L. Blanchard. Volume
     9/428]
__   Heart, fr. Anima Mundi. Hope of the   [R.
     Milnes. Volume 4/110]
__   Wishes. Charles XII, fr. The Vanity of   [S.
     Johnson. Volume 7/7]
Humanity and the Knife-Grinder. The Friend of   [G.
     Canning. Volume 9/398]
Humblebee. To the   [R. Emerson. Volume 5/342]
Humility.   [J. Montgomery. Volume 4/148]
Hunchback in the Park" "The   [D. Thomas. Supp
     2/364]
Hundred Thousand More. Three   [Unknown. Volume
     8/356]
Hunger. The Face of   [M. Mtshali. Supp 6/84]
Hungry. The Wheel of the   [C. Vallejo. Supp 6/189]
Hunt. The Last   [W. Thayer. Volume 8/262]
Hunt, fr. The Lady of the Lake. The Stag   [S.
     Scott. Volume 5/159]
__   fr. The Seasons: Autumn. The Stag   [J.
     Thomson. Volume 5/163]
Hunted Squirrel, fr. Britannia's Pastorals. The
     [W. Browne. Volume 5/157]
Hunter Mountain.   [F. Lima. Supp 4/245]
Hunter's Song. The   [B. Procter. Volume 5/156]
Hunting of the Snark. The Baker's Tale, fr. The
     [C. Dodgson. Volume 9/456]
__   Song.   [S. Scott. Volume 5/154]
__   We Will Go. A   [H. Fielding. Volume 5/158]
Huntington. Lines to Miss Florence   [Unknown.
     Volume 9/453]
Hurricane. The   [W. Bryant. Volume 7/151]
Hurricanes.   [J. Das. Supp 7/51]
Husband. The Wife to Her   [Unknown. Volume 3/146]
Husband, fr. The Contrivances. A Maiden's Ideal of a
     [H. Carey. Volume 2/89]
Hush!   [J. Dorr. Volume 3/400]
Hussar's Song, fr. The Dynasts   [T. Hardy. Supp
     1/159]
Hym That Togyder Wyll Serve Two Maysters. Of   [S.
     Brandt. Volume 4/217]
Hymne in Honor of Beautie. Beauty, fr. An   [E.
     Spenser. Volume 6/282]
__   of Heavenly Love. Love to Christ, fr. An
     [E. Spenser. Volume 4/90]
Hymnes of Astraea, in Acrosticke Verse. To the Spring,
     fr.   [S. Davies. Volume 7/3]

Ianthe, Sleeping. To   [P. Shelley. Volume 7/129]
Ice Age. Past the   [M. Waddington. Supp 5/314]
Icicles Hang by the Wall", fr. Love's Labor 's Lost.
     " When   [W. Shakespeare. Volume
     5/171]
Idea of Ancestry. The   [E. Knight. Supp 4/169]
Ideal of a Husband, fr. The Contrivances. A Maiden's
     [H. Carey. Volume 2/89]
Ideality.   [H. Coleridge. Volume 6/8]
Identity.   [J. Das. Supp 7/48]
Idle Tears", fr. The Princess. " Tears,   [A.
     Tennyson. Volume 3/142]
Idyl. Song of the Brook, fr. The Brook: An   [A.
     Tennyson. Volume 5/194]
Igitur. Gaudeamus   [Unknown. Volume 1/231]
Iliad.   [H. Wolfe. Supp 1/321]
__.   Hector to His Wife, fr. The   [Homer. Volume
     3/122]

Isles of the Amazons. Proem, fr. The   [J. Miller. Volume 6/278]

Islington. The Bailiff's Daughter of   [Unknown. Volume 2/153]

Italiens. Aux   [O. Meredith. Volume 2/214]

Italy. Naples, fr.   [S. Rogers. Volume 7/194]

__. Venice, fr.   [S. Rogers. Volume 7/189]

Ithaca Standing. On   [L. Durrell. Supp 2/260]

Ivan Ivanovitch.   [R. Browning. Volume 9/102]

Ivanhoe. Rebecca's Hymn, fr.   [S. Scott. Volume 4/205]

Ivanovitch. Ivan   [R. Browning. Volume 9/102]

Ivry.   [L. Macaulay; Thomas Babington. Volume 8/226]

Ivy Green. The   [C. Dickens. Volume 5/263]


Jack. Poor   [C. Dibdin. Volume 5/436]

__ Built. The Modern House that   [Unknown. Volume 9/396]

Jackdaw of Rheims. The   [R. Barham. Volume 9/331]

Jackson's Way. Stonewall   [J. Palmer. Volume 8/360]

Jacob. Wrestling   [C. Wesley. Volume 4/79]

Jacobite on Tower Hill. The   [G. Thornbury. Volume 8/17]

Jaffar.   [L. Hunt. Volume 1/350]

James. At the Grave of Henry   [W. Auden. Supp 2/150]

__. Notes Found Near a Suicide: To   [F. Horne. Supp 4/111]

__. Plain Language from Truthful   [B. Harte. Volume 9/374]

January. In   [G. Bottomley. Supp 1/62]

Japanese Lullaby.   [E. Field. Volume 1/15]

Jardin Du Palais Royal.   [D. Gascoyne. Supp 2/384]

Jari. Hakon's Defiance, fr. Hakon   [A. Oehlenschlager. Volume 8/208]

Jason's Grave in Jerusalem.   [D. Pagis. Supp 7/250]

Jazzonia.   [L. Hughes. Supp 4/129]

Jean. I Love My   [R. Burns. Volume 3/126]

Jeanie Morrison.   [W. Motherwell. Volume 3/127]

Jeanie"   " Thou Hast Sworn By Thy God, My   [A. Cunningham. Volume 2/416]

Jerusalem. Hebrew Wedding, fr. The Fall Of   [H. Milman. Volume 2/405]

__. Jason's Grave in   [D. Pagis. Supp 7/250]

__. The New   [Unknown. Volume 4/426]

Jessie Mitchell's Mother.   [G. Brooks. Supp 5/41]

Jester's Plea. The   [F. Locker-Lampson. Volume 6/350]

__ Sermon. The   [G. Thornbury. Volume 6/272]

Jesus Shall Reign.   [I. Watts. Volume 4/96]

__ Villanueva, with Love. To   [A. Villanueva. Supp 4/259]

Jet Flight.   [Agyeya. Supp 7/40]

Jetsam. Flotsam and   [Unknown. Volume 5/387]

Jewish Hymn in Babylon.   [H. Milman. Volume 4/307]

Jhelum"   "The Meandering Current of the   [R. Tagore. Supp 7/71]

Jim's Kids.   [E. Field. Volume 3/290]

Jitterbugs.   [L. Jones. Supp 4/177]

Jo. John Anderson, My   [R. Burns. Volume 2/460]

Joao. The Poem of   [N. Sousa. Supp 5/61]

Joaquin", sels.   " I Am   [R. Gonzales. Supp 4/234]

Jock Johnstone the Tinkler.   [J. Hogg. Volume 7/390]

Joe Hill Listens to the Praying.   [K. Patchen. Supp 2/248]

Joe, fr. Poems of the Class of 'Twenty-nine. Bill and   [O. Holmes. Volume 1/341]

Johannesburgh. City   [M. Serote. Supp 6/90]

John. England, fr. King   [W. Shakespeare. Volume 7/390]

__. Jonathan to   [J. Lowell. Volume 8/346]

__ and the Abbot of Canterbury, fr. Percy's Reliques. King   [Unknown. Volume 9/241]

__ Anderson, My Jo.   [R. Burns. Volume 2/460]

__ Charles Fremont.   [J. Whittier. Volume 8/173]

__ Gilpin. The Diverting History of   [W. Cowper. Volume 9/276]

__ Henry.   [Unknown (African American). Supp 4/54]

__ Milton. Under the Portrait of   [J. Dryden. Volume 7/54]

__ Moore. Burial of Sir   [C. Wolfe. Volume 8/283]

__ Street. 159   [F. Lima. Supp 4/242]

__ Winter.   [L. Binyon. Supp 1/50]

Johnny-Head-In-Air. The Story of   [H. Hoffmann. Volume 1/173]

Johnstone the Tinkler. Jock   [J. Hogg. Volume 7/390]

Join The Choir Invisible!"   " O, May I   [M. Cross. Volume 4/241]

Jonathan to John.   [J. Lowell. Volume 8/346]

Jonathan's Lament for Sister Caroline. Brother   [O. Holmes. Volume 8/344]

Jonson. Ode to Ben   [R. Herrick. Volume 7/47]

__. To the Memory of Ben   [J. Cleveland. Volume 7/46]

Joseph Rodman Drake.   [F. Halleck. Volume 7/91]

Journey. This   [N. Hikmet. Supp 7/312]

__ to Samarkand. The Golden   [J. Flecker. Supp 1/122]

Joy. Today Is a Day of Great   [V. Cruz. Supp 4/276]

__ Forever", fr. Endymion. "A Thing of Beauty is a   [J. Keats. Volume 6/329]

Joy"   " Phillis Is My Only   [S. Sedley. Volume 2/22]

Joys of the Road. The   [B. Carman. Volume 1/253]

Juan," Canto I. First Love, fr. "Don   [G. Byron. Volume 2/256]

Jubilee. The Year of   [Unknown. Volume 8/411]

Judas Iscariot. The Ballad of   [R. Buchanan. Volume 6/90]

Judge Not.   [A. Proctor. Volume 4/319]

Judging Distances. Lessons of the War:   [H. Reed. Supp 2/344]

Judgment.   [T. Carmi. Supp 7/245]

__ on a Wicked Bishop. God's   [R. Southey. Volume 9/52]

Julia Goes"   " Whenas in Silks my   [R. Herrick. Volume 2/38]

Juliet. Queen Mab, fr. Romeo and   [W. Shakespeare. Volume 6/13]

Julius Caesar. Brutus And Portia, fr.   [W. Shakespeare. Volume 2/389]

__ Caesar. Mark Antony, Over the Body of Caesar, fr.   [W. Shakespeare. Volume 9/20]

__ Caesar. Quarrel of Brutus and Cassius, fr.   [W. Shakespeare. Volume 1/381]

July 1936. Toledo,   [R. Campbell. Supp 2/95]

__. Poppies in   [S. Plath. Supp 5/218]

Jumblies. The   [E. Lear. Volume 1/192]

June.   [W. Bryant. Volume 5/102]

__. Knee-deep in   [J. Riley. Volume 5/108]

__ Thunder.   [L. MacNeice. Supp 2/179]

June, fr. Thyrsis. Early   [M. Arnold. Volume 5/252]

Jungle: 001. The   [A. Lewis. Supp 2/375]

__ 002. The   [A. Lewis. Supp 2/375]

__ 003. The   [A. Lewis. Supp 2/376]

__ 004. The   [A. Lewis. Supp 2/377]

**Lad.** Whistle, and I'll Come To You, My    [R. Burns. Volume 2/109]
**Ladder** of Saint Augustine. The    [H. Longfellow. Volume 4/294]
**Laden"** " With Rue My Heart is    [A. Housman. Supp 1/169]
**Ladies.** The Ballad of Dead    [F. Villon. Volume 6/192]
**Lad's** Lament in the Town. The Rustic    [D. Moir. Volume 3/131]
**Lady.** A Court    [E. Browning. Volume 8/146]
__.  For a Dead    [E. Robinson. Supp 1/271]
__.  My    [Dante Alighieri. Volume 2/24]
__.  My Beautiful    [T. Woolner. Volume 2/260]
__.  Portrait of a    [T. Eliot. Supp 1/116]
__.  The Irishman and the    [W. Maginn. Volume 9/320]
__.  To a    [J. Piatt. Volume 2/47]
___  Admiring Herself in a Looking-Glass. To a    [T. Randolph. Volume 2/21]
___  Ann Bothwell's Lament.    [Unknown. Volume 3/47]
___  Clara Vere De Vere" "    [A. Tennyson. Volume 3/4]
___  Clare.    [A. Tennyson. Volume 2/300]
___  in Blue: Homage to Montreal.    [M. Waddington. Supp 5/315]
___  in Milan" " There Lived a    [W. Benet. Supp 1/47]
___  Lazarus.    [S. Plath. Supp 5/213]
___  Lost in the Wood, fr. Comus. The    [J. Milton. Volume 6/64]
___  of Shalott. The    [A. Tennyson. Volume 6/124]
___  of the Lake. Beal' an Dhuine, fr. The    [S. Scott. Volume 8/307]
___  of the Lake. Coronach, fr. The    [S. Scott. Volume 3/309]
___  of the Lake. Fitz-James and Ellen, fr. The    [S. Scott. Volume 7/413]
___  of the Lake. Fitz-James and Roderick Dhu, fr. The    [S. Scott. Volume 7/404]
___  of the Lake. Song of Clan-Alpine, fr. The    [S. Scott. Volume 8/305]
___  of the Lake. Song, fr. The    [S. Scott. Volume 3/101]
___  of the Lake. The Stag Hunt, fr. The    [S. Scott. Volume 5/159]
___  Please" " If Doughty Deeds My    [R. Graham. Volume 2/102]
___  Poverty. The    [A. Meynell. Supp 1/212]
**Laird** O' Cockpen. The    [C. Nairne. Volume 2/205]
**Lake.** Beal' an Dhuine, fr. The Lady of the    [S. Scott. Volume 8/307]
__.  Coronach, fr. The Lady of the    [S. Scott. Volume 3/309]
__.  Fitz-James and Ellen, fr. The Lady of the    [S. Scott. Volume 7/413]
__.  Fitz-James and Roderick Dhu, fr. The Lady of the    [S. Scott. Volume 7/404]
__.  Heavenly    [Pak Tu-Jin. Supp 7/155]
__.  Song of Clan-Alpine, fr. The Lady of the    [S. Scott. Volume 8/305]
__.  Song, fr. The Lady of the    [S. Scott. Volume 3/101]
__.  Souls    [R. Fitzgerald. Supp 2/241]
__.  The Stag Hunt, fr. The Lady of the    [S. Scott. Volume 5/159]
__.  To Seneca    [J. Percival. Volume 5/209]
___  Isle of Innisfree. The    [W. Yeats. Volume 5/211]
___  Leman, fr. Childe Harold. Calm on    [G. Byron. Volume 5/211]
**Lambourne.** Upper    [J. Betjeman. Supp 2/138]
**Lambs.** Sheep and    [K. Hinkson. Volume 1/121]

**Lament.** A    [P. Shelley. Volume 3/172]
__.  Lady Ann Bothwell's    [Unknown. Volume 3/47]
___  for Heliodore.    [Meleager. Volume 3/337]
___  for Sister Caroline. Brother Jonathan's    [O. Holmes. Volume 8/344]
___  in the Town. The Rustic Lad's    [D. Moir. Volume 3/131]
___  of the Irish Emigrant.    [H. Sheridan. Volume 3/343]
**Lament,** fr. Paradise Lost. Eve's    [J. Milton. Volume 4/272]
**Lamentations:** 1. The Logos    [L. Gluck. Supp 5/106]
___  2. Nocturne    [L. Gluck. Supp 5/106]
___  3. The Covenant    [L. Gluck. Supp 5/106]
___  4. The Clearing    [L. Gluck. Supp 5/107]
**Lamp.** Soul    [Li Chi. Supp 7/12]
**Lancashire** Doxology. A    [D. Craik. Volume 4/204]
**Land.** Fog    [I. Bachmann. Supp 5/23]
__.  My Native    [J. O'Reilly. Volume 8/59]
__.  Song of the Silent    [J. Von Salis. Volume 4/388]
___  O' the Leal. The    [C. Nairne. Volume 3/380]
___  of Counterpane. The    [R. Stevenson. Volume 1/107]
___  of Story-Books. The    [R. Stevenson. Volume 1/140]
**Land"** " Bless the Dear Old Verdant    [D. MacCarthy. Volume 8/60]
___  " I Hear an Army Charging Upon the    [J. Joyce. Supp 2/1]
**Land,** fr. In Memoriam. Dead, In a Foreign    [A. Tennyson. Volume 3/349]
___  sel. The    [V. Sackville-West. Supp 1/276]
**Land?** Where Lies the    [A. Clough. Volume 6/231]
**Landing.**    [A. Pozzi. Supp 5/221]
___  of the Pilgrim Fathers in New England. The    [F. Hemans. Volume 8/150]
**Landlady's** Daughter. The    [L. Uhland. Volume 2/335]
**Landor.** In Memory of Walter Savage    [A. Swinburne. Volume 7/75]
**Lands.** Foreign    [R. Stevenson. Volume 1/138]
**Landscape.**    [A. Hebert. Supp 5/112]
__.  Innocent    [E. Wylie. Supp 5/340]
__.  near an Aerodome. The    [S. Spender. Supp 2/228]
**Language** from Truthful James. Plain    [B. Harte. Volume 9/374]
**Laodamia.**    [W. Wordsworth. Volume 2/451]
**Lapland** Longspur. To the    [J. Burroughs. Volume 5/314]
**Larghetto.** Dark Symphony: 5.    [M. Tolson. Supp 4/99]
**Lark** Ascending. The    [G. Meredith. Volume 5/292]
**Lark,** fr. Cymbeline. Hark, Hark! The    [W. Shakespeare. Volume 5/292]
**Larks** and Nightingales.    [N. Dole. Volume 9/447]
**Lass"** " O Wha's Been Here Afore Me,    [H. MacDiarmid. Supp 2/30]
**Lass?** O, Saw Ye The    [R. Ryan. Volume 2/41]
**Lassie.** The Emigrant    [J. Blackie. Volume 3/280]
**Last.** Canada Not    [W. Schuyler-Lighthall. Volume 8/70]
___  Banquet. The Baron's    [A. Greene. Volume 7/300]
___  Hunt. The    [W. Thayer. Volume 8/262]
___  in the Dooryard Bloomed" " When Lilacs    [W. Whitman. Volume 3/362]
___  Leaf. The    [O. Holmes. Volume 3/187]
___  Leaf. The    [A. Pushkin. Volume 3/187]
___  Look at La Plata, Missouri.    [J. Barnes. Supp 4/298]
___  Man. The    [T. Campbell. Volume 4/361]
___  Minstrel. Breathes There the Man?, fr. The Lay of the    [S. Scott. Volume 8/4]

205

Minstrel. Love, fr. Lay of the    [S. Scott.
    Volume 2/70]
Minstrel. Melrose Abbey, fr. The Lay of the
    [S. Scott. Volume 7/208]
Minstrel. Scotland, fr. The Lay of the    [S.
    Scott. Volume 8/33]
Minstrel. The Poet's Death, fr. The Lay of the
    [S. Scott. Volume 6/355]
Night.    [Unknown. Volume 2/339]
Pain. This    [W. Empson. Supp 2/145]
Poem i'm Gonna Write About Us.    [S. Sanchez.
    Supp 4/189]
Ride. Army Correspondents    [G. Townsend.
    Volume 8/408]
Rose of Summer", fr. Irish Melodies. "' Tis
    the    [T. Moore. Volume 5/283]
Sonnet. Keats's    [J. Keats. Volume 2/360]
Time You Saw Miami Smile?"  " When Was the
    [A. Casiano. Supp 4/288]
Toast. The    [A. Akhmatova. Supp 5/8]
Late.    [L. Bogan. Supp 5/32]
___. A Poem too    [N. Zach. Supp 7/256]
___. Too    [D. Craik. Volume 3/335]
I Stayed"  " Too    [W. Spencer. Volume
    1/352]
Latest Decalogue. The    [A. Clough. Volume 9/315]
Latter Rain. The    [J. Very. Volume 5/148]
Laudamus. Te Deum    [American Episcopal Church
    Prayer-Book. Volume 4/9]
Laughed. You Laughed and Laughed and    [G. Okara.
    Supp 6/59]
and Laughed. You Laughed and    [G. Okara.
    Supp 6/59]
and Laughed and Laughed. You    [G. Okara.
    Supp 6/59]
Launcelot And Queen Guinevere. Sir    [A. Tennyson.
    Volume 2/257]
Launfal. The Vision of Sir    [J. Lowell. Volume
    4/172]
Laura. Countess    [G. Boker. Volume 9/55]
Laurell. Mountain    [A. Noyes. Supp 1/243]
Lauriger Horatius.    [Unknown. Volume 1/230]
Lavender.    [Unknown. Volume 3/359]
Laverock In The Lift. Like A    [J. Ingelow. Volume
    2/399]
Lawyer's Invocation to Spring. The    [H. Brownell.
    Volume 9/435]
Lay Down with Deer, February 1973. Where Mountain
    Lion    [L. Silko. Supp 4/335]
of St. Aloy's. City Bells, fr. The    [R.
    Barham. Volume 7/147]
of the Last Minstrel. Breathes There the Man?,
    fr. The    [S. Scott. Volume 8/4]
of the Last Minstrel. Love, fr.    [S. Scott.
    Volume 2/70]
of the Last Minstrel. Melrose Abbey, fr. The
    [S. Scott. Volume 7/208]
of the Last Minstrel. Scotland, fr. The    [S.
    Scott. Volume 8/33]
of the Last Minstrel. The Poet's Death, fr.
    The    [S. Scott. Volume 6/355]
Thy Hand In Mine, Dear!"  " O    [G. Massey.
    Volume 2/445]
Lazarus. Lady    [S. Plath. Supp 5/213]
Lead. The Heaving of the    [C. Dibdin. Volume
    5/402]
Lead, Kindly Light.    [J. Newman. Volume 4/41]
Leader. The Lost    [R. Browning. Volume 7/70]
Leaders. Political    [M. Iqbal. Supp 7/61]
Leaf. The Last    [O. Holmes. Volume 3/187]
___. The Last    [A. Pushkin. Volume 3/187]
Leal. The Land O' the    [C. Nairne. Volume 3/380]
Leander. Love, fr. Hero and    [C. Marlowe. Volume
    2/64]
Leander"  Hero's Beauty, fr. The First Sestiad

of "Hero and    [C. Marlowe. Volume
    2/15]
Leap. Harold's    [S. Smith. Supp 5/284]
Leaps Up"  " My Heart    [W. Wordsworth. Volume 5/8]
Lear. Dover Cliff, fr. King    [W. Shakespeare.
    Volume 5/214]
Learning in America. On the Prospect of Planting Arts
    and    [B. Berkeley. Volume 8/91]
Least. At    [D. Mattera. Supp 6/82]
___. Scorn Not the    [R. Southwell. Volume 4/298]
Leave Here"  " Let's    [C. Anwar. Supp 7/86]
Leave"  " You Cannot    [A. Villanueva. Supp 4/263]
Leaves. Nothing But    [L. Akerman. Volume 4/283]
___. The Turning of the    [V. Watkins. Supp
    2/191]
___. Zacchaeus in the    [V. Watkins. Supp 2/192]
Leavetaking.    [W. Watson. Supp 1/313]
Lecture-room. In a    [A. Clough. Volume 4/132]
Leedle Yawcob Strauss.    [C. Adams. Volume 9/327]
Legacies. Strange    [S. Brown. Supp 4/117]
Legacy: My South.    [D. Randall. Supp 4/154]
Legal Fiction.    [W. Empson. Supp 2/144]
Legend.    [J. Weaver. Supp 1/314]
___. Heather Ale: A Galloway    [R. Stevenson.
    Volume 8/40]
of Good Women. The Daisy, fr.    [G. Chaucer.
    Volume 5/275]
Legendar Storm. The    [L. Inada. Supp 4/3]
Legendary Isle"  " Nearing Again the    [C. Day
    Lewis. Supp 2/117]
Lego Blocks: 001. Kicking    [S. Wong. Supp 4/14]
___. Blocks: 002. Kicking    [S. Wong. Supp 4/15]
___. Blocks: 008. Kicking    [S. Wong. Supp 4/17]
Legs. Four Legs, Three Legs, Two    [W. Empson. Supp
    2/143]
Legs, Three Legs, Two Legs. Four    [W. Empson. Supp
    2/143]
Two Legs. Four Legs, Three    [W. Empson.
    Supp 2/143]
Leigh. That England, fr. Aurora    [E. Browning.
    Volume 7/200]
Leisure.    [W. Davies. Supp 1/105]
Lem. Old    [S. Brown. Supp 2/85]
Leman, fr. Childe Harold. Calm on Lake    [G. Byron.
    Volume 5/211]
Lent. A True    [R. Herrick. Volume 4/303]
Lento Grave. Dark Symphony: 2.    [M. Tolson. Supp
    4/97]
Leonardo's "Mona Lisa".    [E. Dowden. Volume 7/150]
Leonidas. The Death of    [G. Croly. Volume 8/194]
Leper. The    [N. Willis. Volume 7/315]
Leschi of the Nisqually. Chief    [D. Niatum. Supp
    4/303]
Leslie?"  " O, Say Ye Bonnie    [R. Burns. Volume
    3/130]
Lesson. Model    [T. Carmi. Supp 7/242]
___. The    [W. Auden. Supp 2/162]
___. The History    [Unknown. Volume 1/194]
Lessons of the War: Judging Distances.    [H. Reed.
    Supp 2/344]
Letter. Her    [B. Harte. Volume 2/128]
on the Use of Machine Guns at Weddings. A
    [K. Patchen. Supp 2/252]
to a Policeman in Kansas City. A    [K.
    Patchen. Supp 2/253]
to Time.    [C. Alegria. Supp 5/14]
Letters. Tearing Up My Mother's    [D. Wakoski. Supp
    5/324]
Letty's Globe.    [C. Turner. Volume 1/31]
Leveller. Death the    [J. Shirley. Volume 3/254]
Leviathan.    [P. Quennell. Supp 1/254]
Liar. The    [L. Jones. Supp 4/175]
Liberty.    [J. Hay. Volume 8/112]
Tree.    [T. Paine. Volume 8/324]
Liberty!"  " Make Way for    [J. Montgomery. Volume

Living: 001. On   [N. Hikmet. Supp 7/306]
    —   002. On   [N. Hikmet. Supp 7/307]
    —   003. On   [N. Hikmet. Supp 7/308]
Lloyd Garrison. William   [J. Lowell. Volume 7/22]
Local Flora. Note on   [W. Empson. Supp 2/145]
Loch Dan. The Pretty Girl of   [S. Ferguson. Volume 1/220]
Lochaber No More.   [A. Ramsay. Volume 3/105]
Lochinvar, fr. Marmion   [S. Scott. Volume 2/276]
lock. Belinda, fr. rape of the   [A. Pope. Volume 2/14]
Lock. The Toilet, fr. The Rape of the   [A. Pope. Volume 7/135]
Locked Gates. The   [K. Raine. Supp 5/225]
Locksley Hall.   [A. Tennyson. Volume 3/17]
Lodore. The Cataract of   [R. Southey. Volume 7/170]
Logic. Love's   [Unknown. Volume 2/164]
Logos. Lamentations: 1. The   [L. Gluck. Supp 5/106]
Loki. The Wife Of   [L. Elliot. Volume 2/398]
London.   [J. Davidson. Volume 7/230]
    ___. A Refusal to Mourn the Death, by Fire of a Child in   [D. Thomas. Supp 2/368]
    — Bridge.   [F. Weatherly. Volume 6/238]
    — Churches.   [R. Milnes. Volume 3/207]
Lone Fisherman.   [T. Heraty. Supp 7/97]
Lonely Birds Sweep Past Us. Fish and Swimmer and   [M. Berssenbrugge. Supp 4/11]
    — Bugel Grieves. The   [G. Mellen. Volume 8/327]
Long" " Love Me Little, Love Me   [Unknown. Volume 2/188]
Long-Handled Dipper. Dot   [C. Adams. Volume 9/328]
Long-Legged Bait. Ballad of the   [D. Thomas. Supp 2/353]
Longfellow.   [A. Dobson. Volume 7/107]
    ___. To Henry Wadsworth   [J. Lowell. Volume 7/106]
Longing? Why Thus   [H. Seawall. Volume 4/127]
Longings. Summer   [D. MacCarthy. Volume 5/81]
Longspur. To the Lapland   [J. Burroughs. Volume 5/314]
Look %But Look" " But   [N. Sachs. Supp 5/251]
    ___. I Want to Find Desperately I   [B. Peralta. Supp 6/184]
    — at La Plata, Missouri. Last   [J. Barnes. Supp 4/298]
    — in the Past. A   [J. Angira. Supp 6/23]
Look" " But Look %But   [N. Sachs. Supp 5/251]
Looking Into Chapman's Homer. On First   [J. Keats. Volume 6/341]
    — Through the Ground" "A Flower is   [H. Monro. Supp 1/225]
Looking-Glass. To a Lady Admiring Herself in a   [T. Randolph. Volume 2/21]
Lord. The Hills of the   [W. Gannett. Volume 4/19]
    — Lovel.   [Unknown. Volume 7/373]
    — of Butrago. The   [Unknown. Volume 8/206]
    — Ullin's Daughter.   [T. Campbell. Volume 7/399]
    — Walter's Wife.   [E. Browning. Volume 2/392]
Lord! When Those Glorious Lights I See" "   [G. Wither. Volume 4/14]
Lord" " Forever with the   [J. Montgomery. Volume 4/403]
Lord-General Cromwell. To the   [J. Milton. Volume 7/5]
Lord?" " Were You There When They Crucified My   [Unknown (African American). Supp 4/60]
Lore-Lei. The   [H. Heine. Volume 6/77]
Loreine: A Horse.   [A. Ficke. Supp 1/121]
Loss of the Royal George. On the   [W. Cowper. Volume 9/182]
Losse in Delayes.   [R. Southwell. Volume 4/341]

Losses.   [R. Jarrell. Supp 2/331]
Lost. " When Icicles Hang by the Wall", fr. Love's Labor 's   [W. Shakespeare. Volume 5/171]
    ___. Adam and Eve, fr, Paradise   [J. Milton. Volume 7/124]
    ___. Adam Describing Eve, fr. Paradise   [J. Milton. Volume 2/385]
    ___. Adam To Eve, fr. Paradise   [J. Milton. Volume 2/368]
    ___. Battle of the Angels, fr. Paradise   [J. Milton. Volume 8/179]
    ___. Eve to Adam, fr. Paradise   [J. Milton. Volume 4/273]
    ___. Eve's Lament, fr. Paradise   [J. Milton. Volume 4/272]
    ___. Evening in Paradise, fr. Paradise   [J. Milton. Volume 5/56]
    ___. Intercession and Redeoption, Book XI, fr. Paradise   [J. Milton. Volume 4/270]
    ___. Invocation to Light, fr. Paradise   [J. Milton. Volume 5/30]
    ___. Light, fr. Paradise   [J. Milton. Volume 5/30]
    ___. Love and Woman, fr. Love's Labor's   [W. Shakespeare. Volume 2/65]
    ___. The Departure from Paradise, Book XII, fr. Paradise   [J. Milton. Volume 4/273]
    ___. The Faithful Angel, fr. Paradise   [J. Milton. Volume 4/337]
    ___. The Fall, fr. Paradise   [J. Milton. Volume 4/268]
    ___. The Little Boy   [S. Smith. Supp 2/103]
    ___. The Poet's Theme, Book I, fr. Paradise   [J. Milton. Volume 4/262]
    ___. The Temptation, Book IX, fr. Paradise   [J. Milton. Volume 4/263]
    — Cargo in a Ship Called Save: 001. Ode to a   [J. Craveirinha. Supp 6/37]
    — Cargo in a Ship Called Save: 002. Ode to a   [J. Craveirinha. Supp 6/38]
    — Cargo in a Ship Called Save: 003. Ode to a   [J. Craveirinha. Supp 6/39]
    — Cargo in a Ship Called Save: 004. Ode to a   [J. Craveirinha. Supp 6/41]
    — Chord. A   [A. Procter. Volume 6/306]
    — Heir. The   [T. Hood. Volume 1/49]
    — in Sulphur Canyons.   [J. Barnes. Supp 4/299]
    — in the Wilderness. Face   [F. Tuqan. Supp 7/273]
    — in the Wood, fr. Comus. The Lady   [J. Milton. Volume 6/64]
    — Leader. The   [R. Browning. Volume 7/70]
    — Pleiad. The   [W. Simms. Volume 4/347]
    — Sheep. The   [E. Clephane. Volume 4/66]
    — Son: 005. The   [T. Roethke. Supp 2/210]
    — Son: Moss-Gathering. The   [T. Roethke. Supp 2/210]
    — Son: The Flight. The   [T. Roethke. Supp 2/205]
    — Son: The Gibber. The   [T. Roethke. Supp 2/207]
    — Son: The Pit. The   [T. Roethke. Supp 2/207]
    — Son: The Return. The   [T. Roethke. Supp 2/209]
    — Youth. My   [H. Longfellow. Volume 1/260]
Lost, sels. Paradise   [J. Milton. Volume 4/262]
Lots. The Runner with the   [L. Adams. Supp 2/71]
Lot's Wife.   [A. Akhmatova. Supp 5/7]
Lotus-Eaters. The   [A. Tennyson. Volume 6/402]
Lou. Sister   [S. Brown. Supp 2/88]
Louise. Baby   [M. Eytinge. Volume 1/21]
Louse. To a   [R. Burns. Volume 5/348]
Love.   [R. Browning. Volume 2/339]

___ Labor's Lost. Love and Woman, fr.   [W. Shakespeare. Volume 2/65]
___ Logic.   [Unknown. Volume 2/164]
___ Memory, fr. All's Well That Ends Well   [W. Shakespeare. Volume 3/140]
___ Philosophy.   [P. Shelley. Volume 2/106]
___ Silence.   [S. Sidney. Volume 2/73]
___ Young Dream, fr. Irish Melodies   [T. Moore. Volume 2/327]
Loving and Be Living"  " Rest From   [C. Day Lewis. Supp 2/122]
Low. The Fairies of the Caldon   [M. Howitt. Volume 1/148]
___ and Very Bare"  " I Saw a Stable,   [M. Coleridge. Supp 1/87]
___ Spirits.   [F. Faber. Volume 4/338]
Low, Sweet Chariot"  " Swing   [Unknown (African American). Supp 4/50]
Low-Backed Car. The   [S. Lover. Volume 2/54]
Lowell on Himself, fr. A Fable for Critics   [J. Lowell. Volume 7/100]
Lower Classes. The Song of the   [E. Jones. Volume 6/391]
Lowly Plain"  " Were I As Base As Is The   [J. Sylvester. Volume 2/330]
___ Spirit"  " From the Recesses of a   [S. Bowring. Volume 4/132]
Lucem. Per Pacem Ad   [A. Procter. Volume 4/333]
Lucile. Dining, fr.   [O. Meredith. Volume 6/246]
Lucina Schynning in Silence of the Night"  "   [E. Chuilleanain. Supp 5/190]
Lucius Junius Brutus Over the Body of Lucretia, fr. Brutus   [J. Payne. Volume 9/14]
Luck About The House. There's Nae   [J. Adam. Volume 2/442]
Lucknow. The Relief of   [R. Lowell. Volume 8/296]
Lucrece. Cousin   [E. Stedman. Volume 7/131]
Lucretia. To The Princess   [T. Tasso. Volume 2/24]
Lucretia, fr. Brutus. Lucius Junius Brutus Over the Body of   [J. Payne. Volume 9/14]
Lullaby.   [T. Carmi. Supp 7/243]
___   [T. Carmi. Supp 7/244]
___. A Dutch   [E. Field. Volume 1/102]
___. Japanese   [E. Field. Volume 1/15]
Lullaby, fr. A Midsummer Night's Dream. The Fairies' [W. Shakespeare. Volume 6/18]
___ fr. The Princess   [A. Tennyson. Volume 1/11]
Luom. Little   [To Huu. Supp 7/196]
Lust. But for   [R. Pitter. Supp 2/48]
Lute. My Heart Is A   [L. Lindsay. Volume 2/424]
Luve's Like a Red, Red Rose"  " O, My   [R. Burns. Volume 3/99]
Lycidas.   [J. Milton. Volume 3/446]
Lye. The   [S. Raleigh. Volume 6/227]
Lying in the Grass.   [E. Gosse. Volume 1/225]
Lyonnesse"  " When I Set Out for   [T. Hardy. Supp 1/160]

Mab. Night, fr. Queen   [P. Shelley. Volume 5/66]
___. Sunset, fr. Queen   [P. Shelley. Volume 5/48]
Mab, fr. Romeo and Juliet. Queen   [W. Shakespeare. Volume 6/13]
Macaulay as Poet.   [W. Landor. Volume 7/61]
Macaw's Beak. Song of the Three Seeds in the   [E. Coatsworth. Supp 1/85]
Macbeth. A Dagger of the Mind, fr.   [W. Shakespeare. Volume 9/120]
___. The Murder, fr.   [W. Shakespeare. Volume 9/122]
MacBride. The Proud Miss   [J. Saxe. Volume 9/228]

Machine Guns at Weddings. A Letter on the Use of   [K. Patchen. Supp 2/252]
Machree. Charlie   [W. Hoppin. Volume 2/365]
___. Widow   [S. Lover. Volume 2/181]
MacSweeney. Turlough   [A. MacManus. Volume 8/54]
Mad Dog. Elegy on the Death of a   [O. Goldsmith. Volume 9/263]
Made for Freedom. The Hills Were   [W. Brown. Volume 8/139]
___ Of. Dream-life, fr. Such Stuff as Dreams Are   [P. Calderon. Volume 6/324]
___ This Screen"  " He   [M. Moore. Supp 1/233]
Madman's Song.   [E. Wylie. Supp 5/336]
Madness Openly"  " Let Us Have   [K. Patchen. Supp 2/254]
Maevius Reads His Hobbling Verse" Epigram: "Hoarse   [S. Coleridge. Volume 9/287]
Mahmoud.   [L. Hunt. Volume 7/305]
Mahogany-tree. The   [W. Thackeray. Volume 1/391]
Maid. The Old   [G. Barlow. Volume 2/369]
___ of Athens, Ere We Part"  "   [G. Byron. Volume 3/100]
___ of Milan. Home Sweet Home, fr. Clari, the   [J. Payne. Volume 1/335]
Maid?"  " Where Are You Going, My Pretty   [Unknown. Volume 2/155]
Maiden"  " I Fear Thy Kisses, Gentle   [P. Shelley. Volume 2/30]
Maidenhood.   [H. Longfellow. Volume 1/214]
Maiden's Ideal of a Husband, fr. The Contrivances. A   [H. Carey. Volume 2/89]
Maids! O, Fairest of Rural   [W. Bryant. Volume 2/46]
Mailman.   [B. Al-Haydari. Supp 7/226]
Maize. The   [W. Fosdick. Volume 5/267]
Malawi.   [I. Banda. Supp 6/25]
Malcolm's Katie. The Axe, fr.   [I. Crawford. Volume 6/388]
Malinche.   [R. Castellanos. Supp 5/51]
Malindy Sings. When   [P. Dunbar. Supp 4/79]
Malone. Widow   [C. Lever. Volume 2/183]
Mammon. The Kingdom of   [A. Hernandez. Supp 7/176]
Man.   [T. Heraty. Supp 7/93]
___   [W. Landor. Volume 3/151]
___. Fame, fr. An Essay on   [A. Pope. Volume 6/264]
___. God and Man, fr. Essay on   [A. Pope. Volume 4/21]
___. Greatness, fr. An Essay on   [A. Pope. Volume 6/283]
___. Gypsy   [L. Hughes. Supp 1/171]
man. Mariner   [E. Sitwell. Supp 5/271]
Man. Of a Certaine   [S. Harrington. Volume 9/199]
___. Poem to a Young   [L. Bell. Supp 6/108]
___. Woman to   [J. Wright. Supp 5/327]
___ and Jim. The Old   [J. Riley. Volume 8/357]
___ Asks for a Song. The Dead   [Unknown (African American). Supp 6/3]
___ Do But Die?"  " What Can An Old   [T. Hood. Volume 3/174]
___ Dreams. The Old   [O. Holmes. Volume 2/459]
___ Go Free"  " Stone the Woman, Let the   [Unknown. Volume 4/322]
___ Immortal, fr. Night Thoughts. Matter and   [E. Young. Volume 4/406]
___ in the Moon. The   [J. Riley. Volume 1/146]
___ Should Die. The Place Where   [M. Barry. Volume 8/111]
___ Talks of Reaping. A Black   [A. Bontemps. Supp 4/126]
___ Who Boxes. The   [A. Istaru. Supp 6/136]
___ with the Hoe. The   [J. Cheney. Volume 6/395]
___ with the Hoe. The   [E. Markham. Supp 1/205]
___ with the Hoe. The   [E. Markham. Volume

6/393]

Man" "The Goal of Intellectual    [R. Eberhart.
    Supp 2/126]
Man, fr. As You Like It. Seven Ages of    [W.
    Shakespeare. Volume 7/126]
__ fr. Essay on Man. God and    [A. Pope. Volume
    4/21]
Man?, fr. The Lay of the Last Minstrel. Breathes
    There the    [S. Scott. Volume 8/4]
Managua 6:30 P.M.    [E. Cardenal. Supp 6/155]
Manchu. The Insidious Dr. Fu    [L. Jones. Supp
    4/174]
Manchuria.    [W. Rendra. Supp 7/102]
Mandalay.    [R. Kipling. Supp 1/180]
Mandela. Echo of    [Z. Mandela. Supp 6/78]
Mandela's Sermon.    [K. Kgositsile. Supp 6/77]
Manhattan" " Shame on Thee, O    [A. Branch. Supp
    1/71]
Manila. The Battle of    [R. Hovey. Volume 8/421]
Mannahatta.    [W. Whitman. Volume 7/245]
Man's Day, fr. The Sabbath. The Poor    [A. Barbauld.
    Volume 4/193]
__ Free-will, fr. The Diving Comedy. Purgatory:
    [Dante Alighieri. Volume 4/438]
__ Mortality.    [S. Wastell. Volume 3/254]
Mansion. Southern    [A. Bontemps. Supp 4/123]
Many A Glorious Morning" " Full    [W. Shakespeare.
    Volume 2/224]
__ a Thousand Die.    [Unknown (African
    American). Supp 4/52]
Map. The Trout    [A. Tate. Supp 2/76]
Maple and Sumach.    [C. Day Lewis. Supp 2/117]
Marble, Not the Gilded Monuments" " Not    [W.
    Shakespeare. Volume 1/359]
March.    [A. Swinburne. Volume 5/74]
__    [W. Wordsworth. Volume 5/77]
__ to the Sea. Sherman's    [S. Byers. Volume
    8/406]
March-Patrol of the Naked Heroes.    [H. Gorman.
    Supp 1/143]
Marches. The Welsh    [A. Housman. Supp 1/167]
Marcia. Dark Symphony: 6. Tempo di    [M. Tolson.
    Supp 4/400]
Marco Bozzaris.    [F. Halleck. Volume 8/200]
Mare. Tonis Ad Resto    [J. Swift. Volume 9/319]
Margaret. Dolcino To    [C. Kingsley. Volume 2/445]
Mariner. A More Ancient    [B. Carman. Volume 5/345]
__. Rime of the Ancient    [S. Coleridge. Volume
    6/130]
__ man.    [E. Sitwell. Supp 5/271]
Mariners of England!" " Ye    [T. Campbell. Volume
    5/407]
Mariner's Dream. The    [W. Dimond. Volume 5/438]
Marion's Men. Song of    [W. Byrant. Volume 8/330]
Mariposa Lily. The    [I. Coolbrith. Volume 5/280]
Mark Antony, Over the Body of Caesar, fr. Julius
    Caesar    [W. Shakespeare. Volume 9/20]
Marketwoman. The    [A. Neto. Supp 6/14]
Marmion. An Old time Christmas, fr.    [S. Scott.
    Volume 7/210]
__. Flodden Field, fr.    [S. Scott. Volume
    8/312]
__. Lochinvar, fr.    [S. Scott. Volume 2/276]
__. Marmion and Douglas, fr.    [S. Scott. Volume
    7/401]
__. The Knight, fr.    [S. Scott. Volume 7/201]
__ and Douglas, fr. Marmion    [S. Scott. Volume
    7/401]
Marriage Of True Minds" " Let Me Not To The    [W.
    Shakespeare. Volume 2/376]
Marriage-Song, fr. Cella: A Tragical Interlude.
    Minstrels'    [T. Chatterton. Volume
    2/340]
Married And A. Song, fr. Woo'd And    [J. Baillie.
    Volume 2/411]

Marseillaise. The    [C. Lisle. Volume 8/145]
Marshes. Sunrise: A Hymn of the    [S. Lanier.
    Volume 5/257]
Marston.    [S. Spender. Supp 2/229]
Martyr. The    [Adonis. Supp 7/285]
Martyrs' Hymn. The    [M. Luther. Volume 4/334]
Marvel. Yet Do I    [C. Cullen. Supp 4/134]
Mary. Highland    [R. Burns. Volume 3/329]
__. Song of the Milkmaid, fr. Queen    [A.
    Tennyson. Volume 2/107]
__ Donnelly. Lovely    [W. Allingham. Volume
    2/50]
__ in Heaven. To    [R. Burns. Volume 3/339]
__ Stuart. To    [P. Ronsard. Volume 7/4]
Maryland. My    [J. Randall. Volume 8/103]
Masai Harper. We Assume: On the Death of Our Son,
    %Reuben    [M. Harper. Supp 4/205]
Mask. Out from Behind This    [W. Whitman. Volume
    7/100]
__ That Grins and Lies" " We Wear the    [P.
    Dunbar. Supp 4/75]
Masks.    [J. Das. Supp 7/47]
__. Prayer to    [L. Senghor. Supp 6/74]
Masque. The Sirens' Song, fr. Inner Temple    [W.
    Browne. Volume 6/79]
Mast. Choosing a    [R. Campbell. Supp 2/92]
Master, Let Me Walk With Thee" " O    [W. Gladden.
    Volume 4/135]
__ William Shakespeare ... To the Memory of My
    Beloved    [B. Jonson. Volume 7/48]
Masters' Touch. The    [H. Bonar. Volume 4/337]
Match. A    [A. Swinburne. Volume 2/86]
Matches. The Dreadful Story About Harriet and the
    [H. Hoffmann. Volume 1/171]
Mate. The Second    [F. O'Brien. Volume 9/189]
Mater Dolorosa. Stabat    [F. Jacopone. Volume 4/70]
maternity. Seven Times Four;    [J. Ingelow. Volume
    1/36]
Matter. A Rough Rhyme on a Rough    [C. Kingsley.
    Volume 3/191]
__ and Man Immortal, fr. Night Thoughts    [E.
    Young. Volume 4/406]
Matthew Henderson. Elegy on Captain    [R. Burns.
    Volume 1/363]
Maud" " Come Into The Garden,    [A. Tennyson.
    Volume 2/273]
Maurice, sel. Max and    [W. Busch. Volume 1/184]
Mavourneen. Kathleen    [J. Crawford. Volume 3/112]
Max and Maurice, sel.    [W. Busch. Volume 1/184]
May. Baby    [W. Bennett. Volume 1/17]
__ Bright Mushrooms Grow" "    [I. Banda. Supp
    6/29]
__ I Join The Choir Invisible!" " O,    [M.
    Cross. Volume 4/241]
__ Morning.    [C. Thaxter. Volume 5/84]
__ Morning. Song: On    [J. Milton. Volume 5/85]
__ Move", fr. Light of the Harem. " Alas! How
    Light a Cause    [T. Moore. Volume 3/80]
__ My Prison Have No Enclosure" "    [A. Shamlu.
    Supp 7/213]
__ Queen. The    [A. Tennyson. Volume 3/292]
May, fr. The Canterbury Pilgrims. Morning in    [G.
    Chaucer. Volume 5/89]
May-tree. The    [A. Noyes. Supp 1/242]
Mayor of Harlem. Walk with De    [D. Henderson. Supp
    4/207]
Maysters. Of Hym That Togyder Wyll Serve Two    [S.
    Brandt. Volume 4/217]
Mazzini at Genoa. On the Monument Erected to    [A.
    Swinburne. Volume 7/13]
Meadow Invites Me" "A Dark    [J. Lima. Supp 6/140]
Meandering Current of the Jhelum" "The    [R.
    Tagore. Supp 7/71]
Means to Attain Happy Life. The    [H. Howard.
    Volume 1/312]

Medallion. [S. Plath. Supp 5/210]
Medias Res. In [F. Lima. Supp 4/241]
Medicine. [A. Walker. Supp 4/229]
Medicines, fr. The Borough. Quack [G. Crabbe. Volume 6/287]
Meditation. [R. Fuller. Supp 2/264]
Meditation: Part 001, Stanza 013. Stansaz in [G. Stein. Supp 5/290]
— Part 002, Stanza 001. Stansaz in [G. Stein. Supp 5/290]
— Part 005, Stanza 041. Stansaz in [G. Stein. Supp 5/291]
Meditations. Moning [T. Hood. Volume 9/261]
— of a Hindu Prince. [S. Lyall. Volume 4/3]
Mediterranean: 001. [M. Rukeyser. Supp 2/296]
— 002. [M. Rukeyser. Supp 2/297]
— 003. [M. Rukeyser. Supp 2/299]
— 004. [M. Rukeyser. Supp 2/300]
— 005. [M. Rukeyser. Supp 2/301]
— 006. [M. Rukeyser. Supp 2/302]
Medusa. [L. Bogan. Supp 1/61]
Meet on the Buddha's Birthday. The Elephant & the Butterfly [D. Wakoski. Supp 5/320]
Meeting. Ode for a Social [O. Holmes. Volume 9/383]
—. The [J. Whittier. Volume 4/208]
— Above. [W. Leggett. Volume 4/395]
— at Night. [R. Browning. Volume 2/364]
— Of Desires, fr. The Angel In The House. Sweet [C. Patmore. Volume 2/166]
Meg. Muckle-Mou'd [J. Ballantine. Volume 7/418]
Meister. Mignon's Song, fr. Wilhelm [J. Goethe. Volume 6/313]
Melancholy %Away With It, Let It Go" " Away, [S. Smith. Supp 5/281]
Melodies. "'Tis the Last Rose of Summer", fr. Irish [T. Moore. Volume 5/283]
—. Come, Rest In This Bosom, fr. Irish [T. Moore. Volume 2/332]
—. Love's Young Dream, fr. Irish [T. Moore. Volume 2/327]
—. The Destruction of Sennacherib, r. Hebrew [G. Byron. Volume 8/183]
Melrose Abbey. Inscription on [F. Beaumont. Volume 3/269]
— Abbey, fr. The Lay of the Last Minstrel [S. Scott. Volume 7/208]
Memento of Roads. [N. Alterman. Supp 7/235]
Memorabilia. [R. Browning. Volume 7/58]
Memorial Verses. [M. Arnold. Volume 7/72]
Memoriam. " O Yet We Trust That Somehow", fr. In [A. Tennyson. Volume 4/243]
—. " Strong Son of God, Immortal Love", fr. In [A. Tennyson. Volume 4/45]
—. Dead, In a Foreign Land, fr. In [A. Tennyson. Volume 3/349]
—. Death in Life's Prime, fr. In [A. Tennyson. Volume 3/354]
—. Doubt and Faith, fr. In [A. Tennyson. Volume 4/139]
—. Grief Unspeakable, fr. In [A. Tennyson. Volume 3/349]
—. In [L. Senghor. Supp 6/76]
—. L., fr. In [A. Tennyson. Volume 3/353]
—. Personal Resurrection, fr. In [A. Tennyson. Volume 3/352]
—. Spiritual Companionship, fr. In [A. Tennyson. Volume 3/352]
—. Spring: 083, fr. In [A. Tennyson. Volume 5/91]
—. Spring: 114, fr. In [A. Tennyson. Volume 5/91]
—. The Dead Friend: 116, fr. In [A. Tennyson. Volume 1/362]
—. The Dead Friend: 22, fr. In [A. Tennyson.

Volume 1/360]
—. The Dead Friend: 23, fr. In [A. Tennyson. Volume 1/360]
—. The Dead Friend: 25, fr. In [A. Tennyson. Volume 1/361]
—. The Dead Friend: 84, fr. In [A. Tennyson. Volume 1/361]
—. The New Year, fr. In [A. Tennyson. Volume 4/260]
—. The Peace of Sorrow, fr. In [A. Tennyson. Volume 3/350]
—. The Poet's Tribute, fr. In [A. Tennyson. Volume 3/354]
—. Time and Eternity, fr. In [A. Tennyson. Volume 3/351]
— F. A. S. In [R. Stevenson. Volume 3/428]
Memory. Blest Memory, fr. The Pleasures of [S. Rogers. Volume 6/300]
—. Pictures of [A. Cary. Volume 1/76]
—. To a Dog's [L. Guiney. Volume 5/363]
— and Oblivion. [Macedonius. Volume 6/321]
— of Ben Jonson. To the [J. Cleveland. Volume 7/46]
— of My Beloved Master, William Shakespeare ... To the [B. Jonson. Volume 7/48]
— of Sigmund Freud. In [W. Auden. Supp 2/158]
— of the Heart. The [D. Webster. Volume 1/346]
— of Thomas Hood. To the [B. Simmons. Volume 7/62]
— of Walter Savage Landor. In [A. Swinburne. Volume 7/75]
Memory, fr. All's Well That Ends Well. Love's [W. Shakespeare. Volume 3/140]
— fr. The Pleasures of Memory. Blest [S. Rogers. Volume 6/300]
Men. Song of Marion's [W. Byrant. Volume 8/330]
—. Song of the Western [R. Hawker. Volume 8/136]
—. Strong [S. Brown. Supp 4/119]
— Alone. Not [E. Rolfe. Supp 2/217]
— and Boys. [K. Korner. Volume 8/78]
— Behind the Guns. The [J. Rooney. Volume 8/419]
— of the North and West" " [R. Stoddard. Volume 8/97]
Men, Riding Horses" " Strong [G. Brooks. Supp 5/38]
Men? Where Are the [Taliessin. Volume 8/301]
Menagerie. The [W. Moody. Supp 1/228]
Mending Wall. [R. Frost. Supp 1/130]
Merchant and the Stranger. The Gouty [H. Smith. Volume 9/275]
— of Venice. Love, fr. The [W. Shakespeare. Volume 2/62]
— of Venice. Music, fr. The [W. Shakespeare. Volume 6/362]
— of Venice. Portia's Picture, fr. The [W. Shakespeare. Volume 2/11]
Mercy. God of [K. Molodowsky. Supp 5/178]
Merlin and Vivien. Not At All, Or All In All, fr. [A. Tennyson. Volume 2/250]
Merman. The Forsaken [M. Arnold. Volume 6/80]
Merry Summer Months" " They Come! The [W. Motherwell. Volume 5/97]
Mersa. [K. Douglas. Supp 2/406]
Message from the Crane. A [Pak Tu-Jin. Supp 7/154]
Messengers. The Black [C. Vallejo. Supp 6/187]
Messiah. [A. Pope. Volume 4/97]
Metal, 9. Pyrargyrite [C. Meireles. Supp 5/164]
Metamorphoses. A Transformation, fr. The [Ovid (Publius Ovidius Naso). Volume 6/87]
Meting Like This" " And Doth Not a [T. Moore.

Volume 1/366]
**Metrical** Feet. [S. Coleridge. Volume 9/429]
**Mexican** Child. [G. Mistral. Supp 6/128]
___ Quarter. Arizona Poems: [J. Fletcher. Supp 1/127]
**Mexico.** In [E. Stein. Volume 7/257]
**Miami** Smile?" " When Was the Last Time You Saw [A. Casiano. Supp 4/288]
**Michaelmas.** [L. Lee. Supp 2/341]
**Middle** Passage. [R. Hayden. Supp 4/142]
**Midges** Dance Aboon the Burn" "The [R. Tannahill. Volume 5/47]
**Midnight.** [G. Mistral. Supp 6/127]
___ Skaters. The [E. Blunden. Supp 2/45]
**Midsummer.** At [L. Moulton. Volume 6/276]
___ Days and Nights. Ballade of [W. Henley. Volume 5/112]
___ Night's Dream. Compliment to Queen Elizabeth, fr. A [W. Shakespeare. Volume 6/17]
___ Night's Dream. Fairy's Song, fr. A [W. Shakespeare. Volume 6/16]
___ Night's Dream. Imagination, fr. A [W. Shakespeare. Volume 6/12]
___ Night's Dream. The Course of True Love, fr. [W. Shakespeare. Volume 3/3]
___ Night's Dream. The Fairies' Lullaby, fr. A [W. Shakespeare. Volume 6/18]
___ Night's Dream. Young Friends, fr. A [W. Shakespeare. Volume 1/344]
**Midsummer's** Noon in the Australian Forest. A [C. Harpur. Volume 5/44]
**Midway.** [N. Madgett. Supp 4/164]
**Might** Fortress Is Our God" " [M. Luther. Volume 4/33]
___ Of One Fair Face. The [M. Angelo. Volume 2/329]
**Mignon's** Song, fr. Wilhelm Meister [J. Goethe. Volume 6/313]
**Milan.** Home Sweet Home, fr. Clari, the Maid of [J. Payne. Volume 1/335]
**Milan"** " There Lived a Lady in [W. Benet. Supp 1/47]
**Mile** from Eden. A [A. Ridler. Supp 2/275]
**Military** Harpist. The [R. Pitter. Supp 2/48]
**Milk** at the Bottom of the Sea. [O. Williams. Supp 2/79]
___ of the Mothers. The [M. Waddington. Supp 5/310]
**Milking-Maid.** The [C. Rossetti. Volume 2/49]
**Milkmaid.** [L. Lee. Supp 2/336]
___. The [J. Taylor. Volume 9/259]
**Milkmaid,** fr. Queen Mary. Song of the [A. Tennyson. Volume 2/107]
**Milkmaid's** Song. The [S. Dobell. Volume 2/285]
**Mill.** Steel [L. Untermeyer. Supp 1/311]
**Miller's** Daughter. Song, fr. The [A. Tennyson. Volume 2/102]
**Milliner.** The Little [R. Buchanan. Volume 2/135]
**Milton.** To [W. Wordsworth. Volume 7/54]
___. Under the Portrait of John [J. Dryden. Volume 7/54]
**Minaret.** The [Adonis. Supp 7/283]
**Mind.** Freedom of the [W. Garrison. Volume 8/161]
___. Heart and [E. Sitwell. Supp 2/14]
___. Once Again the [F. Faiz. Supp 7/173]
**Mind,** fr. Macbeth. A Dagger of the [W. Shakespeare. Volume 9/120]
**Minde** To Me a Kingdom Is" " My [E. Dyer. Volume 6/325]
**Minds"** " Let Me Not To The Marriage Of True [W. Shakespeare. Volume 2/376]
**Mine,** Dear!" " O Lay Thy Hand In [G. Massey. Volume 2/445]
___ fr. Twelfth Night. O Mistress [W. Shakespeare. Volume 2/79]

**Mine?"** " What Ails This Heart O' [S. Blamire. Volume 3/139]
**Minerva.** On an Intaglio Head of [T. Aldrich. Volume 6/383]
**Ministry** of Angels, fr. The Faerie Queen. The [E. Spenser. Volume 4/415]
**Minnehaha,** fr. The Song of Hiawatha. The Death of [H. Longfellow. Volume 3/319]
**Minstrel.** Breathes There the Man?, fr. The Lay of the Last [S. Scott. Volume 8/4]
___. Love, fr. Lay of the Last [S. Scott. Volume 2/70]
___. Melrose Abbey, fr. The Lay of the Last [S. Scott. Volume 7/208]
___. Morning, fr. The [T. Heywood. Volume 5/42]
___. Scotland, fr. The Lay of the Last [S. Scott. Volume 8/33]
___. The Poet's Death, fr. The Lay of the Last [S. Scott. Volume 6/355]
**Minstrels'** Marriage-Song, fr. Cella: A Tragical Interlude [T. Chatterton. Volume 2/340]
**Minstrel's** Song. [T. Chatterton. Volume 3/340]
**Minute** 26 Seconds. Reading Time: 1 [M. Rukeyser. Supp 2/304]
**Minute-Gun.** The [R. Sharpe. Volume 5/403]
**Miranda's** Song. [W. Auden. Supp 2/164]
**Mirror.** [J. Das. Supp 7/50]
___. Broken [Yung Tzu. Supp 7/35]
___. The [L. Gluck. Supp 5/104]
___ for the Twentieth Century. A [Adonis. Supp 7/278]
**Miscellaneum.** The Fire Of Love, fr. The Examen [C. Sackville. Volume 2/449]
**Missing.** Eros Is [Meleager. Volume 2/17]
___ Dates. [W. Empson. Supp 2/144]
**Missouri.** Last Look at La Plata, [J. Barnes. Supp 4/298]
**Mist.** [H. Thoreau. Volume 7/153]
**Mistake.** A Mortifying [A. Pratt. Volume 1/166]
**Mists.** Night [W. Hayne. Volume 6/179]
**Mitchell's** Mother. Jessie [G. Brooks. Supp 5/41]
**Mite.** The Widow's [F. Locker-Lampson. Volume 3/287]
**Mites.** Brief: The Widow's [R. Crashaw. Volume 4/306]
**Mitherless** Bairn. The [W. Thom. Volume 1/78]
**Mixed** Sketches. [D. Lee. Supp 4/210]
**Mixer.** The [L. MacNeice. Supp 2/180]
**Moan,** Moan, Ye Dying Gales" " [H. Neele. Volume 3/152]
___ Ye Dying Gales" " Moan, [H. Neele. Volume 3/152]
**Mocking-bird.** Moonlight Song of the [W. Hayne. Volume 6/179]
___. The [F. Stanton. Volume 5/319]
**Model** Lesson. [T. Carmi. Supp 7/242]
**Moderato.** Dark Symphony: 1. Allegro [M. Tolson. Supp 4/96]
**Modern** Hiawatha. The [Unknown. Volume 9/414]
___ House that Jack Built. The [Unknown. Volume 9/396]
___ Love. The Family Skeleton, fr. [G. Meredith. Volume 6/247]
___ Muses. The Ancient and [F. Palgrave. Volume 6/337]
___ Poet. The [A. Meynell. Volume 6/347]
**Mole.** The Eagle and the [E. Wylie. Supp 1/326]
**Moment** on Green Grass. A [Agyeya. Supp 7/41]
**Moment,** Passing. Dismal [C. Major. Supp 4/203]
**Moments** of Initiation. [K. Kerpi. Supp 6/45]
**Money.** Worry About [K. Raine. Supp 2/202]
**Moning** Meditations. [T. Hood. Volume 9/261]
**Monk.** The Weak [S. Smith. Supp 2/106]
**Monmouth.** Calvary Song, fr. Alice of [E. Stedman.

Volume 8/365]
Mont Blanc. From    [P. Shelley. Volume 5/217]
Monterey.    [C. Hoffman. Volume 8/336]
Monterrey Sun.    [A. Reyes. Supp 6/149]
Months" " They Come! The Merry Summer    [W. Motherwell. Volume 5/97]
Montreal. Lady in Blue: Homage to    [M. Waddington. Supp 5/315]
Montrose. The Execution of    [W. Aytoun. Volume 8/43]
Monument. The    [E. Bishop. Supp 2/243]
—    Erected to Mazzini at Genoa. On the    [A. Swinburne. Volume 7/13]
Monuments" " Not Marble, Not the Gilded    [W. Shakespeare. Volume 1/359]
Moods. Summer    [J. Clare. Volume 5/136]
Moon.    [N. Alterman. Supp 7/237]
—    [Chong Chi-Yong. Supp 7/149]
—. The Man in the    [J. Riley. Volume 1/146]
—. The Window Frames the    [L. Mar. Supp 4/32]
—. White    [H. Sakutaro. Supp 7/106]
Moon" " Early Evening    [A. Yosano. Supp 7/144]
Mooney. Tom    [C. Leland. Supp 1/186]
Moonlight.    [N. Yushij. Supp 7/202]
—    on the Prairie, fr. Evangeline    [H. Longfellow. Volume 5/61]
—    Song of the Mocking-bird.    [W. Hayne. Volume 6/179]
Moonlight" " Hills Picking Up the    [N. Cassian. Supp 5/45]
Moonlit Apples.    [J. Drinkwater. Supp 1/109]
—    Night. Sad    [H. Sakutaro. Supp 7/104]
Moor. Cleator    [L. Lee. Supp 2/340]
Moore. Burial of Sir John    [C. Wolfe. Volume 8/283]
—. To Thomas    [G. Byron. Volume 7/57]
Moors. Gloucester    [W. Moody. Supp 1/225]
Moral. An Experience and a    [F. Cozzens. Volume 2/58]
—    Essays. The Ruling Passion, fr.    [A. Pope. Volume 6/294]
Morn" " So Sweet Love Seemed That April    [R. Bridges. Supp 1/75]
Morning.    [J. Cunningham. Volume 5/40]
—.    Good Night and Good    [R. Milnes. Volume 1/109]
—.    May    [C. Thaxter. Volume 5/84]
—.    Song: On May    [J. Milton. Volume 5/85]
—.    Sunday    [L. MacNeice. Supp 2/184]
—.    The Sabbath    [J. Leyden. Volume 4/192]
—.    at Cambridge. Autumn    [F. Cornford. Supp 1/91]
—    Bells. Sunday    [D. Craik. Volume 4/190]
—    in May, fr. The Canterbury Pilgrims    [G. Chaucer. Volume 5/89]
—    in Vietnam. The First    [Ho Ch'i-Fang. Supp 7/5]
—    of Christ's Nativity. On the    [J. Milton. Volume 4/51]
—    Song.    [J. Baillie. Volume 5/39]
—    Song.    [S. Plath. Supp 5/212]
—    Thought. A    [E. Sill. Volume 3/267]
—    Walk. Winter Morning, fr. The Winter    [W. Cowper. Volume 5/186]
Morning" " Full Many A Glorious    [W. Shakespeare. Volume 2/224]
—    " Hair All Tangled This    [A. Yosano. Supp 7/145]
—    " I Saw Two Clouds At    [J. Brainard. Volume 2/259]
—    " Listen. Put on    [W. Graham. Supp 2/401]
Morning, fr. The Minstrel    [T. Heywood. Volume 5/42]
—    fr. The Winter Morning Walk. Winter    [W. Cowper. Volume 5/186]

Morning-Glory. The    [M. Lowell. Volume 3/285]
Mornings in Various Years: 001.    [M. Piercy. Supp 5/200]
—    in Various Years: 002.    [M. Piercy. Supp 5/200]
—    in Various Years: 003.    [M. Piercy. Supp 5/201]
Morrison. Jeanie    [W. Motherwell. Volume 3/127]
Mors Et Vita.    [S. Waddington. Volume 1/396]
Mortal Eyes. Fairest Thing in    [D. Charles. Volume 3/356]
Mortality.    [W. Knox. Volume 3/256]
—    [N. Madgett. Supp 4/163]
—. Man's    [S. Wastell. Volume 3/254]
Morte D'Arthur.    [A. Tennyson. Volume 7/352]
Mortifying Mistake. A    [A. Pratt. Volume 1/166]
Morton's Ride. Colorado    [L. Bacon. Supp 1/21]
Moses. Burial of    [C. Alexander. Volume 4/365]
Moses" " Go Down,    [Unknown (African American). Supp 4/48]
Mosque. At the    [C. Anwar. Supp 7/79]
Moss Rose. The    [F. Krummacher. Volume 5/281]
Moss-Gathering.    [T. Roethke. Supp 2/210]
—. The Lost Son:    [T. Roethke. Supp 2/210]
Most Lovely Shade.    [E. Sitwell. Supp 2/15]
Most? fr. The House of Life. When Do I See Thee    [D. Rossetti. Volume 2/251]
Mother.    [N. Kiyoko. Supp 5/135]
—. Jessie Mitchell's    [G. Brooks. Supp 5/41]
—. Notes Found Near a Suicide: To    [F. Horne. Supp 4/108]
—. The Happy    [A. Laing. Volume 1/281]
—. The Song of the Old    [W. Yeats. Volume 1/284]
—. To My    [G. Barker. Supp 2/294]
—    and Child.    [W. Simms. Volume 1/25]
—    and Poet.    [E. Browning. Volume 3/323]
—    Carey's Chicken. Ode to    [T. Watts. Volume 5/333]
—    Pieced Quilts. My    [T. Acosta. Supp 4/285]
—    to Her First-Born. A    [Unknown (African American). Supp 6/5]
—    Tongue. Fataher and    [S. Lover. Volume 8/6]
Mother" " Give Me Three Grains of Corn,    [A. Edwards. Volume 3/197]
Mother, Who Came from China, Where She Never Saw Snow My    [L. Mar. Supp 4/34]
Motherhood.    [C. Calverley. Volume 9/440]
Mothers. The Milk of the    [M. Waddington. Supp 5/310]
—. Tired    [M. Smith. Volume 1/282]
mother's Bible. My    [G. Morris. Volume 1/228]
Mother's Habits.    [N. Giovanni. Supp 4/223]
—    Hope. The    [L. Blanchard. Volume 1/37]
—    Letters. Tearing Up My    [D. Wakoski. Supp 5/324]
—    Picture. My    [W. Cowper. Volume 1/79]
—    Sacrifice. The    [S. Smith. Volume 1/24]
Motif. Second Rose    [C. Meireles. Supp 5/161]
Mount. The Sermon on the    [T. Sayigh. Supp 7/296]
—    Fuji.    [M. Kaneko. Supp 7/113]
Mountain. Hunter    [F. Lima. Supp 4/245]
—. The    [H. Riyong. Supp 6/47]
—. The Time We Climbed Snake    [L. Silko. Supp 4/334]
—    Abbey, Surrounded by Elk Horns.    [C. Forche. Supp 5/83]
—    Daisy. To a    [R. Burns. Volume 5/277]
—    Fern. The    [A. Geoghegan. Volume 5/264]
—    Laurell.    [A. Noyes. Supp 1/243]
—    Lion Lay Down with Deer, February 1973. Where    [L. Silko. Supp 4/335]
—    of the Lovers. Love Scorns Degrees, fr. The    [P. Hayne. Volume 2/77]
Mountains. Sabbath Hymn On the    [J. Blackie.

Volume 4/190]
Mounted Umbrella. A    [G. Stein. Supp 5/292]
Mourn. Blessed Are They That    [W. Bryant. Volume 3/421]
—    the Death, by Fire of a Child in London. A Refusal to    [D. Thomas. Supp 2/368]
Mourning Time. In the    [R. Hayden. Supp 4/138]
Mouse. Poor    [M. Berssenbrugge. Supp 4/10]
—. To a    [R. Burns. Volume 5/350]
Move", fr. Light of the Harem. " Alas! How Light a Cause May    [T. Moore. Volume 3/80]
Moved" " All the World    [J. Jordan. Supp 4/194]
Movement. Slow    [L. MacNeice. Supp 2/182]
Movin'" " Keep Sweet and Keep    [R. Burdette. Volume 6/270]
Moving. What is    [S. Takahashi. Supp 7/128]
Mowers. The    [M. Benton. Volume 7/249]
Muckle-Mou'd Meg.    [J. Ballantine. Volume 7/418]
Muff. On an Old    [F. Locker-Lampson. Volume 9/235]
Muirhevney. Chariot of Cuchullin, fr. Breach of the Plain of    [Unknown. Volume 5/371]
Muller. Maud    [J. Whittier. Volume 3/35]
Multitudinous Stars and Sping Waters: 001.    [Ping Hsin. Supp 5/116]
—    Stars and Sping Waters: 002.    [Ping Hsin. Supp 5/116]
—    Stars and Spring Waters: 003.    [Ping Hsin. Supp 5/116]
—    Stars and Spring Waters: 004.    [Ping Hsin. Supp 5/116]
—    Stars and Spring Waters: 005.    [Ping Hsin. Supp 5/116]
—    Stars and Spring Waters: 006.    [Ping Hsin. Supp 5/117]
—    Stars and Spring Waters: 007.    [Ping Hsin. Supp 5/117]
—    Stars and Spring Waters: 008.    [Ping Hsin. Supp 5/117]
—    Stars and Spring Waters: 009.    [Ping Hsin. Supp 5/117]
Mummy at Belzoni's Exhibition. Address to the    [H. Smith. Volume 6/235]
Mundi. Hope of the Human Heart, fr. Anima    [R. Milnes. Volume 4/110]
Murder. The    [G. Brooks. Supp 5/37]
Murder, fr. Macbeth. The    [W. Shakespeare. Volume 9/122]
Musarum. Lachrymae    [W. Watson. Volume 7/84]
Muse in America: 001. The Tears of a    [F. Prince. Supp 2/267]
—    in America: 002. The Tears of a    [F. Prince. Supp 2/267]
—    in America: 003. The Tears of a    [F. Prince. Supp 2/268]
—    in America: 004. The Tears of a    [F. Prince. Supp 2/269]
Musee des Beaux Arts.    [W. Auden. Supp 2/164]
Muses. The Ancient and Modern    [F. Palgrave. Volume 6/337]
Museum.    [S. Tanikawa. Supp 7/131]
—. Homage to the British    [W. Empson. Supp 2/141]
Museums.    [L. MacNeice. Supp 2/180]
Mushrooms Grow" " May Bright    [I. Banda. Supp 6/29]
Music. Alexander's Feast; or, the Power of    [J. Dryden. Volume 6/372]
—. Broken    [T. Aldrich. Volume 6/346]
—    at the Bar. The Woman Who Disapproved of    [H. Gregory. Supp 2/67]
—    in Camp.    [J. Thompson. Volume 8/389]
Music, fr. King Henry Eighth. Influence of    [W. Shakespeare. Volume 6/362]
—    fr. The Merchant of Venice    [W. Shakespeare. Volume 6/362]

Music-box. On Hearing A Little    [L. Hunt. Volume 7/139]
Music-Stand. The Red Lacquer    [A. Lowell. Supp 1/198]
Musical Instrument. A    [E. Browning. Volume 6/86]
Musician.    [C. Bax. Supp 1/28]
Music's Duel. The Nightingales' Song, fr.    [R. Crashaw. Volume 5/306]
Myrrh-Bearers.    [M. Preston. Volume 4/72]
Myrtle and the Vine. Gluggity Glug, fr. The    [G. Colman. Volume 9/245]
Mysteries. The Two    [M. Dodge. Volume 3/262]
Mystery.    [J. Drinkwater. Supp 1/113]
Mystical Ecstasy. A    [F. Quarles. Volume 4/142]
Mysticism Has Not the Patience to Wait for God's Revelation.    [R. Eberhart. Supp 2/128]
Mystics Vision. The    [M. Blind. Volume 4/142]
Mystified Quaker in New York. The    [Unknown. Volume 9/352]

Naked Heroes. March-Patrol of the    [H. Gorman. Supp 1/143]
Naked" "The Trees Are    [E. Manner. Supp 5/154]
Name. Choosing a    [M. Lamb. Volume 1/97]
—    Blew Like a Horn Among the Payira. My    [O. P'bitek. Supp 6/98]
—    of a Ring. What Is the    [G. Stein. Supp 5/295]
—    of the King. We Do Not Know the    [M. Takahashi. Supp 7/122]
Name!" " O, Breathe Not His    [T. Moore. Volume 7/6]
Name", fr. Amoretti. " One Day I Wrote Her    [E. Spenser. Volume 6/353]
Name" " When I Hear Your    [G. Fuertes. Supp 5/91]
Nancy" " Out of the Old House,    [W. Carleton. Volume 1/268]
Nantucket Shell. With a    [C. Webb. Volume 5/425]
—    Skipper. The    [J. Fields. Volume 9/343]
Nantucket: 001. The Quaker Graveyard in    [R. Lowell. Supp 2/394]
—    002. The Quaker Graveyard in    [R. Lowell. Supp 2/395]
—    003. The Quaker Graveyard in    [R. Lowell. Supp 2/395]
—    004. The Quaker Graveyard in    [R. Lowell. Supp 2/396]
—    005. The Quaker Graveyard in    [R. Lowell. Supp 2/397]
—    006. The Quaker Graveyard in    [R. Lowell. Supp 2/397]
—    007. The Quaker Graveyard in    [R. Lowell. Supp 2/398]
Nap" " When I    [N. Giovanni. Supp 4/219]
Naples, fr. Italy    [S. Rogers. Volume 7/194]
Napoleon.    [V. Hugo. Volume 7/8]
—. The Bronze Statue of    [A. Barbier. Volume 8/232]
—    and the British Sailor.    [T. Campbell. Volume 7/347]
Napoleon, fr. Childe Harold    [G. Byron. Volume 7/9]
Naseby.    [L. Macaulay; Thomas Babington. Volume 8/272]
Nathan Hale.    [F. Finch. Volume 8/328]
Nation. A Holy    [R. Realf. Volume 8/178]
National Anthem.    [R. Newell. Volume 9/415]
—    Anthem.    [R. Newell. Volume 9/416]
—    Anthem.    [R. Newell. Volume 9/417]
—    Anthem.    [R. Newell. Volume 9/418]
—    Anthem.    [R. Newell. Volume 9/419]
Nation's Hand.    [F. Daglarca. Supp 7/303]

— of Henry IV. Sleep, fr. Second [W. Shakespeare. Volume 6/433]
— of Henry VI. A Sheperd's Life, fr. Third [W. Shakespeare. Volume 1/319]
Part" " Ae Fond Kiss Before We [R. Burns. Volume 3/98]
— " Maid of Athens, Ere We [G. Byron. Volume 3/100]
Part." " Till Death Us [A. Stanley. Volume 2/458]
Parte. Come, Let Us Kisse and [M. Drayton. Volume 3/111]
Parted Friends. [J. Montgomery. Volume 1/347]
— In Silence. We [J. Crawford. Volume 3/113]
Parting. [J. Borges. Supp 6/104]
—. [C. Patmore. Volume 3/96]
—. Farewell at the Hour of [A. Neto. Supp 6/13]
— Lovers. [E. Browning. Volume 8/85]
— Lovers. The [Unknown. Volume 3/104]
— of Hector and Andromache, fr. The Iliad [Homer. Volume 3/118]
Party. Hans Breitmann's [C. Leland. Volume 9/325]
Passage. Middle [R. Hayden. Supp 4/142]
—. The [L. Uhland. Volume 3/342]
— in the Life of Saint Augustine. [Unknown. Volume 4/1]
Passed" " How the Days [N. Zach. Supp 7/253]
Passes. Service, fr. Pippa [R. Browning. Volume 4/156]
—. Song, fr. Pippa [R. Browning. Volume 4/1]
Passing. Dismal Moment, [C. Major. Supp 4/203]
— Away. [J. Pierpont. Volume 4/350]
— Bell. The [D. Levertov. Supp 5/145]
Passion, fr. Moral Essays. The Ruling [A. Pope. Volume 6/294]
Passionate Shepherd To His Love. The [C. Marlowe. Volume 2/149]
Passions. The [W. Collins. Volume 6/367]
Past" " Our god, Our help in Ages [I. Watts. Volume 4/32]
Pastoral. Doris: A [A. Munby. Volume 2/169]
Pastorals. The Hunted Squirrel, fr. Britannia's [W. Browne. Volume 5/157]
Pastor's Reverie. [W. Gladden. Volume 4/313]
Patience. [C. Anwar. Supp 7/79]
— [P. Hayne. Volume 4/343]
—. The Angel of [J. Whittier. Volume 3/402]
— to Wait for God's Revelation. Mysticism Has Not the [R. Eberhart. Supp 2/128]
Patience, fr. Poems of Freedom [W. Linton. Volume 8/114]
Patient Grissell. The Happy Heart, fr. [T. Dekker. Volume 6/409]
Patriotic Song. [E. Arndt. Volume 8/76]
Paulina's Appeal, fr. Polyeucte [P. Corneille. Volume 2/396]
Paulinus. Edwon and [Unknown. Volume 4/385]
Pauper's Drive. The [T. Noel. Volume 3/202]
Pay No Rent. Live In My Heart And [S. Lover. Volume 2/180]
Payira. My Name Blew Like a Horn Among the [O. P'bitek. Supp 6/98]
Peace. ' [F. Havergal. Volume 4/250]
— [G. Herbert. Volume 4/248]
— [Unknown. Volume 3/437]
— [H. Vaughan. Volume 4/414]
—. A Certain [N. Giovanni. Supp 4/218]
—. Ode to [W. Tennant. Volume 8/423]
— of Sorrow, fr. In Memoriam. The [A. Tennyson. Volume 3/350]
— on Earth. [W. Williams. Supp 1/319]
Peace" " Come to These Scenes of [W. Bowles. Volume 5/17]
Peacock, fr. Sospiri Di Roma. The White [W. Sharp.

— Volume 7/175]
Pearl. The [Adonis. Supp 7/282]
Pearls of the Faith. After Death, fr. [S. Arnold. Volume 3/452]
Peas. The Pilgrims and the [J. Wolcott. Volume 9/249]
Peasant Women from Cua. The [E. Cardenal. Supp 6/156]
Peasant, fr. The Traveller. The Swiss [O. Goldsmith. Volume 1/321]
Peasants. The [A. Lewis. Supp 2/377]
Peewee. [A. Kreymborg. Supp 1/185]
Peg of Limavaddy. [W. Thackeray. Volume 1/236]
Pelican Island. Birds, fr. The [J. Montgomery. Volume 5/288]
— Island. The Coral Reef, fr. The [J. Montgomery. Volume 5/396]
Pelicans. [R. Jeffers. Supp 1/173]
Pelters of Pyramids. [R. Horne. Volume 6/264]
Penitents, fr. The Diving Comedy. Purgatory: Prayer of [Dante Alighieri. Volume 4/437]
Pennsylvania Dutch Country. [S. Sanchez. Supp 4/192]
Penseroso. Il [J. Milton. Volume 6/251]
Pensioner. The Nobleman and the [G. Pfeffel. Volume 7/303]
People Go. Let My [J. Johnson. Supp 4/68]
— Whose Tongue is Tied?: 001. What Value Has the [N. Qabbani. Supp 7/286]
— Whose Tongue is Tied?: 002. What Value Has the [N. Qabbani. Supp 7/286]
— Whose Tongue is Tied?: 003. What Value Has the [N. Qabbani. Supp 7/286]
— Whose Tongue is Tied?: 004. What Value Has the [N. Qabbani. Supp 7/287]
— Whose Tongue is Tied?: 005. What Value Has the [N. Qabbani. Supp 7/287]
— Whose Tongue is Tied?: 006. What Value Has the [N. Qabbani. Supp 7/287]
— Whose Tongue is Tied?: 007. What Value Has the [N. Qabbani. Supp 7/287]
— Whose Tongue Is Tied?: 008. What Value Has the [N. Qabbani. Supp 7/287]
— Whose Tongue Is Tied?: 009. What Value Has the [N. Qabbani. Supp 7/288]
— Whose Tongue Is Tied?: 010. What Value Has the [N. Qabbani. Supp 7/288]
— Whose Tongue Is Tied?: 011. What Value Has the [N. Qabbani. Supp 7/288]
— Whose Tongue Is Tied?: 012. What Value Has the [N. Qabbani. Supp 7/288]
— Whose Tongue Is Tied?: 013. What Value Has the [N. Qabbani. Supp 7/288]
— Whose Tongue Is Tied?: 014. What Value Has the [N. Qabbani. Supp 7/289]
— Whose Tongue Is Tied?: 015. What Value Has the [N. Qabbani. Supp 7/289]
— Whose Tongue Is Tied?: 016. What Value Has the [N. Qabbani. Supp 7/289]
— Whose Tongue Is Tied?: 017. What Value Has the [N. Qabbani. Supp 7/290]
— Whose Tongue Is Tied?: 018. What Value Has the [N. Qabbani. Supp 7/290]
— Whose Tongue Is Tied?: 019. What Value Has the [N. Qabbani. Supp 7/291]
— Whose Tongue Is Tied?: 020. What Value Has the [N. Qabbani. Supp 7/291]
— Will Have to Understand. A Poem Some [L. Jones. Supp 4/178]
Per Pacem Ad Lucem. [A. Procter. Volume 4/333]
Percy's Reliques. King John and the Abbot of Canterbury, fr. [Unknown. Volume 9/241]
Perfume. [E. Goose. Volume 2/]
Perils of Thinking. [Unknown. Volume 9/380]

**Periods.** The Girl of All    [C. Patmore. Volume 1/242]

**Perished.**    [M. Ritter. Volume 3/169]

**Perseus.**    [L. MacNeice. Supp 2/182]

**Perseverance.**    [L. Da Vinci. Volume 6/284]

**Person.** Long    [G. Cardiff. Supp 4/319]

**Personal** Resurrection, fr. In Memoriam    [A. Tennyson. Volume 3/352]

**Peter.** The Sifting of    [H. Longfellow. Volume 4/290]

__ Quince at the Clavier.    [W. Stevens. Supp 1/289]

**Peter's** at Rome, fr. Childe Harold. Saint    [G. Byron. Volume 7/186]

**Petition.**    [W. Auden. Supp 2/167]

__ to Time. A    [B. Procter. Volume 1/334]

**Petrel.** Lines to the Stormy    [Unknown. Volume 5/332]

**Petrified** Fern. The    [M. Branch. Volume 6/200]

**Phantom** Of Delight" " She Was A    [W. Wordsworth. Volume 2/422]

**Philip** Sidney. Sir    [M. Royden. Volume 7/45]

**Philip,** My King.    [D. Craik. Volume 1/16]

**Philippa** is Gone" " Now    [A. Ridler. Supp 2/276]

**Phillida** and Corydon.    [N. Breton. Volume 2/152]

**Phillis** Is My Only Joy" "    [S. Sedley. Volume 2/22]

**Phillis's** Guest. Aunt    [W. Gannett. Volume 3/239]

**Philomela's** Ode.    [R. Greene. Volume 2/79]

**Philomena.**    [M. Arnold. Volume 5/308]

**Philosopher** Toad. The    [R. Nichols. Volume 4/234]

**Philosophy.** Love's    [P. Shelley. Volume 2/106]

__. Sea, False    [L. Riding. Supp 1/264]

__ of Life. The True    [W. Dunbar. Volume 6/299]

**Photo"** " I Swear %By That Summer    [B. Akhmadulina. Supp 5/3]

**Phycolophon.**    [G. Burgess. Volume 9/456]

**Physics.**    [W. Whewell. Volume 9/434]

**Piange.** La Figlia Che    [T. Eliot. Supp 1/120]

**Piazza** Piece.    [J. Ransom. Supp 1/260]

**Pibroch** of Donuil Dhu" "    [S. Scott. Volume 8/311]

**Picciola"** "    [R. Newell. Volume 8/285]

**Picking** Up the Moonlight" " Hills    [N. Cassian. Supp 5/45]

**Picture.** A    [C. Eastman. Volume 1/315]

__. My Mother's    [W. Cowper. Volume 1/79]

__ of an Infant Playing Near a Precipice. On the    [Leonidas of Alexandria. Volume 1/24]

__ of Death, fr. The Giaour. A    [G. Byron. Volume 3/261]

**Picture,** fr. The Merchant of Venice. Portia's    [W. Shakespeare. Volume 2/11]

**Pictures.** Two    [A. Green. Volume 1/318]

__ of Memory.    [A. Cary. Volume 1/76]

**Piece.** Piazza    [J. Ransom. Supp 1/260]

**Pieced** Quilts. My Mother    [T. Acosta. Supp 4/285]

**Pied** Piper of Hamelin. The    [R. Browning. Volume 6/169]

**Pierced** the Twelve" "The Starlight's Intuitions    [D. Schwartz. Supp 2/309]

**Piero** Della Francesca.    [A. Ridler. Supp 2/276]

**Pigeon.** The Belfry    [N. Willis. Volume 5/325]

**Pilgrim** Fathers in New England. The Landing of the    [F. Hemans. Volume 8/150]

**Pilgrimage.** The    [S. Raleigh. Volume 4/335]

__. The Poet's Impulse, fr. Childe Harold's    [G. Byron. Volume 6/335]

**Pilgrims.** Morning in May, fr. The Canterbury    [G. Chaucer. Volume 5/89]

__ and the Peas. The    [J. Wolcott. Volume 9/249]

**Pilgrims,** fr. The Canterbury Tales. The Canterbury    [G. Chaucer. Volume 7/363]

**Pilot** from the Carrier. A    [R. Jarrell. Supp 2/332]

**Pine.** Palm and the    [H. Heine. Volume 3/40]

**Pine-Needles"** " Now    [S. Smith. Supp 5/286]

**Pine-tree,** fr. Edwin the Fair. The Wind and the    [S. Taylor. Volume 5/219]

**Pines.** Kearny at Seven    [E. Stedman. Volume 8/367]

**Pines"** " Through These    [A. Yosano. Supp 7/145]

__ "The Snowing of the    [T. Higginson. Volume 5/180]

**Pipe.** The Brier-wood    [C. Shanly. Volume 6/317]

**Piper.** The    [W. Blake. Volume 1/96]

__ of Hamelin. The Pied    [R. Browning. Volume 6/169]

**Pippa** Passes. Service, fr.    [R. Browning. Volume 4/156]

__ Passes. Song, fr.    [R. Browning. Volume 4/1]

**Pit.** The Lost Son: The    [T. Roethke. Supp 2/207]

**Pitch** Your Tent?" " O Sister %Where Do You    [N. Sachs. Supp 5/249]

**Pitcher.** The Broken    [W. Aytoun. Volume 7/325]

**Pity** the Garden. I    [F. Farrozkhzad. Supp 7/221]

**Place** Where Man Should Die. The    [M. Barry. Volume 8/111]

__ Ye Lovers. Give    [H. Howard. Volume 2/7]

**Places.** In Waste    [J. Stephens. Supp 1/286]

**Plaidie.** The    [C. Sibley. Volume 2/131]

**Plain** Language from Truthful James.    [B. Harte. Volume 9/374]

__ of Muirhevney. Chariot of Cuchullin, fr. Breach of the    [Unknown. Volume 5/371]

**Plain"** " Were I As Base As Is The Lowly    [J. Sylvester. Volume 2/330]

**Plains.** The    [R. Fuller. Supp 2/265]

**Plane** Tree by the Water. As a    [R. Lowell. Supp 2/387]

**Planet.** The Undiscovered    [L. Lee. Supp 2/343]

**Planets.** Two    [M. Iqbal. Supp 7/57]

**Planners.** The City    [M. Atwood. Supp 5/18]

**Plantation** Ditty. A    [F. Stanton. Volume 9/376]

**Planting** Arts and Learning in America. On the Prospect of    [B. Berkeley. Volume 8/91]

__ of the Apple-tree. The    [W. Byrant. Volume 5/232]

**Plata,** Missouri. Last Look at La    [J. Barnes. Supp 4/298]

**Platform** Dances. The New    [J. Mapanje. Supp 6/34]

**Platonic.**    [W. Terrertt. Volume 1/372]

**Play.** A Good    [R. Stevenson. Volume 1/127]

__. The End of the    [W. Thackeray. Volume 4/256]

__ So Well. That Harp You    [M. Moore. Supp 1/234]

**Playing** Near a Precipice. On the Picture of an Infant    [Leonidas of Alexandria. Volume 1/24]

**Playmate.** The Unseen    [R. Stevenson. Volume 1/131]

**Pleasant** Days of Old" " O, The    [F. Browne. Volume 7/206]

**Pleasure** Arising from Vicissitude. Ode on the    [T. Gray. Volume 5/18]

**Pleasure-Boat.** The    [R. Dana. Volume 5/142]

**Pleasures** of Hope. Hope, fr. The    [T. Campbell. Volume 4/145]

__ of Hope. Poland, fr. The    [T. Campbell. Volume 8/144]

__ of Memory. Blest Memory, fr. The    [S. Rogers. Volume 6/300]

**Pleiad.** The Lost    [W. Simms. Volume 4/347]

**Plena.**    [F. Lima. Supp 4/248]

**Pliocene** Skull. To the    [B. Harte. Volume 9/360]

**Plough.** The    [R. Honrne. Volume 5/96]

**Ploughman.** The    [O. Holmes. Volume 5/94]

**Plucking** Out a Rhythm.    [L. Inada. Supp 4/4]

__. Veteran and    [E. Hazewell. Volume 8/19]
**Red.** Do Not Wash Away the    [Ho Ch'i-Fang. Supp 7/7]
__    Crosse Knight, fr. The Faerie Queene. Una and the    [E. Spenser. Volume 6/108]
__    Lacquer Music-Stand. The    [A. Lowell. Supp 1/198]
__    Lark. The Little    [A. Graves. Volume 2/158]
__    Ridinghood.    [N. Alterman. Supp 7/236]
__    Rose"  " O, My Luve's Like a Red,    [R. Burns. Volume 3/99]
__    Slogan"  " I Am a    [R. Wright. Supp 2/214]
**Red, Red Rose"**  " O, My Luve's Like a    [R. Burns. Volume 3/99]
**Red-gold** Hair. The Youth with    [E. Sitwell. Supp 2/22]
**Redeemed** %From Sleep"  "    [N. Sachs. Supp 5/253]
**Redemption,** fr. The Diving Comedy. Paradise: Sin and    [Dante Alighieri. Volume 4/441]
**Redeoption,** Book XI, fr. Paradise Lost. Intercession and    [J. Milton. Volume 4/270]
**Rediscovery.**    [K. Awoonor. Supp 6/20]
**Redwoods.** Among the    [E. Sill. Volume 5/234]
**Reece.** Captain    [W. Gilbert. Volume 9/297]
**Reef,** fr. The Pelican Island. The Coral    [J. Montgomery. Volume 5/396]
**Reflections.** Lovers, and a    [C. Calverley. Volume 9/409]
__    in an Iron Workds.    [H. MacDiarmid. Supp 2/30]
__    in an Iron Works.    [H. MacDiarmid. Supp 2/30]
**Reformer.** The    [J. Whittier. Volume 8/157]
**Refusal** to Mourn the Death, by Fire of a Child in London. A    [D. Thomas. Supp 2/368]
**Regiment.** The Black    [G. Boker. Volume 8/393]
**Rei.** Panta    [T. Heraty. Supp 7/93]
**Reign.** Jesus Shall    [I. Watts. Volume 4/96]
**Release.** A Frightful    [G. Stein. Supp 5/292]
**Relief** of Lucknow. The    [R. Lowell. Volume 8/296]
**Religion** and Doctrine.    [J. Hay. Volume 4/219]
__    of Hudibras, fr. Hudibras. The    [S. Butler. Volume 4/228]
**Reliques.** King John and the Abbot of Canterbury, fr. Percy's    [Unknown. Volume 9/241]
**Remember.** I    [R. Sanchez. Supp 4/254]
**Remember"**  " I Remember, I    [T. Hood. Volume 1/83]
**Remember,** I Remember"  " I    [T. Hood. Volume 1/83]
**Remembered.** I    [S. Teasdale. Supp 1/294]
**Remembering.**    [Ping Hsin. Supp 5/114]
__    Nat Turner.    [S. Brown. Supp 2/87]
**Reminiscence.**    [Ho Ch'i-Fang. Supp 7/6]
**Remonstrance** with the Snails.    [Unknown. Volume 5/352]
**Remorse.** Conscience and    [P. Dunbar. Volume 4/326]
**Remorse,** fr. Othello. Othello's    [W. Shakespeare. Volume 9/67]
**Renascence.**    [E. Millay. Supp 1/214]
**Rend,** Willie"  " My Heid is Like to    [W. Motherwell. Volume 3/49]
**Renouncement.**    [A. Meynell. Volume 2/338]
**Rent.** Live In My Heart And Pay No    [S. Lover. Volume 2/180]
**Renunciation.** A    [E. Vere. Volume 2/246]
**Repentance,** fr. Hamlet. Prayer and    [W. Shakespeare. Volume 4/118]
**Reply.** The Nymph's    [S. Raleigh. Volume 2/150]
**Report** on Experience.    [E. Blunden. Supp 2/46]
**Reproach.**    [M. Iqbal. Supp 7/60]
**Republic.** Battle-Hymn of the    [J. Howe. Volume 8/172]
**Republic,** fr. The Building of the Ship. The    [H. Longfellow. Volume 8/94]
**Request.** A    [K. Das. Supp 5/58]
**Requiem.**    [G. Lunt. Volume 8/388]

**Requiescat.**    [M. Arnold. Volume 3/307]
**Resignation.**    [H. Longfellow. Volume 3/430]
__. The    [T. Chatterton. Volume 4/368]
**Resolution** of Dependence.    [G. Barker. Supp 2/288]
**Resolution,** In A Sonnet, fr. Fair Virtue. The Author's    [G. Wither. Volume 2/238]
**Rest.**    [M. Howland. Volume 3/397]
__    [M. Woods. Volume 6/431]
__    From Loving and Be Living"  "    [C. Day Lewis. Supp 2/122]
__    In This Bosom, fr. Irish Melodies. Come,    [T. Moore. Volume 2/332]
__    Not! Haste Not!    [J. Goethe. Volume 6/414]
**Resto** Mare. Tonis Ad    [J. Swift. Volume 9/319]
**Restraint"**  " With My Customary    [D. Brutus. Supp 6/101]
**Resurrection** of the Daughter.    [N. Shange. Supp 5/266]
**Resurrection,** fr. In Memoriam. Personal    [A. Tennyson. Volume 3/352]
**Resuscitated** Now. I Am    [E. Gutierrez. Supp 6/174]
**Retort.** The    [G. Morris. Volume 2/431]
**Retribution.**    [F. Logau. Volume 6/226]
**Return.** The    [J. Bishop. Supp 2/27]
__. The Lost Son: The    [T. Roethke. Supp 2/209]
__    of Spring.    [P. Ronsard. Volume 5/78]
**Return:** 001. The    [A. Bontemps. Supp 4/124]
__    002. The    [A. Bontemps. Supp 4/124]
__    003. The    [A. Bontemps. Supp 4/124]
__    004. The    [A. Bontemps. Supp 4/125]
**Returned.** Disdain    [T. Carew. Volume 2/20]
**Returning.** About    [Agyeya. Supp 7/39]
**Returns,** My Bosom Burns"  "The Day    [R. Burns. Volume 2/422]
**Reunion.** About the    [J. Jordan. Supp 4/197]
**Reunited** Love.    [R. Blackmore. Volume 2/425]
**Revelation.**    [E. Gosse. Supp 1/145]
__    [R. Warren. Supp 2/131]
__. Mysticism Has Not the Patience to Wait for God's    [R. Eberhart. Supp 2/128]
**Revelry** of the Dying.    [B. Dowling. Volume 9/170]
**Revenge.**    [C. Anwar. Supp 7/80]
__. The    [A. Tennyson. Volume 7/383]
__. Time's    [Agathias. Volume 3/72]
**Reverie.** Pastor's    [W. Gladden. Volume 4/313]
**Revolutionary** Dreams.    [N. Giovanni. Supp 4/222]
**Revolutionists.** Room with    [E. Rolfe. Supp 2/218]
**Rex.** Guiliemus    [T. Aldrich. Volume 7/53]
**Rheims.** The Jackdaw of    [R. Barham. Volume 9/331]
**Rhine.** Bingen on the    [C. Norton. Volume 8/221]
__. On the    [W. Bowles. Volume 5/207]
__. The Watch on the    [M. Schneckenburger. Volume 8/80]
**Rhine,** fr. Childe Harolde. The    [G. Byron. Volume 7/169]
**Rhodora.** The    [R. Emerson. Volume 5/252]
**Rhoecus.**    [J. Lowell. Volume 6/103]
**Rhubarb.**    [G. Stein. Supp 5/295]
**Rhyme.** Railroad    [J. Saxe. Volume 9/431]
__    on a Rough Matter. A Rough    [C. Kingsley. Volume 3/191]
**Rhythm.** Plucking Out a    [L. Inada. Supp 4/4]
**Rice** Grains.    [A. Hernandez. Supp 7/178]
**Richard** Cory.    [E. Robinson. Supp 1/266]
__    III. End of the Civil War, fr. King    [W. Shakespeare. Volume 8/424]
**Riddle.** A    [C. Fanshawe. Volume 9/450]
**Riddlers.** The    [W. De La Mare. Supp 1/108]
**Ride.** Army Correspondents Last    [G. Townsend. Volume 8/408]
__. Colorado Morton's    [L. Bacon. Supp 1/21]
__. Sheridan's    [T. Read. Volume 8/383]
__. The King of Denmark's    [C. Norton. Volume 3/346]
__. The Lion's    [F. Freiligrath. Volume 5/355]

___. The Wild    [L. Guiney. Volume 6/259]
___. Train    [J. Wheelwright. Supp 2/56]
___. Fast. The Dead    [R. Blackmur. Supp 2/107]
Riding Down.    [N. Perry. Volume 1/206]
___    Horses" " Strong Men,    [G. Brooks. Supp 5/38]
Ridinghood. Red    [N. Alterman. Supp 7/236]
Riel. Herve    [R. Browning. Volume 7/341]
Rienzi. Rienzi to the Romans, fr.    [M. Mitford. Volume 8/123]
___    to the Romans, fr. Rienzi    [M. Mitford. Volume 8/123]
Right Must Win. The    [F. Faber. Volume 4/299]
___    On: Wite America.    [S. Sanchez. Supp 4/187]
Rill" " By Cool Siloam's Shady    [R. Herber. Volume 1/122]
Rime of the Ancient Mariner.    [S. Coleridge. Volume 6/130]
Rimini, fr. Divina Commedia: Inferno. Francesca Da    [Dante Alighieri. Volume 2/99]
Ring. An Etruscan    [J. Mackail. Volume 7/149]
___. The    [D. Wakoski. Supp 5/323]
___. What Is the Name of a    [G. Stein. Supp 5/295]
___    To-Night. Curfew Must Not    [R. Thorpe. Volume 2/303]
Rise of Man. The    [J. Chadwick. Volume 4/311]
Risen" "The Women Thought Christ    [E. Manner. Supp 5/155]
Rita and the Gun.    [M. Darwish. Supp 7/263]
Ritter Hugo.    [C. Leland. Volume 9/324]
Rivalry In Love.    [W. Walsh. Volume 2/225]
River. By the Alma    [D. Craik. Volume 8/292]
___. Islands in the    [Agyeya. Supp 7/45]
___. My    [E. Morike. Volume 5/205]
___. Over the    [N. Priest. Volume 3/406]
___. San-Kan    [Ya Hsuan. Supp 7/31]
___. Song of the    [C. Kingsley. Volume 5/201]
___    an Death. The    [B. Al-Sayyab. Supp 7/233]
___    God. The    [S. Smith. Supp 2/104]
___    of Colors. A    [Liang Shang Ch'uan. Supp 7/21]
River, Hants. Youth and Age on Beaulieu    [J. Betjeman. Supp 2/138]
___    Smile. Brown    [J. Toomer. Supp 4/91]
Rivers. The Negro Speaks of    [L. Hughes. Supp 4/130]
Riverside. Summer Night,    [S. Teasdale. Supp 1/294]
Rizpah.    [A. Tennyson. Volume 9/151]
Roach. St.    [M. Rukeyser. Supp 5/244]
Road. On The    [P. Dunbar. Volume 2/292]
___. The Joys of the    [B. Carman. Volume 1/253]
___. The Rolling English    [G. Chesterton. Supp 1/81]
___. The Southern    [D. Randall. Supp 4/155]
___    from Election to Christmas. The    [O. Williams. Supp 2/80]
___    Sabotage.    [To Huu. Supp 7/194]
___    to Chorrera. On the    [A. Bates. Volume 2/47]
Roads. Memento of    [N. Alterman. Supp 7/235]
___. Old    [E. Chuilleanain. Supp 5/191]
Roadside Stone During the First Eruption. Written on a    [P. Cuadra. Supp 6/161]
Roast Beef of Old England. The    [H. Fielding. Volume 8/13]
Robert Browning.    [W. Landor. Volume 7/89]
___    Browning. The Burial of    [M. Field. Volume 7/89]
___    Haydon. To Benjamin    [J. Keats. Volume 7/69]
___    of Lincoln.    [W. Bryant. Volume 5/310]
___    of Sicily. King    [H. Longfellow. Volume 4/148]

Robin. The English    [H. Weir. Volume 5/327]
___    Adair.    [L. Keppel. Volume 3/134]
___    Gray. Auld    [L. Barnard. Volume 3/32]
___    Hood. " I am a Friar of Orders Gray", fr.    [J. O'Keeffe. Volume 9/247]
___    Hood and Allan-A-Dale.    [Unknown. Volume 7/375]
Robinson Thinks, fr. The Biglow Papers. What Mr.    [J. Lowell. Volume 9/339]
Roc. Ode to the    [W. Courthope. Volume 9/437]
Rock. Colloquy in Black    [R. Lowell. Supp 2/388]
___. The Inchcape    [R. Southey. Volume 5/431]
___    and the Sea. The    [C. Gilman. Volume 5/418]
___    Me to Sleep.    [E. Akers. Volume 1/284]
___    of Ages" "    [E. Rice. Volume 4/85]
___    of Kiltearen. The Black    [A. Young. Supp 2/2]
Rocked in the Cradle of the Deep" "    [E. Willard. Volume 4/30]
Rocks. Among the    [R. Browning. Volume 5/430]
___. Black    [L. Mar. Supp 4/33]
Rod: 006. The Flowering of the    [H. Doolittle. Supp 5/76]
___    007. The Flowering of the    [H. Doolittle. Supp 5/77]
___    008. The Flowering of the    [H. Doolittle. Supp 5/78]
___    009. The Flowering of the    [H. Doolittle. Supp 5/78]
___    010. The Flowering of the    [H. Doolittle. Supp 5/79]
Roderick Dhu, fr. The Lady of the Lake. Fitz-James and    [S. Scott. Volume 7/404]
Rodman Drake. Joseph    [F. Halleck. Volume 7/91]
Roller. To a Steam    [M. Moore. Supp 5/185]
Rolling English Road. The    [G. Chesterton. Supp 1/81]
Roma. The White Peacock, fr. Sospiri Di    [W. Sharp. Volume 7/175]
Roma, fr. Poesie    [G. Carducci. Volume 6/310]
Roman Army, fr. Catiline. Catiline to the    [G. Croly. Volume 8/188]
roman Campagna. A View Across the    [E. Browning. Volume 7/187]
Roman Father, fr. Virginia. The    [L. Macaulay; Thomas Babington. Volume 9/16]
___    Poem Number Thirteen.    [J. Jordan. Supp 4/196]
___    Poem Number Two.    [J. Jordan. Supp 5/124]
Romance of the Swan's Nest. The    [E. Browning. Volume 1/123]
Romans, fr. Rienzi. Rienzi to the    [M. Mitford. Volume 8/123]
Romantic Fool.    [H. Monro. Supp 1/224]
Rome. February in    [E. Gosse. Volume 7/185]
___. To    [F. Quevedo Y. Villegas. Volume 7/177]
Rome, fr. Childe Harold. Saint Peter's at    [G. Byron. Volume 7/186]
Romeo and Juliet. Queen Mab, fr.    [W. Shakespeare. Volume 6/13]
Ronsard. After    [C. Williams. Supp 1/315]
Roof. Rain on the    [C. Kinney. Volume 1/88]
Room. Concerning a    [S. Tanikawa. Supp 7/132]
___. To My Son Parker, Asleep in the Next    [B. Kaufman. Supp 4/185]
___    with Revolutionists.    [E. Rolfe. Supp 2/218]
Roosevelt. To    [R. Dario. Supp 6/163]
Roosters Will Crow When We Die" "The    [C. Meireles. Supp 5/160]
Rory O'More.    [S. Lover. Volume 2/172]
Rosalynd.    [T. Lodge. Volume 2/19]
Rosalynd's Complaint.    [T. Lodge. Volume 2/89]
Rosario Beach House, 001. Bronchitis: The    [A. Rodriguez. Supp 4/279]

Beach House, 002. Bronchitis: The    [A. Rodriguez. Supp 4/280]

Beach House, 003. Bronchitis: The    [A. Rodriguez. Supp 4/280]

Beach House, 004. Bronchitis: The    [A. Rodriguez. Supp 4/281]

Beach House, 005. Bronchitis: The    [A. Rodriguez. Supp 4/282]

**Rose.** Our Wee White    [G. Massey. Volume 1/64]

__. Sea    [H. Doolittle. Supp 5/66]

__. The Moss    [F. Krummacher. Volume 5/281]

__. The Shadow    [R. Rogers. Volume 3/53]

__. The White    [Unknown. Volume 2/36]

__ and the Gauntlet. The    [J. Sterling. Volume 9/131]

__ Aylmer.    [W. Landor. Volume 2/375]

__ Motif. Second    [C. Meireles. Supp 5/161]

__ of Summer. The First    [O. Herford. Volume 1/154]

__ of Summer", fr. Irish Melodies. "' Tis the Last    [T. Moore. Volume 5/283]

**Rose"** " Go, Lovely    [E. Waller. Volume 2/37]

__    " O, My Luve's Like a Red, Red    [R. Burns. Volume 3/99]

**Rose-bush.** The    [Unknown. Volume 6/233]

**Rose?"** " Has Summer Come Without the    [A. O'Shaughnessy. Volume 3/54]

**Roses.** Ashes of    [E. Eastman. Volume 3/51]

__ in the Bosom of Castara. To    [W. Habington. Volume 2/34]

**Rough** Matter. A Rough Rhyme on a    [C. Kingsley. Volume 3/191]

__ Rhyme on a Rough Matter. A    [C. Kingsley. Volume 3/191]

**Rouse.** Give a    [R. Browning. Volume 8/271]

**Rowing.**    [A. Sexton. Supp 5/256]

**Rows.** Fir Trees in    [C. Anwar. Supp 7/86]

**Royal.** Jardin Du Palais    [D. Gascoyne. Supp 2/384]

__ George. On the Loss of the    [W. Cowper. Volume 9/182]

**Rudolph** the Headsman, fr. This Is It    [O. Holmes. Volume 9/293]

**Rue** My Heart is Laden"    " With    [A. Housman. Supp 1/169]

**Ruins.** The Castle    [W. Barnes. Volume 7/213]

__ of a Country Inn. On the    [P. Freneau. Volume 6/315]

**Rule,** Britannia, fr. Alfred    [J. Thomson. Volume 8/11]

**Ruling** Passion, fr. Moral Essays. The    [A. Pope. Volume 6/294]

**Runagate.** Runagate    [R. Hayden. Supp 4/150]

__ Runagate.    [R. Hayden. Supp 4/150]

**Runaway** Slave. Song to the    [Unknown (African American). Supp 4/53]

**Runner** with the Lots. The    [L. Adams. Supp 2/71]

**Runs** into Heaven. 23rd Street    [K. Patchen. Supp 2/255]

**Rural** Maids! O, Fairest of    [W. Bryant. Volume 2/46]

**Rus** in Urbe.    [C. Scott. Volume 5/25]

**Rustic** Lad's Lament in the Town. The    [D. Moir. Volume 3/131]

**Rustum.** Oxus, fr. Sohrab and    [M. Arnold. Volume 5/207]

__. The Slaying of Sohrab, fr. Sohrab and    [M. Arnold. Volume 9/28]

**Ruth.**    [T. Hood. Volume 1/219]

**Rye.** Comin' Through The    [R. Burns. Volume 2/108]

**Ryton** Firs.    [L. Abercrombie. Supp 1/5]

**Sabbath.** Song of the    [K. Molodowsky. Supp 5/173]

__. The Poor Man's Day, fr. The    [A. Barbauld. Volume 4/193]

__ Hymn On the Mountains.    [J. Blackie. Volume 4/190]

__ Morning. The    [J. Leyden. Volume 4/192]

**Sabotage.** Road    [To Huu. Supp 7/194]

**Sack** of Baltimore. The    [T. Davis. Volume 9/127]

__ of the City. The    [V. Hugo. Volume 9/26]

**Sacred** Elegy V: 001.    [G. Barker. Supp 2/290]

__ Elegy V: 002.    [G. Barker. Supp 2/290]

__ Elegy V: 003.    [G. Barker. Supp 2/291]

__ Elegy V: 004.    [G. Barker. Supp 2/291]

**Sacrifice.** The Mother's    [S. Smith. Volume 1/24]

__. Too Great a    [Unknown. Volume 9/394]

__ of Polyxena, fr. Hecuba    [Euripides. Volume 9/5]

**Sad** is Our Youth, For It Is Ever Going"  "    [A. De Vere. Volume 3/225]

__ Moonlit Night.    [H. Sakutaro. Supp 7/104]

__ Soul"  " Sit Down,    [B. Procter. Volume 4/372]

**Saddened** Tramp. A    [Unknown. Volume 9/395]

**Saddest** Fate. The    [Unknown. Volume 3/247]

__ Lines"  " Tonight I Can Write the    [P. Neruda. Supp 6/131]

**Sadness.** Against    [N. Zach. Supp 7/257]

**Saga.** Frithiof at the court of Angantyr, fr. Frithiof    [E. Tegner. Volume 7/289]

**Sage** Counsel.    [A. Quiller-Couch. Volume 1/195]

**Said.** What My Lover    [H. Greene. Volume 2/279]

__ I Not So.    [G. Herbert. Volume 4/282]

**Said"** "The Wooden Horse Then    [J. Mastoraki. Supp 5/157]

**Sailor.** Napoleon and the British    [T. Campbell. Volume 7/347]

**Sailor,** fr. The Tent on the Beach. To Her Absent    [J. Whittier. Volume 3/124]

**Sailor's** Consolation. The    [W. Pitt. Volume 5/435]

**Saint** Agnes.    [A. Tennyson. Volume 4/416]

__ Agnes. The Eve of    [J. Keats. Volume 2/312]

**St.** Aloy's. City Bells, fr. The Lay of    [R. Barham. Volume 7/147]

**Saint** Anthony's Sermon to the Fishes.    [Unknown. Volume 9/239]

__ Augustine. Passage in the Life of    [Unknown. Volume 4/1]

__ Augustine. The Ladder of    [H. Longfellow. Volume 4/294]

**St.** Bartholomew's Eve. For    [M. Cowley. Supp 2/59]

__ Cecilia's Day. Song for    [W. Auden. Supp 2/167]

**Saint** Cecilia's Day, 1687. A Song for    [J. Dryden. Volume 6/364]

__ Christopher.    [D. Craik. Volume 4/296]

**St.** Keyne. Well of    [R. Southey. Volume 9/204]

__ Nicholas. A Visit from    [C. Moore. Volume 1/157]

**Saint** Paul. The Conversion of    [J. Keble. Volume 4/82]

__ Peter's at Rome, fr. Childe Harold    [G. Byron. Volume 7/186]

**St.** Roach    [M. Rukeyser. Supp 5/244]

**Saint"**  " To Heaven Approached a Sufi    [J. Rumi. Volume 4/405]

**Saints** in Glory, fr. The Diving Comedy. Paradise: The    [Dante Alighieri. Volume 4/445]

**Saitire** XIII. Conscience, frm    [Juvenal. Volume 4/329]

**Sake.** For Charlie's    [J. Palmer. Volume 3/411]

**Salutation.**    [T. Eliot. Supp 1/114]

**Salve** Auction. The    [F. Harper. Supp 4/63]

**Salvos** for Randolph Bourne: 001.    [H. Gregory. Supp 2/65]

__    for Randolph Bourne: 002.    [H. Gregory. Supp 2/65]

___.  Morning    [J. Baillie. Volume 5/39]
___.  Morning    [S. Plath. Supp 5/212]
___.  Owl    [M. Atwood. Supp 5/20]
___.  Patriotic    [E. Arndt. Volume 8/76]
___.  Scythe    [A. Lang. Volume 7/248]
___.  Sleigh    [G. Pettee. Volume 5/189]
___.  Somebody's    [D. Parker. Supp 1/248]
___.  Spirit's    [L. Bogan. Supp 5/34]
___.  Spring    [B. Carman. Volume 1/248]
___.  Summer    [G. Barker. Supp 2/293]
___.  Sword    [K. Korner. Volume 8/217]
___.  The    [Ho Ch'i-Fang. Supp 7/4]
___.  The Angels'    [E. Sears. Volume 4/48]
___.  The Cavalier's    [W. Motherwell. Volume 8/270]
___.  The Dead Man Asks for a    [Unknown (African American). Supp 6/3]
___.  The Exile's    [R. Gilfillan. Volume 8/51]
___.  The Hunter's    [B. Procter. Volume 5/156]
___.  The Milkmaid's    [S. Dobell. Volume 2/285]
___.  The Poet's Bridal-Day    [A. Cunningham. Volume 2/414]
___.  The Singer of One    [H. Beers. Volume 6/343]
___.  The Spinning-Wheel    [J. Waller. Volume 2/294]
___.  The Wind's    [W. Rendra. Supp 7/101]
___.  Thread and    [J. Palmer. Volume 1/113]
song.  To J.H.; four years old: a nursery    [L. Hunt. Volume 1/33]
Song.  Walking    [C. Williams. Supp 1/315]
___.  Winter    [L. Holty. Volume 5/186]
___.  at Night.    [L. Lee. Supp 2/341]
___.  For a Slight Voice.    [L. Bogan. Supp 5/33]
___.  for My Father.    [J. Hagedorn. Supp 4/24]
___.  for Saint Cecilia's Day, 1687. A    [J. Dryden. Volume 6/364]
___.  for Simoisius. A Friend's    [L. Guiney. Supp 1/154]
___.  for St. Cecilia's Day    [W. Auden. Supp 2/167]
___.  in the Front Yard. A    [G. Brooks. Supp 5/36]
___.  of Abraham in Fire. The    [A. Shamlu. Supp 7/211]
___.  of Bullets. The    [J. Hagedorn. Supp 4/29]
___.  of Clan-Alpine, fr. The Lady of the Lake    [S. Scott. Volume 8/305]
___.  of Derivations. A    [A. Meynell. Supp 1/213]
___.  of Eglia.    [M. Brooks. Volume 3/138]
___.  of Hiawatha. The Death of Minnehaha, fr. The    [H. Longfellow. Volume 3/319]
___.  of Marion's Men.    [W. Byrant. Volume 8/330]
___.  of Myself. Myself, fr. The    [W. Whitman. Volume 7/102]
___.  of Myself. What is the Grass?, fr. The    [W. Whitman. Volume 6/198]
___.  of One Eleven Years in Prison.    [G. Canning. Volume 9/294]
___.  of Other Lives.    [L. Marechal. Supp 6/105]
___.  of Seasons. A    [E. MacDonald. Volume 5/191]
___.  of the Bell. Labor Done, fr.    [J. Schiller. Volume 6/412]
___.  of the Brook, fr. The Brook: An Idyl    [A. Tennyson. Volume 5/194]
___.  Of The Camp. The    [B. Taylor. Volume 2/362]
___.  of the Chattahoochee.    [S. Lanier. Volume 7/242]
___.  of the Demented Priest. The    [J. Berryman. Supp 2/329]
___.  of the East.    [A. Mutis. Supp 6/133]
___.  of the Emigrants in Bermuda.    [A. Marvell. Volume 5/400]
___.  of the Greek Poet, fr. Don Juan    [G. Byron. Volume 8/130]
___.  of the Greeks.    [T. Campbell. Volume 8/197]

___   of the Lower Classes. The    [E. Jones. Volume 6/391]
___   of the Milkmaid, fr. Queen Mary    [A. Tennyson. Volume 2/107]
___   of the Mocking-bird. Moonlight    [W. Hayne. Volume 6/179]
___   of the Old Mother. The    [W. Yeats. Volume 1/284]
___   of the River.    [C. Kingsley. Volume 5/201]
___   of the Sabbath.    [K. Molodowsky. Supp 5/173]
___   of the Savoyards. The    [H. Blood. Volume 3/248]
___   of the Shirt. The    [T. Hood. Volume 3/199]
___   of the Silent Land.    [J. Von Salis. Volume 4/388]
___   of the Smoke. The    [W. Du Bois. Supp 4/65]
___   of the Summer Winds.    [G. Darley. Volume 5/99]
___   of the Sun.    [J. Toomer. Supp 4/90]
___   of the Three Seeds in the Macaw's Beak.    [E. Coatsworth. Supp 1/85]
___   of the Western Men.    [R. Hawker. Volume 8/136]
___   of Three Friends. The Prairie Fire, fr. The    [J. Neihardt. Supp 1/240]
___   on Autumn Harvest. Short    [Li Chi. Supp 7/11]
___   To His Wife. The Poet's    [B. Procter. Volume 2/421]
___   to the Argentine, sel.    [R. Dario. Supp 6/169]
___   to the Runaway Slave.    [Unknown (African American). Supp 4/53]
___   Without Words.    [P. Pietri. Supp 4/256]
Song"  The " Old, Old    [C. Kingsley. Volume 1/230]
Song,  fr. A Midsummer Night's Dream. Fairy's    [W. Shakespeare. Volume 6/16]
___   fr. Alice of Monmouth. Calvary    [E. Stedman. Volume 8/365]
___   fr. Bitter-Sweet. Cradle    [J. Holland. Volume 1/13]
___   fr. Facade. Dark    [E. Sitwell. Supp 2/12]
___   fr. Idyls of the King. Enid's    [A. Tennyson. Volume 6/266]
___   fr. Inner Temple Masque. The Sirens'    [W. Browne. Volume 6/79]
___   fr. Music's Duel. The Nightingales'    [R. Crashaw. Volume 5/306]
___   fr. Pippa Passes    [R. Browning. Volume 4/1]
___   fr. The Bacchae. Choral    [Euripides. Volume 5/215]
___   fr. The Bell-Founder. Labor    [D. MacCarthy. Volume 1/327]
___   fr. The Dynasts. Hussar's    [T. Hardy. Supp 1/159]
___   fr. The Lady of the Lake    [S. Scott. Volume 3/101]
___   fr. The Miller's Daughter    [A. Tennyson. Volume 2/102]
___   fr. The White Company. The Bowman's    [S. Doyle. Volume 8/12]
___   fr. Wilhelm Meister. Mignon's    [J. Goethe. Volume 6/313]
___   fr. Woo'd And Married And A    [J. Baillie. Volume 2/411]
___   Shall I, Wasting In Despair. Answer To Master Wither's    [B. Jonson. Volume 2/239]
Song:  On May Morning.    [J. Milton. Volume 5/85]
___   Survival. Indian    [L. Silko. Supp 4/331]
Songs.  Sentinel    [A. Ryan. Volume 8/452]
___.  The Cause of the South, fr. Sentinel    [A. Ryan. Volume 8/451]
songs  and Mine. Thy    [J. Dorr. Volume 6/355]
Songs  of Ariel, fr. The Tempest    [W. Shakespeare.

5/99]
__　Wish.　[F. Lima. Supp 4/244]
Summer", fr. Irish Melodies. "' Tis the Last Rose of
　　[T. Moore. Volume 5/283]
Summit.　[Chong Chi-Yong. Supp 7/148]
Sun.　[Pak Tu-Jin. Supp 7/152]
__.　Monterrey　[A. Reyes. Supp 6/149]
__.　Song of the　[J. Toomer. Supp 4/90]
__　Gods Have Sun Spots.　[D. Wakoski. Supp
　　5/321]
__　Spots. Sun Gods Have　[D. Wakoski. Supp
　　5/321]
Sun", fr. Cymbeline. " Fear No More the Heat O' the
　　[W. Shakespeare. Volume 3/328]
Sun-dial. The　[A. Dobson. Volume 3/15]
Sunday. The Dome of　[K. Shapiro. Supp 2/312]
__　Morning.　[L. MacNeice. Supp 2/184]
__　Morning Bells.　[D. Craik. Volume 4/190]
Sunday" " Today Is　[G. Fuertes. Supp 5/95]
Sunday, August 11, 1974.　[M. Algarin. Supp 4/283]
Sunday: The Love Story. When You Have Forgotten
　　[G. Brooks. Supp 4/156]
Sundays. Those Winter　[R. Hayden. Supp 4/149]
Sung to the Tune … We Wait, 3. (To Be　[R.
　　Conley. Supp 4/310]
Sunken City. The　[W. Mueller. ]
Sunlight on the Garden" "The　[L. MacNeice. Supp
　　2/185]
Sunrise.　[C. Turner. Volume 4/20]
__.　Dirge for the New　[E. Sitwell. Supp 5/275]
__　Over the Gobi.　[Li Ying. Supp 7/15]
__　Song. A　[S. Lanier. Volume 6/277]
Sunrise: A Hymn of the Marshes.　[S. Lanier.
　　Volume 5/257]
Sunset City. The　[H. Cornwell. Volume 7/158]
__　of the City. A　[G. Brooks. Supp 5/42]
Sunset, fr. Queen Mab　[P. Shelley. Volume 5/48]
Suppliant. The　[E. Gosse. Supp 1/145]
Suppose and Eyes.　[G. Stein. Supp 5/294]
suppose, Lie Down Together" " In heaven, I　[C.
　　Day Lewis. Supp 2/115]
Supposed Mistress. Wishes For The　[R. Crashaw.
　　Volume 2/83]
Supreme. The Love of God　[G. Tersteegen. Volume
　　4/130]
Supreme, fr. Night Thoughts. Time of the　[E.
　　Young. Volume 6/187]
Sure Help in Sorrow. God's　[A. Ulrich. Volume
　　3/236]
Surprising Conversions. After the　[R. Lowell.
　　Supp 2/386]
Surrounded by Elk Horns. Mountain Abbey,　[C.
　　Forche. Supp 5/83]
Survival. Indian Song:　[L. Silko. Supp 4/331]
__.　To Insure　[S. Ortiz. Supp 4/317]
__.　This Way.　[S. Ortiz. Supp 4/314]
Susan. Black-eyed　[J. Gay. Volume 3/102]
Susan: A Poem of Degrees. Sweet Nature's Voice, fr.
　　[A. Munby. Volume 6/350]
Swallow. The Departure of the　[W. Howitt. Volume
　　5/331]
Swallow, Flying South, fr. The Princess. O Swallow,
　　[A. Tennyson. Volume 2/100]
__　Swallow, Flying South, fr. The Princess. O
　　[A. Tennyson. Volume 2/100]
Swallowed. Cupid　[L. Hunt. Volume 2/91]
Swan. The Bereaved　[S. Smith. Supp 2/102]
__.　The Dying　[A. Tennyson. Volume 5/323]
__.　Winter　[L. Bogan. Supp 5/31]
Swans.　[L. Gluck. Supp 5/105]
Swan's Feet. The　[E. Scovell. Supp 2/188]
__　Nest. The Romance of the　[E. Browning.
　　Volume 1/123]
Swear %By That Summer Photo" " I　[B. Akhmadulina.
　　Supp 5/3]

Sweat. Heat and　[M. Serote. Supp 6/92]
Sweep Past Us. Fish and Swimmer and Lonely Birds
　　[M. Berssenbrugge. Supp 4/11]
Sweet. In the Cellar, fr. Bitter　[J. Holland.
　　Volume 1/317]
__.　The Cost of Worth, fr. Bitter　[J. Holland.
　　Volume 4/300]
__　and Keep Movin'" " Keep　[R. Burdette.
　　Volume 6/270]
__　Chariot" " Swing Low,　[Unknown (African
　　American). Supp 4/50]
__　Home, fr. Clari, the Maid of Milan. Home
　　[J. Payne. Volume 1/335]
__　Love Seemed. So　[R. Bridges. Volume 2/326]
__　Love Seemed That April Morn" " So　[R.
　　Bridges. Supp 1/75]
__　Meeting Of Desires, fr. The Angel In The House
　　[C. Patmore. Volume 2/166]
__　Nature's Voice, fr. Susan: A Poem of Degrees
　　[A. Munby. Volume 6/350]
__　Silent Thought" " When to the Sessions of
　　[W. Shakespeare. Volume 1/348]
__　Spring. Spring, the　[T. Nash. Volume 5/77]
__　Stay-at-Home.　[W. Davies. Supp 1/106]
__　Stream, That Winds" "　[W. Cowper. Volume
　　1/210]
__　Sweeting, fr. A Ms. Temp. Henry 8. My
　　[Unknown. Volume 2/253]
Sweet, fr. Tyrannic Love. Ah, How　[J. Dryden.
　　Volume 2/68]
Sweetheart Of Mine. An Old　[J. Riley. Volume
　　2/372]
Sweetheart's Face. My　[J. Wyeth. Volume 2/43]
Sweeting, fr. A Ms. Temp. Henry 8. My Sweet
　　[Unknown. Volume 2/253]
Sweetly Breathing, Vernal Air" "　[T. Carew.
　　Volume 5/82]
Swell's Soliloquy.　[Unknown. Volume 9/341]
Swimmer and Lonely Birds Sweep Past Us. Fish and
　　[M. Berssenbrugge. Supp 4/11]
Swimmers.　[L. Untermeyer. Supp 1/309]
Swimming, fr. The Two Foscari　[G. Byron. Volume
　　5/141]
Swineherd.　[E. Chuilleanain. Supp 5/188]
Swing. Boy on a　[M. Mtshali. Supp 6/83]
__.　The Grape-vine　[W. Simms. Volume 5/231]
__　Low, Sweet Chariot" "　[Unknown (African
　　American). Supp 4/50]
Swiss Peasant, fr. The Traveller. The　[O.
　　Goldsmith. Volume 1/321]
Switzerland, fr. William Tell　[J. Knowles. Volume
　　8/140]
Sword and Dagger, fr. Hudibras. Hudibras;　[S.
　　Butler. Volume 9/254]
__　Song.　[K. Korner. Volume 8/217]
Sworn By Thy God, My Jeanie" " Thou Hast　[A.
　　Cunningham. Volume 2/416]
Sylphides. Les　[L. MacNeice. Supp 2/185]
Sympathy, fr. Ion　[S. Talfourd. Volume 4/163]
Symphony. Beethoven's Third　[R. Hovey. Volume
　　6/379]
Symphony: 1. Allegro Moderato. Dark　[M. Tolson.
　　Supp 4/96]
__　2. Lento Grave. Dark　[M. Tolson. Supp
　　4/97]
__　3. Andante Sostenuto. Dark　[M. Tolson.
　　Supp 4/97]
__　4. Tempo Primo. Dark　[M. Tolson. Supp
　　4/98]
__　5. Larghetto. Dark　[M. Tolson. Supp 4/99]
__　6. Tempo di Marcia. Dark　[M. Tolson. Supp
　　4/400]

Syne. Auld Lang　[R. Burns. Volume 1/405]

__.  A Morning    [E. Sill. Volume 3/267]
__   a Design. It    [H. Sakutaro. Supp 7/109]
__   Christ Risen"  "The Women    [E. Manner. Supp 5/155]
**Thought"**  " When to the Sessions of Sweet Silent [W. Shakespeare. Volume 1/348]
**Thoughts.** Friendship, fr. Night    [R. Emerson. Volume 1/340]
__.  Matter and Man Immortal, fr. Night    [E. Young. Volume 4/406]
__.  Procrastination, fr. Night    [E. Young. Volume 6/190]
__.  Sly    [C. Patmore. Volume 2/112]
__.  Time of the Supreme, fr. Night    [E. Young. Volume 6/187]
__   About the Christian Doctrine of Eternal Hell. [S. Smith. Supp 5/279]
__   from Abroad. Home    [R. Browning. Volume 5/83]
__   of Heaven.    [R. Nicoll. Volume 4/391]
__   On The Commandments.    [G. Baker. Volume 2/125]
**Thousand** Die. Many a    [Unknown (African American). Supp 4/52]
__   More. Three Hundred    [Unknown. Volume 8/356]
**Thread** and Song.    [J. Palmer. Volume 1/113]
**Threnody.** A    [G. Lanigan. Volume 9/451]
**Thrush.** The Darling    [T. Hardy. Supp 1/156]
**Thrym.** Thor Recovers His Hammer from    [S. Saemund. Volume 7/284]
**Thunder.** June    [L. MacNeice. Supp 2/179]
**Thus** Did I Chide"  "The Forward Violet    [W. Shakespeare. Volume 2/9]
__   Longing? Why    [H. Seawall. Volume 4/127]
**Thusnelda.** Hermann and    [F. Klopstock. Volume 8/215]
**Thyrsis.** Early June, fr.    [M. Arnold. Volume 5/252]
**Tide** at Gettysburg. The High    [W. Thompson. Volume 8/398]
**Tied?:** 001. What Value Has the People Whose Tongue is [N. Qabbani. Supp 7/286]
__   002. What Value Has the People Whose Tongue is [N. Qabbani. Supp 7/286]
__   003. What Value Has the People Whose Tongue is [N. Qabbani. Supp 7/286]
__   004. What Value Has the People Whose Tongue is [N. Qabbani. Supp 7/287]
__   005. What Value Has the People Whose Tongue is [N. Qabbani. Supp 7/287]
__   006. What Value Has the People Whose Tongue is [N. Qabbani. Supp 7/287]
__   007. What Value Has the People Whose Tongue Is [N. Qabbani. Supp 7/287]
__   008. What Value Has the People Whose Tongue Is [N. Qabbani. Supp 7/287]
__   009. What Value Has the People Whose Tongue Is [N. Qabbani. Supp 7/288]
__   010. What Value Has the People Whose Tongue Is [N. Qabbani. Supp 7/288]
__   011. What Value Has the People Whose Tongue Is [N. Qabbani. Supp 7/288]
__   012. What Value Has the People Whose Tongue Is [N. Qabbani. Supp 7/288]
__   013. What Value Has the People Whose Tongue Is [N. Qabbani. Supp 7/288]
__   014. What Value Has the People Whose Tongue Is [N. Qabbani. Supp 7/289]
__   015. What Value Has the People Whose Tongue Is [N. Qabbani. Supp 7/289]
__   016. What Value Has the People Whose Tongue Is [N. Qabbani. Supp 7/289]
__   017. What Value Has the People Whose Tongue Is [N. Qabbani. Supp 7/290]

__   018. What Value Has the People Whose Tongue Is [N. Qabbani. Supp 7/290]
__   019. What Value Has the People Whose Tongue Is [N. Qabbani. Supp 7/291]
__   020. What Value Has the People Whose Tongue Is [N. Qabbani. Supp 7/291]
**Tiger.** The    [W. Blake. Volume 5/354]
**Tigress.** The    [R. Pitter. Supp 2/50]
**Tim.** Banty    [J. Hay. Volume 9/366]
**Time.**    [J. Swift. Volume 6/224]
__     [S. Takahashi. Supp 7/125]
__.  A Petition to    [B. Procter. Volume 1/334]
__.  Byron, fr. The Course of    [R. Pollok. Volume 7/59]
__.  Gleam in    [F. Daglarca. Supp 7/298]
__.  In the Mourning    [R. Hayden. Supp 4/138]
__.  Letter to    [C. Alegria. Supp 5/14]
__.  No    [Nguyen Sa. Supp 7/190]
__.  Ocean, fr. The Course of    [R. Pollok. Volume 5/379]
__.  The Disappointed Lover, fr. The Triumph of [A. Swinburne. Volume 5/378]
__   and Eternity, fr. In Memoriam    [A. Tennyson. Volume 3/351]
__   Caught in a Net.    [D. Ravikovitch. Supp 5/232]
**time** Christmas, fr. Marmion. An Old    [S. Scott. Volume 7/210]
**Time** Coming. The Good    [C. Mackay. Volume 6/399]
__   Eating.    [K. Douglas. Supp 2/407]
__   for Prayer. The    [G. Bennett. Volume 4/112]
__   of the Supreme, fr. Night Thoughts    [E. Young. Volume 6/187]
__   That I Wrote My Will"  " It Is    [W. Yeats. Supp 1/330]
__   to Dance. A    [C. Day Lewis. Supp 2/124]
__   We Climbed Snake Mountain. The    [L. Silko. Supp 4/334]
__   You Saw Miami Smile?"  " When Was the Last [A. Casiano. Supp 4/288]
**Time"**  " In the Course of    [N. Zach. Supp 7/255]
**Time, Son"**  " Once Upon a    [G. Okara. Supp 6/58]
**time."**  " When in the chronicle of wasted    [W. Shakespeare. Volume 2/3]
**Time:** 1 Minute 26 Seconds. Reading    [M. Rukeyser. Supp 2/304]
**Timepiece.** England, fr. The    [W. Cowper. Volume 8/10]
__.  Slavery, fr. The    [W. Cowper. Volume 8/135]
**Times.**    [D. Diop. Supp 6/71]
__.  Good    [L. Clifton. Supp 4/193]
__   Are In Thy Hand"  " My    [C. Hall. Volume 4/140]
__   Four; maternity. Seven    [J. Ingelow. Volume 1/36]
__   Go by Turns.    [R. Southwell. Volume 3/228]
__   One. Seven    [J. Ingelow. Volume 1/48]
__   Six. Seven    [J. Ingelow. Volume 1/290]
__   Three. Seven    [J. Ingelow. Volume 2/282]
__   Two. Seven    [J. Ingelow. Volume 1/204]
**Time's** Revenge.    [Agathias. Volume 3/72]
**Tinkler.** Jock Johnstone the    [J. Hogg. Volume 7/390]
**Tintern** Abbey.    [W. Wordsworth. Volume 5/11]
**Tired.**    [F. Johnson. Supp 4/85]
__   Mothers.    [M. Smith. Volume 1/282]
**Tirzah** and the Wide World.    [D. Ravikovitch. Supp 5/233]
**Titanic** Litany.    [J. Wheelwright. Supp 2/55]
**To---.**    [P. Shelley. Volume 6/363]
**To-day.** If We Knew; or, Blessings of    [M. Smith. Volume 1/278]
__.  The Poet of    [S. Lippincott. Volume 6/338]
**To-Night.** Curfew Must Not Ring    [R. Thorpe. Volume 2/303]

Supp 5/269]
Trooper's Death. The   [G. Herwegh. Volume 8/220]
Tropical Town.   [S. De La Selva. Supp 6/172]
Tropics in New York. The   [C. McKay. Supp 4/86]
Trout Map. The   [A. Tate. Supp 2/76]
Troy, fr. Aeneid. The Fall of   [Virgil (Publius
     Vergillius Maro). Volume 7/261]
Truck in California. Valentine for Ben Franklin Who
     Drives a   [D. Wakoski. Supp 5/322]
True Lent. A   [R. Herrick. Volume 4/303]
—   Love, fr. Midsummer Night's Dream. The Course
     of   [W. Shakespeare. Volume 3/3]
—   Minds"   " Let Me Not To The Marriage Of   [W.
     Shakespeare. Volume 2/376]
—   Philosophy of Life. The   [W. Dunbar. Volume
     6/299]
—   That Any Beauteous Thing"   " If It Be   [M.
     Angelo. Volume 2/72]
True, %This Is the Gift You Gave"   " It's   [Nirala.
     Supp 7/63]
True-Love Hath My Heart. My   [S. Sidney. Volume
     2/330]
Trust That Somehow", fr. In Memoriam. " O Yet We
     [A. Tennyson. Volume 4/243]
Truth, and the Life. The Way, the   [T. Parker.
     Volume 4/92]
Truthful James. Plain Language from   [B. Harte.
     Volume 9/374]
Tryste Noel.   [L. Guiney. Volume 4/61]
Tubal Cain.   [C. Mackay. Volume 8/426]
Tune ...  We Wait, 3. (To Be Sung to the   [R.
     Conley. Supp 4/310]
—   of the Coventry Carol. To the   [S. Smith.
     Supp 2/105]
Tunnel. The   [H. Crane. Supp 1/92]
Turk in Armenia, fr. The Purple East. The   [W.
     Watson. Volume 8/22]
Turlough MacSweeney.   [A. MacManus. Volume 8/54]
Turned. The Tables   [W. Wordsworth. Volume 5/23]
—   Into Wine. Brief: Water   [R. Crashaw.
     Volume 4/306]
Turner. Remembering Nat   [S. Brown. Supp 2/87]
Turning of the Leaves. The   [V. Watkins. Supp
     2/191]
Turns. Times Go by   [R. Southwell. Volume 3/228]
Turquoise"   " Earth and I Gave You   [N. Momaday.
     Supp 4/302]
Turret Gunner. The Death of the Ball   [R. Jarrell.
     Supp 2/330]
Turrets Hear"   " Ears in the   [D. Thomas. Supp
     2/362]
Twa Corbies. The   [Unknown. Volume 9/126]
Twelfth Night. O Mistress Mine, fr.   [W.
     Shakespeare. Volume 2/79]
—   Night. Olivia, fr.   [W. Shakespeare. Volume
     2/10]
—   Night. Unrequited Love, fr.   [W.
     Shakespeare. Volume 3/9]
Twelve"   "The Starlight's Intuitions Pierced the
     [D. Schwartz. Supp 2/309]
Twentieth Century. A Mirror for the   [Adonis. Supp
     7/278]
Twenty Years. After   [F. Tuqan. Supp 5/306]
Twilgiht Fancy. A   [D. Goodale. Volume 5/53]
Twilight. Cradle-song at   [A. Meynell. Supp 1/212]
—   at Sea.   [A. Welby. Volume 5/411]
Twinkle. Twinkle,   [Unknown. Volume 1/104]
Twinkle, Twinkle.   [Unknown. Volume 1/104]
Twos. In   [W. Gannett. Volume 2/403]
Tyrannic Love. Ah, How Sweet, fr.   [J. Dryden.
     Volume 2/68]

Ulalume.   [E. Poe. Volume 6/152]
Ullin's Daughter. Lord   [T. Campbell. Volume
     7/399]
Ultima Veritas.   [W. Gladden. Volume 4/255]
Ulysses.   [A. Tennyson. Volume 6/426]
—.  A Chinese   [S. Kazuko. Supp 5/132]
Umbrella. A Mounted   [G. Stein. Supp 5/292]
Una and the Lion, fr. The Faerie Queene   [E.
     Spenser. Volume 6/110]
—   and the Red Crosse Knight, fr. The Faerie
     Queene   [E. Spenser. Volume 6/108]
Unadorned, fr. Elegies. Beauty   [S. Propertius.
     Volume 6/282]
Uncertainty.   [B. Reyna. Supp 6/146]
Unchanging.   [F. Von Bodenstedt. Volume 3/242]
Unco Guid. To the   [R. Burns. Volume 4/320]
Unconfessed. Forever   [R. Milnes. Volume 2/241]
Understand. A Poem Some People Will Have to   [L.
     Jones. Supp 4/178]
Understand"   " Now I   [T. Heraty. Supp 7/95]
Underworld. Orpheus in the   [D. Gascoyne. Supp
     2/385]
Undeveloped Lives.   [W. Lecky. Volume 6/268]
Undiscovered Country. The   [E. Stedman. Volume
     4/387]
—   Planet. The   [L. Lee. Supp 2/343]
Unfinished Prayer. The   [Unknown. Volume 1/43]
Unillumined Verge"   "The   [R. Bridges. Volume
     3/308]
Unimplored Beloved. To the   [E. Shanks. Supp
     1/284]
Uninhabited City: 001. The   [E. Cardenal. Supp
     6/153]
—   City: 002. The   [E. Cardenal. Supp 6/154]
Universal Prayer. The   [A. Pope. Volume 4/11]
University Student"   " I Am a   [S. Wongthed. Supp
     7/185]
Unknown Bards"   " O Black and   [J. Johnson. Supp
     4/67]
—   Poets, fr. The Excursion   [W. Wordsworth.
     Volume 6/339]
Unlocks the Dirge of the Sea"   " Night's Fall   [W.
     Graham. Supp 2/402]
Unmusical Birds, fr. The Task   [W. Cowper. Volume
     5/309]
Unrequited Love, fr. Twelfth Night   [W.
     Shakespeare. Volume 3/9]
Unseen Playmate. The   [R. Stevenson. Volume 1/131]
—   Spirits.   [N. Willis. Volume 3/204]
Unspeakable, fr. In Memoriam. Grief   [A. Tennyson.
     Volume 3/349]
Upper Lambourne.   [J. Betjeman. Supp 2/138]
Upstate.   [D. Walcott. Supp 4/167]
Urbe. Rus in   [C. Scott. Volume 5/25]
Urn. Ode on a Grecian   [J. Keats. Volume 7/136]
Urn"   " Then They Paraded Pompey's   [J. Mastoraki.
     Supp 5/156]
Ury. Barclay of   [J. Whittier. Volume 7/429]
USA. We Wait, 4.   [R. Conley. Supp 4/310]

V-A-S-E. The   [J. Roche. Volume 9/446]
V-Letter.   [K. Shapiro. Supp 2/323]
V: 001. Sacred Elegy   [G. Barker. Supp 2/290]
—   002. Sacred Elegy   [G. Barker. Supp 2/290]
—   003. Sacred Elegy   [G. Barker. Supp 2/291]
—   004. Sacred Elegy   [G. Barker. Supp 2/291]
Vacations.   [F. Lima. Supp 4/243]
Vagabond. The Old   [P. De Beranger. Volume 3/188]
Vagabonds. The   [J. Trowbridge. Volume 6/260]
Vain Delights", fr. The Nice Valour. " Hence, All Ye
     [J. Fletcher. Volume 3/160]
Vale. Ave Atque   [R. Watson. Volume 6/191]

_ Thus Did I Chide" "The Forward    [W. Shakespeare. Volume 2/9]
**Violets.** To    [R. Herrick. Volume 5/253]
**Viper.** The    [R. Pitter. Supp 2/51]
**Virgil.** To    [A. Tennyson. Volume 7/37]
**Virginal.** A    [E. Pound. Supp 1/251]
**Virgins.** To the    [R. Herrick. Volume 1/229]
**Virgins,** fr. Idyls of the King: Guinevere. The Foolish    [A. Tennyson. Volume 4/331]
**Virtue.** The Author's Resolution, In A Sonnet, fr. Fair    [G. Wither. Volume 2/238]
_ Immortal.    [G. Herbert. Volume 3/254]
**Vision.** The Inner    [W. Wordsworth. Volume 6/322]
_. The Mystics    [M. Blind. Volume 4/142]
_ of a Fair Woman.    [E. Sharp. Volume 2/25]
_ of Beauty. A    [B. Jonson. Volume 2/23]
_ of Delight. Fantasy, fr. The    [B. Johnson. Volume 6/3]
_ of Sir Launfal. The    [J. Lowell. Volume 4/172]
_ of the Cuckoo.    [R. Pitter. Supp 5/206]
**Visit** from St. Nicholas. A    [C. Moore. Volume 1/157]
**Visitants.** The    [M. Waddington. Supp 5/317]
**Visitors.** My    [F. Faiz. Supp 7/174]
**Vita.** Mors Et    [S. Waddington. Volume 1/396]
_. Sic    [H. King. Volume 3/253]
**Vitae.** Curriculum    [I. Bachmann. Supp 5/25]
**Vivien.** Not At All, Or All In All, fr. Merlin and    [A. Tennyson. Volume 2/250]
**Vocables** of Love" " O    [L. Riding. Supp 1/265]
**Voice.** Song For a Slight    [L. Bogan. Supp 5/33]
_. The    [W. Gibson. Supp 1/141]
_ of the Diving Herdsman.    [Unknown (African American). Supp 6/10]
_ of the Grass. The    [S. Roberts. Volume 5/237]
**Voice,** fr. Susan: A Poem of Degrees. Sweet Nature's    [A. Munby. Volume 6/350]
**Voiceless.** The    [O. Holmes. Volume 3/172]
**Vowels:** an Enigma. The    [J. Swift. Volume 9/311]
**Vows.** Not Ours the    [B. Barton. Volume 2/450]
**Voyage.** The    [C. Mason. Volume 4/38]
_. The Second    [E. Chuilleanain. Supp 5/193]
_ of Sleep. The    [A. Eaton. Volume 6/438]
**Vulture.** The Black    [G. Sterling. Supp 1/288]


**Wadsworth** Longfellow. To Henry    [J. Lowell. Volume 7/106]
**Wail** of Prometheus Bound, fr. Prometheus. The    [Aeschylus. Volume 3/156]
**Wait.** The Useless    [G. Mistral. Supp 6/124]
_ for God's Revelation. Mysticism Has Not the Patience to    [R. Eberhart. Supp 2/128]
**Wait,** 1. White Blight. We    [R. Conley. Supp 4/309]
_ 2. The Earth. We    [R. Conley. Supp 4/309]
_ 3. (To Be Sung to the Tune ... We    [R. Conley. Supp 4/310]
_ 4. USA. We    [R. Conley. Supp 4/310]
_ 5. The Old Prophecy. We    [R. Conley. Supp 4/311]
**Waiting.**    [J. Burroughs. Volume 3/238]
_. Hopefully    [A. Randolph. Volume 4/371]
_ for the Grapes.    [W. Maginn. Volume 2/243]
_ in the Children's Hospital.    [C. Major. Supp 4/199]
**Waiting"** Only    [F. Mace. Volume 4/369]
**Waitings.** The Two    [J. Chadwick. Volume 3/409]
**Waitress.** The    [B. Akhmadulina. Supp 5/2]
**Wake.** Kilmeny, fr. The Queen's    [J. Hogg. Volume 6/21]
**Wakefield.** The Hermit, fr. The Vicar Of    [O.

_ Goldsmith. Volume 2/199]
**Walk.**    [F. Horne. Supp 4/106]
_. Winter Morning, fr. The Winter Morning    [W. Cowper. Volume 5/186]
_ in a Crowd. Yearing I    [H. Sakutaro. Supp 7/107]
_ the Way of the New World: 001. We    [D. Lee. Supp 4/213]
_ the Way of the New World: 002. We    [D. Lee. Supp 4/214]
_ with De Mayor of Harlem.    [D. Henderson. Supp 4/207]
_ With Thee" " O Master, Let Me    [W. Gladden. Volume 4/135]
**Walked** Out to the Graveyard to See the Dead" " I    [R. Eberhart. Supp 2/128]
**Walker** of the Snow. The    [C. Shanly. Volume 6/167]
**Walking** Out of Expectation" "    [Hsiung Hung. Supp 7/9]
_ Song.    [C. Williams. Supp 1/315]
**Walks** in Beauty. She    [G. Byron. Volume 2/32]
**Wall.** Mending    [R. Frost. Supp 1/130]
_ of a House" " Near the    [Y. Amichai. Supp 7/240]
_ Street. Pan in    [E. Stedman. Volume 6/381]
**Wall",** fr. Love's Labor 's Lost. " When Icicles Hang by the    [W. Shakespeare. Volume 5/171]
**Wall,** Within and Beyond. The Great    [Liang Shang Ch'uan. Supp 7/19]
**Wallenstein.** Dallying with Temptation, fr.    [S. Coleridge. Volume 4/327]
**Walls** Do Not Fall: 006. The    [H. Doolittle. Supp 5/72]
_ Do Not Fall: 013. The    [H. Doolittle. Supp 5/73]
_ Do Not Fall: 014. The    [H. Doolittle. Supp 5/74]
**Wally,** Waly.    [Unknown. Volume 3/45]
**Walrus** and the Carpenter, fr. Alice in Wonderland. The    [C. Dodgson. Volume 1/180]
**Walter's** Wife. Lord    [E. Browning. Volume 2/392]
**Walton's** Book of Lives, fr. Ecclesiastical Sonnets    [W. Wordsworth. Volume 7/55]
**Waly.** Wally,    [Unknown. Volume 3/45]
**Wan?** Why So Pale And    [S. Suckling. Volume 2/247]
**Wanderer.** Descending Figure: 1. The    [L. Gluck. Supp 5/102]
_. Isis    [K. Raine. Supp 2/199]
_. The    [S. Smith. Supp 5/285]
**Wanderer's** Home. The    [O. Goldsmith. Volume 1/314]
**Wanders** into Old Workings" " As One Who    [C. Day Lewis. Supp 2/110]
**Wanting.** Found    [E. Dickinson. Volume 4/326]
**Wanton** With Those Eyes" " O, Do Not    [B. Jonson. Volume 2/39]
**Wants** of Man. The    [J. Adams. Volume 6/421]
**War.** Civil    [C. Shanly. Volume 8/353]
_. The Holy    [R. Kipling. Supp 1/182]
_ is Over. When This Cruel    [Unknown. Volume 8/382]
**War,** fr. Cato. Sempronius' Speech for    [J. Addison. Volume 8/193]
_ fr. King Richard III. End of the Civil    [W. Shakespeare. Volume 8/424]
_ fr. Tamburlaine. The School of    [C. Marlowe. Volume 8/185]
**War:** 001. A World Within a    [H. Read. Supp 2/36]
_ 002. A World withing a    [H. Read. Supp 2/38]
_ 003. A World withing a    [H. Read. Supp 2/39]
_ 004. A World withing a    [H. Read. Supp 2/41]
_ 005. A World withing a    [H. Read. Supp 2/42]

___ Judging Distances. Lessons of the    [H. Reed. Supp 2/344]
**Ward** Beecher. Henry    [C. Phelps. Volume 7/24]
**Warnings.** The Three    [H. Thrale. Volume 6/289]
**Warpland.** The Second Sermon on the    [G. Brooks. Supp 4/160]
___. The Sermon on the    [G. Brooks. Supp 4/159]
**Warren's** Address.    [J. Pierpont. Volume 8/326]
**Warres** in Ireland, fr. Epigrams. On the    [S. Harrington. Volume 8/237]
**Warrior** Dead, fr. The Princess. Home They Brought Her    [A. Tennyson. Volume 3/345]
**Wars** with the Angels. Nimrod    [A. Branch. Supp 1/67]
**Was"** " That's How I    [C. Conde. Supp 4/291]
**Wash** Away the Red. Do Not    [Ho Ch'i-Fang. Supp 7/7]
**Washington.** George    [Unknown. Volume 7/15]
___ Sends a Pair of Shoebuckles ... George    [D. Wakoski. Supp 5/319]
**Washington,** fr. Under the Elm    [J. Lowell. Volume 7/15]
**Waste** Places. In    [J. Stephens. Supp 1/286]
**wasted** time." " When in the chronicle of    [W. Shakespeare. Volume 2/3]
**Wasting** In Despair. Answer To Master Wither's Song, Shall I,    [B. Jonson. Volume 2/239]
**Watch** Any Day.    [W. Auden. Supp 2/169]
___ on the Rhine. The    [M. Schneckenburger. Volume 8/80]
**Watching.**    [E. Judson. Volume 6/435]
___ for Papa.    [Unknown. Volume 3/414]
**Water.** Afton    [R. Burns. Volume 5/202]
___. As a Plane Tree by the    [R. Lowell. Supp 2/387]
___. The Shaded    [W. Simms. Volume 5/196]
___ From The Well. Fetching    [Unknown. Volume 2/298]
___ Raining.    [G. Stein. Supp 5/293]
___ Turned Into Wine. Brief:    [R. Crashaw. Volume 4/306]
___ Witch. My Brigantine, fr. The    [J. Cooper. Volume 5/402]
**Water"** " Carry Her Over the    [W. Auden. Supp 2/157]
**Water-lily.** The    [J. Tabb. Volume 5/280]
**Water-Colour** of Venice. A    [L. Durrell. Supp 2/261]
**Waterfall.** To a    [Nirala. Supp 7/66]
**Waterfowl.** To a    [W. Bryant. Volume 5/304]
**Waterloo,** fr. Childe Harold    [G. Byron. Volume 8/287]
**Waters.** Living    [C. Spencer. Volume 4/251]
___ Are Wiser Than We" "    [F. Daglarca. Supp 7/298]
**Waters:** 001. Multitudinous Stars and Sping    [Ping Hsin. Supp 5/116]
___ 002. Multitudinous Stars and Sping    [Ping Hsin. Supp 5/116]
___ 003. Multitudinous Stars and Spring    [Ping Hsin. Supp 5/116]
___ 004. Multitudinous Stars and Spring    [Ping Hsin. Supp 5/116]
___ 005. Multitudinous Stars and Spring    [Ping Hsin. Supp 5/116]
___ 006. Multitudinous Stars and Spring    [Ping Hsin. Supp 5/117]
___ 007. Multitudinous Stars and Spring    [Ping Hsin. Supp 5/117]
___ 008. Multitudinous Stars and Spring    [Ping Hsin. Supp 5/117]
___ 009. Multitudinous Stars and Spring    [Ping Hsin. Supp 5/117]
**Wave"** "A Life on the Ocean    [E. Sargent. Volume 5/409]

**Waves.**    [D. Diop. Supp 6/70]
**Waves"** " Our Boat to the    [W. Channing. Volume 5/409]
**Wayfaring** Song. A    [H. Van Dyke. Volume 1/347]
**Weak** Monk. The    [S. Smith. Supp 2/106]
**Wear** the Mask That Grins and Lies" " We    [P. Dunbar. Supp 4/75]
**Wear"** " Nothing to    [W. Butler. Volume 9/213]
**Wearing** of the Green. The    [D. Boucicault. Volume 8/57]
**Weary.** Art Thou    [S. Stephen the Sabaite. Volume 4/87]
___ Blues. The    [L. Hughes. Supp 1/171]
___ Eyes" " Ere Sleep comes Down To Soothe the    [P. Dunbar. Supp 4/78]
**Weaver.** Blanket    [S. Esteves. Supp 4/292]
**Webster.** Daniel    [O. Holmes. Volume 7/20]
**Wedding.** The    [C. Aiken. Supp 1/14]
___. The Bride, fr. A Ballad Upon A    [S. Suckling. Volume 2/410]
___. The Golden    [D. Gray. Volume 2/448]
**Wedding,** fr. The Fall Of Jerusalem. Hebrew    [H. Milman. Volume 2/405]
**Wedding-Day,** fr. Epithalamion. The    [E. Spenser. Volume 2/4068]
**Wedding-Ring.** The Worn    [W. Bennett. Volume 2/438]
**Weddings.** A Letter on the Use of Machine Guns at    [K. Patchen. Supp 2/252]
**Wee** Thing. My Wife's A Winsome    [R. Burns. Volume 2/420]
___ White Rose. Our    [G. Massey. Volume 1/64]
**Weed.** The    [E. Bishop. Supp 2/245]
___. The Indian    [Unknown. Volume 6/249]
**Weeds.**    [E. Millay. Supp 1/223]
**Weehawken** and the New York Bay, fr. Fanny    [F. Halleck. Volume 7/244]
**Weeping"** " Beyond the Smiling and the    [H. Bonar. Volume 3/378]
**Weidersehen,** Summer. Auf    [J. Lowell. Volume 3/114]
**Weighing** the Baby.    [E. Beers. Volume 1/5]
**Weinsberg.** The Wives of    [G. Burger. Volume 9/200]
**Welcome.** The    [F. Attar. Volume 1/380]
___. The    [T. Davis. Volume 2/296]
___ Love. Things to    [J. Pasos. Supp 6/182]
___ the Hour" " Farewell! - But Whenever You    [T. Moore. Volume 3/116]
___ to "Boz" A    [W. Venable. Volume 7/77]
**Welcome,** Do I Sing" " Welcome,    [W. Browne. Volume 2/69]
___ Welcome, Do I Sing" "    [W. Browne. Volume 2/69]
**Wellaway.** Woe and    [N. Yushij. Supp 7/205]
**Welsh** Marches. The    [A. Housman. Supp 1/167]
**Wert** By My Side, My Love" " If Thou    [R. Heber. Volume 2/441]
**Werther.** Sorrows of    [W. Thackeray. Volume 9/204]
**West.** Hymn of the    [E. Stedman. Volume 8/458]
___ Coast Episode.    [J. Jordan. Supp 5/128]
___ Wind. Ode to the    [P. Shelley. Volume 5/128]
**West"** " Men of the North and    [R. Stoddard. Volume 8/97]
**West,** Home's Best, fr. The Traveller. East,    [O. Goldsmith. Volume 8/7]
**Western** Civilization.    [A. Neto. Supp 6/17]
___ Men. Song of the    [R. Hawker. Volume 8/136]
**Westminster.** Lines Found in His Bible in the Gate-house at    [S. Raleigh. Volume 4/352]
___ Abbey. On the Tombs in    [F. Beaumont. Volume 3/269]
**Wet** Sheet and a Flowing Sea" " A    [A. Cunningham. Volume 5/399]
**Whale.** Sojourn in the    [M. Moore. Supp 5/185]
**Wheel.** Carriers of the Dream    [N. Momaday. Supp

4/301]
— of the Hungry. The    [C. Vallejo. Supp
    6/189]
Whenas in Silks my Julia Goes" "    [R. Herrick.
    Volume 2/38]
Whip. Beyong the    [Lo Fu. Supp 7/29]
Whisper. The Angel's    [S. Lover. Volume 1/10]
Whispering Goodnight.    [A. Yosano. Supp 7/144]
Whistle. The    [R. Story. Volume 2/112]
Whistle, and I'll Come To You, My Lad.    [R. Burns.
    Volume 2/109]
White. A Poem in Black and    [M. Serote. Supp 6/91]
— Blight. We Wait, 1.    [R. Conley. Supp
    4/309]
— Company. The Bowman's Song, fr. The    [S.
    Doyle. Volume 8/12]
— Hair. The One    [W. Landor. Volume 6/285]
— Lilies. A Soldier Dreaming of    [M. Darwish.
    Supp 7/265]
— Moon.    [H. Sakutaro. Supp 7/106]
— Night.    [K. Molodowsky. Supp 5/176]
— Peacock, fr. Sospiri Di Roma. The    [W.
    Sharp. Volume 7/175]
— Rose. Our Wee    [G. Massey. Volume 1/64]
— Rose. The    [Unknown. Volume 2/36]
— Squall. The    [B. Procter. Volume 5/408]
— Women. The    [M. Coleridge. Supp 1/87]
Whittling.    [J. Pierpont. Volume 1/89]
Wicked Bishop. God's Judgment on a    [R. Southey.
    Volume 9/52]
Wicklow. Wicklow Winds, fr.    [G. Savage-Armstrong.
    Volume 5/127]
— Winds, fr. Wicklow    [G. Savage-Armstrong.
    Volume 5/127]
Wide Awe and Wisdom of the Night" " In the    [C.
    Roberts. Volume 5/69]
— World. Tirzah and the    [D. Ravikovitch.
    Supp 5/233]
Widow Machree.    [S. Lover. Volume 2/181]
— Malone.    [C. Lever. Volume 2/183]
Widow's Mite. The    [F. Locker-Lampson. Volume
    3/287]
— Mites. Brief: The    [R. Crashaw. Volume
    4/306]
Wife. Farewell to His    [G. Byron. Volume 3/109]
—. Lord Walter's    [E. Browning. Volume 2/392]
—. Lot's    [A. Akhmatova. Supp 5/7]
—. My Ain    [A. Laing. Volume 2/419]
—. The Auld    [C. Calverley. Volume 9/387]
—. The Poet's Song To His    [B. Procter. Volume
    2/421]
—. Were I But His Own    [M. Downing. Volume
    2/400]
— and Child. My    [H. Jackson. Volume 3/228]
— Of Loki. The    [L. Elliot. Volume 2/398]
— to Her Husband. The    [Unknown. Volume
    3/146]
Wife, Children, and Friends.    [W. Spencer. Volume
    1/354]
— fr. The Iliad. Hector to His    [Homer.
    Volume 3/122]
Wife's A Winsome Wee Thing. My    [R. Burns. Volume
    2/420]
Wild Ballad.    [G. Fuertes. Supp 5/93]
— Honey.    [M. Thompson. Volume 5/344]
— Ride. The    [L. Guiney. Volume 6/259]
Wilderness. Face Lost in the    [F. Tuqan. Supp
    7/273]
—. The    [K. Das. Supp 5/57]
—. The    [K. Raine. Supp 5/227]
Wildgoose Tower. Ascending the    [Feng Chih. Supp
    7/2]
Wilhelm Meister. Mignon's Song, fr.    [J. Goethe.
    Volume 6/313]
Will. The    [J. Donne. Volume 6/295]

—. Woman's    [J. Saxe. Volume 2/438]
— Be Done! Father, Thy    [S. Adams. Volume
    4/346]
— Crow When We Die" "The Roosters    [C.
    Meireles. Supp 5/160]
— Go. A Hunting We    [H. Fielding. Volume
    5/158]
— Happen" " And What    [K. Molodowsky. Supp
    5/175]
— Have to Understand. A Poem Some People    [L.
    Jones. Supp 4/178]
— Love Come? When    [P. Beatty. Volume 2/74]
— Not Let Thee Go" " I    [R. Bridges. Supp
    1/72]
— of God. The    [F. Faber. Volume 4/36]
— Take Us. The Wind    [F. Farrozkhzad. Supp
    7/217]
Will"  It Is Time That I Wrote My    [W. Yeats.
    Supp 1/330]
William Lloyd Garrison.    [J. Lowell. Volume 7/22]
— Shakespeare ... To the Memory of My Beloved
    Master,    [B. Jonson. Volume 7/48]
— Tell. Switzerland, fr.    [J. Knowles. Volume
    8/140]
Willie Winkie.    [W. Miller. Volume 1/31]
Willie"  " My Heid is Like to Rend,    [W.
    Motherwell. Volume 3/49]
Willow.    [A. Akhmatova. Supp 5/9]
Win. The Right Must    [F. Faber. Volume 4/299]
Wind.    [A. Yosano. Supp 7/146]
—. Elegy of the    [C. Okigbo. Supp 6/62]
—. Ode to the West    [P. Shelley. Volume 5/128]
—. The    [R. Stevenson. Volume 1/145]
—. The Evening    [W. Bryant. Volume 5/54]
— and the Pine-tree, fr. Edwin the Fair. The
    [S. Taylor. Volume 5/219]
— in a Frolic. The    [W. Howitt. Volume 1/143]
— Sleepers. The    [H. Doolittle. Supp 5/67]
— Will Take Us. The    [F. Farrozkhzad. Supp
    7/217]
Wind", fr. As You Like It. " Blow, Blow, Thou Winter
    [W. Shakespeare. Volume 3/155]
Wind-Up Doll. The    [F. Farrozkhzad. Supp 7/219]
Windmill. The    [R. Bridges. Supp 1/74]
Windmills. Arizona Poems:    [J. Fletcher. Supp
    1/126]
Window. The Triangular    [Yung Tzu. Supp 7/36]
— Frames the Moon. The    [L. Mar. Supp 4/32]
— of the Woman Burning. The    [M. Piercy. Supp
    5/197]
Window"  " Under my    [T. Westwood. Volume 1/139]
Windows. Painted    [G. Fuertes. Supp 5/96]
Winds. Love In The    [R. Hovey. Volume 2/252]
—. Song of the Summer    [G. Darley. Volume
    5/99]
—. The Three    [L. Lee. Supp 2/337]
Winds"  " Sweet Stream, That    [W. Cowper. Volume
    1/210]
— " Tell Me, Ye Winged    [C. Mackay. Volume
    4/411]
Wind's Song. The    [W. Rendra. Supp 7/101]
Winds, fr. Wicklow. Wicklow    [G. Savage-Armstrong.
    Volume 5/127]
Wine. Brief: Water Turned Into    [R. Crashaw.
    Volume 4/306]
Wine"  " This Is My    [I. Shabaka. Supp 7/261]
Winged Winds"  " Tell Me, Ye    [C. Mackay. Volume
    4/411]
— Worshippers. The    [C. Sprague. Volume
    5/330]
Wingless Hours" On His "Sonnets of the    [E. Lee-
    Hamilton. Volume 6/338]
Wings.    [M. Ritter. Volume 1/137]
—. The    [D. Levertov. Supp 5/141]
Winkie. Willie    [W. Miller. Volume 1/31]